Seventy-Five Years

of

German Immigration

to

Ste. Genevieve County, Missouri

1800-1875

Volume I: A-E

Barbara A. McClurkin

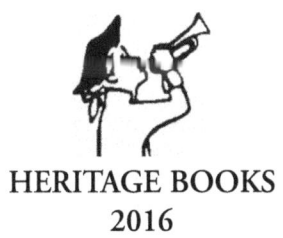

HERITAGE BOOKS
2016

HERITAGE BOOKS
AN IMPRINT OF HERITAGE BOOKS, INC.

Books, CDs, and more—Worldwide

For our listing of thousands of titles see our website
at
www.HeritageBooks.com

Published 2016 by
HERITAGE BOOKS, INC.
Publishing Division
5810 Ruatan Street
Berwyn Heights, Md. 20740

Copyright © 2016 Barbara A. McClurkin

Original cover art by Riza McClurkin.

All rights reserved. No part of this book may be reproduced or transmitted in any form or by any means, electronic or mechanical, including photocopying, recording or by any information storage and retrieval system without written permission from the author, except for the inclusion of brief quotations in a review.

International Standard Book Numbers
Paperbound: 978-0-7884-5749-4
Clothbound: 978-0-7884-5995-5

In memory of

David Lambert Wilder, Jr.

Contents

List of Illustrations and Maps ix
Preface xi
Acknowledgements xiii
Introduction xv

PART I – A
    Paul Abt Family 1
    Joseph Allgire Family 3
    John Amsler Family 6
    Andreas "Andrew" Anderson Family 8
    Andreas "Andrew" Armbruster Family 9
    Ignatz "Ignatius" Armbruster Family 11
    Joseph Armbruster Family 13
    Ludwig "Louis" Armbruster Family 15
    Michael Arnold Family 18
    Ignatius Auer Family 21

PART II – B
    Johann "John" Bach Family 23
    Augustus Bachle Family 25
    Joseph Bader Family 28
    Ludwig "Louis" Bader Family 30
    Maximilian "Max" Bader Family 32
    Joseph Baechle Family 34
    Martin Bahr Family 37
    Benedict Bantz Family 39
    Frederick Bartels Family 40
    Jacob Basler Family 42
    Johann Baptist "John" Basler Family 44
    Joseph Basler Family 47
    Peter Basler Family 48
    Theresia Basler Family 51
    Valentine Basler Family 53
    Wilhelm "William" Basler Family 55
    John Bassler Family 57
    George Bauer Family 58
    Christian Baum Family 61
    Franz Anton Baumann Family 66
    Magdalena Baumann Family 70
    Johann "John" Baumgartner Family 71
    Franz "Frank" Baumstark Family 73
    Wilhelm "William" Baumstark Family 76
    Vincent Bayer Family 78
    Gottlob Bebion Family 80
    Bernard Bechtold Family 82

George Beck Family	84
William Beckemeyer Family	87
George Beckermann Family	90
Anselm Begley Family	93
Franz Jacob Bernays Family	94
John Betten Family	98
Charles Henry Biel Family	100
Anton Bieser Family	103
August Bieser Family	106
Jacob Bieser Family	108
Joseph Bieser Family	110
Joseph Bieser Family	111
Michael Bieser Family	113
Albert Bisch Family	115
Martin B. Bleckler Family	118
Michael Bleifuss Family	120
Herman Bockenkamp Family	121
Lucas Boehle Family	125
Frederick Bolle Family	127
Johann Franz "Frank" Bonnarens Family	130
Franz Xavier Boos Family	133
Franz Jacob Botz Family	134
Heinrich "Henry" Brandel Family	136
Harmony Brands Family	139
Bernard Braun Family	141
Franz Anton "Frank" Braun Family	143
George Braun Family	144
Johann Nepomuk "John" Braun Family	148
Martin Braun Family	150
Francis "Frank" Breckle Family	153
Joseph Breig Family	155
Wilhelm "William" Breig Family	157
Vincent Brischle Family	159
Benedict Bross Family	161
Adam Bube Family	164
Morris Buchholtz Family	166
Francis Charles Buehler Family	168
Herman Buehler Family	171
Joseph Buehler Family	173
Adam Buenniger Family	175
Bartholomew Burgert Family	177
Karl "Charles' Burgert Family	179
Simon Burgert Family	182
Gregor Burkart Family	185
Ulrich Burkart Family	188
Alexander Burle Family	190
Ludwig "Louis" Burle Family	192
Michael Burtcher Family	194
Bernhard Busam Family	196
Michael Busam Family	198

PART III – C

Carl Felix "Charles" Carssow Family 201
Johann Georg Cromer Family 205

PART IV – D

Christopher Dallas Family 207
John Dallas Family 208
Franz Sales Deck Family 211
Johann Ulrich "John" Denler Family 212
Peter Dietzer Family 216
Bernard Difani Family 217
Bertha Doerge Family 222
Carl "Charles" Doerge Family 224
Johann Georg Dold Family 228
Bernard Doll Family 230
Johann George "George" Doll Family 233
Joseph Doll Family 236
Joseph Doll Family 238
Julius Joseph Doll Family 240
Lorenz "Lawrence" Doll Family 241
Meinrad Donze Family 243
Seraphin Donze Family 247
Jacob Duffner Family 249

PART V – E

Jacob Echle Family 253
Severin Eckenfels Family 254
Anton Eckert Family 256
Bernard Benjamin Effrein Family 258
William Ehe Family 261
Gottfried Ehler Family 263
Charles Ehrhard Family 265
Gervais Eichenlaub Family 267
Ferdinand Eisenbeis Family 270
Joseph Endres Family 274
Joseph A. Ernst Family 276
Francis "Frank" Esselman Family 278
Benjamin Etter Family 281

Appendix A, German Confederation, 1815 – 1866 287
Appendix B, Modern German States after 1990 291
Appendix C, Ste. Genevieve County, Missouri 293
Bibliography 295
Index 301

List of Illustrations and Maps

Map of Germany before 1871 287
Map of Modern German States after 1990 291
Map of Ste. Genevieve County, Missouri Towns and Townships 293

Preface

The genesis of this project was accidental. I was nineteen when I asked my dad about the German side of his family and he reluctantly admitted that he didn't know much about his family history beyond his grandparents. I already knew quite a bit about my mother's ancestry since the women in her family had carefully kept family records through the generations. After talking with my father, I wrote down as much information as I could about the family members he had mentioned and then began my research. My original intention was to discover the history of my own German ancestors in Ste. Genevieve County, Missouri. Curiosity and the never-ending thrill of discovery led to my documenting all of the German families in that county.

At the time, I was a sophomore at the University of Missouri on the Columbia campus. I quickly discovered that the State Historical Society of Missouri, which was housed in Ellis Library, contained a treasure trove of books, journals, manuscript collections, microfilmed newspapers and government documents. To my great delight, I started to find information right away. The more information I gathered, the more people I identified who were related to me through both blood and marriage. In time, I found that my lines of relationship extended to include almost every family with German ancestry who had settled in Ste. Genevieve County, Missouri.

One of the best things about conducting research these days is the fact that many repositories of primary vital records have made their collections available on microfilm or in online digital formats. I had access to images of the original documents instead of having to rely on transcribed copies. Accessing the online records was sometimes difficult since the indexing wasn't always accurate and rules for modern, standardized spelling did not exist at the time the records were created, so I learned to be creative in how I constructed my search terms.

The greatest challenge I faced in my research was learning to translate the records into English. Most of the early records of Ste. Genevieve County were written in a multitude of languages including Latin, French, Spanish, German and English. After I had identified the European origins of the German families, I struggled not only to learn both the Latin and German terminology specific to the records, I also had to learn to decipher a number of German Fraktur script styles.

I built a database to organize the information using the Personal Ancestral File application developed by the Church of Jesus Christ of Latter-Day Saints. The files have grown to include over 29,000 individual records and ancestral lines that extend back into the mid-1600s. The information in that database is the foundation for this project.

Acknowledgements

After more than thirty years of collecting information and conducting research, the list of people who have provided assistance and encouragement to me along the way is incredibly long. Numerous relatives shared information and helped to fill in a lot of blank spaces. Librarians and archivists pulled records, processed interlibrary loan requests and made invaluable suggestions as to where I could find the information I needed. Fellow researchers and coworkers listened politely when I enthused over the latest discovery. If I attempted to list all the individuals, I would inevitably leave someone out. But there are some people who I must thank specifically:

Mrs. Gale Nelson and the wonderful volunteer staff of the Church of Jesus Christ of Latter Day Saint Family History Center in Norman, Oklahoma, who became valued friends and research buddies.

My mother, Mary G. Wilder, who provided unending moral support, careful editorial review, and made suggestions for the format of the biographical sketches.

My husband, David, and my daughter, Elizabeth, who both gave me the time and space to work on this project and allowed me to pile books, microfilms and papers all over the house.

Thank you all more than I can say.

Introduction

Ste. Genevieve County, Missouri is one of the most historically significant areas in the United States due to the longevity of its settlement, the completeness of written records available, the well-preserved artifacts, and because of its rich cultural history. Scholars have studied the French colonial era, but most have stopped short of the advent of the Germans into this southeastern Missouri region. The Germans began to arrive in Missouri as the United States expanded westward at the beginning of the nineteenth century. Their numbers increased significantly after Missouri became a state in 1821. By the 1830s there was a steady movement of Germans into Ste. Genevieve County after government lands were made available for settlement.

This project focuses on the immigration of Germanic people into Ste. Genevieve County between 1800 and 1875, and examines their European origins, what routes they followed to get to Ste. Genevieve County, and identifies the family members who came with them. The intent is to provide a comprehensive compilation of German immigrant families in order to complement the scholarly research that has already been accomplished and to establish groundwork for future study.

Inclusive Dates

The period of 1800 to 1875 was chosen for two reasons. First, although there were some German people who settled in Ste. Genevieve County prior to 1800, most of them had moved, been absorbed into the local French families or died out by 1800. Second, the documentation available for most of the earlier Germans is sketchy at best and it is nearly impossible to determine what affect they had on the settlement of Ste. Genevieve County. The year 1875 was chosen as the end date since by that time, most of the original German immigrant families had arrived in the county. A handful of families whose arrival occurred either before or after these two dates have been included since they are within five years of the stated range.

Study Population

Most of the subject families included in this project originated within the borders of what is now modern Germany. However, a number of people who were identified in the U.S. census as Austrian, Bohemian, Swiss, Danish, Russian and some people from Alsace and Lorraine, France, were also included. Germany as a unified nation did not exist before 1871. Prior to that date, the territory claimed by the Germanic people fluctuated considerably in size and governance and included areas that now belong to other modern-day countries. As the borders moved in Europe, immigrants' nations of origin would change in American records.

Under the rule of the Holy Roman Empire (800 – 1806), more than 300 independent Germanic states came into being. Between 1806 and 1808, Napoleon Bonaparte reorganized the German territories after he defeated Austria and Russia in the Battle of Austerlitz, consolidating them into the Confederation of the Rhine. But this organization collapsed in 1813 when Bonaparte was defeated during his campaign against the Russian Empire in the Battle of Leipzig. In 1815 the Congress of Vienna established the German Confederation, a loose association of 39 German-speaking countries whose primary goals were to coordinate mutual defense, to promote economic welfare, and to act as a buffer between Prussia and Austria, the two largest member states who both disputed the right to rule the Confederation. [See Appendix A for a map and comprehensive list of the members of the German Confederation]

During the period between 1815 and 1871, Germans endured the stresses of natural disasters and numerous political, military and religious conflicts.

1816 became known as the Year Without a Summer because of severe climate abnormalities, most likely caused by the eruption of the Indonesian volcano, Mount Tambora. Major food shortages resulted from disrupted or shortened growing seasons across Europe. In addition to the climate woes, Germany also suffered epidemics of typhus and cholera, especially in the early 1830s and late 1840s.

Prussia and Austria were constantly battling for dominance of the Confederation. Prussia, in particular, had expansionist ambitions and slowly annexed more and more territory. In 1848-49, a number of liberal rebellions and revolutions broke out across Europe, and within the Confederation the protests raged against its autocratic political structure. One of the strongest rebellions was the Baden Revolution of 1848. This series of uprisings, including the Hecker Uprising, were all put down by the Confederation military and the reprisals against the rebels and anyone who was suspected to have been a sympathizer were swift and vicious. Thousands of people fled Baden into France and Switzerland. As the punitive actions continued, many refugees left Europe for America. Denmark and the Duchy of Holstein fought two major battles between 1848 and 1852 over the ownership of the Duchy of Schleswig and a wave of people left northern Germany for America. Many of the Germans who settled in Ste. Genevieve County were refugees from these epidemics, battles and rebellions.

In northern parts of the Confederation, there was a schism developing within the Lutheran faith between Rational Reformed Lutherans and "Old Lutherans." In an attempt to mend the breach, Frederick William III of Prussia ordered the two sects to unite, forming the Evangelical Church of the Prussian Union. But dissenters remained strong in their beliefs and many left Europe for the Americas. Many of the dissenting Old Lutheran groups came to Missouri and eventually formed what became the Lutheran Church – Missouri Synod.

Excluded Population

A number of people were deliberately left out of this study. Transient laborers and people who remained in Ste. Genevieve County for less than five years were excluded. While they were members of the community, there is very little recorded information available about these people and, other than their collective general contributions, they had little definable individual impact on the community as members of the society. Roman Catholic clergy assigned to the Ste. Genevieve County parishes [either nuns or priests] who had Germanic ancestry were excluded since none of them had family connections in the county during the inclusive time-frame.

There is one very large, influential family with German ancestry that was excluded from this study: the Joseph Kauffman/Coffman family. They were not included since they were not an immigrant family as defined by the parameters of this project. By the time Joseph Kaufman came to Missouri from Pennsylvania by way of Virginia in the early 1830s, his family had been in the United States for two generations and was therefore no longer considered immigrant. Joseph and his family eventually acquired over 1200 acres of land and owned over one hundred and fifty slaves prior to the Civil War. The Kauffmans founded the town of Coffman in southern Ste. Genevieve County.

Biographical Sketch Design

Although elements of genealogical research are involved in this project, it is not in any way intended to be a genealogy. This study was designed using the principles of prosopography: the intent of learning about patterns of relationships and activities through the study of collective biography by collecting and analyzing statistically relevant quantities of biographical data about a well-defined group of individuals. Robert Charles Anderson's *Great Migration* project was the model for the family sketches in this study.

The families are presented in two-generation biographical sketches in order to provide a logical framework for the information as follows:

If parentage and natal family of the immigrant is known, that information will be included. If a reasonably close relationship to another immigrant is known [i.e., siblings, cousins, in-laws], that information will be stated in the comments section. But if the ancestry is known beyond his parents, that information will not be presented or discussed, although a citation to anything published on the subject may be included in the bibliography.

Not every detail of the life of the immigrant will be incorporated into each sketch. If the subject of the sketch was one of the leaders of a community, his lesser offices and day-to-day activities, as recorded in official records, will not be recorded here.

The children of immigrants will all be identified along with their spouses and vital statistical information. The progeny of this second generation will only be numerated as "number of sons and number of daughters," and not named individually.

Children of a male immigrant with multiple spouses will be numbered sequentially.
For example:
    Male Immigrant
    1) Wife
       Children with 1st wife:
          i.
          ii
    2) Wife
       Children with 2nd wife:
          iii.
          iv.
          v.

Children of female immigrants with multiple spouses will be numbered according to where the children stand in order of birth as children of their fathers. For example:
    Male immigrant B
    1) wife, who was the widow of Male immigrant A
    Children of Male immigrant A and 1) wife:
        i.
        ii.
    Children of Male immigrant B [2nd husband] and 1) wife:
        i.
        ii.
        iii.
    Children of Male Immigrant B and 2) wife:
        iv.
        v.

If more than one sibling in a German family came to the United States they will be identified as follows:

* = subject of the sketch
† = sibling who also immigrated to Ste. Genevieve County, Missouri.
‡ = sibling who also immigrated to the United States, but not to Ste. Genevieve County.

Female immigrants who married another immigrant will be fully described in the biographical sketches of their spouse with a cross reference in the sketch of their natal family. If a woman has more than one spouse, and both spouses are immigrants, she will be described fully in both husbands' sketches. If a woman married a non-German man, she will be fully described in the sketch of her parents and all vital data on her spouse and children will be included. If a female immigrant did not marry, she will be fully described in the sketch of her parents.

Most of the heads of family are male. There are a few notable exceptions to this rule. In the case of a female immigrant who had a significant personal impact on her community, she and her family origins are discussed separately from her husband, if any. A notable example is that of Mrs. Bertha Straube Doerge, a very well-known and beloved midwife in Ste. Genevieve County.

If no information is found for a particular category, then that category does not appear in the biographical sketch (i.e. if no naturalization record is found, then the sketch will not have a section for naturalization.)

Any information enclosed in square brackets, [ ], is an editorial commentary or additional information added by the author.

Conflict Resolution

Surname variations were resolved as follows: The surname of the primary immigrant named in the title of each sketch was the one most commonly found in official records if there was no modern version. Otherwise, the modern form of a surname was used and the original name was given with the parentage of the immigrant and any other variations were noted in the surname variations category.

If a conflict occurred in birth or death dates, such as those found on tombstones versus those in the baptismal or burial records, the dates in the primary records were used. Primary records rule.

As a rule, I avoided using genealogies or collections of records compiled by other authors or published transcriptions of original records as cited sources. With very few exceptions, my sources are all original primary or secondary sources. I used newspaper accounts and some compiled records as indicators as to where I should look for the original records to verify my information. If I could find no authoritative primary source and had doubt as to the veracity of any information, I stated that doubt in the comments section of the biographical information.

Disclaimer

No matter how many times I reviewed this manuscript and had other people double- and triple-check my information, I still found errors. And there are still holes and question marks in my facts and data. It is my hope that readers will gently help me correct the mistakes that were missed and will perhaps be generous enough to share information that could fill in the blank spaces.

A

Paul Abt Family
Surname Variations: Abb, Abp, Apt
European Origin: Harthausen auf der Scheer, Hohenzollern, Germany
Family:
Father: Joseph C. Abt, born 23 August 1834 in Harthausen auf der Scheer, Hohenzollern, Germany. He was baptized on 24 August 1834 in the Catholic Church at Harthausen.
Mother: Agnes Wessner, born 17 May 1839 in Harthausen auf der Scheer, Hohenzollern, Germany. She was baptized on 18 May 1839 in the Catholic Church at Harthausen. She died on 12 February 1912, most likely at Harthausen.
Children:
  i. Paul, born 18 June 1863 in Harthausen auf der Scheer, Hohenzollern, Germany. He was baptized on 19 June 1863 in the Catholic Church at Harthausen. Paul died on 7 February 1866 at Harthausen. No issue.
 * ii. Paul, born 16 February 1867 in Harthausen auf der Scheer, Hohenzollern, Germany. He was baptized on 17 February 1867 in the Catholic Church at Harthausen. [See sketch below.]
  iii. Agatha, born 10 February 1870 in Harthausen auf der Scheer, Hohenzollern, Germany. She was baptized on 11 February 1870 in the Catholic Church at Harthausen. Agatha died on 10 March 1949 at Harthausen. No further information.
  iv. Engelbert, born 8 December 1873 in Harthausen auf der Scheer, Hohenzollern, Germany. He was baptized on 9 December 1873 in the Catholic Church at Harthausen. Engelbert died on 17 October 1947 at Harthausen. No further information.
  v. Jacob, born and baptized on 8 September 1875 in Harthausen auf der Scheer, Hohenzollern, Germany. Jacob died on 31 January 1950 in Harthausen. No further information.
  vi. Andreas, born 1 December 1877 in Harthausen auf der Scheer, Hohenzollern, Germany. He was baptized on 2 December 1877 in the Catholic Church at Harthausen. Jacob died on 5 January 1878 at Harthausen. No issue.

Immigration:
Arrived on 3 November 1884 from Liverpool, England to New York aboard the *Oregon*:
  Abt, Paul, 17   [black]smith   Germany

Biographical:
Husband: Paul Abt
  Birth – 16 February 1867 in Harthausen auf der Scheer, Hohenzollern, Germany.
  Death/Burial – 25 February 1919 in Ste. Genevieve County, Missouri. He was buried in the Valle Spring Cemetery in Ste. Genevieve, Ste. Genevieve County, Missouri.
1) Wife: Frances Philomena Burgert, daughter of Joseph Burgert and Clara Trautmann [See Bartholomew Burgert sketch.]
  Birth – 8 March 1878 in Ste. Genevieve County, Missouri.
  Marriage – 7 August 1893 in Ste. Genevieve, Ste. Genevieve County, Missouri.
  Death/Burial – 15 August 1901 in Ste. Genevieve County, Missouri. She was buried in the Valle Spring Cemetery in Ste. Genevieve, Ste. Genevieve County, Missouri.
  Children:
    1. Clara A., born 2 September 1894 in Ste. Genevieve County, Missouri. She married Francis Xavier "Frank" Stuppy on 21 September 1920 in Ste. Genevieve County, Missouri. Frank was the son of Anton Reinhard Stuppy and Theresia Kuehn, born 3 August 1890 in Ste. Genevieve

County, Missouri. Frank was a fireman in one of the lime plants in Ste. Genevieve County. The couple had two sons and two daughters. Frank died of a coronary occlusion on 15 September 1963 in Ste. Genevieve County, Missouri. Clara died on 26 June 1982 in Ste. Genevieve County, Missouri. They were both buried in the Valle Spring Cemetery in Ste. Genevieve, Ste. Genevieve County, Missouri.

    ii. Joseph Charles, born 4 November 1896 in Ste. Genevieve County, Missouri. He was baptized on 13 December 1896 in the Ste. Genevieve Catholic Church in Ste. Genevieve, Ste. Genevieve County, Missouri. Joseph was a farmer. During World War I, he served in the U.S. Navy aboard the *USS Minneapolis*, and rose to the rank of coxswain. He was discharged from active service in April 1919 and returned to Ste. Genevieve County, Missouri. Joseph married Leona Cornelia Kiefer on 27 April 1931 in Ste. Genevieve County. Leona was the daughter of Peter Kiefer and Laura Blanche Bader, born 16 July 1904 in Ste. Genevieve County. The couple had two sons. Joseph died on 1 December 1986 and Leona died on 15 September 1988, both in Ste. Genevieve County, Missouri. They were both buried in the Valle Spring Cemetery in Ste. Genevieve, Ste. Genevieve County, Missouri.

    iii. Child, born about 1897 in Ste. Genevieve County, Missouri. The child died before June 1900. No issue.

    iv. Peter John, born 4 July 1898 in Ste. Genevieve County, Missouri. He was a quarry worker. Peter married Helena Agnes Bahr on 22 April 1930 in Ozora, Ste. Genevieve County, Missouri. Helena was the daughter of Charles Joseph Bahr and Mary Schweigert, born 2 July 1904 in Ozora, Ste. Genevieve County, Missouri. The couple had one son and three daughters. Peter died on 22 July 1983 and Helena died on 2 October 1987, both in Ste. Genevieve County, Missouri. They were both buried in the Sacred Heart Cemetery in Ozora, Ste. Genevieve County, Missouri.

2) Wife: Mary Josepha Burgert, daughter of Joseph Burgert and Clara Trautmann [See Bartholomew Burgert sketch.]

Birth – 19 March 1879 in Ste. Genevieve County, Missouri.

Marriage – 3 November 1909 in Ste. Genevieve County, Missouri.

Death/Burial – 27 December 1935 in Ste. Genevieve County, Missouri. She was buried in the Valle Spring Cemetery in Ste. Genevieve, Ste. Genevieve County, Missouri.

Children:

    v. Maria Hedwig, born 25 October 1911 in Ste. Genevieve County, Missouri. She was baptized on 29 October 1911 in the Ste. Genevieve Catholic Church in Ste. Genevieve, Ste. Genevieve County, Missouri. Mary married Leonard C. Glaser. Leonard was the son of John Wendolin Glaser and Mary Helena Jokerst, born 26 May 1907 in Ste. Genevieve County. The couple had one son and one daughter. Leonard was a carpenter and was instrumental in starting the Carpenters' Union in Ste. Genevieve. He worked for the R. H. Roth Construction Company and for Herzog Construction. Marie died on 10 October 1989 and Leonard died on 28 August 1999, both in Ste. Genevieve County, Missouri. They were both buried in the Valle Spring Cemetery in Ste. Genevieve, Ste. Genevieve County, Missouri.

    vi. Anton Austin "Tony" [twin], born 13 July 1914 in Ste. Genevieve County, Missouri. He was baptized on 26 July 1914 in the Ste. Genevieve Catholic Church in Ste. Genevieve, Ste. Genevieve County, Missouri. Tony was a farmer. He may never have married and had no known issue. Tony died on 15 August 1984 in Ste. Genevieve County, Missouri.

    vii. Margaret Catherine [twin], born 13 July 1914 in Ste. Genevieve County, Missouri. She was baptized on 26 July 1914 in the Ste. Genevieve Catholic Church in Ste. Genevieve, Ste. Genevieve County, Missouri. Margaret married Xavier Charles Pfaff on 5 November 1934 in Ste. Genevieve County. Xavier was the son of Francis Pfaff and Cecilia Schmidt, born 10 February 1902 in Ste. Genevieve County. He was a farmer. The couple had six sons and two daughters. Xavier died on 18 July 1967 and Margaret died on 26 November 1998. They were both buried in the St. Joseph Cemetery in Zell, Ste. Genevieve County, Missouri.

viii. Alphonse Paul, born 13 June 1916 in Ste. Genevieve County, Missouri. He was baptized on 25 June 1916 in the Ste. Genevieve Catholic Church in Ste. Genevieve, Ste. Genevieve County, Missouri. He was a lime kiln worker. Alphonse married Leona Catherine Wolk on 25 March 1940 in Ste. Genevieve County. Leona was the daughter of Joseph A. Wolk and Mary Anna Denler, born 12 December 1921 in Ste. Genevieve County. Alphonse died on 16 November 1984 and Leona died on 10 October 1990, both in Ste. Genevieve County, Missouri. They were both buried in the Valle Spring Cemetery in Ste. Genevieve, Ste. Genevieve County, Missouri.

ix. Gerald Francis, born 30 March 1918 in Ste. Genevieve County, Missouri. He was baptized on 7 April 1918 in the Ste. Genevieve Catholic Church in Ste. Genevieve, Ste. Genevieve County, Missouri. Gerald married Anna Mary Wolk on 11 June 1947 in Ste. Genevieve County. Anna was the daughter of Joseph A. Wolk and Mary Anna Denler, born 19 November 1924 in Ste. Genevieve County. The couple had three sons and one daughter. Anna died on 22 October 2005 and Gerald died on 8 November 2005, both in Ste. Genevieve County. They were both buried in the St. Joseph Cemetery in Zell, Ste. Genevieve County, Missouri.

Naturalization:

Name	Declaration	Naturalization	Origin
Abt, Paul		28 November 1896 Ste. Genevieve Co.	Germany

Education: Could read, write and speak English
Occupation: Farmer
Religious Affiliation: Roman Catholic
Comments:
Paul Abt left Germany at the age of seventeen in 1884, and appears to have come directly to Ste. Genevieve County, Missouri in late 1884 or early 1885. He worked for several years as a farm laborer before he was able to buy a farm of his own in Jackson Township. He worked and lived on this farm for the rest of his life. His first wife, Frances Burgert, died of typhoid fever in 1901. Eight years later, Paul married Mary Josepha Burgert, the younger sister of his first wife. Paul died of a cerebral hemorrhage [hemiplegia] on 25 February 1919 in Ste. Genevieve County, Missouri. Mary lived with her oldest step-son/nephew, Joseph, until her death in 1935. She died of heart disease and gastroenteritis on 27 December 1935 in Ste. Genevieve County, Missouri. Paul and both of his wives were buried in the Valle Spring Cemetery in Ste. Genevieve, Ste. Genevieve County, Missouri.

Joseph Allgire Family

Surname Variations: Al[l]geier, Al[l]gier, Al[l]gar, Al[l]gayer, Al[l]geyer, Al[l]guire
European Origin: Fautenbach, Baden, Germany
Family:
Father: Lorenz Allgeier, born 13 December 1784 in Fautenbach, Baden, Germany. He died before November 1850, most likely in Indiana.
Mother: Salome Braun, born about 1788 in [possibly Beiertheim, Karlsruhe], Baden, Germany. She died after June 1860 in Allen County, Indiana.
Children:

‡ i. Agatha, born 6 February 1811 in Fautenbach, Baden, Germany. She and her fiancé, Joseph Huber, came to the United States in 1836, and landed in New York. She married Joseph on 29 August 1836 in Buffalo, Erie County, New York. Joseph was the son of Philip Huber and Christina Zimmermann, born 11 March 1810 in Fautenbach, Baden, Germany. Agatha and Joseph had at least two sons, Joseph and Philip, and one daughter, Mary, all born in New York, and possibly other children. Joseph and Philip Huber were living in Ste. Genevieve, Missouri with their uncle, Joseph Allgire in 1860. Mary was married to Alexius Gittinger in Ste.

     Genevieve on 22 November 1859. [See Franz Anton Gittinger sketch.] No further information has been found on Joseph and Agatha Huber.
  ii. Francisca, born 1 August 1813 in Fautenbach, Baden, Germany. No further information.
* iii. Joseph, born 26 January 1816 in Fautenbach, Baden, Germany. [See sketch below.]
‡ iv. Stephen, born 25 December 1818 in Fautenbach, Baden, Germany. He came to the United States in 1836, landing in New York. Stephen was a cooper and farmer. He stayed in Erie County, New York for several years before moving to Allen County, Indiana. He married Augusta Hauser on 18 November 1845 in Fort Wayne, Allen County, Indiana. Augusta was the daughter of Franz Joseph Hauser and Theresia Kaltenbach, born 8 April 1829 in Gamshurst, Baden, Germany. Stephan and Augusta had three sons and four daughters, all born in Allen County, Indiana. Augusta died on 22 July 1854 in Allen County, Indiana. Stephen married Mary Baschob as his second wife on 22 July 1855 in Allen County. Mary was the daughter of Johann Baschob and Barbara Osstheimer, born 25 March 1836 in Northampton County, Pennsylvania. Stephen and Mary had four sons and one daughter, all born in Allen County, Indiana. Stephen died on 26 May 1879 in Allen County, and was buried in the Lindenwood Cemetery at Fort Wayne. Mary died on 28 December 1909 in Allen County, Indiana.
‡ v. Johann Evangelist "John," born 27 December 1821 in Fautenbach, Baden, Germany. John was a farmer in Allen County, Indiana. He married Wilhelmina [Hauser?] about 1847. Wilhelmina was born about 1826 in Baden, Germany. The couple had six sons and two daughters, all born in Allen County. John died in 1887 and Wilhelmina died on 4 April 1898. They are both buried in the Catholic Cemetery at Fort Wayne, Allen County, Indiana.
  vi. Franz Ignatius, born 2 February 1825 in Fautenbach, Baden, Germany. He died on 25 February 1825 at Fautenbach. No issue.
  vii. Franz Carl, born 28 January 1826 in Fautenbach, Baden, Germany. He died on 15 February 1826 at Fautenbach. No issue.
‡ viii. Maria Barbara, born 8 May 1827 in Fautenbach, Baden, Germany. She came to the United States with her parents in 1843, landing in New York. She married Meinrad Seiler on 13 July 1844 in Allen County, Indiana. Meinrad was the son of Joseph Seiler and Franziska Helena Wirtner, born 4 October 1809 in Altdorf, Freiburg, Baden, Germany. He had come to the United States in 1836, landing at New York. Meinrad was a carpenter and farmer and had worked for several years in New York before moving to Indiana. The couple had eight sons and two daughters, all born in Allen County, Indiana. Meinrad died on 27 April 1875 and Barbara died on 14 March 1898, both in Allen County, Indiana.
  ix. Anton, born 19 May 1830 in Fautenbach, Baden, Germany. He died on 4 September 1831 at Fautenbach. No issue.

Immigration:
Arrived on 18 July 1836 from Le Havre, France to New York aboard the *Formosa*:
  Huber, Joseph, 25   Baden
  Algeire, Agatha, 25   Baden
Arrived in 1836 aboard an unknown vessel:
  Allgeier, Stephen
  Seiler, Meinrad
Arrived on 27 April 1841 from Le Havre, France to New York aboard the *Sully*:
  Allgeyer, Joseph, 20   Baden   Farmer
Arrived on 16 May 1843 from Le Havre, France to New York aboard the *Sully*:
  Allgeier, Lorenz, 58   Farmer   Baden
    Salome, 54
    Barbara, 16
Arrived before 1846 marriage aboard an unknown vessel:
  Allgeier, Johann

Biographical:
Husband: Joseph Allgire
   Birth – 26 January 1818 in Fautenbach, Baden, Germany.
   Death/Burial – about 1861 probably in Ste. Genevieve County, Missouri.
Wife: Sophia Frederick
   Birth – about 1820 in Pennsylvania.
   Marriage – 1 June 1847 in Allen County, Indiana.
   Death/Burial – after July 1870, most likely in Ste. Genevieve County, Missouri.
   Children:
   i. John, born 22 June 1848 in Allen County, Indiana. He was a farmer. John married Emelie Marcelite Govro on 28 November 1867 in Ste. Genevieve County, Missouri. Marcelite was the daughter of Etienne Govro [aka Govereau or Govreau] and Mary Belieu [aka Bellew, widow of Jacob Asher], born 11 February 1849 in Ste. Genevieve County, Missouri. The couple had three daughters. Marcelite died before September 1879, probably in Ste. Genevieve County, Missouri. John married Elizabeth Ann "Eliza" Henderson as his second wife on 2 September 1879 in River aux Vases, Ste. Genevieve County, Missouri. Eliza was the daughter of Stokely Henderson and Catherine Bloom, born 23 January 1860 in Ste. Genevieve County, Missouri. The couple had six sons and five daughters. By 1900, John and Eliza had moved to a farm near Lithium, Perry County, Missouri. They stayed there for almost twenty years and then moved to Festus, Jefferson County, Missouri. John died on 6 January 1942 in Ste. Genevieve County when he was hit by a train. Eliza died on 9 October 1942 in St. Louis, Missouri from a combination of kidney and heart disease. They were both buried in the Sacred Heart Cemetery in Crystal City, Jefferson County, Missouri.
   ii. Elisabeth, born September 1850 in Allen County, Indiana. No further mention of her has been found after the 1870 census in Ste. Genevieve County, Missouri.
   iii. Bernard, born 19 August 1851 in Allen County, Indiana. He was a farmer. Bernard married Mary Govro on 17 November 1874 in River aux Vases, Ste. Genevieve County, Missouri. Mary was the daughter of Francis Xavier Govro [aka Govereau or Govreau] and Louise Buyatte, born about 1851 in Ste. Genevieve County, Missouri. The couple had three sons. Mary died before October 1882 and is said to have been buried in the Stone Church Cemetery near Coffman, Ste. Genevieve County, Missouri. Bernard married Mary Mildred Rudloff as his second wife on 17 October 1882 in River aux Vases. Mary was the daughter of Francis "Frank" Rudloff and Nancy Ann Woolford, born 26 December 1865 in Ste. Genevieve County, Missouri. The couple had nine sons, three daughters and one child that died in infancy. The family lived in Ste. Genevieve County until the 1920s when Bernard and Mary moved to a farm near the town of Brewerville, Randolph County, Illinois with their five youngest sons. Mary died on 21 December 1925 in East St. Louis, St. Clair County, Illinois. Bernard died on 18 August 1928 in Ste. Genevieve County, Missouri. They were both buried with several of their children in St. Joseph Cemetery in Prairie du Rocher, Randolph County, Illinois.
   iv. Mary, born about 1852 in Allen County, Indiana. She married Henry Rudloff on 3 March 1870 at River aux Vases, Ste. Genevieve County, Missouri. Henry was the son of Johann Georg "George" Rudloff and Cecilia Winkler, born about 1849 in Ste. Genevieve County, Missouri. [See Johann Georg "George" Rudloff sketch.]

U.S. residence prior to Ste. Genevieve County, Missouri:
   Possibly New York, 1841 – before 1847
   Adams Township, Allen County, Indiana, [1847] – before 1860

Education: Could read and write.
Occupation: Farmer
Religious Affiliation: Roman Catholic

Comments:
Joseph Allgire followed his siblings to the United States in 1841. He may have spent some time in New York before moving to Allen County, Indiana. His parents and younger sister and brother came to Indiana within a few years of his arrival. Joseph and his brothers purchased adjoining land and farmed together. Joseph married Sophia Frederick in Allen County in 1847. Sophia was born of unknown parents about 1820 in Pennsylvania. The couple had two sons and two daughters, all born in Allen County, Indiana. Joseph moved his family to Ste. Genevieve County, Missouri shortly before the Civil War began, but his siblings chose to remain in Indiana. He reportedly died some time in 1861 in Ste. Genevieve County. Sophia remained in Ste. Genevieve County with her children but by 1880, she had either died or moved away. No further information has been found on her after the 1870 census of Ste. Genevieve County.

John Amsler Family
European Origin: Switzerland
Family:
Father: Unknown
Mother: Unknown
   Child:
*   i.   John, born about 1845 in Switzerland. [See sketch below.]

Immigration:
Arrived some time before October 1874 marriage aboard an unknown vessel:
    Amsler, John

Biographical:
Husband: John Amsler
   Birth – About 1845 in Switzerland.
   Death/Burial – 25 August 1895 in Ste. Genevieve County, Missouri. He was buried on the family farm in Ste. Genevieve County, Missouri.
Wife: Louise Roth, daughter of Christian Roth and Genevieve Huck [See Christian Roth sketch.]
   Birth – 3 August 1848 in Missouri.
   Marriage – 8 October 1874 in Zell, Ste. Genevieve County, Missouri. [Possibly the sanctification of an earlier, secular marriage.]
   Death/Burial – 1 April 1919 in St. Louis, Missouri. She was buried in the Calvary Cemetery in St. Louis, Missouri.
Children:
   i. Mary Louise, born 27 March 1871 in Ste. Genevieve County, Missouri. She married Joseph Klein on 26 August 1895 in Ste. Genevieve, at about the same time her father died. Joseph was the son of Anton Klein and Catherina Kohm, born 23 October 1861 in Ste. Genevieve County. He was the widower of Emerencia "Emma" Herzog who had died on 7 May 1895, leaving her husband with two sons and a baby daughter. Emma was the daughter of Bonaventure Herzog and Apollonia Schmiederer, born 10 January 1867 in Ste. Genevieve County, Missouri. Joseph and Mary Louise lived in Ste. Genevieve County for the first few years of their lives together and then moved south to Perry County, Missouri, where Joseph bought a farm. By 1920, the family had moved to St. Louis, Missouri where Joseph was an assembly line worker in an auto factory. The couple had three sons and five daughters. Joseph died of a cerebral hemorrhage on 17 August 1929 in St. Louis, Missouri. He was buried in the Catholic Cemetery at St. Mary, Ste. Genevieve County, Missouri. After her husband's death, Mary remained in St. Louis. She died of heart disease on 23 December 1945 in St. Louis, Missouri. She was buried in the Calvary Cemetery in St. Louis, Missouri.
   ii. William John, born 25 July 1875 in Ste. Genevieve County, Missouri, He married Mary Anna Huber on 10 June 1902 in Zell, Ste. Genevieve County, Missouri. Mary was the daughter of

Andrew Huber and Agatha Harter, born 28 February 1874 in Ste. Genevieve County, Missouri. The couple moved to a farm in Perry County, Missouri where they raised their son and daughter. There may have been some marital conflict between them because when Mary died of tuberculosis on 9 October 1925 in St. Louis, her marital status on her death certificate indicated she was separated from her spouse. She was buried near her parents in the St. Joseph Cemetery in Zell, Ste. Genevieve County, Missouri. William remained in Perry County for the rest of his life. He died of a cerebral apoplexy on 18 April 1956 in Perryville, Perry County, Missouri. He was buried in the Mount Hope Cemetery in Perryville, Perry County, Missouri.

iii. Lorena Caroline, born 28 September 1881 in Ste. Genevieve County, Missouri. She married August William Joggerst on 13 August 1901 in Ste. Genevieve, County, Missouri. August was the son of Nicholas Joggerst and Wilhelmina Klein, born 5 August 1879 in Ste. Genevieve County, Missouri. August was a farmer. He and Lorena had seven sons and three daughters, of whom at least three sons died in infancy or early childhood. Lorena died on 16 July 1964 and August died on 3 April 1965, both in Ste. Genevieve County, Missouri. They were both buried in the Valle Spring Cemetery in Ste. Genevieve, Ste. Genevieve County, Missouri.

iv. Baby boy, stillborn on 2 July 1892 in Ste. Genevieve County, Missouri. No issue.

v. Josephine G., born 25 July 1894 in Ste. Genevieve County, Missouri. She lived in St. Louis, Missouri with her mother and supported them both by working as a telephone operator. She married a man named Henry B. Bockers on 5 November 1919 in Franklin County, Missouri. They had one son and one daughter. Henry died before April 1940. Josephine appears to have moved back to Ste. Genevieve County and was a resident of River aux Vases in 1955. No further information.

U.S. residence prior to Ste. Genevieve County, Missouri:
Possibly St. Louis, Missouri

Education: Could read and write
Occupation: Carpenter
Religious Affiliation: John's wife and children were all Roman Catholic, but he may have been Jewish [information from birth and death record of a stillborn son on 2 July 1892 in Ste. Genevieve County, Missouri.]
Comments:
John Amsler was born in Switzerland about 1845, but nothing is known of his ancestry or when he came to the United States. There were several Swiss Amsler families that settled in St. Louis, Missouri between 1850 and 1870 and there were several John Amslers in those families who were about the same age as the person who settled in Ste. Genevieve County, Missouri. However, they have not yet been sorted out. The John Amsler who settled in Ste. Genevieve County arrived in the area some time between 1870 and 8 October 1874 when he married Louise Roth at Zell, Ste. Genevieve County. The family lived in Beauvais Township where John worked as a carpenter and farmed. The couple had two sons and three daughters, of whom one son was stillborn. On Sunday afternoon, 25 August 1895, John left the house with a rifle and a jug of cider, merely saying, "goodbye" as he went out. It wasn't unusual for him to go out and stay away for several days, so the family didn't miss him for several days. On Thursday morning, Louise found his body lying against a tree in the back pasture of their farm. A coroner's jury determined that he had apparently committed suicide by shooting himself in the head. He was a man with a pleasant disposition, but was known to have been subject to fits of "melancholy." It was believed that he had been in one of those low moods when he died. Since John had mentioned several times that he wished to be buried on the hill near the spot where he had died, the family buried him there. Louise remained on the farm until 1911 when she sold it and moved to St. Louis, Missouri with her youngest daughter. Louise died of valvular heart disease on 1 April 1919 in St. Louis, Missouri. She was buried in Calvary Cemetery in St. Louis, Missouri.

Andreas A. "Andrew" Anderson Family

Surname Variation: Andersen
European Origin: Flensburg, Schleswig-Holstein, Denmark [part of present-day Germany]
Family:
Father: Unknown
Mother: Unknown
    Child:
*   i.   Andreas, born 14 March 1821 in Flensburg, Schleswig-Holstein, Denmark. [part of present-day Germany] [See sketch below.]

Immigration:
Arrived before March 1848 aboard an unknown vessel:
    Anderson, Andreas

Biographical:
Husband: Andreas A. "Andrew" Anderson
    Birth – 14 March 1821 in Flensburg, Schleswig-Holstein, Denmark [part of present-day Germany].
    Death/Burial – 12 May 1877 in Ste. Genevieve, Ste. Genevieve County, Missouri. He was buried in the Memorial Cemetery in Ste. Genevieve, Ste. Genevieve County, Missouri.
Wife: Amelia Sophia Schoenfeld, daughter of Karl Friedrich Schönfeld and Dorothea Lutz [See William Schoenfeld sketch.]
    Birth – 9 July 1827, Kandern, Lörrach, Baden, Germany.
    1) Marriage – 4 February 1853 in St. Louis, Missouri to Andreas "Andrew" Anderson.
    2) Marriage – 14 October 1879 in Ste. Genevieve, Ste. Genevieve County, Missouri to Charles Henry Biel as his second wife. [See Charles Henry Biel sketch.]
    Death/Burial – 16 October 1888 in Ste. Genevieve, Ste. Genevieve County, Missouri. She was buried in the Lutheran Cemetery in Ste. Genevieve, Ste. Genevieve County, Missouri.

There were no children born to Andrew Anderson and Amelia Schoenfeld.

U.S. residence prior to Ste. Genevieve County, Missouri:
    New York City, New York [from Declaration of Intent to become a citizen]

Naturalization:

Name	Declaration	Naturalization	Origin
Anderson, Andrew	2 March 1848 New York City, NY	22 May 1852 Ste. Genevieve Co.	Denmark

Education: He could read and write.
Occupation: Farmer and Grocer
Religious Affiliation: Lutheran
Political Affiliation and/or any Offices Held:
    Collector, Ste. Genevieve County, Missouri
    Sheriff, Ste. Genevieve County, Missouri, 1867
Comments:
Andreas A. "Andrew" Anderson came to the United States some time before March 1848 and appears to have lived in New York City, New York for a time before he came to Missouri. Andrew was living in the household of Henry Wilder in Ste. Genevieve, Missouri in September 1850. In [December?] 1852 Amelia Schoenfeld arrived in the United States with two sisters, landing at New Orleans and traveling by river to St. Louis, Missouri. Andrew and Amelia were married in St. Louis on 4 February 1853. They came directly to Ste. Genevieve County, Missouri and took up residence on a farm near the small village of New Bremen. In 1866 Andrew moved to the town of Ste. Genevieve and opened a hardware and grocery store on Main Street. He

was elected to serve terms as Collector and as Sheriff for Ste. Genevieve County. Amelia's nephew, Frank Jenny, lived in the Anderson household for a short time until he began working as a wagon maker. Emily Hagan, an orphan and Frank's future wife, was also living in the Anderson household. Andrew died of consumption in 1877. Until she married Charles Henry Biel, Sophia continued to successfully run the grocery business that Andrew had established. After her marriage she continued to work in the store as an assistant to Charles. Amelia died from a "complication of diseases" on 16 October 1888. She was buried in the Lutheran Cemetery in Ste. Genevieve.

Andreas "Andrew" Armbruster Family

Surname Variations: Ambruster, Armbuster
European Origin: Sasbach, Achern, Baden, Germany and Lauf, Baden, Germany
Family:
Father: Bernard Armbruster, born 3 February 1772 in Sasbachwalden, Achern, Baden, Germany. He died on 8 June 1835 in Sasbach, Achern, Baden, Germany.
Mother: Maria Brigida Hauser, born 9 January 1769 in Sasbachwalden, Achern, Baden, Germany. She died on 8 June 1835 in Sasbach, Achern, Baden, Germany.
   Children:
       i. Maria Anna, born 10 June 1796 in Sasbach, Achern, Baden, Germany. She married Franz Joseph Raumschuh on 20 March 1817 in Sasbach. He was the son of Josef Raumschuh and Katharina Feist, born 16 March 1780 in Sasbach, [See Bernard Raumschuh sketch.]
† ii. Catherine, born 11 November 1798 in Sasbach, Achern, Baden, Germany. She married Franz Anton Baumann on 23 May 1821 in Sasbach. He was the son of Leonhard Baumann and Maria Anna Schnurr, born 17 September 1798 in Sasbach. [See Franz Anton Baumann sketch.]
       iii. Joseph, born 22 January 1802 in Sasbach, Achern, Baden, Germany. No further information.
       iv. Franz Michael, born 26 May 1806 in Sasbach, Achern, Baden, Germany. He died on 21 November 1814 in Sasbach. No issue.
* v. Andreas, born 9 November 1808 in Sasbach, Achern, Baden, Germany. [See sketch below.]
† vi. Ignatz, born 27 July 1812 in Sasbach, Achern, Baden, Germany. [See Ignatz Armbruster sketch.]

Immigration:
Arrived on 5 April 1852 from Le Havre, France to New Orleans aboard the *Old England*:
   Armbruster, André [Andreas], 43   Farmer   Germany
       Frisca [Franziska], 37
   Kust, Stephania, 15
   Armbruster, Wilhelm, 11
       Josephine, 7

Biographical:
Husband: Andreas "Andrew" Armbruster
   Birth – 9 November 1808 in Sasbach, Achern, Baden, Germany.
   Death/Burial – 13 March 1855 in Ste. Genevieve County, Missouri. He was buried in the St. Joseph Cemetery in Zell, Ste. Genevieve County, Missouri.
1) Wife: Franziska Nesselbosch, daughter of Stefan Nesselbosch and Maria Anna Ernst
   Birth – 5 August 1814 in Lauf, Baden, Germany.
   1) Marriage – 29 November 1834 in Lauf, Baden, Germany to Ignatz Kuest [aka Kist].
   2) Marriage – 6 September 1837 in Lauf, Baden, Germany to Andreas Armbruster.
   Death/Burial – 6 September 1853 in Ste. Genevieve County, Missouri. She was buried in the St. Joseph Cemetery in Zell, Ste. Genevieve County, Missouri.
   Children of Ignatz Kuest and Franziska Nesselbosch:
       i. Joseph Friedrich, born 17 March 1835 in Lauf, Baden, Germany. He died on 16 March 1837 in

Lauf. No issue.
  ii. Stephanie, born 14 April 1837 in Lauf, Baden, Germany. She came to the United States with her mother and stepfather in 1852. She married Johann "John" Boehle on 21 March 1854 in St. Louis, Missouri. John was the son of Lucas Boehle and Balbina Krummer, born 2 June 1828 in Windschläg, Baden, Germany. [See Lucas Boehle sketch.]

Children of Andreas Armbruster and Franziska Nesselbosch:
  i. Wilhelm Michael "William," born 9 February 1839 in Lauf, Baden, Germany. He came to the United States with his parents in 1852. He married Mary Eliza Kobel on 26 October 1865 in Missouri. Mary was the daughter of Jacob Kobel and Elizabeth Hermann, born 24 October 1847 in Switzerland. The couple lived in the northern part of Ste. Genevieve County, Missouri for the first few years of their life together. About 1873 they moved to Jefferson County, Missouri. They had two sons and three daughters. Mary died on 24 February 1879 and was buried in the Avoca Cemetery in DeSoto, Jefferson County, Missouri. William married Vianna Reynolds as his second wife on 3 June 1880 in Missouri. Vianna was the daughter of George Reynolds and Margaret Huff, born 23 March 1851 in Kentucky. William and Vianna had three sons and three daughters. Vianna died of mitral regurgitation on 17 May 1928 and William died of chronic pulmonary tuberculosis on 24 April 1929, both in Jefferson County, Missouri. They were both buried in the Mount Olive Cemetery in DeSoto, Jefferson County, Missouri.
  ii. Ludwig, born 6 October 1840 in Lauf, Baden, Germany. He died on 18 May 1841 in Lauf. No issue.
  iii. Josephine, born 20 February 1845 in Lauf, Baden, Germany. She came to the United States with her parents in 1852. Josephine was still a child when her parents died. She lived first with her uncle, Ignatius Armbruster, and then with the Joseph Sauers family where she worked as a domestic servant until her marriage. She married Benedict Huber on 12 February 1866 in Zell, Ste. Genevieve County, Missouri. Benedict was the son of Benedict Huber and Franziska Weiler, born 13 July 1841 in Ste. Genevieve County, Missouri. [See Benedict Huber sketch.]

2) Wife: Emerentia Scherer
  Birth – about 1822 [from age given in burial record] most likely in Germany.
  1) Marriage – 27 March 1854 in Zell, Ste. Genevieve County, Missouri to Andrew Armbruster.
  2) Marriage – 26 July 1855 in Zell, Ste. Genevieve to Bernard Jokerst. [See Franz Anton Jokerst sketch.]
  Death/Burial – 22 November 1858 in Ste. Genevieve County, Missouri. She was buried in the St. Joseph Cemetery in Zell, Ste. Genevieve County, Missouri.

There were no children born to Andrew Armbruster and Emerentia Scherer.

Land Patents:
Ste. Genevieve County, Missouri

Patentee	Issue Date	Land Office	Cert. No.	Serial No.	Twp	Rng	Sec	Acres
Armbruster, Andrew	1 Dec 1858	Jackson	16332	MO3850_.026	37-N	7-E	28	64.70

Occupation: Farmer
Religious Affiliation: Roman Catholic
Comments:
Andreas "Andrew" Armbruster came to the United States in 1852. He and his wife brought their four children with them. They landed in New Orleans and may have stayed briefly in St. Louis before settling in Ste. Genevieve County, Missouri near the German Settlement [present-day Zell]. Andrew's older sister, Catherine Armbruster Baumann, and her family had settled in Ste. Genevieve County about 1843. Franziska died on 6 September 1853 in Ste. Genevieve County, Missouri. She was buried in St. Joseph Cemetery in Zell. Andreas married Emerentia Scherer as his second wife on 27 March 1854 in Zell. Emerentia was born of unknown parents about 1822, most likely in Germany. The couple had no children together. Andreas died on 13 March

1855 in Ste. Genevieve County, Missouri. He was buried in the St. Joseph Cemetery in Zell. Emerentia married Bernard Jokerst as her second husband on 25 July 1855. Bernard was the widower of Anna Maria Hermann who had died between 1850 and July 1855. Bernard was the son of Franz Anton Jokerst and Anna Maria Siebert, born 28 March 1810 in Bohlsbach, Baden, Germany. He had five sons and four daughters from his first marriage. Bernard died on 29 December 1856 in Ste. Genevieve County about seven months before his only child with Emerentia was born. Emerentia died on 22 November 1858 and her baby died on 20 November 1860. They were both buried in St. Joseph Cemetery in Zell, Ste. Genevieve County, Missouri.

Ignatz "Ignatius" Armbruster Family

Surname Variations: Ambruster, Armbensher, Armbuster
European Origin: Sasbach, Achern, Baden, Germany and Ottersweier, Baden, Germany
Family:
Father: Bernard Armbruster, born 3 February 1772 in Sasbachwalden, Achern, Baden, Germany. He died on
    8 June 1835 in Sasbach, Achern, Baden, Germany.
Mother: Maria Brigida Hauser, born 9 January 1769 in Sasbachwalden, Achern, Baden, Germany. She died
    on 2 January 1837 in Sasbach, Achern, Baden, Germany.
    Children:

Note: For a comprehensive discussion of Bernard Armbruster's children see the Andreas "Andrew" Armbruster family sketch.

Immigration:
Arrived on 21 October 1852 from Le Havre, France to New Orleans aboard the *Old England*:
    Ambensher [Armbruster], Ignaz, 40   farmer   Baden
        Therese, 39
        Euphrosine, 13
        Mathias, 9
        Elisabeth, 8
        Caroline, 7
        Helena, 5
        Catherine, 3 ½
        Bernhard, 11 months

Biographical:
Husband: Ignatz "Ignatius" Armbruster
    Birth – 27 July 1812 in Sasbach, Achern, Baden, Germany.
    Death/Burial – 25 March 1881 in Ste. Genevieve County, Missouri.
1) Wife: Maria Anna Höss, daughter of Andreas Höss and Maria Elisabetha Ams
    Birth/Baptism – 25 May 1816 in Ottersweier, Baden, Germany. She was baptized on 26 May 1816 in the
        Catholic Church at Ottersweier.
    Marriage – 9 May 1838 in Sasbach, Achern, Baden, Germany.
    Death/Burial – 30 October 1846 in Ottersweier, Baden, Germany.
    Children:
        i. Euphrosine, born 11 February 1839 in Sasbach, Achern, Baden, Germany. She came to the
            United States with her father and stepmother in 1852. Euphrosine married Joseph Christian
            Willi on 23 November 1858 in Ste. Genevieve, Ste. Genevieve County, Missouri. Joseph was
            the son of Jacob Willi and Catherine Manchert, born 25 December 1834 in Canton Bern,
            Switzerland. [See Joseph Christian Willi sketch.]
        ii. Mathias "Matthew", born 23 February 1840 in Sasbach, Achern, Baden, Germany. He came to
            the United States with his father and stepmother in 1852. Matthew was a farmer. Matthew
            served during the Civil War in the 78th Enrolled Missouri Militia. After the war, Matthew
            married Christina Wieberg on 5 September 1865 in Ste. Genevieve, Ste. Genevieve County,

Missouri. Christina was the daughter of John Wieberg and Elisabeth Klassner, born about 1848 in Illinois. The couple had four sons and five daughters. Christina died of dropsy on 3 June 1885 in Ste. Genevieve County, Missouri. Matthew died of an apoplectic stroke on 11 July 1912 in Ste. Genevieve County, Missouri. They were both buried in the Valle Spring Cemetery in Ste. Genevieve, Ste. Genevieve County, Missouri.

   iii. Elisabeth, born 30 September 1841 in Ottersweier-Haft, Baden, Germany. She was baptized on 1 October 1841 in the Catholic Church at Ottersweier. Elisabeth came to the United States with her father and stepmother in 1852. Elisabeth married Benedict Bantz on 10 September 1860 in Ste. Genevieve, Ste. Genevieve County, Missouri. Benedict was the son of Florian Benz and Agatha Benz, born 21 March 1828 in Durbach, Baden, Germany. [See Benedict Bantz sketch.]

   iv. Caroline, born 15 January 1844 in Ottersweier-Haft, Baden, Germany. She was baptized on 16 January 1843 in the Catholic Church at Ottersweier. Caroline came to the United States with her father and stepmother in 1852. Caroline married Joseph Christian Willi as his second wife on 20 October 1867 in Ste. Genevieve, Ste. Genevieve County, Missouri. Joseph was the widower of Caroline's older sister, Euphrosine.[See Joseph Christian Willi sketch.]

   v. Bernhard, born 8 April 1845 in Ottersweier-Haft, Baden, Germany. He was baptized in the Catholic Church at Ottersweier on the same day he was born. Bernhard died on 9 November 1845 in Ottersweier. No issue.

   vi. Bernhard [twin], born 15 August 1846 in Ottersweier-Haft, Baden, Germany. He was baptized on 17 August 1846 in the Catholic Church at Ottersweier. Bernhard died on 27 December 1846 in Ottersweier. No issue.

   vii. Helena [twin], born 15 August 1846 in Ottersweier-Haft, Baden, Germany. She was baptized on 17 August 1846 in the Catholic Church at Ottersweier. She came to the United States with her father and stepmother in 1852. When she was in her late teens or early twenties, Helena moved to St. Louis to work as a domestic servant. She married Christian Stamm on 6 December 1870 in St. Louis, Missouri. Christian was born on 24 August 1843 in Switzerland. He had come to the United States about 1869. Christian was a leather tanner in a belt factory in St. Louis. He and Helena had three sons and three daughters, of whom one daughter died in infancy. Christian died on 21 June 1929 from shock after he fell and broke a femur in his leg and Helena died of apoplexy on 27 January 1937, both in St. Louis, Missouri. They were both buried in the Bethany Cemetery in Wellston, St. Louis County, Missouri.

2) Wife: Theresia Streule, daughter of Franz Xavier Streule and Johanna Huber
Birth – 31 January 1823 in Neusatz, Baden, Germany.
Marriage – 21 April 1847 in Ottersweier, Baden, Germany.
Death/Burial – 3 July 1877 in Ste. Genevieve County, Missouri. She was buried in the Memorial Cemetery in Ste. Genevieve, Ste. Genevieve County, Missouri.
Children:

   viii. Catherine Theresa, born 14 February 1849 in Ottersweier-Haft, Baden, Germany. She was baptized in the Catholic Church at Ottersweier on the day she was born. She came to the United States with her parents in 1852. She married George Adam Messenger on 6 August 1872 in Ste. Genevieve, Ste. Genevieve County, Missouri. George was the son of Georg Messenger and Catherine Grither, born 25 December 1841 in Baden, Germany. [See George Adam Messenger sketch.]

   ix. Bernard, born 23 June 1850 in Ottersweier-Haft, Baden, Germany. He was baptized on 25 June 1850 in the Catholic Church at Ottersweier. He came to the United States with his parents in 1852. Bernard may never have married. He remained on the farm that his father had bought in Ste. Genevieve County until at least the census of 1880. He seems to have disappeared after that. No further information at present.

   x. Louisa, born 11 February 1854 in Missouri. She married Severin Basler on 18 May 1875 in Ste. Genevieve, Ste. Genevieve County, Missouri. Severin was the son of Peter Basler and Helena

Sellinger, born 22 September 1851 in Ste. Genevieve County, Missouri. [See Peter Basler sketch.]
xi. Ignatius [aka Nicholas], born on 12 December 1857 in Missouri. He was baptized on 9 May 1858 in the Sts. Philip and James Catholic Church at River aux Vases, Ste. Genevieve County, Missouri. He married Anna Katherine Worley about 1887, probably in St. Louis, Missouri. Anna was the daughter of Jacob Worley and Eliza Ann Kirklin, born in May 1863 in Missouri. Ignatius [or Nicholas as he was later known] was a baker in Kansas City, Wyandotte County, Kansas. He and his wife had three sons, all born in Kansas. Nicholas died in 1911 and Anna died in 1949, both in Kansas. They were both buried in the Mount Hope Cemetery in Kansas City, Wyandotte County, Kansas.
xii. Joseph, born on 15 December 1862 in Ste. Genevieve County, Missouri. He was baptized on 17 June 1863 in the Ste. Genevieve Catholic Church in Ste. Genevieve, Ste. Genevieve County, Missouri. Joseph died on 6 September 1864 in Ste. Genevieve County, Missouri. No issue.
xiii. Mary Theresia, born 19 July 1865 in Ste. Genevieve County, Missouri. She was baptized on 6 October 1865 in the Ste. Genevieve Catholic Church in Ste. Genevieve, Ste. Genevieve County, Missouri. No further information has been found on Mary after she was enumerated in her father's household in Ste. Genevieve County in the 1880 census.

Military:
Served in the U.S. Civil War for the Union:
Private, Company C, 78th Enrolled Missouri Militia
   Mathew Armbruster enlisted 4 October 1862 in Ste. Genevieve, Missouri. He was promoted to corporal on 30 April 1864. He was ordered into active service on 16 October 1864. He was relieved from duty on 25 November 1864 after having served 41 days of actual service. [A note on his service card indicates that he deserted this unit on 2 September 1863 at Cape Girardeau, Missouri.]
Company A, 8th Provisional Regiment Enrolled Missouri Militia
   Matthew Armbruster was temporarily assigned to active duty in this unit on 10 August 1863 at Ste. Genevieve.

Occupation: Farmer
Religious Affiliation: Roman Catholic
Comments:
Ignatius Armbruster and his family followed his older brother, Andreas, to the United States in late 1852. They appear to have gone directly to Ste. Genevieve County, Missouri. Their older sister, Catherine Armbruster Baumann and her family had settled in Ste. Genevieve County about 1843. Ignatius and his family lived for a short time near present-day River aux Vases, before moving closer to what is now the town of St. Mary. Ignatius worked as a farmer. His wife, Theresa, died on 3 July 1877 and was buried in the Memorial Cemetery in Ste. Genevieve, Ste. Genevieve County, Missouri. Ignatius lived with his unmarried son, Bernard, and continued to farm for the remainder of his life. He died on 25 March 1881 and was also buried in the Memorial Cemetery in Ste. Genevieve, Ste. Genevieve County, Missouri.

Joseph Armbruster Family
Surname Variations: Ambruster, Armbuster, Armbrester
European Origin: Baden, Germany
Family:
Father: Unknown
Mother: Unknown
   Child:
*   i.   Joseph, born about 1824 in Baden, Germany. [See sketch below.]

Immigration:
Arrived on 2 December 1848 from Le Havre, France to New Orleans aboard the *Ferriere*:
  Ambruster [Armbruster], Joseph, 23   Farmer   Baden

Biographical:
Husband: Joseph Armbruster
  Birth – about 1824 in Baden, Germany.
  Death/Burial – 14 December 1880 in Ste. Genevieve County, Missouri.
Wife: Catherine Eichenlaub, daughter of Gervais Eichenlaub and Catherine Jokerst. [See Gervais Eichenlaub sketch.]
  Birth – 5 November 1837 in Zell, Ste. Genevieve County, Missouri.
  Marriage – 2 August 1853 in Ste. Genevieve County, Missouri.
  Death/Burial – after June 1900 most likely in Ste. Genevieve County, Missouri.
Children:
  i. Mary, born about 1859 in Missouri. She died before April 1865 in Missouri. No issue.
  ii. Philippine, born about 1861 in Missouri. She married John Holst on 6 February 1879 in Ste. Genevieve County, Missouri. John was the son of Johann Friedrich Holst and Catharina Maria Grimm born 29 December 1852 in Gross Sittensen, Hannover, Germany. [See John Holst sketch.]
  iii. Mary, born 7 April 1865 in Ste. Genevieve County, Missouri. She married John Holst as his second wife on 30 December 1882 in Ste. Genevieve County, Missouri. John was the widower of Mary's sister, Philippine. [See John Holst sketch.]
  iv. Nicholas, born 6 December 1867 in Ste. Genevieve County, Missouri. He was baptized on 5 January 1868 in St. Philomena's Catholic Church in Bloomsdale, Ste. Genevieve County, Missouri. Nicholas died of consumption at the age of twenty-six on 15 February 1893 in Ste. Genevieve County, Missouri. He had been bedridden for the last two months of his life. He never married and had no issue.
  v. John, born 26 June 1871 in Ste. Genevieve County, Missouri. He was baptized on 26 August 1871 in Ste. Genevieve Catholic Church in Ste. Genevieve, Ste. Genevieve County, Missouri. John was a farmer in Ste. Genevieve County with his brother Henry. He married Odelia "Delia" Bieser [aka Delia Basler] on 13 November 1900 in French Village, St. Francois County, Missouri. Delia was the daughter of Joseph Bieser and Maria Anna Bransch, born 2 January 1869 in Ste. Genevieve County, Missouri. Her father died when she was very young and she was raised by Peter Basler and his wife, Victoria Ritter. John and Delia had no children of their own, but adopted a boy named Anton. John died of heart disease on 9 October 1937 in Ste. Genevieve County, Missouri. Delia died of a heart attack on 2 September 1941 in St. Louis, Missouri. They were both buried in St. Philomena's Cemetery in Bloomsdale, Ste. Genevieve County, Missouri.
  vi. Henry, born 12 October 1874 in Ste. Genevieve County, Missouri. He was baptized on 11 April 1875 in St. Philomena's Catholic Church in Bloomsdale, Ste. Genevieve County, Missouri. Henry worked for the Frisco Railroad as a section hand. He married Josephine Maria Eva Basler on 18 November 1902 in Ste. Genevieve County, Missouri. Josephine was the daughter of Peter Basler and Victoria Ritter, born 23 April 1883 in Ste. Genevieve County. The couple had one son and one daughter. Henry died of a cerebral hemorrhage on 1 May 1949 in Ste. Genevieve County, Missouri. Josephine died of thyroid cancer on 6 September 1959 in St. Louis, Missouri. They were both buried in the Valle Spring Cemetery in Ste. Genevieve, Ste. Genevieve County, Missouri.
  vii. William, born 31 January 1879 in Ste. Genevieve County, Missouri. He married Alice M. Aubuchon on 1 May 1905 in Ste. Genevieve County. Alice was the daughter of Leo Aubuchon and Nora E. Carron, born 10 May 1885 in Ste. Genevieve County, Missouri. The couple lived with Alice's maternal grandparents while William worked their land as a farm hand. The couple

had two sons and one daughter. William died of tuberculosis meningitis on 20 December 1919. He was buried in the St. Philomena's Cemetery in Bloomsdale, Ste. Genevieve County, Missouri. Alice married William A. Hicks of Pemiscot County, Missouri on 27 February 1922 in Ste. Genevieve County. William was born about 1891 in Missouri. The couple moved to Festus, Jefferson County, Missouri where William worked as a watchman in a railroad yard. William appears to have died some time between 1930 and 1940 although no record of his death has been found. He did not appear in the 1940 census with Alice who was living with her daughter and son-in-law in Festus. Alice died on 27 December 1959 in Red Bud, Randolph County, Illinois. She was buried in St. Philomena's Cemetery in Bloomsdale, Ste. Genevieve County, Missouri beside her first husband. Her son Lucas, who reportedly hadn't liked his stepfather, had the surname "Armbruster" carved on his mother's headstone.

Land Patents:
Ste. Genevieve County, Missouri

Patentee	Issue Date	Land Office	Cert. No.	Serial No.	Twp	Rng	Sec	Acres
Armbruster, Joseph	2 May 1859	St. Louis	25545	MO1100 .262	39-N	7-E	19	165.00
Armbruster, Joseph	2 May 1859	St. Louis	30558	MO1100 .310	39-N	7-E	30	121.78

Naturalization:

Name	Declaration	Naturalization	Origin
Armbruster, Joseph	5 May 1851	21 May 1853 Ste. Genevieve Co.	Baden

Occupation: Farmer
Religious Affiliation: Roman Catholic
Comments:
Joseph Armbruster was born about 1824 in Baden, Germany of unknown parents. He came to the United States before 1850 and settled in Ste. Genevieve County, Missouri, In 1850 he was living in the household of his future father-in-law, working as a farm laborer. He is definitely *not* the Joseph Armbruster who was the son of Melchior Armbruster and Magdalena Walter, born 10 February 1827 in Berghaupten amt Offenburg, Baden, Germany, as some have stated. That Joseph remained in Germany and married Catharina Lienhard on 10 March 1853 in Berghaupten and had children with her. Joseph Armbruster of Ste. Genevieve County, Missouri married Catherine Eichenlaub on 2 August 1853 in Ste. Genevieve County, Missouri. Joseph was a farmer in Ste. Genevieve County. He and his wife had four sons and three daughters, all born in Ste. Genevieve County. Joseph died on 14 December 1880 in Ste. Genevieve County. Catherine stayed on the farm with her sons John and Henry after her husband died. She died some time after June 1900, most likely in Ste. Genevieve County, Missouri.

Ludwig "Louis" Armbruster Family
Surname Variations: Ambruster
European Origin: Gengenbach, Baden, Germany
Family:
Father: Gottfried Boniface Armbruster, born 28 May 1783 in Gengenbach, Baden, Germany.
Mother: Maria Anna Elisabetha Faessler, born 10 June 1791 in Gengenbach, Baden, Germany.
  Children:
  i. Gottfried, born and baptized on 16 April 1810 in the Catholic Church at Gengenbach, Baden, Germany. He died before July 1815. No issue.
  ii. Johanna, born 21 July 1811 and baptized 22 July 1811 in the Catholic Church at Gengenbach, Baden, Germany. No further information.
  iii. Theresia, born 29 October 1813 and baptized on 30 October 1813 in the Catholic Church at Gengenbach, Baden, Germany. No further information.
  iv. Gottfried, born 24 July 1815 and baptized on 25 July 1815 in the Catholic Church at

Gengenbach, Baden, Germany. He married Amalie Bruederlie on 27 January 1851 at Gengenbach. Amalie was the daughter of Martin Bruederlie and Theresia Wussler, born 26 July 1825. The couple had at least one son and one daughter, both born in Gengenbach. No further information.
- v. Georg, born and baptized 8 September 1817 in the Catholic Church at Gengenbach, Baden, Germany. No further information.
- vi. Franz Xavier, born and baptized on 1 December 1819 in the Catholic Church at Gengenbach, Baden, Germany.
- *vii. Ludwig "Louis", born and baptized 22 August 1822 in the Catholic Church at Gengenbach, Baden, Germany. [See sketch below.]
- viii. Johann Baptist, born 12 September 1824 and baptized on 13 September 1824 in the Catholic Church at Gengenbach, Baden, Germany. He married Genovefa Ganther on 31 January 1853 in Gengenbach. Genovefa was the daughter of Michael Ganther and Regina Heid, born 1 January 1827. The couple had at least two sons and two daughters, all born in Gengenbach. No further information.

Immigration:
Arrived on 29 January 1852 from Le Havre, France to New Orleans aboard the *Sarah Parrington*:
- Armbruster, Elisabeth [first name indexed as Magdaley], 56
- Felicite, 33
- Ludwig, 30
- Kunigunde, 27
- Elisabeth, 25
- Francisca, 5
- Joseph, 4

Biographical:
Husband: Ludwig "Louis" Armbruster
- Birth/Baptism – born and baptized 22 August 1822 in the Catholic Church at Gengenbach, Baden, Germany.
- Death/Burial – 15 August 1884 in Ste. Genevieve, Ste. Genevieve County, Missouri. He was buried in the Valle Spring Cemetery in Ste. Genevieve, Ste. Genevieve County, Missouri.

Child of Louis Armbruster and _____:
- i. Joseph, born about 1848 in Germany. The last mention of him found in the records in Ste. Genevieve County, Missouri is his father's obituary in 1884. No further information.

Wife: Euphrosine Siefert, daughter of Johannes Peter Siefert and Catherine Anastasia Fautz
- Birth – 31 March 1825 in Reichenbach, Baden, Germany.
- Marriage – 17 April 1854 in Zell, Ste. Genevieve County, Missouri.
- Death/Burial – 18 July 1902 in Ste. Genevieve, Ste. Genevieve County, Missouri. She was buried in the Valle Spring Cemetery in Ste. Genevieve, Ste. Genevieve County, Missouri.
- Children:
  - ii. Henry, born 9 February 1855 in Ste. Genevieve County, Missouri. He was baptized on 20 May 1855 in the Ste. Genevieve Catholic Church in Ste. Genevieve, Ste. Genevieve County, Missouri. He was a farmer. He was married in River aux Vases, Ste. Genevieve County, Missouri on 23 October 1876 to Theresa Siebert, widow of Joseph Eichenlaub. Joseph died on 15 November 1875 in Ozora, Ste. Genevieve County. [See Gervais Eichenlaub sketch.] Theresa was the daughter of Henry Siebert and Mary Ann Sucher, born 23 September 1846 in Ste. Genevieve County, Missouri. Henry and Theresa had one son and one daughter. Theresa died on 8 August 1907 in Ste. Genevieve County, Missouri. Henry died of a crushed skull on

31 May 1917 when he was hit by flying debris during a tornado just south of the city of Ste. Genevieve. They were both buried in the Valle Spring Cemetery in Ste. Genevieve, Ste. Genevieve County, Missouri.

iii. Wilhelmina, born 23 October 1856 in Ste. Genevieve County, Missouri. She married Wilhelm "William" Schaaf on 21 May 1877 at River aux Vases, Ste. Genevieve County, Missouri. He was the son of Wolfgang Schaaf and Magdalena Schmiederer, born 25 March 1838 in Önsbach, Baden, Germany. [See William Schaaf sketch.] Wilhelmina married Francis Xavier Eckenfels as her second husband on 7 June 1880 in Ste. Genevieve County, Missouri. Xavier was the son of Severin Eckenfels and Catharina Kiefer, born on 2 January 1853 in Ste. Genevieve County, Missouri. [See Severin Eckenfels sketch.]

iv. Rosine, born 7 August 1859 in Ste. Genevieve County, Missouri. She married Jacob Roth on 6 April 1880 in Ste. Genevieve County, Missouri. Jacob was the son of George Roth and Johanna Roth, born 4 January 1854 in Buffalo, Erie County, New York. [See George Roth sketch.]

v. Charles William, born 5 April 1863 in Ste. Genevieve County, Missouri. He married Josephine Mary Siebert on 13 January 1885 in Ste. Genevieve. She was the daughter of Henry Siebert and Barbara Eichenlaub, born 26 December 1867 in Ste. Genevieve County, Missouri. Charles was a farmer and blacksmith and owned farms in both Ste. Genevieve and Perry Counties in Missouri. Six sons and three daughters were born to this couple, of whom at least one son and two daughters died young. The family moved back to Ste. Genevieve County when Charles retired. He died of bulbar paralysis on 18 January 1937 in St. Mary, Ste. Genevieve County, Missouri. He was buried in the St. Mary's Catholic Cemetery in St. Mary, Ste. Genevieve County, Missouri. Josephine died of congestive heart failure on 19 April 1959 in Ste. Genevieve County, Missouri. She was buried in the Valle Spring Cemetery in Ste. Genevieve, Ste. Genevieve County, Missouri.

vi. Amelia, born 26 March 1866 in Ste. Genevieve, Ste. Genevieve County, Missouri. She was baptized on 22 April 1866 in the Ste. Genevieve Catholic Church in Ste. Genevieve, Ste. Genevieve County, Missouri . Amelia died on 19 January 1867 and was buried in the Memorial Cemetery in Ste. Genevieve, Ste. Genevieve County, Missouri. No issue.

vii. Anthony, born 8 February 1868 in Ste. Genevieve, Ste. Genevieve County, Missouri. He was baptized on 20 February 1868 in the Ste. Genevieve Catholic Church in Ste. Genevieve, Ste. Genevieve County, Missouri. He died on 20 February 1868 and was buried in the Memorial Cemetery in Ste. Genevieve, Ste. Genevieve County, Missouri. No issue.

U.S. residence prior to Ste. Genevieve County, Missouri:
Possibly Alton, Madison County, Illinois
St. Louis, Missouri

Naturalization:

Name	Declaration	Naturalization	Origin
Armbruster, Louis		6 May 1859 Ste. Genevieve Co.	Baden

Military:
Served in the U.S. Civil War for the Union:
Private, Company G, 78th Enrolled Missouri Militia
Louis Armbruster enlisted 30 April 1864 in Ste. Genevieve County, Missouri. He was ordered into active service on 16 October 1864. He was relieved from duty on 25 November 1864 after having served 41 days of actual service.

Occupation: Farmer / Blacksmith
Religious Affiliation: Roman Catholic

Comments:
Ludwig "Louis" Armbruster was born in Gengenbach, Baden, Germany. When he came to the United States, he appears to have traveled as part of a family group. Although no record has been found, it is possible that Louis was married and had children before he left Germany. In both the 1860 and 1870 census in Ste. Genevieve, there is a Joseph Armbruster, born about 1848 in Germany living in Louis Armbruster's household. This Joseph may be the four-year-old boy who traveled with him aboard the *Sarah Parrington*. None of the other members of the family group from the ship's manifest appear on any records in Ste. Genevieve County, Missouri. It is said that Louis went first to Alton, Madison County, Illinois and then to St. Louis, Missouri before he settled in Ste. Genevieve County, Missouri. It is possible that he was escorting relatives to other locations in the United States. In any event, after 1870 the only mention of Joseph Armbruster is in Louis' 1884 death notice as being one of his children, but no location is given for him. Louis and his wife appear to have led quiet, productive lives in Ste. Genevieve County. After Louis died, Euphrosine lived with her daughter Wilhelmina until her own death in 1902. Both Louis and Euphrosine were buried in the Valle Spring Cemetery in Ste. Genevieve, Ste. Genevieve County, Missouri.

Michael Arnold Family

Surname Variations: None
European Origin: [Reistenhausen-Collenberg], Bavaria, Germany
Family:
Father: Joseph Arnold, born about 1790 in Reistenhausen-Collenberg, Bavaria, Germany. He died on 12 June 1852 in Reistenhausen.
Mother: Magdalena Keller, born about 1795 in Bavaria, Germany. She died about 1823 in Germany.
   Children:
*   i.   Michael, born 25 April 1818 in Reistenhausen-Collenberg, Bavaria, Germany. [See sketch below.]
       ii. Sophia, born 9 September 1823 in Reistenhausen-Collenberg, Bavaria, Germany. She married Franz Joseph Arnold on 3 October 1847 in Resitenhausen. Franz was the son of Joseph Anton Arnold and Susan Ulrich, born 28 November 1822 in Reistenhausen. The couple had at least one son who came to New York in 1874, and possibly other children. No further information.

Immigration:
Arrived on 31 March 1852 from Le Havre, France to New Orleans aboard the *Amelia*:
   Arnold, Michel, 33
      Therese, 30
      Antoinette, 8
      Anna Marie, 4

Biographical:
Husband: Michael Arnold
   Birth – 25 April 1818 at [Reistenhausen-Collenberg], Bavaria, Germany.
   Death/Burial – 18 January 1887 in Ste. Genevieve County, Missouri. He was buried in the Valle Spring Cemetery in Ste. Genevieve, Ste. Genevieve County, Missouri.
Wife: Theresia Keller, daughter of Joseph Keller and Magdalena [Keller?]
   Birth – 15 August 1821 in Bavaria, Germany.
   Marriage – 15 June 1843 in Bavaria, Germany.
   Death/Burial – 12 October 1896 in St. Louis, Missouri. She was buried in the Valle Spring Cemetery in Ste. Genevieve, Ste. Genevieve County, Missouri.
   Children:
      i.   Maria Antoinette, born July 1844 in Bavaria, Germany. She married Francis Stocker on 24 February 1868 in Ste. Genevieve, Ste. Genevieve County, Missouri. Francis was the son of Andreas "Andrew" Stocker and Maria Ann _____, born about 1844 in France. Andrew farmed

with his father in Ste. Genevieve County, Missouri. The couple had three sons. Francis died on 8 July 1872 in Ste. Genevieve County, Missouri and was buried in Memorial Cemetery in Ste. Genevieve, Ste. Genevieve County, Missouri. His youngest son was born posthumously the following November and died at the age of eleven months in 1873. Antoinette married Gottfried Basler as her second husband on 27 May 1873 in Ste. Genevieve. Gottfried was the son of Peter Basler and Helena Sellinger, born 13 January 1850 in Ste. Genevieve County, Missouri. [See Peter Basler sketch.]

ii. Maria Anna [aka Nancy], born 3 October 1845 in Bavaria, Germany. Maria married Charles C. Kern on 8 August 1870 in Ste. Genevieve County, Missouri. Charles was the son of John Dominic Kern and Regina Kettinger, born 12 December 1844 in Ste. Genevieve County, Missouri. [See John Dominic Kern sketch.]

iii. Cornelius, born 2 September 1852 in Ste. Genevieve County, Missouri. He married Sophia Basler on 10 November 1874 in Ste. Genevieve County. Sophia was the daughter of Peter Basler and Helena Sellinger, born 15 February 1853 in Ste. Genevieve County, Missouri. For the first years of their married life, the couple remained in Ste. Genevieve County where Cornelius owned a farm. Sophia's widowed father lived with them and helped work the land. In the late 1880s, the family moved to Rawlins County, Kansas, but remained there for only a couple of years. By 1890, the family had moved to Indian Territory [present-day Oklahoma]. The couple had three sons and four daughters. Sophia died on 3 March 1905 in Norman, Cleveland County, Oklahoma. She was buried in the St. Joseph's Catholic Cemetery in Norman. After his wife died, Cornelius lived in Tuttle, Grady County, Oklahoma with his youngest son and daughter, helping his son run his farm. Later, Cornelius moved to Canadian County where he lived with his daughter Lizzie until his death. Cornelius died on 29 December 1927 in El Reno, Canadian County, Oklahoma. He was buried in the St. Joseph's Catholic Cemetery in Norman, Cleveland County, Oklahoma beside his wife.

iv. Joseph, born 16 April 1856 in Ste. Genevieve County, Missouri. Joseph was a farmer. He married Juliana Guethle on 17 September 1878 in Ste. Genevieve, Ste. Genevieve County, Missouri. Juliana was the daughter of Johann "John" Guethle and Cecilia Siebert, born 12 February 1859 in St. Louis, Missouri. The couple had eight sons and two daughters. About 1898, Joseph and Juliana moved to St. Clair County, Illinois. Their oldest daughter and her children lived with them while her husband traveled for his job. Joseph died of dropsy on 28 May 1918 and Juliana died of bowel cancer on 15 October 1925, both in St. Louis, Missouri. They were both buried in the St. Joseph's Cemetery in Freeburg, St. Clair County, Illinois.

v. John Michael, born 13 August 1858 in Ste. Genevieve County, Missouri. John was a farmer in Ste. Genevieve County, Missouri. He married Wilhelmina Basler on 25 May 1880 in Ste. Genevieve County, Missouri. Wilhelmina was the daughter of Peter Basler and Helena Sellinger, born 23 September 1856 in Ste. Genevieve County. The couple had one daughter who died in infancy. Wilhelmina died of heart disease complicated by her pregnancy on 16 February 1881, just two weeks after her daughter's birth. John married Theresia Friedman as his second wife. Theresia was the daughter of John Friedman and Sophia Sucher, born 24 August 1862 in Ste. Genevieve County, Missouri. The couple had four sons and five daughters, of whom two daughters died in infancy. John died of a cerebral hemorrhage on 23 March 1929 and Theresia died of gall bladder cancer on 6 August 1932, both in Ste. Genevieve County, Missouri. They were both buried in the Valle Spring Cemetery in Ste. Genevieve, Ste. Genevieve County, Missouri.

vi. Henry Francis, born 19 February 1862 in Ste. Genevieve County, Missouri. Henry was a farmer in Ste. Genevieve County, Missouri. He married Christina Friedman on 25 May 1885 in Ste. Genevieve. Christina was the daughter of John Friedman and Sophia Sucher, born on 28 September 1866 in Missouri. The couple had two sons and five daughters, of whom one son died in infancy and one daughter died in early childhood. Christina died of blood poisoning on 17 December 1898 in Ste. Genevieve County, Missouri. She was buried in the Valle Spring

Cemetery in Ste. Genevieve, Ste. Genevieve County, Missouri. After his wife's death, the three youngest children were cared for by relatives while Henry kept the three oldest children with him. Henry married Mary Catherine A. "Katie" Friedman as his second wife on 29 August 1899 in St. Mary, Ste. Genevieve County, Missouri. Katie was the younger sister of Henry's first wife, born 1 May 1876 in Ste. Genevieve County, Missouri. After the marriage, Henry's family was reunited. The couple had five sons and one daughter, of whom only the youngest three sons survived childhood. By the turn of the century, Henry wasn't earning enough money as a farmer to support his family. He took a job as a quarryman for the Peerless Lime Company and his sons later worked as laborers in the quarry. Katie died of pneumonia on 14 March 1917 in Ste. Genevieve County, Missouri. She was buried in the Sacred Heart Cemetery in Ozora, Ste. Genevieve County, Missouri. Henry fell and broke the femur of his right leg in July 1937. A few days later, on 31 July 1937, he died of apoplexy at his home in Ste. Genevieve County, Missouri. He was buried in the Valle Spring Cemetery in Ste. Genevieve, Ste. Genevieve County, Missouri.

Land Patents:
Ste. Genevieve County, Missouri

Patentee	Issue Date	Land Office	Cert. No.	Serial No.	Sec	Twp	Rng	Acres
Arnold, Michael	1 Feb 1873	Ironton	268	MO4270_.259	10	37-N	9-E	132.25

Naturalization:

Name	Declaration	Naturalization	Origin
Arnold, Michael	20 May 1854	10 November 1860 Ste. Genevieve Co.	Bavaria

Education: Could read and write
Occupation: Baker and Farmer
Religious Affiliation: Roman Catholic
Comments:
Michael Arnold was born in the small village of Reistenhausen, Bavaria, Germany in 1818. [That village is now a part of the larger city of Collenberg.] He was married to Theresia Keller in 1843 and several of their children were born in Germany before he brought his family to the United States in the spring of 1852. The family settled in Ste. Genevieve County, Missouri where Michael worked as a baker in the town of Ste. Genevieve but he later purchased land a few miles outside the town of Ste. Genevieve and farmed. He and his wife are said to have had nine children; however, records for only four sons and two daughters have been found. It is likely that several children were born and died in Germany before the family emigrated. Although he became a citizen before the outbreak of the Civil War, it does not appear that Michael served in any military units during the conflict. He does appear to have been accident-prone. On one occasion in 1873, he broke his left hip and collar bone when he sleep-walked out of a second story window of a boarding house in Ste. Genevieve. About ten years later he broke his leg at the hip again when he fell from a chair that he was standing on to get something out of a high cupboard. Michael died unexpectedly on 18 January 1887 in Ste. Genevieve County, Missouri. He had been ill for a short time, but was not thought to be in danger of dying. The attending physician was "astonished when the demise of his patient was reported." Theresia died of liver cancer on 12 October 1896 in St. Louis, Missouri. They were both buried in the Valle Spring Cemetery in Ste. Genevieve, Ste. Genevieve County, Missouri.

Ignatius Auer Family

Surname Variations: Our
European Origin: Austria
Family:
Father: Georg Auer, born about 1810 in Austria. He most likely died in Missouri after November 1863.
Mother: Theresia Strobe, born about 1820 in Austria. She died on 31 March 1859 in Ste. Genevieve County, Missouri. She was buried in the St. Philomena's Cemetery in Bloomsdale, Ste. Genevieve County, Missouri.
Children:
†   i.   Theresa, born about 1847 in Austria. She married Anton Vogt in Ste. Genevieve County, Missouri on 27 September 1865. No further information.
*   ii.   Ignatius, born in January 1849 in Austria. [See sketch below.]
    iii.   Anna, born 24 July 1857 in Ste. Genevieve County, Missouri. She was baptized on 4 August 1857 in St. Philomena's Catholic Church in Bloomsdale, Ste. Genevieve County. No further information.

Immigration:
Arrived on 14 January 1850 from Bremen, Germany to New Orleans aboard the *Leontine*:
    Auer, Georg, 42   Farmer   Oestreich [Austria]   Going to Texas
Arrived about 1854 [from 1900 and 1910 census] aboard an unknown vessel:
    Auer, Theresia
          Theresia
          Ignatius

Biographical:
Husband: Ignatius Auer
    Birth – in January 1849 in Austria.
    Death/Burial – Most likely in Randolph County, Illinois between 1920 and 1930.
Wife: Mary Wieberg, daughter of John Wieberg and Elisabeth Klassner [See John Weberg sketch.]
    Birth – August 1858 in Illinois.
    Marriage – 27 May 1879 in Ste. Genevieve, Ste. Genevieve County, Missouri
    Death/Burial – Most likely in Monroe County, Illinois after 1930.
    Children:
       i.   Elisabeth Helen "Lizzie", born in September 1879 in Ste. Genevieve County, Missouri. She married Lawrence Stirnaman on 30 April 1907 in Randolph County, Illinois. Lawrence was the son of Peter Stirnaman and Julia Pariset, born 29 June 1872 in Kaskaskia, Randolph County, Illinois. The couple had two sons and three daughters, all born in Randolph County. Lawrence died on 27 March 1949 and Lizzie died on 14 April 1971, both in Illinois. They were both buried in the St. Marys Catholic Cemetery in Chester, Randolph County, Illinois.
       ii.   Ignatius, born in August 1882 in Ste. Genevieve County, Missouri. He died on 26 August 1882 in Ste. Genevieve County when he was only a few days old. He was buried in the Valle Spring Cemetery in Ste. Genevieve, Ste. Genevieve County, Missouri. No issue.
       iii.   John Nicholas, born 28 September 1886 in Randolph County, Illinois. He married Olivia M. Rauch on 27 October 1908 in Randolph County, Illinois. Olivia was the daughter of Henry Rauch and Emily Phegley, born 21 July 1887 in Randolph County, Illinois. The couple had three sons and two daughters. John died in January 1977 and Olivia died in May 1985, both in Cape Girardeau County, Missouri.
       iv.   Mary, born in March 1889 in Randolph County, Illinois. She married Charles T. Kleinberg on 5 April 1910 in Randolph County, Illinois. Charles was the son of Andrew Kleinberg and Mary E. Marlen, born 15 December 1888 in Evansville, Randolph County, Illinois.
       v.   Theresa, born 18 January 1891 in Randolph County, Illinois. She married Julius William

Linnertz about 1921. Julius was the son of Anton Linnertz and _____, born on 4 August 1888 in Monroe County, Illinois. The couple had two sons and two daughters. Theresa died on 8 April 1964 and Julius died on 25 April 1965, both in Monroe County, Illinois. They were both buried in the St. Mary's Cemetery in Renault, Monroe County, Illinois.

U.S. residence other than Ste. Genevieve County, Missouri:
Texas
Brewerville, Randolph County, Illinois

Naturalization:

Name	Declaration	Naturalization	Origin
Auer, George	28 March 1857	5 November 1863 Ste. Genevieve Co.	Austria

Occupation: Farmer
Religious Affiliation: Roman Catholic

Comments:
Ignatius Auer is said to have come to the United States in 1854, most likely with his mother and sister. His father, Georg, had come earlier, intending to settle in Texas. However, the climate didn't agree with him, so he moved north to Missouri. By 1856, the family was settled in Ste. Genevieve County on a farm near the town of Bloomsdale. Georg's wife, Theresia, died on 31 March 1859 in Ste. Genevieve County, Missouri. She was buried in the St. Philomena's Cemetery in Bloomsdale, Ste. Genevieve County, Missouri. Georg died some time after November 1863, most likely in Ste. Genevieve County, Missouri. Ignatius married Mary Wieberg in Ste. Genevieve County in 1879. The couple had two sons and three daughters, of whom one son died in infancy. Ignatius moved his family across the Mississippi River to Randolph County, Illinois about 1884. They lived on a farm near Brewerville. Ignatius died some time after 1920, most likely in Randolph County. Mary lived the remainder of her life with her youngest daughter in Monroe County, Illinois. She died some time after 1930, most likely in Monroe County, Illinois.

B

Johann "John" Bach Family

Surname Variations: Back, Boch, Buck
European Origin: Württemberg, Germany
Family:
Father: Unknown
Mother: Unknown
   Child:
*   i.   John, born on 1 February 1819 in Württemberg, Germany. [See sketch below.]

Immigration:
Arrived before 1850 aboard an unknown vessel:
    Bach, John and wife Elisabeth _____

Biographical:
Husband: Johann "John" Bach
   Birth – 1 February 1819 in Württemberg, Germany.
   Death/Burial – 12 April 1892 in Perry County, Missouri. He was buried in the Catholic Cemetery in St. Mary, Ste. Genevieve County, Missouri.

1) Wife: Elisabeth "Elise" _____
   Birth – about 1815 in Germany.
   Marriage – in Germany?
   Death/Burial – about 1862, most likely in St. Louis, Missouri.

There do not appear to have been any children born to John Bach and Elise _____.

2) Wife: Wilhelmina Theresia Bangelmann, daughter of Heinrich Andreas Bangelmann and Johanna MariaTheresia Stock
   Birth – 15 December 1831 in Wolfenbüttel, Braunschweig [Brunswick], Germany.
   1) Marriage – to Martin PeterWengert. [See Martin Wengert sketch.]
   2) Marriage – about 1862 most likely in St. Louis, Missouri to Johann "John" Bach.
   Death/Burial – 12 April 1902 in Ste. Genevieve County, Missouri. She was buried in the Catholic Cemetery at St. Mary, Ste. Genevieve County, Missouri.
   Children:
      i.   Frances, born 3 September 1863 in St. Mary, Ste. Genevieve County, Missouri. In her early teens, she worked as a domestic servant in the home of Leon Bogy of St. Mary whose wife was ill. Frances' work took her to Kennebunkport, Maine where she met her future husband. She married Lowell Jacob Marshall on 17 June 1903 in Springvale, York County, Maine. Lowell was the son of Jacob Blake Marshall and Susan Day Alley, born 4 June 1874 in St. George, Knox County, Maine. He was working as a teamster when he met Frances, but shortly after their marriage, the couple moved to Santa Barbara, California. When they first arrived, both of them worked odd jobs to support themselves. Eventually they saved enough money to start a small lunch counter restaurant in Santa Barbara. The couple had one son. Lowell died on 8 May 1941 in Santa Barbara. After her husband's death, Frances moved to San Diego to be near her son. She died there on 15 March 1960.
      ii.   Sophia Friedricka, born 5 April 1867 in St. Mary, Ste. Genevieve County, Missouri. She married Franz Ignatius "Frank" Braun on 25 April 1895 in St. Louis, Missouri. Frank was the

son of Bernard Braun and Crescentia Schweigert, born 16 December 1862 in Ste. Genevieve County, Missouri. [See Bernard Braun sketch.]

iii. Theodore C., born 23 January 1871 Missouri. He was baptized on 19 June 1873 in the Immaculate Conception Catholic Church in St. Mary, Ste. Genevieve County, Missouri. Theodore was a farmer in Perry County, Missouri. He married Emma Rosina Graf on 9 June 1902 in St. Mary, Ste. Genevieve County. Emma was the daughter of Simon Graf and Maria Catherine Fitzkam, born 25 June 1879 in Ste. Genevieve County, Missouri. The couple had one son and three daughters. Theodore died of cerebral thrombosis complicated by diabetes on 20 November 1947 in Perry County, Missouri. Emma died on 28 July 1967 in Perry County, Missouri. They were both buried in the Catholic Cemetery at St. Mary, Ste. Genevieve County, Missouri.

U.S. residence prior to Ste. Genevieve County, Missouri:
St. Louis, Missouri

Naturalization:

Name	Declaration	Naturalization	Origin
Bach, John		7 July 1856 St. Louis, Missouri	Germany

Military:
Served in the U.S. Civil War for the Union:
Private, Company B, 1st Regiment U.S. Reserve Corps, Missouri Infantry
John Bach served from July 1861 to September 1862. Injury noted in 1890 census: "gravel incurred, grows worse all the time."

Occupation: Shoemaker and Farmer
Religious Affiliation: Roman Catholic
Comments:
Johann "John" Bach came to the United States from Germany before 1850 and settled in St. Louis, Missouri. He was married to Elisabeth "Elise" _____, most likely in Germany. The couple does not appear to have had any children. John worked as a shoemaker in St. Louis before the outbreak of the Civil War. He enlisted in the 1st Regiment U.S. Reserve Corps, Missouri Infantry, Company "B," as a private. In May 1861, the regiment took part in the Camp Jackson Affair just outside of St. Louis. John's company supported the Federal troops at Birds' Point, Missouri, directly across the River from Cairo, Illinois, from 29 July to 13 August 1862. He was mustered out on 6 October 1862. Some time between June 1860 and about 1862, John's wife died, probably in St. Louis, Missouri. He married Mrs. Wilhelmina Bangelmann Wengert as his second wife about 1862, most likely in St. Louis. Wilhelmina was the widow of Martin Wengert. She came to the United States in 1856 according to the 1900 census. Very little is known of Martin other than his name and that he was born in Germany. The couple had one son. Martin died between 1859 and 1862, most likely in Missouri. John and Wilhelmina Bach moved south to St. Mary, Ste. Genevieve County, Missouri shortly after they were married. John bought land and worked as a farmer for the rest of his life. Wilhelmina is said to have had six children, however, records have only been found for four, the one son with Martin Wengert and one son and two daughters with John Bach. John moved his family south to Perry County, Missouri after 1880. He died on 12 April 1892 in Perry County and was buried in the Catholic Cemetery at St. Mary, Ste. Genevieve County, Missouri. Wilhelmina lived with her son in Perry County after her husband's death. She later moved back to St. Mary to live with her daughter and her family. She died on 12 April 1902 in St. Mary, Ste. Genevieve County, Missouri. She was buried in the Catholic Cemetery at St. Mary, Ste. Genevieve County, Missouri.

Augustus Bachle Family

Surname Variations: Bächlé, Bachle, Bacle, Baechlé, Baechli, Bechle, Beckle, Beckly, Begley
European Origin: [Remetschweil amt Waldshut], Baden, Germany
Family:
Father: Conrad Bächlé
Mother: Walburga Apollonia Benz [aka Dentz]
   Children:
†   i.   Helena, born 27 March 1827 in Baden, Germany. She married Jacob Meyer on 27 April 1851 in Ste. Genevieve, Ste. Genevieve County, Missouri. [See Jacob Meyer sketch.]
*   ii.   Augustus, born 31 July 1828 in Baden, Germany. [See sketch below.]
†   iii.   Anselm, born about 1830 in Baden, Germany. [See Anselm Begley sktetch.]
†   iv.   Catherine, born 31 May 1832 in Baden, Germany. She came to the United States some time before May 1857. She married Johann Georg "George" Will on 14 May 1857 in Ste. Genevieve, Ste. Genevieve County, Missouri. George was the son of Johann Martin Will and Margaretha Schaefer, born 12 April 1832 in Bellheim, Pfalz, Bavaria, Germany.[See Johann Georg "George" Will sketch.]
†   v.   Elisabeth, born 12 March 1834 in Baden, Germany. She is said to have come to the United States in 1854. She married Hilarius Meyer as his second wife on 12 February 1857 in Ste. Genevieve, Ste. Genevieve County, Missouri. [See Hilarius Meyer sketch.]
†   vi.   Joseph, born in June 1835 in Baden, Germany. [See Joseph Baechle sketch.]

Immigration:
Arrived 21 April 1849 from Le Havre, France to New Orleans aboard the *St. Charles*:
    Baechli, August, 20
        Joseph, 22 [This is most likely Helena listed as a boy.]
        Anselm, 18
    Meier, Jacob, 21 [fiancé of Helena Baechle]
Arrived on 20 April 1854 from Liverpool, England to New York aboard the *Constitution*:
    Beckle, Joseph, 22   Shoemaker   Germany
Arrived some time before 1857 aboard an unknown vessel:
    Baechlé, Catherine
        Elizabeth

Biographical:
Husband: Augustus Baechlé [aka August Bachle]
   Birth – 31 July 1828 in Baden, Germany.
   Death/Burial – 20 July 1905 in Oklahoma City, Oklahoma County, Oklahoma. He was buried in the Fairlawn Cemetery in Oklahoma City, Oklahoma County, Oklahoma.
1) Wife: Franciska Miller [aka Muller or Mueller]
   Birth – September 1828 in Baden Germany.
   Marriage – 4 August 1853 in Ste. Genevieve County, Missouri.
   Death/Burial – 11 October 1865 in Ste. Genevieve County, Missouri. She was buried in the St. Joseph Cemetery in Zell, Ste. Genevieve County, Missouri.
   Children:
         i.   Maria Magdalena, born about 1854 in Ste. Genevieve County, Missouri. She died on 29 December 1855 and was buried in the St. Joseph Cemetery in Zell, Ste. Genevieve County, Missouri. No issue.
         ii.   Francis Joseph "Frank", born 19 March 1857 in Ste. Genevieve County, Missouri. He was a farmer in Ste. Genevieve County. Frank married Josephine Vaeth on 10 April 1888 in Weingarten, Ste. Genevieve County, Missouri. Josephine was the daughter of Peter Andrew Vaeth and Ursula Isenmann, born 19 May 1861 in Ste. Genevieve County. The couple had four

sons and three daughters. Frank and his descendants kept the original "Baechle" surname. Frank died of prostate and rectal cancer on 23 January 1926 in Ste. Genevieve County, Missouri. Josephine died of pneumonia and an abscessed gall bladder on 16 December 1931 in St. Louis, Missouri. They were both buried in the St. Joseph Cemetery in Zell, Ste. Genevieve County, Missouri.

    iii. August, born in February 1860 in Ste. Genevieve County, Missouri. He died on 10 July 1860 and was buried in the St. Joseph Cemetery in Zell, Ste. Genevieve County, Missouri. No issue.

    iv. Johanna Philomena, born 14 May 1863 in Ste. Genevieve County, Missouri. She died on 11 September 1863 and was buried in the St. Joseph Cemetery in Zell, Ste. Genevieve County, Missouri. No issue.

    v. Conrad, born 6 August 1864 in Ste. Genevieve County, Missouri. He was a farmer in Ste. Genevieve County. Conrad married Louisa Philomena Schmelzle on 11 April 1893 in Zell, Ste. Genevieve County, Missouri. Louisa was the daughter of Bernard Schmelzle and Mary Ann Schmutz, born 6 November 1873 in Ste. Genevieve County, Missouri. The couple had three sons and six daughters, of whom three daughters died in infancy or early childhood. Conrad and his descendants kept the original "Baechle" surname. Conrad died of heart disease and cirrhosis of the liver on 24 March 1931 and Louisa died of heart disease on 24 June 1950, both in Ste. Genevieve County, Missouri. They were both buried in the Valle Spring Cemetery in Ste. Genevieve, Ste. Genevieve County, Missouri.

2) Wife: Maria Anna Fallert, daughter of Franz Anton Fallert and Regina Oberle [See Franz Anton Fallert sketch.]

Birth – 31 December 1830 in Achern, Baden, Germany.

1) Marriage – 11 November 1851 in Ste. Genevieve County, Missouri to George Falk. [See George Falk sketch.]

2) Marriage – 12 February 1866 in Zell, Ste. Genevieve County, Missouri to Augustus Baechlé.

Death/Burial – 30 August 1900 in Oklahoma City, Oklahoma County, Oklahoma. She was buried in the Fairlawn Cemetery in Oklahoma City, Oklahoma County, Oklahoma.

Children:

    vi. Mary Louise, born 24 December 1866 in Ste. Genevieve County, Missouri. She died on 30 March 1873 in Ste. Genevieve County and was buried in the St. Joseph Cemetery in Zell, Ste. Genevieve County, Missouri. No issue.

    vii. Anthony August, born 28 September 1868 in Ste. Genevieve County, Missouri. He followed his parents to Oklahoma Territory about 1900. Anthony ran a billiard and beer hall called the Budweiser Saloon in Oklahoma City. He was appointed to serve a term as postmaster for the town of Conception near Oklahoma City in 1895. He married Mary Cimijotti about 1902 in Oklahoma. Mary was the daughter of Frank Cimijotti and Anna [Lucas?], born on 8 February 1879 in Chickasaw County, Iowa. The Cimijotti family were famous circus horse trainers and riders in both the United States and in Europe. Mary and her parents had moved to Oklahoma about 1901. The couple had two sons, both born in Oklahoma. August died on 15 August 1904 in Oklahoma City, Oklahoma Territory [now Oklahoma County, Oklahoma]. He was buried in the Fairlawn Cemetery in Oklahoma City, Oklahoma County, Oklahoma. After her husband's death, Mary and her children lived with her parents in Oklahoma City. Mary died in Oklahoma City on 22 December 1957 and was buried in the Fairlawn Cemetery beside her husband.

    viii. Bernard George, born 30 April 1870 in Ste. Genevieve County, Missouri. He died on 10 September 1870 in Ste. Genevieve County and was buried in the St. Joseph Cemetery in Zell, Ste. Genevieve County, Missouri. No issue.

    ix. Regina R., born 5 April 1871 in Ste. Genevieve County, Missouri. She married Charles E. Brandt about 1896 in Oklahoma Territory. Charles was the son of Adam Brandt and Maria Anna Koenig, born in February 1873 in Wisconsin. He was a farmer and the family lived near Mustang, Canadian County, Oklahoma. The couple had five sons and three daughters, of whom one son died in infancy. Charles died on 15 October 1929 and Regina died in 1959, both in Oklahoma City, Oklahoma County, Oklahoma. They were both buried in the Immaculate Conception Cemetery in Oklahoma City.

    x. Lawrence Alexander, born 15 January 1872 in Ste. Genevieve County, Missouri. He returned to Ste. Genevieve County from Oklahoma to marry Ursula Bertha Wehner on 27 November 1906. Ursula was the daughter of George Wehner and Theresa Vaeth, born 21 November 1884 in Ste. Genevieve County, Missouri. The couple lived in Oklahoma City, Oklahoma County, Oklahoma, where Lawrence was the proprietor of the Oklahoma Wire and Iron Works in Oklahoma City. The couple had four sons and one daughter. Ursula died on 18 February 1936 and Lawrence died on 18 August 1951, both in Oklahoma City. They were both buried in the Rose Hill Burial Park in Oklahoma City, Oklahoma County, Oklahoma.

U.S. residence other than Ste. Genevieve County, Missouri:
Oklahoma Territory [Oklahoma County, Oklahoma]

Land Patents:
Ste. Genevieve County, Missouri

Patentee	Issue Date	Land Office	Cert. No.	Twp	Rng	Sec	Acres
Baechle, Augustin	26 Oct 1885	[Township school land]	173	39	8-E		40.00

Naturalization:

Name	Declaration	Naturalization	Origin
Bechle, Augustus	16 May 1853	24 May 1855 Ste. Genevieve Co.	Baden

Education: Could read and write.
Occupation: Farmer
Religious Affiliation: Roman Catholic
Comments:

Augustus Baechlé [later known as August Bachle in Oklahoma] was born in Germany and came to the United States with two of his siblings in April 1849. He became a farmer in Ste. Genevieve County, Missouri. August married Franciska Miller [aka Mueller] and they had three sons and two daughters. They are said to have had six children, although records for only five have been found. Of their known children, one son and both daughters died in infancy. Franciska died on 11 October 1865 and was buried in the St. Joseph Cemetery in Zell, Ste. Genevieve County, Missouri. August married Mrs. Maria Ann Falk as his second wife on 12 February 1866. Maria was the widow of George Falk and had five surviving children from her first marriage. August and Maria had three sons and two daughters together, of whom one son and one daughter died in infancy. In late 1895, the Bachles made plans to move to Oklahoma Territory in the spring of 1896. In late February 1896, August and Maria sold their property in Ste. Genevieve County, Missouri, and most of their household goods and left for Oklahoma with their youngest children. August's two oldest sons remained in Ste. Genevieve County. The family settled just south of present-day Oklahoma City and remained there the rest of their lives. Maria died on 30 August 1900 in Oklahoma City, Oklahoma County, Oklahoma. August died of sepsis after an operation to repair an aggravated hernia on 20 July 1905 in Oklahoma City. They were both buried in the Fairlawn Cemetery in Oklahoma City, Oklahoma County, Oklahoma.

Note: Descendants of August Bachle and those of his children who moved to Oklahoma before 16 November 1907 are eligible for membership in the First Families of the Twin Territories through the Oklahoma Genealogical Society.

Joseph Bader Family
Surname Variations: Baader, Beader
European Origin: Durbach, Baden, Germany
Family:
Father: Johann Baptist Baader, born about 1804 in Baden, Germany.
Mother: Rosine Winter, born in Baden, Germany.
   Children:
†   i. Caroline, born 14 November 1830 in Durbach, Baden, Germany. She married Paul Palmer on 16 September 1856 in Zell, Ste. Genevieve County, Missouri. Paul was the son of Isfried Palmer and Rosa Heitz, born 22 June 1832 in Ebersweier, Baden, Germany. [See Isfried Palmer sketch.]
    ii. Wilhelm, born 7 June 1833 in Durbach, Baden, Germany. No further information.
†   iii. Ludwig "Louis," born 24 August 1834 in Durbach, Baden, Germany. [See Ludwig "Louis" Bader sketch.]
    iv. Karl, born 2 November 1835 in Durbach, Baden, Germany. No further information.
    v. Friedrich, born 15 January 1837 in Durbach, Baden, Germany. He died 20 February 1838 in Durbach. No issue.
*   vi. Joseph, born 25 March 1838 in Durbach, Baden, Germany. [See sketch below.]
    vii. Crescentia, born 7 March 1841 in Durbach, Baden, Germany. She died on 30 March 1851 in Durbach. No issue.
    viii. Josepha, born 6 July 1845 in Durbach, Baden, Germany. No further information.

Immigration:
Arrived on 13 June 1853 from Le Havre, France to New Orleans aboard the *Isabella*:
    Bader, Caroline, 23
           Louis, 18
Arrived on 23 January 1854 from Le Havre, France to New Orleans aboard the *Wurtemberg*:
    Bada [Bader], Jean Baptiste, 53
           Joseph, 16

Biographical:
Husband: Joseph Bader
    Birth – 25 March 1838 in Durbach, Baden, Germany.
    Death/Burial – 9 September 1915 in Ste. Genevieve County, Missouri. He was buried in the Valle Spring Cemetery in Ste. Genevieve, Ste. Genevieve County, Missouri.
Wife: Mary Witty, daughter of [William or John?] Witty and Catherine Catticoath
    Birth – 13 March 1842 in either Pemiscot County or New Madrid County, Missouri.
    Marriage – 31 July 1869 in Ste. Genevieve, Ste. Genevieve County, Missouri. [This was a sanctification of a civil marriage that had most likely taken place in New Madrid County, Missouri about 1859.]
    Death/Burial – 28 March 1912 in Ste. Genevieve County, Missouri. She was buried in the Valle Spring Cemetery in Ste. Genevieve, Ste. Genevieve County, Missouri.
   Children:
    i. Laura Blanche, born 28 November 1864 in Ste. Genevieve County, Missouri. She married Peter Kiefer on 7 February 1886 in Se. Genevieve County, Missouri. Peter was the son of Philip Kiefer and Josephine C. Schaub, born 2 October 1858 in Ste. Genevieve County, Missouri. [See Philip Kiefer sketch.]
    ii. John Baptist, born 9 August 1866 in Ste. Genevieve County, Missouri. He was baptized in the Ste. Genevieve Catholic Church in Ste. Genevieve, Ste. Genevieve County, Missouri on 22 September 1866. He moved to Texas in the late 1890s, at the same time as his sister Mary Caroline Gittinger, and settled on a farm near Cameron, Milam County, Texas. He later worked as a building contractor. He appears to have married about 1904 in Texas, but nothing is

known about his wife except that she was born in Texas and had died by 1920. The couple had two daughters. John died of uremia and heart disease in Beaumont, Jefferson County, Texas on 13 August 1959. He was buried in the Oak Hill Cemetery in Cameron, Milam County, Texas.

iii. Mary Caroline, born 12 January 1869 in Ste. Genevieve County, Missouri. She was baptized in the Ste. Genevieve Catholic Church in Ste. Genevieve, Ste. Genevieve County, Missouri on 19 February 1869. She married George Felix Gittinger on 13 September 1887 in Ste. Genevieve. George was the son of George Felix Gittinger and Mary Ann Valle, born 22 November 1865 in Ste. Genevieve County, Missouri. He was baptized in the Sts. Philip and James Catholic Church at River aux Vases, Ste. Genevieve County, Missouri on 26 November 1865. The young couple moved to San Antonio, Bexar County, Texas shortly after they were married. Several years later, they settled on a farm near the town of Rockdale, Milam County, Texas. The couple had two sons and four daughters, all born in Texas. One son died in early childhood. George died on 17 February 1902 in Milam County. He was buried in the Hirt-Braun Cemetery near Rockdale, Milam County, Texas. After her husband's death, Mary sold the farm and moved her family back to Ste. Genevieve County, Missouri. She died of chronic myocarditis and senility on 13 July 1949 in St. Louis, Missouri. She was buried in the Valle Spring Cemetery in Ste. Genevieve, Ste. Genevieve County, Missouri.

iv. Joseph M., born 29 September 1871 in Ste. Genevieve County, Missouri. He was baptized in the Ste. Genevieve Catholic Church in Ste. Genevieve, Ste. Genevieve County, Missouri on 2 November 1871. Joseph was a farmer in Ste. Genevieve County. He married Helena Josephine "Lena" Dallas on 12 September 1893 in Ste. Genevieve, Ste. Genevieve County. Lena was the daughter of Christopher Dallas and Franciska Kiefer, born 19 April 1873 in Ste. Genevieve County, Missouri. The couple had six sons and five daughters, of whom two sons and one daughter died in infancy or early childhood. Lena died of a cerebral hemorrhage on 22 June 1946 and Joseph died of acute coronary thrombosis on 11 December 1960, both in Ste. Genevieve County, Missouri. They were both buried in the Valle Spring Cemetery in Ste. Genevieve, Ste. Genevieve County, Missouri.

v. Maximilian Joseph "Max," born 17 October 1873 in Ste. Genevieve County, Missouri. He was a farmer in Ste. Genevieve County. Max married Sophia Louisa Rudloff on 17 October 1894 in Ste. Genevieve, Ste. Genevieve County, Missouri. Sophia was the daughter of Joseph Rudloff and Franciska Kiefer, born 24 March 1876 in Ste. Genevieve County, Missouri. The couple had six sons and three daughters, of whom one son and one daughter died in infancy. Max died of chronic myocarditis on 7 August 1960 and Sophia died on 16 April 1970, both in Ste. Genevieve County. They were both buried in the Valle Spring Cemetery in Ste. Genevieve, Ste. Genevieve County, Missouri.

vi. William Leo "Willie", born 24 April 1882 in Ste. Genevieve County, Missouri. He appears to have traveled to Texas as a young man. He was married about 1905 in Travis County, Texas to Harriet Kristie "Hattie" Eversole. Hattie was the daughter of Barry Abraham Eversole and Melissa Jane Stevens, born 16 January 1889 in Gonzales, Gonzales County, Texas. The couple moved to Missouri shortly after their marriage and Willie worked for a railroad in various capacities, including watchman and bridge carpenter. Three sons and five daughters were born to this couple, of whom one son and two daughters died in infancy. Hattie died of coronary occlusion on 1 January 1962 in Perryville, Perry County, Missouri. Willie died on 12 April 1966. They were both buried in the Valle Spring Cemetery in Ste. Genevieve, Ste. Genevieve County, Missouri.

U.S. residence prior to Ste. Genevieve County, Missouri:
New Madrid, New Madrid County, Missouri

Naturalization:

Name	Declaration	Naturalization	Origin
Bader, Joseph		6 May 1859 Ste. Genevieve Co.	Baden

Military:
Served in the U.S. Civil War for the Union:
Sergeant, Company G, 78th Enrolled Missouri Militia
    Joseph Bader enlisted 30 April 1864 in Ste. Genevieve, Missouri. He was ordered into active service on 22 October 1864 in Ste. Genevieve; mustered out on 25 November 1864. He served 35 days of actual service.
Private, Company K, 21st Regiment, Missouri Infantry
    Joseph Bader enlisted 22 September 1864 in Ironton, Missouri. He mustered in on 15 December 1864 at Benton Barracks, Missouri. He joined the unit as a drafted recruit. Mustered out 3 October 1865 as an extern at Mobile, Alabama. [Indexed in Missouri State Archives records as "Joseph Baden."]

Education: Could read and write
Occupation: Shoemaker and Farmer
Religious Affiliation: Roman Catholic
Comments:

Joseph Bader came to the United States with his father, Johann Baptist, in January 1854. [He was not the Joseph Bader who was a passenger aboard *Westphalia*, which landed at New York from Bremen, Germany on 19 December 1854. That Joseph appears to have remained in the New England area.] They landed in New Orleans and traveled north to Missouri from there. It is not known whether Johann remained in the United States or if he returned to Germany, but he does not appear in any records in Ste. Genevieve County, Missouri. Joseph's older sister Caroline and older brother Ludwig "Louis" had arrived in the United States in June 1853 and come directly to Ste. Genevieve to settle. Joseph settled in New Madrid, New Madrid County, Missouri and worked as a shoemaker for a number of years. He married Mary Witty there in either late 1859 or very early 1860. The young Baders moved to Ste. Genevieve County, Missouri about 1861 where their four sons and three daughters were all born. Joseph enlisted in the 78th Enrolled Missouri Militia in 1864 and served as a sergeant in Company G. He may have also served in Company K of the 21st Regiment, Missouri Infantry. By 1870, Joseph had purchased land in Ste. Genevieve County, Missouri and begun farming. Mary died of pulmonary tuberculosis on 28 March 1912 and Joseph died of cardiac insufficiency and arteriosclerosis on 9 September 1915, both in Ste. Genevieve County. They were both buried in the Valle Spring Cemetery in Ste. Genevieve, Ste. Genevieve County, Missouri.

Note: This Bader family was distantly related to the Maximilian Bader family and to the Hettig family who also came to Ste. Genevieve County, Missouri from Durbach, Baden, Germany.

Ludwig "Louis" Bader Family
Surname Variations: Baader, Beader
European Origin: Durbach, Baden, Germany
Family:
Father: Johann Baptist Baader, born about 1804 in Baden, Germany.
Mother: Rosine Winter, born in Baden, Germany.
    Children:

Note: For a comprehensive discussion of Johann Baptist Baader's children see the Joseph Bader sketch.

Immigration:
Arrived on 13 June 1853 from Le Havre, France to New Orleans aboard the *Isabella*:
    Bader, Caroline, 23
           Louis, 18
Arrived on 31 May 1858 from Le Havre, France to New Orleans aboard the *Zenobia*:
    Oberle, M. Ann, 22

Biographical:
Husband: Ludwig "Louis" Bader
  Birth – 24 August 1834 in Durbach, Baden, Germany.
  Death/Burial – 1 October 1860 in Ste. Genevieve County. He was buried in the St. Joseph Cemetery in Zell, Ste. Genevieve County, Missouri.
Wife: Maria Anna Oberle, daughter of Bernard Oberle and Anna Maria Lipp [See Bernard Oberle sketch.]
  Birth – 13 August 1836 in Obersasbach, Achern, Baden, Germany.
  1) Marriage – 3 January 1859 in Zell, Ste. Genevieve County, Missouri to Ludwig "Louis" Bader.
  2) Marriage – 26 November 1860 in Zell, Ste. Genevieve County, Missouri to Andreas "Andrew" Sewald. [See Andreas "Andrew" Sewald sketch.]
  Death/Burial – 6 October 1901 near Kinsey, Ste. Genevieve County, Missouri. She was buried in the St. Lawrence Cemetery in Lawrenceton, Ste. Genevieve County, Missouri.
  Child:
    i. Joseph, born 12 March 1860 in Ste. Genevieve County, Missouri. His father died when he was an infant and his mother married Andrew Sewald as her second husband. Joseph married Margarette Bayer on 25 September 1883 at Bloomsdale, Ste. Genevieve County. Margarette was the daughter of Vincent Bayer and Elisabeth Rottler, born 12 November 1862 in Ste. Genevieve County, Missouri. Three of Joseph's Sewald half-sisters married brothers of his wife. Joseph and Margarette had four sons and one daughter, of whom one son died in infancy. Joseph was a blacksmith in Bloomsdale. He worked in partnership with William Bieser until 1883 when William moved to Crystal City, Jefferson County, Missouri. In 1896, Joseph sold the blacksmith shop and, with Felix LaRose and Valentine Schilly, bought an established general store in Bloomsdale from Charles and Jules Drury. Joseph eventually bought out his partners and the store became known as the Bader Mercantile. In early 1907, Joseph installed the first telephone in Bloomsdale in his store. The line was later extended to include the Catholic rectory. Margarette died at Bloomsdale on 29 July 1915 from complications due to diabetes. Joseph married Delma Rose Billy on 27 November 1916 at Bloomsdale as his second wife. Delma was the daughter of Joshua Billy and Mary Jane Lalumondiere, born 23 February 1885 in Ste. Genevieve County. The couple had one son and two daughters together. When the switchboard for the Bloomsdale Telephone Company was located in the Bader's store, Delma became one of the first telephone operators in Ste. Genevieve County. Joseph died of heart disease on 20 January 1941 in St. Louis, Missouri. Delma died on 8 July 1969. Joseph and both of his wives were buried in the St. Philomena's Cemetery at Bloomsdale, Ste. Genevieve County, Missouri.

Occupation: Farmer
Religious Affiliation: Roman Catholic
Comments:
Ludwig "Louis" Bader came to the United States with his older sister, Caroline in 1853. They appear to have gone directly to Ste. Genevieve County, Missouri to settle. Louis was a farmer. He married Maria Anna Oberle on 3 January 1859 in the German Settlement [present-day Zell], Ste. Genevieve County, Missouri. The couple had one son who was born only a few months before his father's death. Louis died on 1 October 1860 in Ste. Genevieve County, Missouri. He was buried in the St. Joseph Cemetery in Zell, Ste. Genevieve County,

Missouri. Maria married Andreas "Andrew" Sewald as her second husband on 26 November 1860 in Zell. [See Andreas "Andrew" Sewald sketch.]

Note: This Bader family was distantly related to the Maximilian Bader family and the Hettig family who also came to Ste. Genevieve County from Durbach, Baden, Germany.

Maximilian "Max" Bader Family

Surname Variations: Baader
European Origin: Durbach, Baden, Germany and Fautenbach, Baden, Germany
Family:
Father: Joseph Bader, born about 1800 in [Durbach?], Baden, Germany. He died most likely in Germany before 1858.
Mother: Regina Mueller, born 19 August 1802 in Fautenbach, Baden, Germany. She died 4 July 1876 in Ste. Genevieve County, Missouri. Regina was buried in the Memorial Cemetery in Ste. Genevieve, Ste. Genevieve County, Missouri.
Children:

    i. Anton, born 20 April 1839 in Fautenbach, Baden, Germany, before his parents were married. He was baptized in the Katholisch Church in Durbach, Baden, Germany on 21 April 1839. Anton died on 2 January 1840 in Durbach. No issue.

†   ii. Theresia, born 18 October 1840 in Durbach, Baden, Germany. She married George Braun on 3 September 1860 in Ste. Genevieve County, Missouri. George was the son of Franz Joseph Braun and Maria Ursula Laigast, born 21 April 1829 in Ebersweier, Baden, Germany. [See George Braun sketch.]

    iii. Magdalena, born and died on 10 February 1842 in Durbach, Baden, Germany. No issue.

*   iv. Maximilian, born 29 September 1843 in Durbach, Baden, Germany. He was baptized in the Katholisch Church in Durbach on 1 October 1843. [See sketch below.]

    v. Viktoria, born 9 October 1845 in Durbach, Baden, Germany. She died on 2 February 1847 in Durbach. No issue.

Immigration:
Arrived on 31 May 1858 from Le Havre, France to New Orleans aboard the *Zenobia*:
    Muller [Bader], Regina, 54
        Theresa, 17 [11]
    Barler [Bader], Max[milian], 9 ½

Biographical:
Husband: Maximilian "Max" Bader
    Birth – 29 September 1843 in Durbach, Baden, Germany.
    Death/Burial – 8 May 1927 in Ste. Genevieve County, Missouri. He was buried in the Valle Spring Cemetery in Ste. Genevieve, Ste. Genevieve County, Missouri.
Wife: Julia Margaretha Kern, daughter of John Dominic Kern and Regina Kettinger [See John Dominic Kern sketch.]
    Birth – 14 February 1856 in Ste. Genevieve County, Missouri.
    Marriage – 10 April 1877 in Ste. Genevieve, Ste. Genevieve County, Missouri.
    Death/Burial – 24 August 1914 in Ste. Genevieve County, Missouri. She was buried in the Valle Spring Cemetery in Ste. Genevieve, Ste. Genevieve County, Missouri.
    Children:

    i. William Frederick, born 1 January 1878 in Ste. Genevieve County, Missouri. He was baptized in the Ste. Genevieve Catholic Church in Ste. Genevieve on 4 February 1878. William was a tinner and had a hardware store in Ste. Genevieve. He married Rosina Klein on 8 January 1902 in Ste. Genevieve. Rosina was the daughter of William F. Klein and Christina Roth, born 24 October 1877 in Ste. Genevieve County, Missouri. She was baptized in the Ste. Genevieve

Catholic Church on 4 November 1879. The couple does not appear to have had any children. William died of chronic nephritis and uremia on 12 October 1930 in Ste. Genevieve County. Rosina died on 18 August 1960 of pulmonary edema following a bout of pneumonia on 18 August 1960 in St. Louis, Missouri. They were both buried in the Valle Spring Cemetery in Ste. Genevieve, Ste. Genevieve County, Missouri.

ii. Jessie Josephine, born 28 August 1880 in Ste. Genevieve County, Missouri. She was baptized in the Ste. Genevieve Catholic Church in Ste. Genevieve on 27 September 1880. She married Joseph Gottlieb Rehm on 21 November 1905 in Ste. Genevieve. Joseph was the son of Gottlieb Rehm and Sophia Catherina Wilder, born 23 December 1881 in Ste. Genevieve. Joseph worked as a brakeman for the Illinois South Railroad and later as a house painter. The couple had three sons and one daughter. Jessie died of a cerebral hemorrhage on 17 January 1935 and Joseph died of heart disease complicated by gastric ulcers on 11 January 1954, both in Ste. Genevieve County, Missouri. They were both buried in the Valle Spring Cemetery in Ste. Genevieve, Ste. Genevieve County, Missouri.

iii. Charles Joseph, born 4 January 1883 in Ste. Genevieve County, Missouri. He was baptized in the Ste. Genevieve Catholic Church in Ste. Genevieve on 4 March 1883. He managed a grain elevator in Mendota, LaSalle County, Illinois. Charles married Edith J. Larkin about 1915 in Illinois. Edith was the daughter of Hugh Larkin and Jennie J. Henry, born 3 March 1887 in Lee County, Illinois. The couple had two sons. Charles died in April 1969 and Edith died in December 1984, both in Mendota, LaSalle County, Illinois. They were both buried in the Holy Cross Cemetery in Mendota.

iv. Anna Mary, born 9 May 1885 in Ste. Genevieve County, Missouri. She was baptized in the Ste. Genevieve Catholic Church in Ste. Genevieve on 31 May 1885. Anna married William Andrew Marquis on 3 September 1919 in St. Louis, Missouri. He was the son of John G. Marquis and Clara A. McFarland, born 28 January in Washington County, Pennsylvania. William was an oil field contractor and later owned and operated a gas service station in Carlyle, Clinton County, Illinois. The couple does not appear to have had any children. Anna died on 10 March 1941 in Murphysboro, Jackson County, Illinois. William died on 3 September 1958, in Illinois. They were both buried in the St. Mary Catholic Cemetery in Carlyle, Clinton County, Illinois.

v. August Edwin "Gus", born 19 October 1887 in Ste. Genevieve County, Missouri. He was baptized in the Ste. Genevieve Catholic Church in Ste. Genevieve on 13 November 1887. Gus managed a grain elevator in Mendota, LaSalle County, Illinois with his brother Charles. Gus married Helen A. Bloss about 1916 in Illinois. Helen was the daughter of George Bloss and Hedwig "Hattie" Lett, born 24 January 1895 in Lee County, Illinois. The couple had one son and one daughter. Gus died on 1 January 1959 in Earlville, LaSalle County, Illinois. Helen died on 22 August 1983 in Mendota. They were both buried in the Holy Cross Cemetery in Mendota, LaSalle County, Illinois.

vi. Oliver John, born 8 March 1890 in Ste. Genevieve County, Missouri. He was baptized in the Ste. Genevieve Catholic Church in Ste. Genevieve on 13 April 1890. Oliver moved to Bureau County, Illinois where he worked in the grain industry. He married Winifred B. Donnelly in Illinois about 1925. Winifred was the daughter of James Donnelly and Mary Monahan, born 1 December 1895 in Illinois. The couple had two sons. Oliver died on 13 May 1942 in Princeton, Bureau County, Illinois. Winifred died in January 1975 in Bureau County. They were both buried in the Oakland Cemetery in Princeton, Bureau County, Illinois.

vii. Jules Vincent, born 25 June 1892 in Ste. Genevieve County, Missouri. He was baptized in the Ste. Genevieve Catholic Church in Ste. Genevieve on 10 July 1892. He died of croup on 19 October 1897 in Ste. Genevieve County. He was buried in the Valle Spring Cemetery in Ste. Genevieve, Ste. Genevieve County, Missouri. No issue.

viii. Susan Elisabeth, born 8 July 1894 in Ste. Genevieve County, Missouri. She was baptized in the Ste. Genevieve Catholic Church in Ste. Genevieve on 29 July 1894. Susan married Bernard Leo Schwarz on 13 December 1914 in Ste. Genevieve. Leo was the son of Joseph Schwarz and

Katherine John, born 7 February 1891 in Mendota, LaSalle County, Illinois. The couple lived in Illinois where Leo ran a general store for the first few years they were married. About 1918 they moved to Calhoun County, Michigan where Leo worked in a furniture factory but the climate didn't agree with them and they moved back to Illinois. Leo attended mortuary school and subsequently opened his own undertaking business in Freeport, Stephenson County, Illinois. He became an outspoken advocate for stricter government regulation of the mortuary business, especially calling for training and licensing of morticians. The couple had two sons and one daughter. Susan died on 26 April 1946 in Freeport, Stephenson County, Illinois. She was buried in the Calvary Cemetery in Harlem, Stephenson County. Leo died in 1965.

ix. Mary Helen Regina "Ellen," born 3 December 1898 in Ste. Genevieve County, Missouri. She was baptized in the Ste. Genevieve Catholic Church in Ste. Genevieve on 1 January 1899. Ellen married Benjamin Harrison Miller on 1 April 1929 in Ste. Genevieve, Ste. Genevieve County, Missouri. Ben was the son of John Henry Miller and Cora Alice Henderson, born 27 January 1889 in Fredericktown, Madison County, Missouri. He was a railroad fireman when the couple was first married. He later worked as an engineer at the lime plant in Ste. Genevieve County. The couple does not appear to have had any children. Ben died of coronary thrombosis on 12 July 1949. Ellen died on 18 April 1969, both in Ste. Genevieve County, Missouri. They were both buried in the Valle Spring Cemetery in Ste. Genevieve, Ste. Genevieve County, Missouri.

Naturalization:

Name	Declaration	Naturalization	Origin
Bader, Maximillian		2 May 1868 Ste. Genevieve Co.	Baden

Education: Could read, write and speak English and German
Occupation: Store Clerk and Retail Salesman
Religious Affiliation: Roman Catholic
Political Affiliation and/or Any Offices Held: Max Bader – Democrat
  Ste. Genevieve County Treasurer, 1907 to 1908,
Comments:
Max Bader came to the United States in 1858 with his older sister and widowed mother. They traveled in company with several other Durbachers who were also immigrating to Ste. Genevieve County, Missouri. They settled in the town of Ste. Genevieve where Max worked as a clerk in a general store. His sister lived with the Fidel Hettig family and worked as a household servant until her marriage to George Braun. Max married Julia Margaretha Kern on 10 April 1877 in Ste. Genevieve. The couple had five sons and four daughters, of whom one son died in infancy. In February 1880, Max purchased what is now known as the Jean Baptiste Valle House on the south side of Ste. Genevieve from John L. Bogy and his wife Melanie P. Valle. He owned the property until his death in 1927. Max served as the Ste. Genevieve County Treasurer from 1907 to 1908. He was affiliated with the Democratic Party. Julia died of leukemia on 24 August 1914 and Max died of heart disease and chronic interstitial nephritis on 8 May 1927, both in Ste. Genevieve County, Missouri. They were both buried in the Valle Spring Cemetery in Ste. Genevieve, Ste. Genevieve County, Missouri.

Note: This Bader family was distantly related to the Joseph Bader family and to the Hettig family who also came to Ste. Genevieve County, Missouri from Durbach, Baden, Germany.

Joseph Baechle Family
Surname Variations: Bächlé, Bachle, Bacle, Baechlé, Baechli, Bechle, Beckle, Beckly, Begley
European Origin: [Remetschweil amt Waldshut], Baden, Germany
Family:
Father: Conrad Bächlé
Mother: Walburga Apollonia Benz [aka Dentz]
  Children:

Note: For a comprehensive discussion of Conrad Bächlé's children see the Augustus Bachle sketch.

Immigration:
Arrived on 20 April 1854 from Liverpool, England to New York aboard the *Constitution*:
    Beckle, Joseph, 22   Shoemaker   Germany

Biographical:
Husband: Joseph Baechle
   Birth – June 1835 in Baden, Germany.
   Death/Burial – 5 September 1901 in St. Louis, Missouri. He was buried in the Sts. Peter and Paul Cemetery in St. Louis, Missouri.
1) Wife: Maria Brigita Hauck [or Huck], daughter of Andreas Hauck [or Huck] and Francisca Able
   Birth – about 1841 in Missouri.
   Marriage – 10 October 1859 in Ste. Genevieve, Ste. Genevieve County, Missouri.
   Death/Burial – 25 January 1872 in Ste. Genevieve County, Missouri. She was buried in the Memorial Cemetery in Ste. Genevieve, Ste. Genevieve County, Missouri.
   Children:
      i. Adeline Helen, born 12 September 1860 in Ste. Genevieve County, Missouri. She was baptized on 14 October 1860 in the Ste. Genevieve Catholic Church in Ste. Genevieve, Ste. Genevieve County, Missouri. She died on 14 September 1861 in Ste. Genevieve and was buried in the Memorial Cemetery in Ste. Genevieve, Ste. Genevieve County, Missouri. No issue.
      ii. Joseph, born about 1861 in Missouri. No record of him has been found after he appears in his father's household in the 1880 census.
      iii. Mary Louise, born 21 December 1861 in Ste. Genevieve County, Missouri. She was baptized on 16 February 1862 in the Ste. Genevieve Catholic Church in Ste. Genevieve, Ste. Genevieve County, Missouri. No record of her has been found after she appears in her father's household in the 1880 census.
      iv. Francisca Catherine "Kate," born 9 April 1863 in Ste. Genevieve County, Missouri. She was baptized on 3 May 1863 in the Ste. Genevieve Catholic Church in Ste. Genevieve, Ste. Genevieve County, Missouri. She married Joseph Sexauer on 14 December 1885 in Ste. Genevieve County, Missouri. Joseph was the son of George Sexauer and Francisca "Fanny" Perret, born 18 December 1858 in Missouri. [See George Sexauer sketch.]
      v. Conrad August, born 28 October 1864 in Ste. Genevieve County, Missouri. He was baptized on 20 November 1864 in the Ste. Genevieve Catholic Church in Ste. Genevieve, Ste. Genevieve County, Missouri. He died on 9 September 1877 in Ste. Genevieve County, Missouri. He was buried in Memorial Cemetery in Ste. Genevieve, Ste. Genevieve County, Missouri. No issue.
      vi. Rosine Magdalena, born 20 May 1866 in Ste. Genevieve County, Missouri. She was baptized on 10 June 1866 in the Ste. Genevieve Catholic Church in Ste. Genevieve, Ste. Genevieve County, Missouri. She married John Charles William Humpert. Charles was the son of Hieronymus Humpert and Wilhelmina "Minnie" Pauleke, born 22 January 1860 in Ste. Genevieve County, Missouri. [See Hieronymus Humpert sketch.]
      vii. William Joseph, born 1 March 1869 in Ste. Genevieve County, Missouri. He was baptized on 5 April 1868 in the Ste. Genevieve Catholic Church in Ste. Genevieve. William worked as a bartender in a saloon in St. Louis, Missouri. He married Anna B. Kelleher. The couple may not have had children before William died of tuberculosis on 10 August 1898 in St. Louis, Missouri. He was buried in the Calvary Cemetery and Mausoleum in St. Louis, Missouri. Anna's fate is unknown at present.
      viii. Henry, born 8 February 1870 in Ste. Genevieve County, Missouri. He was baptized on 20 March 1870 in the Ste. Genevieve Catholic Church in Ste. Genevieve, Ste. Genevieve County, Missouri. He moved to St. Louis, Missouri with his father and step-mother and became a butcher. On 26 February 1891, Henry enlisted in the U.S. Army at St. Louis. He became a

career soldier and served in the infantry. He saw duty in the western United States and in the Philippine Islands. Henry retired on 6 September 1915 with the rank of sergeant. He was temporarily returned to active duty during World War I from June 1917 to January 1918. By 1920, Henry was living as a civilian in St. Louis, Missouri. Some time in late 1920, Henry married a woman named Emma Martin. The couple had no children together. Henry died of chronic myocarditis on 16 January 1944 and Emma died of a blocked bile duct and septicemia on 12 June 1948, both in St. Louis, Missouri. They were both buried in the St. John's Cemetery in St. Louis, Missouri.

2) Wife: Wilhelmina "Minnie" Berger, daughter of John Berger and _____
Birth – 29 April 1839 in Baden, Germany.
1) Marriage – John Friedrich Schneider.
2) Marriage – 22 November 1872 in Ste. Genevieve County, Missouri to Joseph Baechlé.
Death/Burial – 7 March 1920 in St. Louis, Missouri. She was buried in the Calvary Cemetery and Mausoleum in St. Louis, Missouri.

Wilhelmina does not appear to have had any surviving children with her first husband.

Child of Joseph Baechle and Wilhelmina Berger:
  ix. Emma K., born 16 February 1878 in Ste. Genevieve County, Missouri. She married Frank S. Donnelly in 26 June 1901 in St. Louis, Missouri, Frank was the son of Michael Donnelly and Mary Coyle, born 26 December 1873 in St. Louis. He was a cooper. The couple had three sons and one daughter, of whom the daughter died in infancy. Frank committed suicide by breathing gas fumes on 26 June 1927 and Emma died of uterine cancer on 4 March 1937, both in St. Louis, Missouri. They were both buried in the Calvary Cemetery and Mausoleum in St. Louis, Missouri.

U.S. residence other than Ste. Genevieve County, Missouri:
St. Louis, Missouri

Naturalization:

Name	Declaration	Naturalization	Origin
Bechle, Joseph	31 May 1858	8 May 1862 Ste. Genevieve Co.	Baden

Military:
Served in the U.S. Civil War for the Union:
Private, Company G, 78th Enrolled Missouri Militia
  Joseph Bechle enlisted on 1 October 1862 in Ste. Genevieve, Missouri.

Education: Could read and write
Occupation: Cooper
Religious Affiliation: Roman Catholic
Comments:
Joseph Baechle came to the United States about 1854 and settled in Ste. Genevieve County, Missouri. He had learned the shoemaker's trade in Germany, but once he arrived in the United States, he worked as a cooper. Joseph seemed to be unusually prone to misfortune. Of his four sons and five daughters, only two sons and two daughters are known to have survived to adulthood. Of those, only the two surviving daughters appear to have had children. In 1882 Joseph was the victim of a counterfeit swindle. He had been in a saloon and accepted a $50.00 bill as payment for some drinks from a man he didn't know. Later inspection revealed that the bill was in fact an altered $5.00 bill. The culprit was caught, but Joseph lost the money. In December 1884, Joseph was nearly killed when an unknown person shot him in the right leg when he was out for a walk in the woods near his home. If a neighbor hadn't been passing by in a wagon, Joseph might have bled to death.

Joseph and his second wife and surviving sons moved to St. Louis, Missouri, some time after 1880. Joseph died from a self-inflicted gunshot wound to the head on 5 September 1901 in St. Louis. Despondency was given as the explanation for his act. Joseph was buried in Saints Peter and Paul Cemetery in St. Louis, Missouri. Wilhelmina died of pneumonia on 7 March 1920 in St. Louis. She was buried in the Calvary Cemetery and Mausoleum in St. Louis, Missouri.

Martin Bahr Family

Surname Variations: Baer, Barr, Bear
European Origin: Ortenberg, Baden, Germany
Family:
Father: Martin Bahr, born in Ortenberg, Baden, Germany. He died 9 December 1812 in Ortenberg.
Mother: Katharina Mueller, born 11 November 1778 in Fessenbach, Baden, Germany. She died on
   31 July 1839 in Ortenberg.
   Children:
*   i. Martin, born 17 October 1802 in Ortenberg, Baden, Germany. [See sketch below.]
    ii. Franziska, born 27 February 1805 in Ortenberg, Baden, Germany. She died on
       28 February 1806 in Ortenberg. No issue.
    iii. Friedrich, born 10 November 1807 in Ortenberg, Baden, Germany. He died on
       6 October 1818 in Ortenberg. No issue.
    iv. Klara, born 17 August 1811 in Baden, Germany. She married Mathias Volk on 6 April
       1835 in Ortenberg. The couple had three sons and six daughters, all born in Ortenberg.
       No further information.

Immigration:
Arrived on 22 February 1847 from Le Havre, France to New Orleans aboard the *Queen Victoria*:
   Bahr, Martin, 42
        Genevieve, 41
        Bartholomew, 18
        Martin, 16
        Cecilia, 10
        Agatha, 9
        [John] Nep., 8
        Franziska, 6

Biographical:
Husband: Martin Bahr
   Birth – 17 October 1802 in Ortenberg, Baden, Germany.
   Death/Burial – is said to have died on 28 March 1875 at an unknown location.
1) **Wife:** Maria Cecilia Leitermann, daughter of Mathias Leitermann and Maria Francisca Rueff
   Birth – 7 February 1802 in Fessenbach, Baden, Germany.
   Marriage – 27 November 1828 in Ortenberg, Baden, Germany.
   Death/Burial – 28 August 1829 in Ortenberg, Baden, Germany.
   Children:
    i. Bartholomew "Bartley", born 22 August 1827 in Fessenbach, Baden, Germany. He married
       Regina Friedmann on 15 July 1856 in Zell, Ste. Genevieve County, Missouri. Regina was the
       daughter of Joseph Friedmann and Rosa Klumpp, born 2 April 1838 in Ottersweier-Haft,
       Baden, Germany. Her family had come to the United States in 1847. Bartley was a farmer in
       Ste. Genevieve County. He and Regina had five sons and four daughters, of whom one daughter
       died in infancy. Some time between 1880 and 1900, the Bahrs and their youngest children
       moved to Chester, Randolph County, Illinois. Bartholomew worked as a nursery man for the
       last few years of his life. He died on 27 May 1905 in Chester, Randolph County, Illinois.

Regina lived with her son Henry for the remainder of her life. She died on 11 November 1914 in Chester. She was buried in the St. Mary of Help Cemetery in Chester, Randolph County, Illinois.
ii. Mathias, born 27 August 1829 in Ortenberg, Baden, Germany. He died on 4 September 1829 in Ortenberg. No issue.

2) Wife: Genevieve Heitz, daughter of Valerian Joseph Heitz and Maria Anna Braun
Birth – 20 December 1803 in Ebersweier, Baden, Germany.
Marriage – 15 October 1829 in Ebersweier, Baden, Germany.
Death/Burial – is said to have died on 27 February 1875 at an unknown location.
Children:
iii. Martin, born 7 November 1830 in Ortenberg, Baden, Germany. He was a farmer in Ste. Genevieve County, Missouri. Martin married Maria Sophina Guethle on 6 November 1855 in Zell, Ste. Genevieve County, Missouri. Sophina was the daughter of Johann "John" Guethle and Cecilia Siebert, born 8 September 1836 in Bohlsbach, Baden, Germany. She had come to the United States with her parents in 1843. The couple had seven sons and five daughters, of whom one daughter died in early childhood. Martin died on 30 July 1901 and Sophina died on 10 February 1907, both in Ste. Genevieve County, Missouri. They were both buried in the Valle Spring Cemetery in Ste. Genevieve, Ste. Genevieve County, Missouri.
iv. Lorenz, born 2 August 1832 in Ortenberg, Baden, Germany. He died on 21 September 1832 in Ortenberg. No issue.
v. Cecilia, born 10 October 1833 in Ortenberg, Baden, Germany. She married Michael Jokerst on 14 January 1850 in Zell, Ste. Genevieve County, Missouri. Michael was the son of Laurence Jokerst and Theresia Siebert, born 21 December 1827 in Bohlsbach, Baden, Germany. [See Laurence Jokerst sketch.]
vi. Agatha, born 20 January 1835 in Ortenberg, Baden, Germany. She married Wendelin Naeger on 23 September 1851 in Zell, Ste. Genevieve County, Missouri. Wendelin was the son of Mathias Naeger and Maria Sophia End, born 5 October 1826 in Rammersweier, Baden, Germany. [See Mathias Naeger sketch.]
vii. Johann Nepomuk, born 9 May 1838 in Ortenberg, Baden, Germany. No information has been found on him after he appears in his father's household in the 1850 census of Ste. Genevieve County, Missouri.
viii. Franciska, born 9 March 1840 in Ortenberg, Baden, Germany. No information has been found on her after she appears in his father's household in the 1850 census of Ste. Genevieve County, Missouri.

Land Patents:
Ste. Genevieve County, Missouri

Patentee	Issue Date	Land Office	Cert. No.	Serial No.	Twp	Rng	Sec	Acres
Bahr, Martin	5 May 1853	St. Louis	54053	MW-0660-375	38-N	8-E	20	54.42

Naturalization:

Name	Declaration	Naturalization	Origin
Bahr, Martin	26 May 1851	1 May 1853 Ste. Genevieve Co.	Baden
Balm [Bahr], Martin, Jr.		24 November 1854 Ste. Genevieve Co.	Baden

Military:
Served in the U.S. Civil War for the Union:
Private, Company G, 78th Enrolled Missouri Militia
Bartholomew Bahr enlisted 4 October 1862 in Ste. Genevieve, Missouri.
Occupation: Shoemaker

Religious Affiliation: Roman Catholic
Comments:
Martin Bahr and his wife brought their family to the United States in 1847. The family settled in Ste. Genevieve County, Missouri on a farm near the German Settlement [present-day Zell]. After the 1850 census, Martin and his wife and their two youngest children have not yet been found in the records of Ste. Genevieve County. Their four oldest surviving children remained in Ste. Genevieve County, married and had families. It has been said that both Martin and Genevieve both died in 1875 within a month of one another, but no record of their death or burial has been found in Ste. Genevieve County, Missouri. It is possible that the parents and youngest children returned to Germany or they moved to another location in the United States.

Benedict Bantz Family
Surname Variations: Banty, Benz, Bentz
European Origin: Durbach, Baden, Germany
Family:
Father: Florian Benz
Mother: Agatha Benz
   Children:
      i. Felix, born 7 July 1826 in Durbach, Baden, Germany. He married Maria Anna Hoferer on 25 November 1861 in Durbach. Maria was the daughter of Michael Hoferer and Theresa Hoferer, born 12 Mar 1836 in Durbach. The couple had at least three sons, all born in Durbach. No further information.

*   ii. Benedict, born 21 March 1828 in Durbach, Baden, Germany. [See sketch below.]

      iii. Georg, born 2 April 1831 in Durbach, Baden, Germany. He married Paula Serrer on 11 July 1859 in Durbach. Paula was the daughter of Joseph Serrer and Kreszentia Benz, born 10 January 1830 in Durbach. The couple had at least two sons and one daughter, all born in Durbach. No further information.

Immigration:
Arrived on 7 November 1857 from Le Havre, France to New Orleans aboard the *Mulhouse*:
    Bentz, Benoit [Benedict], 30   Baden   Farmer

Biographical:
Husband: Benedict Bantz
  Birth – 21 March 1828 in Durbach, Baden, Germany.
  Death/Burial – 17 December 1908 in Ste. Genevieve County, Missouri. He was buried in the Valle Spring Cemetery in Ste. Genevieve, Ste. Genevieve County, Missouri.
Wife: Elisabeth Armbruster, daughter of Ignatz Armbruster and Maria Anna Höss [See Ignatz Armbruster sketch.]
  Birth – born 30 September 1841 in Ottersweier-Haft, Baden, Germany.
  Marriage – 10 September 1860 in Zell, Ste. Genevieve County, Missouri.
  Death/Burial – 23 June 1875 in Ste. Genevieve County, Missouri. She was buried in the Memorial Cemetery in Ste. Genevieve, Ste. Genevieve County, Missouri.
  Children:
     i. Catherine Euphrosine, born 15 September 1864 in Ste. Genevieve County, Missouri. She was baptized in the Ste. Genevieve Catholic Church, Ste. Genevieve, Ste. Genevieve County, Missouri on 30 November 1864. Catherine died before June 1870. No issue.
     ii. Francis Henry, born 1 May 1867 in Ste. Genevieve County, Missouri. He was baptized in the Ste. Genevieve Catholic Church, Ste. Genevieve, Ste. Genevieve County, Missouri on 11 August 1867. Henry was a farmer. He never married and had no issue. He died alone at his home in Ste. Genevieve County of an apparent stroke on 16 January 1933. Henry was buried with his father in the Valle Spring Cemetery in Ste. Genevieve, Ste. Genevieve County,

Missouri.
iii. Anna Mary Magdalena, born 12 January 1870 in Ste. Genevieve County, Missouri. She was baptized in the Ste. Genevieve Catholic Church, Ste. Genevieve, Ste. Genevieve County, Missouri on 6 March 1870. She must have died young since she does not appear in the 1880 census with her father and brother. No further information.

Naturalization:

Name	Declaration	Naturalization	Origin	Remarks
Bantz, Benedict		was naturalized		1880 Census

Military:
Served in the U.S. Civil War for the Union:
Private, Company G, 78th Enrolled Missouri Militia
Benedict Bentz enlisted 1 October 1862 in Ste. Genevieve, Missouri. He was ordered into active service on 16 October 1864. He was relieved from duty on 25 November 1864 after having served 41 days of actual service.

Education: Could read and write
Occupation: General laborer and farmer
Religious Affiliation: Roman Catholic
Comments:
Benedict Bantz was born in Durbach, Baden, Germany and came to the United States in 1857 on the same ship with several other young people from his village. He appears to have come directly to Ste. Genevieve County, Missouri. He worked as a general laborer for a number of years doing any work that needed doing for people in the town in Ste. Genevieve. He married Elisabeth Armbruster on 10 September 1860 in the German Settlement [present-day Zell], Ste. Genevieve County, Missouri. The couple had one son and two daughters, of whom only the son survived to adulthood. Elisabeth died on 23 June 1875 and was buried in the Memorial Cemetery in Ste. Genevieve, Ste. Genevieve County, Missouri. Benedict and his son lived together for the remainder of Benedict's life. He died on 17 December 1908 and was buried in the Valle Spring Cemetery in Ste. Genevieve, Ste. Genevieve County, Missouri. He shares a grave and headstone with his son, Henry.

Frederick Bartels Family
Surname Variations: Bartells
European Origin: Saltzwedel, Hannover, Germany
Family:
Father: Frederick Bartels. He died about 1846, shortly after the birth of his son.
Mother: Dora _____ [See Heinrich "Henry" Otte sketch for her second marriage.]
   Child:
*   i. Johann Frederick, born 22 May 1846 in Saltzwadel, Hanover, Germany. [See sketch below.]

Immigration:
Arrived on 5 November 1865 from Bremen, Germany to New York aboard the *Thiermann* [ship's name was erroneously indexed as *Shinemann* in Ancestry.com]:
    Barnel [Bartels], Fr[iedrich], 19
    Otto [Otte], Aug[ust], 16
    Otto [Otte], Dorot[hea], 20

Biographical:
Husband: Johann Frederick Bartels
   Birth – 22 May 1846 in Saltzwedel, Hanover, Germany.
   Death/Burial – 20 July 1924 in Ste. Genevieve County, Missouri. He was buried in the St. Mary Catholic Cemetery in St. Mary, Ste. Genevieve County, Missouri.

Wife: Mary Louisa Grither, daughter of Johann Baptist "John" Grither and Rosalia Huber [See John Grither sketch.]
Birth – 10 February 1853 in Ste. Genevieve County, Missouri.
Marriage – 28 June 1871 in St. Mary, Ste. Genevieve County, Missouri.
Death/Burial – 12 May 1919 in Ste. Genevieve County, Missouri. She was buried in the St. Mary Catholic Cemetery in St. Mary, Ste. Genevieve County, Missouri.
Children:
　i. John Frederick, born 2 September 1872 in Ste. Genevieve County, Missouri. He was baptized in the Immaculate Conception Catholic Church in St. Mary, Ste. Genevieve County, Missouri on 3 November 1872. As a young man he worked at the Jules Rozier Store in St. Mary. Later, he was employed at the St. Mary's Mill Company from 1900 to 1938. He also served as mayor of St. Mary for two terms and was director and president of the Bank of St. Mary. John married Nora M. Kenner on 24 February 1897 in Murphysboro, Jackson County, Illinois. Nora was the daughter of George W. Kenner and _____, born 3 March 1877 in Missouri. The couple had no children. John became a member of several fraternal organizations, including the Masons and the Shriners. John died of a cerebral embolism on 30 May 1944 in St. Louis, Missouri. Nora died on 26 September 1965. They were both buried in the Catholic Cemetery in St. Mary, Ste. Genevieve County, Missouri.
　ii. Charles Robert, born 29 January 1874 in St. Mary, Ste Genevieve County, Missouri. He was baptized in the Immaculate Conception Catholic Church in St. Mary, Ste. Genevieve County, Missouri on 8 March 1874. He worked with his father in the lumber business and became a skilled carpenter. After a tornado struck St. Louis in 1896, Charles went to the city to help repair the damage. While he was there, he also attended night classes at the St. Louis Business School [Brown's]. He moved to Perryville, Perry County, Missouri where he was employed as manager of the Schaaf's Elevator. Charles married Mary Catherine Lawbaugh on 9 November 1898 in St. Mary, Ste. Genevieve County, Missouri. Mary was the daughter of Emanuel Sylvester Lawbaugh and Mary Adelaide LaVielle, born 8 January 1877 in St. Mary, Ste. Genevieve County, Missouri. The couple had four sons and three daughters, of whom three sons died before the age of two years. In 1901, the Bank of St. Mary was chartered and Charles moved his family back to St. Mary to work as a cashier in the new bank. He served as Secretary of the Board and later as President of the bank. Charles was involved in various other enterprises. He bought government land on Kaskaskia Island and started a farming operation. He bought a printing press and published the *St. Mary's Review* newspaper for several years. He was also owner of a machine shop, a hardware store and an insurance company. He owned various properties that he rented out. In 1918, Charles and Mary bought a home in St. Mary known as Oak Lawn and it became the family home until 1956 when it was destroyed by fire. Mary died Spanish influenza on 14 March 1919 at St. Mary. She was buried in the Catholic Cemetery at St. Mary. Charles married Mary's younger sister, Ella Adelaide Lawbaugh, as his second wife on 7 December 1921 in St. Mary. The couple had no children together. Charles died of a heart attack at his home in St. Mary on 16 December 1957. Ella died on 10 June 1965. They were both buried in the Catholic Cemetery at St. Mary, Ste. Genevieve County, Missouri.
　iii. August Frederick, born 20 April 1878 in St. Mary, Ste. Genevieve County, Missouri. He was baptized in the Immaculate Conception Catholic Church in St. Mary, Ste. Genevieve County, Missouri on 2 June 1878. He married Augusta Keller on 10 April 1901 in Missouri. Augusta was the daughter of Herman Keller and Sybilla Herter, born 16 April 1876 in St. Louis, Missouri. August and Augusta made their home in Farmington, St. Francois County, Missouri. They had two daughters. August worked in various capacities for the Lang Lumber Company in Farmington. Augusta died of lung cancer on 24 January 1944 in Farmington. After his wife's death, August's mental condition slowly deteriorated until he was no longer able to care for himself. He was committed to the State Hospital No. 4 in Farmington where he spent the rest of his life. August died of stomach cancer on 19 September 1950 in Farmington. He and his wife

were both buried in the St. Paul Lutheran Cemetery in Farmington, St. Francois County, Missouri.

U.S. residence other than Ste. Genevieve County, Missouri:
Farmington, St. Francois County, Missouri

Naturalization:

Name	Declaration	Naturalization	Origin	Remarks
Bartells, Fredrick			Germany	1900 Census

Education: Could read and write.
Occupation: Carpenter, Lumber yard owner and operator, Builder
Religious Affiliation: Frederick Bartels was Lutheran. His wife and children were all Roman Catholic.
Comments:
Frederick Bartels was born in Germany. His father is said to have died soon after his birth and his mother married for a second time to Heinrich Otte, a widower with five children of his own. [See the Heinrich "Henry" Otte sketch.] He was apprenticed to a master carpenter at the age of fifteen and stayed with him until he left for the United States in 1865, supposedly to avoid conscription into the army. Frederick traveled with Dorothea and August Otte, his step-sister and half-brother. They all settled in Ste. Genevieve County, Missouri where Frederick's older step-brother, Henry Otte, was already living. Frederick worked as a carpenter in and around the town of Ste. Genevieve and in neighboring counties until his marriage to Mary Louisa Grither in 1871. They settled in the town of St. Mary's Landing [present-day St. Mary] just south of Ste. Genevieve and their three sons were all born there. Frederick helped construct many of the buildings in the town. In 1885 he went into partnership with John W. Tlapek in a lumber yard and construction business known as Tlapek and Bartels. The partnership lasted until 1898 when John sold his share of the business to Frederick. The lumber yard was destroyed by a fire in 1918. Louisa died suddenly on 12 May 1919 of heart disease. After his wife's death, Frederick lived for a few years with his son, August, and his family in Farmington, St. Francois County, Missouri. In the summer of 1920 he returned to St. Mary and made his home with his son Charles. He died of heart disease on 20 July 1924. Both he and his wife are buried in the Catholic Cemetery in St. Mary, Ste. Genevieve County, Missouri.

Jacob Basler Family
Surname Variations: Bassler, Bosler
European Origin: Rammersweier, Baden, Germany
Family:
Father: Sebastian Basler, born 30 December 1772 in Rammersweier, Baden, Germany. He is said to have died about 1823 in Baden, Germany.
Mother: Helena Fitzkam, born 26 November 1776 in Weierbach, Baden, Germany. She is said to have died in 1871 in Ste. Genevieve County, Missouri.
Children:

† i. Maria Anna, born 14 December 1796 in Rammersweier, Baden, Germany. She married Joseph Kiefer on 4 December 1823 in Rammersweier. Joseph was the son of Johann Michael Kiefer and Maria Lutgardis Ehrhard, born 16 March 1799 in Rammersweier. [See Joseph Kiefer sketch.]

† ii. Maria Victoria, born 23 March 1799 in Rammersweier, Baden, Germany. She married Simon May as his second wife on 22 April 1844 in Weingarten Church, Baden, Germany. Simon was the son of Johann May and Katharina Basler, born about 1799 in Baden, Germany. He appears to have been married previously to an unknown woman by whom he had at least two daughters, Franziska and Martha, who survived to adulthood. Victoria does not appear to have had any surviving children of her own. Simon died on 20 October 1852 in Rammersweier. Victoria left Germany with her two step-daughters and with her sister, Franziska, and her family in 1853. They arrived in New Orleans in June 1853 and settled in Ste. Genevieve County, Missouri

shortly after that. Victoria died on 25 August 1855 in Ste. Genevieve County, Missouri. She was buried in the St. Joseph Cemetery in Zell, Ste. Genevieve County. Her step-daughter, Martha, married Franz Kiefer. [See Joseph Kiefer sketch.]

† iii. Johann Baptist "John," born 17 June 1801 in Rammersweier, Baden, Germany. [See John Baptist Basler sketch.]

† iv. Franziska, born 29 Jnauary 1804 in Rammersweier, Baden, Germany. She married Johann Nepomuk "John" Braun on 14 September 1840 in Rammersweier. John was the son of Johann Martin Braun and Catharina Biser, born 10 May 1805 in Rammersweier [See Johann Nepomuk Braun sketch.]

† v. Johanna, born 24 May 1806 in Rammersweier, Baden, Germany. She married Heinrich "Henry" Gremminger on 19 January 1835 in Baden, Germany. Henry was the son of Franz Matthias Gremminger and Helena Hurst, born 30 May 1809 in Ortenberg, Baden, Germany. [See Heinrich Gremminger sketch.]

vi. Michael, born 11 September 1808 in Rammersweier, Baden, Germany. He may have died young. No further information.

† vii. Peter, born 15 June 1811 in Rammersweier, Baden, Germany. [See Peter Basler sketch.]

viii. Joseph, born 8 February 1814 in Rammersweier, Baden, Germany. He died on 18 August 1814 in Rammersweier. No issue.

ix. Theresia, born 23 September 1815 in Rammersweier, Baden, Germany. She married Andreas Braun in Bohlsbach, Baden, Germany on 22 April 1844. Andreas was the son of Johann Braun and Luzia Henn, born 15 May 1819 in Baden, Germany. The couple had at least one son and two daughters, all born in Germany. This family and their descendants remained in Germany.

* x. Jacob, born 27 July 1819 in Rammersweier, Baden, Germany. [See sketch below.]

xi. Euphrosina, born 10 March 1822 in Rammersweier, Baden, Germany. She died on 27 September 1822 in Rammersweier. No issue.

Immigration:
Arrived on 23 March 1846 from Le Harvre, France to New Orleans aboard the *Monument*:
    Basler, Jacob, 27   farmer   from Baden   going to Missouri
        Marianne, 25
        Baumgratz [Pancratius], 1
        Helena, 69 [mother of Jacob]

Arrived on 3 June 1853 from Le Harvre, France to New Orleans aboard the *Statesman*:
    Basler [May], Victoria, 53 [widow of Simon May]
        Martha, 19
        Franciska, 22

Biographical:
Husband: Jacob Basler
    Birth – 27 July 1819 in Rammersweier, Baden, Germany.
    Death/Burial – 14 July 1851 in Zell, Ste. Genevieve County, Missouri. He was buried in the St. Joseph Cemetery in Zell, Ste. Genevieve County, Missouri.
Wife: Maria Anna Braun, daughter of Johann Braun and Luzia Henn
    Birth – 22 February 1821 in [Bohlsbach?], Baden, Germany
    1) Marriage – 20 April 1844 in Bohlsbach, Baden, Germany to Jacob Basler
    2) Marriage – 7 October 1851 in Zell, Ste. Genevieve County, Missouri to Constantine Trautmann [See Constantine Trautmann sketch.]
    Death/Burial – 19 May 1902 in Zell, Ste. Genevieve County, Missouri. She was buried in the St. Joseph Cemetery in Zell, Ste. Genevieve County, Missouri.
Children:
    i. Pancratius, born 12 May 1843 in Baden, Germany. He was a farmer near Bloomsdale, Ste.

Genevieve County, Missouri. Pancratius married Mary Rehm on 17 December 1867 in Zell, Ste. Genevieve County, Missouri. Mary was the daughter of Joseph Richard Rehm and Christina Kempf, born 24 November 1844 in Zell, Ste. Genevieve County. The couple had five sons and four daughters, of whom, one daughter died at the age of nine years. In his last few years, Pancratius began to suffer from senile dementia and he was committed to the State Hospital No. 4 in Farmington, St. Francois County, Missouri. He died there on 30 September 1915 of heart disease. Mary died of chronic nephritis and dropsy on 7 May 1817 in Bloomsdale, Ste. Genevieve County. They were both buried in St. Philomena's Cemetery in Bloomsdale, Ste. Genevieve County, Missouri.

ii. Joseph, born 14 June 1848 in Zell, Ste. Genevieve County, Missouri. He was a farmer in Ste. Genevieve County, Missouri. Joseph married Maria Anna Schweiss on 21 November 1871 in Zell, Ste. Genevieve County. Maria was the daughter of Francis Xavier Schweiss and Genovefa Kiefer, born 11 March 1852 in Ste. Genevieve County, Missouri. The couple had five sons and six daughters, of whom two sons and one daughter died in infancy or early childhood. Maria died of la grippe [influenza] on 27 March 1909 in Bloomsdale, Ste. Genevieve County. Joseph lived his last years with his youngest son and daughter. He died of heart disease on 10 April 1932. They were both buried in St. Philomena's Cemetery in Bloomsdale, Ste. Genevieve County, Missouri.

iii. Regina, born 8 February 1850 in Zell, Ste. Genevieve County, Missouri. She married William Schwent on 21 November 1871 in Zell, Ste. Genevieve County, Missouri. William was the son of Joseph Schwent and Maria Magdalena Jokerst, born 17 February 1847 in Ste. Genevieve County, Missouri. [See Joseph Schwent sketch.]

Military:
Served in the U.S. Civil War for the Union:
Private, Company K, 78th Enrolled Missouri Militia
  Bangratius Bosler [Pancratius Basler] enlisted 1 August 1863 in Ste. Genevieve, Missouri. He was ordered into active service on 16 October 1864. He was relieved from duty on 25 November 1864 after having served 41 days of actual service.

Occupation: Farmer
Religious Affiliation: Roman Catholic
Comments:
Jacob Basler came to the United States with his wife, son and mother and three siblings and their families aboard the same vessel. They settled in Ste. Genevieve County, Missouri near the German Settlement [present-day Zell]. Jacob was a farmer. Within a few years of having settled in Missouri, Jacob died on 14 July 1851 in Ste. Genevieve County. He was buried in the St. Joseph Cemetery in Zell, Ste. Genevieve County, Missouri. Maria was left with three small children to raise alone. She married Constantine Trautmann as her second husband on 7 October 1851 in Ste. Genevieve County. [See Constantine Trautmann sketch.] The three Basler children were raised by their step-father.

Johann Baptist "John" Basler Family
Surname Variations: Bassler, Bosler
European Origin: Rammersweier, Baden, Germany
Family:
Father: Sebastian Basler, born 30 December 1772 in Rammersweier, Baden, Germany. He is said to have died about 1823 in Baden, Germany.
Mother: Helena Fitzkam, born 26 November 1776 in Weierbach, Baden, Germany. She is said to have died in 1871 in Ste. Genevieve County, Missouri.
  Children:

Note: For a comprehensive discussion of Sebastian Basler's children see the Jacob Basler sketch.

Immigration:
Arrived on 23 March 1846 from Le Harvre, France to New Orleans aboard the *Monument*:
    Barler [Basler], Johann, 45   Farmer from Baden   going to Missouri
        Marie, 44
        Julie, 17
        Regina, 9 ½ [13]
        Catherine, 8 ½
        Favian, 6
        Jacob, 5
        Nobert, 1

Biographical:
Husband: Johann Baptist "John" Basler
    Birth – 17 June 1801 in Rammersweier, Baden, Germany.
    Death/Burial – 23 November 1871 in Ste. Genevieve County, Missouri. He was buried in the St. Joseph Cemetery in Zell, Ste. Genevieve County, Missouri.
Wife: Maria Anna Giesler, daughter of Georg Giesler [aka Gissler] and Anna Maria Basler [See George Giesler sketch.]
    Birth – 21 March 1802 in Rammersweier, Baden, Germany.
    Marriage – 3 June 1835 in Baden, Germany.
    Death/Burial – 22 October 1872 in Ste. Genevieve County, Missouri. She was buried in the St. Joseph Cemetery in Zell, Ste. Genevieve County, Missouri.
Children:
    i.   Juliana, born 15 February 1828 in Rammersweier, Baden, Germany. She married Joseph Fallert on 11 November 1851 in Zell, Ste. Genevieve County, Missouri. Joseph was the son of Franz Anton Fallert and Regina Oberle, born 12 March 1825 in Achern, Bühl, Baden, Germany. [See Franz Anton Fallert sketch.]
    ii.   Regina, born 7 September 1830 in Rammersweier, Baden, Germany. She married Lawrence Kirchner on 5 November 1850 in Zell, Ste. Genevieve County, Missouri. Lawrence was the son of Michael Anton Kirchner and Elisabeth Haeffner, born 10 October 1827 in Freudenberg amt Wertheim, Baden, Germany. [See Michael Anton Kirchner sketch.]
    iii.   Catherine, born 26 November 1835 in Rammersweier, Baden, Germany. She married Ignatius Myers on 2 December 1858 in Zell, Ste. Genevieve County, Missouri. Ignatius was the son of Joseph Myers and Catherine [Conrad?], born April 1837 in France. [See Ignatius Myers sketch.]
    iv.   Fabian, born 19 January 1838 in Rammersweier, Baden, Germany. He was a farmer in Ste. Genevieve County, Missouri. Fabian married Gertrude Weiler on 2 December 1858 in Zell, Ste. Genevieve County, Missouri. Theirs was a double wedding with Fabian's sister, Catherine. Gertrude was the daughter of Anton Weiler and Salome Deck, born 1 August 1840 in Mörsch, Baden, Germany. Fabian and Gertrude had two sons and seven daughters, of whom one daughter, a twin, died in infancy. Gertrude died on 24 March 1872 in Ste. Genevieve County, Missouri. She was buried in the St. Joseph Cemetery in Zell, Ste. Genevieve County, Missouri. Fabian married Catherine Schweiss as his second wife on 17 September 1872 in Ste. Genevieve County, Missouri. Catherine was the daughter of Francis Xavier Schweiss and Genovefa Kiefer, born 18 April 1849 in Ste. Genevieve County. Fabian and Catherine had three sons and four daughters, of whom one daughter died in infancy and one daughter died of typhoid fever at the age of nineteen. Some time between 1880 and 1900, Fabian moved his family to St. Louis, Missouri where he worked in a brewery. He died of heart disease and dropsy on 8 June 1905 in St. Louis. Catherine died of a heart attack on 10 November 1921 in St. Louis. They were both buried in Saints Peter and Paul Cemetery in St. Louis, Missouri.
    v.   Jacob, born 25 July 1840 in Rammersweier, Baden, Germany. He was a farmer in Ste. Genevieve County, Missouri. Jacob married Maria Magdalena Braun in Ste. Genevieve County,

Missouri on 25 November 1861. Magdalena was Jacob's first cousin, the daughter of Johann Nepomuk Braun and Franziska Basler, born 22 July 1841 in Baden, Germany. The couple had eleven sons and three daughters, of whom two sons died in infancy and one son died at the age of nineteen. Jacob died on heart disease and senile dementia on 21 March 1925 and Magdalena died of heart disease and chronic nephritis on 2 January 1931, both in Ste. Genevieve County. They were both buried in the Saints Philip and James Cemetery in River aux Vases, Ste. Genevieve County, Missouri.

vi. Norbert, born 24 June 1844 in Rammersweier, Baden, Germany. He was a farmer in Ste. Genevieve County, Missouri. Norbert married Maria Theresa Ruh on 16 April 1867 in Zell, Ste. Genevieve County, Missouri. Theresa was the daughter of Conrad Ruh and Agatha Hurst, born 14 October 1849 in Staufen, Freiburg, Baden, Germany. Norbert and Theresa had four sons and six daughters, of whom two sons and one daughter died in infancy. During the Civil War, Norbert enlisted in the 78th Enrolled Missouri Militia, but it is doubtful that he ever served active duty. Some time around the turn of the century, Norbert moved his family to Crystal City, Jefferson County, Missouri. He died there on 31 October 1905 and was buried in the Sacred Heart Cemetery in Crystal City. After her husband's death, Theresa moved to St. Louis, Missouri. She later lived for a time with her daughter, Philomena, in Indiana. Theresa died on 4 April 1926 and was buried beside her husband in the Sacred Heart Cemetery in Crystal City, Jefferson County, Missouri.

Land Patents:
Ste. Genevieve County, Missouri

Patentee	Issue Date	Land Office	Cert. No.	Serial No.	Twp	Rng	Sec	Acres
Barler, John	1 Jan 1852	Jackson	12519	MO3610_.122	37-N	8-E	5	40.00
Barler, John	1 Jan 1852	Jackson	12618	MO3610_.229	37-N	8-E	5	42.80
Basler, John	1 Mar 1848	Jackson	9904	MO3550_.164	37-N	8-E	5	40.00
Basler, John	1 Jan 1850	Jackson	11564	MO3590_.216	37-N	8-E	5	40.00
Basler, John	15 Apr 1853	Jackson	13234	MO3620_.345	37-N	8-E	5	80.00
Basler, John	3 Jan 1856	Jackson	17967	MO3700_.080	37-N	8-E	6	80.00

Naturalization:

Name	Declaration	Naturalization	Origin
Basler, John	9 November 1849	22 May 1852 Ste. Genevieve Co.	Baden

Military:
Served in the U.S. Civil War for the Union:
Private, Company K, 78th Enrolled Missouri Militia
  Robert Boster [Norbert Basler] enlisted 30 April 1864 in Ste. Genevieve, Missouri.

Occupation: Farmer
Religious Affiliation: Roman Catholic
Comments:
Johann Baptist "John" Basler came to the United States with his family in 1846. All but one sister of his surviving siblings also came to the United States, either aboard the same vessel or on later ships. John settled his family on a farm near the German Settlement [present-day Zell] in Ste. Genevieve County, Missouri. He purchased a sizable amount of land which he and his sons farmed and the family prospered. John died on 23 November 1871 and Maria died on 22 October 1872, both near the German Settlement [present-day Zell] in Ste. Genevieve County. They were both buried in the St. Joseph Cemetery in Zell, Ste. Genevieve County, Missouri.

Joseph Basler Family

Surname Variations: Besler, Bosler
European Origin: Zell (Offenburg), Baden, Germany
Family:
Father: Joseph Litterst [From Joseph Basler's marriage record in Ste. Genevieve County, Missouri.]
Mother: Maria Antonia Basler, born 12 December 1792 in Fessenbach, Baden, Germany. She died on 29 July 1867 in Riedle, Baden, Germany.
  Child:
* i. Joseph, born 7 March 1820 in Zell (Offenburg), Baden, Germany. [See sketch below.]

Immigration:
Arrived 24 February 1855 from Le Havre, France to New Orleans aboard the *Lexington*:
  Besler [Basler], Joseph, 32
  [Bantz], Suzanne, 24

Note: Susanna was listed as a member of Michael Busam's family with her surname left blank. Joseph Basler is listed immediately after her name. This is most likely Susanna Bantz based on age and date of arrival.

Biographical:
Husband: Joseph Basler [aka Joseph Litterst from marriage record in Ste. Genevieve County, Missouri.]
  Birth – 7 March 1820 in Zell (Offenburg), Baden, Germany.
  Death/Burial – 18 June 1881 in Ste. Genevieve County, Missouri. He was buried in Our Lady Help of Christians Cemetery in Weingarten, Ste. Genevieve County, Missouri.
Wife: Susanna "Susan" Bantz, daughter of M. Bantz and Theresia _____
  Birth – about 1831 in Baden, Germany.
  Marriage – 5 February 1856 in Ste. Genevieve County, Missouri.
  Death/Burial – 17 November 1879 in Weingarten, Ste. Genevieve County, Missouri. She was buried in Our Lady Help of Christians Cemetery in Weingarten, Ste. Genevieve County, Missouri.
  Children:
  i. Joseph, born 22 November 1856 in Ste. Genevieve County, Missouri. He died some time before February 1867 in Missouri. No issue.
  ii. Elisabeth, born 6 November 1858 in Ste. Genevieve County, Missouri. She married William Raumschuh on 28 September 1875 in Ste. Genevieve, Ste. Genevieve County, Missouri. William was the son of Bernard Raumschuh and Barbara Müller, born 12 January 1849 in Sasbach, Achern, Baden, Germany. [See Bernard Raumschuh sketch.]
  iii. Nicholas, born 2 January 1861 in Ste. Genevieve County, Missouri. He died on 5 April 1861 in Ste. Genevieve County. He was buried in St. Joseph Cemetery in Zell, Ste. Genevieve County, Missouri. No issue.
  iv. Mary Ann, born 28 May 1863 in Ste. Genevieve County, Missouri. She married Louis Andrew Wilder on 19 June 1883 in Ste. Genevieve, Ste. Genevieve County, Missouri. Louis was the son of Peter Nicolaj Georg Weide [aka Wilder] and Ludwina Johanna Klein, born 16 February 1860 in Ste. Genevieve County, Missouri. [See Peter Wilder sketch.]
  v. Katherine, born 7 November 1865 in Ste. Genevieve County, Missouri. She died 16 April 1866 in Ste. Genevieve County, Missouri. She was buried in St. Joseph Cemetery in Zell, Ste. Genevieve County, Missouri. No issue.
  vi. Joseph, born 22 February 1867 in Ste. Genevieve County, Missouri. No further information has been found after he appears in his father's household in the 1880 census in Ste. Genevieve County, Missouri.
  vii. George Philip, born 22 April 1873 in Ste. Genevieve County, Missouri. He was a farmer. He married Regina Johanna Guethle on 3 September 1895 in Zell, Ste. Genevieve County, Missouri. Regina was the daughter of Felix Guethle and Maria Anna Herzog, born 19 July 1873

in Ste. Genevieve County, Missouri. The couple lived the first years of their married life together in Ste. Genevieve County. Seven sons and four daughters were born to this couple. About 1905, George moved his family to Salisbury, Chariton County, Missouri, where he worked as a general blacksmith. By 1913, the family had returned to Ste. Genevieve County. On the afternoon of 14 June 1913, George was helping Robert Herter load hay into a wagon on his farm near Lawrenceton. George accidentally dropped his hay fork which fell on one of the horses and startled the team into bolting. George was thrown forward onto the double tree and his foot was caught in the harness. He was dragged under the wagon for almost a half-mile before the team stopped. His upper body and head were badly mangled and he died of the injuries. George was buried in the Our Lady Help of Christians Cemetery in Weingarten, Ste. Genevieve County. Regina remained on the farm with her youngest children until after 1920 when she sold the farm and moved to Festus, Jefferson County, Missouri. She died of myocarditis on 22 March 1960 in Festus. She was buried in the Sacred Heart Cemetery in Crystal City, Jefferson County, Missouri.

viii. Francis, born and died on 9 January 1875 in Ste. Genevieve County, Missouri. He was buried in St. Joseph Cemetery in Zell, Ste. Genevieve County, Missouri. No issue.

Military:
Served in the U.S. Civil War for the Union:
Private, Company K, 78th Enrolled Missouri Militia
  Joseph Bosler enlisted on 30 April 1864 in Ste. Genevieve, Missouri. He was ordered into active service on 16 October 1864. He was relieved from duty on 25 November 1864 after having served 41 days of actual service.

Occupation: Farmer
Religious Affiliation: Roman Catholic
Comments:
Joseph Basler was born in Fessenbach, Baden, Germany. His mother married a man named Joseph Litterst in 1829 and Joseph Basler sometimes used his step-father's surname. Joseph Basler and his fiancé, Susanna Bantz, traveled together to the United States in 1855. They were married shortly after they arrived in Ste. Genevieve County Missouri and settled on a farm between the German Settlement [present-day Zell] and Weingarten. They had five sons and three daughters, of whom only two sons and two daughters survived infancy. Susanna died of heart disease on 17 November 1879 and Joseph died of heart disease on 18 June 1881, both in Ste. Genevieve County. They were both buried in the Our Lady Help of Christians Cemetery in Weingarten, Ste. Genevieve County, Missouri.

Peter Basler Family
Surname Variations: Bassler, Be[s]sler, Bo[s]sler
European Origin: Rammersweier, Baden, Germany
Family:
Father: Sebastian Basler, born 30 December 1772 in Rammersweier, Baden, Germany. He is said to have died about 1823 in Baden, Germany.
Mother: Helena Fitzkam, born 26 November 1776 in Weierbach, Baden, Germany. She is said to have died in 1871 in Ste. Genevieve County, Missouri.
  Children:

Note: For a complete discussion of Sebastian Basler's children see the Johann Baptist "John" Basler sketch.

Immigration:
Arrived 30 January 1843 from Le Harvre, France to New Orleans aboard the *Mozart*:
  Basler, Peter, 31
  [Sellinger], Helena, 24

Biographical:
Husband: Peter Basler
  Birth – 15 June 1811 in Rammersweier, Baden, Germany
  Death/Burial – 31 March 1881 in Ste. Genevieve County, Missouri. He was most likely buried in the Memorial Cemetery in Ste. Genevieve, Ste. Genevieve County, Missouri.
Wife: Helena Sellinger, daughter of Bernard Sellinger and Franziska Litterst [See George Sellinger sketch.]
  Birth – 6 May 1819 in Weierbach, Baden, Germany.
  Marriage – 18 February 1843 in Ste. Genevieve County, Missouri.
  Death/Burial – 5 February 1874 in Zell, Ste. Genevieve County, Missouri. She was buried in the St. Joseph Cemetery in Zell, Ste. Genevieve County, Missouri.
Children:
  i. Peter, born 15 August 1843 in Ste. Genevieve County, Missouri. He was baptized on 19 November 1843 in the Ste. Genevieve Catholic Church in Ste. Genevieve, Ste. Genevieve County, Missouri. He was a farmer in Ste. Genevieve County. Peter married Victoria Ritter on 28 July 1868 in Ste. Genevieve County. Victoria was the daughter of Paul Ritter and Catharina Metz, born 27 October 1846 in Ste. Genevieve County, Missouri. The couple had three sons and four daughters. They also fostered a girl named Odelia "Delia" Bieser. She was the daughter of Joseph Bieser and Maria Anna Bransch. [See Joseph Bieser sketch.] Peter died of pneumonia on 15 December 1917 in Ste. Genevieve County. He was buried in the St. Anne's Cemetery in French Village, St. Francois County, Missouri. Victoria lived with her youngest son until she died of cirrhosis of the liver on 12 February 1922 in Ste. Genevieve County. She was buried in the St. Anne's Cemetery in French Village, St. Francois County, Missouri.
  ii. Joseph, born 2 December 1845 in Ste. Genevieve County, Missouri. He was baptized on 14 June 1846 in the Ste. Genevieve Catholic Church in Ste. Genevieve, Ste. Genevieve County, Missouri. Joseph married Louisa Guethle on 24 November 1868 in Ste. Genevieve County. Louisa was the daughter of Johann "John" Guethle and Cecilia Siebert, born 5 January 1848 in Ste. Genevieve County. The couple had two sons and three daughters of whom the youngest two daughters died in infancy. Louisa died in childbirth on 5 May 1876 in Ste. Genevieve County. She was buried in the St. Joseph Cemetery in Zell, Ste. Genevieve County, Missouri. Joseph married Catharina Magdalena Waller as his second wife on 23 April 1877 in Lawrenceton, Ste. Genevieve County. Catherine was the daughter of Joseph Anton Waller and Magdalena Dauer, born 4 August 1843 in Louisville, Quebec, Canada. She was widowed twice before her marriage to Joseph Basler. She had been married first on 15 November 1865 in Ste. Genevieve County to Peter Ludwig Haxel who had died before December 1871 and by whom she had a son and a daughter. Catherine was married second to Henry F. Hammert on 19 December 1871 in Ste. Genevieve. They do not appear to have had any children before Henry died on 7 March 1875. He was buried in the Oddfellows Cemetery in Farmington, St. Francois County, Missouri. Shortly after they were married, Joseph and Catherine moved to Lawrence County, Arkansas where Joseph farmed for a while with his youngest brother, Isidore. Two more children, a son and a daughter, were born while the family was living in Arkansas. By 1900, Joseph had moved his family to a farm in Oklahoma Territory in present-day Custer County. Joseph died on 11 May 1923 and Catherine died on 30 May 1924, both in Oklahoma. They were both buried in the Rhea Cemetery in Leedy, Dewey County, Oklahoma.
  iii. Theresa, born 29 December 1847 in Ste. Genevieve County, Missouri. She was baptized on 13 February 1848 in the Ste. Genevieve Catholic Church in Ste. Genevieve, Ste. Genevieve County, Missouri. Theresa married Lawrence Werner on 3 September 1872 in Ste. Genevieve County. Lawrence was the son of George Werner and Maria Eva Ritter, born 12 August 1852 in Ste. Genevieve County. [See George Werner sketch.]
  iv. Gottfried, born 13 January 1850 in Ste. Genevieve County, Missouri. Gottfried married Maria Antoinette Arnold on 27 May 1873 in Ste. Genevieve. She was the daughter of Michael Arnold and Theresia Keller, born in July 1844 in Bavaria, Germany. She had come to the United States

49

with her parents in 1852. Antoinette was the widow of Francis Stocker who had died on 8 July 1872 and left her with three small sons to raise. Gottfried and Antoinette had two daughters. Antoinette died on 15 March 1877 in Ste. Genevieve County, Missouri and was buried in Memorial Cemetery in Ste. Genevieve, Ste. Genevieve County, Missouri. Gottfried married Mary Suzanne Felicite Léon as his second wife on 22 January 1878 in Ste. Genevieve. Felicite was the daughter of Joseph Amabile Léon and Leocadia Labruyere, born 8 December 1857 in Ste. Genevieve County, Missouri. Gottfried and Felicite had six sons and four daughters. About 1886, Gottfried moved his family to Rawlins County, Kansas with several other families from Ste. Genevieve County, Missouri. He settled a farm near the town of Atwood. The climate was harsh and his crops failed several years in a row and the family struggled financially. Felicite died on 25 March 1898 after suffering for several years from a liver complaint. She was buried in the Saint Marys Cemetery in Rawlins County. Gottfried married Marguerite Gibson as his third wife on 31 August 1898 in Herndon, Rawlins County. Marguerite was born in January 1838 in Illinois. Nothing further is known of her ancestry. There were no children born to this union. Margaret died in April 1912 and was buried in the Atwood (Fairview) Cemetery in Atwood, Rawlins County, Kansas. Gottfried is said to have died about 1917 in Florida. [Note: After 1880, Gottfried used the surname "Bosler" and his descendants are known by that name.]

v. Severin, born 22 September 1851 in Ste. Genevieve County, Missouri. He married Louisa Armbruster on 18 May 1875 in Ste. Genevieve County, Missouri. Louisa was the daughter of Ignatius Armbruster and Theresia Streule, born 11 February 1854 in Missouri. Severin was a farmer, but he was not content to stay in Missouri. He moved his family first to Hamilton County, Nebraska in the early 1880s, and then to Rawlins County, Kansas, where they remained. The couple had four sons and two daughters. Louisa died on 24 February 1921 and Severin died three days later on 27 February 1921, both in Rawlins County, Kansas. They were both buried in the Rose Hill Cemetery at Ludell, Rawlins County.

vi. Sophia, born 15 February 1853 in Ste. Genevieve County, Missouri. She married Cornelius Arnold on 10 November 1874 in Ste. Genevieve County. Cornelius was the son of Michael Arnold and Theresia Keller, born 2 September 1852 in Ste. Genevieve County, Missouri. [See Michael Arnold sketch.]

vii. Wilhelmina, born 23 September 1856 in Ste. Genevieve County, Missouri. She married John Michael Arnold on 25 May 1880 in Ste. Genevieve County, Missouri. John was the son of Michael Arnold and Theresia Keller, born in August 1858 in Ste. Genevieve County, Missouri. [See Michael Arnold sketch.]

viii. Isidore, born 4 April 1859 in Ste. Genevieve County, Missouri. He was a farmer. In the early 1880s, Isidore lived and worked with his older brother, Joseph in Lawrence County, Arkansas. When Joseph moved to Oklahoma, Isidore went to Kansas. For a few short years in the 1890s, he lived in Rawlins County, Kansas with his brothers Gottfried and Severin. But by the late 1890s, he had followed Joseph south to Oklahoma. It is possible that Isidore married a widow whose last name was King as his first wife. It appears that she had at least one son, William J. "Willie" King, from her first marriage. Willie remained in Isidore's household until Isidore's death in 1917. Nothing further is known of the first wife other than that she must have died before 1897. Isidore married Mary Haxel about 1897, most likely in Oklahoma. Mary was the daughter of Peter Ludwig Haxel and Catharina Magdalena Waller, born 1 October 1870 in Missouri. She was also the step-daughter of Isidore's older brother, Joseph. The couple had one son and two daughters, all born in Oklahoma. Mary died on 29 August 1909 and Isidore died on 15 August 1917, both in Oklahoma. They were both buried in the Fairview Cemetery in Tuttle, Grady County, Oklahoma.

Land Patents:
Rawlins County, Kansas

Patentee	Issue Date	Land Office	Cert. No.	Serial No.	Twp	Rng	Sec	Acres
Bosler, Godfried	20 Jun 1891	Oberlin	8393	KS0500_.420	35	32-W	32	160.00
Basler, Gotftried	12 Nov 1894	Oberlin	546	TC-0072-160	35	32-W	29	160.00
Basler, Isidor	16 May 1890	Oberlin	1761	KS0670_.122	25	32-W	5	160.25
Basler, Severin	6 Sep 1890	Oberlin	1864	KS0570_.297	25	32-W	8	160.00

Custer County, Oklahoma

Patentee	Issue Date	Land Office	Cert. No.	Serial No.	Twp	Rng	Sec	Acres
Bosler, Joseph	7 Jun 1905	Kingfisher	9395	OK1610_.467	15-N	20-W	1	160.00
	4 Apr 1911	Guthrie	02144	187859	15-N	20-W	1	159.72

Naturalization:

Name	Declaration	Naturalization	Origin
Basler, Peter	23 May 1849	24 May 1851 Ste. Genevieve Co.	Baden

Military:
Served in the U.S. Civil War for the Union:
Private, Company F, 78th Enrolled Missouri Militia
  Joseph Basler enlisted in August 1862 in Ste. Genevieve, Missouri. He was ordered into active service on 16 October 1864. He was relieved from duty on 25 November 1864 after having served 41 days of actual service.

Occupation: Farmer
Religious Affiliation: Roman Catholic
Comments:
Peter Basler came to the United States with his fiancé in 1843. All but one sister of his surviving siblings also came to the United States on later voyages. Peter and Helena Sellinger were married within weeks of their arrival in Ste. Genevieve County, Missouri. They settled on a farm near the town of Ste. Genevieve. Peter purchased a sizable amount of land which he and his sons farmed and the family prospered. Helena died on 5 February 1874 and Peter lived his last years in the household of his daughter, Sophia. He died on 31 March 1881 in Ste. Genevieve County. After their father's death, most of Peter's children left Ste. Genevieve County, Missouri and settled in Kansas and Oklahoma.

Theresia Basler Family
Surname Variations: Bosler
European Origin: Bohlsbach, Fessenbach and Rammersweier, Baden, Germany
Family:
Father: Johann Georg Basler, born 29 February 1784 in Fessenbach, Baden, Germany. He died on
  19 March 1868 in Fessenbach.
Mother: Walburga Höpf, born 10 February 1790 in Weierbach, Baden, Germany. She died on
  15 January 1861 in Fessenbach.
  Children:
*   i. Valentin, born 4 February 1813 in Rammersweier, Baden, Germany. [See sketch below.]
   ii. Helena, born 19 March 1815 in Rammersweier, Baden, Germany. She married Franz
    Bartholomew Kiefer on 20 November 1837 in Baden, Germany. He was born on 6 October
    1810 in Weierbach, Baden, Germany. The couple had five sons and six daughters, of whom two
    daughters, Louisa and Franziska, came to Ste. Genevieve County, Missouri. Franz
    Bartholomew died on 31 March 1879 and Helena died on 19 December 1896, both in
    Fessenbach, Baden, Germany.

iii. Simon, born 16 October 1817 in Fessenbach, Baden, Germany. He married Anastasia Riehle on 10 July 1844 in Baden, Germany. No further information.
iv. Isidor, born 3 April 1820 in Rammersweier, Baden, Germany. He married Franziska Zoller on 10 September 1861 in Baden, Germany. No further information.

Immigration:
Arrived 13 December 1860 from Le Harve, France to New Orleans aboard the *Pequot*:
    Bossler [Basler], Theresa Burgert, 46 [widow of Valentin]
        Veronika, 20
        Franciska, 17
        Andreas, 14
        Joseph, 12
    Kiefer, Louise, 21 [niece of Theresia]
Arrived 2 September 1869 from Le Havre, France to New York aboard the *Cella*:
    Kafer [Kiefer], Franciska, 22 [niece of Theresia]

Biographical:
Husband: Valentin Basler
    Birth – 4 February 1813 in Rammersweier, Baden, Germany.
    Death/Burial – 24 July 1849 in Fessenbach, Baden, Germany.
Wife: Theresia Burgert, daughter of Joseph Burgert and Genovefa Kempf [See Karl "Charles" Burgert sketch.]
    Birth – 21 September 1814 in Bohlsbach, Baden, Germany.
    Marriage – 23 September 1839 in Baden, Germany.
    Death/Burial – 7 July 1881 in Zell, Ste. Genevieve County, Missouri. She was buried in the St. Joseph Cemetery in Zell, Ste. Genevieve County, Missouri.
Children:
i. Veronica, born 3 September 1840 in Fessenbach, Baden, Germany. She worked with her mother as a maid and cook in the St. Joseph parish rectory in Zell, Ste. Genevieve County, Missouri and for another nearby household to help support the family. She married William Roth as his second wife on 12 May 1863 in Ste. Genevieve County, Missouri. William was the son of Anton Roth and Maria Elisabeth Kuntz, born 21 November 1829 in Sasbach, Achern, Baden, Germany. [See William Roth sketch.]
ii. Franziska, born 2 April 1843 in Fessenbach, Baden, Germany. She married Andreas "Andrew" Baumann as his second wife on 20 May 1862 in Zell, Ste. Genevieve County, Missouri. Andrew was the son of Franz Anton Baumann and Catherine Armbruster, born 11 November 1798 in Sasbach, Achern, Baden, Germany. [See Franz Anton Baumann sketch.]
iii. Andreas "Andrew," born 16 July 1846 in Fessenbach, Baden, Germany. Andrew was a farmer. He married Johanna Palmer on 4 May 1869 in Ste. Genevieve County, Missouri. Johanna was the daughter of Pius Palmer and Johanna Hug [aka Huck], born 22 January 1850 in Ste. Genevieve County, Missouri. For the first few years of their married life, Andrew and Johanna lived and farmed in Ste. Genevieve County where the couple's first two sons and three daughters were born. By late 1882, Andrew moved his family to Otis, Hamilton County, Nebraska. The family later moved to Grand Island, Hall County, Nebraska where Andrew operated a dairy farm. Their youngest son and two daughters were all born in Nebraska. In Nebraska, Andrew and his descendants are all known by the surname "Bosler." Johanna died on 2 June 1910 and Andrew died on 23 October 1916, both in Hall County, Nebraska. They were both buried in the Grand Island Cemetery in Grand Island, Hall County, Nebraska.
iv. Joseph, born 26 March 1848 in Fessenbach, Baden, Germany. His whereabouts for his first ten years in the United States is uncertain, but most likely he lived in Ste. Genevieve County with the rest of his family. However, by 1872 he was living in Illinois. He married Mary Magdalena

Zopf on 10 September 1872 in Madison County, Illinois. Mary was the daughter of Jacob Zopf and Elisabeth _____, born 12 December 1853 in Highland, Madison County, Illinois. Joseph was a wagon maker and carpenter in Bond County, Illinois. The couple is said to have had twelve children; however, records for only three sons and five daughters have been found. Joseph died on 13 August 1913 in Pierron, Bond County, Illinois. Mary died on 12 February 1931 in Highland, Madison County. Their burial locations are unknown at present.

Military:
Served in the U.S. Civil War for the Union:
Private, Company K, 78th Enrolled Missouri Militia
 Andrew Bosler enlisted on 30 April 1864 in Ste. Genevieve, Missouri. He was ordered into active service on 16 October 1864. He was relieved from duty on 25 November 1864 after having served 41 days of actual service.

Occupation: Rectory housekeeper for the St. Joseph parish in Zell, Ste. Genevieve County, Missouri.
Religious Affiliation: Roman Catholic
Comments:
Theresia Burgert married Valentin Basler in Baden, Germany in 1839. Valentin supported his family by tending vineyards in a monastery near their home in Fessenbach. He died in 1849 when he fell out of a hayloft and was impaled on a hay rake. After her husband's death, Theresia kept her family together, but struggled financially. In 1860, Theresia moved to the United States with her four children and a niece. She reportedly had a relative in Missouri who had told her about a vacant housekeeper's position in the local priest's home in Zell, Ste. Genevieve County, Missouri. [This relative could also have been Theresia's older sister Magdalena who had come to Ste. Genevieve County in 1852 with her husband, Joseph Satory, and their three children, or her brother Karl "Charles" Burgert who was also in Ste. Genevieve County.] Theresia took the position as housekeeper and her daughter Veronica worked as maid and cook in a neighbor's household. Theresia did very fine handwork and intricate sewing and helped to make vestments and altar cloths for the church to supplement her income. She maintained a lifelong correspondence with her family and friends in Germany and many of her letters have been preserved. Theresia died on 7 July 1881 in Ste. Genevieve County, Missouri. She was buried in the St. Joseph Cemetery in Zell, Ste. Genevieve County, Missouri.

Valentine Basler Family
Surname Variations: Bosler
European Origin: Rammersweier, Baden, Germany
Family:
Father: Franz Michael Basler, born 6 September 1767 in Rammersweier, Baden, Germany. He died on 11 December 1843 in Rammersweier.
Mother: Gertrud Litterst, born 4 March 1775 in Weierbach, Baden, Germany.
 Children:
  i. Ursula, born 19 October 1798 in Rammersweier, Baden, Germany. She died on 21 October 1799 in Rammersweier. No issue.
  ii. Agatha, born 6 February 1800 in Rammersweier, Baden, Germany. She died on 26 September 1800 in Rammersweier. No issue.
† iii. Cornelius, born 12 September 1801 in Rammersweier, Baden, Germany. He came to the United States with his brothers and sister in 1846 and settled with them in Ste. Genevieve County, Missouri. It is possible that the Genevieve Basler who came with the family was his wife, although he is listed as single in all records found in Ste. Genevieve. Cornelius lived with his sister Maria and her husband and helped his brother-in-law work his farm. Cornelius' history is unknown after the 1860 census of Ste. Genevieve County. He had no known issue.
  iv. Bernhard, born 26 July 1803 in Rammersweier, Baden, Germany. He married Theresia Lehmann on 25 November 1830 in Baden, Germany. Theresia was the daughter of Franz

Michael Lehmann and Maria Ursula Neger, born 5 August 1797 in Rammersweier. The couple had at least one son and three daughters, all born in Rammersweier. This family remained in Germany. Theresia died on 27 April 1869 and Bernhard died on 2 January 1870, both in Rammersweier.

    v. Georg, born 25 March 1806 in Rammersweier, Baden, Germany. No further information.

    vi. Joseph, born 17 February 1809 in Rammersweier, Baden, Germany. He died on 21 June 1811 in Rammersweier. No issue.

†   vii. Wilhelm, born 21 May 1812 in Rammersweier, Baden, Germany. [See William Basler sketch.]

*   viii. Valentine, born 23 December 1815 in Rammersweier, Baden, Germany. [See sketch below.]

†   ix. Maria Anna, born 24 January 1819 in Rammersweier, Baden, Germany. Maria married Charles Humpert on 24 July 1846 in Ste. Genevieve, Ste. Genevieve County. Charles was the son of Franz Michael Humpert and Theresa Hahn, born 26 December 1809 in Fessenbach, Baden, Germany. [See Charles Humpert sketch.]

Immigration:
Arrived on 30 January 1843 from Le Harvre, France to New Orleans aboard the *Mozart*:
    Basler, Valentine

Biographical:
Husband: Valentine Basler
    Birth – 23 December 1815 in Rammersweier, Baden, Germany.
    Death/Burial – before March 1859 most likely in Ste. Genevieve County, Missouri.
Wife: Maria Anna Cleopha Falk, daughter of Peter Falk and Maria Anna Benz [See Peter Falk sketch.]
    Birth – 4 April 1828 in Rammersweier, Baden, Germany.
    1) Marriage – 26 April 1847 in Ste. Genevieve, Ste. Genevieve County, Missouri to Valentine Basler.
    2) Marriage – 7 March 1859 in River aux Vases, Ste. Genevieve County, Missouri to Lawrence Klumpp. [See Lawrence Klumpp sketch]
    Death/Burial – 23 March 1881 in River aux Vases, Ste. Genevieve County, Missouri. She was buried in the Sts. Philip and James Cemetery in River aux Vases, Ste. Genevieve County, Missouri.
Children:

    i. Sophia, born 5 February 1848 in Ste. Genevieve County, Missouri. She was baptized on 21 May 1848 in the Ste. Genevieve Catholic Church in Ste. Genevieve. She married Marquart Hess on 12 November 1866 in River aux Vases, Ste. Genevieve County, Missouri. Marquart was the son of Marquart Hess and Elisabeth _____, born about 1842 in Germany. [See Marquart Hess sketch.]

    ii. Agatha, born 5 February 1850 in Ste. Genevieve County, Missouri. She married Francis Kreitler on 5 February 1876 in Weingarten, Ste. Genevieve County, Missouri. Francis was the son of Ferdinand Kreitler and Maria Anna See, born 10 September 1851 in Rammersweier, Baden, Germany. [See Ferdinand Kreitler sketch.]

    iii. Joseph, born 19 March 1852 in Ste. Genevieve County, Missouri. He was a farmer. Joseph married Paulina Dold on 19 February 1878 in Weingarten, Ste. Genevieve County, Missouri. Paulina was the daughter of Johann Georg Dold and Eleanora Seitz, born 30 November 1855 in Ste. Genevieve County. The couple had four daughters and one child that died in infancy. They also adopted Frank Hess after Joseph's sister, Sophia and her husband died. Paulina died from the complications of childbirth in 1887 in Ste. Genevieve County. She was buried in the Sts. Philip and James Cemetery in River aux Vases, Ste. Genevieve County, Missouri. Joseph raised his children with the assistance of his widowed mother-in-law after his wife's death. He continued to work his farm until shortly before his death. Joseph died of Bright's disease on 20 April 1926 in Ste. Genevieve County, Missouri. He was buried in the Sts. Philip and James Cemetery in River aux Vases, Ste. Genevieve County, Missouri.

    iv. William V., born 10 March 1854 in Ste. Genevieve County, Missouri. He was a farmer.

William married Maria Anna "Mary" Friedrich [aka Frederick] on 7 January 1880 in River aux Vases, Ste. Genevieve County, Missouri. Mary was the daughter of Johann Friedrich and Maria Anna Rosebach, born 17 March 1861 in Newark, Essex County, New Jersey. The couple is said to have had eight children but records for only four sons and two daughters have been found. William died of heart disease on 13 November 1930 and Mary died of heart disease on 17 September 1938, both in Ste. Genevieve County, Missouri. They were both buried in the St. Catherine's Cemetery in Coffman, Ste. Genevieve County, Missouri.

v. Andrew, born 6 February 1856 in Ste. Genevieve County, Missouri. He was baptized on 13 April 1856 in Sts. Philip and James Catholic Church in River aux Vases, Ste. Genevieve County. Andrew was a farmer. He married Catherine Eleanor Dold on 9 August 1881 in Weingarten, Ste. Genevieve County, Missouri. Catherine was the daughter of Johann Georg Dold and Eleanora Seitz, born 30 July 1862 in Ste. Genevieve County, Missouri. The couple had four sons and one daughter. Andrew died of winter fever on 2 December 1889 in Ste. Genevieve County. Catherine married for a second time to Francis Joseph Gegg on 23 April 1895 in River aux Vases. Francis was the son of Severin Gegg and Rosina Ehret, born 28 November 1861 in Pennsylvania. [See Severin Gegg sketch.]

vi. Henry, born 1 September 1858 in Ste. Genevieve County, Missouri. He died of pneumonia on 18 March 1881 in Ste. Genevieve County. He was buried in the Sts. Philip and James Cemetery in River aux Vases, Ste. Genevieve County, Missouri. He never married and had no issue.

Occupation: Farmer
Religious Affiliation: Roman Catholic
Comments:
Valentine Basler came to the United States with a group of families who were intent on settling in Ste. Genevieve County, Missouri. He married Maria Anna Cleopha Falk within a few years of his arrival in Missouri. The couple settled on a farm in Saline Township, Ste. Genevieve County, Missouri with Valentine's brothers, Cornelius and William, and brother-in-law Charles Humpert. Maria had come to the United States with her parents in 1846. Valentine does not appear to have lived long enough to have become a naturalized citizen. He died some time before 7 March 1859 when his widow married Lawrence Klumpp. His place of death and burial location are unknown, but most likely he died in Ste. Genevieve County, Missouri.

Wilhelm "William" Basler Family
Surname Variations: Basley, Bassler, Bosler
European Origin: Rammersweier, Baden, Germany
Family:
Father: Franz Michael Basler, born 6 September 1767 in Rammersweier, Baden, Germany. He died on 11 December 1843 in Rammersweier.
Mother: Gertrud Litterst, born 4 March 1775 in Weierbach, Baden, Germany.
    Children:

Note: For a comprehensive discussion of Franz Michael Basler's children see the Valentine Basler sketch.

Immigration:
Arrived on 26 May 1846 from Le Harvre, France to New Orleans aboard the *Ancona*:
    Basler, William, 23 [31]
        Ursula [Gisi], 21
        Genevieve, 35 [relative of William?]
        Corneli[us], 40
        Marie, 27 [sister of William, fiancé of Carl Humpert]
    Humbert [Humpert], Carl, 36 [fiancé of Maria Basler]

Biographical:
Husband: Wilhelm "William" Basler
  Birth – 21 May 1812 in Rammersweier, Baden, Germany.
  Death/Burial – 27 May 1892 in Ste. Genevieve County, Missouri. He was buried in the Sts. Philip and James Cemetery in River aux Vases, Ste. Genevieve County, Missouri.
Wife: Ursula Gisi, daughter of Joseph Gisi and Walburga Goering [See Joseph Gisi sketch.]
  Birth – 13 October 1825 in Zell amt Offenburg, Baden, Germany.
  Marriage – 26 February 1846 in Baden, Germany.
  Death/Burial – 1 April 1881 in Ste. Genevieve County, Missouri. She was buried in the Sts. Philip and James Cemetery in River aux Vases, Ste. Genevieve County, Missouri.
Children:
    i. John, born 20 September 1847 in Ste. Genevieve County, Missouri. He was baptized on 19 December 1847 in the Ste. Genevieve Catholic Church in Ste. Genevieve, Ste. Genevieve County. He was a farmer near River aux Vases in Ste. Genevieve County. John married Sophia Roth on 11 June 1872 in River aux Vases. Sophia was the daughter of Anton Roth and Maria Eva Roth, born 1 October 1852 in Ste. Genevieve County, Missouri. The couple had one son and two daughters, of whom the son and one daughter had died in by 1880. John died on 11 February 1876 in Ste. Genevieve County, Missouri. He was buried in the Memorial Cemetery in Ste. Genevieve, Ste. Genevieve County, Missouri.
    ii. George, born 24 February 1849 in Ste. Genevieve County, Missouri. He was a farmer. George married Sophia Roth, his older brother's widow, on 3 August 1880 in River aux Vases, Ste. Genevieve County, Missouri. George and Sophia had six sons and two daughters. Sophia died of heart disease and uremia on 20 March 1917 in Ste. Genevieve County. After his wife's death, George lived with his oldest son and helped him on his farm. He died of pneumonia caused by influenza on 20 January 1941 in Ste. Genevieve County. Both he and Sophia were buried in the Valle Spring Cemetery in Ste. Genevieve, Ste. Genevieve County, Missouri.
    iii. Caroline, born 7 July 1853 in River aux Vases, Ste. Genevieve County, Missouri. She married Albert Gegg on 24 September 1878 in Weingarten, Ste. Genevieve County, Missouri. Albert was a farmer. He was the son of Francis Xavier Gegg and Maria Anna Grither, born 9 December 1854 in Ste. Genevieve County, Missouri. The couple had five sons and two daughters, of whom one daughter died in infancy. Caroline died of pneumonia and chronic interstitial nephritis on 25 March 1920 and Albert died of pneumonia and intestinal trouble on 6 June 1923, both in Ste. Genevieve County, Missouri. They were both buried in Our Lady Help of Christians Cemetery in Weingarten, Ste. Genevieve County, Missouri.
    iv. Sophia [aka Josephine], born 31 May 1855 in Ste. Genevieve County, Missouri. She married Anton Roth on 28 September 1880 in River aux Vases, Ste. Genevieve County, Missouri. Anton was a farmer. He was the son of Anton Roth and Maria Eva Roth, born 21 March 1859 in Ste. Genevieve County, Missouri. The couple had eight daughters and one son, of whom four daughters died in infancy. Anton died of chronic myocarditis and nephritis on 1 February 1935 in Ste. Genevieve County, Missouri. Sophia died on 22 December 1943. They were both buried in the Valle Spring Cemetery in Ste. Genevieve, Ste. Genevieve County, Missouri.
    v. Henry, born 1 September 1858 in Ste. Genevieve County, Missouri. He was baptized on 14 November 1858 in the Sts. Philip and James Catholic Church in River aux Vases, Ste. Genevieve County. He was a farmer. Henry married Agatha Herzog on 20 November 1883 in River aux Vases. Agatha was the daughter of Bonaventure Herzog and Apollonia Schmiederer, born 2 February 1862 in Ste. Genevieve County, Missouri. The couple had four sons and four daughters, of whom the youngest son died in infancy. Henry and Agatha both died of influenza and pneumonia on 13 March 1928 in Ste. Genevieve County. They were both buried in the Sts. Philip and James Cemetery in River aux Vases, Ste. Genevieve County, Missouri.
    vi. Joseph, born 9 July 1859 in Ste. Genevieve County, Missouri. He was baptized on 14 August 1859 in the Sts. Philip and James Catholic Church in River aux Vases, Ste. Genevieve County.

Joseph died on 30 August 1860 in Ste. Genevieve County, Missouri. No issue.
vii. Louise Ursula, born 18 April 1864 in Ste. Genevieve County, Missouri. She was baptized on 15 May 1864 in the Sts. Philip and James Catholic Church in River aux Vases, Ste. Genevieve County. Louise married Theodore Joseph Stoll on 22 May 1888 in River aux Vases, Ste. Genevieve County, Missouri. Theodore was the son of Michael Stoll and Philippine Staab, born 1 October 1838 in Hofweier, Baden, Germany. [See Michael Stoll sketch.]

Land Patents:
Ste. Genevieve County, Missouri

Patentee	Issue Date	Land Office	Cert. No.	Serial No.	Twp	Rng	Sec	Acres
Basler, William	15 Nov 1854	Jackson	15804	MO3670_.328	36-N	8-E	22	40.00
Basler, William	1 Sep 1856	Jackson	16547	MO3730_.385	36-N	8-E	22	200.00
Basler, William	30 Oct 1857	Jackson	23354	MO3810_.463	36-N	8-E	22	40.00

Occupation: Farmer
Religious Affiliation: Roman Catholic
Comments:
Wilhelm "William" Basler came to the United States in 1846 with several of his siblings and settled near the village of River aux Vases in Ste. Genevieve County, Missouri. He and his brother Valentine and his brother-in-law, Carl Humpert, purchased adjoining land and farmed together. It does not appear that William ever became a naturalized citizen or that he took part in the Civil War. He may have been too old and his sons too young to participate. William and Ursula had four sons and three daughters, of whom one son died in infancy. Ursula died on 1 April 1881 and William died on 27 May 1892, both in Ste. Genevieve County. They were both buried in the Sts. Philip and James Cemetery in River aux Vases, Ste. Genevieve County, Missouri.

John Bassler Family
Surname Variations: Basler, Bosler
European Origin: Baden, Germany
Family:
Father: Unknown
Mother: Unknown
   Child:
* i. John, born in September 1822 in Baden, Germany. [See sketch below.]

Immigration:
Arrived some time before the 1860 census aboard an unknown vessel:
    Bassler, John

Biographical:
Husband: John Bassler
   Birth – September 1822 in Baden, Germany.
   Death/Burial – 28 February 1882 in Ste. Genevieve, Ste. Genevieve County, Missouri. He was buried in the Valle Spring Cemetery in Ste. Genevieve, Ste. Genevieve County, Missouri.
Wife: Salome "Sally" Berke
   Birth – about 1829 in Oberkirchen, Baden, Germany.
   1) Marriage – 9 April 1865 in Ste. Genevieve County, Missouri to Joseph Panter [aka Pander, Ponder]
   2) Marriage – between 1865 and 1870 in Missouri to John Bassler.
   Death/Burial – 6 March 1882 in Ste. Genevieve, Ste. Genevieve County, Missouri. She was buried in the Valle Spring Cemetery in Ste. Genevieve, Ste. Genevieve County, Missouri.

There were no children born to John Bassler and Salome Berke.

Military:
Served in the U.S. Civil War for the Union:
Private, Company G, 78th Enrolled Missouri Militia
    John Basler enlisted on 4 October 1862 in Ste. Genevieve, Missouri. He was ordered into active service on 16 October 1864. He was relieved from duty on 25 November 1864 after having served 41 days of actual service.

Education: Could read and write
Occupation: General laborer and teamster
Religious Affiliation: Roman Catholic
Comments:
Very little is known about this John Bassler. He may have been related to the Baslers from Rammersweier, but so far no evidence has come to light to support that speculation. He appears to have come to Ste. Genevieve County before 1860 and lived with Joseph Panter and his wife Salome who had no children. The three settled in the city of Ste. Genevieve where Joseph was a butcher and John worked as a general laborer. This Joseph Panter is not to be confused with the Joseph Ponder [aka Panther, Panter] who married Mary Giesler in Ste. Genevieve County, Missouri in 1856. That Joseph Ponder was the son of Lorenz Panther and Magdalena Panther, born 26 May 1828 in Butschbach, Offenburg, Baden, Germany. [See Joseph Ponder sketch.] During the Civil War, John Bassler enlisted in the 78th Enrolled Missouri Militia, but it is doubtful that he ever saw active service. Joseph Panter died at the age of 40 on 12 December 1865 in Ste. Genevieve. He was buried in the Memorial Cemetery in Ste. Genevieve, Ste. Genevieve County, Missouri. John Bassler and Salome were married in Missouri some time between 1865 and 1870. The couple does not appear to have had any children. John died on 28 February 1882 and Salome died on 6 March 1882 [her headstone erroneously gives her date of death as 10 March 1882], both in Ste. Genevieve. They were both buried in the Valle Spring Cemetery in Ste. Genevieve, Ste. Genevieve County, Missouri.

George Bauer Family
Surname Variations: Baur, Bower[s], Power
European Origin: Niederseebach, Bas-Rhin, Alsace, France
Family:
Father: Unknown
Mother: Unknown
    Child:
*   i.   George A. B., born 2 February 1834 in Niederseebach, Bas-Rhin, Alsace, France. [See sketch below.]

Immigration:
Arrived about 1840 aboard an unknown vessel:
    Bauer, George

Biographical:
Husband: George A. B. Bauer
    Birth – 2 February 1834 in Niederseebach, Bas-Rhin, Alsace, France.
    Death/Burial – 12 April 1898 in Ste. Genevieve County, Missouri. He was buried in the Lutheran Cemetery in Ste. Genevieve, Ste. Genevieve County, Missouri.
Wife: Anna Barbara Seibold
    Birth – 17 March 1834 in Bavaria, Germany.
    Marriage – about 1851 in New York.
    Death/Burial – 11 September 1898 in River aux Vases, Ste. Genevieve County, Missouri. She was buried in the Lutheran Cemetery in Ste. Genevieve, Ste. Genevieve County, Missouri.
    Children:
      i.   Magdalena, born in November 1852 in New York. She married Ferdinand Kuehne as his

second wife on 10 April 1871 in Ste. Genevieve County, Missouri. Ferdinand was born in October 1845 in Germany. [See Ferdinand Kuehne sketch.]

ii. Margarethe Mary, born 12 April 1854 in Erie County, New York. She married Henry Vogt on 2 April 1872 in River aux Vases, Ste. Genevieve County, Missouri. Henry was the son of Anton Vogt and Regina Hoog, born 14 July 1848 in Ste. Genevieve County, Missouri. [See Anton "Anthony" Vogt sketch.]

iii. Barbara, born 16 November 1855 in Erie County, New York. She married Andreas "Andrew" Flieg on 25 November 1875 in River aux Vases, Ste. Genevieve County, Missouri. Andrew was the son of Anton Flieg and Catharina Strobel, born 17 February 1852 in Germany. [See Anton Flieg sketch.]

iv. Elizabeth, born 27 March 1857 in Erie County, New York. She died on 7 July 1877 near River aux Vases, Ste. Genevieve County. Her death was attributed to her having over exerted herself at the 4th of July celebrations earlier that week. Elizabeth was buried in the Lutheran Cemetery in Ste. Genevieve, Ste. Genevieve County, Missouri. No issue.

v. Henry B., born 18 April 1858 in Erie County, New York. Henry was a farmer in Ste. Genevieve County. He married Genevieve Rosine "Jennie" Rudloff on 23 November 1880 in River aux Vases, Ste. Genevieve County, Missouri. Jennie was the daughter of Johann Georg "George" Rudloff and Cecilia Winkler, born 4 May 1860 in Missouri. The couple had one daughter who died of tuberculosis at the age of fourteen. Jennie died of consumption on 28 January 1885 in Ste. Genevieve County, Missouri. She was buried in the Sts. Philip and James Cemetery in River aux Vases. Henry married for a second time to Lila Anna "Lillie" Brown on 19 March 1888 in Ste. Genevieve County. Lillie was the daughter of William Brown and Margaret Jennings, born 5 August 1867 in Missouri. Henry and Lillie had five sons and three daughters, of whom one son and one daughter died before 1907. Lillie died of "lung trouble" near River aux Vases on 9 September 1907. She was buried in the Lutheran Cemetery in Ste. Genevieve, Ste. Genevieve County, Missouri. Henry married for a third time to Mrs. Louise Roth, widow of Peter Roth, on 19 October 1908 in River aux Vases. Louise was the daughter of Andreas "Andrew" Baumann and Fidelia Herzog, born 11 May 1858 in Ste. Genevieve County. Henry and Louise had no children together. Henry died of aortic stenosis on 27 October 1928 and Louise died of a cerebral hemorrhage on 31 October 1943, both in Ste. Genevieve County. Henry was buried in the Lutheran Cemetery in Ste. Genevieve, Ste. Genevieve County, Missouri, and Louise was buried in the St. Joseph Cemetery in Zell, Ste. Genevieve County, Missouri.

vi. Andrew F., born 17 September 1860 in Buffalo, Erie County, New York. He was a farmer in Ste. Genevieve County, Missouri. Andrew married Louisa Rosalie Langelier on 13 January 1885 in River aux Vases, Ste. Genevieve County, Missouri. Louisa was the daughter of Jean Baptiste "John" Langelier and Judithe Zoe Lalumondiere, born 24 October 1864 in River aux Vases. The couple had three sons and three daughters. Andrew died of heart disease on 8 April 1939 and Louisa died of a cerebral hemorrhage on 6 July 1946, both in Ste. Genevieve County, Missouri. They were both buried in the Valle Spring Cemetery in Ste. Genevieve, Ste. Genevieve County, Missouri.

vii. Michael John, born 28 November 1862 in Buffalo, Erie County, New York. Michael was a famer and farm laborer in Missouri. He married Pelagie Juliette "Julia" Langelier on 14 July 1885 in River aux Vases, Ste. Genevieve County, Missouri. She was the daughter of Jean Baptiste "Jean" Langelier and Judithe Zoe Lalumondiere, born in December 1854 in River aux Vases, Ste. Genevieve County, Missouri. Julia was twice a widow when she married Michael. Her first husband was Louis Anton Bernard Labruyere whom she married on 5 February 1878. Louis died on 19 March 1879 in Ste. Genevieve County and was buried in the Sts. Philip and James Cemetery in River aux Vases. Julia married her second husband, _____ McNabb, some time between March 1879 and July 1885. She had one daughter with her second husband. Mr. McNabb appears to have died some time before July 1885. Michael and Julia are said to have had five children together; however, records for only two daughters have been found. Julia died of heart disease and septicemia on 13 January 1925 in Ste. Genevieve County, Missouri. She was buried in the Sts. Philip and James Cemetery in River aux Vases. Michael died of pneumonia on 26 May 1944 in St. Louis. He was buried in the Saint Trinity Cemetery in Lemay, St. Louis County, Missouri.

viii. Mary Agnes, born 28 November 1863 in Buffalo, Erie County, New York. She married Gustave Joseph Schmitt on 8 September 1885 in Ste. Genevieve, Ste. Genevieve County, Missouri. Gustave was the son of Bernard Schmitt and Theresia Doll, born 20 November 1859 in Ste. Genevieve County, Missouri. [See Bernard Schmitt sketch.]

ix. John Peter, born 4 December 1867 in Missouri. He was a blacksmith in St. Louis County, Missouri. He married Frances A. Boos about 1894 in Missouri. Frances was the daughter of George Boos and Margaret Koester, born 4 February in St. Louis, Missouri. The 1910 census record indicates that the couple had nine children, but records for only four sons and one daughter have been found. John died of heart disease on 19 January 1935 and Frances died of diabetes on 18 November 1945, both in St. Louis, Missouri. They were both buried in the Calvary Cemetery and Mausoleum in St. Louis, Missouri.

x. George H., born 9 February 1870 in Missouri. On the afternoon of Saturday, 11 April 1884, fourteen-year-old George was driving an empty wagon on his brother Henry's farm after dropping off a load of wood. The wagon hit a stump as it went down a hill and the boy was thrown out onto the ground. A rear wheel ran over his abdomen, causing severe bruising. But he got back into the wagon and went to the house, shrugging off the pain. His brother took him home to his parents' house and the doctor was sent for. The doctor found no external evidence of any dangerous injury but suspected that the boy was bleeding internally for which he could do nothing. During that evening, George ate dinner and sat with his family but became increasingly uncomfortable. The boy continued to get worse during the night and in the early morning hours, he began to vomit blood and finally died at about 4 o'clock on Sunday morning. George was buried in the Lutheran Cemetery in Ste. Genevieve, Ste. Genevieve County, Missouri. No issue.

xi. Charles Lawrence, born 28 January 1872 in River aux Vases, Ste. Genevieve County, Missouri. He was a blacksmith. He married Lucinda Julia Rigdon on 12 October 1897 in River aux Vases, Ste. Genevieve County, Missouri. Lucinda was the daughter of James Abijah Rigdon and Christina Josephine Kirchner, born 2 December 1860 in Ste. Genevieve County, Missouri. She was a widow when she married Charles. Her first husband was George Walter Shearlock whom she married on 2 February 1882 in Ste. Genevieve County, Missouri. George died on 1 August 1882 in Ste. Genevieve County and was buried in the Sts. Philip and James Cemetery in River aux Vases, Ste. Genevieve County, Missouri. George and Lucinda had one son who was born two months after his father's death. Charles and Lucinda had three sons and one daughter, all born in Ste. Genevieve County, Missouri. Lucinda died of abdominal lympho-sarcoma on 11 September 1921 in Ste. Genevieve County, Missouri. She was buried in the St. Catherine's Cemetery in Coffman, Ste. Genevieve County, Missouri. After his wife's death, Charles moved to Detroit, Michigan where he worked in construction. He married a widow named Delilah Mathes in Detroit on 9 February 1929. Delilah had one son from a previous marriage. The couple remained in Detroit and Charles died there on 18 June 1942. According to his wishes, his body was taken back to Ste. Genevieve County, Missouri, and was buried beside his first wife in the St. Catherine's Cemetery in Coffman. Delilah's ultimate fate is not known.

xii. Katharina, born 22 November 1873 in Missouri. She died on 11 September 1876 in Missouri. Katharina was buried in the Lutheran Cemetery in Ste. Genevieve, Ste. Genevieve County, Missouri. No issue.

xiii. Emile William, born 6 July 1877 in River aux Vases, Ste. Genevieve County, Missouri. In his father's will, Emile is described as "crippled and not as able as his siblings to make a living." However, he does appear to have had a full life. Emile married Mary Anna Anderson on 4 June

1901 in Farmington, St. Francois County, Missouri. Mary Anna was the daughter of Brooks Anderson and Margaret Bowling, born 20 July 1880 in St. Francois County, Missouri. The couple lived in Farmington for the first ten years of their married life. Emile worked in an ice plant in the city of Farmington and later worked as a miner for the Doe Run Lead Company. By 1920, the family had moved to St. Louis where Emile worked as a machinist in a brick factory. The couple had three sons and two daughters. Mary Anna died of heart disease on 20 June 1962 in St. Louis, Missouri. Emile died of heart disease on 6 August 1963 in St. Francois County, Missouri. They were both buried in the Laurel Hill Cemetery in St. Louis, Missouri.

U.S. residence prior to Ste. Genevieve County, Missouri:
Erie County, New York

Military:
Served in the U.S. Civil War for the Union:
1st Lieutenant, Company G, 15th Regiment Missouri Volunteer Infantry
    George A. Bauer enlisted on 9 September 1862 in St. Louis, Missouri. Mustered out on 16 November 1864.

Education: Could read and write
Occupation: Farmer
Religious Affiliation: Lutheran
Comments:
According to his obituary, George Bauer was born in Niederseebach, Bas-Rhin, Alsace, France. He is said to have come to the United States as a young boy with his family in 1840 and settled in Erie County, New York near the town of Eden. George married Anna Barbara Seibold in Buffalo, Erie County, New York about 1851. Barbara had come to the United States from her native Bavaria about 1850 at the age of 17. George was a farmer. In the spring of 1867, the family moved to Ste. Genevieve County, Missouri where George purchased a farm near Staabtown [present-day River aux Vases]. The couple had seven sons and six daughters, of whom two daughters and one son died in adolescence. In the late 1890s, Barbara's health began to fail and eventually she became bedridden. It was thought that she would die before her husband, but George died unexpectedly of heart disease on 12 April 1898 in Ste. Genevieve County, Missouri. Barbara soon followed him, dying of Bright's disease on 11 September 1898. They were both buried in the Lutheran Cemetery in Ste. Genevieve, Ste. Genevieve County, Missouri.

Christian Baum Family

European Origin: Lauchröden, Sachsen-Weimar [Lauchröden, Wartburgkreis, Thuringia, Germany]
Family:
Father: Johann Kaspar Baum, born 20 December 1775 in Lauchröden, Sachsen-Weimar. He died on
    9 March 1854 in Lauchröden.
Mother: Anna Margaretha Radloff, 16 June 1797 in Fernbreitenbach, Sachsen-Weimar. She died on
    15 December 1839 in Lauchröden.
    Child:
*   i.   Christian, born 7 January 1836 in Lauchröden, Sachsen-Weimar. [See sketch below.]

Immigration:
Arrived 28 June 1858 from Bremen, Germany to New Orleans aboard the *Edmund*:
        Baum, Christian, 22   Shoemaker   from Sachsen-Weimar   going to St. Merry, Mo

Biographical:
Husband: Christian Baum
    Birth – 7 January 1836 in Lauchröden, Sachs-Weimar, Germany.
    Death/Burial – 2 December 1927 in Ste. Genevieve, Ste. Genevieve County, Missouri. He was buried in

the Valle Spring Cemetery in Ste. Genevieve, Ste. Genevieve County, Missouri.

1) Wife: Caroline Klein, daughter of Michael Klein and Helena Catherina Schindler [See Michael Klein sketch.]

Birth – 27 January 1838 in Ste. Genevieve County, Missouri.

Marriage – 9 April 1860 in Ste. Genevieve, Ste. Genevieve County, Missouri.

Death/Burial – 24 March 1877 in Ste. Genevieve, Ste. Genevieve County, Missouri. She was buried in the Memorial Cemetery in Ste. Genevieve, Ste. Genevieve County, Missouri.

Children:

i. Henry, born 30 July 1861 in Ste. Genevieve, Ste. Genevieve County, Missouri. He was baptized on 15 September 1861 in the Ste. Genevieve Catholic Church in Ste. Genevieve, Ste. Genevieve County, Missouri. Henry was a barber. As a young man he went west to Colorado, settling first in Teller County and later he moved to Boulder County. Henry married Maud Union Whitehead about 1892, most likely in Colorado. Maud was the daughter of George E. Whitehead and Jane Winn, born 4 February 1869 at sea aboard the *American Union* while her family was enroute to the United States from England. The couple had one son and a child that died in infancy. Maud died on 20 May 1941 and Henry died on 29 April 1946, both in Boulder County, Colorado. They were both buried in the Green Mountain Cemetery in Boulder, Boulder County, Colorado.

ii. Anthony Christian, born 18 September 1863 in Ste. Genevieve, Ste. Genevieve County, Missouri. He was baptized on 18 October 1863 in the Ste. Genevieve Catholic Church in Ste. Genevieve, Ste. Genevieve County, Missouri. He died on 6 April 1864 in Ste. Genevieve County, Missouri. No issue.

iii. Anthony Christian, born 8 February 1865 in Ste. Genevieve, Ste. Genevieve County, Missouri. He was baptized on 16 February 1865 in the Ste. Genevieve Catholic Church in Ste. Genevieve, Ste. Genevieve County, Missouri. Anton was a bricklayer. He married Anna Mary Falk on 20 November 1895 in Ste. Genevieve County. Anna was the daughter of Jacob Falk and Thekla Deck, born 30 July 1869 in Ste. Genevieve County, Missouri. The couple had one son and seven daughters. The family moved to Pueblo, Pueblo County, Colorado where Anton worked in construction. Anna died on 1 December 1914 and Anton died on 1 July 1917, both in Pueblo, Pueblo County, Colorado. They were both buried in the Roselawn Cemetery in Pueblo, Pueblo County, Colorado.

iv. Charles Albert, born 16 July 1866 in Ste. Genevieve, Ste. Genevieve County, Missouri. He was baptized on 12 August 1866 in the Ste. Genevieve Catholic Church in Ste. Genevieve, Ste. Genevieve County, Missouri. Charles was a bricklayer. He married Mary Alice Boyer on 10 October 1894 in Ste. Genevieve County, Missouri. Alice was the daughter of Eli P. Boyer and Jane M. Hammer, born 11 October 1871 in Ste. Genevieve, Ste. Genevieve County, Missouri. The couple moved to Pueblo, Pueblo County, Colorado where Charles worked as a contract bricklayer. Alice died three days after giving birth to her only child, a son, on 23 July 1895 in Pueblo. Charles brought her body back to Ste. Genevieve and she was buried in the Valle Spring Cemetery in Ste. Genevieve, Ste. Genevieve County, Missouri. Charles left his infant son in the care of his grandparents in Ste. Genevieve and returned to Colorado. He lived for a time with his brother, Henry, in Teller County, and then returned to Pueblo. Charles married Elizabeth May _____ some time after 1900 in Colorado. Elizabeth was born of unknown parents about 1877 in Indiana. Charles and Elizabeth do not appear to have had any children together, but raised Charles' son and two of his orphaned nieces. Charles died on 13 February 1956 and Elizabeth died on 1 April 1974, both in Colorado. They were both buried in the Roselawn Cemetery in Pueblo, Pueblo County, Colorado.

v. Louisa Anna, born 20 July 1868 in Ste. Genevieve, Ste. Genevieve County, Missouri. She was baptized on 16 August 1868 in the Ste. Genevieve Catholic Church in Ste. Genevieve, Ste. Genevieve County, Missouri. Louisa was married about 1891 to Henry H. Wood. Henry was the son of unknown parents, born in England in May 1866. He came to the United States about

1886. For the first years of their married life, Henry and Louisa lived in St. Louis, Missouri where Henry worked as a clerk in a dairy. About 1908 they moved to Trenton, Clinton County, Illinois where Henry had a job as a milk buyer for a dairy. Henry and Louisa had one son and six daughters. There is no further mention of Henry after the 1910 census entry in Clinton County, Illinois. His ultimate fate is unknown. By 1920, Louise had moved her family to Pueblo, Pueblo County, Colorado. She remained there until after 1940 and then moved to Los Angeles, California where she died on 28 July 1954. Louisa was buried in the Roselawn Cemetery in Pueblo, Pueblo County, Colorado.

    vi. George Francis "Frank," born 18 July 1870 in Ste. Genevieve, Ste. Genevieve County, Missouri. He was baptized on 14 August 1870 in the Ste. Genevieve Catholic Church in Ste. Genevieve, Ste. Genevieve County, Missouri. Frank became an electrical engineer. He married Mary Elizabeth Dawson on 19 July 1901. Mary was the daughter of Frederic "Fred" Dawson and Victoria Adelaide "Ada" Pyle, born 12 January 1882 in Wickes, Jefferson County, Montana. Frank and Mary lived in various locations in California as Frank's work took them from place to place. Several times he went overseas to study hydroelectric facilities. The couple had three daughters. Frank and Mary were divorced about 1925 and Mary's widowed father came to live with her and her daughters. Frank reportedly died in Pueblo, Pueblo County, Colorado in 1933. Mary died on 19 June 1962 in San Francisco, San Francisco County, California.

    vii. Anna Caroline, born 19 September 1872 in Ste. Genevieve, Ste. Genevieve County, Missouri. She was baptized on 3 November 1872 in the Ste. Genevieve Catholic Church in Ste. Genevieve, Ste. Genevieve County, Missouri. She was a dressmaker. Anna married rather late in life to George Henry Barnum. George was the son of _____ Barnum and Mary Akers, born 9 June 1874 in California. George worked a variety of jobs, mostly manual labor. The couple had one daughter. George died on 4 June 1949 in Ventura County, California. Anna died on 24 January 1952 in Alameda, California.

    viii. Mary Odelia, born 13 December 1875 in Ste. Genevieve, Ste. Genevieve County, Missouri. She was baptized on 9 January 1876 in the Ste. Genevieve Catholic Church in Ste. Genevieve, Ste. Genevieve County, Missouri. Mary lived with various siblings for most of her adult life and does not appear to have ever had a job or profession. She died on 25 July 1960 in San Bernardino County, California. She was buried in the Queen of Heaven Cemetery in Rowland Heights, Los Angeles County, California. Mary never married and had no known issue.

2) Wife: Louise Genevieve Ringwald, daughter of Franz Xavier Ringwald and Maria Anna Sellinger [See Franz Xavier Ringwald sketch.]

Birth – 8 November 1848 in Baden, Germany.

1) Marriage – 10 April 1866 in Ste. Genevieve, Ste. Genevieve County, Missouri to John N. Schneider. [See John N. Schneider sketch.]

2) Marriage – 7 April 1878 in Ste. Genevieve, Ste. Genevieve County, Missouri to Christian Baum.

Death/Burial – 4 February 1934 in Ste. Genevieve, Ste. Genevieve County, Missouri. She was buried in the Valle Spring Cemetery in Ste. Genevieve, Ste. Genevieve County, Missouri.

Children:

    ix. Hedwig Olympia Maria, born 13 February 1879 in Ste. Genevieve, Ste. Genevieve County, Missouri. She was baptized on 23 February 1879 in the Ste. Genevieve Catholic Church in Ste. Genevieve, Ste. Genevieve County, Missouri. She died on 3 February 1880 in Ste. Genevieve. No issue.

    x. Genevieve Catherine, born 15 February 1880 in Ste. Genevieve County, Missouri. She was baptized on 7 March 1880 in the Ste. Genevieve Catholic Church in Ste. Genevieve, Ste. Genevieve County, Missouri. She married Adolph Christian Okenfuss on 30 April 1900 in Ste. Genevieve County, Missouri. Adolph was the son of Maximilian Okenfuss and Barbara Harter, born 4 July 1871 in Ste. Genevieve County, Missouri. [See Maximilian Okenfuss sketch.]

xi. Odelia Estella, born 27 February 1881 in Ste. Genevieve County, Missouri. She was baptized on 27 March 1881 in the Ste. Genevieve Catholic Church in Ste. Genevieve, Ste. Genevieve County, Missouri. Odelia worked as a sales clerk in a dry goods store in Ste. Genevieve. She and her youngest brother, Robert, lived with and supported their mother after their father's death. Odelia died on 1 May 1970 and was buried in the Valle Spring Cemetery in Ste. Genevieve, Ste. Genevieve County, Missouri. She never married and had no known issue.

xii. John Francis Xavier, born 28 February 1882 in Ste. Genevieve County, Missouri. He was baptized on 21 March 1882 in the Ste. Genevieve Catholic Church in Ste. Genevieve, Ste. Genevieve County, Missouri. He died of typhoid fever in December 1898 at the age of seventeen. He was buried in the Valle Spring Cemetery in Ste. Genevieve, Ste. Genevieve County, Missouri. He never married and had no issue.

xiii. Oliver Louis, born 17 September 1883 in Ste. Genevieve, Ste. Genevieve County, Missouri. He was baptized on 12 October 1883 in the Ste. Genevieve Catholic Church in Ste. Genevieve, Ste. Genevieve County, Missouri. As a young man, Oliver enlisted in the U.S. Army and served in the western states between 1901 and 1904. He returned to Missouri and married Charlotte Louisa Jokerst on 9 October 1907 in Ste. Genevieve. Charlotte was the daughter of Charles Conrad Jokerst and Theresia Regina Hettig, born 5 November 1885 in Ste. Genevieve County, Missouri. The couple moved to St. Louis, Missouri where Oliver worked as a pharmacist in a drug store. Oliver and Charlotte had three sons and four sons. About 1928, Oliver began to suffer from physical and mental debility and was committed to the State Hospital No. 4 in Farmington, St. Francois County, Missouri. Charlotte remained in St. Louis and raised her children by herself. She worked as a practical nurse for a private family in order to support her family. Oliver died of paresis with psychosis [a form of neurosyphilis in which chronic meningoencephalitis causes gradual loss of cortical function, progressive dementia, and generalized paralysis] on 12 October 1947 in the State Hospital No. 4 in Farmington, St. Francois County, Missouri. Charlotte died on 3 October 1973 in St. Louis, Missouri. They were both buried in the Valle Spring Cemetery in Ste. Genevieve, Ste. Genevieve County, Missouri.

xiv. Hilda Helen, born 3 December 1884 in Ste. Genevieve, Ste. Genevieve County, Missouri. She was baptized on 28 January 1885 in the Ste. Genevieve Catholic Church Church in Ste. Genevieve, Ste. Genevieve County, Missouri. She married Edward Leo Sexauer on 19 October 1906 in Ste. Genevieve County, Missouri. Edward was the son of George Sexauer and Elizabeth Sauer, born 23 June 1871 in Ste. Genevieve County, Missouri. Edward was a tavern keeper. Before Prohibition, he sold beer and hard liquor. During and after Prohibition, he served mostly soft drinks. The couple had seven sons and one daughter. Edward died of cancer of the penis complicated by heart disease and cirrhosis of the liver on 1 July 1939 in St. Louis, Missouri. Hilda died on 1 November 1963. They were both buried in the Valle Spring Cemetery in Ste. Genevieve, Ste. Genevieve County, Missouri.

xv. Frieda Gertrude, born 12 December 1886 in Ste. Genevieve, Ste. Genevieve County, Missouri. She was baptized on 7 January 1887 in the Ste. Genevieve Catholic Church in Ste. Genevieve, Ste. Genevieve County, Missouri. She married Eugene Beauregarde Joseph Stanton on 9 June 1909 in Ste. Genevieve County, Missouri. Eugene was the son of Samuel Stewart Stanton and Marie Louise Moreau, born 2 May 1881 in Ste. Genevieve County, Missouri. He managed a garage in Ste. Genevieve. Eugene and Frieda had four sons and three daughters, of whom the two oldest sons died of diphtheria in the spring of 1921. Eugene died of an apoplectic stroke on 3 April 1959 in Ste. Genevieve. Frieda died in 1970. They were both buried in the Valle Spring Cemetery in Ste. Genevieve, Ste. Genevieve County, Missouri.

xvi. Walter Joseph, born 21 May 1889 in Ste. Genevieve, Ste. Genevieve County, Missouri. He was baptized on 16 June 1889 in the Ste. Genevieve Catholic Church in Ste. Genevieve, Ste. Genevieve County, Missouri. He was a bartender. He married Tossie Mary Beauchamp on 24 October 1912 in Ste. Genevieve County, Missouri. Tossie was the daughter of Michael Andrew "Mike" Beauchamp and Mary Genevieve "Jennie" Berry, born 29 February 1890. The couple had one son and one daughter. Walter died of coronary thrombosis on 22 April 1949 in St. Louis, Missouri. He was buried in the Valle Spring Cemetery in Ste. Genevieve, Ste. Genevieve County, Missouri. After her husband died, Tossie moved around. In the 1940s, she worked as a housemother for St. Monica's Hospital in Phoenix, Arizona. She later moved to Alaska. Tossie died on 8 June 1969 in Kenai, Kenai Peninsula, Alaska.

xvii. Alma Josephine, born 21 September 1891 in Ste. Genevieve, Ste. Genevieve County, Missouri. She was baptized on 12 October 1891 in the Ste. Genevieve Catholic Church in Ste. Genevieve, Ste. Genevieve County, Missouri. Alma was a grade school teacher in Oakland, Alameda County, California. She married Charles Hana Lusk about 1923, most likely in California. Charles was the son of Salmon Brooks Lusk and Isabelle Walton, born 7 March 1871 in North Bloomfield, Nevada County, California. He was almost twenty years older than Alma. Charles worked for a gas and electric company. The couple had one daughter, born in California. Charles died on 16 May 1956 in San Mateo, California. Alma died on 30 October 1975 in Santa Clara, California. Their burial location is unknown at present.

xviii. Robert Joseph, born 30 May 1893 in Ste. Genevieve, Ste. Genevieve County, Missouri. He was baptized on 23 June 1893 in the Ste. Genevieve Catholic Church in Ste. Genevieve, Ste. Genevieve County, Missouri. Robert was an auto mechanic in Ste. Genevieve. During World War I, he served in the U.S. Army in the Mechanical Support Company, 354 Infantry. Robert married rather late in life on 25 November 1941 in Ste. Genevieve, Ste. Genevieve County, Missouri to Mildred C. Rutledge. Mildred was the daughter of Dr. George M. Rutledge and Angie Patrick, born 27 August 1901 in Missouri. She was a pharmacist in Ste. Genevieve before her marriage. The couple had one son and one daughter. Their son was born with hydrocephalus and died at the age of seven years. Their daughter died at the age of nineteen. Robert suffered from cirrhosis of the liver for about ten years before he died after aspirating the contents of his stomach on 6 April 1962 in St. Louis, Missouri. Mildred died on 18 September 1974. They were all buried in the Valle Spring Cemetery in Ste. Genevieve, Ste. Genevieve County, Missouri.

Naturalization:

Name	Declaration	Naturalization	Origin	Remarks
Baum, Christian			Baden	1900 Census

Military:
Served in the U.S. Civil War for the Union:
Private, Company G, 78th Enrolled Missouri Militia
    Christian Baum enlisted on 4 October 1862 in Ste. Genevieve, Missouri.

Education: Could read and write
Occupation: Boot and Shoemaker
Religious Affiliation: Christian was Lutheran and his wives and children were all Roman Catholic.
Comments:
Christian Baum was reportedly the youngest and only surviving child in a large family, a child of his father's third wife. At the age of fourteen he began learning the shoemaker's trade, and in 1858 he came to the United States, landing in New Orleans. He traveled by boat up the Mississippi River to Ste. Genevieve, where he opened a boot and shoe business. He was twice married. His first wife, Caroline Klein, bore him five sons and three daughters. She died in 1877. In April 1878, Christian married Mrs. Louisa Schneider, the widow of John N. Schneider. She had two daughters with her first husband, and four sons and six daughters with Christian. It is interesting to note that none of the children of his first marriage remained in Missouri and that all but one daughter of the surviving children of his second marriage did stay in Ste. Genevieve County. Christian was a member of the Holy Cross Evangelical Lutheran Church in Ste. Genevieve. Both of his wives and all of his children were Roman Catholic.

Franz Anton Baumann Family

Surname Variations: Bauman, Bawman, Bowman
European Origin: Sasbach, Achern, Baden, Germany
Family:
Father: Leonhard Baumann, born 1 March 1770 in Obersasbach, Achern Baden, Germany. He died on 13 May 1814 in Sasbach, Achern, Baden, Germany.
Mother: Maria Anna Schnurr, born 20 February 1775 in Sasbach, Achern, Baden, Germany. She died on 18 May 1814 in Sasbach.
Children:
  i. Franz Anton, born 14 September 1796 in Sasbach, Achern, Baden, Germany. He died on 10 May 1797 in Sasbach. No issue.
* ii. Franz Anton, born 17 September 1798 in Sasbach, Achern, Baden, Germany. [See sketch below.]
  iii. Maria Magdalena, born 2 January 1801 in Sasbach, Achern, Baden, Germany. She died on 29 February 1820. No further information.
  iv. Maria Anna, born 24 March 1803 in Sasbach, Achern, Baden, Germany. She married Ignatz Rudolphi on 25 February 1824 in Sasbach. Ignatz was the son of Fidel Rudolphi and Maria Anna Ernst. No further information.
  v. Catharina, baptized on 28 April 1805 in the Katholisch Church at Sasbach, Achern, Baden, Germany. She died on 15 June 1808 in Sasbach. No issue.
  vi. Francisca, baptized on 11 September 1807 in the Katholisch Church at Sasbach, Achern, Baden, Germany. She married Joseph Werner on 27 November 1827 in Sasbach. Joseph was the son of Ignatz Werner and Christina Fallert, baptized on 20 May 1797 in Obersasbach, Achern, Baden, Germany. No further information.
  vii. Joseph, baptized on 6 February 1809 in the Katholisch Church at Sasbach, Achern, Baden, Germany. He most likely died before February 1810. No issue.
  viii. Joseph, baptized on 6 February 1810 in the Katholisch Church at Sasbach, Achern, Baden, Germany. He married Maria Anna Schnurr on 8 February 1832 in Sasbach. Maria was the daughter of Joseph Schnurr and Maria Anna Früh. No further information.
  ix. Johannes, baptized on 2 October 1812 in the Katholisch Church at Sasbach, Achern, Baden, Germany. No further information.

Immigration:
Arrived on 22 September 1831 from Le Havre, France to New York aboard the *James*:
  Baumann, [Franz] Anton, 33
    Rosine [Catherine], 30
    Bernard, 8
    Leonard, 7
    Anton, 5
    Andreas, 3
    Brigitta, 1

Biographical:
Husband: Franz Anton Baumann
  Birth – 17 September 1798 in Sasbach, Achern, Baden, Germany.
  Death/Burial – 6 March 1850 in Ste. Genevieve County, Missouri. He was buried in the St. Joseph Cemetery in Zell, Ste. Genevieve County, Missouri.
Wife: Catherine Armbruster, daughter of Bernard Armbruster and Maria Brigida Hauser [See Andreas "Andrew" Armbruster sketch.]
  Birth – 11 November 1798 in Sasbach, Achern, Baden, Germany.
  Marriage – 23 May 1821 in Sasbach, Achern, Baden, Germany.

Death/Burial – 6 December 1876 in Ste. Genevieve County, Missouri. She was buried in the St. Joseph Cemetery in Zell, Ste. Genevieve County, Missouri.

Children:
  i. Bernard, born 2 March 1822 in Sasbach, Achern, Baden, Germany. As a young man in Ohio, he learned the wagon maker's trade, but he was a farmer in Ste. Genevieve County, Missouri. He married Maria Barbara Fallert on 11 August 1846 in Ste. Genevieve, Ste. Genevieve County, Missouri. Barbara was the daughter of Franz Anton Fallert and Regina Oberle, born 13 March 1823 in Achern, Baden, Germany. She had come to the United States with her parents in 1832, landing in New York. Bernard and Barbara had five sons and three daughters, of whom one son died in infancy. Barbara died from complications following the birth of her eighth child on 16 January 1863 in Ste. Genevieve County. She was buried in the St. Joseph Cemetery in Zell, Ste. Genevieve County, Missouri. Bernard married Barbara's younger, widowed sister, Caroline Fallert Echle, as his second wife on 19 May 1863. Caroline was born 8 December 1839 in Ste. Genevieve County, Missouri. She had married Jacob Echle as her first husband on 17 January 1856 in Zell, Ste. Genevieve County, Missouri. Jacob was the son of [Andreas?] Echle and Cecilia Breig, born about 1829 in Baden, Germany. The couple had two sons and two daughters, of whom both sons died in infancy. Jacob died in 1861 by drowning in the Mississippi River. [See Jacob Echle sketch.] Bernard and Caroline had six sons and four daughters, of whom one son and one daughter died in infancy. In the summer of 1870, Caroline was pregnant with her seventh child and she was dealing with a house full of children. The census shows that she and Bernard [erroneously named "Andrew" by the census taker] were living on the Baumann farm with Bernard's oldest children and Caroline's youngest daughter. The four youngest Baumann children were living with the oldest Echle daughter several miles down the road on the Echle farm. The baby daughter that was born that July died six days after birth. Bernard died on 30 December 1893 in Ste. Genevieve County. He was buried in St. Joseph Cemetery in Zell, Ste. Genevieve County, Missouri. Caroline died of arteriosclerosis and an intestinal hemorrhage on 27 May 1915 in Ste. Genevieve County. She was buried in the Sts. Philip and James Cemetery in River aux Vases, Ste. Genevieve County, Missouri.
  ii. Leonard, born 3 December 1823 in Sasbach, Achern, Baden, Germany. He was a farmer. Leonard married Francisca Schwent on 25 November 1851 at Zell, Ste. Genevieve County, Missouri. Francisca was the daughter of Joseph Schwent and Maria Magdalena Jokerst, born 24 July 1833 in Ste. Genevieve County, Missouri. The couple had four sons and six daughters, of whom one daughter died in infancy. During the Civil War, Leonard served in the Union forces in Company F of the 78th Enrolled Missouri Militia. Leonard died in Ste. Genevieve County on 7 July 1879. Francisca died of consumption on 3 March 1895. They were both buried in Our Lady Help of Christians Cemetery in Weingarten, Ste. Genevieve County, Missouri.
  iii. Anton, born 2 September 1824 in Sasbach, Achern, Baden, Germany. He reportedly died aboard ship while the family was enroute to the United States. However, there was no note to that effect made on the ship's manifest. It is more likely that he died shortly after the family arrived in the United States. He had definitely died by January 1840. No issue.
  iv. Andreas "Andrew," born 28 November 1827 in Sasbach, Achern, Baden, Germany. He was a farmer in Ste. Genevieve County, Missouri. Andrew married Fidelia Herzog on 6 May 1861 in Zell, Ste. Genevieve County, Missouri. Fidelia was the daughter of Joseph Herzog and Josephine Barth, born 8 February 1829 in Baden, Germany. She is said to have been orphaned in Germany and to have come to the United States about 1838 with the family of Johann Paul Fischer and Gertrud Littenecker who were from Hofweier, Baden, Germany. Andrew and Fidelia lived near Zell and had four sons and three daughters. Their oldest son died at the age of four in 1857. Some disease or illness seems to have affected the family in 1861. Fidelia died on 26 November 1861, the day after giving birth to her seventh child. Within a week, the newborn baby and three older children had also died. They were all buried together in the same grave in

the St. Joseph Cemetery in Zell, Ste. Genevieve County, Missouri. Andrew was left with one son and one daughter to raise. He married Francisca Basler as his second wife on 20 May 1862 in Zell. Francisca was the daughter of Valentin Basler and Theresia Burgert, born 2 April 1843 in Fessenbach, Baden, Germany. She had come to the United States with her widowed mother and three siblings in December 1860. Andrew and Francisca had two sons and five daughters. During the Civil War, Andrew served in the Union forces in Company K of the 78th Enrolled Missouri Militia. Andrew died on 14 April 1879 and Francisca died of uterine cancer on 19 June 1927, both in Ste. Genevieve County. They were both buried in St. Joseph Cemetery at Zell, Ste. Genevieve County, Missouri.

v. Brigitta "Bridget," born 17 January 1830 in Sasbach, Achern, Baden, Germany. She married Michael Bleifuss on 6 May 1851 in Zell, Ste. Genevieve County, Missouri. Michael was the son of Mathaus Bleifuss and Anna Maria Haefner, born about 1812 in Bavaria, Germany. [See Michael Bleifuss sketch.]

vi. William, born 15 February 1832 in Stark County, Ohio. He was a farmer in Ste. Genevieve County, Missouri. William married Sophia Doll on 17 June 1856 at Zell, Ste. Genevieve County, Missouri in a double wedding with his sister Louisa and Roman Huck, Sophia's half-brother. Sophia was the daughter of Joseph Doll and Johanna Lang, born 20 January 1839 in Obersasbach, Achern, Baden, Germany. Sophia had come to the United States with her parents from Germany in 1847. William enlisted in Company G of the 78th Enrolled Missouri Militia during the Civil War. It is doubtful whether he ever saw active service. William and Sophia had five sons and six daughters, of whom the youngest four children, all daughters, died in infancy or early childhood. Sophia died on 28 June 1898 in Ste. Genevieve County, Missouri. She was buried in the Valle Spring Cemetery in Ste. Genevieve, Ste. Genevieve County, Missouri. After his wife died, William lived with his son, Henry, for the remainder of his life. William died of chronic nephritis and uremia on 24 May 1921 in Ste. Genevieve County, Missouri. He was buried in the Valle Spring Cemetery in Ste. Genevieve, Ste. Genevieve County, Missouri.

vii. Louisa, born 11 February 1834 in Stark County, Ohio. She married Roman Huck on 17 June 1856 at Zell, Ste. Genevieve County, Missouri in a double wedding with her brother William and Roman's half-sister, Sophia Doll. Roman was the son of Johann Hug and Johanna Lang, born 14 January 1833 in Obersasbach, Achern, Baden, Germany. [See Roman Huck sketch.]

viii. Johanna, born 8 February 1836 in Stark County, Ohio. She died on 2 August 1853 in Ste. Genevieve County, Missouri. No issue.

ix. John B., born 25 June 1837 near Canton, Stark County, Ohio. He was baptized in September 1837 in St. John the Baptist Catholic Church in Canton, Stark County, Ohio. As a young man he learned the wagon maker's trade and worked as a wagon maker for about five years. He purchased a farm about six miles south of the town of Ste. Genevieve and worked the land for the rest of his life. John married Amelia Hoog on 3 November 1863 at River aux Vases, Ste. Genevieve County. Amelia was the daughter of Thomas Hoog and Anastasia Grieshaber, born 25 September 1845 in Ste. Genevieve County, Missouri. The couple had four sons and five daughters. Amelia died on 29 March 1882 in Ste. Genevieve County, Missouri. She was buried in the St. Joseph Cemetery in Zell, Ste. Genevieve County, Missouri. John married Catherine Schilli Kettinger, widow of Joseph Kettinger, as his second wife on 30 October 1883. Catherine was the daughter of Joseph Schilli and Anna Maria Jaeger, born 30 April 1848 in Ste. Genevieve County, Missouri. Catherine had married Joseph Huck as her first husband on 8 December 1865 in Ste. Genevieve County, Missouri. Joseph was the son of Florian Huck and Maria Ursula Fischer, born 20 December 1844 in Ste. Genevieve County. Catherine and Joseph had three sons and two daughters before Joseph died on 19 March 1875. She married Joseph Kettinger as her second husband on 13 April 1880 in Ste. Genevieve County. Joseph was the son of Franz Joseph Kettinger and Maria Anna Bauer, born 1 October 1838 in Ste. Genevieve County. Joseph died on 16 July 1880, only a few months after his marriage. The couple's only child, a son, was born the following January, after his father's death. John Baumann and

Catherine Schilli had two sons and two daughters together. With the multiple marriages and numerous step- and half-siblings, the relationships in John's family were very complex. John died of a cerebral hemorrhage on 14 April 1927 and Catherine died of heart disease aggravated by a fractured thigh, both in Ste. Genevieve County, Missouri. They were both buried in the Valle Spring Cemetery in Ste. Genevieve, Ste. Genevieve County, Missouri.

x. Anton, born 18 January 1840 in Stark County, Ohio. He was a farmer near St. Mary's, Ste. Genevieve County, Missouri. During the Civil War, Anton served in the Union forces in Company K of the 78th Enrolled Missouri Militia. He married Justine Schweigert on 29 January 1866 at River aux Vases, Ste. Genevieve County, Missouri. Justine was the daughter of Andreas "Andrew" Schweigert and Helena Lehmann, born 6 June 1840 in Nordrach, Baden, Germany. She had come to the United States with her parents in 1845. Anton and Justine had three sons and one daughter. Justine died on 17 August 1902 and Anton died of an abdominal growth on 18 August 1924, both in Ste. Genevieve County, Missouri. They were both buried in the Sacred Heart Cemetery in Ozora, Ste. Genevieve County, Missouri.

xi. Joseph, born about 1842 in Stark County, Ohio. He was a schoolteacher before he married and lived with his sister Bridget. Joseph later worked as an administrator for the city of Ste. Genevieve and served as clerk of the Ste. Genevieve County Circuit Court. He married Louisa Belle Harris on 10 June 1868 in Ste. Genevieve. Louisa was the daughter of Oliver Harris and Mary Catherine Dudley, born 5 June 1844 in St. Louis, Missouri. The couple had one son. Joseph died unexpectedly of apoplexy on 26 April 1874 in Ste. Genevieve. He was buried in the Memorial Cemetery in Ste. Genevieve, Ste. Genevieve County, Missouri. After her husband's death, Louisa remained single and lived with her son and widowed mother in the town of Ste. Genevieve. She died of a cerebral hemorrhage on 30 July 1921 in Ste. Genevieve County. She was buried in the Valle Spring Cemetery in Ste. Genevieve, Ste. Genevieve County, Missouri.

xii. Francis Xavier, born 22 March 1845 in Ste. Genevieve County, Missouri. He was baptized in the Ste. Genevieve Catholic Church in Ste. Genevieve, Ste. Genevieve County, Missouri. Xavier was a farmer in Ste. Genevieve County. He married Anna Maria "Mary" Palmer on 4 May 1869 in Ste. Genevieve County, Missouri. Mary was the daughter of Pius Palmer and Johanna Huck, born 11 January 1849 in Ste. Genevieve County, Missouri. Xavier served in Company G of the 78th Enrolled Missouri Militia during the Civil War. It is doubtful whether he ever saw active service. Xavier and Mary had four sons and three daughters. Xavier died of nephritis and heart disease on 15 Apr 1920 in Ste. Genevieve County. He was buried in the Valle Spring Cemetery in Ste. Genevieve, Ste. Genevieve County, Missouri. Mary died of chronic myocarditis on 3 November 1925 in Lebanon, Laclede County, Missouri. She was also buried in the Valle Spring Cemetery in Ste. Genevieve, Ste. Genevieve County, Missouri.

U.S. residence prior to Ste. Genevieve County, Missouri:
Stark County, Ohio 1832-1843

Military:
Served in the U.S. Civil War for the Union:
Private, Compnay K, 78th Enrolled Missouri Militia
   Anton Baumann enlisted on 1 August 1863 in Ste. Genevieve, Missouri.
Private, Company C, 8th Provisional Enrolled Missouri Militia
   Anton Bauman was transferred into this unit on 5 August 1863 in Ste. Genevieve, Missouri. He was relieved from active service on 8 November 1863 in Ste. Genevieve. His name appears on the rolls with a credit of 61 days of active service.
Private, Company K, 78th Enrolled Missouri Militia
   Bernard Bauman enlisted on 1 August 1863 in Ste. Genevieve, Missouri. According to unit records, he was ordered into active service between 16 October and 25 November 1864. But the record states that he did not report for duty.

Private, Company F, 78th Enrolled Missouri Militia
: Leonard Bauman enlisted on 30 April 1864 in Ste. Genevieve County, Missouri. He was ordered into active service on 16 October 1864. He was relieved from duty on 25 November 1864 after having served 41 days of actual service.

Private, Company G, 78th Enrolled Missouri Militia
: William Bauman enlisted on 30 April 1864 in Ste. Genevieve, Missouri. He was ordered into active service on 16 October 1864. He was relieved from duty on 25 November 1864 after having served 41 days of actual service.

Private, Company G, 78th Enrolled Missouri Militia
: Xavier Bauman enlisted on 30 April 1864 in Ste. Genevieve, Missouri. He was ordered into active service on 16 October 1864. He was relieved from duty on 25 November 1864 after having served 41 days of actual service.

Corporal, Company K, 78th Enrolled Missouri Militia
: Andrew Bowman [Bauman] enlisted on 1 August 1863 in Ste. Genevieve, Missouri. According to unit records, he was ordered into active service between 16 October and 25 November 1864. But the record states that he did not report for duty.

Land Patents:
Ste. Genevieve County, Missouri

Patentee	Issue Date	Land Office	Cert. No.	Serial No.	Twp	Rng	Sec	Acres
Bauman, Andrew	3 Jan 1856	Jackson	17747	MO3690_.380	37-N	8-E	13	105.50
Bauman, Bernard	1 Aug 1853	Jackson	14347	MO3640_.325	37-N	7-E	33	80.00
Bauman, Barnkard	1 Dec 1858	Jackson	16326	MO3850_.025	7-N	7-E	32/33	80.00
Bauman, Barnhard	20 Aug 1867	Ironton	43088	MO4200_.397	37-N	9-E	7	69.40
Bauman, Barnard	15 Nov 1870	Ironton	43555	MO4210_.206	37-N	9-E	7	6.65
Bauman, William	1 Dec 1853	Jackson	15070	MO3660_.011	37-N	7-E	33	80.00
Bowman, William	10 Jun 1856	Jackson	16327	MO3720_.206	37-N	7-E	34	120.00

Occupation: Wheelwright and farmer
Religious Affiliation: Roman Catholic
Comments:
Franz Anton Baumann was a wheelwright and farmer. He brought his family to America in 1832 and originally settled near Massillon, Stark County, Ohio. In 1843 the Baumanns moved to Ste. Genevieve County, Missouri and settled on a farm near Zell. His wife's two brothers, Andreas and Ignatz Armbruster, also brought their families to Ste. Genevieve County from Germany in 1852. Anton died on 6 March 1850 and was buried in the St. Joseph Cemetery in Zell, Ste. Genevieve County, Missouri. Six of the eight surviving sons of Anton and Catherine served in the 78th Enrolled Missouri Militia during the Civil War. Catherine lived the remainder of her life with her son, Andrew, helping to care for his children. She died on 6 December 1876 and was buried in the St. Joseph Cemetery in Zell, Ste. Genevieve County, Missouri.

Magdalena Baumann Family
Surname Variations: Bauman
European Origin: Baden, Germany
Family:
Father: Unknown
Mother: Unknown
   Child:
*   i.   Peter, born in Germany. [See sketch below.]

Immigration:
Arrived on 29 December 1860 from Le Havre, France to New York aboard the *Zurich*:
    Grieshober, Fabian, 18   from Baden
    Kempff, Madgalena, 46
        Amelia, 18
        Victoria, 14

Biographical:
Husband: Peter Baumann
  Birth – in Germany.
  Death/Burial – before December 1860 in Germany.
Wife: Magdalena Kempf
  Birth – about 1814 in Germany.
  1) Marriage – in Germany to Peter Bauman.
  2) Marriage – 11 May 1862 in River aux Vases, Ste. Genevieve County, Missouri to Michael Feist. [See Michael Feist sketch.]
  Death/Burial – 2 August 1874 in Ste. Genevieve County, Missouri. She was buried in the Sts. Philip and James Cemetery in River aux Vases, Ste. Genevieve County, Missouri.
  Children:
    i.   Amelia, born about 1842 in Baden, Germany. She married Fabian Grieshaber on 15 April 1861 in Ste. Genevieve County, Missouri. Fabian was the son of Brigitta Grieshaber, born 18 January 1842 in Niederschopfhiem, Baden, Germany. [See Fabian Grieshaber sketch.]
    ii.   Victoria, born about 1846 in Baden, Germany. According to her mother's will, she married a man named Constantine Hiney.
    iii.   Paulina. According to her mother's will, she married a man named John Bohise.

Religious Affiliation: Roman Catholic
Comments:
Nothing is known of Peter Baumann other than that he did not come to the United States with his family. It is presumed that he died some time before December 1860 in Germany. His widow, Magdalena, and two daughters traveled to the United States in company with Fabian Grieshaber, the fiancé of Magdalena's oldest daughter. The family appears to have come directly to Ste. Genevieve County, Missouri to settle. Magdalena married Michael Feist as his second wife in the summer of 1862 in Ste. Genevieve County. The couple did not have any children together.

Johann "John" Baumgartner Family
Surname Variations: Baumgertner
European Origin: Switzerland
Family:
Father: Unknown
Mother: Unknown
  Child:
*   i.   Johann "John," born 25 March 1827 in Switzerland. See sketch below.

Immigration:
Arrived in 1849 [1900 census] in an unknown vessel:
    Baumgartner, Johann

Biographical:
Husband: Johann "John" Baumgartner
  Birth – 25 March 1827 in Switzerland.
  Death/Burial – 15 December 1905 in Ste. Genevieve, Ste. Genevieve County, Missouri. He was buried in

the Lutheran Cemetery in Ste. Genevieve, Ste. Genevieve County, Missouri.

Wife: Maria Eva Siebert, daughter of Augustin Siebert and Ludgard Jokerst

Birth – 26 December 1836 in Bohlsbach, Baden, Germany.

Marriage – 16 August 1852 in St. Louis, Missouri.

Death/Burial – 5 July 1910 in Ste. Genevieve, Ste. Genevieve County, Missouri. She was buried in the Lutheran Cemetery in Ste. Genevieve, Ste. Genevieve County, Missouri.

Children:
- i. Lena, born about 1853 in Missouri. She may have died young. No further information.
- ii. John Henry, born 18 January 1854 in St. Louis, Missouri. He was a farmer in Ste. Genevieve County, Missouri. John married Mary Elizabeth Deckert on 10 July 1877 in Ste. Genevieve, Ste. Genevieve County, Missouri, Mary was the daughter of John Deckert and Johanna Anstedt, born 1 January 1862 in Millstadt, St. Clair County, Illinois. The couple had seven sons and three daughters. John died of chronic heart disease on 11 January 1933 and Mary died of heart disease and nephritis on 1 May 1947, both in Ste. Genevieve. They were both buried in the Valle Spring Cemetery in Ste. Genevieve, Ste. Genevieve County, Missouri.
- iii. Augustus, born 9 March 1856 in Missouri. He lived with his parents and worked on his father's farm as a general farm laborer for all of his life. August died of cancer on 22 May 1904 in Ste. Genevieve. He was buried in the Lutheran Cemetery in Ste. Genevieve, Ste. Genevieve County, Missouri. He does not appear to have ever married and had no known issue.
- iv. Henry John [twin], born 14 February 1859 in St. Louis, Missouri. As a young man, he worked as a laborer on his father's farm. Henry married Philomena Mary Kiefer on 3 April 1888 in Ste. Genevieve, Ste. Genevieve County, Missouri. Philomena was the daughter of Joseph Sebastian Kiefer and Catherine Palmer, born 12 August 1870 in Zell, Ste. Genevieve County, Missouri. The couple had seven sons and four daughters, of whom one son died in infancy. After his marriage, Henry worked as a general laborer in the city of Ste. Genevieve. By 1910, he had moved his family to St. Louis where he worked as a laborer in a foundry. In the early 1920s, Henry moved his family to Toledo, Lucas County, Ohio where he worked as a grave digger and maintenance man in the Calvary Cemetery. He died of prostate cancer on 2 September 1924 in Toledo and was buried in the Woodlawn Cemetery in that city. Philomena remained in Toledo after her husband's death and lived with her two youngest sons. She died of senility on 5 July 1947 in Toledo and was buried in the Woodlawn Cemetery in Toledo, Lucas County, Ohio.
- v. Anna C. [twin], born 14 February 1859 in St. Louis, Missouri. She married Charles Schuler on 19 August 1883 in Ste. Genevieve County, Missouri. Charles was the son of Johann Jacob Schuler and Caroline Sparmeyer, born 26 January 1842 in Barr, Alsace, Bas-Rhin, France. [See Johann Jacob Schuler sketch.]
- vi. William, born about 1862 in Missouri. As a young man, he worked as a farm hand in Ste. Genevieve County, Missouri. No further record of him has been found after 1921..
- vii. Clara Therese, born 5 September 1864 in Ste. Genevieve County, Missouri. She married Charles Anton Stauss on 5 January 1882 in Ste. Genevieve County. Charles was born of unknown parents in February 1855 in Germany. He had come to the United States in 1872. He worked as a teamster in a brick yard in Jefferson County, Missouri and later worked in the glass factory in Crystal City. The couple had one son and two daughters. Clara died of ovarian cancer on 29 April 1921 in Festus, Jefferson County, Missouri. She was buried in the Gamel Cemetery in Festus. After his wife's death, Charles lived with his oldest daughter in California. He most likely died there some time after 1930.
- viii. Ursuala, born about 1867 in Missouri. No mention of her has been found after the 1880 census when she was living in her father's household in Ste. Genevieve, Ste. Genevieve County, Missouri. She may have married a man named Charles Wenger.
- ix. Anton, born 20 October 1869 in Ste. Genevieve County, Missouri. He lived in St. Louis, Missouri and worked in a candy factory. Anton married Frances _____ about 1896, most likely in St. Louis. Frances was born of unknown parents on 12 July 1875 in St. Louis. The couple

had one son and two daughters, all born in St. Louis. Anton died of heart disease on 18 January 1953 in St. Louis. Frances died of a gastric hemorrhage from a peptic ulcer on 13 May 1960 in St. Louis. They were both buried in the Oak Grove Cemetery in St. Louis, Missouri.

 x. Eva, born 22 February 1873 in Ste. Genevieve County, Missouri. She married John Demsky about 1893 in Missouri. John was the son of Johann "John" Demsky and Johanna Ziegler, born 11 December 1873 in St. Louis, Missouri. John was a saloon bartender in St. Louis, Missouri. The couple had two children: a daughter and a child who died in infancy before June 1900. John died of a cerebral hemorrhage on 2 December 1939 in St. Louis. Eva died of a heart attack on 18 June 1956 in St. Louis. They were both buried in the Sunset Burial Park in St. Louis.

 xi. Sophia M. , born 10 April 1877 in Ste. Genevieve County, Missouri. She married Andrew Doering. Andrew was a baker in St. Louis, Missouri. Andrew was the son of Ignatz Doering and Maria Frederich, born 21 August 1877 in Marktleugast, Bavaria, Germany. He had come to the United States about 1891. The couple had one daughter. Sophia died of ovarian cancer on 28 May 1929 in St. Louis. Andrew died on 18 August 1934 in St. Louis when he stepped off a curb and was accidentally struck by a car which fractured his skull and broke a leg. They were both buried in the Sunset Burial Park in St. Louis, Missouri.

U.S. residence prior to Ste. Genevieve County, Missouri:
St. Louis, Missouri

Naturalization:

Name	Declaration	Naturalization	Origin	Remarks
Baumgartner, John			Switzerland	1900 U.S. Census

Military:
Served in the U.S. Civil War for the Union:
Private, Company K, 1st Missouri Infantry
 John Baumgartner enlisted 7 May 1861 in St. Louis, Missouri for a 3-month tour of duty.
 He mustered out on 20 August 1861 in St. Louis, Missouri.
Private, Company A, 2nd Missouri Infantry
 John Baumgartner

Education: Could read and write
Occupation: Farmer
Religious Affiliation: Lutheran and Roman Catholic
Comments:
Johann "John" Baumgartner was born in Switzerland and came to the United States about 1849. He settled in St. Louis, Missouri where he married Maria Eva Siebert. Nothing is known of John's ancestry. There were several other Swiss Baumgartner families living in St. Louis and it is possible that they were his relatives. Eva had come to the United States with her parents about 1840 and settled in Ste. Genevieve County, Missouri. John served in the Union army during the Civil War. The family remained in St. Louis until about 1866 when they moved to a farm near Zell, Ste. Genevieve County, Missouri. John died on 15 December 1905 and Eva died of senile dementia on 5 July 1910, both in Ste. Genevieve County, Missouri. They were both buried in the Lutheran Cemetery in Ste. Genevieve, Ste. Genevieve County, Missouri.

Franz "Frank" Baumstark Family
Surname Variations: Burnstock
European Origin: Oberweier amt Rastatt, Baden, Germany
Family:
Father: Boniface Baumstark, born 12 May 1819 in Oberweier amt Rastatt, Baden, Germany. He died on
 13 March 1884 in Oberweier amt Rastatt, Baden, Germany.
Mother: Theresia Wipfler, born 20 October 1812 in Oberweier amt Rastatt, Baden, Germany. She died on

2 April 1896 in Oberweier amt Rastatt, Baden, Germany.

Children:
- i. Ludwig, born 12 May 1851 in Oberweier amt Rastatt, Baden, Germany. He married Maria Eva Ball on 3 June 1884 in Oberweier. Maria was the daughter of Anton Ball and _____, born 28 April 1860 in Oberweier. The couple had five sons and three daughters. Maria died on 5 November 1922 and Ludwig died on 7 September 1934, both in Oberweier.
- * ii. Franz "Frank," born 1 June 1853 in Oberweier amt Rastatt, Baden, Germany. [See sketch below.]
- † iii. Wilhelm "William," born 15 October 1855 in Oberweier amt Rastatt, Baden, Germany. [See William Baumstark sketch.]
- iv. Anton, born 6 November 1857 in Oberweier amt Rastatt, Baden, Germany. He married Franziska Jungling on 12 May 1889 in Oberweier. No further information.
- v. Augustin, born 23 August 1860 in Oberweier amt Rastatt, Baden, Germany. He may have never married. He is said to have died in Oberweier in 1896.
- vi. Ameliana, born and died on 25 January 1863 in Baden, Germany. No issue.
- vii. Thomas, born 22 October 1864 in Oberweier amt Rastatt, Baden, Germany. He died on 1 June 1866. No issue.
- ‡ viii. Thomas, born 22 July 1872 in Oberweier amt Rastatt, Baden, Germany. He came to the United States in 1888 and settled in Perryville, Perry County, Missouri. He died on 8 July 1889 in Perryville. He was buried in the St. Boniface Cemetery in Perryville, Perry County, Missouri. No known issue.

Immigration:
Arrived 7 April 1880 from Le Harvre, France to New York aboard the *Labrador*:
Baumstark, Francois, 26

Biographical:
Husband: Franz "Frank" Baumstark
  Birth – 1 June 1853 in Oberweier amt Rastatt, Baden, Germany.
  Death/Burial – 24 February 1912 in Ste. Genevieve, Ste. Genevieve County, Missouri. He was buried in the Valle Spring Cemetery in Ste. Genevieve, Ste. Genevieve County, Missouri.
Wife: Rosina Rottler, daughter of Valentine Rottler and Maria Anna Isenmann [See Valentine Rottler sketch.]
  Birth – 2 January 1859 in New Offenburg, Ste. Genevieve County, Missouri.
  Marriage – 9 June 1884 in Ste. Genevieve, Ste. Genevieve County, Missouri.
  Death/Burial – 2 May 1946 in Ste. Genevieve, Ste. Genevieve County, Missouri. She was buried in the Valle Spring Cemetery in Ste. Genevieve, Ste. Genevieve County, Missouri.

Children:
- i. Mary Theresa "Mamie," born 6 July 1886 in Valley Forge, St. Francois County, Missouri. She remained single all of her life and after her mother was widowed, she lived with and cared for her. Mamie supported herself by working as a sales clerk in a clothing store. She died on 17 August 1977 and was buried in the Valle Spring Cemetery in Ste. Genevieve, Ste. Genevieve County, Missouri. No issue.
- ii. Emile Valentine, born 6 January 1889 in Valley Forge, St. Francois County, Missouri. He worked as a clerk for an express company in Ste. Genevieve. Emile married Anna Agnes Grieshaber on 23 September 1913 in Ste. Genevieve County, Missouri. Anna was the daughter of John Grieshaber and Mary Ann Will, born 3 November 1889 in Ste. Genevieve County, Missouri. The couple had two sons, both born in Ste. Genevieve County. Emile died of heart disease on 13 November 1931 in Ste. Genevieve County, Missouri. Anna died of leukemia on 2 November 1962 in Ste. Genevieve. They were both buried in the Valle Spring Cemetery in Ste. Genevieve, Ste. Genevieve County, Missouri.

iii. Irene Catherine, born 16 October 1893 in Valley Forge, St. Francois County, Missouri. She was baptized in the St. Joseph's Catholic Church in Farmington, St. Francois County, Missouri on 22 October 1893. Irene remained single all her life. She supported herself by working as a sales clerk in a store. Irene died on 14 December 1986 in Ste. Genevieve County, Missouri. She was buried in the Valle Spring Cemetery in Ste. Genevieve, Ste. Genevieve County, Missouri. No issue.

iv. Herbert Friedrich, born 27 October 1897 in Valley Forge, St. Francois County, Missouri. He was baptized in the St. Joseph's Catholic Church in Farmington, St. Francois County on 11 November 1897. Herbert graduated from St. Louis University in June 1919 with a degree in dentistry. He began practice in Ste. Genevieve with Dr. Henry S. Rehm. Herbert moved to Cape Girardeau, Cape Girardeau County, Missouri in late 1920 where he took over the practice of Dr. Charles B. Ruff. He married Helen Louise Spann on 9 June 1925 in Cape Girardeau. Helen was the daughter of John Naill Spann and Edna Earle Speak, born 13 December 1903 in Union County, Illinois. The couple had one son and two daughters. Helen died unexpectedly of heart failure on 12 July 1940 in Cape Girardeau. She was buried in the St. Marys Cemetery in Cape Girardeau. Herbert married for a second time on 9 April 1942 in Cape Girardeau to Vernice Alvina Vogelsang. Vernice was the daughter of Ervin C. R. Vogelsang and Emelie Franck, born 31 August 1917 in Gordonville, Cape Girardeau County. She was a registered nurse and continued her career after her marriage. The couple had one son. During their lifetimes, both Herbert and Vernice were active members of a number of charitable and civic organizations and worked to improve their community. Herbert died on 16 July 1979 and Vernice died on 5 July 2011, both in Cape Girardeau. They were both buried in the St. Marys Cemetery in Cape Girardeau, Cape Girardeau County, Missouri.

v. Genevieve Lorina, born 29 March 1900 in Valley Forge, St. Francois County, Missouri. She was baptized in the St. Joseph's Catholic Church in Farmington, St. Francois County on 8 April 1900. Genevieve attended the Mullanphy School of Nursing at the Mullanphy Hospital in St. Louis, Missouri. Genevieve married James Jonathan Downs on 23 November 1925 in Ste. Genevieve. James was the son of Michael Downs and Bridget Glynn, born 13 July 1885 in County Westmeath, Ireland. He had arrived in the United States with his parents aboard the *City of Rome*, landing at New York on 26 April 1889. James was a railroad locomotive engineer for the Chicago, Milwaukee, St. Paul and Pacific Railroad. He was based in Mason City, Cerro Gordo County, Iowa. The couple ad four sons and four daughters, all born in Mason City. James died unexpectedly of a heart attack on 18 March 1954 in Mason City. Genevieve is said to have died in 1983. Their burial locations are unknown at present.

U.S. residence Other Than Ste. Genevieve County, Missouri:
Valley Forge, St. Francois County, Missouri

Naturalization:

Name	Declaration	Naturalization	Origin	Remarks
Baumstark, Frank			Baden	1910 Census

Education: Could read and write
Occupation: Shoemaker, Miller, Bartender
Religious Affiliation: Roman Catholic
Comments:

Frank Baumstark came to the United States in 1880. He had been trained as a shoemaker in Germany. However, in Missouri he became a miller and worked in several flour mills in both Ste. Genevieve and St. Francois Counties. He married Rosina Rottler in 1884. The couple had two sons and three daughters, all born in St. Francois County. Frank died from a ruptured abdominal aortic aneurism on 24 February 1912 and Rosine died of a cerebral hemorrhage on 2 May 1946, both in Ste. Genevieve. They were both buried in the Valle Spring Cemetery in Ste. Genevieve, Ste. Genevieve County, Missouri.

Wilhelm "William" Baumstark Family

Surname Variations: Baumstork, Baumeister, Braunstark
European Origin: Oberweier amt Rastatt, Baden, Germany
Family:
Father: Boniface Baumstark, born 12 May 1819 in Oberweier amt Rastatt, Baden, Germany. He died on 13 March 1884 in Oberweier amt Rastatt, Baden, Germany.
Mother: Theresia Wipfler, born 20 October 1812 in Oberweier amt Rastatt, Baden, Germany. She died on 2 April 1896 in Oberweier amt Rastatt, Baden, Germany.
Children:

Note: For a comprehensive discussion of Boniface Baumstark's children see the Frank Baumstark sketch.

Immigration:
Arrived 30 May 1879 from Bremen, Germany to New York aboard the *Main*:
    Braunstark, Wilhelm, 24   Farmer   Germany

Biographical:
Husband: Wilhelm "William" Baumstark
    Birth – 15 October 1855 in Oberweier amt Rastatt, Baden, Germany.
    Death/Burial – 3 July 1932 in Ste. Genevieve, Ste. Genevieve County, Missouri. He was buried in the Valle Spring Cemetery in Ste. Genevieve, Ste. Genevieve County, Missouri.
Wife: Mary Wehner, daughter of Nicholas Wehner and Clara Schneider [See Nicholas Wehner sketch.]
    Birth – 13 September 1854 in Ste. Genevieve, Ste. Genevieve County, Missouri.
    1) Marriage – 3 June 1873 in Ste. Genevieve, Ste. Genevieve County, Missouri to Martin Meyer. [See Martin Meyer sketch.]
    2) Marriage – 10 December 1884 in Ste. Genevieve, Ste. Genevieve County, Missouri to William Baumstark.
    Death/Burial – 13 March 1932 in Ste. Genevieve, Ste. Genevieve County, Missouri. She was buried in the Valle Spring Cemetery in Ste. Genevieve, Ste. Genevieve County, Missouri.
Children:
    i. Augusta Maria Theresa, born 1 October 1885 in Ste. Genevieve, Ste. Genevieve County, Missouri. She was baptized in the Ste. Genevieve Catholic Church on 1 November 1885. Augusta died of congestive chills at the age of eight years on 11 June 1894 in Ste. Genevieve. She was buried in the Valle Spring Cemetery in Ste. Genevieve, Ste. Genevieve County, Missouri. No issue.
    ii. Marie Antoinette "Tony", born 4 September 1887 in Ste. Genevieve, Ste. Genevieve County, Missouri. She was baptized in the Ste. Genevieve Catholic Church on 25 September 1887. She married Leslie Earl Miller on 28 November 1907 in Ste. Genevieve. Leslie was the son of William H. Miller and Carrie A. Delcour, born in August 1886 in [St. Francois County?], Missouri. He was an engineer at the railroad depot at the Little Rock ferry landing in Ste. Genevieve County, Missouri. The couple had twins, a son and a daughter, born on 26 July 1908. Tony had been seriously ill during the last two months of her pregnancy and the birth of the twins was too much for her frail body. She died within two weeks of the birth of her children on 10 September 1908 at the home of her parents. Her infant son died on 26 October 1908 and the two of them were buried in the same grave in the Valle Spring Cemetery in Ste. Genevieve, Ste. Genevieve County, Missouri. The surviving twin daughter was raised by her Baumstark grandparents in Ste. Genevieve. After the death of his wife, Leslie moved to St. Francois County, Missouri where he worked as a bartender in a saloon for a time. He married Lydia Josephine Hannauer on 19 January 1910 in St. Louis, Missouri. Lydia was the daughter of Charles Edward Hannauer and Mary L. Ottenad, born 24 June 1889 in St. Louis, Missouri. She may have been previously married to a man named Arthur Rolffes, but nothing is known of

him. Leslie and Lydia had no children together. By 1920, Leslie and Lydia had moved to Chicago, Illinois with his parents and sister. Lydia died on 23 December 1963 in St. Louis, Missouri. She was buried in the Resurrection Cemetery in St. Louis. No record has been found of Leslie after 1920 and his ultimate fate is unknown.

iii. Olivia Theresa "Illma," born 17 July 1889 in Ste. Genevieve, Ste. Genevieve County, Missouri. She was baptized in the Ste. Genevieve Catholic Church on 25 August 1889. Illma married George Washington Huck on 10 June 1908 in Ste. Genevieve. George was the son of Francis John Florian "Frank" Huck and Walburga Grass, born 22 February 1888 in Ste. Genevieve County, Missouri. George was a baker. The couple lived the first few years of their married life in Ste. Genevieve and then moved to Crystal City, Jefferson County, Missouri where George quickly established a new bakery. The couple had two sons and one daughter. George died of a ruptured appendix on 30 September 1925 in St. Louis, Missouri. He was buried in the Valle Spring Cemetery in Ste. Genevieve, Ste. Genevieve County, Missouri. After her husband's death, Illma was unable to keep her family together and the two boys were sent to live with two different families in Ste. Genevieve. Illma and her daughter remained in Crystal City. Illma died on 15 December 1966 in Festus, Jefferson County, Missouri. She was buried in the Valle Spring Cemetery in Ste. Genevieve, Ste. Genevieve County, Missouri.

iv. Anna Helena, born 22 December 1891 in Ste. Genevieve, Ste. Genevieve County, Missouri. She was baptized in the Ste. Genevieve Catholic Church on 24 January 1892. She married August John Birsner on 12 October 1914 in Ste. Genevieve. August was the son of John Nepomuk Birsner and Johanna Neidhardt, born 2 December 1888 in St. Louis, Missouri. August was a master brewer. He took his wife to New Orleans, Louisiana early in their marriage and their two children, a son and a daughter, were both born there. In the mid-1920s, the family left the country to escape Prohibition by moving to Cristobal, Canal Zone [Panama]. They returned to the United States in July 1927. Within six months, August moved to Regina, Saskatchewan, Canada, to work in a brewery. Anna and the children followed him nine months later. August died in St. Boniface, Manitoba, Canada on 2 April 1932. His burial location is unknown. Anna and the children remained in Canada until about 1935 when they moved to Los Angeles, California. Anna died in May 1969 in New Orleans, Louisiana.

v. Eulalia Margareta, born 6 January 1894 in Ste. Genevieve, Ste. Genevieve County, Missouri. She was baptized in the Ste. Genevieve Catholic Church on 4 February 1894. Eulalia was a registered nurse and worked in one of the hospitals in St. Louis, Missouri for a number of years. She married a man named [Vernon?] Jones some time after 1930. Very little is known about him other than his name. The couple lived in St. Louis. Eulalia died of congestive heart failure on 26 July 1972 in St. Louis. She was buried in the St. Matthew's Cemetery in St. Louis, Missouri. Mr. Jones' fate is unknown. No issue.

Naturalization:

Name	Declaration	Naturalization	Origin
Baumstark, William		1889	Baden

Education: Could read and write
Occupation: Locksmith, Farmer, Flour Mill Engineer, Hotel Keeper
Religious Affiliation: Roman Catholic
Political Affiliation and/or Any Offices Held: Alderman, City of Ste. Genevieve, 1908
Comments:

Wilhelm "William" Baumstark was born in Germany in 1855. He learned the trade of locksmith, at which he worked for a number of years before coming to the United States in 1879. He came directly to Ste. Genevieve County, where he raised sheep and farmed for a number of years. In 1883, he moved into the city of Ste. Genevieve where he was employed as a mill engineer in the Cone Mills. A year later he married Mrs. Mary Wehner Meyer, widow of Martin Meyer who had been killed in an explosion at the Cone Mills in 1880. Mary was an entrepreneur in her own right. The year after her first marriage, she opened a boarding house at the Little Rock landing just north of Ste. Genevieve in order to house the workers of the newly opened government rock quarry. After her husband's death, Mary designed and built what became known as the Meyer's Hotel in Ste. Genevieve. It opened for business in December 1882. After William Baumstark and Mary Wehner Meyer were married, William took over the management of the Meyer's Hotel while Mary raised their large combined family of children and grandchildren. He added a livery stable and omnibus service and later added an additional wing to the hotel building, greatly increasing its capacity. The couple ran the hotel until 1921 when they leased the business to two women from Bismarck, St. Francois County, Missouri. Mary died of heart failure on 13 March 1932 and William died of pneumonia on 2 July 1932, both in Ste. Genevieve. They were both buried in the Valle Spring Cemetery in Ste. Genevieve, Ste. Genevieve County, Missouri.

Vincent Bayer Family

Surname Variations: Baier, Byer[s], Boyer
European Origin: Hofweier, Baden, Germany
Family:
Father: Amand Bayer, born 25 October 1804 in Hofweier, Baden, Germany. He died on 11 October 1839 in Ste. Genevieve, Ste. Genevieve County, Missouri. He was buried in the Memorial Cemetery in Ste. Genevieve, Ste. Genevieve County, Missouri.
Mother: Margaretha Neff, born 28 June 1803 in Hofweier, Baden, Germany. She died on 26 October 1880 near Zell, Ste. Genevieve County, Missouri. She was buried in the St. Joseph Cemetery in Zell, Ste. Genevieve County, Missouri. [See Michael Kempf sketch for her second marriage to Simon Kempf.]
Child:
*   i.   Vincent, born 13 January 1827 in Hofweier, Baden, Germany. [See sketch below.]

Immigration:
Arrived on 3 May 1839 from Le Havre, France to New York aboard the *Poland*:
    Bayer, Amand, 34
        Margarite, 35
        Vincenz, 12

Biographical:
Husband: Vincent Bayer
    Birth – 13 January 1827 in Hofweier, Baden, Germany.
    Death/Burial – 13 February 1893 in Lawrenceton, Ste. Genevieve County, Missouri. He was buried in the St. Lawrence Cemetery in Lawrenceton, Ste. Genevieve County, Missouri.
1) Wife: Elisabeth Rottler, daughter of Wendelin Rottler and Katharina Eisenbeis [See Valentine Rottler sketch.]
    Birth – 1 August 1829 in Oberweier bei Lahr, Baden, Germany.
    1) Marriage – 29 January 1852 in the German Settlement [present-day Zell], Ste. Genevieve County, Missouri to Joseph Seitz. [See Joseph Seitz sketch.]
    2) Marriage – 30 November 1854 in the German Settlement [present-day Zell], Ste. Genevieve County, Missouri to Vincent Bayer.
    Death/Burial – 15 March 1886 in Lawrenceton, Ste. Genevieve County, Missouri. She was buried in the St. Lawrence Cemetery in Lawrenceton, Ste. Genevieve County, Missouri.
Children:
    i.   Simon, born 26 November 1855 in Ste. Genevieve County, Missouri. He farmed land near the town of Bloomsdale. He married Mary Ann Kirchner on 13 November 1877 at Lawrenceton, Ste. Genevieve County, Missouri. Mary was the daughter of Peter Kirchner and Anastasia Schweiss, born 18 November 1857 in Ste. Genevieve County, Missouri. The couple had six sons and six daughters. Simon died of a cancerous growth on his face on 9 October 1927 and

Mary died of heart disease on 30 November 1939, both in St. Louis. They were both buried in the St. Lawrence Cemetery at Lawrenceton, Ste. Genevieve County, Missouri.

ii. Charles "Carl," born 21 August 1857 in Ste. Genevieve County, Missouri. He farmed land near the town of Bloomsdale. He married Caroline Sewald on 7 September 1885 at Bloomsdale. She was the daughter of Andrew Sewald and Mary Ann Oberle, born 12 November 1867 in Ste. Genevieve County, Missouri. The couple had three sons and three daughters. Carl died of apoplexy on 13 May 1935 and Caroline died of pernicious anemia on 10 June 1940, both in Bloomsdale. They are both buried in the St. Lawrence Cemetery at Lawrenceton, Ste. Genevieve County, Missouri.

iii. Valentine, born 12 March 1859 in Ste. Genevieve County, Missouri. He was a farmer near Bloomsdale, Ste. Genevieve County. He married Mary Ann Sewald on 30 January 1883 at Lawrenceton, Ste. Genevieve County, Missouri. She was the daughter of Andrew Sewald and Mary Ann Oberle, born 12 October 1865 in Ste. Genevieve County, Missouri. The couple had three sons and two daughters. Valentine died in Lawrenceton, Ste. Genevieve County, Missouri on 21 January 1920 from stomach cancer which had spread to his liver and intestines. Mary died of chronic nephritis on 17 April 1936 in DeSoto, Jefferson County, Missouri. They are both buried in the St. Lawrence Cemetery at Lawrenceton, Ste. Genevieve County, Missouri.

iv. Fridolin Mathias "Fred," born 28 December 1860 in Ste. Genevieve County, Missouri. He was a farmer near Bloomsdale, Ste. Genevieve County, Missouri. He was baptized on 24 February 1861 in St. Anne's Catholic Church in French Village, St. Francois County, Missouri. He married Elizabeth M. Sewald on 3 May 1886 at Bloomsdale, Ste. Genevieve County, Missouri. She was the daughter of Andrew Sewald and Mary Ann Oberle, born on 9 January 1870 in Ste. Genevieve County, Missouri. The couple had two sons and three daughters. Fred died of a cerebral hemorrhage on 22 May 1937 and Elizabeth died of chronic heart disease on 6 August 1941, both in Lawrenceton. They were both buried in the St. Lawrence Cemetery at Lawrenceton, Ste. Genevieve County, Missouri.

v. Margarette, born 12 November 1862 in Ste. Genevieve County, Missouri. She was baptized on 29 November 1862 in St. Philomena's Catholic Church at Bloomsdale, Ste. Genevieve County, Missouri. She married Joseph Bader on 25 September 1883 at Bloomsdale, Ste. Genevieve County, Missouri. Joseph was the son of Ludwig "Louis" Bader and Maria Anna Oberle, born 12 March 1860 Ste. Genevieve County, Missouri. [See Ludwig "Louis" Bader sketch.]

2) Wife: Katharina Rottler, daughter of Wendelin Rottler and Katharina Eisenbeis [See Valentine Rottler sketch.]

Birth – 1 December 1825 in Oberweier bei Lahr, Baden, Germany.

1) Marriage – 27 November 1848 in Gengenbach, Baden, Germany to Martin Braun. [See Martin Braun sketch.]

2) Marriage – 3 May 1887 in Ste. Genevieve, Ste. Genevieve County, Missouri to Vincent Bayer.

Death/Burial – 22 February 1925 in St. Louis, Missouri. She was buried in Calvary Cemetery in St. Louis, Missouri.

Children:

Vincent Bayer and Katharina Rottler had no children together.

Land Patents:
Ste. Genevieve County, Missouri

Patentee	Issue Date	Land Office	Cert. No.	Serial No.	Twp	Rng	Sec	Acres
Bayer, Vincent	15 Jan 1856	St. Louis	23374	MO0980_.083	38-N	6-E	23	320.0
					38-N	6-E	24	
					38-N	6-E	13	
					38-N	6-E	14	

Naturalization:

Name	Declaration	Naturalization	Origin
Byer, Vincent	7 March 1852	21 May 1853 Ste. Genevieve Co.	Baden

Military:
Served in the U.S. Civil War for the Union:
Private, Company F, 78th Enrolled Missouri Militia
    Vincent Bayer enlisted August 1862 in Ste. Genevieve, Missouri. He was enrolled as a Sergeant on 30 April 1864. He was ordered into active service on 16 October 1864. He was relieved from duty on 25 November 1864 after having served 41 days of actual service.

Education: Could read and write
Occupation: Farmer
Religious Affiliation: Roman Catholic
Comments:
Vincent Bayer came to Ste. Genevieve County, Missouri with his parents in 1839. His father died within a few months of their arrival and his mother married for a second time on 24 February 1840 in Ste. Genevieve to Simon Kempf. Simon and Margaretha had no children of their own, but raised Vincent and the orphaned son and daughter of Simon's sister, Theresa Kempf Siebert. Vincent married Elisabeth Rottler in Zell, Ste. Genevieve County, Missouri on 30 November 1854. Elizabeth was the widow of Joseph Seitz, son of Joseph Seitz and Maria Josepha Rheinhardt, born 7 January 1826 in Oberweier bei Lahr, Baden, Germany. She had come to the United States in 1851 in the company of her future husband, Joseph Seitz, and his sister, Elisabeth. They landed at New Orleans and traveled up the Mississippi River to Ste. Genevieve. Joseph and Elisabeth were married on 29 January 1852 at the German Settlement [present-day Zell], Ste. Genevieve County. Elisabeth was almost nine months pregnant with her first child when her husband died on 31 August 1853 at Zell. She lived with her brother Valentine until her marriage to Vincent Bayer. Shortly after they were married, Vincent and Elisabeth bought a farm near Punjaub [present-day Lawrenceton] in the northern part of Ste. Genevieve County. Their five children were all born there. During the Civil War, Vincent enlisted as a private under Captain Andrew Miller in Company F, 78th Enrolled Missouri Militia in August 1862. On 30 April 1864, he was promoted to sergeant. Elisabeth died of erysipelas [an acute streptococcus bacterial infection of the skin] in Lawrenceton on 15 March 1886 and was buried in the St. Lawrence Cemetery at Lawrenceton, Ste. Genevieve County, Missouri. Vincent married for a second time in Ste. Genevieve on 3 May 1887 to Katharina Rottler Braun, his wife's widowed older sister. The wedding took place at the home of Valentine Rottler and a large wedding dinner followed. The couple lived the rest of their lives on the farm west of Lawrenceton. Vincent died at Lawrenceton on 13 February 1893 and was buried in the St. Lawrence Cemetery next to his first wife. Katharina died of nephritis on 22 February 1925 in St. Louis, Missouri. She was buried in the Calvary Cemetery in St. Louis, Missouri.

Gottlob Bebion Family
Surname Variations: Babeon, Babion, Bebian, Bebron
European Origin: Fellbach, Neckarkreis, Wuerttemberg, Germany
Family:
Father: Michael Bebion, born about 1796 in Wuerttemberg, Germany. He died some time between 1850 and 1860 [in Louisiana? Missouri?].
Mother: Anna Ernst, born 15 May 1797 in Fellbach, Wuerttemberg, Germany. She died on 11 January 1875 in Ste. Genevieve, Ste. Genevieve County, Missouri. She was buried in the Memorial Cemetery in Ste. Genevieve, Ste. Genevieve County, Missouri.
    Children:
        i.   Anna Louisa, born in October 1824 in Fellbach, Neckarkreis, Wuerttemberg, Germany. She was christened in the Evangelical [Lutheran] Church in Fellbach on 28 October 1824. Anna died on 11 April 1825 in Fellbach. No issue.

‡ ii. Johanna Friedericka, born in January 1826 in Fellbach, Neckarkreis, Wuerttemberg, Germany. She was christened in the Evangelical [Lutheran] Church in Fellbach on 4 January 1826. She married Christian Klein about 1850. The couple had one son, born in Hermann, Gasconade County, Missouri, before Christian died. Fredericka married Gottlieb Koch as her second husband. Gottlieb was the son of unknown parents, born about 1835 in Germany. He was a farmer. The couple had at least two sons and possibly other children. About 1874, Gottlieb moved his family to Johnson County, Kansas. Eventually, they moved to Eudora, Douglas County, Kansas where both Gottlieb and Fredericka died. Their place of burial is unknown.

‡ iii. Georg Friederich "Fred," born in September 1827 in Fellbach, Neckarkreis, Wuerttemberg, Germany. He was christened in the Evangelical [Lutheran] Church in Fellbach on 5 September 1827. He was a barkeeper in Hermann, Gasconade County, Missouri. Fred married Mary _____ about 1856. Mary was the daughter of unknown parents, born about 1836 in Ohio. The couple had at least one daughter and possibly other children. No further record of this family has been found after the record of Fred's naturalization in Gasconade County in 1862.

iv. Johann Michael, born in November 1828 in Fellbach, Neckarkreis, Wuerttemberg, Germany. He was christened in the Evangelical [Lutheran] Church in Fellbach on 28 November 1828. No further information.

v. Johann Georg, born in June 1830 in Fellbach, Neckarkreis, Wuerttemberg, Germany. He was christened in the Evangelical [Lutheran] Church in Fellbach on 27 June 1830. Johann died on 9 April 1831. No issue.

vi. Johann Georg, born in April 1832 in Fellbach, Neckarkreis, Wuerttemberg, Germany. He was christened in the Evangelical [Lutheran] Church in Fellbach on 6 April 1832. Johann died on 7 April 1832. No issue.

‡ vii. Anna Elisabetha, born in July 1834. She was christened in the Evangelical [Lutheran] Church in Fellbach on 6 July 1834. No further record of her has been found after she appears on the ship's manifest in 1849.

‡ viii. Euphrosine Caroline, born in September 1837 in Fellbach, Neckarkreis, Wuerttemberg, Germany. She was christened in the Evangelical [Lutheran] Church in Fellbach on 3 September 1837. Caroline married Henry Hohmann on 25 May 1864 in Gasconade County, Missouri. Henry was the son of Caspar Hohmann and Barbara Duebner, born 18 February 1840 in Saxony, Germany. [See Henry Hohmann sketch.]

* ix. Gottlob, born 14 February 1843 in Fellbach, Neckarkreis, Wuerttemberg, Germany. He was christened in the Evangelical [Lutheran] Church in Fellbach on 19 February 1843. [See sketch below.]

Immigration:
Arrived 10 July 1849 from Le Havre, France to New Orleans aboard the *Manteo*:
Bebron [Bebion], Michel, 52   from Germany
    Anna, 54
    Frederic, 23
    Elisa, 15
    Caroline, 11
    Gotlob, 6

Biographical:
Individual: Gottlob Bebion
  Birth – 14 February 1843 in Fellbach, Neckarkreis, Wuerttemberg, Germany.
  Death/Burial – 27 June 1873 in Ste. Genevieve County, Missouri. He was buried in the Memorial Cemetery in Ste. Genevieve, Ste. Genevieve County, Missouri.
Wife: Gottlob does not appear to have ever married.

U.S. residence prior to Ste. Genevieve County, Missouri:
Jefferson Parish, Louisiana

Naturalization:

Name	Declaration	Naturalization	Origin
Bebion, Frederick	1856 Gasconade Co.	1862 Gasconade Co.	Wurtemberg

Military:
Served in the U.S. Civil War for the Union:
Private, Company B, 34th Regiment Enrolled Missouri Militia
Frederick Bebion enlisted 18 August 1862 in Hermann, Gasconade County, Missouri. Relieved from duty on 27 May 1863.

Religious Affiliation: Lutheran

Comments:
Gottlob Bebion came to the United States with his parents and three siblings in 1849. The family lived for a short period of time in Louisiana before moving north to Hermann, Gasconade County, Missouri. Gottlob's father, Michael, died some time between 1850 and 1860. His widowed mother, Anna, lived first with her oldest son in Hermann and then with her youngest daughter in St. Louis, Missouri. Gottlob's whereabouts and occupation are unknown between 1850 and 1873. He may never have married and had no known issue. He moved to Ste. Genevieve, Ste. Genevieve County, Missouri, possibly to live with his youngest sister. His mother came to Ste. Genevieve County in 1871 with her youngest daughter and son-in-law, Henry Hohmann. Henry had come to Ste. Genevieve to establish a seltzer and soda water factory. Gottlob died on 27 June 1873 in Ste. Genevieve. He was buried in the Memorial Cemetery in Ste. Genevieve, Ste. Genevieve County, Missouri. Anna died on 11 January 1875 in Ste. Genevieve and was buried beside her son in the Memorial Cemetery.

Bernard Bechtold Family

Surname Variations: Becktold, Beckdolt, Bechtoldt, Beicktold, Betsteald
European Origin: Freudenberg amt Wertheim, Baden, Germany
Family:
Father: Andreas Bechtold, baptized on 30 November 1745 in Freudenberg amt Wertheim, Baden, Germany.
Mother: Maria Anna Will, baptized on 11 March 1742 in Freudenberg amt Wertheim, Baden, Germany.
Children:
* i. Johann Bernard, born 18 February 1781 in Freudenberg amt Wertheim, Baden, Germany. [See sketch below.]
† ii. Barbara, born 25 October 1783 in Freudenberg amt Wertheim, Baden, Germany. She married Peter Vaeth on 24 November 1814 in Freudenberg amt Wertheim, Baden, Germany. Peter was the son of Bernard Vaeth and Margaretha Hauk, born 25 December 1783 in Freudenberg. [See Peter Vaeth sketch.]

Immigration:
Arrived before December 1853 aboard an unknown vessel:
    Bechtold, Margaretha
        Dominicus
        Thecla
        Maria Theresia

Biographical:
Husband: Johann Bernard Bechtold
    Birth – 18 February 1781 in Freudenberg amt Wertheim, Baden, Germany.

Death/Burial – Most likely in Germany before December 1853.
Wife: Margaretha Knapp, daughter of Nikolaus Knapp and Eva Clara Kerchner
Birth – 15 March 1789 in Freudenberg amt Wertheim, Baden, Germany.
Marriage – 6 February 1810 in Freudenberg amt Wertheim, Baden, Germany.
Death/Burial – She died in 1864 in Ste. Genevieve County, Missouri. She was buried in the St. Joseph Cemetery in Zell, Ste. Genevieve County, Missouri.
Children:
  i. Clara Barbara, born 28 August 1811 in Freudenberg amt Wertheim, Baden, Germany. She died before June 1819. No issue.
  ii. Johann Sebastian, born 28 November 1812 in Freudenberg amt Wertheim, Baden, Germany. No further information.
  iii. Johann Andreas, born on 16 December 1815 in Freudenberg amt Wertheim, Baden, Germany. He died on 20 December 1815 in Freudenberg. No issue.
  iv. Johann Nicholas, born 5 December 1816 in Freudenberg amt Wertheim, Baden, Germany. He left Freudenberg to come to America in 1848. No further information.
  v. Clara Barbara, born 30 June 1819 in Freudenberg amt Wertheim, Baden, Germany. No further information.
  vi. Johann Bernard, born 26 January 1822 in Freudenberg amt Wertheim, Baden, Germany. He died on 28 December 1822 in Freudenberg. No issue.
  vii. Dominicus, born 1 February 1828 in Freudenberg amt Wertheim, Baden, Germany. He came to the United States with his family and became a farmer in Ste. Genevieve County, Missouri near present-day Lawrenceton. He never married. After the death of his mother, Dominic lived with his sister Theresa and helped her husband Joseph Endres run his farm. He died on 12 April 1899 in Ste. Genevieve County, Missouri and was buried in the St. Lawrence Cemetery at Lawrenceton. No issue.
  viii. Maria Elisabetha, born 12 June 1827 in Freudenberg amt Wertheim, Baden, Germany. She died on 21 March 1828 in Freudenberg amt Wertheim, Baden, Germany. No issue.
  ix. Thecla, born 1 November 1829 in Freudenberg amt Wertheim, Baden, Germany. She was married to Gerhard Charles Guethle [aka Gidley] on 4 September 1857 at Zell, Ste. Genevieve County, Missouri. Gerhard was the son of Heinrich "Henry" Guethle and Barbara Huber, born 23 February 1828 at Ebersweier, Baden, Germany. [See Heinrich Guethle sketch.]
  x. Maria Theresia, born 13 October 1832 in Freudenberg amt Wertheim, Baden, Germany. She married Joseph Michael Endres on 9 May 1858 in Petite Canada [present-day French Village, St. Francois County, Missouri.] Joseph was the son of Valentin Endres and Maria Anna Kunzmann, born 5 February 1827 in Freudenberg amt Wertheim, Baden, Germany. [See Joseph Endres sketch.]

Land Patents:
Ste. Genevieve County, Missouri

Patentee	Issue Date	Land Office	Cert. No.	Serial No.	Sec	Twp	Rng	Acres
Becktold, Thomas	1 Dec 1853	Jackson	14858	MO3650_.311	19	37-N	7-E	40.00
Becktold, Dominick	10 Jun 1856	Jackson	16347	MO3720_.209	19	37-N	7-E	110.50
Becktold, Dominick	1 Sep 1856	Jackson	21076	MO3740_.155	19/20	37-N	7-E	87.39

Naturalization:

Name	Declaration	Naturalization	Origin
Bectold, Dominick	7 June 1858	8 May 1862 Ste. Genevieve Co.	Baden

Military:
Served in the U.S. Civil War for the Union:
Private, Company I, 78th Enrolled Missouri Militia
   Dominicus Bechtold enrolled on 12 June 1863 in New Offenburg, Missouri.
Private, Company F, 78th Enrolled Missouri Militia
   Domeniteus Bechholt enrolled on 30 April 1864 in Ste. Genevieve County, Missouri. Transferred from Company I by order of Lt. Col. Rond on 1 October 1864. He was ordered into active service on 16 October 1864. He was relieved from duty on 25 November 1864 after having served 41 days of actual service.

Occupation: Farmer
Religious Affiliation: Roman Catholic
Comments:
Bernard Bechtold and Margaretha Knapp were married in Freudenberg amt Wertheim, Baden, Germany and all of their children were born there. Bernard appears to have died in Germany before December 1853. Margaretha came to the United States with one son and two daughters and settled in Ste. Genevieve County, Missouri about 1853. An older son, Nicholas, left Freudenberg in 1848, but no record of his ever reaching America has been found. Margaretha's son Dominic purchased land near present-day Lawrenceton in Ste. Genevieve County and established a farm to support the family. During the Civil War, Dominic served in the 78th Enrolled Missouri Militia. After the war, Dominic and his mother remained on the farm. Margaretha died in September 1864, within a week of her granddaughter, Regina Guethle, and of Barbara Guethle, her daughter Thecla's mother-in-law. The two grandmothers and their infant granddaughter all share a grave in the St. Joseph Cemetery in Zell, Ste. Genevieve County, Missouri.

George Beck Family
Surname Variations: Boeck
European Origin: Oberweier bei Lahr, Baden, Germany
Family:
Father: Franz Anton Beck, born about 1774 in Seelbach, Baden, Germany. He died on 12 February 1830 in Oberweier bei Lahr, Baden, Germany.
Mother: Magdalena Hugelmann, born 7 May 1783 in Oberweier bei Lahr , Baden, Germany. She died on 4 December 1852 in Oberweier bei Lahr, Baden, Germany.
   Children:
   i. Anselm, born 9 April 1802 in Oberweier bei Lahr, Baden, Germany. He was a nail maker in Oberweier. Anselm married Franziska Haas on 9 January 1832 in Oberweier. Franziska was the daughter of Michael Haas and Magdalena Hug, born 19 July 1806 in Oberweier. The couple had three sons and four daughters, all born in Oberweier. Franziska died on 2 February 1844 in Oberweier. Anselm married Aloisia Nock as his second wife on 5 June 1844 in Oberweier. She was the daughter of Josef Nock and Elisabeth Kopf, born 19 June 1799 in Oberweier bei Lahr, Baden, Germany. The couple may not have had any children. Aloisia died on 23 October 1858 and Anselm died on 4 March 1885, both in Oberweier bei Lahr, Baden, Germany.
   ii. Bonifaz, born 5 June 1804 in Oberweier bei Lahr, Baden, Germany. He was a nail maker in Oberweier. Bonifaz married Ludgardis Hess on 18 July 1836. She was the daughter of Peter Hess and Ludgardis Herz, born 22 March 1811 in Oberweier bei Lahr, Baden, Germany. They had one stillborn child. Bonifaz died on 8 March 1837 and Ludgardis died on 5 May 1837, both in Oberweier bei Lahr, Baden, Germany.
   iii. Apollonia, born 6 February 1806 in Oberweier bei Lahr, Baden, Germany. She married Joseph Pfundstein on 26 January 1837 in Oberweier. Joseph was the son of Anton Pfundstein and Luitgard Tränkle, born on 26 January 1805 in Kuhbach, Baden, Germany. The couple had three sons and three daughters, all born in Oberweier. Joseph died on 23 December 1846 and Apollonia died on 13 May 1865, both in Oberweier bei Lahr, Baden, Germany.

iv. Mathias, born 22 February 1808 in Oberweier bei Lahr, Baden, Germany. He married Agatha Haas on 5 October 1841 in Oberweier. Agatha was the daughter of Michael Haas and Magdalena Hug, born on 16 November 1819 in Oberweier bei Lahr, Baden, Gerrmany. The couple had eight sons and three daughters, all born in Oberweier. Mathias died on 28 December 1872 and Agatha died on 31 January 1893, both in Oberweier bei Lahr, Baden, Germany.

v. Liborius, born 15 August 1809 in Oberweier bei Lahr, Baden, Germany. He died 1 November 1831 in Oberweier bei Lahr, Baden, Germany.

vi. Anton, born 23 May 1812 in Oberweier bei Lahr, Baden, Germany. He died on 30 January 1835 in Oberweier bei Lahr, Baden, Germany.

vii. Elisabeth, born 25 June 1814 in Oberweier bei Lahr, Baden, Germany. She died on 1 April 1818 in Oberweier bei Lahr, Baden, Germany. No issue.

viii. Karl, born 25 January 1817 in Oberweier bei Lahr, Baden, Germany. He died 1 April 1818 in Oberweier bei Lahr, Baden, Germany. No issue.

ix. Karl, born 23 October 1819 in Oberweier bei Lahr, Baden, Germany. He died on 28 July 1847 in Oberweier bei Lahr, Baden, Germany.

x. Ottilia, born 17 August 1821 in Oberweier bei Lahr, Baden, Germany. She died 25 December 1822 in Oberweier bei Lahr, Baden, Germany. No issue.

xi. Amelia, born 27 July 1826 in Oberweier bei Lahr, Baden, Germany. She died on 21 April 1841 in Oberweier bei Lahr, Baden, Germany.

* xii. Georg, born 2 April 1828 in Oberweier bei Lahr, Baden, Germany. [See sketch below.]

Immigration:
Arrived 26 May 1851 from Le Havre, France to New Orleans aboard the *Y. I. Roger*:
    Beck, Georg, 23

Biographical:
Husband: George Beck
    Birth – 2 April 1828 in Oberweier bei Lahr, Baden, Germany.
    Death – 1 May 1862 in Ste. Genevieve County, Missouri. He was buried in St. Joseph Cemetery in Zell, Ste. Genevieve County, Missouri.
Wife: Maria Albertina Gegg, daughter of Joseph Gegg and Josepha Wörter [See Joseph Gegg sketch.]
    Birth/Baptism – 6 March 1830 in Hofweier bei Offenburg, Baden, Germany.
    1) Marriage – 29 August 1852 in the German Settlement [present-day Zell], Ste. Genevieve County, Missouri to George Beck.
    2) Marriage – 17 November 1863 in River aux Vases, Ste. Genevieve County, Missouri to George Fritsch. [See George Fritsch sketch.]
    3) Marriage – 17 October 1876 in Zell, Ste. Genevieve County, Missouri to Roman Vogt. [See Anton Vogt sketch.]
    Death/Burial – 12 February 1888 in River aux Vases, Ste. Genevieve County, Missouri. She was buried in the Sts. Philip and James Cemetery in River aux Vases, Ste. Genevieve County, Missouri.
Children:
    i. Joseph, born 2 February 1853 in Zell, Ste. Genevieve County, Missouri. He was a farmer. Joseph married Clara Guethle on 6 September 1874 in Ste. Genevieve, Ste. Genevieve County, Missouri, Clara was the daughter of Andreas Saturnin "Andrew" Guethle and Theresia Seckinger, born 24 October 1853 in Ste. Genevieve County, Missouri. Joseph and Clara had one son who died in infancy. Clara died a week after her son was born from complications of the birth. She was buried in the Memorial Cemetery in Ste. Genevieve, Ste. Genevieve County, Missouri. Joseph married for a second time to Maria Josephine Ketterer on 21 November 1876 in Weingarten, Ste. Genevieve County, Missouri. Josephine was the daughter of Engelbert Ketterer and Crescentia Basler, born 12 October 1854 in Ste. Genevieve County, Missouri. Joseph and Josephine lived in Ste. Genevieve County for the first few years of their married

lives. By 1910, they had moved to St. Francois County, Missouri. The couple had four sons and five daughters, of whom one son and two daughters died in infancy or early childhood. In their old age, Joseph and Josephine lived with one of their daughters near the small town of French Village in St. Francois County. Josephine died of heart failure on 26 August 1937 and Joseph died of chronic heart disease on 9 August 1939, both in French Village, St. Francois County, Missouri. They were both buried in the St. Anne's Cemetery in French Village, St. Francois County, Missouri.

ii. Rosina, born 7 March 1855 in Zell, Ste. Genevieve County, Missouri. She married Leo Kreitler on 21 November 1876 in River aux Vases, Ste. Genevieve County. Leo was the son of Daniel Kreitler and Tharsilla Joggerst, born 7 August 1853 in Ste. Genevieve County, Missouri. [See Daniel Kreitler sketch.]

iii. Maria Magdalena, born 21 July 1857 in Zell, Ste. Genevieve County, Missouri. She married William Hurst on 18 May 1880 in River aux Vases, Ste. Genevieve County. William was the son of Isidore Hurst and Victoria Kist, born 25 May 1857 in Ste. Genevieve County, Missouri. [See Isidore Hurst sketch.]

iv. Juliana [twin], born 5 December 1859 in Zell, Ste. Genevieve County, Missouri. She died within a few days of her birth. No issue.

v. Sophia [twin], born 5 December 1859 in Zell, Ste. Genevieve County, Missouri. She married William Andrew Huber on 12 June 1883 in Zell. William was the son of Andreas "Andrew" Huber and Agatha Harter, born 19 February 1854 in Boston, Erie County, New York. [See Andreas "Andrew" Huber sketch.]

vi. George, born 27 January 1862 in Zell, Ste. Genevieve County, Missouri. He was a wagon maker and undertaker. George married Regina Kirchner on 3 May 1887 in River aux Vases, Ste. Genevieve County. Regina was the daughter of Peter Kirchner and Anastasia Schweiss, born 4 April 1860 in Ste. Genevieve County, Missouri. For the first ten years of their lives together, George and Regina lived in Lawrenceton, Ste. Genevieve County, where George worked in a wagon shop. By early 1898, the family had moved to Jefferson County, Missouri, where George established his own wagon making business and later became an undertaker in Festus. The couple had four sons and five daughters. George died of chronic nephritis on 16 May 1927 and Regina died of heart disease on 23 November 1958, both in Festus, Jefferson County. They were both buried in the Catholic Cemetery in Festus, Jefferson County, Missouri.

Land Patents:
Ste. Genevieve County, Missouri

Patentee	Issue Date	Land Office	Cert. No.	Serial No.	Twp	Rng	Sec	Acres
Beck, George	15 Nov 1854	Jackson	15689	MO3670_.215	37N	8E	21	40.00
Beck, George	15 Nov 1854	Jackson	15690	MO3670_.216	37N	8E	22	40.00
Beck, George	1 Dec 1858	Jackson	16292	MO3850_.022	37N	8E	21	120.00

Naturalization:

Name	Declaration	Naturalization	Origin
Beck, George	14 December 1852	21 November 1856 Ste. Genevieve Co.	Baden

Occupation: Farmer
Religious Affiliation: Roman Catholic
Comments:
George Beck was the youngest child of a very large family. He was the only member of his family to have come to the United States. He arrived in 1851, traveling in company with several other German families from Oberweier bei Lahr, and came directly to Ste. Genevieve County, Missouri. George married Maria Albertina Gegg and the couple purchased a farm near the German Settlement [present-day Zell]. Their six children were all born there. George died of consumption on 1 May 1862 in Ste. Genevieve County, Missouri. He was buried

in the St. Joseph Cemetery in Zell, Ste. Genevieve County, Missouri. His wife was left with five surviving children to raise alone. She married George Fritsch as her second husband on 17 November 1863 at River aux Vases, Ste. Genevieve County. The couple had three sons, of whom one died in infancy. George died some time between 1871 and October 1876. Maria married Roman Vogt as her third husband on 17 October 1876 in Zell. They had no children together. Maria died on 12 February 1888 in River aux Vases and was buried in the Sts. Philip and James Cemetery in River aux Vases, Ste. Genevieve County, Missouri.

William Beckemeyer Family

Surname Variations: Beckelmire, Beckemeier, Beckenmeyer, Beckermeyer, Beckmere, Beckmeyer, Beckmier, Begelmeyer, Beggemeyer, Bekmeier, Bickmire, Boekemeyer, Bokemeier, Bökemeier

European Origin: Germany

Family:
Father: Unknown
Mother: Unknown
   Children:
‡   i.   Carl, born about 1833 in Germany.
*   ii.   Wilhelm "William," born 19 September 1835 in Germany. [See sketch below.]
‡   iii. Heinrich, born about 1836 in Germany.

Immigration:
Arrived 8 December 1853 from Bremen, Germany to New Orleans aboard the *Ocean*:
   Boeckemeyer, Carl, 18   Shoemaker   Prussia   going to St. Louis, Mo
      Wilhelm, 15
      Heinrich, 14

Biographical:
Husband: William Beckemeyer
   Birth – 19 September 1835 in Germany.
   Death/Burial – 10 October 1910 in Ste. Genevieve County, Missouri. He was buried in the Beckemeyer
      Cemetery [aka McClanahan Cemetery] in Ste. Genevieve County, Missouri.
1) Wife: Mary A. Bellisime [daughter of Charles Bellisime and Barbara _____ ?]
   Birth – about 1847 in Ste. Genevieve County, Missouri.
   Marriage – 8 February 1866 in Ste. Genevieve County, Missouri to William Beckemeyer.
   Death/Burial – before June 1869 in Missouri.

There were no known children born to William Beckemeyer and Mary A. Bellisime.

2) Wife: Rachel Byington, daughter of James Byington and Esther Seals
   Birth – about 1833 in Missouri.
   1) Marriage – 5 October 1849 in Ste. Genevieve County, Missouri to Samuel Guitar.
   2) Marriage – 19 June 1869 in Ste. Genevieve County, Missouri to William Beckemeyer.
   Death/Burial – [5 May 1871 in Missouri?]
   Children of Samuel Guitar and Rachel Byington:
      i.   James L., born about 1850 in Missouri.
      ii.   Minerva., born about 1852 in Missouri. She married William Brent Reeder in 1866.
      iii. Josephine., born about 1854 in Missouri.
      iv. Mary Elizabeth., born about 1856 in Missouri. She married William Felix Carron.
      v.   Missouri Ellen., born about 1860 in Missouri.

There were no known children born to William Beckemeyer and Rachel Byington.

3) Wife: Artemissa Martha Jane Lutman, daughter of Jacob Franklin Lutman and Harriet Elizabeth Schmitt
Birth – 21 January 1858 in Calhoun County, Illinois.
Marriage – 25 April 1872 in Ste. Genevieve County, Missouri.
Death/Burial – 17 August 1917 in Ste. Genevieve County, Missouri. She was buried in the Beckemeyer Cemetery [aka McClanahan Cemetery] in Ste. Genevieve County, Missouri.
Children:
  i. Mary Elizabeth, born 25 November 1873 in Ste. Genevieve County, Missouri. She married William M. Parker on 5 November 1890 in Ste. Genevieve County, Missouri. William was the son of Timothy Parker and Sarah Elizabeth Frent, born in October 1859 in Ste. Genevieve County, Missouri. He was a farmer. The couple had at least one son and one daughter. No further information after the 1900 census.
  ii. Charles F. , born 4 October 1876 in Ste. Genevieve County, Missouri. Charles died on 24 October 1876 in Ste. Genevieve County, Missouri. No issue.
  iii. John W. , born 24 January 1878 in Ste. Genevieve County, Missouri. John died on 5 February 1878 in Ste. Genevieve County, Missouri. No issue.
  iv. Margaret Theresa "Maggie," born 30 January 1879 in Ste. Genevieve County, Missouri. She married Robert Theodore Bradfield on 8 January 1903 in Festus, Jefferson County, Missouri. Robert was the son of Charles R. Bradfield and Elizabeth Ann Perkins, born 25 September 1875 in Jefferson County, Missouri. He worked at the Pittsburgh Plate Glass Company in Crystal City, Jefferson County, Missouri. The couple had three sons and four daughters, of whom one son died in early childhood. Robert died of pulmonary tuberculosis on 23 September 1935 in St. Louis, Missouri. After her husband's death, Maggie supported her family by running a boarding house in St. Louis. Her brother, George, lived with her for a time. Maggie died of pulmonary thrombi on 30 May 1959 in St. Louis, Missouri. They were both buried in the Gamel Cemetery in Festus, Jefferson County, Missouri.
  v. Edward August, born 23 January 1882 in Ste. Genevieve County, Missouri. He worked at the Pittsburgh Plate Glass Company in Crystal City, Jefferson County, Missouri. Edward married Josephine Carron on 12 November 1902 in Bloomsdale, Ste. Genevieve County, Missouri. Josephine was the daughter of William Felix Carron and Mary Elizabeth Guitar, born in December 1884 in Ste. Genevieve County, Missouri. The couple had one son. Josephine died some time between 1903 and 1910. Edward married Rose Regina Weber as his second wife on 18 December 1917 in Ste. Genevieve County, Missouri. Rose was the daughter of John J. Weber and Josephine Rogers Rugg, born 13 November 1899 in Missouri. The couple had one son and four daughters, of whom one daughter died in infancy. Edward died of coronary thrombosis on 8 August 1962 in Crystal City, Jefferson County, Missouri. Rose died on 1 May 1980 in Missouri. They were both buried in the Gamel Cemetery in Festus, Jefferson County, Missouri.
  vi. Martin Luther, born 15 March 1885 in Ste. Genevieve County, Missouri. He was a farmer. Luther married Ida Agnes Carron on 1 June 1909 in Ste. Genevieve County, Missouri. Ida was the daughter of Theodore F. Carron and Ellen M. [Pullen?], born 20 July 1888 in Ste. Genevieve County, Missouri. The couple had three sons and two daughters. Ida died about 1926, most likely in Missouri. Luther died of cardio vascular disease on 1 September 1955 in Jefferson County, Missouri. They were both buried in the Beckemeyer Cemetery [aka McClanahan Cemetery] in Ste. Genevieve County, Missouri.
  vii. Richard Franklin "Frank" [twin], born 30 July 1886 in Ste. Genevieve County, Missouri. During World War I, Frank served as a private in Company G of the 349th Infantry Division. He married Lola Hester Stanford on 28 January 1919 in Hillsboro, Jefferson County, Missouri. Lola was the daughter of Thomas Stanford and Amanda Jane Derrick, born 14 May 1891 in Washington County, Missouri. For the first few years of their marriage, Frank worked in the Pittsburgh Plate Glass Company in Crystal City. By 1930, the family had moved to St. Louis, Missouri. The couple had four daughters. Richard died on 22 October 1957. Lola died on

16 March 1971. They were both buried in the Jefferson Barracks National Cemetery in Lemay, St. Louis County, Missouri.
viii. Robert Samuel [twin], 30 July 1886 in Ste. Genevieve County, Missouri. Robert died on 10 September 1886 in Ste. Genevieve County, Missouri. No issue.
ix. James Ara [aka James Ira], born 15 January 1889 in Ste. Genevieve County, Missouri. He married Hattie Boyer on 14 May 1912 in Bloomsdale, Ste. Genevieve County, Missouri. Hattie was the daughter of Solomon C. Boyer and Mary Clementine Charleville, born 12 December 1894 in Ste. Genevieve County, Missouri. The couple had three sons and five daughters, of whom one daughter died in early childhood. Hattie died on 27 September 1947 in Redondo Beach, Los Angeles County, California. James died on 5 March 1967 in Soledad, Monterey County, California. They were both buried in the Pacific Crest Cemetery in Redondo Beach, Los Angeles County, California.
x. Mary Ella Sarah, born 16 September 1891 in Ste. Genevieve County, Missouri. She married George Francis Boyer on 9 April 1907 in Bloomsdale, Ste. Genevieve County, Missouri. George was the son of Theodule Cyprian Boyer and Mary Louise Carron, born 21 September 1878 in Ste. Genevieve County, Missouri. He was a farmer. The couple had two sons and two daughters. Ella died on 12 January 1955 in Ste. Genevieve County, Missouri. George died of pneumonia and chronic myocarditis on 16 December 1957 in Ste. Genevieve County, Missouri. They were both buried in the St. Agnes Cemetery in Bloomsdale, Ste. Genevieve County, Missouri.
xi. George Philip, born 25 March 1895 in Ste. Genevieve County, Missouri. George married Bertha Layton on 21 August 1920 in Ste. Genevieve, Ste. Genevieve County. There is no further information on Bertha after the marriage record for this couple. [She may be the Bertha A. Layton, who was the daughter of Clement Layton and Elizabeth _____, born about 1903 in Jefferson County, Missouri.] According to George's death certificate, he was divorced. George died of cerebral thrombosis on 1 May 1952 in St. Louis, Missouri. He was buried in the Beckemeyer Cemetery [aka McClanahan Cemetery] in Ste. Genevieve County, Missouri. George had no known issue.
xii. Val, born 19 November 1897 in Ste. Genevieve County, Missouri. Val died on 22 November 1897 in Ste. Genevieve County, Missouri. No issue.
xiii. Rose Ann, born 25 March 1901 in Ste. Genevieve County, Missouri. She married Arthur Marion Spradling on 29 December 1917 in Bloomsdale, Ste. Genevieve County, Missouri. Arthur was the son of George Lincoln Spradling and Annie Wehrle, born 16 January 1891 in Mulberry Grove, Bond County, Illinois. The couple had two sons and two daughters. Arthur and Rose may have been divorced some time between 1920 and 1930. Arthur was living in Manito, Mason County, Illinois with a woman named Emma _____ by 1930. They appear to have had a daughter together. Rose died on 7 April 1973.

U.S. residence prior to Ste. Genevieve County, Missouri:
Nashville, Washington County, Illinois
St. Louis, Missouri [probably]

Naturalization:

Name	Declaration	Naturalization	Origin	Remarks
Beckemeyer, William			Germany	1900, 1910 Census

Military:
Served in the U.S. Civil War for the Union:
Private, Company C, 49th Illinois Volunteer Infantry
William Beckemeyer enlisted 1 November 1861 in Nashville, Washington County, Illinois. He was mustered out on 9 September 1865 in Paducah, Kentucky.

Education: Could neither read nor write, but could speak English.
Occupation: Famer
Religious Affiliation: Lutheran
Comments:
Wilhelm "William" Beckemeyer came to the United States in 1853 and appears to have originally settled in Washington County, Illinois. During the Civil War he served as a private in Company C of the 49th Illinois Volunteer Infantry and remained on active duty for the duration of the war. Less than a year after the end of the war, William had moved to Ste. Genevieve County, Missouri. He married his first wife, Mary A. Bellisime, on 8 February 1866 in Ste. Genevieve County, Missouri. The couple does not appear to have had any surviving children. Mary appears to have died some time before June 1869, most likely in Missouri. William married Mrs. Rachel Guitar on 19 June 1869 in Ste. Genevieve County, Missouri. Rachel was the widow of Samuel Guitar whom she had married in 1849. Samuel was born about 1828 in Missouri. He was a farmer. The Guitars had one son and four daughters together before Samuel died. William and Rachel Beckemeyer had no known surviving children. Rachel is said to have died on 5 May 1871, presumably in Missouri. William married Artemissa Martha Jane Lutman on 25 April 1872 in Ste. Genevieve County, Missouri. They couple had nine sons and four daughters, of whom four sons died in infancy or early childhood. William died from Bright's disease and chronic bronchitis on 10 October 1910 in Ste. Genevieve County, Missouri. Jane died of overexcitement and heart failure on 17 August 1917 in Ste. Genevieve County. They were both buried in the Beckemeyer Cemetery [aka McClanahan Cemetery] in Ste. Genevieve County, Missouri.

Note: There are Beckemeyer families that settled in both Washington County, Illinois and in St. Louis, Missouri in the mid-1800s. It is possible that these families are connected to the Beckemeyer family of Ste. Genevieve County, Missouri.

George Beckermann Family
Surname Variations: Bakerman, Beckerman, Beckmann, Bekerman, Bickerman
European Origin: [Badbergen?], Hanover, Germany
Family:
Father: Johann Heinrich "John Henry" Beckermann, born 22 April 1812 in Badbergen, Hanover, Germany. He died on 25 January 1897 in Ste. Genevieve, Ste. Genevieve County, Missouri. He was buried in the Lutheran Cemetery in Ste. Genevieve, Ste. Genevieve County, Missouri.
Mother: Maria Kleibecker, born about 1816 in Germany. She died of brain fever on 25 August 1860 in St. Louis, Missouri. She was buried in the Holy Ghost Cemetery in St. Louis, Missouri.
Children:
‡   i. Hermann, born about 1843 in Germany. He came to the United States with his parents in 1859. He enlisted as a private in Company F of the 4th Regiment Missouri Cavalry in August 1861 at St. Louis, Missouri. The unit took part in Curtis' Campaign in Missouri and Arkansas, the Battles of Pea Ridge, Fox Creek March, and Mountain Grove March. In late 1862, they were sent to Mississippi where they took part in the Battle of Corinth. Company F took part in the Siege of Vicksburg from 18 May to 4 July 1863. Hermann died of fever and dysentery on 25 July 1863 at Vicksburg, Warren County, Mississippi. He was buried in Section H, Grave 441 in the Vicksburg National Cemetery in Vicksburg, Warren County, Mississippi. He never married and had no known issue.
*   ii. George, born 18 September 1847 in Germany. [See sketch below.]
‡   iii. Johann Heinrich "Henry", born about 1851 in Germany. At the time of his father's death he was living in St. Louis, Missouri. He died after January 1897. No further information.
‡   iv. William, born about 1853 in Germany. He died before January 1897. No further information.
    v. Margaret. She was named in her father's obituary, but no other mention has been found. She may have been an older child who remained in Germany. She died some time before January 1897. No further information.

Immigration:
Arrived 7 November 1859 from Bremen, Germany to New York aboard the *Stella*:
    Beckermann, John, 42   from Hanover   going to Missouri
        Mary, 40
        Hermann, 16
        Gerhard [George], 14
        Henry, 8
        William, 6

Biographical:

Husband: George Beckermann
  Birth – 18 September 1847 in Hanover, Germany.
  Death/Burial – 15 March 1917 in Ste. Genevieve, Ste. Genevieve County, Missouri. He was buried in the Valle Spring Cemetery in Ste. Genevieve, Ste. Genevieve County, Missouri.

Wife: Mary C. Hauck, daughter of Nicholas Hauck and Catherine Barbara Keck [or Heck] [See Nicholas Hauck sketch.]
  Birth – 18 January 1851 in St. Louis, Missouri.
  Marriage – 19 August 1873 in St. Louis, Missouri.
  Death/Burial – 15 July 1923 in St. Louis, Missouri. She was buried in the Valle Spring Cemetery in Ste. Genevieve, Ste. Genevieve County, Missouri.

Children:
    i. Emma Clothilde, born about 1871 in Missouri. No further information.
    ii. Henrietta Catherine "Etta," born 6 January 1875 in Missouri. She married Henry Ernest Ploeger on 1 May 1912 in St. Charles County, Missouri. Henry was a fireman in St. Louis. He was the son of Ernst Ploeger and Wilhelmina Bush, born 23 February 1874 in Missouri. The couple does not appear to have ever had children. Henry died of heart disease on 30 June 1946 and Etta died of degenerative heart disease complicated by pneumonia on 15 April 1947, both in St. Louis, Missouri. They were both buried in the Memorial Park Cemetery in Jennings, St. Louis County, Missouri.
    iii. John Nicholas, born 11 December 1879 in Ste. Genevieve, Ste. Genevieve County, Missouri. As a young man, he left Ste. Genevieve to be a cowboy in the Dakota Territory and Nebraska. He married Mabel E. McGee in Hartington, Cedar County, Nebraska in September 1903. Mabel was the daughter of Robert W. McGee and Jennie Kemp, born 11 January 1889 in Iowa. The couple remained in Nebraska until about 1909 when they moved back to Ste. Genevieve County, Missouri where John worked as an oven cleaner at the lime plant. The couple had three sons and two daughters. Mabel died of nephritis two months after the birth of her fifth child on 8 July 1917 in Ste. Genevieve. She was buried in the Valle Spring Cemetery in Ste. Genevieve. John married Regina C. Meyer as his second wife on 27 August 1919 in Ste. Genevieve. Regina was the daughter of Conrad Meyer and Helen A. Klein, born 21 July 1891 in St. Louis, Missouri. Regina had a daughter who was born about two years before her marriage to John. John and Regina had three sons and two daughters, of whom one son died in infancy. John died of chronic nephritis on 8 April 1960 and Regina died on 19 June 1973, both in Ste. Genevieve County. John was buried between both of his wives in the Valle Spring Cemetery in Ste. Genevieve, Ste. Genevieve County, Missouri.
    iv. William Henry "Bunk," born 3 July 1881 in Ste. Genevieve County, Missouri. William worked as a house plasterer and in various capacities at the lime kiln. He married Mary Elizabeth "Libbie" Mentier on 18 November 1907 in Ste. Genevieve. Libbie was the daughter of Robert Mentier and Josephine Maurice, born 15 April 1891 in Ste. Genevieve County, Missouri. William and Libbie had one son and one daughter. William died of chronic heart disease on 17 November 1953 in Ste. Genevieve. He was buried in the Valle Spring Cemetery in Ste. Genevieve, Ste. Genevieve County, Missouri. Libbie died on 9 April 1957 of shock from

injuries she sustained when she was accidentally struck by an automobile as she was crossing the street at the corner of 5th and Market streets in Ste. Genevieve. She was buried in the Valle Spring Cemetery in Ste. Genevieve, Ste. Genevieve County, Missouri.

v. Louise, born in September 1884 in Missouri. She married a man named Edward Loeb and may have married a second man named Miller. She was living in St. Louis at the time of her mother's death in 1923. No further information.

vi. Antoinette Sophia "Nettie," born 19 September 1887 in Missouri. Nettie worked as a housekeeper for various families in St. Louis, Missouri. She may never have married. No further information.

vii. George Edward, born 18 October 1888 in Ste. Genevieve County, Missouri. He worked as a laborer in the lime kiln. George married Stella Martha Meyer on 8 September 1913 in Ste. Genevieve. Stella was the daughter of Frank Jacob Meyer and Elizabeth Williams, born 19 December 1891 in Ste. Genevieve County, Missouri. The couple had three sons and three daughters, of whom one daughter died in early childhood. Stella died of influenza complicated by bronchio pneumonia on 26 January 1928 in Ste. Genevieve. After his wife's death, George raised his children alone. In his final years, he lived with his son, Floyd. George died of tuberculosis on 8 February 1941 in Ste. Genevieve County, Missouri. Both he and his wife were buried in the Valle Spring Cemetery in Ste. Genevieve, Ste. Genevieve County, Missouri.

U.S. residence prior to Ste. Genevieve County, Missouri:
St. Louis, Missouri

Naturalization:

Name	Declaration	Naturalization	Origin	Remarks
Beckerman, George		before October 1876	Germany	from 1900 census
Beckerman, John Henry		18 October 1876 St. Louis, MO	Germany	son George was his witness

Military:
Served in the U.S. Civil War for the Union:
Private, Company F, 30th Regiment, Missouri Volunteer Infantry
  George Beckermann enlisted 21 Aug 1862 at St. Louis, Missouri; mustered in 29 April 1862 at Benton Barracks. Remarks: Transferred to Company C and Company G
Private, Company D, 3rd Regiment, Missouri Volunteer Reserve Corps
  Henry Beckermann enlisted for 3 months on 1 June 1961 in St. Louis, Missouri; mustered in on 1 June 1861 in St. Louis. He was mustered out on 17 August 1861 at St. Louis.
Private, Company F, 4th Regiment, Missouri Cavalry
  Herman Beckermann enlisted 2 August 1861 at St. Louis, Missouri. Mustered in on 23 September 1861 at St. Louis, Missouri. Remarks: Original Company C of the Benton Hussars, then 5th Cavalry. Died of fever and diarrhea on 26 July 1863 in a floating hospital at Vicksburg, Mississippi.

Education: Could read and write English and German
Occupation: Truck Gardener
Religious Affiliation: Lutheran and Roman Catholic
Political Affiliation and/or Any Offices Held:
  Post Commander, J. Felix St. James Post of the G.A.R., 1891 - 1893
Comments:
George Beckermann was born in Hanover, Germany on 18 September 1847 to Johann Heinrich "John" Beckermann and Maria Kleibecker. In 1859 the family moved to the United States and settled in St. Louis, Missouri. Maria died of brain fever on 25 August 1860 in St. Louis. She was buried in the Holy Ghost Cemetery in St. Louis, Missouri. John was left with four sons to raise on the eve of the Civil War. In June 1861, John enlisted in a reserve unit that was tasked to patrol the St. Louis area. His enlistment ended after

three months and he didn't reenlist. His oldest son Herman also enlisted in 1861 and served in some of the fiercest battles of the war until he died of dysentery at Vicksburg, Warren County, Mississippi. At age 16, George enlisted in Company G of the 30th Missouri He took part in action through the south and also served at Vicksburg, Mississippi during the Siege of Vicksburg. He was a guard on the steamship *Gladiator* for a time and while transferring a horse on board the vessel, was kicked in the groin which caused a severe injury. George was discharged from the military due to that disability. After his discharge George returned to St. Louis, Missouri. He married Mary C. Hauck on 19 August 1873 in St. Louis. By 1880, George had moved his family to Ste. Genevieve where he started a truck gardening business. He owned most of the land from Jefferson to Washington streets, and Seventh to Eighth streets in Ste. Genevieve, with only one other house in the block. His most profitable crop was horseradish. His wife spent hours grinding it for sauces. George died of pneumonia on 15 March 1917 in Ste. Genevieve. He was buried in the Valle Spring Cemetery in Ste. Genevieve, Ste. Genevieve County, Missouri. Mary lived with her son George after her husband died. However, she developed senile dementia and was placed in the St. Vincent's Institution in St. Louis, Missouri where she remained until she died of dysentery on 15 July 1923 in St. Louis, Missouri. She was buried in the Valle Spring Cemetery in Ste. Genevieve, Ste. Genevieve County, Missouri.

Anselm Begley Family
Surname Variations: Bächlé, Bachle, Bacle, Baechlé, Baechli, Bechle, Beckle, Beckly, Begly
European Origin: [Remetschweil amt Waldshut], Baden, Germany
Family:
Father: Conrad Bächlé
Mother: Walburga Appollonia Benz [aka Dentz]
   Children:

Note: For a comprehensive discussion of Conrad Bächlé's children see the Augustus Bachle sketch.

Immigration:
Arrived 21 April 1849 from Le Havre, France to New Orleans aboard the *St. Charles*:
    Baechli, Anselm, 18

Biographical:
Husband: Anselm Baechle [aka Anselm Begley]
   Birth – 17 April 1830 in Baden, Germany.
   Death/Burial – 28 January 1910 in Ironton, Iron County, Missouri. He was buried in the Masonic
     Cemetery in Ironton, Iron County, Missouri.
Wife: Theresia Spitzmiller, daughter of Michael Spitzmiller and Scholastica Schwartz
   Birth – 5 May 1836 in Nordrach, Baden, Germany.
   Marriage – 1 January 1858 in Iron County, Missouri.
   Death/Burial – 20 June 1895 in Ironton, Iron County, Missouri. She was buried in the Masonic Cemetery
     in Ironton, Iron County, Missouri.
   Children:
     i. George, born 6 November 1858 in Iron County, Missouri. He married Mary A. Reynolds in Poplar Bluff, Butler County, Missouri on 6 January 1881. Mary was the daughter of Benjamin F. Reynolds and Elizabeth Baird, born 1 January 1861 in Fredericktown, Madison County, Missouri. George was an undertaker in Poplar Bluff. The couple had four sons and three daughters, of whom two sons and two daughters died in infncy or early childhood. Mary died of heart disease and senile dementia on 3 June 1934 and George died of coronary occlusion on 12 January 1941, both in Poplar Bluff. They were both buried in the Poplar Bluff City Cemetery in Poplar Bluff, Butler County, Missouri.
     ii. Child, born in Iron County, Missouri. Died in infancy. No issue.
     iii. Theresa, born 15 December 1862 in Iron County, Missouri. She married John Sylvester Norman on 26 March 1890 in Ironton, Iron County. John was the son of Willis Norman and

Sarah Tinker, born 1 March 1860 in Marion, Williamson County, Illinois. The couple first lived in Murphysboro, Jackson County, Illinois where John was a banker. By 1910 they had moved to Kelso, Scott County, Missouri. The couple had one daughter, born in Illinois. John died unexpectedly of an attack of acute indigestion complicated by angina pectoris on 13 July 1912 in Kelso. His body was taken back to Murphysboro, Jackson County, Illinois where he was buried in the Tower Grove Cemetery. Theresa and her daughter moved to St. Louis, Missouri between 1910 and 1920. Theresa died of coronary thrombosis on 24 February 1943 in St. Louis, Missouri. She was buried in the Tower Grove Cemetery in Murphysboro, Jackson County, Illinois.

U.S. residence other than Ste. Genevieve County, Missouri:
Iron County, Missouri

Naturalization:

Name	Declaration	Naturalization	Origin
Beckly, Anselm		21 November 1856 Ste. Genevieve Co.	Baden

Military:
Served in the U.S. Civil War for the Union:
Private, Company C, 68th Enrolled Missouri Militia
   Anselm Baechle enlisted 2 April 1862 at Ironton, Iron County, Missouri. He mustered out in late 1863.

Education: Could read and write.
Occupation: Brickmaker, Livery Stable owner, Undertaker
Religious Affiliation: Roman Catholic
Comments:
Anselm Baechle came to Ste. Genevieve County, Missouri in 1849 with two of his siblings. When the Pilot Knob Iron Company began operations in the early 1850s in Iron County, Missouri, Anselm was hired to drive a wagon between Ste. Genevieve and Pilot Knob. He transported goods to Iron County and hauled iron pigs back to Ste. Genevieve for shipment back east. Anselm continued to work as a teamster until the completion of the Iron Mountain Railroad in 1856. At that time he became a resident of Pilot Knob. He married Theresia Spitzmiller on 1 January 1858 in Iron County, Missouri. Her family had come to the United States in 1851, locating first in Ste. Genevieve County and then removing to Pilot Knob, Iron County, Missouri. Shortly after their marriage, the couple moved to Ironton, Iron County, Missouri. The couple had three children: one son and one daughter and a child who died in infancy. Anselm served as a private in Company C of the 68th Enrolled Missouri Militia during the Civil War, enlisting at Ironton, Iron County, Missouri on 2 April 1862 and mustering out the following year. After the war Anselm became known as "Anselm Begley." He was engaged in the manufacture of brick and building materials until about 1874 when he became an undertaker and operated a livery stable. Theresa died on 20 June 1895 and Anselm died of facial erysipelas and heart failure on 28 January 1910, both in Iron County. They were both buried in the Masonic Cemetery at Ironton, Iron County, Missouri.

Franz Jacob Bernays Family
Surname Variations: Bernass, Bernay
European Origin: Mainz, Rheinland-Pfalz, Germany
Family:
Father: Clemens Bernays, born 14 February 1773 in Weisenau, Mainz, Rheinland-Pfalz, Germany. He died
   on 15 July 1837 in Frankenthal, Rheinland-Pfalz, Germany.
Mother: Theresia Creizenach, born in February 1788 in Mainz, Rheinland-Pfalz, Germany. She died on
   2 August 1863 in Frankenthal, Rheinland-Pfalz, Germany.
   Children:

‡   i. Friedrich Bernard, born about 1813 in Mainz, Rheinland-Pfalz, Germany. Bernard had been crippled as a baby by a nurse who had dropped him and so severely injured one leg that it was much shorter than the other. In spite of his affliction, he became a rabid supporter of the German Revolution of 1848. When the revolution failed, he fled to the Netherlands and then joined his brother Jacob when he left for the United States in 1854. Bernard bought a small house in Highland, Madison County, Illinois that was surrounded by a large garden which he cultivated. Bernard had a law degree and had opened a small practice and acted as a notary public. He also wrote freelance articles, mostly for the radical Milwaukee *Friedenker*. Bernard had a great love of art and had managed to acquire a few very valuable paintings while he was a refugee in the Netherlands. He died of old age in Highland, Madison County, Illinois on 24 March 1891. He was cremated in the Missouri Crematory. He never married and had no known issue.

‡   ii. Karl Ludwig "Charles Louis," born 10 November 1815 in Mainz, Rheinland-Pfalz, Germany. As a young man Charles studied law at Heidelberg University, but spent his leisure hours acting as a freelance correspondent for several newspapers. In 1840, he became the editor of a Mannheim newspaper where he remained until 1842 when he ran afoul of censorship authorities. He fled to Paris, France where he met Heinrich Boernstein, an Austrian radical, and began to collaborate with him on *Vorwaertz!*, an anti-government cultural newspaper which eventually became the principal mouthpiece of Karl Marx and his associates. The paper survived for two years before the French government shut it down after Charles authored an article which appeared to endorse the political assassination of monarchs. Charles was arrested and spent two months in the St. Pélagie prison which left him bitter and humiliated. Boernstein invited Charles to live in his home to recuperate and while there he met and fell in love with Boernstein's foster daughter. He married Josephine "Pepi" Wolf [in Paris, France?]. Josephine was the daughter of unknown parents, born 1 January 1822 in Linz, Austria. In early 1849 the couple came to the United States, coming directly to St. Louis, Missouri. At that time, a cholera epidemic was raging in the city, so Charles moved his family across the Mississippi River to Highland, Madison County, Illinois. The couple had three sons and two daughters. For about nine years, the family remained in Illinois where Charles founded a brewery and had interest in a mercantile business. He sold the brewery to the Schott brothers and moved his family back to St. Louis in 1858 to accept a position as the assistant editor of the St. Louis newspaper *Anzeiger des Westens* which had been started up by his former associate, Heinrich Boernstein. The paper failed in 1863 when political pressure and wartime economic woes caused advertising sales to drop disastrously. In 1861, Charles was appointed Consul to Zurich and then to Helsingoerd by President Abraham Lincoln. He served in these positions for nearly three years, returning to St. Louis in 1863. He then became paymaster for the U.S. Army in Missouri. At the end of the war, Charles accepted a position on the literary staff of the *Missouri Republican*, which post he held for the rest of his life. Charles died of heart disease complicated by dropsy on 22 June 1879 in St. Louis, Missouri. He was buried in the Bellefountaine Cemetery in St. Louis, Missouri. Josephine died on 30 May 1889 in Berlin, Germany where she had gone to visit her son who was studying music. She was cremated in the Gotha Crematory in Berlin and the ashes were buried in Bellefountaine Cemetery in St. Louis, Missouri next to her husband.

*   iii. Franz Jacob, born 18 June 1818 in Mainz, Rheinland-Pfalz, Germany. [See sketch below.]

      iv. Michael. He is said to have died at the age of 64 years. No further information.

      v. Son.

‡   vi. Johann Georg "George John," born 4 April 1824 in Oggersheim, Bavaria, Germany. He was a pharmacist and physician. George began his medical studies at the Universities of Heidelberg and Wurzburg in Germany. He completed his medical training in St. Thomas' Hospital in England. He had gone to England in order to be close to Wilhelmina "Minna" Doering whom he had met while he was working in a pharmacy owned by her uncle. She had gone to England to teach in St. Mary's Hall in London. George followed his older brother to the United States in

early 1853 and Minna came later with her brother Heinrich in the fall of 1853. George married Minna Doering on 5 November 1853 in St. Louis, Missouri. Minna was the daughter of Friedrich Doering and Louisa Bertrand, born about 1834 in Germany. The couple had three sons and two daughters. The whole family moved to Heidelburg, Germany when their oldest son entered Heidelburg University to study medicine. George wanted to personally supervise his sons curriculum. Minna died in December 1874, three weeks after giving birth to her fifth child, in Heidelberg, Germany. She was buried in Heidelburg. George returned home to St. Louis, Missouri and raised his children alone He died of erysipelas on 16 December 1888 in St. Louis, Missouri. He had contracted the disease while working on an infected cadaver as a young medical student. He had suffered from intermittent bouts of the disease for the rest of his life. George, a charter member of the St. Louis Cremation Society, was cremated and his ashes were taken to Heidelberg, Germany to be buried in his wife's grave.

vii. Amalia Mathilde, born about 1825 in Germany. She married Joseph Forthuber. The couple lived in Lauterecken, Pfalz, Bavaria, Germany. They had two sons and three daughters. Amelia died on 11 October 1869 in Landstuhl, Baveria, Germany.

viii. Helen, born 15 December 1827 in Germany. She may be the daughter who remained in Germany and lived in Frankfurt am Main. She is said to have died on 8 January 1913.

Immigration:
Arrived 30 January 1849 from Le Havre, France to New Orleans aboard the *Scyane*:
    Bernays, C[harles] H., 45
        Madam [Josephine], 30
        Henry, 5
        Marie, 3
        Louis, 1
Arrived 9 October 1854 from Bremen, Germany to New York aboard the *Hansa*:
    Bernays, Friedr Mich [Friedrich Bernard], 41   from Frankenthal
        Franz Jacob, 35
        Amalie, 28
        Clementine, 6

Biographical:
Husband: Franz Jacob Bernays
   Birth – 18 June 1818 in Mainz, Rheinland-Pfalz, Germany
   Death/Burial – 20 January 1894 in Ste. Genevieve, Ste. Genevieve County, Missouri. He was
      buried in the Valle Spring Cemetery in Ste. Genevieve, Ste. Genevieve County, Missouri.
Wife: Amelia Adelmann
   Birth – 1 August 1825 in Germany.
   Marriage – about 1845 in Germany.
   Death/Burial – 23 April 1895 in Ste. Genevieve, Ste. Genevieve County, Missouri. She was
      buried in the Valle Spring Cemetery in Ste. Genevieve, Ste. Genevieve County, Missouri.
Children:

i. Clementine, born 21 February 1847 in Germany. She married Maurice André on 20 November 1866 in Ste. Genevieve, Ste. Genevieve County, Missouri. He was a physician in Ste. Genevieve. Maurice was the son of Jean Jacques Louis André and Marie Francoise Revillod, born 30 August 1834 in Thrônes, Savoy, France. He had come to the United States with his parents in 1848. For a short time, he was enrolled at St. Mary's of the Barrens Seminary in Perry County, Missouri. However, he soon decided that the priesthood was not his vocation. He went to St. Louis where he attended the Washington University School of Medicine, graduating in 1866. Maurice went into practice with Dr. Charles Hertich in Ste. Genevieve where he met his wife. The couple had one son and two daughters, of whom one daughter died at the age of nineteen. Maurice died of heart disease on 23 January 1914 in St. Louis. He was buried in the Valle Spring Cemetery in Ste. Genevieve, Ste. Genevieve County, Missouri. In 1920, Clementine was living in Newark, Essex County, New Jersey where she had gone to visit a grandson. Clementine died on 23 July 1927, most likely in Connecticut at the home of her daughter. She was buried in the Valle Spring Cemetery in Ste. Genevieve, Ste. Genevieve County, Missouri.

ii. Anna Cecilia, born 23 June 1859 in Highland, Madison County, Illinois. She was well known for her knowledge of music and for an exceptional singing voice. She died of a paralytic stroke on 16 December 1896 in Ste. Genevieve, Ste. Genevieve County, Missouri. She was buried in the Valle Spring Cemetery in Ste. Genevieve, Ste. Genevieve County, Missouri. Anna never married and had no issue.

iii. Helen Genevieve, born 6 February 1860 in Highland, Madison County, Illinois. She married Charles Brandon Fischer on 14 May 1884 in Ste. Genevieve. He was a machinist in St. Louis, Missouri. Charles was the son of George W. Fischer and Edith G. Wood, born August 1855 in Missouri. The couple had one son and one daughter. Helen died of a blocked bile duct and liver cancer on 23 December 1931 and Charles died of a heart attack on 15 March 1947, both in St. Louis, Missouri. They were both cremated in the Missouri Crematory in St. Louis.

U.S. residence prior to Ste. Genevieve County, Missouri:
Highland, Madison County, Illinois

Military:
Served in the U.S. Civil War for the Union:
Surgeon, Medical Corps, Hospital #14, Nashville, Tennessee
Dr. Francis J. Bernays enlisted on 14 August 1862. He was mustered out in December 1866.

Education: Universities of Heidelberg and Wurzburg in Germany
Occupation: Physician
Religious Affiliation: Jewish born; Baptized Lutheran
Comments:
Franz Jacob Bernays was born into a family of religious, political, musical, literary and medical giants. His cousin, Martha Bernays, became the wife of Sigmund Freud. An uncle, Adolphus Bernays, was the first professor of German in King's College in London, England and the second professor of German in all of England. Another cousin, Jacob Bernays was a Jewish rabbi of considerable reputation for his philosophical writings on ancient classical literature. His father Clemens, a grain merchant, married Theresia Creizenach, the divorced former wife of another Jewish rabbi, Leo Ehlinger. Franz Jacob was the third son in a family of six sons and two daughters. His parents were liberal in their religious views and had all of their children christened in the Lutheran church. The conversion to Christianity was a pragmatic move on the part of his parents, as Jews were not allowed to attend secular colleges or universities at that time. Franz Jacob and his brothers attended a Catholic primary school in Oggersheim, Bavaria, Germany and studied at home with a private tutor. He studied medicine with a specialty in chemistry at the Universities of Heidelberg and Wurzburg. At the age of 27 Franz Jacob married Amelia Adelmann. The couple had one daughter who was born in Germany before they followed Charles to the United States. The family settled in Highland, Madison County, Illinois where two more daughters were born. Jacob served as an army surgeon during the Civil War and then moved his family to Ste. Genevieve, Ste. Genevieve County, Missouri in 1865. Franz Jacob died of uremia on 20 January 1894 and Amelia died of pneumonia on 23 April 1895, both in Ste. Genevieve. They were both buried in the Valle Spring Cemetery in Ste. Genevieve, Ste. Genevieve County, Missouri.

John Betten Family

Surname Variations: Baden, Betton
European Origin: [Enkhausen?], Westphalia, Germany
Family:
Father: Johannes Christoph Betten
Mother: Anna Theodora Pieper
　Children:
　　i.　Maria Catherina, born 11 February 1819 in Westphalia, Germany.
　　ii.　Maria Anna, born 14 May 1822 in Westphalia, Germany. She married Peter Maas on 27 January 1842 in Enkhausen, Westphalia, Germany. Peter was the son of Joducus Maas and Elisabeth Correck, born about 1809 in Germany. They had three sons and one daughter and possibly others, all born in Enkhausen. No further information.
*　　iii.　Johann "John," born 18 May 1825 in Westphalia, Germany. [See sketch below.]
‡　　iv.　Christoph, born 21 March 1830 in Westphalia, Germany. He came to the United States with his brother and a cousin named Johann Schulte. They settled in Madison County, Missouri, near the Valle Mines where they worked as miners. Christoph later bought a farm in Madison County, near Fredericktown, where he raised his family. Christoph married Elizabeth Catherine "Katie" Belken on 14 February 1855 in Madison County. She was the daughter of Caspar Belken and Gertrud Freiburg, born on 22 February 1832 in Affeln, Markisher Kreis, Nordrhein-Westphalen, Germany. The couple had three sons and five daughters. Christoph died of bronchitis and senile debility on 7 September 1912 in Madison County. Catherine died of heart disease and acute gastritis on 3 January 1921 in Madison County. They were both buried in the Calvary Cemetery [St. Michael's Catholic Church Cemetery] in Fredericktown, Madison County, Missouri.

Immigration:
Arrived 5 November 1849 from Antwerp, Belgium to New Orleans aboard the *George Stevens*:
　　Schulte, Johann, 27
　　Bettin, Christoph, 22　　[surname indexed as "Rebbin"]
Arrived some time in early 1850 aboard an unknown vessel:
　　Betten, Johann

Biographical:
Husband: Johann "John" Betten
　Birth – 18 May 1825 in Westphalia, Germany.
　Death/Burial – 20 November 1883 in Rock Haven, Ste. Genevieve County, Missouri. He was buried in the Valle Spring Cemetery in Ste. Genevieve, Ste. Genevieve County, Missouri.
Wife: Antoinette Zoellner, daughter of Wilhelm Zoellner and Maria Beule
　Birth – 11 January 1831 in Germany.
　Marriage – 29 December 1853 in Madison County, Missouri.
　Death/Burial – 14 July 1898 in Cape Girardeau County, Missouri. She was buried in the Old Lorimier Cemetery in Cape Girardeau, Cape Girardeau County, Missouri.
　Children:
　　i.　John, born about 1855 in Mine La Motte, Madison County, Missouri. He died suddenly at the age of twenty-six on 16 October 1881 in Ste. Genevieve County. He was buried in the Valle Spring Cemetery in Ste. Genevieve, Ste. Genevieve County, Missouri. No known issue.
　　ii.　Christopher F., born 12 April 1857 in Mine La Motte, Madison County, Missouri. He attended St. Benedict College in Atchison, Kansas [present-day Benedictine College] for four years, graduating in 1871. He then took a position as a bookkeeper in the Carondelet Savings Bank in St. Louis, Missouri for five years. In 1878 he moved to Cape Girardeau County, Missouri and served as United States deputy collector until 1884. He married Mary Julia Hawkins on

25 November 1880 in Cape Girardeau, Cape Girardeau County, Missouri. Julia was the daughter of Judge David Lewis Hawkins and Tiporah S. "Tippie" Knott, born 28 May 1863 in Missouri. The couple had one son and two daughters, of whom one daughter died at the age of two years. On the afternoon of 11 May 1883, a fire started in the Fuerth & Smith Foundry in Cape Girardeau which was partly owned by Christopher's brother-in-law, Joseph Fuerth. A strong southwest wind was blowing and the fire quickly spread to a livery stable and several nearby residences, including the home of the Bettens, which had just recently been completed. Many of the occupants of the businesses and homes were able to save only a few items before the fire overtook them. Christopher had insured his new house, but only for about half of its value. Christopher was a city clerk in Cape Girardeau for over 25 years and also served as manager of the St. Charles Hotel for a short time. He later worked for his father-in-law as a personal secretary while the judge was the Assistant Secretary of the Interior under President Grover Cleveland. Christopher died of carcinoma of the tongue on 7 March 1918 in Cape Girardeau, Cape Girardeau County, Missouri. He was buried in the Old Lorimier Cemetery in Cape Girardeau. Julia died some time after the 1920 census, most likely in Cape Girardeau County, Missouri.

iii. Elizabeth, about 1859 in Mine La Motte, Madison County, Missouri. She may have died after 1860, most likely in Madison County. There is no mention of her after the 1860 census.

iv. Francis J. "Frank," born 16 September 1860 in Mine La Motte, Madison County, Missouri. Frank owned and operated a flour mill in Lebanon, St. Clair County, Illinois. He married Mary T. Schultz on 2 January 1892 in Cape Girardeau, Cape Girardeau County, Missouri. Mary was the daughter of Richard Schultz and Adelia Bridget Sullivan, born 9 April 1864 in Missouri. Frank and Mary had no children of their own, but adopted a boy who they named Frank Schultz Betten. Mary died on 9 February 1943 and Frank died on 14 December 1943, both in Lebanon. They were both buried in the St. Joseph Cemetery in Lebanon, St. Clair County, Illinois.

v. Emma Louise, born 12 May 1864 in Mine La Motte, Madison County, Missouri. She married Joseph Francis Fuerth on 20 September 1887 in Cape Girardeau, Cape Girardeau County, Missouri. Joseph was the son of Charles Christian Fuerth and Walburga Stauss, born 4 October 1862 in Cape Girardeau County, Missouri. Joseph was a machinist, foundry owner and farmer in Cape Girardeau County. Joseph was a part-owner of the Fuerth & Smith Foundry in Cape Girardeau which was destroyed by fire on the afternoon of 11 May 1883. The couple had six sons, two daughters and one child that died in infancy. Joseph died of chronic valvular heart disease and nephritis on 14 February 1939 and Emma died of myocarditis and nephritis on 22 April 1944, both in Cape Girardeau. They were both buried in the St. Marys Cemetery in Cape Girardeau, Cape Girardeau County, Missouri.

vi. Joseph, born about 1866 in Missouri. He died by drowning in the Mississippi River on 5 June 1874 in Rock Haven, Ste. Genevieve County, Missouri. Joseph had been playing with another boy on the river bank when he fell into the water. His father found the boy's lifeless body about five hours later. Joseph was buried in the Memorial Cemetery in Ste. Genevieve, Ste. Genevieve County, Missouri. No issue.

vii. Maria Anna, born 16 September 1869 in Ste. Genevieve County, Missouri. She was a nurse. Maria died of myocarditis and nephritis on 5 April 1954 in Cape Girardeau, Cape Girardeau County, Missouri. She was buried in the St. Marys Cemetery in Cape Girardeau, Cape Girardeau County, Missouri. She never married and had no issue.

viii. Clara Ernestina, born 17 January 1871 in Ste. Genevieve County, Missouri. She died on 27 June 1871 in Ste. Genevieve County. She was buried in the Memorial Cemetery in Ste. Genevieve, Ste. Genevieve County, Missouri. No issue.

U.S. residence prior to Ste. Genevieve County, Missouri:
Mine La Motte, Madison County, Missouri

Land Patents:
Ste. Genevieve County, Missouri

Patentee	Issue Date	Land Office	Cert. No.	Serial No.	Twp	Rng	Sec	Acres
Betten, Christoph	30 Oct 1857	Jackson	23823	MO3820_.387	34-N	6-E	34	40.00

Military:
Served in the U.S. Civil War for the Union:
Private, Company I, 68th Enrolled Missouri Militia
  Christian [Christoph] Betten enlisted 2 October 1862 at Fredericktown, Madison County, Missouri.
Corporal, Company I, 68th Enrolled Missouri Militia
  John Betten enlisted 2 October 1862 at Fredericktown, Madison County, Missouri.

Education: Could read and write
Occupation: Miner, Farmer
Valle, Betten & Valle – Mill owner/operator with Francis L. and L. Bert Valle.

Religious Affiliation: Roman Catholic
Comments:
Johann "John" Betten was born in Westphalia, Germany and came to the United States as a young man in company with his younger brother and a cousin. They all settled in Madison County, Missouri and worked in the lead mines near Mine La Motte. John eventually bought part of a mine in partnership with Francis L. Valle and J. A. Weber. In 1868, John sold his share of the mine for a good profit and moved his family to Ste. Genevieve County where he, Francis L. and L. Bert Valle established a flour mill at Rock Haven. In 1872 John bought out his two partners and continued to run the mill as sole proprietor with limited success. From that time on, misfortune seemed to follow him. Two of his sons died and John began to suffer from debilitating rheumatism. He leased the mill to two men named Frederick Wunning and William Koeneman in the mid-1870s, but poor management and competition from other mills in the area gradually caused the Rock Haven Mill to fail. In May 1880 John sold the mill to John S. Stevens of Memphis, Tennessee for the sum of $14,000. About 10 months later, on the evening of 5 March 1881, the Betten home at Rock Haven caught fire and burned to the ground. John, who was home sick, had been in an upstairs bedroom when the fire broke out. He was able to save only a few items and suffered a severe burn on one arm. The house was not insured, and a large portion of the cash that John had received from the sale of his mill was also destroyed in the fire. His health declined rapidly after these losses. John died of dropsy complicated by induration of the liver [hardening as a result of inflammation] on 20 November 1883 at Rock Haven. He was buried in the Valle Spring Cemetery in Ste. Genevieve, Ste. Genevieve County, Missouri. After her husband's death, Antoinette sold the remaining personal property in a public auction and moved to Cape Girardeau, Cape Girardeau County, Missouri to live with her son Christopher. She died on 14 July 1898 in Cape Girardeau. She was buried in the Old Lorimier Cemetery in Cape Girardeau, Cape Girardeau County, Missouri.

Charles Henry Biel Family
Surname Variations: Beal, Bial
European Origin: Bad Gandersheim, Niedersachsen, Braunschweig, Germany
Family:
Father: Wilhelm Biel
Mother: Caroline Shuppe
  Children:
‡   i.   Wilhelm "William," born 8 January 1828 in Bad Gandersheim, Niedersachsen, Braunschweig, Germany. He was a shoemaker. William married Henrietta Pförtner on 9 July 1857 in Iron County, Missouri. Henrietta was the daughter of Heinrich Pförtner and Henrietta [Ewel?], born 23 November 1831 in Hahausen, Braunschweig, Germany. She had come to the United States

with her family in 1854 aboard the *Ernestine*. The couple had three sons and two daughters. Henrietta died on 4 March 1909 in Pilot Knob, Iron County, Missouri. William died of peritonitis due to a strangulated hernia on 11 November 1914 in Bismarck, St. Francois County, Missouri. They were both buried in the Pilot Knob Cemetery in Pilot Knob, Iron County, Missouri.

*   ii. Carl Heinrich "Charles Henry," was born 17 November 1838 in Bad Gandersheim, Niedersachsen, Braunschweig, Germany. [See sketch below.]

Immigration:
Arrived 5 June 1855 from Bremen, Germany to New Orleans aboard the *Auguste*:
    Biel, Wilhelm, 27   from Brunswick   going to Missouri   Shoemaker
Arrived 4 November 1857 from Bremen, Germany to New Orleans aboard the *New Orleans*:
    Biel, Carl, 18   from Gandersheim   going to Missouri   Shoemaker

Biographical:
Husband: Carl Heinrich "Charles Henry" Biel
    Birth – 17 November 1838 in Bad Gandersheim, Niedersachsen, Braunschweig, Germany.
    Death/Burial – 10 May 1910 in Ste. Genevieve, Ste. Genevieve County, Missouri. He was buried in the Lutheran Cemetery in Ste. Genevieve, Ste. Genevieve County, Missouri.
1) Wife: Caroline Faulkner
    Birth – about 1841 in Missouri.
    Marriage – 4 January 1864 in Ste. Genevieve, County, Missouri.
    Death/Burial – January 1871 in Ste. Genevieve County, Missouri.
    Children:
        i. Minnie Ida, born 19 April 1866 near Avon, Ste. Genevieve County, Missouri. She married Elza B. Burgess on 20 April 1896 in St. Francois County, Missouri. Elza was the son of Gilliam Washington Burgess and Amanda Elizabeth Dicus, born 1 October 1865 in Missouri. The couple had no children of their own, but fostered a boy named Harold Miller. Minnie died of pulmonary tuberculosis on 16 November 1938 in Farmington, St. Francois County, Missouri. She was buried in the Parks Family Cemetery in St. Francois County, Missouri. Elza died of heart disease complicated by asthma on 16 April 1939 in Farmington at the home of his foster son. He was buried in the Chestnut Ridge Cemetery in Ste. Genevieve County, Missouri.
        ii. Jennie Ruth, born 2 February 1868 in Coffman, Ste. Genevieve County, Missouri. Jennie married Joseph Henry Vorst on 18 September 1889 in Ste. Genevieve. Joseph was the son of Joseph Vorst and Maria Anna Scherer, born 9 October 1866 in Ste. Genevieve County, Missouri. [See Joseph Vorst sketch.]
        iii. Frances A. , born 24 December 1870 in [Ste. Genevieve County?], Missouri. She married George Grant "Grover" Clevlen on 21 May 1891 in Ste. Genevieve. George was the son of Charles Clevlen and Eliza M. Miller, born 13 July 1864 in Ironton, Iron County, Missouri. He was a restaurant manager in Festus when they married. The couple had two sons and one daughter, of whom one son died in infancy. Frances died on 17 May 1901 in Festus, Jefferson County, Missouri. She was buried in the Fairview Christian Church Cemetery [adjoining the Gamel Cemetery] in Festus. George married Lou V. McDaniel as his second wife on 31 August 1902 in Crystal City, Jefferson County, Missouri. Lou was the daughter of James McDaniel and Henrietta Albright, born in September 1896 in Madison County, Missouri. The couple had no children together. After his second marriage George worked as a carpenter and as a fireman in the boiler room of an electrical company. George died of chronic myocarditis on 29 June 1944 in St. Louis, Missouri. He was buried in the Fairview Christian Church Cemetery [adjoining the Gamel Cemetery] in Festus. Lou's date and place of death are unknown.

2) Wife: Amelia Sophia Schoenfeld, daughter of Karl Friedrich Schönfeld and Dorothea Lutz [See William Schoenfeld sketch.]

Birth – 9 July 1827, Kandern, Lörrach, Baden, Germany.
1) Marriage – 4 February 1853 in St. Louis, Missouri to Andreas A. Anderson. [See Andreas "Andrew" Anderson sketch.]
2) Marriage – 14 October 1879 in Ste. Genevieve, Missouri to Charles Henry Biel.
Death/Burial – 16 October 1888, Ste. Genevieve, Missouri. She was buried in the Lutheran Cemetery in Ste. Genevieve, Ste. Genevieve County, Missouri.

There were no children from the marriage between Charles Henry Biel and Amelia Schoenfeld.

3) Wife: Sophia Petrequin, daughter of Frederick Petrequin and Catherine Guilloz
Birth – 5 February 1852 in France.
Marriage – 20 November 1894 in St. Louis, Missouri.
Death/Burial – 2 January 1922 in Ste. Genevieve, Ste. Genevieve County, Missouri. She was buried in the Lutheran Cemetery in Ste. Genevieve, Ste. Genevieve County, Missouri.

There were no children from the marriage between Charles Henry Biel and Sophia Petrequin.

U.S. residence prior to Ste. Genevieve County, Missouri:
Iron County, Missouri
Perry County, Missouri

Land Patents:
Ste. Genevieve County, Missouri

Patentee	Issue Date	Land Office	Cert. No.	Serial No.	Twp	Rng	Sec	Acres
Beal, Charles H.	7 Jan 1893	Ironton	1844	MO4360_.149	36-N	7-E	27	40.00

Naturalization:

Name	Declaration	Naturalization	Origin	Remarks
Biel, William		26 May 1860 Iron County, MO	Germany	Passport Appl. 18 May 1897

Military:
Served in the U.S. Civil War for the Confederacy:
Private, Company B, Missouri Confederate Cavalry
    Charles Biel
Private, Company C, 68th Enrolled Missouri Militia
    William Biel enlisted 26 September 1862 in Ironton, Iron County, Missouri. He was mustered out on 4 October 1862 in Ironton. Enrolled again on 1 May 1864.

Education: Could read and write German and English
Occupation: Shoemaker, Farmer, Merchant
Religious Affiliation: Lutheran, Presbyterian
Political Affiliation and/or Any Offices Held:
Ste. Genevieve County Coroner for 15 years
Deputy Sheriff and Sheriff
County Collector
Member, Ste. Genevieve Board of Education

Comments:
Charles Henry Biel was born in Germany and came to the United States as a young man, only a few years after his older brother William had arrived. They had both been trained as shoemakers in Germany, but only William continued in the trade in Missouri. William had settled in Iron County, Missouri, and for the first few years he was in America, Charles lived with him. During the Civil War, Charles served briefly for the Confederacy as a private in Company B, Missouri Confederate Cavalry. After the war, He moved to Perry

County, Missouri and worked as a farm laborer. He married Caroline Faulkner on 4 January 1864 in Ste. Genevieve County, Missouri. Caroline was the daughter of unknown parents, born about 1841 in Missouri. The couple lived on a farm near the present-day town of Coffman where their three daughters were born. Caroline died from complications after the birth of her third child in January 1871. Her burial location is unknown. After his wife's death, Charles moved to the town of Ste. Genevieve where he was a clerk in the general store owned by Andrew Anderson. Andrew died of consumption in 1877. Charles married Andrew's widow, Amelia Sophia Schoenfeld, as his second wife on 14 October 1879 in Ste. Genevieve County, Missouri. Until she married Charles Henry Biel, Sophia successfully ran the grocery business that Andrew Anderson had established. After her marriage she continued to work in the store as an assistant to Charles. Amelia died of tuberculosis on 16 October 1888 in Ste. Genevieve County, Missouri. She was buried in the Lutheran Cemetery in Ste. Genevieve, Ste. Genevieve County, Missouri. Charles married Sophia Petrequin as his third wife on 20 November 1894 in St. Louis, Missouri. Charles died of cirrhosis of the liver on 10 May 1910 and Sophia died of a cerebral hemorrhage on 2 January 1922, both in Ste. Genevieve, Ste. Genevieve County, Missouri. They were both buried in the Lutheran Cemetery in Ste. Genevieve, Ste. Genevieve County, Missouri.

Anton Bieser Family

Surname Variations: Beezer, Biser, Buesser
European Origin: Ortenberg, Baden, Germany and Gengenbach, Baden, Germany
Family:
Father: Franz Anton Biser, born 15 January 1787 in Riedle, Baden, Germany. He died on 1 December 1867 in Fessenbach, Baden, Germany.
Mother: Ottilia Rieble, born 10 December 1791 in Ortenberg, Baden, Germany. She died on 3 October 1845 in Ortenberg.
Children:
- i. Rosina, born 25 Jun 1815 in Ortenberg, Baden, Germany. She died on 27 June 1817 in Ortenberg. No issue.
- ii. Sabina, born 27 October 1816 in Ortenberg, Baden, Germany.
- iii. Cecilia, born 13 November 1818 in Ortenberg, Baden, Germany.
- iv. Helena, born 18 Aug 1820 in Ortenberg, Baden, Germany. She married Peter Buss on 3 July 1859 in Pforzheim, Baden, Germany. Peter was the son of Xavier Buss and Theresia Oehler, born 28 June 1825 in Hofweier, Baden, Germany.
- * v. Anton, born 30 December 1821 in Riedle, Baden, Germany. [See sketch below.]
- vi. Johann Baptist, born 1 June 1824 in Ortenberg, Baden, Germany.
- vii. Bartholomew, born 23 August 1826 in Ortenberg, Baden, Germany.
- viii. Carolina, born 13 January 1828 in Ortenberg, Baden, Germany.
- ix. Viktoria, born 21 August 1830 in Ortenberg, Baden, Germany. She married Simon Hurst on 7 April 1863 in Weingarten Church, Baden, Germany. Simon was the son of Karl Joseph Franz Hurst and Sophia Giesler, born 28 October 1837 in Fessenbach, Baden, Germany. The couple had at least two sons and one daughter. Viktoria died on 19 December 1899 and Simon died on 9 September 1908, both in Fessenbach.
- x. Anastasia, born 31 March 1833 in Ortenberg, Baden, Germany.
- xi. Maria Anna, born 6 September 1834 in Ortenberg, Baden, Germany.
- xii. Richardis, born 15 January 1837 in Ortenberg, Baden, Germany.

Immigration:
Arrived about 1852 aboard an unknown vessel:
    Bieser, Anton and wife Caroline
        Ferdinand
        Ellen

Biographical:

Husband: Anton Bieser
   Birth – 30 December 1821 in Riedle, Baden, Germany.
   Death/Burial – 30 May 1879 in Ste. Genevieve County, Missouri. He was buried in the Our Lady Help of
      Christians Cemetery in Weingarten, Ste. Genevieve County, Missouri.

1) Wife: Caroline Saar, daughter of Mathias Saar and Katharina Feist [See Michael Feist sketch.]
   Birth/Baptism – 25 October 1826 in Gengenbach, Baden, Germany. She was baptized on 26 October
      1826 in the Catholic Church in Gengenbach.
   Marriage – 28 September 1848 in Ortenberg, Ortenaukreis, Baden, Germany.
   Death/Burial – 16 March 1857 in Ste. Genevieve County, Missouri. She was buried in the St. Joseph
      Cemetery in Zell, Ste. Genevieve County, Missouri.
   Children:
      i.   Ferdinand, born 25 January 1846 in Baden, Germany. He was baptized on 25 September 1848 in the Catholic Church in Gengenbach. Ferdinand was a cooper. He married Louisa Eder on 24 February 1868 in Ste. Genevieve County, Missouri. Louisa was the daughter of Anton Eder and Louisa Weiss, born 4 July 1845 in New York. The couple had four sons and one daughter. Ferdinand died of stomach cancer on 9 July 1896 in Ste. Genevieve County. He was buried in the Valle Spring Cemetery in Ste. Genevieve, Ste. Genevieve County, Missouri. Louisa died of heart disease and chronic nephritis on 28 September 1928 in Ste. Genevieve County. She was buried in the Sacred Heart Cemetery in Ozora, Ste. Genevieve County, Missouri.
      ii.   Theresia, born 29 August 1848 in Gengenbach, Baden, Germany. She was baptized on 26 September 1848 in the Catholic Church in Gengenbach. She died young and had no issue.
      iii.   Ellen, born about 1850 in Baden, Germany. No further mention of her has been found after the 1860 census.
      iv.   Sophia, born in March 1854 in Ste. Genevieve County, Missouri. She married Lawrence Ruh on 11 September 1877 in Ste. Genevieve, Ste. Genevieve County, Missouri. Lawrence was the son of Anton Ruh and Maria Anna Schneider, born about 1852 in Baden, Germany. [See Lawrence Ruh sketch.]
      v.   Louisa, born 7 April 1856 in Ste. Genevieve County, Missouri. She married Nicholas Schwent on 23 November 1876 in Weingarten, Ste. Genevieve County, Missouri. Nicholas was the son of Joseph Schwent and Maria Magdalena Jokerst, born 6 December 1842 in Ste. Genevieve County, Missouri. [See Joseph Schwent sketch.] Louisa married Jacob Hurka as her second husband on 10 April 1894 in Weingarten. Jacob was the son of Ignatius Hurka and Maria Loida, born 14 June 1840 in Schwechen, Bohemia. [See Jacob Hurka sketch.]

2) Wife: Maria Anna Stutz, daughter of Mathias Stutz and Magdalena Feist [See Mathias Stutz sketch.]
   Birth – 24 May 1840 in Hofweier bei Offenburg, Baden, Germany.
   Marriage – 23 April 1857 in the Germany Settlement [Zell], Ste. Genevieve County, Missouri.
   Death/Burial – 17 January 1920 in St. Francois County, Missouri. She was buried in the Old Calvary
      Cemetery in Farmington, St. Francois County, Missouri.
   Children:
      vi.   Maria Anna, born in February 1858 in Ste. Genevieve County, Missouri. She died on 9 June 1858 in Ste. Genevieve County and was buried in St. Joseph Cemetery in Zell, Ste. Genevieve County, Missouri. No issue.
      vii.   Joseph, born 13 August 1859 in Ste. Genevieve County, Missouri. He was a farmer. Joseph married Adeline Durlbaw on 2 February 1891 in Farmington, St. Francois County, Missouri. Adeline was the daughter of Nicholas Burlbaw and Monica Weldesofer, born 2 August 1867 in Cincinnati, Hamilton County, Ohio. The couple had three sons and five daughters. Joseph died of apoplexy on 3 April 1919 in Ste. Genevieve County. Adeline died of a gangrenous foot caused by diabetes and complicated by pneumonia and heart disease on 3 June 1944 in Ste. Genevieve County, Missouri. They were both buried in the Our Lady Help of Christians

Cemetery in Weingarten, Ste. Genevieve County, Missouri.

viii. Anthony, born 13 November 1863 in Ste. Genevieve County, Missouri. He was baptized on 6 December 1863 in the Sts. Philip and James Catholic Church in River aux Vases, Ste. Genevieve County, Missouri. Anton was a farmer. He married Anna Regina Schwent on 29 January 1889 in Weingarten, Ste. Genevieve County. Anna was the daughter of Joseph Schwent and Franziska Stoetzle, born 3 January 1870 in Zell, Ste. Genevieve County. The couple had two sons and five daughters, of whom one daughter died as a toddler. Joseph died of an apoplectic stroke on 18 April 1918 in Ste. Genevieve County. Anna died of apoplexy on 20 December 1941 in Ste. Genevieve County. They were both buried in the Our Lady Help of Christians Cemetery in Weingarten, Ste. Genevieve County, Missouri.

ix. Maria Theresa, born 26 March 1866 in Ste. Genevieve County, Missouri. She married Joseph Nicholas Kohler on 30 March 1889 in Zell, Ste. Genevieve County, Missouri. Joseph was the son of Joseph Kohler and Maria Adelaide Gegg, born 11 March 1861 in Ste. Genevieve County, Missouri. Joseph was a farmer in Ste. Genevieve County. The couple had six sons and three daughters, of whom one son and one daughter died in infancy. Joseph died of influenza on 27 April 1919 in Ste. Genevieve County. Theresa died of heart disease on 1 February 1939 in Ste. Genevieve County. They were both buried in the Our Lady Help of Christians Cemetery in Weingarten, Ste. Genevieve County, Missouri.

x. Child, born 2 March 1868 in Ste. Genevieve County, Missouri. The child died on 3 March 1868 and was buried in the St. Joseph Cemetery in Zell, Ste. Genevieve County, Missouri. No issue.

xi. Rosina Caroline, born 28 January 1869 in Ste. Genevieve County, Missouri. She married Francis Xavier "Frank" Steffan on 1 June 1889 in Weingarten, Ste. Genevieve County. Frank was the son of Sylvester Steffan and Barbara Schmidt, born 3 April 1864 in Erie County, Pennsylvania. [See Sylvester Steffan sketch.]

xii. Charles Paul, born 26 June 1871 in Ste. Genevieve County, Missouri. He was a farmer. Charles married Katherine Barbara Burlbaw on 18 November 1895 in Missouri. Katherine was the daughter of Nicholas Burlbaw and Monica Weldesofer, born 27 March 1873 in Scott County, Indiana. The couple had no children. Charles died of choleocystitis and hemiplegia on 1 April 1936 in Bonne Terre, St. Francois County, Missouri. Katherine died of arteriosclerosis and senile dementia on 15 April 1944 in Farmington, St. Francois County. They were both buried in the Calvary Cemetery in St. Francois County, Missouri.

xiii. Francis William "Frank," born 27 May 1873 in Ste. Genevieve County, Missouri. He was a stock farmer. Frank married Salome Katherine "Sally" Weiler on 17 January 1899 in Weingarten, Ste. Genevieve County. Sally was the daughter of Wendelin Weiler and Caroline Busam, born 1 August 1875 in Zell, Ste. Genevieve County, Missouri. The couple had two daughters. Frank died on 29 December 1943. Sally died on 4 January 1969 in Farmington, St. Francois County, Missouri. They were both buried in the Old Calvary Cemetery in Farmington, St. Francois County, Missouri.

xiv. Edward Henry, born 14 October 1875 in Ste. Genevieve County, Missouri. He was baptized on 23 November 1875 in the Sts. Philip and James Catholic Church in River aux Vases, Ste. Genevieve County, Missouri. He worked with his brother Frank as a stock farmer. Henry married Elizabeth Theresa Weiler. Elizabeth was the daughter of Wendelin Weiler and Caroline Busam, born 17 June 1888 in Weingarten, Ste. Genevieve County, Missouri. The couple had one son and one daughter. Henry died on 30 January 1953. Elizabeth died on 1 March 1977 in Farmington, St. Francois County, Missouri. They were both buried in the Old Calvary Cemetery in Farmington, St. Francois County, Missouri.

xv. Katherine Josephine, born 30 April 1878 in Ste. Genevieve County, Missouri. She was baptized on 4 May 1878 in Our Lady Help of Christians Catholic Church in Weingarten, Ste. Genevieve County, Missouri. She married Charles Buhlinger on 30 April 1901 in St. Francois County, Missouri. Charles was the son of Cyriac Buhlinger and Matilda Krauch, born 22 March 1875 in Knoblick, St. Francois County, Missouri. The couple had one son and one daughter. Charles died of a cerebral accident on 11 November 1960 in St. Louis, Missouri. He was buried in the Calvary Cemetery in St. Louis, Missouri. Katherine's date and place of death are unknown.

Land Patents:
Ste. Genevieve County, Missouri

Patentee	Issue Date	Land Office	Cert. No.	Serial No.	Twp	Rng	Sec	Acres
Bieser, Anthony	10 Jun 1856	Jackson	17847	MO3720_.311	37-N	8-E	17	120.00
Bieser, Ferdinand	10 Jun 1856	Jackson	15295	MO3720_.181	37-N	8-E	17	40.00

Military:
Served in the U.S. Civil War for the Union:
Corporal, Company F, 78th Enrolled Missouri Militia
    Anton Bieser enlisted in August 1862 in St. Genevieve County, Missouri
Private, Company K, 78th Enrolled Missouri Militia
    Anton Beiser enlisted on 30 April 1864 in St. Genevieve County, Missouri. He was ordered into active service on 16 October 1864. He was relieved from duty on 25 November 1864 after having served 41 days of actual service.

Occupation: Farmer
Religious Affiliation: Roman Catholic
Comments:
Anton Bieser came to the United States about 1852 with his family. They apparently came directly to Ste. Genevieve County, Missouri after they arrived. Anton purchased land in Ste. Genevieve County and began to farm. His first wife, Caroline Saar, died in 1857 and was buried in the St. Joseph Cemetery in Zell, Ste. Genevieve County, Missouri. Anton married Maria Anna Stutz as his second wife on 23 April 1857 in the German Settlement [Zell], Ste. Genevieve County. Anton died of apoplexy on 30 May 1879 and was buried in the Our Lady Help of Christians Cemetery in Weingarten, Ste. Genevieve County, Missouri. His oldest son, Ferdinand, inherited the farm and took over operations. Maria moved to St. Francois County, Missouri with her two youngest sons and lived with them for the rest of her life. She died of hemiplegia on 17 January 1920 in St. Francois County. She was buried in the Old Calvary Cemetery in Farmington, St. Francois County, Missouri.

August Bieser Family
Surname Variations: Baser, Beezer, Buser
European Origin: [Nesselried?], Baden, Germany
Family:
Father: Georg Bieser, born about 1797 in Baden, Germany. He died at sea on 20 November 1857 aboard the *Emily A. Hall*. He was buried at sea.
Mother: Catherina Jaeger
    Children:
†   i.   Michael, born about 1821 in Baden, Germany. [See Michael Bieser sketch.]
†   ii. Joseph, born about 1824 in Baden, Germany. [See Joseph Bieser sketch.]
*   iii. August, born about 1834 in Baden, Germany. [See sketch below.]

Immigration:
Arrived 17 December 1857 from Le Havre, France to New Orleans aboard the *Emily A. Hall*:
    Buser [Bieser], Georg, 60 [died at sea 20 November 1857]
        Joseph, 31
        August, 23

Biographical:
Husband: August Bieser
   Birth – about 1834 in Baden, Germany.
   Death/Burial – after 1880, possibly in St. Louis, Missouri.
Wife: Elisabeth Weitmann
   Birth – about 1838 in Germany.
   Marriage – about 1860.
   Death/Burial – after 1880, possibly in St. Louis, Missouri.
   Children:
   i. William, born about 1862 in Missouri. No record of him has been found after the 1880 census.
   ii. August, born about 1863 in Missouri. He died on 7 May 1873 in Ste. Genevieve County, Missouri. He was buried in the St. Lawrence Cemetery in Lawrenceton, Ste. Genevieve County, Missouri. No issue.
   iii. Andrew, born 2 January 1867 in Ste. Genevieve County, Missouri. He was baptized on 18 July 1867 in St. Anne's Catholic Church in French Village, St. Francois County, Missouri. No record of him has been found after the 1880 census.
   iv. Wendolin George, born 10 October 1867 in Ste. Genevieve County, Missouri. He was baptized on 1 March 1868 in St. Anne's Catholic Church in French Village, St. Francois County, Missouri. George moved to St. Louis, Missouri with his parents in the late 1870s. However, as a young man, he returned to Ste. Genevieve County and became a farmer. He never married and had no known issue. George died of heart disease on 15 April 1942 in Ste. Genevieve County. He was buried in the St. Lawrence Cemetery in Lawrenceton, Ste. Genevieve County, Missouri.
   v. Charles Joseph, born 25 May 1870 in Ste. Genevieve County, Missouri. He was baptized on 25 May 1870 in St. Anne's Catholic Church in French Village, St. Francois County, Missouri. No record of him has been found after the 1880 census.
   vi. John, born 23 January 1873 in Ste. Genevieve County, Missouri. He was baptized on 15 February 1873 in St. Lawrence Catholic Church in Lawrenceton, Ste. Genevieve County, Missouri. John worked as a river man, landing barges in St. Louis, Missouri. He was married to Mary Pohlmann. Mary was born of unknown parents about 1885 in Missouri. The couple had two sons and possibly others, of whom the oldest son died in early childhood. John died of multiple myeloma and anemia on 26 February 1939 in St. Louis, Missouri. Mary died in 1971. They were both buried in the St. Matthews Cemetery in St. Louis, Missouri.
   vii. Elizabeth "Lizzie," born about 1876 in Missouri. No record of her has been found after the 1880 census.
   viii. August, born about 1879 in Missouri. He was a machinist in St. Louis, Missouri. August married a woman named Edith _____. They were divorced. It is unknown whether or not they had children. August died of heart disease on 27 July 1928 in Crystal City, Jefferson County, Missouri. He was buried in Festus, Jefferson County, Missouri.

U.S. residence other than Ste. Genevieve County, Missouri:
   St. Louis, Missouri

Education: Could read and write.
Occupation: Farmer, Lumber yard worker
Religious Affiliation: Roman Catholic
Comments:
August Bieser came to the United States with his father and brother in 1857 to join his eldest brother, Michael, who had settled in the northern part of Ste. Genevieve County, Missouri. The father died at sea during the journey. The three brothers lived and worked on a farm owned by Michael. August married Elisabeth Weitmann about 1860 and soon started a family. Some time in the late 1870s, August moved his family to St.

Louis, Missouri, where he and his two oldest surviving sons worked in a lumber yard. No record has been found of August or his wife after the 1880 census. At least two of their sons remained in the St. Louis area and one son moved back to Ste. Genevieve County, Missouri.

Jacob Bieser Family

Surname Variations: Beezer, Beiser
European Origin: Rammersweier, Baden, Germany
Family:
Father: Johannes Georg Biser, born 30 March 1786 in Rammersweier, Baden, Germany.
Mother: Katharina Kieffer, born 21 November 1781 in Weierbach, Baden, Germany.
   Children:
*   i. Jacob, born 12 July 1810 in Rammersweier, Baden, Germany. [See sketch below.]
      ii. Wilhelm, born 23 May 1812 in Rammersweier, Baden, Germany. He died on 27 July 1812 in Rammersweier. No issue.
      iii. Bernhard, born 18 July 1813 in Rammersweier, Baden, Germany. He married Elisabeth End on 23 August 1841 in Weingarten Church, Baden, Germany. Elisabeth was the daughter of Franz Joseph End and Franziska Falk, born 18 November 1813 in Rammersweier. The couple had five sons and four daughters, all born in Rammersweier.
      iv. Helena, born 8 May 1815 in Rammersweier, Baden, Germany. She married Ferdinand Kiefer on 9 October 1837 in Weingarten Church, Baden, Germany. Ferdinand was the son of Philip Jacob Kiefer and Maria Magdalena Omeis, born 16 October 1812 in Rammersweier. The couple had five sons and four daughters, all born in Rammersweier. Helena died on 30 June 1890 and Ferdinand died on 24 March 1891, both in Rammersweier.
†   v. Joseph, born 19 January 1817 in Rammersweier, Baden, Germany. [See Joseph Bieser sketch.]
      vi. Magdalena, born and died 11 January 1821 in Rammersweier, Baden, Germany. No issue.

Immigration:
Arrived 30 December 1854 from Le Havre, France to New Orleans aboard the *John Hancock*:
   Bieser, Jacob, 52
      Maria Anna, 40
      Monica, 14
      Ursula, 13
      Anton, 9
      Balthasar [Bartholomew], 6
      Maria, 5
      Bernhard, 4
      Caroline, 3
      Henry [Helena], 3/12

Biographical:
Husband: Jacob Bieser
   Birth – 12 July 1810 in Rammersweier, Baden, Germany.
   Death/Burial – 3 December 1883 in Weingarten, Ste. Genevieve County, Missouri. He was buried in the Our Lady Help of Christians Cemetery in Weingarten, Ste. Genevieve County, Missouri.
Wife: Maria Anna Litterst, daughter of Jacob Litterst and Monica Ockenfuss
   Birth – 26 July 1813 in Rammersweier, Baden, Germany.
   Marriage – 8 July 1839 in Baden, Germany.
   Death/Burial – 17 February 1902 in Ste. Genevieve, Ste. Genevieve County, Missouri. She was buried in the Valle Spring Cemetery in Ste. Genevieve, Ste. Genevieve County, Missouri.
   Children:
      i. Monica, born about 1840 in Baden, Germany. She married Francis Xavier "Frank" Huber on

7 November 1859 in Zell, Ste. Genevieve County, Missouri. He was the son of Benedict Huber and Franziska Weiler, born 11 April 1836 in Ste. Genevieve County. [See Benedict Huber sketch.]

ii. Ursula, born 21 October 1841 in Rammersweier, Baden, Germany. She married Francis Xavier "Frank" Huber, her older sister's widower, on 26 August 1862 in Zell, Ste. Genevieve County, Missouri. [See Benedict Huber sketch.]

iii. Johann Evangelist, born 8 December 1842 in Rammersweier, Baden, Germany. He died on 13 August 1843 in Rammersweier. No issue.

iv. Anton, born 14 January 1845 in Rammersweier, Baden, Germany. He moved to Canada in 1891 to farm and became a naturalized Canadian citizen in 1901. Anton was living in Vancouver, British Columbia, Canada at the time of his sister Ursula's death on 28 October 1911. He does not appear to have ever married and has no known issue. He died on 27 October 1927 in Vancouver, British Columbia, Canada.

v. Bartholomew, born 24 August 1846 in Rammersweier, Baden, Germany. He married Catherine Baumann on 14 November 1876 in Weingarten, Ste. Genevieve County. Catherine was the daughter of Leonard Baumann and Francisca Schwent, born 25 September 1856 in Ste. Genevieve County. The couple had five sons and one daughter. As a young man, Bart had served an apprenticeship as a shoemaker. He worked as a shoemaker in Bismarck and Farmington in St. Francois County, Missouri. Bart also owned and operated a farm in that county where he raised his family. In later years, he and his wife retired to Coffman, Ste. Genevieve County, Missouri. Bart died of chronic heart disease on 18 March 1934 and Catherine died of coronary thrombosis on 13 May 1938, both in Ste. Genevieve County. They were both buried in the St. Catherine Cemetery in Coffman, Ste. Genevieve County, Missouri.

vi. Maria Anna, born 17 April 1848 in Rammersweier, Baden, Germany. She married Joseph Firmin Siebert on 4 February 1868 in Ste. Genevieve County, Missouri. Joseph was the son of Carl Aloysius Siebert and Maria Anna Hurst, born 4 February 1843 in Ste. Genevieve County, Missouri. [See Carl Aloysius Siebert sketch.]

vii. Bernhard, born 16 July 1849 in Rammersweier, Baden, Germany. He died on 25 October 1870 in Ste. Genevieve County, Missouri. He was buried in the St. Joseph Cemetery in Zell, Ste. Genevieve County, Missouri. No known issue.

viii. Caroline, born 15 January 1851 in Rammersweier, Baden, Germany. She married Francis "Frank" Rehm on 23 May 1871 in Ste. Genevieve County, Missouri. Frank was the son of Joseph Rehm and Christina Kempf, born 9 December 1846 in Ste. Genevieve County, Missouri. [See Joseph Rehm sketch.]

ix. Helena, born 5 August 1854 in Rammersweier, Baden, Germany. She married George Meyer. George was born of unknown parents in Mississippi. The couple had two sons. George must have died some time between 1890 and 1900 since Helena is listed as a widow in the 1900 census. Her mother, Maria Anna, lived with her and helped her raise her two sons. Helena and her two sons moved to Los Angeles County, California about 1921. Helena died on 4 September 1926 in Los Angeles County, California.

Education: Could read and write
Occupation: Farmer
Religious Affiliation: Roman Catholic
Comments:
Jacob Bieser brought his family to the United States in 1854. They appear to have come directly to Ste. Genevieve County, Missouri where Jacob's younger brother, Joseph, and his family were already settled. The family lived on a farm near Weingarten, Ste. Genevieve County. Jacob died of pneumonia on 3 December 1883 in Weingarten, Ste. Genevieve County, Missouri. He was buried in Our Lady Help of Christians Cemetery in Weingarten, Ste. Genevieve County, Missouri. After her husband's death, Maria Anna turned the farm over to her sons and moved to the city of Ste. Genevieve to live with her widowed youngest daughter,

Helena, to help her raise her two sons. Maria died on 17 February 1902 in Ste. Genevieve, Ste. Genevieve County, Missouri. She was buried in the Valle Spring Cemetery in Ste. Genevieve, Ste. Genevieve County, Missouri.

Joseph Bieser Family
Surname Variations: Beser, Buser
European Origin: [Nesselried?], Baden, Germany
Family:
Father: Georg Bieser, born about 1797 in Baden, Germany. He died at sea on 20 November 1857 aboard the *Emily A. Hall*. He was buried at sea.
Mother: Catherina Jaeger
   Children:

Note: For a comprehensive discussion of Georg Bieser's children see the August Bieser sketch.

Immigration:
Arrived 17 December 1857 from Le Havre, France to New Orleans aboard the *Emily A. Hall*:
   Buser [Bieser], Georg, 60 [died at sea on 20 November 1857]
      Joseph, 31
      August, 23

Biographical:
Husband: Joseph Bieser
   Birth – about 1824 in Baden, Germany.
   Death/Burial – about 1880, most likely in Ste. Genevieve County, Missouri.
Wife: Maria Anna Bransch, daughter of Franz Bransch and Elisabeth Basso
   Birth – 5 August 1845 in Germany.
   Marriage – 24 April 1866 in Ste. Genevieve County, Missouri.
   Death/Burial – 6 August 1901 in Jefferson County, Missouri. She was buried in the Charter Baptist Church Cemetery in Festus, Jefferson County, Missouri.
   Children:
   i. Sophia Caroline, born 27 December 1865 in Ste. Genevieve County, Missouri. She was baptized on 22 April 1866 in the Ste. Genevieve Catholic Church in Ste. Genevieve, Ste. Genevieve County, Missouri. She must have died in infancy as no record has been found for her other than her baptismal record. No issue.
   ii. Catherine, born 29 May 1867 in Ste. Genevieve County, Missouri. She was baptized on 7 July 1867 in the St. Ann's Catholic Church in French Village, St. Francois County, Missouri. Catherine must have died as a toddler after July 1870. No record of her has been found after the 1870 census. No issue.
   iii. Odelia "Delia," born 26 January 1869 in Ste. Genevieve County, Missouri. She was baptized on 22 August 1869 in the St. Ann's Catholic Church in French Village, St. Francois County, Missouri. She married John Armbruster on 13 November 1900 in French Village, St. Francois County, Missouri. John was the son of Joseph Armbruster and Catherine Eichenlaub, born 26 June 1871 in Ste. Genevieve County, Missouri. [See Joseph Armbruster sketch.]
   iv. Philip August, born 23 March 1870 in Ste. Genevieve County, Missouri. He was baptized on 13 April 1871 in the St. Lawrence Catholic Church in Lawrenceton, Ste. Genevieve County, Missouri. Philip was a farmer. He married Wilhelmina "Minnie" Koester on 6 April 1899 in St. Francois County, Missouri. Minnie was the daughter of John Charles Edward Koester and Anna Sophia Elisabeth Hammenstedt, born 31 December 1876 in Jefferson County, Missouri. The couple had three sons. Philip died of diabetes on 25 July 1941 and Minnie died on 7 July 1966, both in Missouri. They were both buried in the Charter Baptist Church Cemetery in Festus, Jefferson County, Missouri.

    v. Elisabeth Maria, born 11 April 1873 in Ste. Genevieve County, Missouri. She was baptized on 15 June 1873 in the St. Lawrence Catholic Church in Lawrenceton, Ste. Genevieve County, Missouri. She must have died young. No record of her has been found after her baptismal record.

    vi. George Joseph, born 9 January 1877 in Ste. Genevieve County, Missouri. He was baptized on 18 March 1877 in the St. Lawrence Catholic Church in Lawrenceton, Ste. Genevieve County, Missouri. George was a farmer. He married Augusta Rosetta Koester on 4 February 1901 in Jefferson County, Missouri. Augusta was the daughter of John Charles Edward Koester and Anna Sophia Elisabeth Hammenstedt, born 1 January 1882 in Jefferson County, Missouri. The couple had one son and four daughters, of whom one daughter died in infancy. George died on 16 November 1945 in Madison County, Illinois. He was buried in the Sunset Burial Park in St. Louis, Missouri. Augusta died on 15 November 1971 in Festus, Jefferson County, Missouri.

    vii. Maria J. "Mary," born 23 March 1880 in Ste. Genevieve County, Missouri. She lived with her brother, George, and helped with the household chores. She never married and had no known issue. Mary died of facial erysipelas and chronic myocarditis on 18 March 1935 in St. Louis, Missouri. She was buried in the Charter Baptist Church Cemetery in Festus, Jefferson County, Missouri.

Occupation: Farmer
Religious Affiliation: Roman Catholic
Comments:
Joseph Bieser came to the United States with his father and younger brother in 1857 to join his older brother Michael who had settled in the northern part of Ste. Genevieve County, Missouri. The father died at sea during the journey. The three bothers lived and worked on a farm owned by Michael. Joseph married Maria Anna Bransch in 1866 and soon started a family. This Joseph Bieser family is definitely not to be confused with the Joseph Bieser family that resided near present-day River aux Vases, Ste. Genevieve County, Missouri. That family is discussed in a separate sketch. The Joseph Bieser of this sketch appears to have operated a distillery in addition to farming. In August 1878 he was arrested for failing to pay taxes on distilled spirits. He was released on a bond of $1000, a very high sum for that time. Joseph appears to have died about 1880, most likely in Ste. Genevieve County, Missouri. His surviving daughters were fostered out to neighboring families and the two sons remained with their mother. Maria lived with her son George until her death on 6 August 1901. She was buried in the Charter Baptist Church Cemetery in Festus, Jefferson County, Missouri.

Joseph Bieser Family
Surname Variations: Beezer, Biser, Boazer, Boser
European Origin: Rammersweier, Baden, Germany
Family:
Father: Johannes Georg Biser, born 30 March 1786 in Rammersweier, Baden, Germany.
Mother: Katharina Kieffer, born 21 November 1781 in Weierbach, Baden, Germany.
   Children:

Note: For a comprehensive discussion of Johannes Georg Bieser's children see the Jacob Bieser sketch.

Immigration:
Arrived about 1841 aboard an unknown vessel:
    Bieser, Joseph and wife Elisabeth
        Mathias

Biographical:
Husband: Joseph Bieser
   Birth – 19 January 1817 in Rammersweier, Baden, Germany.
   Death/Burial – After June 1900 [in Colorado?].

Wife: Elisabeth Oehler, daughter of Joseph Oehler and Franziska Bürck
Birth – 8 June 1810 in Rammersweier, Baden, Germany.
Marriage – 18 June 1838 in Weingarten Church, Baden, Germany.
Death/Burial – 15 February 1888 in Weingarten, Ste. Genevieve County, Missouri. She was buried in Our Lady Help of Christians Cemetery in Weingarten, Ste. Genevieve County, Missouri.
Children:
  i. Katharina, born 7 December 1838 in Rammersweier, Baden, Germany. She died young, before 1850. No issue.
  ii. Mathias, born 24 February 1840 in Rammersweier, Baden, Germany. He came to the United States with his parents about 1841. There is no record of Mathias after the 1880 census of Ste. Genevieve County, Missouri.
  iii. Theresia, born 6 September 1842 in Ste. Genevieve County, Missouri. She was baptized on 16 October 1842 in the Ste. Genevieve Catholic Church in Ste. Genevieve. She married Conrad Isenmann on 1 April 1861 in Zell, Ste. Genevieve County. Conrad was the son of Joseph Isenmann and Maria Richardis Schimpf, born 25 November 1832 at Hofweier, Baden, Germany. [See Conrad Isenmann sketch.] She married Francis Brichle as her second husband on 28 November 1861 in Zell, Ste. Genevieve County. Francis was the son of Francis Brichle and Walburga Braching, born 10 November 1840 in Germany. [See Francis Breckle sketch.]
  iv. Bernard, born 8 January 1844 in Ste. Genevieve County, Missouri. He was baptized on 28 April 1844 in the Ste. Genevieve Catholic Church in Ste. Genevieve. He served as a private in Company F of the 78th Enrolled Missouri Militia, a reserve unit, during the Civil War. It is doubtful whether he was ever called to active service in that unit. However, he later enlisted in the 47th Regiment Missouri Infantry Volunteers and served in southeastern Missouri and then in Tennessee until March 1865. He must have become seriously ill either before he mustered out or shortly thereafter. He died on 21 April 1865 in Ste. Genevieve County, Missouri. He was buried in the St. Joseph Cemetery in Zell, Ste. Genevieve County. He does not appear to have ever married and had no known issue.
  v. Joseph, born 5 September 1846 in Ste. Genevieve County, Missouri. He was baptized on 20 April 1847 in the Ste. Genevieve Catholic Church in Ste. Genevieve. Joseph moved to Mesa County, Colorado as a young man and became a stockman, working cattle on a ranch. He married Minna Amelia Splettstoser on 29 December 1886 in Mesa County, Colorado. Minna was the daughter of unknown parents, born 11 January 1867 in Rohrbach, Baden, Germany. The couple had eight sons and one daughter. Joseph died on 29 February 1932 and Minna died on 19 July 1951. They were both buried in the Mesa [Fairview] Cemetery in Mesa, Mesa County, Colorado. [Note: Their headstone gives Joseph's date of birth incorrectly as 5 February 1847.]
  vi. Louise, born 20 September 1849 in Ste. Genevieve County, Missouri. She married William S. Baumann on 23 November 1875 in Ste. Genevieve County. William was the son of Leonard Baumann and Francisca Schwent, born 28 April 1853 in Ste. Genevieve County, Missouri. William was a carpenter. The couple had one son and three daughters. Louise died on 20 February 1897 in Ste. Genevieve County. William died on 2 November 1938 in Elvins, St. Francois County, Missouri. Their burial location is unknown.
  vii. Valentine, born about 1853 in Ste. Genevieve County, Missouri. He married Cornelia Josephine Langelier on 8 August 1876 in River aux Vases, Ste. Genevieve County. Josephine was the daughter of Jean Baptist Langelier and Judithe Zoe Lalumondiere, born 24 November 1856 in Ste. Genevieve County. The couple had two sons. Valentine died some time before August 1887, most likely in Ste. Genevieve County. Josephine married Edward F. Lalumondiere as her second husband on 23 August 1887 in River aux Vases, Ste. Genevieve County. Edward was the son of Henry Lalumondiere and Eulalia Valle, born in April 1849 in Missouri. He was a stone mason. Edward was the widower of Leah Marie Boyer who died on 15 March 1886 in Bloomsdale, Ste. Genevieve County, and left Edward with an infant son to

raise alone. Edward and Josephine had one son who died in infancy. Edward died about 1920, most likely in Ste. Genevieve County. Josephine died of acute dysentery on 26 December 1934 at the County Poor Farm in Ste. Genevieve County.

Land Patents:
Ste. Genevieve County, Missouri

Patentee	Issue Date	Land Office	Cert. No.	Serial No.	Twp	Rng	Sec	Acres
Bieser, Joseph	10 Apr 1849	Jackson	10285	MO3570_.020	37-N	7-E	30	40.00
Bieser, Joseph	15 Nov 1854	Jackson	15978	MO3670_.429	37-N	8-E	20	40.00
Bieser, Joseph	15 Nov 1854	Jackson	15979	MO3670_.430	37-N	8-E	30	40.00

Naturalization:

Name	Declaration	Naturalization	Origin
Bieser, Joseph	8 May 1852	23 November 1855 Ste. Genevieve Co.	Baden

[Note: There is another Joseph Bieser, son of Georg Bieser and Catherine Jaeger, born in 1824, who lived near Bloomsdale. The Joseph of this sketch lived near Zell. The naturalization record could be for either one, but more likely for this person, based on the dates and places of birth of his children.]

Military:
Served in the U.S. Civil War for the Union:
Corporal, Company F, 78th Enrolled Missouri Militia
   Joseph Bieser enlisted on 18 August 1862 in Ste. Genevieve County, Missouri.
Private, Company F, 78th Enrolled Missouri Militia
   Bernhart Bieser enlisted on 18 August 1862 in Ste. Genevieve County, Missouri.
Private, Company K, 47th Regiment Missouri Infantry Volunteers
   Bernard Buser [Bieser] enlisted on 30 August 1864 in Ste. Genevieve, Missouri. He was mustered out on 29 March 1865 at Benton Barracks, Missouri.

Education: Could read and write
Occupation: Farmer
Religious Affiliation: Roman Catholic
Comments:
Joseph Bieser came to the United States with his family about 1841. They appear to have come directly to Ste. Genevieve County, Missouri. Joseph bought a farm near what became the present-day village of River aux Vases. His older brother, Jacob, brought his family to Ste. Genevieve County in 1854 and settled near him. Both Joseph and his son Bernard served in Company F of the 78th Enrolled Missouri Militia during the Civil War. Joseph's wife Elizabeth died in 1888 and was buried in the Our Lady Help of Christians Cemetery in Weingarten, Ste. Genevieve County, Missouri. Shortly after his wife's death, Joseph sold his farm and most of his household goods with the intention of moving out to Colorado to live with his son Joseph for the remainder of his years. His trip must have been delayed or he had returned for a visit as he was living in the household of his son-in-law, William Baumann, in 1900. His date and place of death are unknown.

Michael Bieser Family
Surname Variations: Beiser, Beizer
European Origin: [Nesselried?], Baden, Germany
Family:
Father: Georg Bieser, born about 1797 in Baden, Germany. He died at sea on 20 November 1857 aboard the *Emily A. Hall*. He was buried at sea.
Mother: Catherina Jaeger
   Children:

Note: For a comprehensive discussion of Georg Bieser's children see the August Bieser sketch.

Immigration:
Arrived 10 December 1853 from Le Havre, France to New Orleans aboard the *Heidelberg*:
> Bieser, Michel, 28

Arrived 8 April 1856 from Le Havre, France to New Orleans aboard the *Susan Hinks*:
> Rieser [Bieser], Magdal[ena], 36
>> Emma, 8

Biographical:
Husband: Michael Bieser
  Birth – about 1821 in Baden, Germany.
  Death/Burial – 28 November 1894 in Ste. Genevieve County, Missouri. He was buried in the Valle Spring Cemetery in Ste. Genevieve, Ste. Genevieve County, Missouri.
1) **Wife:** Magdalena Steinle
  Birth – about 1818 in Baden, Germany.
  Marriage – in Baden, Germany.
  Death/Burial – 15 May 1872 in Ste. Genevieve County, Missouri.
  Children:
  i. Emma, born 31 December 1846 in Baden, Germany. She married Michael Sewald on 9 December 1865 in Hillsboro, Jefferson County, Missouri. Michael was the son of Anton Seewald and Verena Herrmann, born 10 September 1839 in Durbach, Baden, Germany. [See Michael Sewald sketch.]
  ii. William M., born 4 May 1857 in Ste. Genevieve County, Missouri. He was baptized on 17 May 1857 in St. Ann's Catholic Church in French Village, St. Francois County, Missouri. He was a blacksmith and worked in a shop near Bloomsdale, Ste. Genevieve County in partnership with Joseph Bader. William married Selma Clare Hacke on 21 December 1879 in Jefferson County, Missouri. Selma was the daughter of Fred Hacke and Pauline Helbig, born in April 1858 in Germany. She had come to the United States with her parents about 1868. William and Selma had four sons and one daughter, of whom one son died in infancy. In the spring of 1883, William left his partnership with Joseph Bader and went to Jefferson County, Missouri to take over operation of his own smithy. By 1910, he had moved his family to Pine Bluff, Jefferson County, Arkansas where he and his three surviving sons had all gotten jobs working in a railroad shop, maintaining and repairing train cars and engines. William died on 16 July 1932 in Pine Bluff. Selma's date of death is unknown.
  iii. Charles Michael, born 26 March 1863 in Ste. Genevieve County, Missouri. He was baptized on 19 May 1863 in St. Ann's Catholic Church in French Village, St. Francois County, Missouri. He was a blacksmith. Charles married Elizabeth Sephronia Vaughn on 16 March 1898 in Jefferson County, Missouri. Elizabeth was the daughter of James Edward Vaughn and Martha Ann Whitehead, born in October 1878 in Missouri. The couple had two daughters. Charles died of pneumonia complicated by chronic alcoholism on 30 July 1925 in Festus, Jefferson County, Missouri. He was buried in the Gamel Cemetery in Festus. Elizabeth married Charles Raymond Thompson as her second husband on 17 March 1927 in Hillsboro, Jefferson County, Missouri. Charles was born about 1893 in Missouri. They had no children together. Elizabeth married Otto Joseph Young as her third husband on 3 July 1954 in Festus, Jefferson County, Missouri. Otto was born on 3 November 1883 in DeSoto, Jefferson County. He may have been previously married. Elizabeth and Otto had no children together. Otto died on 16 March 1961 in DeSoto and was buried in the Calvary Cemetery in DeSoto. Elizabeth died in 1965 and was buried in the Methodist Cemetery in Festus, Jefferson County, Missouri.

2) Wife: Walburga Manchert, daughter of Christoph Manchert and Theresia Wipfler
Birth – 17 December 1833 in Waldprechtsweier, Baden, Germany.
1) Marriage – 1 March 1859 in Zell, Ste. Genevieve County, Missouri to Meinrad Kuehn. [See Meinrad Kuehn sketch.]
2) Marriage – 1 December 1873 in Ste. Genevieve, Ste. Genevieve County, Missouri to Michael Bieser.
Death/Burial – 5 September 1907 in Ste. Genevieve, Ste. Genevieve County, Missouri. She was buried in the Valle Spring Cemetery in Ste. Genevieve, Ste. Genevieve County, Missouri.
Children:
- iv. Caroline, born 31 December 1874 in Ste. Genevieve County, Missouri. She was baptized on 28 February 1875 in St. Philomena's Catholic Church in Bloomsdale, Ste. Genevieve County. Caroline died in infancy. No issue.
- v. Michael, born about 1878 in Ste. Genevieve County, Missouri. He died on 11 September 1883 in Ste. Genevieve County, Missouri. He was buried in the Valle Spring Cemetery in Ste. Genevieve, Ste. Genevieve County, Missouri. No issue.

Land Patents:
Ste. Genevieve County, Missouri

Patentee	Issue Date	Land Office	Cert. No.	Serial No.	Twp	Rng	Sec	Acres
Biser, Michael	10 Jun 1857	St. Louis	27769	MO1080_.140	39-N	6-E	33	320.00

Occupation: Farmer and Blacksmith
Religious Affiliation: Roman Catholic
Comments:
Michael Bieser came to the United States by himself in 1853. It is uncertain whether or not he came directly to Ste. Genevieve County, Missouri. His wife, Magdalena, and daughter, Emma, followed him about two and a half years later in 1856. Michael bought a substantial parcel of land in northern Ste. Genevieve County where he established a farm. He also operated a blacksmith shop to supplement his income. Magdalena died some time between March 1863 and December 1873, most likely in Ste. Genevieve County. Michael married Walburga Manchert as his second wife on 1 December 1873 in Ste. Genevieve. Walburga was the widow of Meinrad Kuehn and had children from her first marriage. Michael and Walburga had one son and one daughter together, but both children died young. Michael died at the County Poor Farm of general debility from old age on 28 November 1894. He was buried in the Valle Spring Cemetery in Ste. Genevieve, Ste. Genevieve County, Missouri. Walburga returned to the city of Ste. Genevieve to live with her oldest surviving son and was commonly known as "Mrs. Kuehn" until her death on 5 September 1907 in Ste. Genevieve. She was buried in the Valle Spring Cemetery in Ste. Genevieve, Ste. Genevieve County, Missouri.

Albert Bisch Family
Surname Variations: Beisch, Bische, Bish, Bitsch, Buesch
European Origin: Frankenthal, Rheinland-Pfalz, Germany
Family:
Father: Andreas Bisch
Mother: Magdalena Schaf
Children:
- * i. Albert, born 12 September 1779 in Frankenthal, Rheinland-Pfalz, Germany. [See sketch below.]
- † ii. Maria Anna, born 11 September 1785 in Frankenthal, Rheinland-Pfalz, Germany. She married Conrad Norwein on 11 May 1805 in Frankenthal. [See Conrad Norwine sketch.]

Immigration:
Arrived some time before 1800 and possibly landed in Philadelphia aboard an unknown vessel:
Bisch, Albert

Biographical:
Husband: Albert Bisch
  Birth – 12 September 1779 in Frankenthal, Rheinland-Pfalz, Germany.
  Death/Burial – 30 January 1845 in St. Louis, Missouri. He was buried in the Memorial Cemetery in Ste. Genevieve, Ste. Genevieve County, Missouri.

Wife: Johanna "Hannah" Kraft [aka Krafft]
  Birth – about 1787 in Philadelphia, Pennsylvania.
  Marriage – about 1804 in Philadelphia, Pennsylvania.
  Death/Burial – 14 March 1849 in Ste. Genevieve, Ste. Genevieve County, Missouri. She was buried in the Memorial Cemetery in Ste. Genevieve, Ste. Genevieve County, Missouri.

Children:

  i. Mary Ann, born 3 May 1805 in Philadelphia, Pennsylvania. She died on 20 May 1826 in Ste. Genevieve, Ste. Genevieve County, Missouri. She is buried next to her parents in the Memorial Cemetery in Ste. Genevieve, Ste. Genevieve County, Missouri. Mary Ann never married and had no issue.

  ii. Albert, born about 1806 in Philadelphia, Pennsylvania. He was one of the founders of the Bisch Mines, located in Jefferson and St. Francois Counties. In 1850, Albert was listed as a slave owner in the Ste. Genevieve County census. At that time he owned two adult female slaves, five female slaves aged ten years or younger, and one infant male slave. He died "suddenly" from an unknown cause on 19 January 1856 in Ste. Genevieve, Ste. Genevieve County, Missouri. He was buried in the Memorial Cemetery in Ste. Genevieve, Ste. Genevieve County, Missouri. Albert never married and does not appear to have had any issue.

  iii. Theodore, born 18 April 1809 in Philadelphia, Pennsylvania. He was a lead miner and smelter and was very well off financially. He married Marie Felicite St. Vrain on 3 November 1840 in Ste. Genevieve, Ste. Genevieve County, Missouri. Marie was the daughter of Felix Auguste de Hault de Lassus St. Vrain and Marie Pauline Gregoire, born 16 August 1823 in Ste. Genevieve. Her father's family were French nobility who had fled the French Revolution and come to America in 1790. They came to Ste. Genevieve County in 1793. By virtue of political connections rather than any special knowledge or expertise, young Felix St. Vrain was appointed to serve as the United States Indian agent to the Sauk and Fox nations of the Rock Island region of Illinois during William Clark's service as superintendent of the St. Louis Indian Agency. When the Black Hawk War began in 1832, St. Vrain was stationed at Fort Armstrong, located at the foot of Rock Island in the Mississippi River between present-day Illinois and Iowa. While on a mission to deliver dispatches to Galena, Illinois, St. Vrain and other members of his party were killed by a band of Pro-Sauk Winnebago Indians. The event, known as the St. Vrain Massacre, occurred on 24 May 1832. In January 1834, Congress passed a bill that provided for the relief of Felix's widow and children – in the form of a 640 acre land grant in the state of Missouri. Felix's older brother, Ceran, acted as guardian for the orphaned St. Vrain children. Legend has it that when Marie St. Vrain was about sixteen years old [about 1837], she went to Bent's Fort, Colorado with her uncle. While there, she met and fell in love with Kit Carson, the famous scout. Ceran objected to a match between the two, even though he personally liked Carson. Marie was sent back to St. Louis, Missouri to a convent school where she remained until her marriage to Theodore Bisch. The couple had ten sons and five daughters, of whom, only two sons and two daughters lived beyond the age of 26 and only three of the survivors married and had children. Of the children who died, the oldest daughter died at the age of sixteen when she caught pneumonia at the convent school in Dubuque, Iowa where she was studying. Four children died in infancy. Six others died within two weeks of each other in the fall of 1874 when they were either poisoned by bad well water or suffered from an unusual strain of typhoid fever. Theodore was a slave owner before emancipation and in the 1860 census of St. Francois County, he was listed as the owner of two adult male slaves, two adult female slaves, and two toddler female slaves. After selling his interest in the lead mines,

Theodore moved his family to Bonne Terre, St. Francois County, Missouri. Theodore died on 10 March 1878 and Marie died on 22 May 1902, both in Bonne Terre. They were most likely buried in the old Catholic Cemetery at Bonne Terre, St. Francois County, Missouri.

iv. Charles, born about 1811 in Philadelphia, Pennsylvania. He married Mary L. Alexandre about 1850. Mary was born on 28 September 1830 in [Napoleon, Desha County?], Arkansas. The couple had one son who was born in Ste. Genevieve. Mary died on 27 March 1853 in Ste. Genevieve and was buried in the Memorial Cemetery in Ste. Genevieve, Ste. Genevieve County, Missouri. Charles married Estelle Ricketts as his second wife about 1856. Estelle was born about 1842 in Missouri. The couple had three sons and one daughter. In the 1860 census of Ste. Genevieve County, Charles was listed as the owner of one adult female slave, two adolescent female slaves and one three-year-old male slave. Charles died of apoplexy on 5 June 1874 in Ste. Genevieve, Missouri. Estelle moved to St. Louis with her children where she ran a boarding house. She married a man named _____ Jones some time after 1880. She died of pneumonia on 9 April 1909 in St. Louis, Missouri and was buried in the Calvary Cemetery.

v. Henry, born 29 June 1815 in Philadelphia, Pennsylvania. He married Theresa Orilla Pratte on 13 April 1841 in Washington County, Missouri. Theresa was the daughter of Pierre Auguste Bernard Pratte and Emilie Reine Janis, born 9 March 1820 in Ste. Genevieve County, Missouri. The couple had one son, born in St. Francois County, who survived to adulthood. In 1850, Henry was listed as a slave owner in the St. Francois County census. At that time he owned three adult female slaves, six adult male slaves aged fifteen years or older, four female slaves aged eleven years or younger, and one infant male slave. By 1860, Henry had only one adult male slave in his household. He was in the mercantile business in Jefferson and St. Francois counties during the Civil War and his entire stock of goods was confiscated by General Sterling Price's Confederate soldiers. After the war Henry spent a fortune prosecuting claims for damages against the government, but never succeeded in winning his case. Theresa died on 26 October 1874 and was buried in St. Anne's Cemetery in French Village, St. Francois County, Missouri. Henry married Liona Moon as his second wife on 21 July 1880 in Jefferson County, Missouri. Liona was the daughter of James Moon and Lucinda Long, born 20 July 1859 in Jefferson County, Missouri. In spite of his rather advanced age, Henry and Liona had one son, born in Jefferson County when Henry was about 67 years old. Henry died on 28 August 1913 in DeSoto, Jefferson County, Missouri. He was buried in St. Anne's Cemetery in French Village, St. Francois County, Missouri next to his first wife. After her husband's death, Liona worked as a domestic servant for a family in St. Louis. By 1930, she was an inmate of the St. Louis City Infirmary where she died of lung and heart disease on 9 September 1932. She was buried in Lakewood Park Cemetery in Affton, St. Louis County, Missouri.

U.S. residence prior to Ste. Genevieve County, Missouri:
Philadelphia, Pennsylvania

Land Patents:
Ste. Genevieve County, Missouri

Patentee	Issue Date	Land Office	Cert. No.	Serial No.	Twp	Rng	Sec	Acres
Bisch, Albert, Jr	1 Feb 1848	St. Louis	15577	MO0830_.239	38-N	8-E	27	80.00
Bisch, Albert, Jr	1 Feb 1848	St. Louis	15578	MO0830_.240	38-N	8-E	34	80.00
St. Francois County, Missouri								
Bisch, Albert	15 Jul 1825	St. Louis	846	MO0020_.349	38-N	5-E	18	150.92
Bisch, Albert	15 Jul 1825	St. Louis	966	MO0020_.469	38-N	5-E	18	150.40
Bisch, Albert, Jr	1 Nov 1851	St. Louis	18417	MO0880_.470	38-N	5-E	20	80.00
Jefferson County, Missouri								
Bisch, Albert	1 Oct 1840	St. Louis	6876	MO0660_.012	38-N	4-E	12	80.00
Bisch, Theo.	1 Oct 1840	St. Louis	6885	MO0660_.208	38-N	4-E	12	80.00

Jefferson and St. Francois Counties, Missouri

Bisch, Albert	1 Oct 1840	St. Louis	6884	MO0660_.207	38-N	4-E	13	40.00
Bisch, Albert, Jr	15 Nov 1854	St. Louis	22333	MO0960_.331	38-N	4-E	13	120.00

Naturalization:

Name	Declaration	Naturalization	Origin	Remarks
Bisch, Albert		12 October 1807 Philadelphia, PA		Quarter Sessions Court

Education: Could read and write
Occupation:
   Grocer and retail merchant
   Ste. Genevieve Rope Walk (1820s)
   Keil, Bisch & Roberts (trading company, 1820s-1832)
Religious Affiliation: Roman Catholic
Comments:
Albert Bisch came to the United States some time before 1802. He most likely landed in Philadelphia and then settled in that city. He married Johanna "Hannah" Kraft there about 1804. Nothing is known of her ancestry. By 1808 Albert had established a grocery business on the corner of Spruce and 5th Streets in Philadelphia which he moved to High Street by 1810. According to the Philadelphia city directories, his business remained at this location until about 1816. Albert moved his family to Ste. Genevieve, Ste. Genevieve County, Missouri about 1818. He became a partner in the trading firm of Keil, Bisch and Roberts [Henry Keil, Albert Bisch and Edmund Roberts]. They used a building which had been built by Parfait Dufour on the corner of Second and Merchant streets in Ste. Genevieve as a warehouse. Edmund Roberts, the last remaining partner in the business, sold the building to Senator Louis Linn in 1831. Albert also established a rope walk in Ste. Genevieve in the 1820s and most likely operated it with his brother-in-law, Conrad Norwine, a rope maker. Albert and his sons were all slave owners before the Civil War. After emancipation, some of the former slave families kept the Bisch surname and continued to live with and work for the Bisch family. The Bisch [lead] Mines, located near Valles Mines, Jefferson County, Missouri, were owned by Albert's four sons and opened in 1824. A public stock corporation was formed in December 1855 known as the Rozier and Bisch Mining and Smelting Company. The founding members were the four Bisch brothers and Francis C., Firmin A., and Felix Rozier of Ste. Genevieve. The Bisch family sold their interest in the mines to the St. Francois Lead and Zinc Mining Company in March 1871. Albert died on 30 January 1845 in St. Louis. Hannah died on 14 March 1849 in Ste. Genevieve. They were both buried in the Memorial Cemetery in Ste. Genevieve, Ste. Genevieve County, Missouri.

Martin B. Bleckler Family
Surname Variations: Baechle, Bechler, Beckler, Blaechler, Blachler, Blechler
European Origin: Baden, Germany
Family:
Father: Bernard [Baechle?], born in Baden, Germany
Mother: Maria Damers, born in Baden, Germany
   Child:
*   i.   Martin B., born 13 November 1870 in Baden, Germany.

Immigration:
Arrived about 1890 aboard an unknown vessel:
   Baehle, Martin

Biographical:
Husband: Martin B. Bleckler
  Birth – 13 November 1870 in Baden, Germany.
  Death/Burial – 2 September 1923 in Ste. Genevieve County, Missouri. He was buried in the Valle
    Spring Cemetery, Ste. Genevieve, Ste. Genevieve County, Missouri.
1) Wife: Margaret Courtois, daughter of Henry Courtois and Mary Melissa Simpson
  Birth – December 1875 in Ste. Genevieve County, Missouri.
  Marriage – 15 April 1891 in Ste. Genevieve County, Missouri.
  Death/Burial – 22 January 1902 in Ste. Genevieve County, Missouri. She was buried in the Valle
    Spring Cemetery, Ste. Genevieve, Ste. Genevieve County, Missouri.
  Children:
    i. Joseph Edgar, born 6 March 1894 in Ste. Genevieve County, Missouri. He was baptized on 25 March 1894 in the Ste. Genevieve Catholic Church in Ste. Genevieve. He married Clara Perman in March 1920 in Crystal City, Jefferson County, Missouri. No further information.
    ii. Mary Myrtle, born 15 June 1897 in Ste. Genevieve County, Missouri. She was baptized on 4 July 1897 in the Ste. Genevieve Catholic Church in Ste. Genevieve. She is said to have married a man named Erwin White. The couple lived in St. Louis, Missouri. No further information.
    iii. Henry Dudley, born 4 March 1900 in Ste. Genevieve County, Missouri. He was baptized on 1 April 1900 in the Ste. Genevieve Catholic Church in Ste. Genevieve. He married Edna Mae Miller on 3 September 1922 in Festus, Jefferson County, Missouri. Edna was the daughter of Hugh H. Miller and Susan Elizabeth Minks, born 14 March 1903 in Sullivan, Franklin County, Missouri. The couple had five sons and one daughter. Henry died of heart disease on 26 September 1961 in Flat River, St. Francois County, Missouri. He was buried in the St. Francois Memorial Park in Bonne Terre, St. Francois County, Missouri. After Henry died, Edna married Dorsey T. Swafford as her second husband. Dorsey was born of unknown parents on 28 January 1897. He had been married once before he married Edna. Dorsey and Edna had no children together. Dorsey died on 24 July 1970. He was buried near his first wife in the Bismarck Masonic Cemetery in Bismarck, St. Francois County, Missouri. Edna died on 28 September 1979 in Farmington, St. Francois County, Missouri. She was buried in the Parkview Cemetery in Farmington, St. Francois County, Missouri.

2) Wife: Odile Philomena Maurice, daughter of Felix Maurice and Eleanora LaRose
  Birth – 2 October 1862 in Bloomsdale, Ste. Genevieve County, Missouri.
  1) Marriage – 5 February 1883 in Ste. Genevieve County, Missouri to Joseph Stanislaus LaRose
  2) Marriage – 23 February 1903 in Ste. Genevieve County, Missouri to Martin B. Bleckler
  Death/Burial – 8 August 1946 in Ste. Genevieve County, Missouri. She was buried in the Valle Spring
    Cemetery, Ste. Genevieve, Ste. Genevieve County, Missouri.
  Children:
    iv. Russel Francis Benedict, born 3 December 1903 in Ste. Genevieve County, Missouri. He was baptized on 6 December 1903 in the Ste. Genevieve Catholic Church in Ste. Genevieve. He married Margaret Pearl Tinker. She may have been previously married to a man named Lampman. Margaret was the daughter of James Tinker and Isabelle Shappo, born 8 November 1906 in St. Francois County, Missouri. The couple had three daughters. They were eventually divorced. Russell died 11 August 1951 in Perryville, Perry County, Missouri. He fell under a moving house trailer which rolled over him and crushed his chest. He was buried in the Valle Spring Cemetery, Ste. Genevieve, Ste. Genevieve County, Missouri. Margaret died on 24 April 1987 in Ste. Genevieve County, Missouri.
    v. Gerald Joseph Martin "Jerry," born 15 November 1905 in Ste. Genevieve County, Missouri. He was baptized on 21 November 1905 in the Ste. Genevieve Catholic Church in Ste. Genevieve. He married Louise Elizabeth Scherer. Louise was the daughter of Anton Scherer

and Mary Judith Thomure, born 24 January 1910 in Ste. Genevieve County. The couple had five sons and four daughters. Jerry died on 27 March 1966 and Louise died on 17 March 1996, both in Ste. Genevieve County. They were both buried in the Valle Spring Cemetery, Ste. Genevieve, Ste. Genevieve County, Missouri.

Naturalization:

Name	Declaration	Naturalization	Origin
Baechle [Bleckler], Martin		25 October 1894 Ste. Genevieve Co.	Germany

Occupation: Cooper at lime kiln
Religious Affiliation: Roman Catholic
Comments:
Martin B. Bleckler came to the United States about 1890 and settled in Ste. Genevieve County, Missouri. He found work as a cooper at the lime kiln near Ste. Genevieve. He married Margaret Courtois in 1891 in Ste. Genevieve. The couple had two sons and one daughter, all born in Ste. Genevieve. Margaret died of consumption on 22 January 1902 in Ste. Genevieve. She was buried in the Valle Spring Cemetery in Ste. Genevieve, Ste. Genevieve County, Missouri. Martin married Odile Philomena Maurice as his second wife on 23 February 1903 in Ste. Genevieve. Odile was the widow of Joseph Stanislaus LaRose who died 20 June 1896 and was buried in the Valle Spring Cemetery in Ste. Genevieve, Ste. Genevieve County, Missouri. Odile and Stanislaus had three sons and three daughters. Martin and Odile had two sons together. Martin died of pulmonary tuberculosis on 2 September 1923 in Ste. Genevieve. Odile died of chronic heart disease on 8 August 1946 in Ste. Genevieve County, Missouri. They were both buried in the Valle Spring Cemetery in Ste. Genevieve, Ste. Genevieve County, Missouri.

Note: Up until the death of his first wife, all of the records in Ste. Genevieve refer to Martin and his family using the surname "Baechle." After 1902, the family surname gradually evolved to the present-day "Bleckler."

Michael Bleifuss Family
Surname Variations: Bleifus, Bleyfus[s]
European Origin: Bavaria, Germany
Family:
Father: Mathaus "Matthew" Bleifuss, born about 1782 in Bavaria, Germany. He died between 4 March 1853 and 23 June 1853, most likely in Ste. Genevieve County, Missouri.
Mother: Anna Maria Haefner
    Child:
*   i.   Michael, born about 1812 in Bavaria, Germany. [See sketch below.]

Immigration:
Arrived on 14 June 1847 from Antwerp, Belgium to New York aboard the *Louis de Geer*:
    Bleifuss, Michael, 34   Farmer
Arrived before the 1850 census of Ste. Genevieve County, Missouri aboard an unknown vessel:
    Bleifuss, Mathaus

Biographical:
Husband: Michael Bleifuss
    Birth – about 1812 in Bavaria, Germany.
    Death/Burial – 30 June 1853 in Ste. Genevieve, Ste. Genevieve County, Missouri. He was buried in the Memorial Cemetery in Ste. Genevieve, Ste. Genevieve County, Missouri.
Wife: Brigitta "Bridget" Baumann, daughter of Franz Anton Baumann and Catherine Armbruster [See Franz Anton Baumann sketch.]
    Birth – 17 January 1830 in Sasbach bei Achern, Baden, Germany.

Marriage – 6 May 1851 in Zell, Ste. Genevieve County, Missouri.
Death/Burial – 23 June 1908 in Ste. Genevieve, Ste. Genevieve County, Missouri. She was buried in the Valle Spring Cemetery in Ste. Genevieve, Ste. Genevieve County, Missouri.
Child:
  i. Mary Louise, born 11 June 1852 in Ste. Genevieve County, Missouri. She was baptized in the Ste. Genevieve Catholic Church in Ste. Genevieve on 27 June 1852. Mary married Leon Sebastian Yealy on 31 January 1883 in Ste. Genevieve. Leon was the son of Jacob Yealy and Maria Anna Winkler, born 7 September 1848 in Ste. Genevieve County, Missouri. [See Jacob Yealy sketch.]

U.S. residence prior to Ste. Genevieve County, Missouri:
New York for a short time before moving to Ste. Genevieve County, Missouri.

Occupation: Merchant – M. Bleifuss & Co. [general store in Ste. Genevieve]
Religious Affiliation: Roman Catholic
Comments:
Michael Bleifuss came to the United States in 1841. He may have spent some time in the state of New York before moving west to Ste. Genevieve County, Missouri. He and his father, Mathaus "Matthew" Bleifuss, were living together in Ste. Genevieve County by 1850. Michael was a merchant and ran a general store in the town of Ste. Genevieve. He married Brigitta "Bridget" Baumann on 6 May 1851 in Zell, Ste. Genevieve County. The couple had one daughter before Michael died on 30 June 1853 in Ste. Genevieve. He left provisions for his wife and daughter and for his "aged father" in his will, dated 4 March 1853. But a codicil dated 23 June 1853 removed the provision for his father. It is most likely that Matthew died some time between those two dates. Michael died on 30 June 1853 and was buried in the Memorial Cemetery in Ste. Genevieve, Ste. Genevieve County, Missouri. Bridget kept the general store going at least until 1858, but by 1860, she had sold the business and become housekeeper for Father Francis Xavier Weiss, the much-revered pastor of the Ste. Genevieve Catholic Church. She continued to work as the rectory housekeeper until March 1901 when Father Weiss died. Bridget spent her remaining years with her daughter, helping to care for the Yealy family. She died on 23 June 1908 and was buried in the Valle Spring Cemetery in Ste. Genevieve, Ste. Genevieve County, Missouri.

Herman Bockenkamp Family
Surname Variations: Bockencamp, Boekenkamp, Buckencamp
European Origin: Brunswick, Germany
Family:
Father: Julius Bockenkamp, born about 1822 in Brunswick, Germany. He died on 17 November 1894 in Ste. Genevieve County, Missouri. He was buried in the Bockenkamp Cemetery in Ste. Genevieve County, Missouri.
Mother: Wilhelmina Donnerberg, born in June 1831 in Prussia, Germany. She died some time after the 1900 census, most likely in Missouri. [She may be the Wilhelmina Bockenkamp who died in St. Louis, Missouri in May 1906.] She is said to have been buried in the Bockenkamp Cemetery in Ste. Genevieve County, Missouri.
Children:
*   i. Herman Frederick, born 18 January 1854 in New Braunfels, Comal County, Texas. [See sketch below.]
    ii. Helena, born 1 July 1856 in New Braunfels, Comal County, Texas. She married Paul Oberle on 16 February 1874 in Crystal City, Jefferson County, Missouri. Paul was the son of Bernard Oberle and Maria Anna Lipp, born 28 June 1848 in Germany. [See Bernard Oberle sketch.]
    iii. Wilhelmina, born about 1858 in Texas. No further mention has been found of her after the 1870 census in Ste. Genevieve County, Missouri.
    iv. Mary Bertha, born 1 October 1859 in Comal County, Texas. She married Charles G. Hambel

about 1879, most likely in Missouri. Charles was the son of Charles Hambel and Josephine Brandel, born in February 1857 in Pittsburgh, Allegheny County, Pennsylvania. The couple had two sons and three daughters and one child that died in infancy. Charles and Bertha may have been divorced. By 1910, Charles was living in Fresno, California. No further mention of him has been found after the 1910 census. Bertha lived the rest of her live in St. Louis, Missouri where she died of apoplexy and bronchio pneumonia on 12 August 1950. She was buried in the Lakewood Park Cemetery in Affton, St. Louis County, Missouri.

v. Richard J., born about 1861 in Missouri. He married Elizabeth Jane "Eliza" Reed on 21 April 1885 in French Village, St. Francois County, Missouri. Eliza was the daughter of James Reed and Christine Petrie, born 9 January 1864 in Ste. Genevieve County, Missouri. The couple had one son and two daughters. Richard died of typhoid malaria and hemorrhaging from the lungs on 1 July 1899 in Kinsey, Ste. Genevieve County, Missouri. He is said to have been buried in the Bockenkamp Cemetery in Ste. Genevieve County, Missouri. Eliza married Adam Buenniger as her second husband on 14 October 1900 in Ste. Genevieve County. Adam was a widower with six children of his own. Adam and Eliza had no children together. He died of typhoid fever in mid-December 1901 in Kinsey, Ste. Genevieve County, Missouri. [See Adam Buenniger sketch.] By 1910, Eliza had moved to St. Louis with her children. Eliza died of myocarditis on 5 September 1941 in St. Louis, Missouri. She was buried in the Sunset Memorial Park and Mausoleum in Affton, St. Louis County, Missouri.

vi. Emma, born 27 May 1867 in Missouri. She married Harry F. Burleigh. Harry was the son of Samuel W. Burley and Araminta Gray, born 19 May 1855 in Missouri. He was a blacksmith and fireman. The couple had one son and two daughters. Emma died of biliary calculi [gall stones] on 6 August 1900 in St. Louis, Missouri. She was buried in the Gatewood Gardens Cemetery in St. Louis, Missouri. Harry married for a second time to Jennie L. Morebock about 1901 and had two sons and four daughters with her. He died of chronic valvular heart disease on 5 September 1916 in St. Louis, Missouri and was buried in the Gatewood Gardens Cemetery in St. Louis, Missouri.

vii. Caroline, born about 1869 in Missouri. No mention of her has been found after the 1880 census in Ste. Genevieve County, Missouri.

viii. Gustave, born 11 April 1875 in Ste. Genevieve County, Missouri. He was a tinner. Gustave married Lizetti "Sadie" Ebinger. Sadie was the daughter of August Ebinger and Sophie Milz, born about 1880 in Missouri. The couple had two sons. Gustave died of chronic heart disease on 20 July 1936 in St. Louis, Missouri. He was cremated in the Valhalla Crematory in St. Louis, Missouri.

Immigration:
Said to have arrived about 1851 from [Bremerhaven, Germany?] to Galveston, Texas aboard the *Suwa*:
    Bockenkamp, Julius

Biographical:
Husband: Herman Frederick Bockenkamp
    Birth – 18 January 1855 in New Braunfels, Comal County, Texas.
    Death/Burial – 26 May 1935 in Ste. Genevieve County, Missouri. He was buried in the Bockenkamp Cemetery in Ste. Genevieve County, Missouri.

1) Wife: Caroline Maria Uding, daughter of Friedrich Wilhelm August Uding and Caroline W. Lange. [See Friedrich Uding sketch.]
    Birth – 26 August 1859 in Ste. Genevieve County, Missouri.
    Marriage – 23 February 1875 in Missouri.
    Death/Burial – 13 July 1887 in Ste. Genevieve County, Missouri. She was buried in the Bockenkamp Cemetery in Ste. Genevieve County, Missouri.
    Children:

i. Wilhelmina "Minnie," born 13 June 1876 in Missouri. She married Friedrich "Fred" Eckert some time between 1930 and 1940, most likely in St. Louis, Missouri. Fred was the son of Friedrich Eckert and Catherine Humke, born 1 December 1886 in St. Louis, Missouri. Fred died on 16 February 1945 and Minnie died on 16 June 1957, both in Alameda County, California. The couple does not appear to have had any children.
ii. Henry Julius, born 6 April 1878 in Missouri. He married Susan "Susie" Summers. She was born of unknown parents on 28 January 1880 in De Soto, Jefferson County, Missouri. The couple had two daughters. They moved to Cincinnati, Hamilton County, Ohio, where Henry was a metal worker in a kitchen equipment manufacturing company. Henry died on 9 October 1949 and Susie died on 31 January 1962, both in Cincinnati. They were both buried in the Spring Grove Cemetery in Cincinnati, Hamilton County, Ohio.
iii. August Gustav "Gus," born 18 August 1880 in Ste. Genevieve County, Missouri. He married Alta Mavis Moody on 23 May 1905 in Chicago, Cook County, Illinois. Alta was the daughter of William Moody and Jane D. Henderson, born 1 January 1886 in Benton County, Iowa. Within a few years of their marriage, the family moved to Montana where Gus worked first as a machinist and then tried his hand at farming. The couple had one son and five daughters. Alta died on 3 July 1925 in Great Falls, Cascade County, Montana. August died in July 1975 in Seattle, King County, Washington. They were both buried in the Old Highland Cemetery in Great Falls, Cascade County, Montana.
iv. Bertha, born 30 May 1884 in Missouri. She married Ernest S. Vineyard on 25 February 1908 in Ste. Genevieve County, Missouri. Ernest was the son of Steve Vineyard and Sarah J. McDonnell, born 14 March 1884 in Jefferson County, Missouri. The couple had twin daughters. Ernest died on 14 October 1911 in Great Falls, Cascade County, Montana. He was buried in the Old Highland Cemetery in Great Falls, Cascade County, Montana. Bertha married James Joseph Healy as her second husband on 21 January 1914 in Great Falls. James was the son of Michael Healy and Catherine Moran, born 19 July 1872 in Bastard Township, Ontario, Canada. He had come to the United States in 1903. He was a mine worker and later became foreman in a smelting company. James and Bertha had no children together. Bertha died on 7 October 1920 in Cascade County, Montana. She was buried in the Old Highland Cemetery in Great Falls, Cascade County, Montana. James died on 23 October 1956 in Cascade County. He was buried in the Mount Olivet Cemetery in Great Falls, Cascade County, Montana.
v. Edwin, born 8 February 1885 in Ste. Genevieve County, Missouri. No mention has been found of him after the 1900 census.
vi. Leonard, born August 1886 in Ste. Genevieve County, Missouri. He is said to have died of an accidental gunshot wound some time between 1900 and 1910. He is said to have been buried in the Bockenkamp Cemetery in Ste. Genevieve County, Missouri. No issue.

2) Wife: Mary Ann Reed, daughter of James Reed and Christine Petrie
Birth – 15 October 1866 in Ste. Genevieve County, Missouri.
Marriage – 28 January 1890 in Kinsey, Ste. Genevieve County, Missouri.
Death/Burial – 19 December 1933 in Missouri. She was buried in the St. Anne's Cemetery in French Village, St. Francois County, Missouri.
Children:
vii. Elva Leona, born 12 December 1890 in Ste. Genevieve County, Missouri. Elva may have suffered from some significant health problems. She lived at home with her parents and never married. She had no issue. Elva died of mitral and aortic regurgitation complicated by nephritis on 11 November 1913 in St. Louis, Missouri. She was buried in the St. Anne's Cemetery in French Village, St. Francois County, Missouri.
viii. Jessie Ellen, born 26 March 1892 in Ste. Genevieve County, Missouri. She married Harry Robert Gamel. Harry was the son of Elias Theodore Gamel and Mary Jane Medley, born 6 May 1883. The couple had two sons. Harry died in 1966 and Jessie died in March 1989. They were

both buried in the Gamel Cemetery in Festus, Jefferson County, Missouri.
   ix. Georgiana Edith, born 23 December 1895 in Kinsey, Ste. Genevieve County, Missouri. She suffered an attack of polio when she was a child and was partially paralyzed on her right side. As she grew older, Georgiana began to show signs of rapid mental degeneration. She was committed to the State Hospital No. 4 in Farmington, St. Francois County, Missouri. She died there on 10 December 1934 of exhaustion from dementia praecox which had caused her to suffer from chronic excitement. She was buried in the St. Anne's Cemetery in French Village, St. Francois County. She never married and had no issue.
   x. Blanche Agnes, born in December 1893. She married Edward Bayer on 20 February 1917 in French Village, St. Francois County, Missouri. Edward was the son of Charles Bayer and Caroline Sewald, born 14 April 1890 in Ste. Genevieve County, Missouri. He was a farmer. The couple had one son and one daughter. Agnes died of coronary thrombosis complicated by anemia and a brain tumor on 13 May 1951 in Ste. Genevieve County, Missouri. She was buried in the St. Philomena's Cemetery in Bloomsdale, Ste. Genevieve County, Missouri. Edward died on 5 October 1988 in Festus, Jefferson County, Missouri.
   xi. Irene Virgie, born 5 February 1898 in Ste. Genevieve County, Missouri. She married Clyde Primo on 1 September 1923 in Festus, Jefferson County, Missouri. Clyde was the son of Louis Valle Primo and Florence McCarthy, born 13 June 1902 in Missouri. Both Irene and Clyde were life-long teachers. They had no children of their own. Clyde died in May 1979 in Jefferson County, Missouri. Irene married Ralph Claude Primo as her second husband on 23 June 1981 in Ironton, Iron County, Missouri. Ralph was the younger brother of her first husband, born 30 September 1910 in Missouri. Ralph died in January 1986 and Irene died on 29 May 2002, both in Festus. Irene and both of her husbands were buried in the Charter Baptist Church Cemetery in Festus, Jefferson County, Missouri.

U.S. residence prior to Ste. Genevieve County, Missouri:
New Braunfels, Comal County, Texas

Naturalization:

Name	Declaration	Naturalization	Origin
Bockenkamp, Julius	18 November 1851	Spring, 1854 Comal County, TX	Germany
Bockenkamp, Frederick		3 May 1881 Ste. Genevieve Co.	Prussia

Military:
Served in the U.S. Civil War for the Confederacy:
Private, Company A, Texas State Troops, 31st Brigade (Infantry) [Captain Fritz Heidemeyer's Company]
   Julius Bockenkamp enlisted 13 October 1864 in Comal County, Texas

Education: Could read and write
Occupation: Farmer
Religious Affiliation: [Lutheran?]
Political Affiliation and/or Any Offices Held: Herman F. Bockenkamp – Republican
   Judge of County Court, 1st District [Ste. Genevieve and Jackson Townships]
   Chairman, People's Central Committee, 1892
   Election Judge, Kinsey, Fall 1919
Comments:
Julius Bockenkamp and Wilhelmina Donnerberg were married on 26 December 1852 in New Braunfels, Comal County, Texas. Julius is said to have worked his passage from Bremen, Germany to Galveston, Texas aboard the bark *Suwa* in 1851. Wilhelmina came to the United States as a young girl in 1846. The couple farmed for a time in Comal County, Texas and then moved their family north to Ste. Genevieve County,

Missouri about 1865 after the end of the Civil War. Herman, their oldest son, married Caroline Maria Uding in 1875. Herman and Caroline had four sons and three daughters. Caroline died on 13 July 1887 when she was struck by lightning while driving a wagon on the family farm. Herman married for a second time on 28 January 1890 at Ste. Genevieve County to Mary Ann Reed. She was born 5 October 1866 and it is believed her parents were born in Scotland and Ireland. Herman and Mary had five daughters. Mary died of pneumonia and chronic myocarditis on December 1934 in Ste. Genevieve County. She was buried in St. Anne's Cemetery, French Village, St. Francois County, Missouri. Herman died of pulmonary tuberculosis and chronic nephritis on 26 April 1935 at Kinsey, Ste. Genevieve County. He was buried in the Bockenkamp Cemetery on the R. J. Bockenkamp Farm.

Lucas Boehle Family

Surname Variations: Bahle, Bailey, Baley, Bayley, Bhaly, Bohle, Böhle
European Origin: Windschläg, Baden, Germany
Family:
Father: Martin Böhle
Mother: Agatha Bross
   Children:
      i. Mathais, born 16 February 1801 in Windschläg, Baden, Germany. He married Balbina Rendler on 16 June 1829 in Windschläg. No further information.
      ii. Francisca, born 12 March 1803 in Windschläg, Baden, Germany.
      iii. Elisabetha, born 22 June 1804 in Windschläg, Baden, Germany. She married Lorenz Gass on 26 November 1833 in Windschläg. No further information.
*   iv. Lucas, born 15 October 1806 in Windschläg, Baden, Germany. [See sketch below.]
      v. Anna Maria, born 5 August 1811 in Windschläg, Baden, Germany.
      vi. Agnes, born 9 January 1814 in Windschläg, Baden, Germany.

Immigration:
Arrived on 22 February 1847 from Le Havre, France to New Orleans aboard the *Queen Victoria*:
   Boehle, Lucas, 40
        Balvina, 38
        Johann, 18
        Regina, 17
        Balbina, 10
        Michael, 9
        Franz, 6
        Paul, 1
   Fell, Marie Eve, 35 [age should be 65]

Biographical:
Husband: Lucas Boehle
   Birth – 15 October 1806 in Windschläg, Baden, Germany.
   Death/Burial – 17 April 1853 in Ste. Genevieve County, Missouri. He was buried in the St. Joseph Cemetery in Zell, Ste. Genevieve County, Missouri.
Wife: Balbina [aka Paulina] Krummer, daughter of Mathias Krummer and Maria Eva Foell
   Birth – 7 April 1808 in Windschläg, Baden, Germany.
   Marriage – 8 May 1828 in Windschläg, Baden, Germany.
   Death/Burial – 4 April 1891 in Ste. Genevieve County, Missouri. She was buried in the Our Lady Help of Christians Cemetery in Weingarten, Ste. Genevieve County, Missouri.
   Children:
      i. Johann "John," born 2 June 1828 in Windschläg, Baden, Germany. John was a farmer in Ste. Genevieve County, Missouri. He married Stephanie Kist on 21 March 1854 in St. Louis,

Missouri. Stephanie was the daughter of Ignatz Kuest and Franziska Nesselbosch and stepdaughter of Andreas Armbruster, born 14 April 1837 in Lauf, Baden, Germany. She came to the United States with her mother and stepfather in 1852. The couple had two sons and four daughters, of whom one daughter died in infancy. John died of "rheumatic troubles" on 14 May 1899 and Stephanie died of chronic asthma on 30 September 1918, both in Ste. Genevieve County. They were both buried in the Our Lady Help of Christians Cemetery in Weingarten, Ste. Genevieve County, Missouri.

ii. Regina, born 9 September 1829 in Windschläg, Baden, Germany. She married Joseph Schwaab on 11 September 1860 in Zell, Ste. Genevieve County, Missouri. Joseph was the son of Anton Schwaab and Elisabeth Müller, born about 1834 in Germany. [See Joseph Schwaab sketch.]

iii. Balbina [aka Paulina], born 18 June 1832 in Windschläg, Baden, Germany. She married Bernard Kenosha about 1851 in St. Louis, Missouri. Bernard was the son of unknown parents, born on 29 August 1829 in St. Louis, Missouri. He worked various jobs, including bar tending and working in a lumber planing mill in St. Louis. The couple had three sons and six daughters, of whom one daughter died in infancy. Paulina died of pneumonia on 11 October 1897 in St. Louis. Bernard died of heart disease on 2 February 1911 in St. Louis. They were both buried in the Calvary Cemetery in St. Louis, Missouri.

iv. Michael, born 23 June 1835 in Windschläg, Baden, Germany. Michael appears to have died some time between September 1859 and 1860. The last known record of him was when he purchased land in Ste. Genevieve County in 1859. He may never have married and had no known issue.

v. Franz "Frank," born 19 September 1839 in Windschläg, Baden, Germany. He was called a musician but worked with his brother John on the family farm. He froze to death after suffering an epileptic seizure on 30 December 1880 near Bieser's Distillery. Frank was buried in the Our Lady Help of Christians Cemetery in Weingarten, Ste. Genevieve County, Missouri. He never married and had no known issue.

vi. Paul, born 15 June 1845 in Windschläg, Baden, Germany. After his mother and older brothers had died, Paul lived with the Wendel Isenmann family and worked as a farm laborer. He never married and had no known issue. He died some time after the 1900 census, most likely in Missouri.

vii. Joseph, born about 1849 in Ste. Genevieve County, Missouri. He was a carpenter and farmer. He married rather late in life to Mrs. Catherine Gegg, the young widow of William Gegg. Catherine was the daughter of Friedrich Yonk and Eva Gibel, born 25 November 1870 in Lawrenceton, Ste. Genevieve County, Missouri. William was the son of Joseph Gegg and Victoria Brischle, born 11 January 1864 in Ste. Genevieve County. William Gegg and Catherine Yonk had one daughter.

William died of an accidental gunshot wound on 28 January 1889 when he dropped a loaded shotgun. The blast hit him in the leg just above his knee and he bled to death before medical aid could arrive. He was buried in the Our Lady Help of Christians Cemetery in Weingarten, Ste. Genevieve County, Missouri. Joseph Boehle and Catherine Yonk had two sons and one premature stillborn child. Catherine died from complications after the birth of the premature child on 5 May 1893 in Ste. Genevieve County, Missouri. She and the baby were both buried together in the Our Lady Help of Christians Cemetery in Weingarten, Ste. Genevieve County, Missouri. After his wife's death, Joseph gave his step-daughter to his wife's family to raise. He and his two sons moved to St. Francois County, Missouri where they worked as farm laborers. Joseph died in 1906. He was buried in the Old Calvary Cemetery in Farmington, St. Francois County, Missouri.

Land Patents:
Ste. Genevieve County, Missouri

Patentee	Issue Date	Land Office	Cert. No.	Serial No.	Twp	Rng	Sec	Acres
Bohle, John	1 Dec 1851	Jackson	12022	MO3600_.172	37-N	7-E	29	40.00
	1 Dec 1851	Jackson	12023	MO3600_.173	37-N	7-E	30	40.00
	15 Nov 1854	Jackson	15735	MO3670_.261	37-N	7-E	29	40.00
	15 Nov 1854	Jackson	16088	MO3680_.036	37-N	7-E	30	40.00
	10 Jun 1856	Jackson	11154	MO3720_.216	37-N	7-E	29	120.00
Bohle, Michael	1 Sep 1859	Jackson	31071	MO3930_.110	37-N	7-E	22, 27	95.90

Naturalization:

Name	Declaration	Naturalization	Origin
Bahle [Boehle], John		21 May 1853 Ste. Genenvieve Co.	Baden
Bailey [Boehle], Michael		21 November 1856 Ste. Genenvieve Co.	Baden

Military:
Served in the U.S. Civil War for the Union:
Private, Company F, 78th Enrolled Missouri Militia
  Frank Boehle enlisted in August 1862 in Ste. Genevieve County, Missouri. He was ordered into active service on 16 October 1864. He was relieved from duty on 25 November 1864 after having served 41 days of actual service.
Private, Company F, 78th Enrolled Missouri Militia
  John Boehle enlisted in August 1862 in Ste. Genevieve County, Missouri. He was ordered into active service on 16 October 1864. He was relieved from duty on 25 November 1864 after having served 41 days of actual service.
Private, Company F, 78th Enrolled Missouri Militia
  Paul Boehle enlisted 30 April 1864 in Ste. Genevieve County, Missouri. He was ordered into active service on 16 October 1864. He was relieved from duty on 25 November 1864 after having served 41 days of actual service.

Occupation: Farmer
Religious Affiliation: Roman Catholic
Comments:
Lucas Boehle brought his family, including his mother-in-law Maria Eva Foell, to the United States in 1847 and came directly to Ste. Genevieve County, Missouri. He bought a farm near present-day Weingarten which his sons expanded considerably within a few years. Lucas died in 1853, leaving his wife Balbina to raise their children by herself with the help of her mother. Three of the Boehle sons enlisted in 78th Enrolled Missouri Militia during the Civil War. Balbina's mother died at the age of 93 on 15 February 1873 in Ste. Genevieve County, Missouri. She was buried in the St. Joseph Cemetery in Zell, Ste. Genevieve County, Missouri. [The burial records list her name as "Maria Eva Cramer, wife of Mathew."] Balbina lived the remainder of her life on the farm which her sons operated. She died of old age in 1891 and was buried in the Our Lady Help of Christians Cemetery in Weingarten, Ste. Genevieve County, Missouri.

Frederick Bolle Family
Surname Variations: Balle
European Origin: Sattenhausen, Hanover, Germany
Family:
Father: Heinrich Christoph Bolle, born about 1791 in Germany. He is said to have died in 1863 in Germany at the age of 72.

Mother: Regina Elisabeth Baurmann, born about 1805 in Germany. She is said to have died after 1888 in Germany.
Child:
* i. Frederick G. A., born 13 August 1845 in Sattenhausen, Hanover, Germany. [See sketch below.]

Immigration:
Arrived 30 July 1866 from Bremen, Germany to New York aboard the *Hansa*:
    Bolle, C., 56
        W., 23
        F[rederick], 21   Farmer

Biographical:
Husband: Frederick G. A. Bolle
    Birth – 13 August 1845 in Sattenhausen, Hanover, Germany.
    Death/Burial – 26 May 1900 in Ste. Genevieve County, Missouri. He was buried in the Valle Spring Cemetery in Ste. Genevieve, Ste. Genevieve County, Missouri.
Wife: Theresa Wehner, daughter of Nicholas Wehner and Clara Schneider [See Nicholas Wehner sketch.]
    Birth – 2 October 1856 in Ste. Genevieve County, Missouri.
    Marriage – 2 July 1878 in Ste. Genevieve County, Missouri.
    Death/Burial – 1 December 1940 in St. Louis, Missouri. She was buried in the Valle Spring Cemetery in Ste. Genevieve, Ste. Genevieve County, Missouri.
Children:
    i. George Henry, born 6 February 1880 in Ste. Genevieve County, Missouri. He was baptized in the Ste. Genevieve Catholic Church on 24 February 1880. Georgie was a curious little boy and was particularly fascinated by the idea of fishing. He had seen his uncle George Wehner fish and wanted to try the sport himself. On the afternoon of 26 August 1886, Georgie and his parents were visiting his grandfather Nicholas Wehner and Georgie was allowed to play out in the yard. He apparently rigged himself a fishing pole using tackle from his grandfather's shed. His mother checked on him while he was in the process of getting his equipment prepared and thought nothing of his activity. The boy squeezed through a hole in the fence around the yard and made his way down to the nearby North Gabouri Creek. A short time later, his mother came out to check on him again and this time when she didn't receive an answer to her call, she started to search for her son. She spotted Georgie's hat floating in the creek and raised an alarm. A neighbor found the boy's lifeless body a short distance down the creek. The doctor was called, but his efforts to revive the child were in vain. Georgie was buried in the Valle Spring Cemetery in Ste. Genevieve, Ste. Genevieve County, Missouri. No issue.
    ii. Flora Eleonora, born 13 September 1882 in Ste. Genevieve County, Missouri. She was baptized in the Ste. Genevieve Catholic Church on 1 October 1882. Flora married Theodore Mitchell on 23 May 1918 in St. Louis, Missouri. He was a general laborer in St. Louis. Theodore was the son of John Mitchell and Eunice Jarrard, born 14 October 1858 in Illinois. Flora was Theodore's second wife. His first wife, Lena Schmelzle, had died of heart disease on 17 September 1914 in St. Louis. She was cremated. Lena was the daughter of August Schmelzle and Amelia Frezensunski, born 24 May 1864 in Illinois. Theodore and Lena are said to have had eight children together. Theodore and Flora do not appear to have had any children. Theodore died of a cerebral hemorrhage on 10 January 1933 in St. Louis. He was cremated in St. Louis. After her husband's death, Flora's mental state apparently began to deteriorate. By 1940, she was a patient of the State Sanatorium on Arsenal Street in St. Louis. Flora died in the Sanatorium of bronchio-pneumonia on 20 November 1953 in St. Louis, Missouri. She was buried in the Valle Spring Cemetery in Ste. Genevieve, Ste. Genevieve County, Missouri.
    iii. Nicholas Frederick, born 20 October 1884 in Ste. Genevieve County, Missouri. He was baptized in the Ste. Genevieve Catholic Church on 9 November 1884. Nicholas was a machinist

and worked on automobiles. Nicholas committed suicide by swallowing carbolic acid on the evening of 9 November 1908. He had gone to the saloon of A. W. Sickburg at the corner of Vandeventer and Cottage Avenues near his home in St. Louis. He drank a glass of soda and talked for a while with the bartender and some of the other bar patrons. Without any warning, he pulled a bottle of carbolic acid out of his pocket and drank it before anyone could interfere. He died in the ambulance on the way to the hospital. He was buried in the Valle Spring Cemetery in Ste. Genevieve, Ste. Genevieve County, Missouri. He never married and does not appear to have had any issue.

iv. Felix Frederick, born 2 November 1886 in Ste. Genevieve County, Missouri. He was baptized in the Ste. Genevieve Catholic Church on 21 November 1886. Felix died on 30 December 1886 in Missouri. He was buried in the Valle Spring Cemetery in Ste. Genevieve. No issue.

v. Bertha Alvina Alma, born 10 March 1889 in Ste. Genevieve County, Missouri. She was baptized in the Ste. Genevieve Catholic Church on 7 April 1889. Alvina married Samuel Campbell Russell on 26 May 1917 in St. Louis, Missouri. Samuel was the son of John Alfred Russell and Amelia Sephronia Gebhardt, born 19 August 1893 in Canton, Stark County, Ohio. The couple lived in Chicago, Illinois where Samuel was a piano salesman. They had two sons, both born in Chicago. Samuel and Alvina were divorced some time in the mid-1930s and Alvina supported herself and her sons by demonstrating cars for the Ford Motor Company. Samuel married a woman named Lucille _____ as his second wife and had a son and a daughter with her. Alvina moved to California after 1940. She died on 21 August 1979 in Los Angeles, Los Angeles County, California.

vi. Herman Thomas, born 8 August 1891 in Ste. Genevieve County, Missouri. He was baptized in the Ste. Genevieve Catholic Church on 6 September 1891. He was a pharmaceutical salesman in St. Louis, Missouri. Herman married Louise Hahn on 17 September 1913 in St. Louis, Missouri. Louise was the daughter of John Hahn and Margaret Lang, born 30 March 1889 in St. Louis, Missouri. The couple had one daughter. Louise died of ovarian cancer on 13 May 1952 in St. Louis. She was buried in the Resurrection Cemetery in Affton, St. Louis County, Missouri. Herman married Mrs. Wilhelmina "Minnie" Wolf as his second wife in 1952. Minnie was the daughter of Conrad Flori and Katherine Stumpf, born 18 May 1890 in St. Louis. Minnie died of a heart attack on 23 January 1956 in St. Louis. She was buried in the Sunset Burial Park in St. Louis, Missouri. Herman died in 1963. He was buried in the Resurrection Cemetery in Affton, St. Louis, County, Missouri.

vii. Augusta Elisabeth [aka Augusta Grace], born 2 July 1893 in Ste. Genevieve County, Missouri. She was baptized in the Ste. Genevieve Catholic Church on 22 July 1893. Augusta married Peter B. Harris in 1912 in St. Louis, Missouri. It is possible that the couple divorced. She married Carlyle Marshall Terry as her second husband on 20 July 1931 in Cook County, Illinois. Carlyle was the son of Eugene P. Terry and Hattie A. Bennett, born 15 July 1894 in New York. Augusta does not appear to have ever had any children. Augusta died on 29 March 1978 and Carlyle died on 7 January 1981, both in Los Angeles County, California.

U.S. residence prior to Ste. Genevieve County, Missouri:
Louisville, Jefferson County, Kentucky
Bowling Green, Warren County, Kentucky
Belleville, St. Clair County, Illinois

Naturalization:

Name	Declaration	Naturalization	Origin	Remarks
Bolle, Friedrich				St. Louis, MO

Education: Could read and write
Occupation: Mill Operator
Religious Affiliation: Roman Catholic

Political Affiliation and/or Any Offices Held: Was said to have been a Republican
Comments:
Frederick Bolle was born in Sattenhausen, Hanover, Germany. His father is said to have been a merchant and grain dealer. Frederick came to the United States in 1866 and was most likely the F. Bolle who was listed on the manifest of the *Hansa* which landed in New York in 1866. It is not known if he was related to the other two Bolle passengers, but it is likely. Frederick is said to have gone first to Louisville and Bowling Green, Kentucky before moving to Belleville, St. Clair County, Illinois. He was a skilled miller by the time he arrived in Ste. Genevieve County, Missouri in the mid-1870s. He was hired as a miller in the Ste. Genevieve Cone Mills. Frederick married Theresa Wehner in 1878 in Ste. Genevieve. The couple had four sons and three daughters, of whom one son died in infancy and another son died in early childhood. Frederick remained at the Cone Mills until about 1883 when he went into partnership in building and operating the City Mill with his brother-in-law, George Wehner. Frederick was said to have had an unusual personality, combining excellent business acumen with a kind and sympathetic nature. He died of a throat and lung disease on 26 May 1900 in Ste. Genevieve. He was buried in the Valle Spring Cemetery in Ste. Genevieve, Ste. Genevieve County, Missouri. After her husband's death, Theresa lived in Chicago, Illinois with her daughter Alvina. Her health deteriorated after 1930 and she went to the Altheim Home for the Aged in St. Louis, Missouri, where she spent the remainder of her life. Theresa died of a cerebral hemorrhage on 1 December 1940 in St. Louis, Missouri. She was buried in the Valle Spring Cemetery in Ste. Genevieve, Ste. Genevieve County, Missouri.

Johann Franz "Frank" Bonnarens Family
Surname Variations: Bonarens, Bonarns
European Origin: Hebelemeer (Wesuwe), Hanover, Germany
Family:
Father: Franz Ignatius Bonarens, born about 1812 in Hebelemeer (Wesuwe), Hanover, Germany. He died on
  24 January 1891 in Hebelemeer.
Mother: Catharina Margaretha Brands [aka Brandt], born about 1822 in Rühle, Germany. She died on
  28 August 1867 in Hebelemeer.
  Children:
	i.	Martin, born 8 October 1845 in Hebelemeer (Wesuwe), Hanover, Germany. No further information.
‡	ii.	Maria Elisabeth, born 24 March 1848 in Hebelemeer (Wesuwe), Hanover, Germany. She married Bernard Everhard Meyer on 30 May 1871 in Hebelemeer. Bernard was the son of Johann Heinrich Meyer and Susanna Maria Cramer, born 22 August 1845 in Hebelemeer. The couple had three sons and two daughters, all born in Hebelemeer. Two of their sons and one daughter married and lived their lives in Hebelemeer. The oldest son and oldest daughter are said to have come to the United States with their parents, but when they came and where they settled is unknown.
	iii.	Anna Margaretha, born 7 June 1850 in Hebelemeer (Wesuwe), Hanover, Germany. She married Johann Heinrich Meyer on 27 April 1875 in Hebelmeer. Heinrich was the son of Gerard Heinrich Meyer and Maria Helena Schröer, born 24 October 1843 in Hebelemeer. The couple had one son and one daughter and possibly others. Anna died in 1911 and Heinrich died on 16 October 1916, both in Hebelemeer.
‡	iv.	Gerhard Herman, born 28 September 1852 in Hebelemeer (Wesuwe), Hanover, Germany. He came to the United States about 1874. He married Helena Moorman on 29 November 1883 in Pike County, Missouri. Helena was the daughter of Lambert Moorman and Maria Catherine Deters, born 8 July 1861 in Vinnen (Holte), Germany. She came to the United States with her parents in 1881. The couple had six sons and two daughters, of whom one daughter died in childhood. Helena died of heart failure and apoplexy on 12 November 1923 and Gerhard died of chronic myocarditis on 23 June 1931, both in St. Clement, Pike County, Missouri. They were both buried in the St. Clement Cemetery in St. Clement, Pike County, Missouri.
	v.	Maria Adleheid, born 22 January 1855 in Hebelemeer (Wesuwe), Hanover, Germany. She died

on 16 June 1855 in Hebelemeer. No issue.
* vi. Johann Franz "Frank," born 20 March 1856 in Hebelemeer (Wesuwe), Hanover, Germany. [See sketch below.]
‡ vii. Maria Adelheid, born 12 November 1858 in Hebelemeer (Wesuwe), Hanover, Germany. She came to the United States with her two younger brothers in 1882 aboard the *Pollux*. No further information.
† viii. Johann Heinrich "John Henry," born 12 January 1862 in Meppen, Germany. He lived and worked most of his life with his older brother Frank on their farm in Ste. Genevieve County, Missouri. He never married and had no known issue. John died on 29 October 1930 in Ste. Genevieve County, Missouri, from cancer which spread from his left ear to his brain. He was buried in the Our Lady Help of Christians Cemetery in Weingarten, Ste. Genevieve County, Missouri.
‡ ix. Johann Bernard "Ben," born 13 April 1865 in Hebelemeer (Wesuwe), Hanover, Germany. Ben was a farmer in Pike County, Missouri. He married Maria Gesina Thyen on 22 April 1890 in St. Clement, Pike County. Gesina was the daughter of Johann Bernard Thyen and Anna Margaretha Bruns, born 19 July 1867 in Lastrup (Holte), Hanover, Germany. The couple had four sons and two daughters. Gesina died of angina pectoris and arterio sclerosis on 18 December 1941 and Ben died of pneumonia on 29 January 1953, both in Franklin County, Missouri. They were both buried in the St. Ann Cemetery in Clover Bottom, Franklin County, Missouri.

Immigration:
Arrived 1874 [1910 Census] aboard an unknown vessel:
    Bonarens, Frank
        Herman
Arrived 7 April 1882 from Amsterdam, Netherlands to New York aboard the *Pollux*:
    Bonarns, H[einrich], 20   from Hebelemeer   laborer
        J[ohann] B[ernard], 17
        Adelh[eid], 24

Biographical:
Husband: Johann Franz "Frank" Bonnarens
   Birth – 20 March 1856 in Hebelemeer (Wesuwe), Hanover, Germany.
   Death/Burial – 7 May 1939 in Ste. Genevieve County, Missouri. He was buried in the Our Lady Help of Christians Cemetery in Weingarten, Ste. Genevieve County, Missouri.
Wife: Gertrude Krieger, daughter of Theodore Krieger and Anna Maria Berkemeier [aka Brockmeyer]
   Birth – 2 March 1861 in St. Louis, Missouri.
   Marriage – about 1881, most likely in St. Louis, Missouri.
   Death/Burial – 11 April 1938 in Ste. Genevieve County, Missouri. She was buried in the Our Lady Help of Christians Cemetery in Weingarten, Ste. Genevieve County, Missouri.
   Children:
    i. Theodore George, born 15 November 1881 in St. Louis, Missouri. He was a farmer. Theodore married Louisa Frances Baumann on 12 May 1908 in Weingarten, Ste. Genevieve County, Missouri. Louisa was the daughter of Leonard Baumann and Francisca Schwent, born 8 February 1869 in Ste. Genevieve County, Missouri. The couple had no children. Francisca died of breast cancer on 5 October 1940 in Ste. Genevieve County, Missouri. Theodore died on 13 September 1967 in Ste. Genevieve County. They were both buried in the Our Lady Help of Christians Cemetery in Weingarten, Ste. Genevieve County, Missouri.
    ii. Frank, born in July 1883 in Missouri. He appears to have been a wanderer. His mother advertised in several newspapers in 1921, hoping to find him when Frank's brother Bernard was killed. At that time, she had not heard from him for about two years. No record of him has been found after the 1939 mention of him in his father's obituary as living in Belleville, St.

Clair County, llinois.

iii. John Henry, born on 13 October 1885 in Missouri. He was a farmer with his two brothers in Ste. Genevieve County, Missouri. He may never have married. No record of him has been found after the 1940 census.

iv. Martin Herman, born 24 August 1887 in St. Louis, Missouri. He married Theresia Sophia Schwent on 6 April 1915 in Weingarten, Ste. Genevieve County, Missouri. Theresa was the daughter of John Schwent and Francisca Jokerst, born 9 December 1896 in Missouri. For the first few years of their married life, the couple lived in St. Francois County, Missouri where Martin worked as a laborer in a lead mine. By 1930, the family had moved to Denver, Colorado where Martin worked on a poultry farm. The couple had one daughter. Martin died on 28 October 1961 and Theresa died on 14 March 1982, both in Denver, Colorado.

v. Bernard John, born 20 November 1894 in St. Louis, Missouri. Bernard was killed on 7 March 1921 when he was run over by the Lead-Belt Railroad Engine No. 2 in the train yard south of the Federal Office in Flat River, St. Francois County, Missouri. He was buried in the Our Lady Help of Christians Cemetery in Weingarten, Ste. Genevieve County, Missouri. He may never have married and had no known issue.

vi. Edward Bernhard, born 20 December 1896 in St. Louis, Missouri. He married Anna Elisabeth Baumann on 18 November 1935 in Weingarten, Ste. Genevieve County. Anna was the daughter of Joseph F. Baumann and Sophia Clara Muessig, born 2 December 1902 in Weingarten. The couple may never have had children. Edward was a farmer and worked with his brothers Henry and Theodore on the land they had inherited from their parents. Edward died on 15 November 1974 and Anna died on 17 May 1986, both in Ste. Genevieve County. They were both buried in the Valle Spring Cemetery in Ste. Genevieve, Ste. Genevieve County.

vii. Joseph Nicolaus, born 11 March 1898 in Ste. Genevieve County, Missouri. He was baptized in Our Lady Help of Christians Catholic Church in Weingarten, Ste. Genevieve County, Missouri on 17 April 1898. Joseph married Leona Louise Baumann. Leona was the daughter of Nicholas Baumann and Caroline Winter, born 13 May 1900 in Farmington, St. Francois County, Missouri. The couple had three daughters. Joseph died on 4 November 1970. Leona died on 26 August 1991 in Clayton, St. Louis County, Missouri. They were both buried in the Our Lady Help of Christians Cemetery in Weingarten, Ste. Genevieve County, Missouri.

viii. Mary Anna, born 20 August 1900 in Ste. Genevieve County, Missouri. She was baptized in Our Lady Help of Christians Catholic Church in Weingarten, Ste. Genevieve County, Missouri on 9 September 1900. She married Lawrence Joseph Schmidt on 6 September 1921 in Weingarten, Ste. Genevieve County. Lawrence was the son of Lawrence Schmidt and Elizabeth Kraenzle, born 29 March 1891 in Weingarten. He was a farmer. The couple had one son and five daughters. Lawrence died on 23 December 1972 and Mary Ann died on 6 February 1991, both in Ste. Genevieve County, Missouri. They were both buried in the Valle Spring Cemetery in Ste. Genevieve, Ste. Genevieve County, Missouri.

ix. John Herman, born 26 June 1903 in Ste. Genevieve County, Missouri. He was baptized in Our Lady Help of Christians Catholic Church in Weingarten, Ste. Genevieve County, Missouri on 13 July 1903. He was an auto assembly worker in St. Louis, Missouri. John married Veronica Josephine Huber on 6 August 1927 in St. Louis, Missouri. Veronica was the daughter of William Anton Huber and Anna Maria Theresa Naeger, born on 12 March 1905 in Weingarten. The couple had one daughter. John died on 12 January 1988 and Veronica died on 14 July 1996, both in Florissant, St. Louis, County, Missouri.

U.S. residence prior to Ste. Genevieve County, Missouri:
St. Louis, Missouri

Occupation: Farmer
Religious Affiliation: Roman Catholic

Comments:
Johann Franz "Frank" Bonnarens came to the United States about 1874 and originally settled in St. Louis, Missouri. Several of his siblings also came to Missouri at about the same time; all but one brother settled in Pike County, Missouri. Frank married Gertrude Krieger about 1881, most likely in St. Louis. About 1897, Frank moved his family to Ste. Genevieve County, Missouri where he and his brother Henry bought a farm near the village of Weingarten. Frank and Gertrude are said to have had twelve children, but records for only eight sons and one daughter have been found. Gertrude died of a cerebral hemorrhage on 11 April 1938 and Frank died of heart disease and stomach cancer on 7 May 1939, both in Ste. Genevieve County, Missouri. They were both buried in the Our Lady Help of Christians Cemetery in Weingarten, Ste. Genevieve County, Missouri.

Franz Xavier Boos Family

Surname Variations: Boas, Boss
European Origin: [Renchen, Achern], Baden, Germany
Family:
Father: Unknown
Mother: Unknown
   Children:
*   i. Franz Xavier, born about 1797 in Baden, Germany. [See sketch below.]
†   ii. Joseph, born about 1800 in Baden, Germany. He died on 14 February 1858 in Ste. Genevieve County, Missouri. He was buried in the St. Joseph Cemetery in Zell, Ste. Genevieve County, Missouri.

Immigration:
Arrived 1 July 1850 from Le Havre, France to New York aboard the *Connecticut*:
    Boas, A[mbrose], 21   farmer   from Germany
Arrived 2 September 1850 from Le Havre, France to New York aboard the *St. Nicholas*:
    Roos, Haver [Boos, Franz Xavier], 53   farmer   from Baden
        Auguste, 19
    Sibler, Odilia, 27

Biographical:
Husband: Franz Xavier Boos
   Birth – about 1797 in Baden, Germany.
   Death/Burial – 18 March 1861 in Ste. Genevieve County, Missouri. He was buried in the St. Joseph Cemetery in Zell, Ste. Genevieve County, Missouri.
1) Wife: Katharina Schmiderer
   Birth – about 1788 in Baden, Germany.
   Marriage – 21 July 1828 in Renchen, Achern, Baden, Germany.
   Death/Burial – 16 February 1846 in Renchen, Achern, Baden, Germany.
   Children:
     i. Ambrose, born 2 April 1829 in Renchen, Achern, Baden, Germany. He was a farmer in Perry County, Missouri. Ambrose married Mary Ann Hodapp about 1855 in Missouri. Mary Ann was the daughter of Paul Joseph Hodapp and Juliana Eleanora Fischer, born 26 December 1832 in Missouri. The couple had one son. Ambrose died on 1 June 1905 and Mary Ann died on 28 December 1906. They were both buried in the St. Joseph Cemetery in Apple Creek, Perry County, Missouri.
     ii. August, born 18 August 1831 in Renchen, Achern, Baden, Germany. He remained in Cincinnati, Hamilton County, Ohio while the rest of his family moved south to Missouri. He was a machinist. August married Caroline _____. Caroline was born about 1832 in Baden, Germany. The couple had at least one son and one daughter. August died on 4 January 1876 in

Hamilton County, Ohio. He was buried in the Walnut Hills Cemetery in Cincinnati, Hamilton County, Ohio.

2) Wife: Ottilia Siebler
Birth – about 1820 in Baden, Germany.
1) Marriage – October 1850 in Hamilton County, Ohio to Franz Xavier Boos.
2) Marriage – 6 June 1861 in Zell, Ste. Genevieve County, Missouri to Joseph Fisher [See Joseph Fisher sketch.]
Death/Burial – between 1885 and 1892 in Hamilton County, Nebraska.
Children:
- iii. Mary Josephine, born about 1853 in Missouri. She died on 14 August 1860 in Ste. Genevieve County, Missouri. She was buried in the St. Joseph's Cemetery in Zell, Ste. Genevieve County, Missouri. No issue.
- iv. Emilia, born 10 March 1855 in Perry County, Missouri. She married Richard Samson on 24 November 1874 in Ste. Genevieve, Ste. Genevieve County, Missouri. Richard was the son of Karl "Charles" Samson and Josephine Feist, born 5 February 1851 in Oberschopfheim, Baden, Germany. [See Karl "Charles" Samson sketch.]
- v. Infant, born about March 1860 in Ste. Genevieve County, Missouri. The baby died on 30 May 1860 in Ste. Genevieve County, Missouri. The child was buried in the St. Joseph Cemetery in Zell, Ste. Genevieve County, Missouri. No issue.

U.S. residence prior to Ste. Genevieve County, Missouri:
Perry County, Missouri

Military:
Served in the U.S. Civil War for the Union:
Private, Company G, 78th Enrolled Missouri Militia
Francis Broos enlisted on 30 April 1864 at Ste. Genevieve, Missouri. He was ordered into active service on 14 November 1864. He was relieved from duty on 25 November 1864 after having served 12 days of actual service.

Occupation: Carpenter
Religious Affiliation: Roman Catholic
Comments:
Franz Xavier Boos was born in Germany and came to the United States in 1850. He brought his two sons from his first marriage and his fiancé with him. He and Ottilia Siebler were married in Hamilton County, Ohio while they were enroute to Missouri. Xavier also appears to have had a brother named Joseph who came to America with him. Xavier was a carpenter. He may have settled in Perry County, Missouri before moving to Ste. Genevieve County, based on the place of birth given for his daughter, Emilia. His oldest son Ambrose was a farmer in Perry County. Xavier died on 18 March 1861 in Ste. Genevieve County, Missouri, and was buried in the St. Joseph Cemetery in Zell, Ste. Genevieve County, Missouri. His widow remarried within months of her husband's death to a man named Joseph Fisher. Ottilia's second husband died some time before 1880 and she went to live with her daughter Emilia. Ottilia died some time after 1885, most likely in Hamilton County, Nebraska.

Franz Jacob Botz Family
Surname Variations: Botts
European Origin: Baden, Germany
Family:
Father: Unknown
Mother: Unknown
  Child:

  *   i.   Franz Jacob, born about 1821 in Baden, Germany.

Immigration:
Arrived some time before 1850 aboard an unknown vessel:
    Botz, Franz Jacob

Biographical:
Husband: Franz Jacob Botz
    Birth/Baptism – about 1821 in Baden, Germany.
    Death/Burial – 30 September 1875 in Ste. Genevieve, Ste. Genevieve County, Missouri.
1) Wife: Francisca Spietz
    Birth/Baptism – about 1822 in Germany.
    1) Marriage – to _____ Schlichter.
    2) Marriage – to Franz Jacob Botz.
    Death/Burial – 22 August 1866 in St. Louis, Missouri. She was buried in the Holy Ghost Cemetery in St. Louis, Missouri.

    Child of _____ Schlichter and Francisca Spietz:

        i.   Alexander, born 14 June 1849 in either Missouri or Germany. He worked a variety of odd jobs in and around St. Louis, Missouri his whole life. He died of acute peritonitis on 10 October 1920 in St. Louis, Missouri. He was buried in the Park Lawn Cemetery in Lemay, St. Louis County, Missouri. Alexander never married and had no known issue.

Franz Jacob Botz and Francisca Spietz do not appear to have had any children.

2) Wife: Maria Josephine Schmidt, daughter of Michael Schmidt and Eva Margaretha Hirsch
    Birth – 24 March 1831 in Oberamt Brushsal, Baden, Germany.
    1) Marriage – 27 August 1854 in St. Louis, Missouri to Hermann Kastner [See Hermann Kastner sketch.]
    2) Marriage – 22 December 1867 in Ste. Genevieve County, Missouri to Franz Jacob Botz
    Death/Burial – 15 December 1886 in Ste. Genevieve County, Missouri. She was buried in the Valle Spring Cemetery in Ste. Genevieve, Ste. Genevieve County, Missouri.
    Child:
        i.   Johanna Christine "Anna," born 11 April 1869 in Ste. Genevieve, Missouri. She married Adolph Petrequin on 25 November 1890 in Ste. Genevieve. Adolph was the son of Frederick Petrequin and Catherine Guilloz, born 17 June 1858 in Ste. Genevieve. Adolph and Johanna had one son and two daughters. Adolph died on 16 May 1936 and Johanna died on 23 April 1955, both in Ste. Genevieve. They were both buried in the Valle Spring Cemetery in Ste. Genevieve, Ste. Genevieve County, Missouri.

U.S. residence prior to Ste. Genevieve County, Missouri:
    New Orleans, Orleans Parish, Louisiana
    St. Louis, Missouri

Military:
Served in the U.S. Civil War for the Union:
2nd Lieutenant, Company H, 4th Regiment Missouri Volunteer Infantry
    Francis Jacob Botz enlisted on 1 May 1861 at St. Louis, Missouri (for three months).
Private, Company K, 4th Regiment Enrolled Missouri Militia
    Francis Botz enlisted 27 September 1862 at St. Louis, Missouri. He was ordered into active service on 26 April 1863 at St. Louis. Relieved from duty 15 May 1863.
    Remarks: Deserted 6 July 1863.

Occupation: Proprietor, Champion Saloon in Ste. Genevieve
Religious Affiliation: Roman Catholic
Comments:
Franz Jacob Botz was born in Baden, Germany and came to the United States some time before 1850. He appears to have lived in New Orleans for a time before he moved north to St. Louis, Missouri. During the Civil War, he served for the Union and briefly saw active service in 1863. He married Mrs. Francisca Schlichter most likely in St. Louis, Missouri. Francisca had one son from her first marriage. Franz and Francisca had no children together. Francisca died of cholera at the age of 45 years in 1866. By 1868, Franz had moved south to Ste. Genevieve County, Missouri where he became the proprietor of the Champion Saloon in the city of Ste. Genevieve. He married Mrs. Mary Josephine Kastner on 15 January 1869 in Ste. Genevieve County, Missouri. The marriage record indicates that Franz was the widower of Francisca Spietz. This is the only mention that has been found of Franz's first wife's maiden name. Josephine was the widow of Hermann Kastner and had six children with him. Franz and Josephine had one daughter. Franz Jacob died on 30 September 1875 and Josephine continued to run the saloon and a boarding house until shortly before her death. She died of edema of the lungs complicated by fatty degeneration of the heart [congestive heart failure?] on 15 December 1886 in Ste. Genevieve.

Heinrich "Henry" Brandel Family
Surname Variations: Brandle, Brendel, Brendle, Prandel
European Origin: Schieldberg, Oberamt Ettlingen, Baden, Germany
Family:
Father: Joseph Brandel, born 18 March 1831 in Schieldberg, Oberamt Ettlingen, Baden, Germany. He died on 26 March 1896 in St. Joseph, Buchanan County, Missouri. He was buried in the Mount Olivet Cemetery in St. Joseph, Buchanan County, Missouri.

1) Mother: Karoline Schmoll, born in Baden, Germany. She died some time between February 1862 and 22 October 1863 [marriage date for Joseph Brandel and Louisa Schmoll] in Baden, Germany.
   Children:
   * i. Heinrich "Henry," born 14 October 1856 in Neusatz, Baden, Germany. [See sketch below.]
   ‡ ii. Philipp, born 1 May 1859 in Karlsruhe, Baden, Germany. He was a bartender in St. Joseph, Buchanan County, Missouri. Philipp died on 7 September 1899 in St. Joseph. He was buried in the Mount Olivet Cemetery in St. Joseph, Buchanan County, Missouri. He may have never married and had no known issue.
   iii. Maria Anna, born 20 June 1860 in Baden, Germany. She died on 5 April 1861 in Baden, Germany. No issue.
   iv. Louisa, born 15 February 1862 in Baden, Germany. She died on 8 May 1862 in Baden, Germany. No issue.

2) Mother: Louisa Schmoll, born 22 October 1837 in Baden, Germany. [She is believed to have been the sister of Karoline Schmoll, above.] She died on 8 September 1908 in in St. Joseph, Buchanan County, Missouri. She was buried in the Mount Olivet Cemetery in St. Joseph, Buchanan County, Missouri.
   Children:
   ‡ v. Katharina "Katie," born 9 August 1864 in Achern, Baden, Germany. She married Sylvester James "Silas" Fuson on 29 January 1890 in St. Joseph, Buchanan County, Missouri. Sylvester was the son of James C. Fuson and Amanda Red Dean, born 11 July 1863 in Princeton, Mercer County, Missouri. The couple had three sons and two daughters. Katherine died of diabetes mellitus on 21 May 1935 and Sylvester died of chronic myocarditis and partial bowel obstruction on 11 November 1943, both in St. Joseph, Buchanan County, Missouri. They were both buried in the Mount Olivet Cemetery in St. Joseph, Buchanan County, Missouri.
   ‡ vi. Anton, born 12 August 1865 in Achern, Baden, Germany. He died on 26 September 1869 in Ste. Genevieve County, Missouri. He was buried in the St. Joseph Cemetery in Zell, Ste. Genevieve County, Missouri. No issue.

vii. Louisa, born 7 March 1867 in Ste. Genevieve County, Missouri. She married Henry G. Felling on 17 May 1888 in St. Joseph, Buchanan County, Missouri. Henry was the son of Gerhardt Felling and Mary Kaiser, born 17 February 1862 in Platte County, Missouri. The couple had two sons and one daughter and two children who died in infancy. Henry died of lobar pneumonia and chronic gastritis on 19 January 1917 and Louisa died of a cerebral apoplexy on 29 November 1932, both in Buchanan County. They were both buried in the Mount Olivet Cemetery in St. Joseph, Buchanan County, Missouri.

Immigration:
Arrived 14 December 1866 from Le Havre, France to New York aboard the *William Penn*:
    Brandel, Joseph, 35   Oldenbourg, Prussia   Farmer
        Louisa, 34
        Heinrich, 9
        Philippe, 7
        Catherine, 2
        Anton, 9/12

Biographical:
Husband: Heinrich "Henry" Brandel
  Birth – 14 October 1856 in Neusatz, Baden, Germany.
  Death/Burial – 17 March 1930 in Ste. Genevieve County, Missouri. He was buried in the Catholic Cemetery in St. Mary, Ste. Genevieve County, Missouri
Wife: Sophia Rudloff, daughter of Johann Georg "George" Rudloff and Cecilia Winkler [See George Rudloff sketch.]
  Birth – 11 April 1855 in Ste. Genevieve County, Missouri.
  Marriage – 26 August 1879 in River aux Vases, Ste. Genevieve County, Missouri.
  Death/Burial – 15 May 1936 in Perry County, Missouri. She was buried in the Brown Cemetery in Perry County, Missouri.
  Children:
    i. Joseph Andrew, born 16 February 1880 in Perry County, Missouri. He was baptized on 21 March 1880 in the Immaculate Conception Catholic Church in St. Mary, Ste. Genevieve County, Missouri. He was a farmer in Perry County, Missouri. Joseph married Mrs. Lucinda Adaline "Cindy" Holliday on 13 November 1904 in Perry County, Missouri. Cindy was the widow of Milton Holliday with one son and one daughter from her first marriage. She was the daughter of William Biggs and Frances A. Gooch, born 19 May 1879 in Ste. Genevieve County, Missouri. Joseph and Cindy had two sons and one daughter, of whom the daughter died of typhoid fever at the age of fifteen years. Cindy died of pneumonia and influenza on 13 March 1919 in Perry County, Missouri. Joseph married Minnie Cureton on 3 July 1923 in Perry County, Missouri. Minnie was the widow of David Wright with whom she had four sons and one daughter. She was the daughter of Richard Cureton and Sarah Jane Basher, born 3 November 1889 in Patton, Bollinger County, Missouri. Joseph and Minnie had two daughters together. Joseph died on 28 August 1963 in Farmington, St. Francois County, Missouri. Minnie died on 11 February 1967. They were both buried in the Three Rivers Cemetery in Farmington, St. Francois County, Missouri.
    ii. August, born 30 August 1884 in Missouri. He was a farmer in Perry County, Missouri. August married Nettie Biggs on 2 April 1927 in Perryville, Perry County, Missouri. Nettie was the daughter of William Biggs and Frances A. Gooch, born 17 June 1881 in Ste. Genevieve County, Missouri. The couple does not appear to have ever had children. Nettie died of injuries she suffered in an automobile accident on 14 December 1945 in Perry County. August died of pulmonary thrombosis on 12 April 1953 in the State Hospital No. 4 at Farmington, St. Francois County, Missouri. They were both buried in the Brown Cemetery in Perry County, Missouri.

iii. George Bernard "Bernie," born 13 September 1887 in Missouri. He was baptized on 18 December 1887 in the Immaculate Conception Catholic Church in St. Marys, Ste. Genevieve County, Missouri. No further information has been found on him after the 1900 census.

iv. Richard, born 13 October 1887 in Perry County, Missouri. He was a lead miner and farmer. He married Tiney _____ about 1909, most likely in St. Francois County, Missouri. The couple had one son. Nothing further is known of Tiney or of the son after the 1920 census. Richard married Anna Lualen Crawford in St. Francois County, Missouri about 1926. Anna was the daughter of William Washington Crawford and Caroline Owens, born 29 May 1894 in Missouri. Anna had been previously married on 30 March 1914 to Clarence Henderson Kidd. Richard and Anna had one daughter. Richard died of pulmonary tuberculosis on 3 July 1936 in Perry County, Missouri. He was buried in the Brown Cemetery in Perry County, Missouri. Anna married for a third time on 21 September 1963 in St. Francois County, Missouri to Harry Russell Lane. Anna died on 15 October 1981 in Desloge, St. Francois County, Missouri. She was buried in the St. Francois Memorial Park in St. Francois County, Missouri.

v. Mary Louisa, born 30 March 1891. She was baptized on 28 June 1891 in the Immaculate Conception Catholic Church in St. Mary, Ste. Genevieve County, Missouri. She died in infancy. No issue.

vi. Rowena, born 28 May 1892 in Missouri. She was baptized on 14 August 1892 in the Immaculate Conception Catholic Church in St. Mary, Ste. Genevieve County, Missouri. She died in infancy. No issue

vii. Ann Myrtle, born 17 February 1895 in Missouri. She was baptized on 28 April 1895 in the Immaculate Conception Catholic Church in St. Mary, Ste. Genevieve County, Missouri. She married Lloyd F. Proctor on 3 September 1911 in Chaffee, Scott County, Missouri. Lloyd was the son of George Powell Proctor and Mariah Ann Brown, born 26 August 1879 in Missouri. The couple had three sons and four daughters of whom one daughter died in infancy. The couple appears to have divorced before 1930. Lloyd died on 22 February 1950 in South Charleston, Clark County, Ohio. Myrtle married Samuel Adolph "Dalph" Ward as her second husband on 30 December 1935 in Marble Hill, Bollinger County, Missouri. Dalph was born 15 February 1868 in Missouri. He was the widower of Eliza Clara Collier. Dalph died on 7 January 1943 in Bollinger County. He was buried with his first wife in the Kinder Cemetery near Lutesville, Bollinger County, Missouri. Myrtle died of cerebral hemorrhage on 15 October 1961 in Perry County, Missouri. She was buried in the Cambron Cemetery in Perry County, Missouri.

viii. Matilda Elizabeth, born 15 September 1896 in Missouri. She was baptized on 16 February 1897 in the Immaculate Conception Catholic Church in St. Mary, Ste. Genevieve County, Missouri. She died in infancy. No issue.

ix. John Henry, born 22 June 1898 in Missouri. He was baptized on 20 August 1898 in the Immaculate Conception Catholic Church in St. Mary, Ste. Genevieve County, Missouri. He married Gertrude Catherine Holliday on 4 May 1922 in Perryville, Perry County, Missouri. Gertrude was the daughter of Thomas King Holliday and Lena Margaret Mattingly, born on 10 December 1902 in Perry County, Missouri. The couple had two sons and one daughter. John died on 4 November 1974. Gertrude married for a second time on 25 November 1981, to Leonard Elder. He died before November 2004. Gertrude died on 18 November 2004 in Farmington, St. Francois County, Missouri. She and her first husband were both buried in the Brown Cemetery in Perry County, Missouri.

U.S. residence other than Ste. Genevieve County, Missouri:
St. Joseph, Buchanan County, Missouri
St. Francois County, Missouri
Chaffee, Scott County, Missouri
Perry County, Missouri

Naturalization:

Name	Declaration	Naturalization	Origin
Brandel, Joseph		11 March 1882 Circuit Court of Buchanan Co., MO	Baden

Education: Could read and write
Occupation: Farmer
Religious Affiliation: Roman Catholic
Comments:
Heinrich "Henry" Brandel was born in Germany and came to the United States with his family when he was a small boy. His father initially settled in Ste. Genevieve County, Missouri when they came to the United States, but within ten years, they had moved west to St. Joseph, Buchanan County, Missouri. As a young man, Henry returned to Ste. Genevieve County where he married Sophia Rudloff in 1879. Henry was a farmer in Perry County, Missouri. For a short time, he ran a butcher shop in Chaffee, Scott County, Missouri, but eventually returned to Perry County. Henry died of apoplexy on 17 March 1930 in Ste. Genevieve County, Missouri. He is said to have been buried in the Catholic Cemetery in St. Mary, Ste. Genevieve County, Missouri, but no stone has been found. Sophia died of mitral regurgitation on 15 May 1936 in Perry County, Missouri. She is said to have been buried in the Brown Cemetery in Perry County, Missouri, but no stone has been found.

Harmony Brands Family
Surname Variations: Brance, Brantz, Brends
European Origin: Westphalia, Prussia, [Germany]
Family:
Father: Unknown
Mother: Unknown
   Child:
*   i.   Harmony Thomas, born 2 November 1815 in Westphalia, Prussia. [See sketch below.]

Immigration:
Arrived on 24 November 1845 from Bremen, Germany to New Orleans aboard the *Cordova*:
   Brands, Hermany, 28

Biographical:
Husband: Harmony Thomas Brands
   Birth – 2 November 1815 in Westphalia, Prussia [Germany].
   Death/Burial – 31 May 1893 in Ste. Genevieve County, Missouri. He was buried in the Concord
      Cemetery in Ste. Genevieve County, Missouri.
Wife: Emeline Wells
   Birth – 30 December 1822 in Clermont County, Ohio.
   Marriage – 20 April 1853 in Ste. Genevieve County, Missouri.
   Death/Burial – 26 January 1916 in St. Louis, Missouri. She was buried in the Gamel Cemetery in
      Festus, Jefferson County, Missouri.
   Children:
      i.   Franklin Wolcott "Frank," born 19 January 1854 in Ste. Genevieve County, Missouri. He married Nancy A. Poston on 23 August 1877 in Jefferson County, Missouri. Nancy was the daughter of Felix Grundy Poston and Martha Ann Berry, born 18 February 1850 in Missouri. The Postons lived on the next farm over from the Brands. Nancy died on 6 January 1880 in Ste. Genevieve County. She was buried in the Concord Cemetery in Ste. Genevieve County, Missouri. The couple had no children. Frank married for a second time on 25 October 1882 in Rush Tower, Jefferson County, Missouri to Alice Harriet Waggener. She was the daughter of Reuben Garnett Waggener and Mary Moore, born 15 October 1855 in Rush Tower. The couple

had three daughters, the youngest of whom was born five months after her father's death. Frank spent nine years teaching in Ste. Genevieve County schools and then accepted a job with the St. Joe Lead Company in St. Francois County, Missouri. Shortly after he moved to St. Francois County, his health began to decline. He was diagnosed as suffering from Progressive Locomotor Ataxia. His brother Albert was his physician for a time, but eventually he entered the Missouri Baptist Sanitarium in St. Louis. When treatment in that institution failed, he decided to return to his home in Festus, Jefferson County, Missouri. He died there on 8 March 1892. He was buried in the Gamel Cemetery in Festus, Jefferson County, Missouri. Alice died of stomach cancer on 18 April 1913 in Howard County, Missouri. She was buried in the Gamel Cemetery in Festus, Jefferson County, Missouri.

    ii. Albert Lorenzo, born 26 April 1856 in Ste. Genevieve County, Missouri. He attended the St. Louis School of Medicine, graduating in 1880. He moved to Randolph County, Illinois where he established his medical practice. He married Margaret M. "Maggie" Bliler on 28 July 1886 in Chester, Randolph County, Illinois. Maggie was the daughter of Emereuth Bliler and Catherine Allerding, born 10 October 1860 in Carlyle, Clinton County, Illinois. The couple had four sons and one daughter, all born in Randolph County, Illinois. In 1892, Albert was the Democratic nominee from his district for Illinois State Senator and was elected to serve in the Illinois Senate in the 38th General Assembly. In 1895, Albert served a two-year term as postmaster for the town of Prairie du Rocher. Albert died on 20 April 1910 in Prairie du Rocher, Randolph County, Illinois. Maggie raised her five children alone in Prairie du Rocher. She died on 26 December 1947 in Red Bud, Randolph County, Illinois. She was buried in the St. Joseph Cemetery in Prairie du Rocher, Randolph County, Illinois.

    iii. Peter Herman, born 26 April 1857 in Ste. Genevieve County, Missouri. He married Annie Lillie Funk. Annie was the daughter of Christian Funk and Ernestine Kuntz, born 1 December 1863 in Jefferson County, Missouri. The couple had two daughters. Peter died of blood poisoning on 2 April 1889 in Bonne Terre, St. Francois County, Missouri. He was buried in the Concord Cemetery in Ste. Genevieve County, Missouri. After her husband's death, Anna moved to St. Louis where she lived with a cousin. She worked as a nurse in the Bethesda Home for Foundlings, but in her last few years, she lived with her widowed youngest daughter. Annie died of colon cancer on 12 August 1939 in St. Louis, Missouri. She was buried in the Emanuel [Western] Lutheran Cemetery in St. Louis, Missouri.

U.S. residence prior to Ste. Genevieve County, Missouri:
Jefferson County, Missouri

Land Patents:
Ste. Genevieve County, Missouri

Patentee	Issue Date	Land Office	Cert. No.	Serial No.	Twp	Rng	Sec	Acres
Brands, Harmony	1 Mar 1854	St. Louis	21382	MO0940_.249	39-N	7-E	28	80.0
Brands, Harmony	15 Nov 1854	St. Louis	22282	MO0960_.285	39-N	7-E	28	40.0
Brands, Harmoni	1 Oct 1856	St. Louis	23546	MO1020_.249	39-N	7-E	22	200.0

Naturalization:

Name	Declaration	Naturalization	Origin
Brance, Harmony	5 March 1851	21 May 1853 Ste. Genevieve Co.	Prussia

Education: Could read and write
Occupation: Farmer
Religious Affiliation: Unknown

Comments:
Harmony Brands was born in Westphalia, Prussia of unknown parents. As a young man he reportedly served for seven years in the German army. He came to the United States in 1845, landing in New Orleans and traveling up the Mississippi River to Missouri. For the first few years he was in the state, he worked as a farm laborer for other people. By 1854, he had settled in Ste. Genevieve County where he purchased land and began to farm. He married Emeline Wells in 1853 in Ste. Genevieve County and the couple had three sons. Harmony was a firm believer in education and all three of his sons received a better than average education. He died on 31 May 1893 in Ste. Genevieve County. He was buried in the Concord Cemetery in Ste. Genevieve County, Missouri. After her husband's death, Emeline moved to Festus to help her son Frank as his health failed. She died on 26 January 1916 in St. Louis, Missouri of a concussion after she fell and hit her head on a radiator in the Bethesda Old Ladies' Home where she lived. She was buried in the Gamel Cemetery in Festus, Jefferson County, Missouri.

Bernard Braun Family

Surname Variations: Brown
European Origin: Obersasbach and Sasbach, Achern, Baden, Germany
Family:
Father: Franz Ignatius Braun, born 2 April 1795 in Obersasbach, Achern, Baden, Germany. He died on 25 September 1839 in Obersasbach.
Mother: Catherine Oberle, born 14 April 1802 in Sasbachwalden, Achern, Baden, Germany.
   Children:
   i. Regina, baptized 18 September 1822 in Sasbach, Achern, Baden, Germany. She married Meinrad Zink on 7 July 1842 in Lauf, Baden, Germany. Meinrad was the son of Joseph Zink and Walburga Nesselhof.
   ii. Joseph, baptized 29 August 1824 in Sasbach, Achern, Baden, Germany.
† iii. Franz Anton, baptized 17 February 1827 in Sasbach, Achern, Baden, Germany. [See Franz Anton Braun sketch.]
   iv. Christina, baptized 21 July 1829 in Sasbach, Achern, Baden, Germany. She married Ignaz Zink on 18 May 1854 in Lauf, Baden, Germany.
* v. Bernard, baptized 4 September 1831 in Sasbach, Achern, Baden, Germany. [See sketch below.]
   vi. Ignaz, baptized 20 April 1834 in Sasbach, Achern, Baden, Germany. He married Ottilia Wörner on 4 February 1862 in Achern, Bühl, Baden, Germany. Ottilia was the daughter of Joseph Wörner and Elisabetha Fallert.
   vii. Maria Anna, baptized 23 July 1836 in Sasbach, Achern, Baden, Germany. She married Raimund Frueh on 27 August 1857 in Baden, Germany. Raimund was the son of Joseph Frueh and Maria Anna Ullrich.
   viii. Catharina, baptized 3 September 1838 in Sasbach, Achern, Baden, Germany. She married Jonas Wörner on 22 September 1863 in Achern, Bühl, Baden, Germany. Jonas was the son of Joseph Wörner and Elisabetha Fallert.

Immigration:
Arrived 5 July 1853 from Le Havre, France to New York aboard the *Isaac Bell*:
   Braun, Berhardt, 19

Biographical:
Husband: Bernard Braun
   Birth – 7 September 1831 in Obersasbach, Achern, Baden, Germany.
   Death/Burial – 23 October 1881 in River aux Vases, Ste. Genevieve County, Missouri. He was buried in the Sts. Philip and James Cemetery in River aux Vases, Ste. Genevieve County, Missouri.
Wife: Crescentia Schweigert, daughter of Andreas "Andrew" Schweigert and Helena Lehmann [See Andreas Schweigert sketch.]

Birth – 16 April 1838 in Ernsbach, Baden, Germany.
Marriage – 27 December 1859 in Zell, Ste. Genevieve County, Missouri.
Death/Burial – 12 February 1919 in Ste. Genevieve County, Missouri. She was buried in the Sacred Heart Cemetery in Ozora, Ste. Genevieve County, Missouri.
Children:
  i. Andrew, born 21 October 1860 in Ste. Genevieve County, Missouri. He was a farmer near Ozora, Ste. Genevieve County. He married Brigitta Roth on 20 November 1888. Brigitta was the daughter of Roman Roth and Magdalena Dietmeyer, born 3 January 1864 in Ste. Genevieve County, Missouri. The couple had two sons and five daughters. Brigitta died of typhoid fever on 20 July 1912 and Andrew died of chronic heart disease on 15 October 1950, both in Ste. Genevieve County. They were both buried in the Sacred Heart Cemetery in Ozora, Ste. Genevieve County, Missouri.
  ii. Francis Ignatius "Frank," born 16 December 1862 in Ste. Genevieve County, Missouri. He was a wagon maker. He married Sophia Fredricka Bach on 25 April 1895 in St. Louis, Missouri. Sophia was the daughter of Johann "John" Bach and Wilhelmina Theresia Bangelmann, born 5 April 1867 in St. Mary, Ste. Genevieve County, Missouri. The couple had two sons and one daughter. Frank died of heart disease on 9 June 1935 and Sophia died of heart disease complicated by influenza on 13 February 1954, both in Ste. Genevieve County. They were both buried in the Catholic Cemetery in St. Mary, Ste. Genevieve County, Missouri.
  iii. Catherine "Katie," born 29 March 1865 in Ste. Genevieve County, Missouri. She was baptized on 28 May 1865 in the Sts. Philip and James Catholic Church in River aux Vases, Ste. Genevieve County, Missouri. Katie married Joseph Breig on 25 January 1887 in St. Mary, Ste. Genevieve County, Missouri. Joseph was the son of Michael Joseph Breig and Cecilia Hertig, born 19 March 1863 in Oberharmersbach, Baden, Germany. [See Joseph Breig sketch.]
  iv. Joseph Henry, born 28 January 1868 in Ste. Genevieve County, Missouri. He was baptized on 18 March 1868 in the Sts. Philip and James Catholic Church in River aux Vases, Ste. Genevieve County, Missouri. Joseph married Frances Carolyn Bahr on 2 August 1892 in Ste. Genevieve, Ste. Genevieve County, Missouri. The ceremony was a double wedding with the bride's brother, Charles Bahr. Frances was the daughter of Martin Bahr and Maria Sophia Guethle, born 14 June 1870 in Zell, Ste. Genevieve County. The couple had two daughters, of whom one died as a toddler. Joseph died of typhoid fever on 21 August 1894 in Ste. Genevieve County. He was buried in the Catholic Cemetery in St. Mary, Ste. Genevieve County, Missouri. Frances married for a second time to August William "Gus" Striebel on 10 January 1898 in Ste. Genevieve County. [See Stephen Striebel sketch.]
  v. Xavier Bernard, born 8 February 1871 in Ste. Genevieve County, Missouri. He was baptized on 2 April 1871 in the Sts. Philip and James Catholic Church in River aux Vases, Ste. Genevieve County, Missouri. Xavier was a farmer. He died of heart disease complicated by pneumonia on 15 April 1960 in Ste. Genevieve County. Xavier never married and had no known issue. He was buried in the Sacred Heart Cemetery in Ozora, Ste. Genevieve County, Missouri.
  vi. Mary Ann, born 13 March 1874 in Ste. Genevieve County, Missouri. She was baptized on 1 May 1874 in the Sts. Philip and James Catholic Church in River aux Vases, Ste. Genevieve County, Missouri. She died on 16 April 1893 in Ste. Genevieve County. Mary was buried in the Catholic Cemetery in St. Mary, Ste. Genevieve County, Missouri. She never married and had no issue.
  vii. William, born 14 June 1877 in Ste. Genevieve County, Missouri. He was baptized on 22 July 1877 in the Sts. Philip and James Catholic Church in River aux Vases, Ste. Genevieve County, Missouri. He was a farmer. William never married and had no known issue. He died of heart disease complicated by pneumonia on 23 November 1957 in Ste. Genevieve County, Missouri. He was buried in the Sacred Heart Cemetery in Ozora, Ste. Genevieve County, Missouri.
  viii. Christina, born 14 August 1881 in Ste. Genevieve County, Missouri. She died on 24 August 1881 in River aux Vases, Ste. Genevieve County, Missouri. She was buried in the Sts. Philip and James Cemetery in River aux Vases, Ste. Genevieve County, Missouri. No issue.

Land Patents:
Ste. Genevieve County, Missouri

Patentee	Issue Date	Land Office	Cert. No.	Serial No.	Twp	Rng	Sec	Acres
Brown, Bernard	1 Sep 1859	Jackson	80135	MW-1124-500	37-N	9-E	9	149.10
					37-N	9-E	10	

Naturalization:

Name	Declaration	Naturalization	Origin
Braun, Bernard		5 November 1863 Ste. Genevieve Co.	Baden

Military:
Served in the U.S. Civil War for the Union:
Private, Company D, 78th Enrolled Missouri Militia
  Bernard Brown enlisted on 30 April 1864 at St. Mary's, Ste. Genevieve County, Missouri. He was ordered into active service on 16 October 1864. He was relieved from duty on 25 November 1864 after having served 41 days of actual service.

Occupation: Farmer
Religious Affiliation: Roman Catholic
Comments:
Bernard Braun came to the United States and settled in Ste. Genevieve County, Missouri. His older brother Franz "Frank" had come to Missouri a few years earlier and the two men bought a farm near Staabtown [present-day River aux Vases.] Bernard enlisted in the 78th Enrolled Missouri Militia during the Civil War. Bernard died on 23 October 1881 in River aux Vases, Ste. Genevieve County, Missouri. He was buried in the Sts. Philip and James Cemetery in River aux Vases, Ste. Genevieve County, Missouri. After her husband's death, Cresentia moved to Ozora, Ste. Genevieve County, where she lived with her two unmarried sons. She died of heart disease and old age on 12 February 1919 in Ste. Genevieve County, Missouri. She was buried in the St. Joseph Cemetery at Zell, Ste. Genevieve County, Missouri.

Franz Anton "Frank" Braun Family
Surname Variations: Brown
European Origin: Sasbach and Sasbachwalden, Achern, Baden, Germany
Family:
Father: Franz Ignatius Braun, born 2 April 1795 in Obersasbach, Achern, Baden, Germany. He died
  on 25 September 1839 in Obersasbach.
Mother: Catherine Oberle, born 14 April 1802 in Sasbachwalden, Achern, Baden, Germany.
  Children:

Note: For a comprehensive discussion of Franz Ignatius Braun's children see the Bernard Braun sketch.

Immigration:
Arrived 28 November 1851 from Le Havre, France to New Orleans aboard the *State of Maine*:
  Braun, Franz, 24
Arrived 30 January 1871 from Bremerhaven, Germany to New York aboard the *Main*:
  Doll, Cath[erine], 22   from Baden

Biographical:
Husband: Franz Anton "Frank" Braun
  Birth – 17 February 1827 in Sasbach, Achern, Baden, Germany.
  Death/Burial – 27 February 1879 in Ste. Genevieve County, Missouri. He was buried in the Sts. Philip and James Cemetery in River aux Vases, Ste. Genevieve County, Missouri.

Wife: Catherine Doll, daughter of Bernard Doll and Katherine Fallert
Birth – 25 November 1848 in Sasbachwalden, Achern, Baden, Germany.
1) Marriage – about 1872, most likely in Missouri, to Franz Anton "Frank" Braun.
2) Marriage – 26 August 1880 in Weingarten, Ste. Genevieve County, Missouri to Philip Jacob Wolk. [See Philip Jacob Wolk sketch.]
Death/Burial – 23 October 1941 in Ste. Genevieve County, Missouri. She was buried in the Our Lady Help of Christians Cemetery in Weingarten, Ste. Genevieve County, Missouri.
Children:
   i. Francis Charles, born 21 March 1873 in Ste. Genevieve County, Missouri. He was baptized on 20 April 1873 in the Sts. Philip and James Catholic Church in River aux Vases, Ste. Genevieve County, Missouri. Charles left Missouri as a young man and moved west to Ford County, Kansas, where he worked as a farm laborer near the town of Spearville. He died on 23 May 1969 and was buried in the St Johns Cemetery in Spearville, Ford County. Kansas. Charles does not appear to have married and has no known issue.
   ii. Mary Theresia, born 18 January 1875 in Ste. Genevieve County, Missouri. She died on 24 January 1875 in Ste. Genevieve County and was buried in the Sts. Philip and James Cemetery in River aux Vases, Ste. Genevieve County, Missouri. No issue.
   iii. Infant, born in 1877 in Ste. Genevieve County, Missouri. The baby boy died on 25 February 1877 in Ste. Genevieve County and was buried in the Sts. Philip and James Cemetery in River aux Vases, Ste. Genevieve County, Missouri. No issue.
   iv. Mary Elisabeth, born 3 March 1878 in Ste. Genevieve County, Missouri. She was baptized on 31 March 1878 in the Sts. Philip and James Catholic Church in River aux Vases, Ste. Genevieve County, Missouri. Elisabeth married Charles Buchholtz on 21 November 1899 in Weingarten, Ste. Genevieve County, Missouri. Charles was the son of Morris Buchholtz and Elisabeth Sellinger, born 25 April 1866 in Ste. Genevieve County, Missouri. [See Morris Buchholtz sketch.]

Occupation: Farmer
Religious Affiliation: Roman Catholic
Comments:
Franz Anton "Frank" Braun was born in Germany and came to the United States two years before his brother Bernard. They both settled in Ste. Genevieve County, Missouri where they bought a farm near Staabtown [present-day River aux Vases]. Unlike his brother, Frank does not appear to have served in any capacity during the Civil War. He married Catherine Doll about 1872, most likely in Missouri. The couple had two sons and two daughters, of whom one son and one daughter died in infancy. Frank died in February 1879 and was buried in the Sts. Philip and James Cemetery in River aux Vases, Ste. Genevieve County. After her husband's death, Catherine worked as a domestic servant to support her children. She married Philip Jacob Wolk as her second husband in August 1880 in Weingarten, Ste. Genevieve County. [See Philip Jacob Wolk sketch.]

George Braun Family
Surname Variations: Brown
European Origin: Ebersweier, Baden, Germany
Family:
Father: Franz Joseph Braun, born 13 February 1893 in Ebersweier, Baden, Germany.
Mother: Maria Ursula Laigast, born 20 October 1798 in Ebersweier, Baden, Germany.
   Children:
   i. Angelina Paulina, born 30 June 1826 in Ebersweier, Baden, Germany.
* ii. Georg[e] , born 21 April 1829 in Ebersweier, Baden, Germany. [See sketch below.]
   iii. Regina Euphemia, born 13 September 1832 in Ebersweier, Baden, Germany.
   iv. Regina, born 7 May 1835 in Ebersweier, Baden, Germany
   v. Karolina, born 25 January 1840 in Ebersweier, Baden, Germany. She died on 4 February

1840 in Ebersweier. No issue.

vi. Hedwig, born 13 October 1841 in Ebersweier, Baden, Germany. She died on 19 April 1844 in Ebersweier. No issue.

Immigration:
Arrived about 1850 aboard an unknown vessel:
   Braun, George

Biographical:
Husband: George Braun
   Birth/Baptism – 21 April 1829 in Ebersweier, Baden, Germany. He was baptized in the Ebersweier Katholisch Church on the same day.
   Death/Burial – 9 March 1911 in Milam County, Texas. He was buried in the Hirt-Braun Cemetery in Rockdale, Milam County, Texas.
Wife: Theresia Bader, daughter of Joseph Bader and Regina Mueller [See Maximilian Bader sketch.]
   Birth – 18 October 1840 in Durbach, Baden, Germany.
   Marriage – 3 September 1860 in Ste. Genevieve County, Missouri.
   Death/Burial – 13 June 1893 in Milam County, Texas. She was buried in the Hirt-Braun Cemetery in Rockdale, Milam County, Texas.
   Children:
   i. Josephine, born 4 May 1861 in Ste. Genevieve County, Missouri. She was baptized in the Ste. Genevieve Catholic Church in Ste. Genevieve on 3 July 1861. Josephine married Joseph Walter on 18 May 1880 in Ste. Genevieve. Joseph was the son of Peter Walter and Maria Weiger, born in September 1839 in Germany. He had come to the United States about 1852. Joseph was a farmer. The couple had one son. They also fostered several orphaned nephews and nieces. The family first lived in Ruma, Randolph County, Illinois and then, by 1900, they moved to Milam County, Texas with Josephine's family. Joseph apparently died some time between 1910 and 1920, most likely in Texas. By 1920, Josephine was a widow and was living in Runnels County, Texas where she worked as the housekeeper for a Catholic priest. She died of heart disease and chronic nephritis on 26 May 1926 in Poth, Wilson County, Texas. She was buried in the Saint Joseph Cemetery in Rowena, Runnels County, Texas.
   ii. Emma, born 17 August 1862 in Ste. Genevieve County, Missouri. She was baptized in the Ste. Genevieve Catholic Church in Ste. Genevieve on 19 September 1862. Emma married William Lehr on 16 October 1882 in Ste. Genevieve. William was the son of George Lehr and Magdalena Grieg, born 15 November 1859 in Ste. Genevieve County, Missouri. [See George Lehr sketch.]
   iii. Joseph, born 16 February 1864 in Ste. Genevieve County, Missouri. He was baptized in the Ste. Genevieve Catholic Church in Ste. Genevieve on 27 May 1864. Joseph married Caroline Palmer on 10 January 1887 in Rockdale, Milam County, Texas. Caroline was the daughter of Paul Palmer and Caroline Bader, born 3 October 1867 in Ste. Genevieve County, Missouri. Joe was a farmer in Texas. The couple had four sons and six daughters. After 1900, Joe anglicized his surname to "Brown" and all of his descendants are known by that name. Joe died of bronchio pneumonia complicated by heart disease on 14 March 1939 in Rockdale, Milam County. After her husband's death, Caroline lived with her youngest son and his family. She died of pneumonia on 23 December 1951 in Cameron, Milam County. They were both buried in the Hirt-Braun Cemetery in Rockdale, Milam County, Texas.
   vi. Regina, born 26 January 1866 in Ste. Genevieve County, Missouri. She was baptized in the Ste. Genevieve Catholic Church in Ste. Genevieve on 2 March 1866. Regina married Charles Albert Samson on 17 November 1886 in Ste. Genevieve. Charles was the son of Anton Samson and Magdalena Roth, born 17 November 1864 in Ste. Genevieve County, Missouri. Charles was a farmer in Ste. Genevieve County. The couple had two sons and two daughters and one child

who died in infancy. They also fostered an orphan boy named Anton Gerstner. [See Joseph Gerstner sketch.] Regina died of acute cardiac dilation and pneumonia on 12 November 1943 and Charles died of chronic myocarditis and chronic nephritis on 8 February 1947, both in Ste. Genevieve County. They were both buried in the Valle Spring Cemetery in Ste. Genevieve, Ste. Genevieve County, Missouri.

    v.   Theresa, born 17 July 1867 in Ste. Genevieve County, Missouri. She was baptized in the Ste. Genevieve Catholic Church in Ste. Genevieve on 15 August 1867. Theresa married Gustav "August" Baumann on 11 September 1889 in Ste. Genevieve. Gustav was the son of William Baumann and Sophia Doll, born 18 February 1861 in Ste. Genevieve County, Missouri. August was a farmer. The couple had eight sons and two daughters, of whom two sons died in early childhood. They also fostered an orphaned boy named William Bayer. August died of chronic myocarditis on 31 August 1949 in Ste. Genevieve County, Missouri. Theresa died of cardio-vascular disease complicated by a fractured femur and a gangrenous right heel on 17 June 1957 in Jefferson County, Missouri. They were both buried in the Valle Spring Cemetery in Ste. Genevieve, Ste. Genevieve County, Missouri.

    vi.   George, born 19 March 1869 in Ste. Genevieve County, Missouri. He was baptized in the Ste. Genevieve Catholic Church in Ste. Genevieve on 2 September 1869. George appears to have died between 1870 and 1880, most likely in Ste. Genevieve County, Missouri. No issue.

    vii.   Mary Ann, born 12 March 1871 in Ste. Genevieve County, Missouri. She was baptized in the Ste. Genevieve Catholic Church in Ste. Genevieve on 16 April 1871. Mary Ann married Francis Anthony "Frank" Baumann on 3 September 1890 in Ste. Genevieve. Frank was the son of William Baumann and Sophia Doll, born 16 January 1863 in Ste. Genevieve County, Missouri. The couple had one son who died at the age of one year. Mary Ann died of complications within half an hour of the birth of her child on 3 June 1891 in Ste. Genevieve. She was buried in the Valle Spring Cemetery in Ste. Genevieve, Ste. Genevieve County, Missouri. Frank married Mary Ann Viox as his second wife on 13 June 1892 in Ste. Genevieve. Mary was the daughter of John Viox and Catherine Schott, born 14 April 1868 in Ste. Genevieve. Mary died on 15 April 1900 in Ste. Genevieve. She was buried in the Valle Spring Cemetery in Ste. Genevieve, Ste. Genevieve County, Missouri. After Mary's death, Frank worked as a hired man for several local farmers. He spent his last years with his brother, William. He died on 16 February 1932 in Ste. Genevieve County. He had been suffering from senile dementia and wandered off one day. He was found dead seven days later. Frank's burial location is unknown.

    viii.   Francis Xavier, born 31 October 1872 in Ste. Genevieve County, Missouri. He was baptized in the Ste. Genevieve Catholic Church in Ste. Genevieve on 15 December 1872. Frank married Selma "Sallie" Peiser about 1898 in Texas. Sallie was the daughter of Ernst Peiser and Johanna Josephine Schubert, born on 20 October 1879 in Germany. She had arrived in New York with her parents, siblings and maternal grandmother on 26 May 1882 aboard the *Braunschweig*. The family traveled directly to Rockdale, Milam County, Texas. Frank and Sallie had one son and five daughters. Frank died of cancer on 14 June 1930 in Rowena, Runnels County, Texas. He was buried in the Saint Joseph Cemetery in Rowena, Runnels County, Texas. Sallie died of cancer on 16 December 1933 in San Angelo, Tom Green County, Texas. She was buried in the Rowena Protestant Cemetery in Rowena, Runnels County, Texas.

    ix.   Victoria Rosine "Dora," born 3 May 1874 in Ste. Genevieve County, Missouri. She was baptized in the Ste. Genevieve Catholic Church in Ste. Genevieve on 31 May 1874. She moved to Milam County, Texas with her parents. She married Karl "Charles" Hirt about 1896 in Texas. Charles was the son of Bernard "Ben" Hirt and _____, born 8 May 1872 in Germany. He had arrived in New York with his widowed father, an uncle, aunt and several cousins on 9 March 1881 aboard the *Labrador*. Charles and Dora had one son and two daughters, of whom one daughter died at the age of two and a half years. On the day she died, some workmen had been in the family home making some repairs when one of the men knocked over a bottle of strychnine which fell to the floor and broke. The little girl discovered the poison and ate some before it could be cleaned up. She died before the doctor could arrive. In early March 1902, the family was stricken with influenza. Charles died on 11 March 1902 and Dora died on 12 March 1902, both in Milam County. They were both buried in the Hirt-Braun Cemetery in Milam County, Texas. The two surviving children were raised by their uncle and aunt, Joseph and Josephine [née Braun] Walter.

    x. Catherine Ursula, born 14 September 1876 in Ste. Genevieve County, Missouri. She was baptized in the Ste. Genevieve Catholic Church in Ste. Genevieve on 12 October 1876. Catherine married Charles Brackenbusch in Texas. Charles was the son of Charles Brackenbusch and Emma Meyer, born 20 April 1878 in Texas. Charles was a farmer. The couple had one son. Catherine died on 12 December 1901 in Milam County. She was buried in the Hirt-Braun Cemetery in Milam County, Texas. Charles died of septic indigestion on 31 December 1915 in Rockdale, Milam County. He was buried in the Odd Fellows Cemetery in Rockdale, Milam County, Texas. Their orphaned son was raised by his uncle and aunt, Joseph and Josephine [née Braun] Walter.

    xi. Maximillian Anthony Sylvester "Max", born 11 March 1878 in Ste. Genevieve County, Missouri. He was baptized in the Ste. Genevieve Catholic Church in Ste. Genevieve on 21 April 1878. Max died on 14 May 1893 in Milam County, Texas. He was buried in the Hirt-Braun Cemetery, Milam County, Texas. He never married and had no known issue.

    xii. Henry George, born 23 April 1880 in Ste. Genevieve County, Missouri. He was baptized in the Ste. Genevieve Catholic Church in Ste. Genevieve on 20 June 1880. Henry married Anna Caroline Menn on 14 May 1900 in Bushdale, Milam County, Texas. Anna was [possibly the daughter of Ludwig Menn and Christine Louise Lucas?] born in October 1880 in [Bushdale, Milam County?], Texas. The couple had one son. Henry died in 1901 in Texas. He was buried in the Hirt-Braun Cemetery in Milam County, Texas. Anna's fate is unknown.

U.S. residence other than Ste. Genevieve County, Missouri:
Milam County, Texas

Naturalization:

Name	Declaration	Naturalization	Origin	Remarks
Braun, George			Germany	1900 Census Milam Co., TX

Military:
Served in the U.S. Civil War for the Union:
Private, Company G, 78th Enrolled Missouri Militia
    George Brown enlisted on 30 April 1864 at St. Mary's, Ste. Genevieve County, Missouri. He was ordered into active service on 6 November 1864. He was relieved from duty on 25 November 1864 after having served 20 days of actual service.

Education: Could read and write
Occupation: Farmer
Religious Affiliation: Roman Catholic
Comments:
George Braun was born in Ebersweier, Baden, Germany and appears to be the only member of his immediate family to have come to America. He is said to have come to the United States in early 1850. By 1860, he was a resident of Ste. Genevieve County, Missouri. George married Theresia Bader on 3 September 1860 in Ste. Genevieve County, Missouri. George was a farmer and owned land in Ste. Genevieve Township near the city of Ste. Genevieve. The couple had five sons and seven daughters, of whom one son died in early childhood and another son died at the age of sixteen. By the early 1890s, George had moved to Milam County, Texas with most of his family. They bought land near the small town of Rockdale and farmed. Two of their sons anglicized their surnames to "Brown," so there are both Braun and Brown descendants in Texas. Theresa died

on 13 June 1893 and George died on 9 March 1911, both in Milam County, Texas. They were both buried in the Hirt-Braun Cemetery in Rockdale, Milam County, Texas.

Johann Nepomuk "John" Braun Family

Surname Variations: Brown
European Origin: Rammersweier, Baden, Germany
Family:
Father: Johann Martin Braun, born 5 November 1769 in Rammersweier, Baden, Germany.
Mother: Catharina Biser [Bieser], born 15 November 1775 in Rammersweier, Baden, Germany. She died on 2 August 1814 in Rammersweier.
Children:
- i. Viktoria, born 28 August 1803 in Rammersweier, Baden, Germany.
- * ii. Johann Nepomuk, born 10 May 1805 in Rammersweier, Baden, Germany. [See sketch below.]
- iii. Gertrud, born 20 February 1807 in Rammersweier, Baden, Germany.
- iv. Franziska, born 18 February 1809 in Rammersweier, Baden, Germany.
- v. Maria Anna, born 12 January 1811 in Rammersweier, Baden, Germany.
- vi. Bernhard, born 21 May 1813 in Rammersweier, Baden, Germany.

Immigration:
Arrived 3 June 1853 from Le Harvre, France to New Orleans aboard the *Statesman*:
  Braun, Jean, 48
    Francisca, 49
    Carl, 19
    Marianne, 17
    Anton, 15
    Madelaine, 9
    Silvester, 5

Biographical:
Husband: Johann Nepomuk Braun
  Birth – 10 May 1805 in Rammersweier, Baden, Germany.
  Death/Burial – 21 March 1890 in Ste. Genevieve County, Missouri. He was buried in the St. Joseph Cemetery in Zell, Ste. Genevieve County, Missouri.
1) Wife: Thekla Hauser, daughter of Franz Anton Hauser and Maria Ursula Kieffer
  Birth – 12 September 1802 in Rammersweier, Baden, Germany.
  Marriage – 25 May 1830 in Rammersweier, Baden, Germany.
  Death/Burial – 23 June 1840 in Rammersweier, Baden, Germany.
  Children:
  - i. Karl "Charles," born 3 November 1833 in Rammersweier, Baden, Germany. He died on 20 February 1858 in Ste. Genevieve County, Missouri and was buried in the St. Joseph Cemetery in Zell, Ste. Genevieve County, Missouri. He may never have married and had no known issue.
  - ii. Maria Anna, born 29 July 1836 in Rammersweier, Baden, Germany. She married Mathias "Mathew" Schweigert on 2 May 1859 in Zell, Ste. Genevieve County, Missouri. Mathew was the son of Andreas "Andrew Schweigert and Helena Lehmann, born 5 February 1832 in Baden, Germany. [See Andreas Schweigert sketch.]
  - iii. Michael, born 28 September 1837 in Rammersweier, Baden, Germany. He died on 28 September 1837 in Rammersweier, Baden, Germany. No issue.
  - iv. Anton, born 18 January 1839 in Rammersweier, Baden, Germany. He was a farmer in Ste. Genevieve County, Missouri. He married Mathilda Weiler on 25 November 1861 in Zell, Ste. Genevieve County. Mathilda was the daughter of Anton Weiler and Salome Deck, born

30 January 1843 in Mörsch, Baden, Germany. The couple had three sons and one daughter, of whom, one son died in early childhood. Mathilda died on 11 April 1872 in Ste. Genevieve County, Missouri. She was buried in the St. Joseph Cemetery in Zell, Ste. Genevieve County, Missouri. Anton married Maria Eva "Mary" Jacob as his second wife on 30 December 1872 in Zell, Ste. Genevieve County. Mary was the daughter of Franz Kilian Jacob and Maria Eva Berninger, born 7 April 1849 in Louisville, Jefferson County, Kentucky. Anton and Mary had three sons and two daughters, of whom one son died in infancy. Mary died on 5 April 1882 in Ste. Genevieve County. She was buried in the St. Joseph Cemetery in Zell. Anton married Josephine Eckenfels as his third wife on 3 September 1888 in Zell. Josephine was the daughter of Severin Eckenfels and Catharina Kiefer, born 6 May 1849 in Zell, Ste. Genevieve County, Missouri. She was the widow of Lawrence Schwent and had six surviving children from her first marriage. [See Joseph Schwent sketch.] Anton and Josephine had one son and one daughter together. Anton died of acute paranchymatious nephritis on 6 April 1917 in Ste. Genevieve County, Missouri. Josephine died of chronic myocarditis and nephritis on 11 October 1945 in Ste. Genevieve County. They were both buried in the St. Joseph Cemetery in Zell, Ste. Genevieve County, Missouri.

2) Wife: Franziska Basler, daughter of Sebastian Basler and Helena Fitzkam [See Jacob Basler sketch.]
Birth/Baptism – 29 January 1804 in Rammersweier, Baden, Germany.
Marriage – 14 September 1840 in Weingarten Church, Baden, Germany.
Death/Burial – 14 May 1895 in Ste. Genevieve County, Missouri. She was buried in the St. Joseph Cemetery in Zell, Ste. Genevieve County, Missouri.
Children:
- v. Maria Magdalena, born 22 July 1841 in Rammersweier, Baden, Germany. Magdalena married her first cousin Jacob Basler on 25 November 1861 in Ste. Genevieve County, Missouri. Jacob was the son of Johann Baptist "John" Basler and Maria Anna Giesler, born 25 July 1840 in Rammersweier, Baden, Germany. [See Jacob Basler sketch.]
- vi. Victoria, born 11 December 1842 in Rammersweier, Baden, Germany. She died on 20 December 1842 in Rammersweier. No issue.
- vii. Valentin Constantin, born 27 February 1844 in Rammersweier, Baden, Germany. He died on 6 August 1848 in Rammersweier. No issue.
- viii. Silvester, born 6 January 1848 in Rammersweier, Baden, Germany. He married Mary Anna Eckenfels on 23 November 1869 in Zell, Ste. Genevieve County, Missouri. Mary was the daughter of Severin Eckenfels and Catharina Kiefer, born 28 March 1851 in Ste. Genevieve County, Missouri. The couple had four sons and six daughters, of whom three daughters died in childhood. Mary died on 12 January 1890. She was buried in the St. Joseph Cemetery in Zell, Ste. Genevieve County, Missouri. Sylvester married Mrs. Sophia Jokerst as his second wife on 10 September 1895 in Zell, Ste. Genevieve County, Missouri. Sophia was the daughter of Leopold Winter and Catherine Kohler, born 2 November 1858 in Ste. Genevieve County, Missouri. She was the widow of Henry Jokerst. Henry was the son of Joseph Jokerst and Kunigunda Schwent, born 15 August 1854 in Ste. Genevieve County, Missouri. Henry and Sophia had three sons and three daughters. Henry died of bronchitis and neuralgia of the heart on 14 April 1893 in Ste. Genevieve County. Sylvester and Sophia had two sons and one daughter. Sophia died of chronic nephritis and an impacted gall stone on 9 October 1913 in Ste. Genevieve County, Missouri. She was buried in the Our Lady Help of Christians Cemetery in Weingarten, Ste. Genevieve County, Missouri. Sylvester died of a cerebral hemorrhage on 10 December 1924 in Farmington, St. Francois County, Missouri. He was buried beside his first wife in the St. Joseph Cemetery in Zell, Ste. Genevieve County, Missouri.

Land Patents:
Ste. Genevieve County, Missouri

Patentee	Issue Date	Land Office	Cert. No.	Serial No.	Twp	Rng	Sec	Acres
Braun, Sylvester	3 Apr 1893	Ironton	2691	MO4360_.219	37-N	9-E	15	34.67

Naturalization:

Name	Declaration	Naturalization	Origin
Braun, John	16 March 1857	6 May 1859 Ste. Genevieve Co.	Baden

Education: Could read and write
Occupation: Farmer
Religious Affiliation: Roman Catholic
Political Affiliation and/or Any Offices Held:
  Is said to have served a term as the Burgermeister in Rammersweier
  Is said to have served as village accountant in Rammersweier
Comments:
Johann Nepomuk "John" Braun was born in Rammersweier, Baden, Germany. He received an excellent education in his home village and as a young man became a famer and learned the art of grape culture. He married Thekla Hauser and had four children with her, three of whom survived to adulthood. Thekla died in 1840 in Rammersweier and John was left with three children to raise alone. He married Franziska Basler as his second wife and had four more children, of whom two died in infancy. John appears to have prospered and is said to have served in more than one municipal office in Rammersweier. However, in the spring of 1853, he moved with his family to the United States. Several other families from the vicinity of Rammersweier left at the same time and they all traveled directly to Ste. Genevieve County, Missouri. John purchased a farm near the German Settlement [present-day Zell], and once again established a vineyard. John became very well known for the Catawba wine he produced. During and after the Civil War, he was noted as having filled the canteens of thirsty soldiers with wine from his cellar, free of charge. In the last three years of his life, John's health began to fail and he became quite frail. He was completely bedridden for his last two weeks. John died at almost 85 years of age on 21 March 1890 at his home near Zell. He was buried in the St. Joseph Cemetery in Zell, Ste. Genevieve County, Missouri. His funeral was attended by an unusually large number of people, in spite of unpleasantly inclement weather. After her husband's death, Franziska lived with her step-son, Anthony. She was known as a cheerful, helpful soul and enjoyed remarkably good health until the last year of her life when she began to complain of a strange growth on her breast [cancer?]. Franziska died at the age of 91 years on 14 May 1895. She was buried in the St. Joseph Cemetery in Zell, Ste. Genevieve County, Missouri.

Martin Braun Family
Surname Variations: Brown
European Origin: Ohlsbach and Gengenbach, Baden, Germany
Family:
Father: Johann Braun, born 16 December 1791 in Hinterohlsbach, Baden, Germany. He died on
  10 June 1863 in Ohlsbach, Baden, Germany.
Mother: Franziska Hurst [Hoerst], born about 1795 in Baden, Germany. She died on 10 April 1857 in
  Ohlsbach, Baden, Germany.
  Children:
    i. Kunigunda, born 27 February 1823 in Hinterohlsbach, Baden, Germany. She was baptized in the Catholic Church at Gengenbach, Baden, on the same day. She married Georg Suhm on 28 January 1847 in Gengenbach, Baden, Germany. Georg was the son of Michael Suhm and Creszentia Spaeth, born 24 April 1823 in Baden, Germany. No further information.
  * ii. Martin, born 10 November 1824 in Ohlsbach, Baden, Germany. He was baptized in the

Catholic Church at Gengenbach, Baden on 11 November 1824. [See sketch below.]
  iii. Victoria, born 13 December 1830 in Hinterohlsbach, Baden, Germany. She was baptized in the Catholic Church at Gengenbach, Baden, on 14 December 1830. Victoria died on 16 July 1847 in Gengenbach. No issue.

Immigration:
Arrived on 18 September 1852 from Le Havre, France to New York aboard the *Dublin*:
  Braun, Martin, 27
    Catherine, 26
    Catherine, 2 – daughter of Martin
    [Wendel, 1, must have been left off of the manifest]

Biographical:
Husband: Martin Braun
  Birth/Baptism – 10 November 1824 in Ohlsbach, Baden, Germany. He was baptized in the Catholic Church at Gengenbach, Baden on 11 November 1824.
  Death/Burial – 19 September 1883 in Ste. Genevieve, Ste. Genevieve County, Missouri. He was buried in the Valle Spring Cemetery in Ste. Genevieve, Ste. Genevieve County, Missouri.
Wife: Katharina Rottler, daughter of Wendelin Rottler and Katharina Eisenbeis [See Valentine Rottler sketch.]
  Birth – 1 December 1825 in Oberweier bei Lahr, Baden, Germany.
  1) Marriage – 27 November 1848 in Gengenbach, Baden, Germany to Martin Braun.
  2) Marriage – 3 May 1887 in Ste. Genevieve, Ste. Genevieve County, Missouri to Vincent Bayer as his second wife. [See Vincent Bayer sketch.]
  Death/Burial – 22 February 1925 in St. Louis, Missouri. She was buried in Calvary Cemetery in St. Louis, Missouri.
Children:
  i. Catherine, born 31 October 1849 in Ohlsbach, Baden, Germany. She was married to Joseph Glaser in Bloomsdale, Ste. Genevieve Co., Missouri on 6 February 1868. Joseph was the son of Franz Glaser and Rosalia Glaser, born on 9 January 1845 in Fautenbach, Achern, Baden, Germany. [See Franz Glaser sketch.]
  ii. Wendelin, born 16 November 1851 in Ohlsbach, Baden, Germany. He died of smallpox on 25 December 1872 in Ste. Genevieve County, Missouri and was buried in the St. Lawrence Cemetery at Lawrenceton, Ste. Genevieve County, Missouri. No issue.
  iii. Child, born and died in Germany about 1852.
  iv. Maria, born 4 April 1856 in Ste. Genevieve County, Missouri. She was baptized at St. Anne's Catholic Church, French Village, St. Francois County, Missouri on 21 June 1856. Maria died of smallpox on 7 January 1873 and was buried in the St. Lawrence Cemetery in Lawrenceton, Ste. Genevieve County, Missouri. No issue.
  v. Louisa Maria, born 25 January 1859 in Ste. Genevieve County, Missouri. She was baptized in the St. Lawrence Catholic Church in Lawrenceton, Ste. Genevieve County, on 3 April 1859. Louisa died of smallpox on 16 January 1873 and was buried in the St. Lawrence Cemetery in Lawrenceton, Ste. Genevieve County, Missouri. No issue.
  vi. Elizabeth, born 25 November 1861 in Ste. Genevieve County, Missouri. She was baptized at Anne's Catholic Church, French Village, St. Francois County, Missouri on 22 December 1861. Elizabeth died some time before 1870 in Missouri. No issue.
  vii. Valentine, born 5 June 1864 in Ste. Genevieve County, Missouri. He was baptized in the St. Lawrence Catholic Church in Lawrenceton, Ste. Genevieve County on 26 June 1864. Valentine died of smallpox on 11 January 1873 and was buried in the St. Lawrence Cemetery at Lawrenceton, Ste. Genevieve County, Missouri. No issue.
  viii. Sophia, born 30 May 1867 in Ste. Genevieve County, Missouri. She was baptized at St. Anne's

Catholic Church, French Village, St. Francois County, Missouri on 18 July 1867. Sophia died of smallpox on 17 January 1873 and was buried in the St. Lawrence Cemetery in Lawrenceton, Ste. Genevieve County, Missouri. No issue.

   ix. John, born 10 June 1870 in Ste. Genevieve County, Missouri. He survived the smallpox epidemic that killed most of his siblings in 1873. He grew to young manhood near Lawrenceton and then went to St. Louis to work. He contracted typhoid fever in the fall of 1888 and was taken to the city hospital to be treated. As he began to convalesce, relatives took him to their home in order to be able to take better care of him. He seemed to have recovered, but suffered a relapse and died of congestive chills on 11 October 1888. His mother had his body brought home to Ste. Genevieve County and he was buried in the St. Lawrence Cemetery in Lawrenceton, Ste. Genevieve County, Missouri. No issue.

Land Patents:
Ste. Genevieve County, Missouri

Patentee	Issue Date	Land Office	Cert. No.	Serial No.	Twp	Rng	Sec	Acres
Braun, Martin	10 Jun 1857	St. Louis	28091	MO1080_.258	38-N	6-E	22	120.0

Military:
Served in the U.S. Civil War for the Union:
Corporal, Company F, 78 Enrolled Missouri Militia
Martin Braun enlisted on 8 August 1862 in Ste. Genevieve, Missouri. He was ordered into active service on 16 October 1864. He was relieved from duty on 25 November 1864 after having served 41 days of actual service.

Education: Could read and write
Occupation: Farmer, Superintendent of the Ste. Genevieve County Poor Farm
Religious Affiliation: Roman Catholic
Comments:
Martin Braun, with his wife and two children, left Europe for the United States from Le Havre, France on the ship *Dublin,* arriving in New York on 18 September 1852. They settled in Ste. Genevieve County, Missouri in late 1852 near Punjaub [present-day Lawrenceton] where Martin bought a farm. Martin later became the Superintendent of the Ste. Genevieve County Poor Farm. Katherina and Martin had nine children, but only one of them reached adulthood. One child died in Germany before they came to America. One daughter died before 1870 in Missouri when she was less than 10 years old. Five others died between 25 December 1872 and 17 January 1873 of smallpox. There was a small epidemic in the northern part of Ste. Genevieve County that winter. Their youngest son died from complications of typhoid fever in 1888. Only their oldest daughter survived to have a family of her own. Martin died at Lawrenceton on 19 September 1883 and was buried in the Valle Spring Cemetery in Ste. Genevieve, Ste. Genevieve County, Missouri. He had purchased a $3000 life insurance policy through Home Insurance Company, a company in Burlington, Iowa, some time before his death. However, Katherina only received $1,005 of it for some unknown reason. She took over the management of the poor farm after her husband's death to support her family. The Ste. Genevieve County Court authorities attempted to find a successor for Martin to superintend the Poor Farm since "the work of the superintendent at the county farm [was], in the first place, not fit work for a lady and secondly, too arduous a task for her..." After several weeks of receiving no bids for the job, the County Court asked Katherina to stay on temporarily while they continued to seek applicants. The following year [August 1884] after no one else stepped forward, the court formally appointed Katharina as superintendent. She continued on at the County Farm until 1887, leaving shortly after she remarried. Katherina married for a second time at Ste. Genevieve, Ste. Genevieve County, Missouri on 3 May 1887 to Vincent Bayer, her younger sister Elizabeth's widower. They had no children together. He died on 13 February 1893 and was buried in the St. Lawrence Cemetery at Lawrenceton, Ste. Genevieve County, Missouri, beside his first wife. Shortly after the turn of the century, Katharina moved to St. Louis with her daughter, son-in-law, and most of her grandchildren. She lived to be 99 years 2 months and 22 days old and was reportedly somewhat unhappy that she was not going to live to be

100. She died of nephritis on 22 February 1925 and her grandson, Dr. Martin J. Glaser, was the attending physician. She was buried in the Calvary Cemetery in St. Louis, Missouri.

Francis "Frank" Breckle Family
Surname Variations: Breckley, Brichle, Brickle, Brickley, Brickly
European Origin: Germany
Family:
Father: Franz Xavier Brichle
Mother: Walburga Braching
   Child:
*   i. Francis, born 10 November 1840 in Germany. [See sketch below.]

Immigration:
Arrived about 1841 aboard an unknown vessel:
    Brichle, Francis

Biographical:
Husband: Francis Brichle [aka Francis Breckle]
   Birth – 10 November 1840 in Germany.
   Death/Burial – 19 November 1906 in Ste. Genevieve County, Missouri. He was buried in the Sts. Philip and James Cemetery in River aux Vases, Ste. Genevieve County, Missouri.
1) Wife: Theresia Bieser, daughter of Joseph Bieser and Elisabeth Oehler [See Joseph Bieser sketch.]
   Birth – 6 September 1842 in Ste. Genevieve County, Missouri.
   1) Marriage – 1 April 1861 in Zell, Ste. Genevieve County to Conrad Isenmann. [See Conrad Isenmann sketch.]
   2) Marriage – 28 November 1861 in Zell, Ste. Genevieve County to Francis Brichle.
   Death/Burial – 8 December 1877 in Ste. Genevieve County, Missouri. She was buried in the Sts. Philip and James Cemetery in River aux Vases, Ste. Genevieve County, Missouri.
   Children:
    i. Frank, born about 1864 in Missouri. No further mention of him has been found after the 1880 census in Ste. Genevieve County, Missouri.
    ii. Bernard, born 19 July 1865 in Ste. Genevieve County, Missouri. He was baptized on 27 August 1865 in Sts. Philip and James Catholic Church in River aux Vases, Ste. Genevieve County. No further mention of him has been found after he is named in his father's will in 1906.
    iii. Elisabeth, born 17 August 1867 in Ste. Genevieve County, Missouri. She died of brain trouble on 15 August 1896 in River aux Vases. She knew that she was dying and was reportedly unhappy about not living to see her 29th birthday. She was buried in the Sts. Philip and James Cemetery in River aux Vases, Ste. Genevieve County, Missouri. No issue.
    iv. Sophia, born 16 February 1871 in Ste. Genevieve County, Missouri. She was baptized on 2 April 1871 in Sts. Philip and James Catholic Church in River aux Vases, Ste. Genevieve County. After her parents died, she lived with her half-brother, August, and helped with household chores. When August became the superintendent of the County Poor Farm, she moved there with him and became an inmate of the institution. Sophia died of carcinoma of the stomach on 24 March 1954 in Ste. Genevieve County. She was buried in the Valle Spring Cemetery in Ste. Genevieve, Ste. Genevieve County, Missouri. She never married and had no issue.
    v. Maria Magdalena, born 13 February 1873 in Ste. Genevieve County, Missouri. She was baptized on 6 April 1873 in Sts. Philip and James Catholic Church in River aux Vases, Ste. Genevieve County. No mention of her has been found after she was named in her father's will in 1906.
    vi. Anna Catherine, born 26 January 1875 in Ste. Genevieve County, Missouri. She was baptized on 28 February 1875 in Sts. Philip and James Catholic Church in River aux Vases, Ste.

Genevieve County, Missouri. She died young. No issue.

    vii. Louise, born 30 September 1876 in Ste. Genevieve County, Missouri. She was baptized on 12 November 1876 in Sts. Philip and James Catholic Church in River aux Vases, Ste. Genevieve County. Louise died in November 1878 in Ste. Genevieve County. She was buried in the Sts. Phillip and James Cemetery in River aux Vases, Ste. Genevieve County, Missouri. No issue.

2) Wife: Catherine Elisabeth Roth, daughter of Heinrich Roth and Magdalena Schott
Birth – 24 April 1862 in Sasbach, Achern, Baden, Germany.
1) Marriage – 17 June 1879 in River aux Vases, Ste. Genevieve County, Missouri to Francis Brichle.
2) Marriage – to Fred Schneider.
Death/Burial – 17 March 1956 in Howell County, Missouri. She was buried in the Oak Lawn Cemetery in West Plains, Howell County, Missouri.
Children:

    viii. Joseph Henry, born 17 September 1880 in Ste. Genevieve County, Missouri. He was baptized on 10 October 1880 in Sts. Philip and James Catholic Church in River aux Vases, Ste. Genevieve County. He married Laura Alta Hynds on 20 August 1917 [in Arkansas?]. Laura was the daughter of David Henry Hynds and Frances Elizabeth Jones, born 19 February 1899 in Arkansas. The couple had five sons and two daughters. The family lived in Memphis, Tennessee and in Lebanon, Sharp County, Arkansas. Joseph died on 27 March 1972. Laura died on 8 September 1991 in Poinsett County, Arkansas. They were both buried in the Oak Lawn Cemetery in West Plains, Howell County, Missouri.

    xi. August William "Gus," born 18 June 1882 in Ste. Genevieve County, Missouri. He was baptized on 6 August 1882 in Sts. Philip and James Catholic Church in River aux Vases, Ste. Genevieve County. August was a farmer. He married Blanche Kennard on 7 January 1902 in Ste. Genevieve County. Blanche was the daughter of James Kennard and Agatha Kempf, born 14 August 1881 in Ste. Genevieve County, Missouri. The couple had no children of their own, but eventually fostered three boys. By 1930, Gus had been appointed Superintendent of the County Poor Farm. He moved there with his wife and half-sister, Sophia. He continued to run the farm until after his wife's death. Blanche died of a cerebral hemorrhage on 17 January 1948. August died on 2 March 1969. They were both buried in the Valle Spring Cemetery in Ste. Genevieve, Ste. Genevieve County, Missouri.

    xi. Child. Died in infancy.

Naturalization:

Name	Declaration	Naturalization	Origin	Remarks
Brechle, Francis				[1900 census]

Military:
Served in the U.S. Civil War for the Union:
1st Lieutenant, Company F, 78th Enrolled Missouri Militia
    Francis Brickley enlisted on 1 September 1862 in Jackson Twp., Ste. Genevieve County, Missouri.

Education: Could read and write.
Occupation: Farmer
Religious Affiliation: Roman Catholic
Comments:
Francis Brichle is said to have come to the United States about 1840. The first record of his presence in Ste. Genevieve County, Missouri is that of his 1861 marriage to Theresia Bieser, widow of Conrad Isenmann. The couple settled on a farm near present-day River aux Vases and raised their family. Francis and Theresia had two sons and five daughters, of whom the two youngest daughters died young. Francis served in the 78th Enrolled Missouri Militia during the Civil War, but it is doubtful whether he ever saw active service since the

militias were reserve units. Theresia died on 8 December 1877 in Ste. Genevieve County, Missouri. She was buried in the Sts. Philip and James Cemetery in River aux Vases, Ste. Genevieve County, Missouri. Francis married Catherine Elisabeth Roth as his second wife on 17 June 1879 in River aux Vases, Ste. Genevieve County, Missouri. Catherine was considerably younger than Francis. The couple had two sons and one child that died in infancy. In 1901, Francis opened a saloon near River aux Vases and made a respectable living for himself and his family. He died 17 November 1906 at his home in River aux Vases, Ste. Genevieve County, Missouri. He was buried next to his first wife in the Sts. Philip and James Cemetery in River aux Vases. According to her death certificate, Catherine married a man named Fred Schneider as her second husband, but nothing further is known of him. She died of congestive heart failure on 17 March 1956 in Howell County, Missouri after she fell and fractured her left hip. She was buried in the Oak Lawn Cemetery in West Plains, Howell County, Missouri.

Joseph Breig Family

Surname Variations: Braig, Brieg
European Origin: Oberharmersbach, Baden, Germany
Family:
Father: Michael Breig, born 1 May 1822 in Oberharmersbach, Baden, Germany. He died on 5 December 1894 in Oberharmersbach.
Mother: Cecilia Hertig, born 29 May 1824 in Oberharmersbach, Baden, Germany. She died on 1 April 1889 in Oberharmersbach.
Children:
 i. Cecilia, born 5 July 1846 in Oberharmersbach, Baden, Germany. She died on 15 July 1846 in Oberharmersbach. No issue.
‡ ii. Leonard, born 29 August 1847 in in Oberharmersbach, Baden, Germany. He came to the United States in 1881 and settled in Milwaukee, Wisconsin where he worked as a general laborer. Leonard died on 17 April 1905 in Milwaukee, Wisconsin. He does not appear to have ever married and had no known issue.
 iii. Agatha, born 2 February 1849 in Oberharmersbach, Baden, Germany. She died on 19 December 1857 in Oberharmersbach. No issue.
 iv. Ludwig, born 8 October 1850 in Oberharmersbach, Baden, Germany.
 v. Stephan, born 23 October 1853 in Oberharmersbach, Baden, Germany. He died on 16 March 1857 in Oberharmersbach. No issue.
 vi. Katharina, born 1 December 1853 in Oberharmersbach, Baden, Germany.
 vii. Magdalena, born 11 May 1855 in Oberharmersbach, Baden, Germany. She died on 29 January 1928 in Oberharmersbach.
 viii. Karolina, born 27 June 1857 in Oberharmersbach, Baden, Germany. She died on 21 February 1858 in Oberharmersbach. No issue.
 ix. Augustine, born 28 April 1859 in Oberharmersbach, Baden, Germany.
 x. Joseph, born in January 1861 in Oberharmersbach, Baden, Germany. He died on 18 August 1861 in Oberharmersbach. No issue.
* xi. Joseph, born 18 March 1863 in Oberharmersbach, Baden, Germany. [See sketch below.]
† xii. Wilhelm "William," born in April 1867 in Oberharmersbach, Baden, Germany. [See Wilhelm "William" Breig sketch.]

Immigration:
Arrived 14 June 1881 from Antwerp, Belgium to New York aboard the *Hecla*:
 Breig, Leonh[ard], 33
Arrived 4 May 1882 from Le Havre, France to New York aboard the *Canada*:
 Braig, Joseph, 19 shoemaker   Baden, Germany

Biographical:
Husband: Joseph Breig
- Birth – 18 March 1863 in Oberharmersbach, Baden, Germany.
- Death/Burial – 7 February 1920 in Perry County, Missouri. He was buried in the Catholic Cemetery in St. Mary, Ste. Genevieve County, Missouri.

Wife: Catherine "Katie" Braun, daughter of Bernard Braun and Crescentia Schweigert [See Bernard Braun sketch.]
- Birth – 29 March 1865 in Ste. Genevieve County, Missouri.
- Marriage – 25 January 1887 in St. Mary, Ste. Genevieve County, Missouri.
- Death/Burial – 17 February 1920 in Perry County, Missouri. She was buried in the Catholic Cemetery in St. Mary, Ste. Genevieve County, Missouri.

Children:
  i. Mary Magdalena, born 20 October 1887 in Perry County, Missouri. She died on 1 November 1887 and was buried in the Catholic Cemetery in St. Mary, Ste. Genevieve County, Missouri. No issue.
  ii. Josephine Catherine, born 18 February 1889 in Perry County, Missouri. She was baptized on 17 March 1889 in the Immaculate Conception Catholic Church in St. Mary, Ste. Genevieve County, Missouri. She married Martin Lewis Wengert on 18 March 1910 in St. Mary, Ste. Genevieve County. Martin was the son of Charles Ambrose Wengert and Christina Mary Cambron, born 29 October 1884 in Perry County, Missouri. He was a farmer. By 1930, the family had moved to St. Mary where Martin opened a general store. Martin and Josephine had two sons and four daughters. Martin died in January 1968 and Josephine died on 3 December 1978, both in St. Mary, Ste. Genevieve County. They were both buried in the Catholic Cemetery in St. Mary, Ste. Genevieve County, Missouri.
  iii. Emily Louisa "Emma," born 20 November 1891 in Perry County, Missouri. She was baptized on 6 December 1891 in the Immaculate Conception Catholic Church in St. Mary, Ste. Genevieve County, Missouri. She married Earl Francis Esselman on 17 October 1910 in St. Mary. Earl was the son of Francis John Nepomuk "Frank" Esselman and Matilda Gertrude "Tillie" Layton, born 12 February 1889 in Claryville, Perry County, Missouri. [See Frank Esselman sketch.]
  iv. Elizabeth Bridget, born 6 March 1894 in Perry County, Missouri. She was baptized on 14 March 1894 in the Immaculate Conception Catholic Church in St. Mary, Ste. Genevieve County, Missouri. She married Leo August Valle on 20 April 1927 in St. Mary. Leo was the son of Francis Joseph Valle and Mary Anna Baumann, born 14 August 1891 in Missouri. He was a farmer. The couple had three sons and two daughters. Elizabeth died on 24 October 1977 and Leo died on 1 November 1986, both in Ste. Genevieve. They were both buried in the Valle Spring Cemetery in Ste. Genevieve, Ste. Genevieve County, Missouri.
  v. John Augustin, born 22 August 1896 in Perry County, Missouri. He was baptized on 30 August 1896 in the Immaculate Conception Catholic Church in St. Mary, Ste. Genevieve County, Missouri. He married Magdalena "Maggie" Esselman on 26 November 1917 in St. Mary. Maggie was the daughter of Francis John Nepomuk "Frank" Esselman and Matilda Gertrude "Tillie" Layton, born 12 May 1896 in Perry County, Missouri. John was a farmer. The couple had one son and two daughters. John died on 23 August 1976 and Maggie died on 13 October 1992 in St. Mary, Ste. Genevieve County. They were both buried in the Catholic Cemetery in St. Mary, Ste. Genevieve County, Missouri.
  vi. Henry Joseph, born 1 May 1899 in Perry County, Missouri. He was baptized on 7 May 1899 in the Immaculate Conception Catholic Church in St. Mary, Ste. Genevieve County, Missouri. He married Dora Agnes Giesler on 8 November 1920 in St. Mary. Dora was the daughter of Gideon Giesler and Henrietta Weiberg, born 29 June 1899 in Perry County. Henry was a farmer. The couple had two sons and two daughters. Henry died on 4 February 1876 and Dora died on 20 February 1984, both in Missouri. They were both buried in the Catholic Cemetery in

      St. Mary, Ste. Genevieve County, Missouri.
- vii. Edward Laurence [twin] , born 11 December 1902 in Perry County, Missouri. He was baptized on 16 December 1902 in the Immaculate Conception Catholic Church in St. Mary, Ste. Genevieve County, Missouri. He died of lobar pneumonia complicated by influenza on 7 February 1920 in Perry County. He was buried in the Catholic Cemetery in St. Mary, Ste. Genevieve County, Missouri. Edward never married and had no issue.
- viii. William Matthew [twin] , born 11 December 1902 in Perry County, Missouri. He was baptized on 16 December 1902 in the Immaculate Conception Catholic Church in St. Mary, Ste. Genevieve County, Missouri. He died on 8 November 1965 in St. Louis, Missouri.
- ix. Clara Genevieve, born 2 May 1905 in Perry County, Missouri. She was baptized on 7 May 1905 in the Immaculate Conception Catholic Church in St. Mary, Ste. Genevieve County, Missouri. She died of bronchial pneumonia complicated by influenza on 9 February 1920 in Perry County. She was buried in the Catholic Cemetery in St. Mary, Ste. Genevieve County, Missouri. No issue.

Naturalization:

Name	Declaration	Naturalization	Origin	Remarks
Breig, Joseph			Baden	1900 Census
Breig, Leonhard		5 June 1896 Milwaukee, WI	Germany	

Education: Could read and write
Occupation: Farmer
Religious Affiliation: Roman Catholic
Comments:
Joseph Breig was born in Germany and learned the shoemakers' trade as a young man. He came to the United States in 1882 and appears to have gone directly to Missouri. He married Catherine "Katie" Braun and the couple settled on a farm in Saline Township, Perry County, Missouri, just south of the Ste. Genevieve County line near the town of St. Mary. Joseph's brother, William, followed him to Missouri in 1891. Joseph and Katie had four sons and five daughters, of whom the oldest daughter died in infancy. In the years between 1918 and 1920, the Spanish influenza epidemic raged across America. In February 1920, Joseph and his entire family fell ill with the disease. Both he and his son Edward died on 7 February 1920. His daughter Clara died on 9 February and his wife Katie succumbed on 17 February. These four were all buried in the Catholic Cemetery in St. Mary, Ste. Genevieve County, Missouri. The rest of the family members eventually recovered.

Wilhelm "William" Breig Family
Surname Variations: Braig, Brieg
European Origin: Oberharmersbach, Baden, Germany
Family:
Father: Michael Breig, born 1 May 1822 in Oberharmersbach, Baden, Germany. He died on 5 December 1894 in Oberharmersbach.
Mother: Cecilia Hertig, born 29 May 1824 in Oberharmersbach, Baden, Germany. She died on 1 April 1889 in Oberharmersbach.
    Children:

Note: For a comprehensive discussion of Michael Breig's children see the Joseph Breig family sketch.

Immigration:
Arrived 23 March 1891 from Le Havre, France to New York aboard the *Russia*:
    Braig, Wilh[elm], 25   worker   Oberharmersbach

Biographical:
Husband: Wilhelm "William" Breig
  Birth – 9 April 1867 in Oberharmersbach, Baden, Germany.
  Death/Burial – 30 August 1945 in Ste. Genevieve County, Missouri. He was buried in the Catholic Cemetery in St. Mary, Ste. Genevieve County, Missouri.
Wife: Anna Catherine Jokerst, daughter of Francis Xavier Jokerst and Catherine Schmidt
  Birth/Baptism – 3 December 1874 in Ste. Genevieve County, Missouri. She was baptized in the Sts. Philip and James Catholic Church in River aux Vases, Ste. Genevieve County, Missouri.
  Marriage – 17 February 1896 in River aux Vases, Ste. Genevieve County, Missouri.
  Death/Burial – 1 December 1956 in St. Mary, Ste. Genevieve County, Missouri. She was buried in the Catholic Cemetery in St. Mary, Ste. Genevieve County, Missouri.
  Children:
   i. Francis Joseph, born 18 March 1897 in Missouri. He was baptized on 25 March 1897 in the Immaculate Conception Catholic Church in St. Mary, Ste. Genevieve County, Missouri. Frank was a general construction worker. He married Esther Mary Roth on 24 November 1931 in Ozora, Ste. Genevieve County. Esther was the daughter of Louis Wendel Roth and Genevieve Jokerst, born 8 September 1909 in Ste. Genevieve County, Missouri. The couple had three sons and three daughters. Frank died on 26 May 1976 and Esther died on 16 April 1987. They were both buried in the Catholic Cemetery in St. Mary, Ste. Genevieve County, Missouri.
   ii. Mary Magdalena, born 30 November 1898 in Missouri. She was baptized on 8 December 1898 in the Immaculate Conception Catholic Church in St. Mary, Ste. Genevieve County, Missouri. She married Edward Albert Otte on 15 April 1918 in St. Mary. Edward was the son of August Friedrich Otte and Theresa Isenmann, born 20 May 1892 in Ste. Genevieve County, Missouri. He was a farmer. The couple had three sons. Edward died of pulmonary tuberculosis complicated by chronic myocarditis on 28 March 1935 in Ste. Genevieve County, Missouri. Mary married _____ Grifford as her second husband. Mary died in June 1976 in Perryville, Perry County, Missouri.
   iii. August Lorenz, born 2 April 1901 in Missouri. He was baptized on 7 April 1901 in the Immaculate Conception Catholic Church in St. Mary, Ste. Genevieve County, Missouri. He worked as a truck driver and helped his father on his farm before 1940. August enlisted in the U.S. Army in September 1942 during World War II. He served until 15 January 1944. He married Letty Lucille Griffey on 24 November 1949 in Cape Girardeau, Cape Girardeau County, Missouri. Letty was the daughter of unknown parents, born 12 June 1919 in Missouri. The couple may never have had children. August died on 29 January 1978. He was buried in the Catholic Cemetery in St. Mary, Ste. Genevieve County, Missouri. Letty died on 9 July 1995 in Cape Girardeau, Cape Girardeau County, Missouri.
   iv. George William, born 28 August 1903 in Missouri. He was baptized on 6 September 1903 in the Immaculate Conception Catholic Church in St. Mary, Ste. Genevieve County, Missouri. George married Roberta Agnes Basler on 9 May 1939 in Bloomsdale, Ste. Genevieve County, Missouri. Roberta was the daughter of Francis Xavier Basler and Marie Ida Carron, born 4 February 1916 in Bloomsdale. The couple had one son and one daughter. George died on 22 August 1974 and Roberta died on 28 December 2007, both in Perryville, Perry County, Missouri. They were both buried in the Mount Hope Cemetery in Perryville, Perry County, Missouri.
   v. Joseph Xavier, born 22 April 1906 in Missouri. He was baptized on 29 April 1906 in the Immaculate Conception Catholic Church in St. Mary, Ste. Genevieve County, Missouri. He married Hildagarde Apollonia "Hilda" Schmiederer on 1 July 1950 in Weingarten, Ste. Genevieve County. Hilda was the daughter of Anthony Joseph Schmiederer and Mary Cecilia Jokerst, born 9 February 1911 in Ste. Genevieve County, Missouri. Hilda died on 7 February 1970 and Joseph died on 24 September 1995. They were both buried in the Catholic Cemetery in St. Mary, Ste. Genevieve County, Missouri.

vi. Emma Catherine, born 2 November 1908 in Missouri. She was baptized on 8 November 1908 in the Immaculate Conception Catholic Church in St. Mary, Ste. Genevieve County, Missouri. Emma became a teacher and lived for a while in Poplar Bluff, Butler County, Missouri, teaching in a Catholic school. She entered the Ursuline novitiate in Alton, Madison County, Illlinois in July 1957 and took the religious name, Sister Honora. The mission of the Ursuline order is to educate young girls. She became the prioress of the Galveston, Texas Ursuline Community in the 1970s. She died on 31 October 1996 in Alton, Madison County, Illinois. She was buried in the Saint Peter Cemetery in Kirkwood, St. Louis County, Missouri. No issue.

vii. Leonard Edgar, born 17 August 1911 in Missouri. He was baptized on 3 September 1911 in the Immaculate Conception Catholic Church in St. Mary, Ste. Genevieve County, Missouri. He was a construction worker. During World War II, Leonard served in the U.S. Army, enlisting in July 1942 at Jefferson Barracks in St. Louis. He was mustered out on 13 March 1946. He married Wilma Magdalena Flieg on 4 November 1950 in Ste. Genevieve, Ste. Genevieve County. Wilma was the daughter of Thomas Flieg and Dora Theresa Baumann, born 21 February 1921 in Ste. Genevieve. Leonard died on 1 July 1986 and Wilma died on 3 August 1986, both in Ste. Genevieve County, Missouri.

viii. Josephine Cecilia [twin], born 15 February 1914 in Missouri. She was baptized on 15 March 1914 in the Immaculate Conception Catholic Church in St. Mary, Ste. Genevieve County, Missouri. She married Clarence C. Pustmueller. Clarence was the son of unknown parents, born 16 March 1912 in Missouri. He died on 19 April 1991 and Josephine died on 27 June 2002, both in St. Louis, Missouri. It is not known whether the couple had children.

ix. Rosa [twin], born and died on 15 February 1914 in Missouri. She was buried in the Catholic Cemetery in St. Mary, Ste. Genevieve County, Missouri. No issue.

Naturalization:

Name	Declaration	Naturalization	Origin
Breig, William		26 April 1920 Ste. Genevieve Co.	Baden

Education: Could read and write
Occupation: Farmer
Religious Affiliation: Roman Catholic
Comments:
Wilhelm "William" Breig followed his brother Joseph to the United States in 1891. He married Anna Catherine Jokerst and settled on a farm in Ste. Genevieve County, Missouri near the town of St. Mary. The family lived relatively quiet, productive lives. William died of cerebral schlerosis and old age on 30 August 1945 and Anna died of congestive heart failure and senility on 1 December 1956. They were both buried in the Catholic Cemetery in St. Mary, Ste. Genevieve County, Missouri.

Vincent Brischle Family
Surname Variations: Brichle, Brishley, Brueschle
European Origin: Weier, Baden, Germany
Family:
Father: Caspar Brueschle
Mother: Maria Eva Matz
  Children:
* i. Vincent, born 1 February 1811 in Weier, Baden, Germany. [See sketch below.]
† ii. Maria Johanna, born 24 May 1813 in Weier, Baden, Germany. She married Franz Ignatz Joggerst [aka Jokerst] on 20 November 1832 in Weier. Franz was the son of Joseph Joggerst and Ursula Schneider, born 29 January 1808 near Offenburg, Baden, Germany. [See Franz Ignatz Joggerst sketch.]

    iii. Linus, born about 1813 in Baden, Germany. He married **Rosalia Neffon**. Rosalia was born about 1817 in Baden, Germany. The couple had at least two sons and one daughter. Their daughter, Sophia, came to Ste. Genevieve County, Missouri with her uncle, Vincent Brischle. Sophia married Joseph Isenmann on 2 February 1858 in Zell, Ste. Genevieve County, Missouri. Joseph was the son of Johann Baptist "John" Isenmann and Maria Anna Littenecker, born 4 January 1833 in Bucyrus, Crawford County, Ohio. [See Johann Baptist "John" Isenmann sketch.]

†   iv. Clara, born 12 August 1815 in Weier, Baden, Germany. She married Ferdinand Stolzer on 12 November 1837 in Griesheim, Baden, Germany. Ferdinand was the son of Martin Stolzer and Viktoria Schneider, born 2 May 1811 in Griesheim. [See Ferdinand Stolzer sketch.]

    v. Magdalena, born in Baden, Germany. She married Karl Geck on 25 September 1837 in Griesheim, Baden, Germany. Karl was the son of Johann Adam Geck and Catharina Siegrist, born 29 October 1809 in Griesheim. The couple lived in Griesheim and had at least three sons.

Immigration:
Arrived 24 January 1857 from Le Havre, France to New Orleans aboard the *Wurtemberg*:
    Brischle, Vincent, 45
        Magdalena, 46
        Victoria, 19
        Sophie, 18   [daughter of Linus Brischle, niece of Vincent]
        Theresa, 16
        Veronica, 13
        Ignace, 8
        Joseph, 6

Biographical:
Husband: Vincent Brischle
    Birth – 1 February 1811 in Weier, Baden, Germany.
    Death/Burial – 10 October 1896 in Ste. Genevieve County, Missouri. He was buried in the Our Lady Help of Christians Cemetery in Weingarten, Ste. Genevieve County, Missouri.

Wife: Magdalena Kurfurst
    Birth – 27 June 1809 in Weier, Baden, Germany.
    Marriage – 25 November 1836 in Baden, Germany.
    Death/Burial – 18 May 1895 in Ste. Genevieve County, Missouri. She was buried in the Our Lady Help of Christians Cemetery in Weingarten, Ste. Genevieve County, Missouri.

Children:
    i. Victoria, born 6 September 1837 in Weier, Baden, Germany. She married Joseph Gegg on 13 April 1858 in Zell, Ste. Genevieve County, Missouri. Joseph was the son of Joseph Gegg and Josepha Wörter, born 25 December 1834 in Ste. Genevieve County, Missouri. [See Joseph Gegg sketch.]

    ii. Theresa, born 15 October 1840 in Baden, Germany. She married August Schwent on 29 May 1860 in Zell, Ste. Genevieve County, Missouri. August was the son of Joseph Schwent and Maria Magdalena Jokerst, born 13 April 1835 in Ste. Genevieve County, Missouri. [See Joseph Schwent sketch.]

    iii. Veronica, born about 1844 in Baden, Germany. She married Johann "John" Sinz on 21 February 1871 in River aux Vases, Ste. Genevieve County, Missouri. John was the son of Augustin Sinz and Philippine Bayer, born 1 January 1840 in Hofweier, Baden, Germany. [See Augustin Sinz sketch.]

    iv. Ignatius, born 21 January 1847 in Baden, Germany. He was a farmer and lived near the town of Weingarten, Ste. Genevieve County. Ignatius married Theresia Hogenmiller on 24 November 1874 in River aux Vases, Ste. Genevieve County, Missouri. Theresia was the daughter of

Joseph Hogenmiller and Crescentia Fritsch, born 22 January 1854 in Ste. Genevieve County, Missouri. The couple had two sons and six daughters, of whom one son died in infancy. Ignatius died of heart disease and chronic interstitial nephritis on 29 September 1930. Theresa died on 24 November 1939, several weeks after she fell and fractured a thigh. They were both buried in Our Lady Help of Christians Cemetery in Weingarten, Ste. Genevieve County, Missouri.

   v. Joseph, born 23 March 1849 in Weier, Baden, Germany. As a young man, Joseph learned the wagon maker's trade under the tutelage of David Karl, his future brother-in-law. He remained in New Offenburg for a time, working for John Isenmann. He married Mary Karl on 27 November 1877 in Weingarten, Ste. Genevieve County, Missouri. Mary was the daughter of Caspar Karl and Johanna Hogenmiller, born 2 July 1855. The couple had five sons and four sons, of whom one son died in infancy. In 1882 Joseph entered into a partnership with his brother-in-law, Henry Karl, in a lumber and sawmilling business under the name of Brischle & Karl. The business was in operation until about 1896. In 1897, Joseph moved his family to Bloomsdale, Ste. Genevieve County where he built a flour mill and a wagon shop. The wagon shop was destroyed by fire in 1929. Mary died of cardio vascular renal disease on 30 June 1929 and Joseph died of chronic myocarditis and arterio-sclerosis on 9 September 1932, both in Ste. Genevieve County, Missouri. They were both buried in the St. Philomena Cemetery in Bloomsdale, Ste. Genevieve County, Missouri.

Naturalization:

Name	Declaration	Naturalization	Origin	Remarks
Brischle, Joseph			Germany	1900 Census
Brischle, Vincent	12 May 1856 Ste. Genevieve Co.			

Education: Could read and write
Occupation: Farmer
Religious Affiliation: Roman Catholic
Comments:
Vincent Brischle brought his family to the United States and traveled directly to Ste. Genevieve County, Missouri where two of his younger sisters had already settled with their families. His niece, Sophia Brischle, traveled to Missouri with Vincent and his family. Vincent bought a farm near the German Settlement [present-day Zell]. He was an industrious man and he prospered. Vincent was especially successful growing grapes and the wine he produced was considered among the best in the region. The family was widely respected for their honesty and fair dealing. Vincent was a favorite in the neighborhood for his good sense of humor. When Vincent retired, his son Ignatius took over the operation of the family farm and the old couple helped as much as they could in the household. Magdalena died on 18 May 1895 and Vincent died on 10 October 1896, both in Ste. Genevieve County, Missouri. They were both buried in the Our Lady Help of Christians Cemetery in Weingarten, Ste. Genevieve County, Missouri.

Benedict Bross Family
Surname Variations: Broce, Bruse
European Origin: Elgersweier, Baden, Germany
Family:
Father: Franz Joseph Bross
Mother: Apollonia Weisskopf
   Children:
     i. Amandus, born 26 October 1789 in Elgersweier, Baden, Germany.
     ii. Johannes Chrysostomus, born 25 January 1791 in Elgersweier, Baden, Germany. He married Walburga Lotspeich on 16 February 1817 in Elgersweier. Walburga was the daughter of Franz

Lotspeich and Elisabeth Ruf, born about 1793 in Baden, Germany. Johannes died on 3 September 1859 in Germany.
- iii. Joseph, born 10 February 1793 in Elgersweier, Baden, Germany.
- iv. Maria Anna, born 7 December 1795 in Elgersweier, Baden, Germany.
* v. Benedict, born 13 August 1799 in Elgersweier, Baden, Germany. [See sketch below.]
- vi. Dominicus, born 19 August 1801 in Elgersweier, Baden, Germany.
- vii. Eleanora, born 30 December 1803 in Elgersweier, Baden, Germany. She died before February 1807 in Elgersweier. No issue.
- viii. Eleanora, born 2 February 1807 in Elgersweier, Baden, Germany. She married Peter Kessler on 28 June 1833 in Elgersweier. Peter was the son of Simon Kessler and Cecilia Messberger.

Immigration:
Arrived before February 1834 marriage in St. Louis, Missouri aboard an unknown vessel:
    Bross, Benedict

Biographical:
Husband: Benedict Bross
   Birth – 13 August 1799 in Elgersweier, Baden, Germany.
   Death/Burial – 23 December 1878 in Ste. Genevieve County, Missouri. He was buried in the old City Cemetery in Ste. Genevieve, Ste. Genevieve County, Missouri.
Wife: Maria Anna Kast, daughter of Aloysius Kast and Catharina Spring
   Birth – 28 June 1816 in Ebersweier, Baden, Germany.
   Marriage – 11 February 1834 in St. Louis, Missouri.
   Death/Burial – 23 December 1876 in Ste. Genevieve County, Missouri. She was buried in the old City Cemetery in Ste. Genevieve, Ste. Genevieve County, Missouri.
   Children:
   - i. Priscilla Margaretha, born in November 1836 in St. Louis, Missouri. She married Joseph Thomure as his third wife on 18 January 1855 in Ste. Genevieve, Ste. Genevieve County, Missouri. Joseph was the son of Joseph Thomure and Celeste Boyer, born on 25 December 1815 in Ste. Genevieve. The couple had at least six sons and four daughters. Joseph died some time between 1880 and 1889, most likely in Missouri. Priscilla died on 2 June 1901 in St. Louis, Missouri. She was buried in the St. Peter's Cemetery in Normandy, St. Louis County, Missouri.
   - ii. Maria Barbara, born 2 May 1839 in Ste. Genevieve County, Missouri. She was baptized on 19 May 1839 in the Ste. Genevieve Catholic Church in Ste. Genevieve, Ste. Genevieve County, Missouri. She may be the Maria Barbara Bross who was married to a man named Fred. Wm. [Thomann? The name is difficult to read in the record.] on 10 December 1882 in Washington, Franklin County, Missouri. No further information.
   - iii. Francis Joseph, born 22 June 1841 in Ste. Genevieve County, Missouri. He was baptized on 4 July 1841 in the Ste. Genevieve Catholic Church in Ste. Genevieve, Ste. Genevieve County, Missouri. Francis died on 1 August 1841 in Ste. Genevieve. He was buried in the Memorial Cemetery in Ste. Genevieve, Ste. Genevieve County, Missouri. No issue.
   - iv. Maria Rosalie "Mary," born 2 February 1843 in Ste. Genevieve County, Missouri. She was baptized on 7 May 1843 in the Ste. Genevieve Catholic Church in Ste. Genevieve, Ste. Genevieve County, Missouri. She married Joseph Rinehart, possibly in Missouri. Joseph was born of unknown parents about 1842 in either New York or Canada. Joseph was a builder. The couple had two sons and three daughters. Some time between 1877 and 1880, the family moved to Chicago, Cook County, Illinois. Joseph died some time between 1883 and 1900, most likely in Chicago, Cook County, Illinois. Mary died in 1910 in Chicago, Cook County, Illinois. She was buried in the Oak Woods Cemetery in Chicago, Cook County, Illinois.
   - v. Josephine Emily, born 26 August 1848 in Ste. Genevieve County, Missouri. She was baptized

on 10 September 1848 in the Ste. Genevieve Catholic Church in Ste. Genevieve, Ste. Genevieve County, Missouri. Josephine married Laurence Herzog on 29 December 1868 in Ste. Genevieve. Laurence was the son of Joseph Herzog and Maria Trautmann, born 10 November 1844 in Ste. Genevieve County, Missouri. The couple had a son and a daughter, of whom the son died in infancy. Josephine died on 19 February 1873 in Ste. Genevieve and was buried in Memorial Cemetery in Ste. Genevieve. Laurence married Mary Ann Leitterman as his second wife on 3 July 1873 in Ste. Genevieve, Ste. Genevieve County, Missouri. Mary Ann was the daughter of Joseph Leitterman and Franziska Burgert, born 26 December 1852 in Ste. Genevieve County, Missouri. Joseph and Mary Ann had four sons and two daughters. Laurence died of peritonitis following an operation for bowel obstruction on 14 September 1913 in St. Louis, Missouri. Mary Ann died of heart disease on 14 April 1941 in Ste. Genevieve County, Missouri. They were both buried in the Catholic Cemetery in St. Mary, Ste. Genevieve County, Missouri.

vi. Benedict Xavier, born 23 August 1851 in Ste. Genevieve County, Missouri. He was baptized on 31 August 1851 in the Ste. Genevieve Catholic Church in Ste. Genevieve, Ste. Genevieve County, Missouri. Benedict married Annie Elizabeth Kelly about 1874. Annie was the daughter of unknown parents, born in August 1858 in Louisiana. The couple had eight children, four of whom died in infancy. Benedict moved his family to Memphis, Shelby County, Tennessee where he worked as a shoemaker. Benedict died of chronic nephritis and senility on 14 February 1933 in Memphis, Shelby County, Tennessee. He was buried in Elmwood Cemetery in Memphis, Shelby County, Tennessee. Annie died of myocarditis and pneumonia on 15 September 1936 in Memphis. She was buried in the Calvary Cemetery in Memphis, Shelby County, Tennessee.

vii. Catherine Victoria Felicity, born 22 January 1854 in Ste. Genevieve County, Missouri. She was baptized on 9 February 1854 in the Ste. Genevieve Catholic Church in Ste. Genevieve, Ste. Genevieve County, Missouri. Catherine married Henry B. Jokerst on 19 February 1878 in Ste. Genevieve. Henry was the son of Bernard Jokerst and Anna Maria Hermann, born 14 August 1851 in Ste. Genevieve County, Missouri. The couple had six sons and one daughter. Henry died of heart disease and chronic rheumatism on 7 April 1917 and Catherine died of chronic interstitial nephritis and chronic myocarditis on 2 July 1928, both in Ste. Genevieve County. They were both buried in the Valle Spring Cemetery in Ste. Genevieve.

viii. Anna Christina Catherine, born 15 April 1857 in Ste. Genevieve County, Missouri. She was baptized on 3 May 1857 in the Ste. Genevieve Catholic Church in Ste. Genevieve, Ste. Genevieve County, Missouri. She died on 6 December 1858 and was buried in theMemorial Cemetery in Ste. Genevieve, Ste. Genevieve County, Missouri. No issue.

U.S. residence prior to Ste. Genevieve County, Missouri:
St. Louis, Missouri

Land Patents:
Ste. Genevieve County, Missouri

Patentee	Issue Date	Land Office	Cert. No.	Serial No.	Twp	Rng	Sec	Acres
Bross, Benedict	8 Oct 1835	St. Louis	4101	MO 0090__.068	35	38-N	8-E	40

Naturalization:

Name	Declaration	Naturalization	Origin
Bross, Benedict		30 July 1838 Ste. Genevieve Co.	Baden

Education: Could read and write.
Occupation: Brick Maker
Religious Affiliation: Roman Catholic

Comments:
Benedict Bross was born in Germany and immigrated to the United States some time before his marriage to Maria Anna Kast in 1834 in St. Louis, Missouri. Her sister Victoria was married to Heinrich "Henry" Maennle. The Maennles also settled in Ste. Genevieve County, Missouri. [See the Heinrich Maennle sketch.] Benedict was a brick maker and the couple remained in St. Louis for the first few years of their marriage. By 1839 the Bross family had moved to Ste. Genevieve County, shortly before the birth of their second daughter. Benedict worked as a brick maker in the city of Ste. Genevieve and Maria was a midwife. After he retired from brick making, Benedict took up gardening. Maria died on 23 December 1876 and Benedict died on 23 December 1878, both in Ste. Genevieve, Ste. Genevieve County, Missouri. They were both buried in the old City Cemetery in Ste. Genevieve, Ste. Genevieve County, Missouri, but no stones exist to mark their graves.

Adam Bube Family

Surname Variations: Bove, Bovie, Bub
European Origin: [Miltenberg, Bavaria?], Germany
Family:
Father: Unknown
Mother: Unknown
   Child:
*   i.   Adam Johann Gottfried, born 24 November 1844 in Germany. [See sketch below.]

Immigration:
Arrived 11 August 1869 from Hamburg, Germany to New York aboard the *Silesia*:
    Bube, Joh[ann] Ad[am], 24   Farmer   from Miltenberg
Also aboard the same vessel [a relative?]:
    Bube, Carl Jos[eph], 28   Farmer   from Miltenberg

Biographical:
Husband: Adam Johann Gottfried Bube
  Birth – 24 November 1844 in [Miltenberg, Bavaria?], Germany.
  Death/Burial – 5 July 1924 in Ste. Genevieve County, Missouri. He was buried in the Valle Spring
     Cemetery in Ste. Genevieve, Ste. Genevieve County, Missouri.
Wife: Maria Katherina "Mary" Guschwa, daughter of Peter Guschwa and Maria Eva Hendrich [aka
     Kendrich]
  Birth/Baptism – 21 August 1850 in Ruchheim, Pfalz, Bavaria, Germany. She was baptized on
     25 August 1850 in the Evangelisch [Lutheran] Church in Ruchheim.
  1) Marriage – 13 January 1872 in St. Louis, Missouri to John P. Allen.
  2) Marriage – 24 November 1872 in St. Louis, Missouri to Adam Bube.
  Death/Burial – 18 June 1918. She was buried in the Valle Spring Cemetery in Ste. Genevieve, Ste.
     Genevieve County, Missouri.

There were no children from the marriage between John P. Allen and Maria Katherina Guschwa.

Children of Adam Bube and Maria Katherina Guschwa:
    i.   Emma, born about 1873 in Missouri. No further information has been found after the
         1880 U.S. Census.
    ii.   Henry, born 24 August 1876 in Missouri. As a young man, he went to Peoria, Illinois where he
         worked for several years as a laborer in a brick yard. By 1905, Henry had moved to St. Louis
         where he worked for the Anheuser Busch Brewery as a brewer and maltman. Henry married
         Anna _____ about 1905. Anna was born 24 November 1881 in Missouri. The couple does not
         appear to have had any children. Henry died of rectal and prostate cancer on 22 November
         1952 in St. Louis, Missouri. He was buried in the Immaculate Conception Cemetery in Arnold,
         Jefferson County, Missouri. Anna's date of death and place of burial are unknown.

iii. Caroline, born 12 July 1878 in Ste. Genevieve County, Missouri. She was baptized on 27 October 1878 in the St. Philomena's [present-day St. Agnes'] Catholic Church in Bloomsdale, Ste. Genevieve County. She was born with "congenital imbecility" and was deaf and mute. She lived at the Ste. Genevieve County Poor Farm for most of her adult life. She died of a cerebral vascular accident on 22 October 1963 in Ste. Genevieve County, Missouri. She was buried in the Valle Spring Cemetery in Ste. Genevieve, Ste. Genevieve County, Missouri. She never married and had no issue.

iv. Catherine Elizabeth "Katie," born 11 October 1880 in Ste. Genevieve County, Missouri. She was baptized on 2 January 1881 in the St. Lawrence Catholic Church in Lawrenceton, Ste. Genevieve County, Missouri. She may have had some mental impairment. Katie lived at the Ste. Genevieve County Poor Farm for most of her adult life. She died on 22 November 1944 on the County Poor Farm in Ste. Genevieve County of chronic myocarditis and from a fractured right hip she suffered in a fall three weeks previous to her death. She was buried in the Valle Spring Cemetery in Ste. Genevieve, Ste. Genevieve County, Missouri. She never married and had no issue.

v. Peter Joseph, born 9 December 1883 in Ste. Genevieve County, Missouri. He was baptized on 3 February 1884 in the St. Philomena's [present-day St. Agnes'] Catholic Church in Bloomsdale, Ste. Genevieve County. He may have had some mental impairment. Peter lived at the Ste. Genevieve County Poor Farm for most of his adult life. He died of influenza on 11 February 1934 in Ste. Genevieve County, Missouri. Peter was buried in the Valle Spring Cemetery in Ste. Genevieve, Ste. Genevieve County, Missouri. He never married and had no known issue.

vi. Mary Theresa, born 30 December 1885 in Ste. Genevieve County, Missouri. She was baptized on 25 March 1886 in the St. Lawrence Catholic Church in Lawrenceton, Ste. Genevieve County, Missouri. She died on 20 February 1890 in Ste. Genevieve County. No issue.

vii. Mary Johanna., born 19 September 1891 in Ste. Genevieve County, Missouri. She was baptized on 11 October 1891 in the St. Lawrence Catholic Church in Lawrenceton, Ste. Genevieve County, Missouri. No further information has been found after the 1910 U.S. census.

U.S. residence prior to Ste. Genevieve County, Missouri:
St. Louis, Missouri

Naturalization:

Name	Declaration	Naturalization	Origin
Bube, John Adam Gottfried		27 April 1891 Ste. Genevieve Co.	Bavaria

Education: Could read and write
Occupation: Farmer
Religious Affiliation: Adam Bube was Roman Catholic.
Maria Katharina Guschwa raised Lutheran. She converted to the Roman Catholic faith and was baptized on 15 April 1877 in the St. Lawrence Catholic Church in Lawrenceton, Ste. Genevieve County, Missouri.
Comments:
Adam Bube was born in Germany and came to the United States in 1869. He appears to have come directly to St. Louis, Missouri where he married Mrs. Maria "Mary" Allen, the widow of a man named John P. Allen. Mary was born in Germany and came to the United States with her mother and possibly a brother. Very little is known of Mary's first husband other than their date of marriage and that he died of brain fever in Kansas City, Missouri on 3 June 1872. He was buried in the Bellefountaine Cemetery in St. Louis, Missouri. Mary's mother, Maria Eva Guschwa [neé Hendrich or Kendrich] married John Henry Weber of Ste. Genevieve in 1875 in St. Louis. [See Henry Weber sketch.] Adam and Mary remained in St. Louis until about 1877 when they moved to Ste. Genevieve County, Missouri where Adam rented a farm from a Mr. Charleville. The couple had two sons and five daughters, of whom two daughters died young. By 1910, Adam could no longer

support his family. His two oldest surviving daughters, who had physical and mental impairments, were sent to live in the Ste. Genevieve County Poor Farm. The youngest daughter boarded with Mary's stepbrother, Henry W. Weber. After Mary's death on 18 June 1918, the younger son, Peter, was also sent to the County Poor Farm. Adam died of chronic interstitial nephritis on 5 July 1924 in Ste. Genevieve County, Missouri. He was buried in the Valle Spring Cemetery in Ste. Genevieve, Ste. Genevieve County, Missouri.

Morris Buchholtz Family
Surname Variations: Bogoltz, Bookholtz, Buch[h]olz, Buckholtz
European Origin: Baden, Germany
Family:
Father: Unknown
Mother: Unknown
   Child:
*   i.   Moritz, born 12 September 1814 in Baden, Germany. [See sketch below.]

Immigration:
Arrived 2 June 1852 from Le Havre, France to New Orleans aboard the *Brunswick*:
    Buchholz, Maurice, 38   from Baden
        Eva, 32
        Catherine, 10
        Victoria, 8
        Wendel, 7
        Caroline, 3

Biographical:
Husband: Morris [aka Moritz, Mauritz and Maurice] Buchholtz
   Birth – 12 September 1814 in Germany.
   Death/Burial – 23 September 1902 in Ste. Genevieve County, Missouri. He was buried in the St. Lawrence Cemetery in Lawrenceton, Ste. Genevieve County, Missouri.
1) Wife: Eva _____
   Birth – about 1820 in Baden, Germany.
   Marriage – in Germany.
   Death/Burial – 4 July 1854 in Ste. Genevieve County, Missouri. She was buried in the Memorial Cemetery in Ste. Genevieve, Ste. Genevieve County, Missouri.
   Children:
      i.   Catherine, born about 1842 in Baden, Germany. She came to the United States with her parents in 1852. No further information has been found.
      ii. Victoria, born about 1844 in Baden, Germany. She came to the United States with her parents in 1852. No further information has been found.
      iii. Franz Wendelin, born 28 October 1845 in Baden, Germany. He served as a private in Company F of the 78th Enrolled Missouri Militia during the Civil War. After the war, Wendelin became a farmer. He married Nancy Ellen Skaggs on 17 January 1869 in Bloomsdale, Ste. Genevieve County, Missouri. Nancy was the daughter of Jeremiah P. Skaggs and Esther _____ [Hester Ann Elmore?], born 4 March 1851 in [Jefferson County?], Missouri. She and her sisters were orphaned as young children and were raised by Edward and Elizabeth Coats in Ste. Genevieve County, Missouri. The couple had six sons and three daughters. Frank moved his family to a farm in Hopkins County, Texas about 1886. In Texas Wendelin was known by the name of Frank Wallace Buckholt. All of his descendants use the Buckholt surname. Nancy died on 28 June 1924 and Frank died of influenza on 4 March 1929, both in Brashear, Hopkins County, Texas. They were both buried in the Brashear Cemetery in Brashear, Hopkins County, Texas.
      iv. Caroline, born about 1849 in Baden, Germany. She came to the United States with her parents

in 1852. No further information has been found.

2) Wife: Elisabeth Sellinger, daughter of Bernard Sellinger and Fransiska Litterst [See George Sellinger sketch.]

Birth – 25 March 1826 in Germany.

Marriage – 25 July 1856 in Bloomsdale, Ste. Genevieve County, Missouri.

Death/Burial – 5 November 1918 in Ste. Genevieve County, Missouri. She was buried in the St. Lawrence Cemetery in Lawrenceton, Ste. Genevieve County, Missouri. [Note: the date of death given on her tombstone is incorrect. Her death certificate gives the correct date.]

Children:
- v. Joseph, born 11 February 1857 in Ste. Genevieve County, Missouri. He was baptized on 27 February 1857 in St. Philomena's Catholic Church in Bloomsdale, Ste. Genevieve County. Joseph died 1 November 1880 in Ste. Genevieve County. He may never have married and had no known issue.
- vi. Sophia Catherine, born 1 April 1858 in Ste. Genevieve County, Missouri. She was baptized on 20 June 1858 in St. Philomena's Catholic Church in Bloomsdale, Ste. Genevieve County. Catherine died on 12 May 1882 in Ste. Genevieve County, Missouri. She was buried in the St. Lawrence Cemetery in Lawrenceton, Ste. Genevieve County, Missouri. She never married and had no known issue.
- vii. George, born 28 February 1860 in Ste. Genevieve County, Missouri. George was a farmer. He married Mary Susan Rosener on 6 November 1888 in Ste. Genevieve County. Mary was the daughter of Valentine Rosener and Susan Cottner, born 1 August 1866 in French Village, St. Francois County, Missouri. The couple had four sons and six daughters. George died of heat prostration and acute gastro enteritis on 17 July 1936 and Mary died of heart disease on 28 December 1950, both in Ste. Genevieve County, Missouri. They were both buried in the St. Lawrence Cemetery in Lawrenceton, Ste. Genevieve County, Missouri.
- viii. Franciska, 28 January 1862 in Ste. Genevieve County, Missouri. She was baptized on 23 February 1862 in St. Philomena's Catholic Church in Bloomsdale, Ste. Genevieve County. Franciska married Andrew Rendler on 19 September 1887 in Ste. Genevieve, Ste. Genevieve County, Missouri. Andrew was the son of Francis Rendler and Agnes Laible. [See Andrew Rendler sketch.]
- ix. Peter, born 13 February 1864 in Ste. Genevieve County, Missouri. He was baptized on 13 March 1864 in St. Philomena's Catholic Church in Bloomsdale, Ste. Genevieve County. Peter was a farmer. He had bought a farm near Lawrenceton from his uncle, George Sellinger. Peter married Mary Helena "Ellen" Werner on 3 October 1894 in Lawrenceton, Ste. Genevieve County. Ellen was the daughter of George Marx Werner and Maria Philippine Guethle, born 26 November 1869 in Ste. Genevieve County, Missouri. The couple had four sons and two daughters, of whom one daughter died in infancy. Their oldest son, George, was killed in action in France during World War I. The Ste. Genevieve Buchholtz-Kiefer American Legion Post No. 150 was named partly in his honor. Ellen died of cardio vascular renal disease on 27 November 1927 in St. Louis, Missouri. Peter died of coronary thrombosis and acute diarrhea on 29 August 1949 in St. Francois County, Missouri. They were both buried in the St. Lawrence Cemetery in Lawrenceton, Ste. Genevieve County, Missouri.
- x. Charles, born 25 April 1866 in Ste. Genevieve County, Missouri. He married Mary Elisabeth Braun on 21 November 1899 in Weingarten, Ste. Genevieve County, Missouri. Elisabeth was the daughter of Franz Anton "Frank" Braun and Catherine Doll, born 3 March 1878 in Ste. Genevieve County, Missouri. The couple had five sons and four daughters. Charles died of a cerebral hemorrhage on 22 January 1926 and Elisabeth died in an automobile accident on 2 December 1930, both in Ste. Genevieve County. They were both buried in the Sacred Heart Cemetery in Ozora, Ste. Genevieve County.
- xi. Mary Philippine, born 15 March 1870 in Ste. Genevieve County, Missouri. She never married.

Mary lived with her brother Lawrence until at least 1920. No further information.
- xii. Lawrence, born 15 March 1872 in Ste. Genevieve County, Missouri. He was a farmer. Lawrence never married and had no known issue. He died of apoplexy on 8 July 1949 in Missouri. He was buried in the St. Lawrence Cemetery in Lawrenceton, Ste. Genevieve County, Missouri.

Land Patents:
Ste. Genevieve County, Missouri

Patentee	Issue Date	Land Office	Cert. No.	Serial No.	Twp	Rng	Sec	Acres
Buckholtz, Moritz	10 Jun 1857	St. Louis	28472	MO1080_.362	38-N	7-E	17	293.46

Naturalization:

Name	Declaration	Naturalization	Origin
Buchholz, Morris	17 June 1856	5 November 1863 Ste. Genevieve Co.	Baden

Military:
Served in the U.S. Civil War for the Union:
Private, Company F, 78th Enrolled Missouri Militia
  Wendelin Buckholz enlisted 30 April 1864 in Ste. Genevieve County, Missouri. He was ordered into active service on 16 October 1864. He was relieved from duty on 25 November 1864 after having served 41 days of actual service.

Education: Could read and write and speak English
Occupation: Farmer
Religious Affiliation: Roman Catholic
Comments:
Morris Buchholtz was born in Baden, Germany. He married a woman named Eva _____ in Germany and had at least four children with her. He and his family came to the United States aboard the *Brunswick* in 1853. Some time between June 1852 and July 1856, Morris' three daughters either died or otherwise disappeared, possibly before the family settled in Ste. Genevieve County, Missouri. Eva died in 1854 in Ste. Genevieve County, Misouri. Morris bought land in the northern part of Ste. Genevieve County and began to farm. He married Elisabeth Sellinger in 1856 in Bloomsdale, Ste. Genevieve County, Missouri. His son from his first marriage, Franz Wendelin, remained in his household until 1869. Morris and Elisabeth had five sons and three daughters. Morris died on 23 September 1902 in Ste. Genevieve County, Missouri. Elisabeth died on 5 November 1918, after she had fallen and severely injured her back and hip. Her date of death is incorrect on her tombstone. They were both buried the St. Lawrence Cemetery in Lawrenceton, Ste. Genevieve County, Missouri.

Francis Charles Buehler Family
Surname Variations: Beehler, Behler, Biehler, Bieler, Biler, Bueler, Bühler
European Origin: Sasbach, Achern, Baden, Germany
Family:
Father: Georg Bühler
Mother: Maria Anna Eisenmann
  Children:
- i. Leopold, born 15 November 1821 in Sasbach, Achern, Baden, Germany. He married Rosalia Schnurr on 29 July 1844 in Sasbach. Rosalia was the daughter of Johann Evangelist Schnurr and Rosalia Röck, born 1 June 1824 in Sasbach. Their son, Anton, came to Ste. Genevieve County, Missouri before June 1874. He married Magdalena Decker in Ste. Genevieve County on 4 November 1874 in Ste. Genevieve County, but there is no further mention of this couple after the record of their marriage.
- ii. Joseph, born 19 January 1823 in Sasbach, Achern, Baden, Germany.

	iii.	Franz Karl "Charles," born 19 January 1826 in Sasbach, Achern, Baden, Germany. [See sketch below.]
	iv.	Eduard, born 16 April 1828 in Sasbach, Achern, Baden, Germany.
	v.	Arnold Willibald, born 7 July 1830 in Sasbach, Achern, Baden, Germany.
†	vi.	Herman, born 7 July 1833 in Sasbach, Achern, Baden, Germany. [See Herman Buehler sketch.]

Immigration:
Arrived some time before the 1850 census aboard an unknown vessel:
    Buehler, Franz Karl

Biographical:
Husband: Franz Karl "Charles" Buehler
    Birth – 19 January 1826 in Sasbach, Achern, Baden, Germany.
    Death/Burial – 5 February 1882 in Ste. Genevieve County, Missouri. He was buried in the Valle
        Spring Cemetery in Ste. Genevieve, Ste. Genevieve County, Missouri.
1) Wife: Mathilda Schaaf, daughter of Wolfgang Schaaf and Magdalena Schmiederer [See Wilhelm
    "William" Schaaf sketch.]
    Birth – 19 March 1828 in Önsbach, Baden, Germany.
    Marriage – 13 May 1850 in Zell, Ste. Genevieve County, Missouri.
    Death/Burial – about 1863, most likely in Missouri.
    Children:
        i. Charles A. , born about 1861 in Missouri. He married Josephine Lohmann on 6 October 1885 in St. Louis, Missouri. Josephine was the daughter of William Lohmann and Josephine Kauflin, born 21 December 1865 in St. Louis, Missouri. The couple had one son and one daughter. Charles died of pneumonia on 26 December 1898 in St. Louis. He was buried in St. Matthew Cemetery in St. Louis, Missouri. After her husband's death, Josephine and her two children lived with her mother's family. Her widowed brother-in-law, William E. Buehler, was also living in the house with his two daughters. Josephine married Charles' younger brother, William Buehler, as her second husband in 1901 in St. Louis, Missouri.
        ii. Josephine, born about 1862 in Missouri. She died on 9 June 1862 in Ste. Genevieve County, Missouri. She was buried in the St. Joseph Cemetery in Zell, Ste. Genevieve County, Missouri. No issue.

2) Wife: Pauline Graf[f], daughter of Fidel Graf and Elisabeth Heidel [See Fidel Graf sketch.]
    Birth – 1 August 1842 in Baden, Germany.
    Marriage – 9 April 1864 in St. Louis, Missouri.
    Death/Burial – 9 March 1922 in Ste. Genevieve County, Missouri. She was buried in the Valle Spring
        Cemetery in Ste. Genevieve, Ste. Genevieve County, Missouri.
    Children:
        iii. Pauline Elisabeth, born 5 January 1865 in Ste. Genevieve County, Missouri. She was baptized on 17 February 1865 in the Ste. Genevieve Catholic Church in Ste. Genevieve, Ste. Genevieve County, Missouri. Pauline died on 29 June 1865 in Ste. Genevieve County. She was buried in the Memorial Cemetery in Ste. Genevieve, Ste. Genevieve County, Missouri. No issue.
        iv. Joseph, born 26 October 1866 in Ste. Genevieve County, Missouri. He was baptized on 7 April 1867 in the Ste. Genevieve Catholic Church in Ste. Genevieve, Ste. Genevieve County, Missouri. Joseph was a butcher. He married Wilhelmina Bertha "Minnie" Schroeder [Schraeder?] on 8 May 1889 in Ste. Genevieve County, Missouri. Minnie was the daughter of Henry Schroeder and Mary Ann Hering, born 5 April 1866 in Cape Girardeau County, Missouri. The couple had two sons and two daughters, of whom one son died in infancy. They also adopted a nephew, William Engelmeier. Minnie died of apoplexy on 26 April 1939 in Perryville, Perry County, Missouri. Joseph died on 12 April 1953 in Perryville, Perry County, Missouri, of cerebral thrombosis and a broken femur he had sustained when he fell three weeks prior to his

death. They were both buried in the St. Boniface Cemetery in Perryville, Perry County, Missouri.
- v. Mary, born 15 August 1868 in Ste. Genevieve County, Missouri. She was baptized on 24 November 1868 in the Ste. Genevieve Catholic Church in Ste. Genevieve, Ste. Genevieve County, Missouri. Mary died on 8 August 1870 in Ste. Genevieve County. She was buried in the Memorial Cemetery in Ste. Genevieve, Ste. Genevieve County, Missouri. No issue.
- vi. Emily Sophia "Emma," born 6 November 1869 in Ste. Genevieve County, Missouri. She was baptized on 9 January 1870 in the Ste. Genevieve Catholic Church in Ste. Genevieve, Ste. Genevieve County, Missouri. Emma died on 19 July 1870 in Ste. Genevieve County. She was buried in the Memorial Cemetery in Ste. Genevieve, Ste. Genevieve County, Missouri. No issue.
- vii. William E., born 25 November 1871 in Ste. Genevieve County, Missouri. He was baptized on 14 April 1872 in the Ste. Genevieve Catholic Church in Ste. Genevieve, Ste. Genevieve County, Missouri. William was a butcher. He married Mary Lohmann on 24 May 1893 in St. Louis, Missouri. Mary was the daughter of William Lohmann, also a butcher, and Josephine Kauflin, born 19 July 1972 in St. Louis, Missouri. The couple had two daughters. Mary died of spinal meningitis on 18 May 1899 in St. Louis. She was buried in the St. Matthew Cemetery in St. Louis, Missouri. After his wife's death, William and his two daughters lived with his wife's parents. He married Josephine Lohmann Buehler, the widow of his half-brother, Charles, in 1901 in St. Louis. The couple had no children together, but raised their combined family of four children in St. Louis. William died of a septic abscess on 4 December 1915 and Josephine died of heart disease and chronic interstitial nephritis on 16 April 1934, both in St. Louis. They were both buried in the St. Matthew Cemetery in St. Louis, Missouri.
- viii. Julius, born 12 April 1874 in Ste. Genevieve County, Missouri. He was baptized on 24 May 1874 in the Ste. Genevieve Catholic Church in Ste. Genevieve, Ste. Genevieve County, Missouri. Julius died on 2 August 1875 in Ste. Genevieve County. He was buried in the Memorial Cemetery in Ste. Genevieve, Ste. Genevieve County, Missouri. No issue.
- ix. Pauline Amelia "Lena," born 18 September 1875 in Ste. Genevieve County, Missouri. She was baptized on 6 February 1876 in the Ste. Genevieve Catholic Church in Ste. Genevieve, Ste. Genevieve County, Missouri. Lena married Peter Edward Hipes on 20 October 1896 in St. Louis, Missouri. Peter was the son of Bartholomew "Bartley" Hipes and Mary Benham, born 25 March 1872 in Ste. Genevieve County, Missouri. The couple had five sons and two daughters, of whom one son died in infancy. Peter died of heart disease on 15 November 1941 in Ste. Genevieve County and Lena died of vascular disease on 9 August 1959 in Crystal City, Jefferson County, Missouri.
- x. Edward, born 13 August 1880 in Ste. Genevieve County, Missouri. He was baptized on 31 October 1880 in the Ste. Genevieve Catholic Church in Ste. Genevieve, Ste. Genevieve County, Missouri. Edward died of malarial fever on 25 January 1883 in Ste. Genevieve County, Missouri. He was buried in the Valle Spring Cemetery in Ste. Genevieve, Ste. Genevieve County, Missouri. No issue.

Naturalization:

Name	Declaration	Naturalization	Origin
Buehler, Charles	16 May 1853	24 May 1855 Ste. Genevieve Co.	Baden

Education: Could read and write
Occupation: Shoemaker, Butcher
Religious Affiliation: Roman Catholic
Comments:
Franz Karl "Charles" Buehler was born in Sasbach, Achern, Baden, Germany, and came to the United States as a young man, about 1850. He and his younger brother, Herman, settled in Ste. Genevieve County, Missouri.

Charles may have been trained as a shoemaker in Germany, but once he settled in Ste. Genevieve County, he became a butcher. He was married twice. His first wife was Mathilda Schaaf who he married shortly after his arrival in Ste. Genevieve County. The couple had at least one son and one daughter, and possibly other children, of whom only one son survived. Mathilda died between 1862 and mid-1863, most likely in Missouri. Charles married Pauline Graf[f] as his second wife. Charles and Pauline had four sons and four daughters, of whom two sons and three daughters died in infancy or early childhood. Charles died suddenly on 5 February 1882 in Ste. Genevieve. Pauline died of cardiac incompetency and arteriosclerosis on 9 March 1922 in Ste. Genevieve County, Missouri. They were both buried in the Valle Spring Cemetery in Ste. Genevieve, Ste. Genevieve County, Missouri.

Herman Buehler Family
Surname Variations: Beehler, Behler, Biehler, Biler, Bueler, Bühler
European Origin: Sasbach, Achern, Baden, Germany
Family:
Father: Georg Bühler
Mother: Maria Anna Eisenmann
  Children:

Note: For a comprehensive discussion of Georg Bühler's children see the Francis Charles Buehler sketch.

Immigration:
Arrived 5 May 1853 from London, England to New York aboard the *Patrick Henry*:
   Biler [Buehler], Herman, 19   copper smith   from Germany

Biographical:
Husband: Herman Buehler
   Birth – 7 July 1833 in Sasbach, Achern, Baden, Germany.
   Death/Burial – 13 February 1901 in Ste. Genevieve County, Missouri. He was buried in the Valle Spring Cemetery in Ste. Genevieve, Ste. Genevieve County, Missouri.
Wife: Amelia "Emily" Roth, daughter of Franz Joseph Roth and Maria Anna Kunz [See Franz Joseph Roth sketch.]
   Birth – 30 November 1836 in New York.
   Marriage – 19 February 1855 in Zell, Ste. Genevieve County, Missouri.
   Death/Burial – 3 August 1901 in Ste. Genevieve County, Missouri. She was buried in the Valle Spring Cemetery in Ste. Genevieve, Ste. Genevieve County, Missouri.
   Children:
   i. Louisa, born 16 November 1855 in Missouri. She married Conrad Yeagle on 3 October 1888 in Ste. Genevieve County, Missouri. He was a farmer. Conrad was the son of Henry Yeagle and Elisabeth Singer, born about 1856 in Missouri. [See Conrad Yeagle sketch.] Louisa married Joseph Doll as her second husband on 27 November 1895 in St. Mary, Ste. Genevieve County. Joseph was the son of Joseph Doll and Frances Klumpp, born 30 April 1862 in Ste. Genevieve County, Missouri. [See Joseph Doll sketch.]
   ii. Pauline, born 31 December 1857 in Missouri. No further information.
   iii. Rosina, born 22 January 1861 in Missouri. She died on 13 February 1866 in Ste. Genevieve County. She was buried in the Memorial Cemetery in Ste. Genevieve, Ste. Genevieve County, Missouri. No issue.
   iv. Henry Herman, born 1 June 1863 in Ste. Genevieve County, Missouri. He was baptized on 5 July 1863 in the Ste. Genevieve Catholic Church in Ste. Genevieve, Ste. Genevieve County, Missouri. Henry fell on a log during the winter of 1885 and his abdomen was punctured by a large splinter. He never complained or told his family of the injury, but his health gradually began to fail. He died of the internal injuries he received in the fall on 11 July 1886 in Ste. Genevieve County, Missouri. He never married and had no known issue.

- v. Mary Ann Elisabeth, born 27 October 1866 in Ste. Genevieve County, Missouri. She was baptized on 6 January 1867 in the Ste. Genevieve Catholic Church in Ste. Genevieve, Ste. Genevieve County, Missouri. She married Joseph Henry Meyers on 25 October 1887 in St. Mary, Ste. Genevieve County. Joseph was the son of John Meyers and Genevieve Palmer. [See John Christian Meyers sketch.]
- vi. Philomena Josephine, born 22 October 1869 in Ste. Genevieve County, Missouri. She was baptized on 21 November 1869 in the Ste. Genevieve Catholic Church in Ste. Genevieve, Ste. Genevieve County, Missouri. No further information.
- vii. John George, born 14 May 1873 in Ste. Genevieve County, Missouri. He was baptized on 25 May 1873 in the Ste. Genevieve Catholic Church in Ste. Genevieve, Ste. Genevieve County, Missouri. He was a farmer. John married Anna Catherine Armbruster on 8 January 1895 in Ste. Genevieve. Catherine was the daughter of Mathias Armbruster and Christina Wieberg, born 31 July 1871 in Ste. Genevieve County, Missouri. The couple had six sons and four daughters, of whom one son died in infancy. Catherine died of a heart attack on 15 March 1958 and John died of general heart disease and pernicious anemia on 2 April 1959, both in Ste. Genevieve County. They were both buried in the Valle Spring Cemetery in Ste. Genevieve, Ste. Genevieve County, Missouri.
- viii. Charles Francis, born 21 March 1875 in Ste. Genevieve County, Missouri. He was baptized on 22 April 1877 in the Ste. Genevieve Catholic Church in Ste. Genevieve, Ste. Genevieve County, Missouri. He married Elizabeth Veronica Wieberg on 31 July 1900 in Ozora, Ste. Genevieve County. Veronica was the daughter of Nicholas Wieberg and Veronica Siebert, born 17 July 1883 in Ste. Genevieve County. Shortly after they were married, Charles moved his family to St. Louis, Missouri, where he first worked as a city forester, trimming trees. He later went into the hauling business, driving a truck. The couple had one son and four daughters. Charles died of metastatic carcinoma of the liver on 19 September 1938 in St. Louis, Missouri. Veronica died on 23 August 1967. They were both buried in the Park Lawn Cemetery in St. Louis, Missouri.

Naturalization:

Name	Declaration	Naturalization	Origin
Behler, Herman	14 June 1858 Ste. Genevieve Co.	10 November 1860 Ste. Genevieve Co.	Baden

Military:
Served in the U.S. Civil War for the Union:
Private, Company G, 78th Enrolled Missouri Militia
  Herman Behler enlisted on 30 April 1864 in Ste. Genevieve, Missouri. He was ordered into active service on 16 November 1864. He was relieved from duty on 25 November 1864 after having served 10 days of actual service.

Education: Could read and write
Occupation: Farmer
Religious Affiliation: Roman Catholic
Comments:
Herman Buehler was born in Sasbach, Achern, Baden, Germany, and came to the United States as a young man. He may have been trained as a copper smith in Germany, but once he settled in Ste. Genevieve County, he became a farmer. Herman married Amelia Roth whose family had also come to America from Sasbach. Herman settled in the southern part of Ste. Genevieve County, near the town of St. Mary. The couple had three sons and five daughters, of whom three daughters died in infancy or early childhood. During the Civil War, Herman served in the 78th Enrolled Missouri Militia as a private in Company G. He also applied to the Union Provost Marshall for a permit to sell and keep wine and liquors, but not to sell to soldiers. Herman died on 13

February 1901 and Amelia died on 3 August 1901, both in Ste. Genevieve County, Missouri. They were both buried in the Valle Spring Cemetery in Ste. Genevieve, Ste. Genevieve County, Missouri.

Joseph Buehler Family
Surname Variations: Beehler, Bühler
European Origin: Gamshurst, Baden, Germany
Family:
Father: Joseph Bühler, born 29 January 1777 in Gamshurst, Baden, Germany. He died on 12 January 1840 in Gamshurst.
Mother: Isabella Weis, born 7 June 1787 Gamshurst, Baden, Germany. She died on 20 January 1848 in Gamshurst.
Children:
  i. Maria Anna, born 14 May 1811 in Gamshurst, Baden, Germany. She died on 14 May 1811 in Gamshurst. No issue.
  ii. Nikolaus [aka Nicholas Beehler], born 15 May 1813 in Gamshurst, Baden, Germany. He was a farmer. Nicholas married Amalia Brunner on 15 February 1841 in Gamshurst. Amalia was the daughter of Felix Brunner and Maria Antonia Scheer, born 28 September 1820 in Gamshurst. The couple had five sons and two daughters, all born in Gamshurst. Nicholas moved his family to Ontario, Canada in the fall of 1854. Once they arrived in Canada, the family surname evolved into "Beehler," the name by which most of their descendants are known. In October 1870, Nicholas purchased a 50-acre farm near the town of Connaught, Ontario. The farm was sold in July 1895 when Amelia became ill and the couple took up residence with their son in Crysler, Stormont, Ontario. Amalia died 5 October 1895 and Nicholas died on 26 September 1899, both in Crysler, Ontario, Canada. They were both buried in the St. Mary Catholic Cemetery in Crysler.
  iii. Viktor, born 12 March 1815 in Gamshurst, Baden, Germany. He was a weaver. Viktor married Rosamunda Meyer on 6 December 1837 in Gamshurst. Rosamunda was the daughter of Franz Anton Meyer and Magdalena Weis, born 28 September 1818 in Gamshurst. The couple had one daughter. Viktor died on 15 July 1839 in Gamshurst. Rosamunda married for a second time to Nikolaus Schmitt on 6 May 1841 in Gamshurst and had one son and two daughters with him.
  iv. Ignaz, born 9 December 1817 in Gamshurst, Baden, Germany. He was a farmer. Ignaz married Regina Allgeier on 6 February 1843 in Gamshurst. Regina was the daughter of Joseph Allgeier and Maria Elisabetha Weis, born 30 June 1819 in Gamshurst. The couple had three sons and one daughter, of whom the youngest son and daughter died in infancy. Regina died giving birth to her fourth child on 2 October 1847 in Gamshurst. Ignaz married Elisabetha Köppel as his second wife on 11 February 1850 in Gamshurst. Elisabetha was the daughter of Sylvester Köppel and Catharina Mundi, born about 1818 in Oberachern, Baden, Germany. The couple had four sons, of whom two died in infancy. All of Ignaz's surviving sons eventually moved to America. Ignaz died on 19 February 1865 and Elisabetha died on 13 December 1867, both in Gamshurst.
  v. Alois [twin], born 22 August 1819 in Gamshurst, Baden, Germany. Alois died on 20 April 1848 in Gamshurst. He never married and had no known issue.
* vi. Joseph [twin], born 22 August 1819 in Gamshurst, Baden, Germany. [See sketch below.]
‡ vii. Kornelius [aka Cornelius], born 16 September 1821 in Gamshurst, Baden, Germany. He came to the United States about 1846. Cornelius worked as a drayman and general laborer in New Orleans, Orleans Parish, Louisiana. He married Anastasia Ruschmann about 1846 in Louisiana. Anastasia was born about 1825 in Germany. The couple had two sons and one daughter. Anastasia died in 1853 in New Orleans. Cornelius married Anna Maria Hans as his second wife about 1856 in Louisiana. Anna Maria was the daughter of Georg Jacob Hans and Barbara Endres, born 10 January 1833 in Germersheim, Langenkandel, Bayern, Germany. She had come to the United States with her parents about 1849. Cornelius and Anna Maria had five sons and seven daughters. Cornelius died on 9 February 1892 and Anna Maria died on 27 March

1901, both in New Orleans, Orleans Parish, Louisiana.

‡ viii. Theresia, born 21 October 1823 in Gamshurst, Baden, Germany. She is said to have died in 1890 in the United States. No further information.

ix. Katharina, born 26 February 1826 in Gamshurst, Baden, Germany. No further information.

x. Stillborn Child, born and died on 20 June 1828 in Gamshurst, Baden, Germany.

‡ xi. Leopold, born 25 October 1830 in Gamshurst, Baden, Germany. He was a furniture mover. Leopold married Elisabeth Mohr on 19 October 1856 in St. Louis, Missouri. Elisabeth was born about 1837 in Germany. The couple had three sons and two daughters. Leopold died of an acute bladder infection on 27 November 1889 in St. Louis, Missouri. He was buried in the Holy Ghost Cemetery in St. Louis, Missouri. Elisabeth may have remarried. She is said to have died about 1910.

xii. Adelgunde, born 30 January 1831 in Gamshurst, Baden, Germany. She died on 11 April 1834 in Gamshurst. No issue.

Immigration:
Arrived some time before July 1863 aboard an unknown vessel:
   Buehler, Joseph

Biographical:
Husband: Joseph Buehler
   Birth – 22 August 1819 in Gamshurst, Baden, Germany.
   Death/Burial – 28 October 1873 in Ste. Genevieve County, Missouri. He was buried in the Memorial Cemetery in Ste. Genevieve, Ste. Genevieve County, Missouri.
Wife: Catherine Schnurr, daughter of Anton Schnurr and Rosalia Godfried
   Birth – 1 December 1834 in France.
   1) Marriage – 10 March 1855 in St. Louis, Missouri to Paul Hoffman. [See Paul Peter Hoffman sketch.]
   2) Marriage – 13 July 1863 in Ste. Genevieve, Ste. Genevieve County, Missouri to Joseph Buehler.
   3) Marriage – 4 October 1875 in Ste. Genevieve County, Missouri to Leopold Winter. [See Leopold Winter sketch.]
   Death/Burial – 19 November 1907 in Ste. Genevieve County, Missouri. She was buried in the St. Mary Cemetery in St. Mary, Ste. Genevieve County, Missouri.
   Children:
      i. Louise Wilhelmina Mary "Mina," born 1 October 1864 in Ste. Genevieve County. She was baptized on 16 October 1864 in the Ste. Genevieve Catholic Church in Ste. Genevieve, Ste. Genevieve County, Missouri. Wilhelmina married Henry Ignatius Kohm on 11 June 1889 in St. Mary. Henry was the son of Franz "Frank" Kohm and Bertha Klein, born 17 December 1865 in Ste. Genevieve County, Missouri. [See Franz "Frank" Kohm sketch.]
      ii. Mary Louise Catherine, born 20 October 1869 in Ste. Genevieve County. She was baptized on 7 November 1869 in the Ste. Genevieve Catholic Church in Ste. Genevieve, Ste. Genevieve County, Missouri. Louise married Herman Gerhardt Roseman on 3 February 1892 in St. Mary, Ste. Genevieve County. Herman was the son of Heinrich "Henry" Roseman and Anna Margaretha Leiner, born 23 May 1860 in Sparta, Randolph County, Illinois. [See Heinrich Roseman sketch.]

Military:
Served in the U.S. Civil War for the Union:
Private, Company G, 78th Enrolled Missouri Militia
   Joseph Behler enlisted on 30 April 1864 in Ste. Genevieve, Missouri. He was ordered into active service on 5 November 1864. He was relieved from duty on 25 November 1864 after having served 21 days of actual service.

Occupation: General laborer
Religious Affiliation: Roman Catholic
Comments:
Joseph Buehler was born in Gamshurst, Baden, Germany. As a young man, he came to the United States and appears to have traveled directly to Ste. Genevieve County, Missouri, about 1858. Several of his siblings also came to North America, but only one other brother settled in Missouri. Joseph married Catherine Hoffman, the widow of Paul Peter Hoffman, on 13 July 1863 in Ste. Genevieve, Ste. Genevieve County. Catherine had two sons and a daughter from her first marriage and she and Joseph had two more daughters together. During the Civil War, Joseph served as a private in Company G of the 78th Enrolled Missouri Militia. Joseph died at the age of 54 years on 28 October 1873 in Ste. Genevieve County, Missouri. He was buried in the Memorial Cemetery in Ste. Genevieve, Ste. Genevieve County, Missouri.

Adam Buenniger Family
Surname Variations: Ben[n]iger, Bineger, Boenniger, Bon[n]iger, Bönniger Bonniker, Buenneger
European Origin: [Nidfurn, Canton Glarus], Switzerland
Family:
Father: Balthasar Bönniger, born 28 June 1823 in [Nidfurn, Canton Glarus], Switzerland. He is said to have
   died on 16 December 1861 in St. Louis, Missouri.
Mother: Elsabeth Weber, born 9 July 1820 in [Netsal, Canton Glarus], Switzerland. She is said to have died on
   26 April 1895 in Ste. Genevieve County, Missouri. [See Christian Jacobs sketch for her second marriage.]
   Child:
* i. Adam, born in May 1858 in Switzerland. [See sketch below.]

Immigration:
Arrived 6 May 1861 from Le Havre, France to New York aboard the *Havre*:
    Boniger, Adam, 23   Switzerland   [relative of Balthasar?]
    Boniger, Balthasar, 37   Switzerland
        Elisabeth, 41
        Adam, 2

Biographical:
Husband: Adam Buenniger
   Birth – May 1858 in Switzerland
   Death/Burial – mid-December 1901 in Kinsey, Ste. Genevieve County, Missouri.
1) Wife: Lydia Bodner [aka Bodmer]
   Birth – about 1860 in Missouri
   Marriage – 22 May 1879 in Ste. Genevieve County, Missouri.
   Death/Burial – 31 July 1899 in Kinsey, Ste. Genevieve County, Missouri.
   Children:
   i. Elsabeth, born 12 May 1881 in Ste. Genevieve County, Missouri. She married Charles
      Frederick "Carl" Sewald on 10 February 1902 in Ste. Genevieve County, Missouri. Carl was
      the son of Michael Sewald and Emma Bieser, born 30 August 1878 in Ste. Genevieve County,
      Missouri. [See Michael Sewald sketch.]
   ii. Mary, born 20 November 1883 in Ste. Genevieve County, Missouri. She married Andrew Elias
      Sewald on 16 November 1904 in Ste. Genevieve County, Missouri. Andrew was the son of
      Michael Sewald and Emma Bieser, born 16 December 1880 in Ste. Genevieve County,
      Missouri. [See Michael Sewald sketch.]
   iii. Christian John, born 4 April 1886 in Ste. Genevieve County, Missouri. He was a farmer at the
      time of his marriage. He later went into partnership with his Sewald brothers-in-law in their
      butcher shop in Festus, Jefferson County, Missouri. He married Mary Ann Sewald on
      7 February 1911 in Jefferson County, Missouri. Mary was the daughter of Valentine Sewald

and Caroline Trautmann, born 10 December 1884 in Missouri. The couple had three sons and one daughter. Christian died of chronic myocarditis on 30 August 1945 in Festus, Jefferson County, Missouri. Mary died in April 1978 in Festus, Jefferson County, Missouri.

    iv. Edward Adam, born 21 September 1888 in Ste. Genevieve County, Missouri. Edward died of phthisis pulmonalis [consumption] on 8 October 1913 in Carondelet, St. Louis County, Missouri. He never married and had no known issue.

    v. Lydia E. , born 6 January1891 in Ste. Genevieve County, Missouri. As a young woman, Lydia began her working life as a domestic servant for a family in St. Louis, Missouri. By 1920, she had moved to Chicago, Cook County, Illinois where she worked as a clerk for a packing company. By 1930, she had moved to Bronx, New York where she was an office manager for an insurance company. Lydia died of coronary thrombosis on 13 October 1957 in Festus, Jefferson County, Missouri. She was buried in the Sacred Heart Catholic Cemetery in Crystal City, Jefferson County, Missouri. Lydia never married and had no known issue.

    vi. Hobart George [twin] , born 11 September 1897 in Ste. Genevieve County, Missouri. He lived with his sister Elsabeth and her family in Jefferson County, Missouri. He worked for a while in the Pittsburgh Plate Glass company as a laborer and then worked as a butcher in a slaughter-house in Festus. Hobart died of a cerebral hemorrhage on 6 June 1958 in Jefferson County, Missouri. He was buried in the Sacred Heart Catholic Cemetery in Crystal City, Jefferson County, Missouri. He never married and had no known issue.

    vii. Garfield [twin] , born and died on 11 September 1897 in Ste. Genevieve County, Missouri. No issue.

2) Wife: Elizabeth Jane "Eliza" Reed, daughter of James Reed and Christine Petrie
Birth – January 1864 in Ste. Genevieve County, Missouri.
1) Marriage – 21 April 1885 in French Village, St. Francois County, Missouri to Richard J. Bockenkamp. [See Herman Bockenkamp sketch.]
2) Marriage – 14 October 1900 in Ste. Genevieve County, Missouri to Adam Buenniger.
Death/Burial – 5 September 1941 in St. Louis, Missouri. She was buried in the Sunset Memorial Park and Mausoleum in Affton, St. Louis County, Missouri.

There were no children from the marriage between Adam Buenniger and Eliza Reed.

U.S. residence prior to Ste. Genevieve County, Missouri:
Possibly St. Louis, Missouri.

Naturalization:

Name	Declaration	Naturalization	Origin	Remarks
Buenniger, Adam			Switzerland	1900 Census

Military:
Served in the U.S. Civil War for the Union:
Private, Company K, 2nd Regiment, U.S. Reserve Corps, Missouri Infantry
    Balzer Bonniker [aka Balz, Balzer, Balthaser Bonninger] is said to have died of cholera on 16 December 1861 in St. Louis, Missouri.
Private, Company I, 40th Missouri Volunteer Infantry
    Adam Bueniger [aka Adam Benecke, Boenecke, Boeneger] enlisted on 31 August 1864 in St. Louis, Missouri. He died of typhoid fever on 12 October 1864 at the P.H. Schofield Barracks in St. Louis, Missouri.

Education: Could read and write.
Occupation: Farmer / Saw mill operator
Religious Affiliation: Unknown

Comments:
Adam Buenniger came to the United States from Switzerland with his parents when he was two years of age. A young man, also named Adam Buenniger, appears to have come with them and may have been a relative. The family settled in Missouri and both Adam's father, Balthasar, and Adam Buenniger enlisted in the Union Army. Ironically, they both lost their lives to disease rather than to wounds. Adam's mother Elsabeth married Christian Jacobs as her second husband some time between 1861 and 1870. By 1870, the family had settled in northern Ste. Genevieve County, Missouri where Christian bought a farm. Adam married Lydia Bodner in 1879 in Ste. Genevieve County and the young couple lived with Adam's parents on their farm. They had four sons and three daughters, of whom one son was stillborn. The family appears to have been plagued by some bad luck. On the afternoon of 8 May 1883, a fire broke out in the Buenniger home and quickly spread to the outbuildings. The house, a barn and a smokehouse were a complete loss. The buildings were insured, but all of their furnishings, tools and personal belongings were lost. Later that same year, Adam's stepfather, Christian Jacobs, cut his foot so severely that he almost bled to death. Adam married Mrs. Elizabeth Jane "Eliza" Bockenkamp as his second wife in 1900. She was the widow of Richard J. Bockenkamp. Adam died just over a year later of typhoid fever in mid-December 1901. He was buried beside is first wife in the Kinsey Cemetery in Kinsey, Ste. Genevieve County, Missouri. By 1910, Eliza had moved to St. Louis with her children from her first marriage. She died of myocarditis on 5 September 1941 in St. Louis, Missouri. She was buried in the Sunset Memorial Park and Mausoleum in Affton, St. Louis County, Missouri.

Bartholomew Burgert Family
Surname Variations: Burget[t], Burkert
European Origin: Rammersweier, Baden, Germany
Family:
Father: Joseph Burgert, born 18 March 1785 in Rammersweier, Baden, Germany. He died on 29 August 1817 in Weingarten, Baden, Germany.
Mother: Genovefa Berger, born 19 May 1791 in Rammersweier, Baden, Germany. She died on 25 March 1840 in Rammersweier.
    Child:
*   i. Bartholomaus, born 2 October 1814 in Rammersweier, Baden, Germany. [See sketch below.]

Immigration:
Arrived 25 January 1854 from Le Havre, France to New Orleans aboard the *Rome*:
    Burgert, Bartholomé, 38
        Victoire, 40
        Joseph, 9
        Sophie, 8
        Charles, 6
        Gustav, 3

Biographical:
Husband: Bartholomew Burgert
  Birth – 2 October 1814 in Rammersweier, Baden, Germany.
  Death/Burial – 7 February 1888 in Ste. Genevieve County, Missouri. He was buried in the Valle Spring Cemetery in Ste. Genevieve, Ste. Genevieve County, Missouri.
Wife: Victoria Busam, daughter of Johann Evangelist Karl Busam and Maria Ursula Fey
  Birth – 31 August 1811 in Rammersweier, Baden, Germany.
  Marriage – 17 May 1842 in Weingarten, Baden, Germany.
  Death/Burial – 18 December 1895 in Ste. Genevieve County, Missouri. She was buried in the Valle Spring Cemetery in Ste. Genevieve, Ste. Genevieve County, Missouri.
  Children:

i. Joseph, born 1 March 1843 in Rammersweier, Baden, Germany. He was a farmer. Joseph served as a private in Company F of the 78th Enrolled Missouri Militia during the Civil War. In August 1863, he was temporarily assigned to Company G of the 8th Provisional Regiment Enrolled Missouri Militia. The unit was given the task of putting down protests of Confederate sympathizers in the Missouri boot heel. Joseph was released from active service in November 1863. After the war, Joseph resumed his life as a farmer in Ste. Genevieve County. He married Clara Trautmann on 8 February 1875. Clara was the daughter of Peter Paul Trautmann and Monica Fallert, born 28 November 1852 in Ste. Genevieve County, Missouri. The couple had one son and six daughters, of whom two daughters died in infancy. Clara died of apoplexy on 14 May 1910 in Ste. Genevieve County. On the afternoon of 11 June 1918, just a few weeks after his brother Gustave's death, Joseph drove his wagon into the path of an oncoming train at a crossing on the west side of Ste. Genevieve. He apparently either didn't hear or notice the danger. One of his mules was killed outright and the other was badly injured. Joseph was thrown about thirty feet and suffered a broken arm and severe trauma to his head and back. He died of his injuries on 17 June 1918. Joseph and his wife were both buried in the Valle Spring Cemetery in Ste. Genevieve, Ste. Genevieve County, Missouri.

ii. Sophia, born in 1845 in Rammersweier, Baden, Germany. She married Valerian Gisi as his second wife on 16 January 1866 in Ste. Genevieve County, Missouri. Valerian was the son of Joseph Gisi and Barbara Goering, born 29 January 1836 in Fessenbach, Baden, Germany. [See Joseph Gisi sketch.]

iii. Charles B., born 17 November 1847 in Rammersweier, Baden, Germany. He was a blacksmith. Charles married Mary Emily Will on 8 October 1878 in Ste. Genevieve County, Missouri. Emily was the daughter of George Will and Catherine Baechle, born 11 February 1859 in Ste. Genevieve County. The couple had two sons and three daughters. Charles died of jaundice and kidney failure on 25 May 1909 in Ste. Genevieve. Emily died of chronic myocarditis on 21 February 1937 in Ste. Genevieve. They were both buried in the Valle Spring Cemetery in Ste. Genevieve, Ste. Genevieve County, Missouri.

iv. Gustav [aka August], born 16 May 1850 in Rammersweier, Baden, Germany. He was a farmer. Gustav married Mary Anna Stuppy on 10 November 1874 in Ste. Genevieve County, Missouri. Mary was the daughter of Jacob Stuppy and Francisca Huck, born 11 April 1855 in Ste. Genevieve County, Missouri. The couple had five sons and four daughters. Gustav died of electrocution on 22 May 1918 in Ste. Genevieve when he stepped on a live wire which had been blown down during a storm. Mary died of chronic nephritis and heart disease on 14 July 1933 in St. Louis, Missouri. They were both buried in Valle Spring Cemetery in Ste. Genevieve, Ste. Genevieve County, Missouri.

Land Patents:
Ste. Genevieve County, Missouri

Patentee	Issue Date	Land Office	Cert. No.	Serial No.	Twp	Rng	Sec	Acres
Burgert, Bart.	10 Apr 1875	Booneville	41969	MO3280_.408	38-N	8-E	24	0.65

Naturalization:

Name	Declaration	Naturalization	Origin
Burgett, Bertholemy	15 May 1854	6 May 1859 Ste. Genevieve Co.	Baden

Military:
Served in the U.S. Civil War for the Union:
Private, Company G, 8th Provisional Regiment Enrolled Missouri Militia
  Joseph Burgert was transferred temporarily from Company F of the 78th Enrolled Missouri Militia on 10 August 1863 in Ste. Genevieve, Missouri. He was relieved from active duty 8 November 1863 by General Fisk.

Education: Could read and write.
Occupation: Tailor and Farmer
Religious Affiliation: Roman Catholic
Comments:
Bartholomew Burgert was born in Rammersweier, Baden, Germany. His father died when he was a small boy and his mother later remarried. He was trained as a tailor as a young man. In 1842 he married Victoria Busam. The couple had three sons and one daughter, all born in Rammersweier. In 1854 Bartholomew moved to the United States with his family, landing in New Orleans, Louisiana where they intended to stay for several weeks to purchase supplies. But somehow they had the misfortune to lose all of their cash, $175 in gold, which had been secured for safe keeping in a leather girdle fastened around Victoria's waist. They arrived in Ste. Genevieve County, Missouri without any money, but with a large supply of clothing and some household items. With a determination to succeed, Bartholomew was slowly able to recover his financial standing. He was a good tailor and quickly obtained employment and worked twelve years for Mr. C. W. Hamm who owned a haberdashery and general store in Ste. Genevieve. Bartholomew also bought land, purchasing a small farm at first, but gradually adding to it until at his death, he possessed between 250 and 300 acres. Bartholomew died of pneumonitis on 7 February 1888 and Victoria died on 18 December 1895, both in Ste. Genevieve County, Missouri. They were both buried in the Valle Spring Cemetery in Ste. Genevieve, Ste. Genevieve County, Missouri.

Karl "Charles" Burgert Family
Surname Variations: Burget[t], Burkert, Burkett
European Origin: Bohlsbach, Baden, Germany
Family:
Father: Joseph Burgert, born 9 February 1780 in Bohlsbach, Baden, Germany. He died on 22 April 1839 in Bohlsbach.
Mother: Genovefa Kempf, born 2 March 1779 in Windschläg, Baden, Germany. She died on 7 February 1858 in Bohlsbach.
Children:
- i. Bartholomew, born 1 May 1808 in Bohlsbach, Baden, Germany. He died on 18 May 1808 in Bohlsbach. No issue.
- ii. Magdalena, born 5 June 1809 in Bohlsbach, Baden, Germany. She died on 8 July 1809 in Bohlsbach. No issue.
- iii. Andreas, born 26 July 1810 in Bohlsbach, Baden, Germany.
† iv. Magdalena, born 1 July 1811 in Bohlsbach, Baden, Germany. She married Joseph Satory on 9 December 1844 in Bohlsbach. Joseph was the son of Joseph Satory and Maria Anna Müller, born 8 February 1819 in Bohlsbach. [See Joseph Satory sketch.]
- v. Karl, born 7 June 1813 in Bohlsbach, Baden, Germany. He died on 5 August 1813 in Bohlsbach. No issue.
† vi. Theresia, born 21 September 1814 in Bohlsbach, Baden, Germany. She married Valentin Basler on 23 September 1839 in Baden, Germany. Valentin was the son of Johann Georg Basler and Walburga Höpf, born 4 February 1813 in Rammersweier, Baden, Germany. [See Theresia Basler sketch.]
- vii. Sophia, born 13 May 1816 in Bohlsbach, Baden, Germany. She died on 12 July 1816 in Bohlsbach. No issue.
- viii. Johannes, born 10 June 1817 in Bohlsbach, Baden, Germany. He died on 19 June 1817 in Bohlsbach. No issue.
- ix. Genovefa, born 13 September 1818 in Bohlsbach, Baden, Germany. She died on 23 May 1819 in Bohlsbach. No issue.
- x. Paul, born 3 March 1820 in Bohlsbach, Baden, Germany. No further information.
- xi. Andreas, born 24 November 1821 in Bohlsbach, Baden, Germany. He died on 9 December 1821 in Bohlsbach. No issue.

xii. Genovefa, born 12 December 1822 in Bohlsbach, Baden, Germany. She died on 19 December 1822 in Bohlsbach. No issue.

xiii. Mathias, born 27 February 1824 in Bohlsbach, Baden, Germany. He died on 5 May 1824 in Bohlsbach. No issue.

* xiv. Karl "Charles," born 29 June 1825 in Bohlsbach, Baden, Germany. [See sketch below.]

xv. Mathias, born 24 February 1827 in Bohlsbach, Baden, Germany. He died on 2 March 1827 in Bohlsbach. No issue.

xvi. Maria Anna, born 16 August 1829 in Bohlsbach, Baden, Germany. She married Theodor Lienert on 25 November 1850 in Bohlsbach. Theodor was the son of Anton Lienert and Cecilia Jokerst, born 30 October 1824 in Bohlsbach. The couple had five sons and six daughters, of whom two sons and one daughter died in infancy. Their oldest son Paul, born 3 July 1853 in Bohlsbach, and his wife Sophia Bahr, came to the United States in 1880 and lived in Zell, Ste. Genevieve, Missouri briefly while on their way to Nebraska. They had three sons and five daughters, of whom the oldest son died in infancy. Paul and Sophia died within six weeks of each other in 1926 and both were buried in the St. Stephens Cemetery in Nuckolls County, Nebraska. Paul's parents and most of his siblings remained in Bohlsbach.

xvii. Bertinus, born 5 September 1831 in Bohlsbach, Baden, Germany. He died on 6 October 1831 in Bohlsbach. No issue.

Immigration:
Arrived before December 1844 aboard an unknown vessel:
    Burgert, Carl
Arrived 19 November 1880 from Antwerp, Belgium to New York aboard the *Belgenland*:
    Lienert, Paul, 27
        Sophia, 27

Biographical:
Husband: Karl "Charles" Burgert
    Birth – 29 June 1825 in Bohlsbach, Baden, Germany.
    Death/Burial – 21 December 1878 in Ste. Genevieve County, Missouri. He was buried in the Memorial Cemetery in Ste. Genevieve, Ste. Genevieve County, Missouri.
1) Wife: Elizabeth Cissell, daughter of Clement Cissell and Anne Layton
    Birth – about 1815 in Missouri.
    1) Marriage – 22 April 1833 in Perry County, Missouri to Michael Tucker.
    2) Marriage – 26 December 1844 in Perry County, Missouri to Karl "Charles" Burgert.
    Death/Burial – 26 February 1868 in Ste. Genevieve County, Missouri. She was buried in the Memorial Cemetery in Ste. Genevieve, Ste. Genevieve County, Missouri.
    Children of Michael Tucker and Elizabeth Cissell:
        i. Martina, born 26 November 1834 in Perry County, Missouri. She died in 1850. No issue.
        ii. Catherine, born 20 August 1836 in Perry County, Missouri. She married Peter James Gibbar on 18 October 1853 in Perry County. Peter was the son of James Nicholas Gibbar and Mary Mattingly, born in 1831. The couple had four sons. Peter died in January 1861 in Perry County, Missouri. He was buried in the St. Mary Cemetery in Perryville, Perry County, Missouri. Catherine died on 27 December 1884 in Perry County, Missouri. She was buried in the Mount Hope Cemetery in Perryville, Perry County, Missouri.
        iii. Martin Francis, born 8 August 1838 in Perry County, Missouri. He died on 4 December 1857 in in Perry County, Missouri. He was buried in the St. Mary Cemetery in Perryville, Perry County, Missouri. No known issue.
        iv. Leo Severin, born 5 June 1840 in Perry County, Missouri. He died on 29 January 1862 in Perry County, Missouri. No known issue.
        v. Clement Camilus, born 11 April 1842 in Perry County, Missouri. He died on 27 September

1859 in Perry County, Missouri. No known issue.

Children of Charles Burgert and Elizabeth Cissell:
  i. Joseph, born about 1846 in Perry County, Missouri. He died on 14 August 1847 in Perry County, Missouri. No issue.
  ii. Joseph, born 21 March 1848 in Perry County, Missouri. He may have died young. No issue.
  iii. Mary Ann, born about 1850 in Perry County, Missouri. She may have died young. No issue.
  iv. Evariste, born 15 May 1852 in Perry County, Missouri. He was a farmer and broom maker. As an adult, Evarise began to use the surname "Burkert" and all of his descendants use that name. He married Mary Clara Bequette on 12 December 1875 in Ste. Genevieve County, Missouri. Mary was the daughter of Augustine Bequette and Marie Louise Carron, born in November 1851 in Missouri. The couple had three sons and ten daughters. Evariste died of acute cardiac dilation on 14 April 1930 and Mary died of chronic myocarditis and nephritis on 26 October 1933, both in Ste. Genevieve, Ste. Genevieve County, Missouri. They were both buried in the Valle Spring Cemetery in Ste. Genevieve, Ste. Genevieve County, Missouri.
  v. Theresia, born about September 1854 in Perry County, Missouri. She died in December 1861 in Ste. Genevieve County, Missouri. Theresia was buried in the Memorial Cemetery in Ste. Genevieve, Ste. Genevieve County, Missouri. No issue.
  vi. Rosalie, born in September 1858 in Perry County, Missouri. She died on 11 October 1860 in Ste. Genevieve County, Missouri. She was buried in the Memorial Cemetery in Ste. Genevieve, Ste. Genevieve County, Missouri. No issue.

2) Wife: Mary Ann Braun, daughter of Moritz Braun and Catherine Herr
Birth – 8 September 1845 in Erlach, Baden, Germany.
1) Marriage – 27 March 1870 in Ste. Genevieve, Ste. Genevieve County, Missouri to Karl "Charles" Burgert.
2) Marriage – 30 March 1879 in Perry County, Missouri to Frank Weber.
Death/Burial – 18 July 1898 in Perry County, Missouri.
Children of Charles Burgert and Mary Ann Braun:
  vii. Francis Charles, born 25 February 1871 in Ste. Genevieve County, Missouri. He was baptized in the Ste. Genevieve Catholic Church in Ste. Genevieve on 23 April 1871. Charles worked as a clerk in a department store in Perryville, Perry County, Missouri. He married Anna Paulina Hunt on 2 September 1895 in Perry County, Missouri. Anna was the daughter of Cornelius Hunt and Frances Habig, born 15 February 1874 in Perry County, Missouri. The couple had six daughters, of whom the oldest died of influenza in 1918. Anna died of liver cancer on 30 August 1945 and Charles died of pyelo nephritis and pneumonia on 23 February 1955, both in Perryville, Perry County, Missouri. They were both buried in the St. Boniface Cemetery in Perryville, Perry County, Missouri.
  viii. Mary Josephine, born 18 March 1873 in Ste. Genevieve County, Missouri. She was baptized in the Ste. Genevieve Catholic Church in Ste. Genevieve on 27 April 1873. She took the religious name Sister Hermina of the Ursuline Order. She died of an ovarian abscess (tubercular) on 12 November 1919 in St. Louis, Missouri. She was buried in the Ursuline Convent Cemetery in Arcadia, Iron County, Missouri. No issue.
  ix. Pauline Catherine Theresa, born 19 November 1874 in Ste. Genevieve County, Missouri. She was baptized in the Ste. Genevieve Catholic Church in Ste. Genevieve on 28 February 1875. She took the religious name Sister Dorothy of the Ursuline Order. No further information.
  x. Mary Magdalena, born 13 September 1876 in Ste. Genevieve County, Missouri. She was baptized in the Ste. Genevieve Catholic Church in Ste. Genevieve on 12 November 1876. She took the religious name Sister Domatilla of the Ursuline Order. She died on 18 August 1903 and was buried in the Ursuline Convent Cemetery in Arcadia, Iron County, Missouri. No issue.

Children of Frank Weber and Mary Ann Braun:
- i. Francis Anthony, born 2 December 1879 in Perry County, Missouri. He married Mary Irene "Rena" Layton on 5 February 1900 in Perry County. Rena was the daughter of Thomas A. Layton and Maria May. The couple had five sons and seven daughters. Rena died of puerperal convulsions on 6 April 1927 in Perryville, Perry County, Missouri shortly after the birth of her last child. Frank died of heart disease on 4 April 1957 in Perryville, Perry County, Missouri. They were both buried in the Mount Hope Cemetery in Perryville, Perry County, Missouri.
- ii. Anna R., born 7 October 1882 in Perry County, Missouri. She took the religious name Sister Mary Anthony of the Ursuline Order. She died on 4 October 1912 and was buried in the Ursuline Convent Cemetery in Arcadia, Iron County, Missouri. No issue.
- iii. Henry W., born 1883 in Perry County, Missouri. He died young. No issue.
- iv. Emma R., born 1886 in Perry County, Missouri. She took the religious name Sister Leoba of the Ursuline Order. She died in 1965 and was buried in the Ursuline Convent Cemetery in Arcadia, Iron County, Missouri. No issue.
- v. Joseph August, born 17 March 1889 in Perry County, Missouri. He died young. No issue.

U.S. residence other than Ste. Genevieve County, Missouri:
Perry County, Missouri

Occupation: Farmer
Religious Affiliation: Roman Catholic
Comments:
Karl "Charles" Burgert was born into a family that suffered a very high rate of infant mortality. Of the seventeen children born to his parents, only Charles and three of his sisters are known to have survived to adulthood. Charles left Germany in 1844 and appears to have come directly to Missouri. He settled in Perry County near the village of Cinque Hommes where he married Elizabeth Cissell, the widow of Michael Tucker. Elizabeth had five children from her first marriage. Of these children, only one daughter survived to marry and have a family. Michael Tucker was the son of Nicholas Tucker and Mary Miles. He had died in Perry County on 1 March 1844 and was buried in the St. Mary Cemetery in Perryville, Perry County, Missouri. Charles and Elizabeth had three sons and three daughters, of whom only one son survived to adulthood. Charles moved his family to Ste. Genevieve County about 1859. Elizabeth died 26 February 1868 in Ste. Genevieve County, Missouri. She was buried in the Memorial Cemetery in Ste. Genevieve, Ste. Genevieve County, Missouri. Charles married for a second time to Mary Ann Braun on 27 March 1870 in Ste. Genevieve, Ste. Genevieve County, Missouri. Mary Ann had come to the United States from Germany to join two older brothers and an older sister who had settled in Perry County, Missouri. Charles and Mary Ann had one son and three daughters. Charles died on 21 December 1878 in Ste. Genevieve County, Missouri. He was buried in the Memorial Cemetery in Ste. Genevieve, Ste. Genevieve County, Missouri beside his first wife. Within months of her husband's death, Mary Ann moved her family back to Perry County. She married a man named Frank Weber there on 30 March 1879. Frank was a farmer. Mary Ann and Frank had three sons and two daughters, of whom two sons died in infancy. It appears that Mary Ann died shortly after having given birth to her last child. She died on 18 July 1898 in Perry County, Missouri. It is interesting to note that all five of Mary Ann's daughters became nuns in the Ursuline Order. Only two of Charles' ten children married and had children of their own.

Simon Burgert Family
Surname Variations: Burger, Burget
European Origin: Bohlsbach, Baden, Germany
Family:
Father: Michael Burgert, born 16 September 1803 in Bohlsbach, Baden, Germany. He died on 10 November 1837 in Bohlsbach.
Mother: Apollonia Fischer, born 8 February 1805 in Windschläg, Baden, Germany. She died on

8 April 1876 in Ste. Genevieve County, Missouri. She was buried in the Memorial Cemetery, Ste. Genevieve, Ste. Genevieve County, Missouri. [See Johann Kraft sketch for her second marriage.]
Children:
* i. Simon, born 1 November 1833 in Bohlsbach, Baden, Germany. [See sketch below.]
  ii. Ludwig, born 18 March 1835 in Bohlsbach, Baden, Germany. No further mention of him has been found after the record of his arrival.
† iii. Balbina, born 24 April 1837 in Bohlsbach, Baden, Germany. She married Ludwig "Louis" Burle on 15 February 1859 in Zell, Ste. Genevieve County, Missouri. Louis was the son of Joseph Burle and Maria Anna Ganter. [See Louis Burle sketch.]

Immigration:
Arrived 13 March 1852 from Le Havre, France to New Orleans aboard the *Middlesex*:
>Kraft, Johann, 39
>>Appelonia, 45
>
>Burger[t], Simon, 18
>>Ludwig, 16
>>Balbina, 15
>
>Kraft, Caroline, 2

Biographical:
Husband: Simon Burgert
>Birth – 1 November 1833 in Bohlsbach, Baden, Germany.
>Death/Burial – 22 January 1896 in Ste. Genevieve County, Missouri. He was buried in the Valle Spring Cemetery in Ste. Genevieve, Ste. Genevieve County, Missouri.

1) Wife: Louisa Fitzkam, daughter of Philip Jacob Fitzkam and Theresia Gallus [See Philip Fitzkam sketch.]
>Birth – about June 1836 in [Zell-Weierbach?], Baden, Germany.
>Marriage – 10 November 1857 in Zell, Ste. Genevieve County, Missouri.
>Death/Burial – 21 January 1880 in Ste. Genevieve County, Missouri. She was buried in the Valle Spring Cemetery in Ste. Genevieve, Ste. Genevieve County, Missouri.

Children:
  i. Jacob, born 26 July 1858 in Zell, Ste. Genevieve County, Missouri. He died on 10 August 1858 in Ste. Genevieve County. Jacob was buried in the St. Joseph Cemetery in Zell, Ste. Genevieve County, Missouri. No issue.
  ii. Infant, born about November 1859 in Ste. Genevieve County, Missouri. The child died on 3 December 1859 in Ste. Genevieve County, Missouri and was buried in the St. Joseph Cemetery in Zell, Ste. Genevieve County, Missouri. No issue.
  iii. Theresa, born 10 October 1860 in Zell, Ste. Genevieve County, Missouri. She married Anthony Grieshaber on 28 September 1887 in Ste. Genevieve County, Missouri. Anthony was the son of Kilian Grieshaber and Paulina Schilli, born 17 July 1860 in Ste. Genevieve County, Missouri. [See Kilian Grieshaber sketch.]
  iv. Maria Elizabeth "Lizzie," born 1 September 1862 in Bloomsdale, Ste. Genevieve County, Missouri. She was baptized on 21 September 1862 in St. Philomena's Catholic Church in Bloomsdale, Ste. Genevieve County, Missouri. Lizzie married Herman Weber on 29 May 1884 in Ste. Genevieve County, Missouri. Herman was the son of Ignatius Weber and Helena Kern [or Kerm?], born 18 March 1852 in Baden, Germany. [See Herman Weber sketch.]
  v. Ursula, born 22 October 1863 in Ste. Genevieve County, Missouri. She married John Burle on 15 November 1887 in Ste. Genevieve County, Missouri. John was the son of Alexander Burle and Magdalena Feist, born 10 November 1863 in Ste. Genevieve County, Missouri. [See Alexander Burle sketch.]
  vi. Maria Apollonia, born 1 August 1866 in Ste. Genevieve County, Missouri. She was baptized on

8 September 1866 in the Ste. Genevieve Catholic Church in Ste. Genevieve, Ste. Genevieve County, Missouri. She married William Loida on 29 August 1887 in Ste. Genevieve, Ste. Genevieve County, Missouri. William was the son of Albert Loida and Anna Worajeck, born 1 April 1864 in Missouri. [See Albert Loida sketch.]

   vii. Francis Joseph "Frank," born 17 September 1870 in Ste. Genevieve County, Missouri. He was baptized on 23 October 1870 in the Ste. Genevieve Catholic Church in Ste. Genevieve, Ste. Genevieve County, Missouri. Frank was a farmer. He married Elizabeth M. Grieshaber on 23 February 1897 in Ste. Genevieve, Ste. Genevieve County, Missouri. Elizabeth was the daughter of Kilian Grieshaber and Paulina Schilli, born 19 April 1875 in Ste. Genevieve County, Missouri. The couple had two sons and one daughter. Frank died of chronic myocarditis on 20 June 1943 in Ste. Genevieve County, Missouri. Elizabeth died on 12 July 1966. They were both buried in the Valle Spring Cemetery in Ste. Genevieve, Ste. Genevieve County, Missouri.

   viii. Mary Louisa [twin], born 29 November 1873 in Ste. Genevieve County, Missouri. She was baptized on 21 December 1873 in the Ste. Genevieve Catholic Church in Ste. Genevieve, Ste. Genevieve County, Missouri. She may have died in infancy.

   ix. Anna Maria [twin], born 29 November 1873 in Ste. Genevieve County, Missouri. She was baptized on 21 December 1873 in the Ste. Genevieve Catholic Church in Ste. Genevieve, Ste. Genevieve County, Missouri. She married Charles Andrew Grieshaber on 17 April 1900 in Ste. Genevieve, Ste. Genevieve County, Missouri. Charles was the son of Kilian Grieshaber and Paulina Schilli, born 28 November 1875 in Ste. Genevieve County, Missouri. [See Kilian Grieshaber sketch.]

   x. Monica Barbara, born 3 May 1876 in Ste. Genevieve County, Missouri. She was baptized on 28 May 1876 in the Ste. Genevieve Catholic Church in Ste. Genevieve, Ste. Genevieve County, Missouri. She died on 5 February 1877 in Ste. Genevieve County, Missouri. She was buried in Memorial Cemetery in Ste. Genevieve, Ste. Genevieve County, Missouri. No issue.

   xi. Mary Josephine, born 1 February 1878 in Ste. Genevieve County, Missouri. She was baptized on 3 March 1878 in the Ste. Genevieve Catholic Church in Ste. Genevieve, Ste. Genevieve County, Missouri. No record of her has been found after the 1900 census when she was living with her brother Frank in Ste. Genevieve.

2) Wife: Catherine Jokerst, daughter of Andreas "Andrew" Jokerst and Kunigunda Grass
   Birth – 12 January 1844 in Ste. Genevieve County, Missouri.
   1) Marriage – 11 September 1866 in Ste. Genevieve County, Missouri to Severin Busam. [See Michael Busam sketch.]
   2) Marriage – 22 February 1881 in Ste. Genevieve, Ste. Genevieve County, Missouri to Simon Burgert.
   Death/Burial – 23 February 1914 at the County Farm in Ste. Genevieve County, Missouri. She was buried in the Valle Spring Cemetery in Ste. Genevieve, Ste. Genevieve County, Missouri.

There were no children born to Simon Burgert and Catherine Jokerst.

Naturalization:

Name	Declaration	Naturalization	Origin
Bargert, Simon		22 October 1866 Ste. Genevieve Co.	Baden

Military:
Served in the U.S. Civil War for the Union:
78th Enrolled Missouri Militia
Private, Company K, 78th Enrolled Missouri Militia
   Simon Burgert enlisted 1 August 1863 in Ste. Genevieve, Ste. Genevieve County, Missouri.

Education: Could read and write.
Occupation: Farmer
Religious Affiliation: Roman Catholic
Comments:
Simon Burgert came to the United States as a young man with his mother, step-father and siblings. The family came directly to Missouri and settled on a farm near Zell, Ste. Genevieve County, Missouri. Simon worked with his step-father on the family farm. He married Louisa Fitzkam in 1857 in Zell. The couple is said to have had twelve children, but records for only eleven children have been found. During the Civil War, Simon enlisted as a private in Company K of the 78th Enrolled Missouri Militia but it is doubtful that he ever saw active duty. After his step-father died, Simon sold the farm near Zell and moved his family to a farm about five miles north of the city of Ste. Genevieve. His widowed mother lived in his household until her death in 1876. Louisa died in 1880 and was buried in the Valle Spring Cemetery in Ste. Genevieve, Ste. Genevieve County, Missouri. Simon married Mrs. Catherine Busam, the widow of Severin Busam, as his second wife on 22 February 1881 in Ste. Genevieve, Ste. Genevieve County. Simon and Catherine had no children together. In the summer of 1895, Simon began to make some improvements on his farm. On the afternoon of 1 July 1895, he was driving a wagonload of lumber to his farm when he was thrown from the bench. The fully loaded wagon passed over Simon's head and broke his lower jaw and severely bruised his neck and back. He was slow to recover. Simon died of inflammation of the bowels on 22 January 1896 in Ste. Genevieve County, Missouri. He was buried in the Valle Spring Cemetery in Ste. Genevieve, Ste. Genevieve County, Missouri. After her husband's death, Catherine lived with her step-son, Frank, and his family until Frank's wife began to suffer from health problems. In August 1912, she moved into her brother, Andrew Jokerst's, household, but due to Andrew's declining health, she was moved to the Ste. Genevieve County Poor Farm only a few months later. She spent her last years on the farm and died there on 23 February 1914. She was buried in the Valle Spring Cemetery in Ste. Genevieve, Ste. Genevieve County, Missouri.

Gregor Burkart Family
Surname Variations: Burghart, Burkert
European Origin: Mörsch, Baden, Germany
Family:
Father: Ludwig Burkart, born 22 August 1824 in Mörsch, Baden, Germany.
Mother: Lucia Laier [aka Layer], born 2 June 1825 in Mörsch, Baden, Germany.
　Children:
* 　　i.　Gregor, born 20 July 1848 in Mörsch, Baden, Germany. [See sketch below.]
　　ii.　Barbara, born 18 October 1849 in Mörsch, Baden, Germany.
　　iii.　Clementine, born 5 May 1852 in Mörsch, Baden, Germany.
　　iv.　Joseph, born 21 November 1854 in Mörsch, Baden, Germany.
　　v.　Katharina, born 9 October 1857 in Mörsch, Baden, Germany.
　　vi.　Jacob, born 15 December 1859 in Mörsch, Baden, Germany.
　　vii.　Maria Luisa, born 27 July 1862 in Mörsch, Baden, Germany.

Immigration:
Arrived 14 November 1879 from Bremen, Germany to New York aboard the *Main*:
　　Burkart, Gregor, 31　　　　Bricklayer　　　Germany
　　　　Marie, 30
　　　　Felix, 5
　　　　Therese, 2
　　　　[Julia, 4 mos.]

Biographical:
Husband: Gregor Burkart
　　Birth – 20 July 1848 in Mörsch, Baden, Germany.

Death/Burial – 9 January 1916 in St. Louis, Missouri. He was buried in the Calvary Cemetery in St. Louis, Missouri.

Wife: Maria Anna Heil, daughter of Joseph Heil and Juliana Fitterer [See John Heil sketch.]

Birth – 8 December 1849 in Rheinstetten, Baden, Germany.

Marriage – about 1872 in Baden, Germany.

Death/Burial – 19 July 1922 in St. Louis, Missouri. She was buried in the Calvary Cemetery in St. Louis, Missouri.

Children:
- i. Felix, born 16 December 1873 in Ettlingen, Baden, Germany. He was a butcher. Felix died of chronic nephritis and heart disease on 15 June 1952 in St. Louis, Missouri. He was buried in the Calvary Cemetery in St. Louis, Missouri. Felix never married and had no known issue.
- ii. Theresa, born in 1877 in Ettlingen, Baden, Germany. She died before 1900 in Missouri. No issue.
- iii. Julia L. , born 16 July 1879 in Ettlingen, Baden, Germany. She married William Frederick Loehring about 1907 as his second wife. William was the son of Frederick Loehring and Dora Burkdorf, born 3 March 1860 in St. Louis, Missouri. He was a carpenter. The couple had one son. William died of tuberculosis on 20 May 1920 in St. Louis, Missouri. He was buried in the Calvary Cemetery in St. Louis, Missouri. After her husband's death, Julia lived with her brother Felix. Julia died of rectal cancer on 31 March 1952 in St. Louis, Missouri. She was buried in the Lake Charles Park Cemetery in St. Louis, Missouri.
- iv. Caroline [twin] , born 4 April 1881 in Ste. Genevieve County, Missouri. She was baptized on 5 April 1881 in the Our Lady Help of Christians Catholic Church in Weingarten, Ste. Genevieve County. Caroline married John H. Ryan. John was the son of Thomas Ryan and Caroline Wulf, born in November 1876 in St. Louis, Missouri. He was a railroad streetcar painter. The couple had two sons and two daughters. John died of pulmonary tuberculosis on 3 August 1919 in St. Louis. After her husband's death, Caroline moved her family into the home of her widowed mother-in-law in St. Louis. She worked as a labeler in a drug company and then in a school cafeteria to support her children. Caroline died in May 1969 in St. Louis, Missouri. John and Caroline were both buried in the Calvary Cemetery in St. Louis, Missouri.
- v. Regina "Jennie" [twin] , born 4 April 1881 in Ste. Genevieve County, Missouri. She was baptized on 5 April 1881 in the Our Lady Help of Christians Catholic Church in Weingarten, Ste. Genevieve County. Jennie worked as a domestic servant for the family of Norman and Augusta Lincoln in St. Louis for over thirty years. Jennie died on 31 August 1965 in St. Louis, Missouri. She never married and had no known issue.
- vi. Katherine Philomena, born 13 August 1883 in Ste. Genevieve County, Missouri. She was baptized on 19 August 1883 in the Our Lady Help of Christians Catholic Church in Weingarten, Ste. Genevieve County. Katherine may have had an affair with [or been married to?] a man named Charles A. Burke some time before 1904. She had a son from this relationship. Nothing is known of this man, other than his name on the birth record of Katherine's son. After the birth of her son, Katherine left the child with her parents and went to St. Louis where she worked as a domestic servant. She married William Martin Drury, most likely in St. Louis, about 1920 as his second or third wife. William was the son of Charles Albert Drury and Sarah Jane Barnett, born on 16 July 1884 in Kentucky. He was a railroad motorman. Almost immediately after their marriage, William and Katherine moved to California, where William worked in a fruit stand. Eventually Katherine's son came to live with them. William died on 21 May 1943 and was buried in the Forest Lawn Memorial Park in Glendale, Los Angeles County, California. Katherine died on 1 July 1951 in Los Angeles County, California.
- vii. Peter Paul Aloysius, born 26 June 1888 in Ste. Genevieve County, Missouri. He was a shoe salesman in St. Louis, Missouri. Peter married Lillian P. Schulz on 8 June 1910 in St. Louis, Missouri. Lillian was the daughter of Carl Schulz and Wilhelmina "Minnie" Ackerman, born 8 June 1889 in New York. The couple had a son who was born in 1912 in St. Louis and another

child which was born in 1916 and may have died in infancy. By the time they were expecting their second child, Peter had begun to have an affair with a woman named Rose Hultrop. Rose was the daughter of Frederick Hultrop and Clara Shine, born 6 December 1892 in St. Louis, Missouri. She may not have been aware that Peter was already married when he began his liaison with her. In November 1916, some six weeks after the birth of her child, Lillian discovered Peter's affair and that he had purchased furniture for Rose's apartment. He had lied to Lillian about the amount of his salary and it wasn't until she found a receipt for the purchase of a piano for Rose that the facts of the affair came to light. In February 1918, Peter and Rose eloped to Alton, Madison County, Illinois supposedly so that Peter could avoid the draft, and federal agents were brought in to investigate. Oddly, Peter sent a post card to Lillian to let her know where he was. Shortly after they moved to Illinois, the relationship between Peter and Rose began to deteriorate. By the middle of 1918, Rose was pregnant, but still unmarried. She died of septicemia from a botched self-induced abortion on 12 September 1918 in St. Louis. She was buried in Calvary Cemetery in St. Louis. Peter returned to St. Louis and was reunited with Lillian by 1920, but their relationship was strained. They were divorced in late 1930. Lillian remained single for the rest of her life and worked as a seamstress in a factory to support herself. She died on 10 April 1972 in St. Louis. She was buried in the Mount Hope Cemetery in St. Louis, Missouri. Peter married Marie J. "Mamie" Katke as his second wife on 18 August 1931 in St. Louis. Mamie was born 19 March 1901 in Missouri. The couple had no children together. Peter died on 25 December 1965 in St. Louis, Missouri. Mamie died on 17 July 1992 in Florissant, St. Louis County, Missouri. They were both buried in the Calvary Cemetery in St. Louis, Missouri.

viii. Mary Theresa, born 2 December 1892 in Ste. Genevieve County, Missouri. She was baptized on 8 December 1892 in the Ste. Genevieve Catholic Church in Ste. Genevieve, Ste. Genevieve County, Missouri. Mary married Thomas Green Hootselle. Thomas was the son of Joseph N. Hootselle and Elizabeth Cagle, born 17 August 1891 in Clayton, Louisiana. He was a machinist. The couple had four sons and two daughters. Thomas died of cancer of the sigmoid and liver on 11 March 1951 in St. Louis, Missouri. Mary died on 9 June 1966. They were both buried in the Calvary Cemetery in St. Louis, Missouri.

ix. Josephine Mary, born 28 May 1896 in Ste. Genevieve County, Missouri. She was baptized on 7 June 1896 in the Ste. Genevieve Catholic Church in Ste. Genevieve, Ste. Genevieve County, Missouri. Josephine [may have] married August Mathias Rossmann. August was the son of Mathias Henry Rossmann and Anna E. Schlicht, born 20 July 1884 in Carlinville, Macoupin County, Illinois. August was married to a woman named Margaret E. Schonder about 1906 in Illinois. Margaret was the daughter of Martin Schonder and Bertha Klagus, born 9 December 1884 in Illinois. At the time of their marriage, August was working as a miner in Macoupin County. The couple had one son and three daughters. Some time before 1920, August moved his family to St. Louis, Missouri where he found work as a streetcar conductor. By 1920, August was living with Josephine in a house on Grand Avenue in St. Louis while Margaret and the children lived separately on North Jefferson Avenue. Margaret supported her family by working as a cook in a restaurant. By 1930, August was once again living with Margaret and their children in a house on Coleman Street in St. Louis and Josephine was living as a single lady in a boarding house. But by 1940, the Rossmanns had divorced and Margaret was living with her daughter and son-in-law in the house on Coleman Street. August and Josephine were once again living together on Washington Boulevard in St. Louis. August and Josephine had no children together. August died of heart disease and chronic interstitial nephritis on 1 April 1944 in St. Louis, Missouri. He was buried in the Gatewood Gardens Cemetery in St. Louis, Missouri. Josephine died in December 1970 in St. Louis, Missouri. She was buried in the Calvary Cemetery in St. Louis, Missouri. Margaret died on 21 February 1965, most likely in Missouri.

U.S. residence other than Ste. Genevieve County, Missouri:
St. Louis, Missouri

Naturalization:

Name	Declaration	Naturalization	Origin	Remarks
Burkart, Gregorie			Germany	[1900 census]

Education: Could read and write.
Occupation: Bricklayer and stonemason
Religious Affiliation: Roman Catholic
Comments:
Gregor Burkart was a bricklayer. He brought his young family to the United States and settled in Ste. Genevieve County, Missouri where some distant relatives had already settled. He and his wife had two sons and seven daughters, of whom one daughter died in infancy. Gregor worked as a bricklayer and stonemason in St. Mary, Ste. Genevieve County, Missouri. As his children grew to adulthood, they all moved to St. Louis to find work. Eventually, Gregor and his wife Mary both moved to St. Louis where they spent their final years. Gregor died of lobar pneumonia on 9 January 1916 in St. Louis. Mary died of chronic nephritis on 19 July 1922 in St. Louis. They were both buried in the Calvary Cemetery in St. Louis, Missouri.

Note: This family is distantly related to the Ulrich Burkart family, and to the Gerstner, Heil, Benedict Huber, Joseph Rehm and Weiler families of Ste. Genevieve County, Missouri.

Ulrich Burkart Family
Surname Variations: Burkert, Burkhardt, Burgert, Burgart
European Origin: Mörsch, Baden, Germany
Family:
Father: Cornel Burkart, born in Mörsch, Baden, Germany.
Mother: Magdalena Weiler, born in Mörsch, Baden, Germany.
  Children:
      i. Franziska, born 21 May 1847 in Mörsch, Baden, Germany.
      ii. Anton, born 28 August 1849 in Mörsch, Baden, Germany. He died on 29 August 1849 in Mörsch. No issue.
*   iii. Ulrich, born 3 July 1853 in Mörsch, Baden, Germany. [See sketch below.]
      iv. Katharina, born and died on 9 January 1856 in Mörsch, Baden, Germany. No issue.
      v. Crispin, born 22 May 1857 in Mörsch, Baden, Germany.
      vi. Magdalena, born 16 July 1859 in Mörsch, Baden, Germany. She died on 18 July 1859 in Mörsch. No issue.

Immigration:
Arrived 9 March 1881 from Le Havre, France to New York aboard the *Labrador*:
    Burkardt, Aldrich [Ulrich], 27   Stone Mason   Germany
        Regina, 26
        M. Magdaline, 1 mo.

Biographical:
Husband: Ulrich Burkart
    Birth – 14 July 1853 in Mörsch, Baden, Germany.
    Death/Burial – 28 December 1918 in St. Louis, Missouri. He was buried in Sts. Peter and Paul Cemetery in St. Louis, Missouri.
Wife: Regina Deck, daughter of Xavier Deck and Aloisia Burkart
    Birth – 7 September 1854 in Mörsch, Baden, Germany.
    Marriage – about 1880 in [Mörsch?], Baden, Germany.

Death/Burial – 10 September 1920 in St. Louis, Missouri. She was buried in Sts. Peter and Paul Cemetery in St. Louis, Missouri.

Children:
    i. Maria Magdalena "Lena," born about 1881 in Baden, Germany. She married Charles Hurley on 1 June 1904 in Ste. Genevieve County, Missouri. Charles was born 13 June 1878 in Missouri. He was a switchman for the St. Louis streetcar railway. The couple does not appear to have had any children. In November 1908, Charles was severely injured when he was jammed between two rail cars while he was helping to couple them. He died of pulmonary tuberculosis and influenza on 31 January 1920 in St. Louis. He was buried in the Steelville Cemetery in Steelville, Crawford County, Missouri. Lena may have married a man named _____ Binder as her second husband. She was still alive and living in St. Louis in 1967 at the time of her sister Alice's death.

    ii. Mary Louise, born 2 August 1882 in Ste. Genevieve County, Missouri. She was baptized on 7 August 1882 in the Ste. Genevieve Catholic Church in Ste. Genevieve, Ste. Genevieve County, Missouri. She married Joseph Hubert about 1904. Joseph was the son of Anthony Hubert and Eva Caine, born 1 June 1878 in St. Louis, Missouri. He was a teamster. The couple had one daughter. Joseph died of encephalomalacia [localized softening of brain due to hemorrhage or inflammation], heart disease and cancer of the prostate and sigmoid on 21 December 1960 in St. Louis, Missouri. Louise died in January 1969. They were both buried in Sts. Peter and Paul Cemetery in St. Louis, Missouri.

    iii. George Anthony, born 10 July 1884 in Ste. Genevieve County, Missouri. He was baptized on 15 July 1884 in the Ste. Genevieve Catholic Church in Ste. Genevieve, Ste. Genevieve County. Anthony died on 5 September 1884 in Ste. Genevieve County. No issue.

    iv. George Aloysius, born 6 September 1885 in Ste. Genevieve County, Missouri. He was baptized on 20 September 1885 in the Ste. Genevieve Catholic Church in Ste. Genevieve, Ste. Genevieve County. George worked as a punch press operator in an auto factory. He married Margaret _____. She was born about 1895 in Missouri. Margaret died some time before July 1951. George died of lung cancer on 5 July 1951 in St. Louis, Missouri. He was buried in the Sts. Peter and Paul Cemetery in St. Louis, Missouri. The couple does not appear to have had any children.

    v. Alice Cecilia, born 2 June 1888 in Ste. Genevieve County, Missouri. She was baptized on 17 June 1888 in the Ste. Genevieve Catholic Church in Ste. Genevieve, Ste. Genevieve County. She married Clyde McCann Carr in January 1907 in St. Louis, Missouri. Clyde was the son of Charles S. Carr and Maria D. Young, born in July 1882 in Ohio. He was a railroad switchman. The couple had one daughter. Clyde moved his family to Fort Scott, Bourbon County, Kansas between 1910 and 1920. Clyde died there in 1944. He was buried in the Evergreen Cemetery in Fort Scott. After her husband's death, Alice supported herself by working as a bookkeeper in a bank in Fort Scott. She married for a second time on 3 April 1951 in Fort Scott to Fred C. Thompson. This was also Fred's second marriage and he had one son and three daughters with his first wife. Fred died in February 1958 and Alice died in August 1967, both in Fort Scott. They were both buried in the Evergreen Cemetery in Fort Scott, Bourbon County, Kansas.

    vi. Cornelius Xavier, born 29 August 1891 in Ste. Genevieve County, Missouri. He was baptized on 10 September 1891 in the Ste. Genevieve Catholic Church in Ste. Genevieve, Ste. Genevieve County, Missouri. He died some time before June 1900. No issue.

    vii. Leo Joseph, born 13 March 1893 in Ste. Genevieve County, Missouri. He was baptized on 19 March 1893 in the Ste. Genevieve Catholic Church in Ste. Genevieve, Ste. Genevieve County, Missouri. Leo worked odd jobs in St. Louis. He died from a brain hemorrhage caused by a fractured skull [manner and cause unknown] on 20 November 1932 in St. Louis, Missouri. Leo never married and had no known issue.

    viii. Odile Genevieve, born 27 December 1895 in Missouri. She was baptized on 29 December 1895 in the Ste. Genevieve Catholic Church in Ste. Genevieve, Ste. Genevieve County, Missouri. Odile married Robert W. Hickey about 1920. Robert was the son of Robert Hickey and Celine Vallet, born 26 August 1894 in St. Louis, Missouri. The couple had two daughters. The family owned and operated a grocery store in the St. Louis area. Robert died of a cerebral hemorrhage and arteriosclerosis on 23 January 1959 in St. Louis. Odile died in October 1977 in St. Louis. They were both buried in the Calvary Cemetery in St. Louis, Missouri.

U.S. residence other than Ste. Genevieve County, Missouri:
St. Louis, Missouri

Naturalization:

Name	Declaration	Naturalization	Origin
Burkhard, Ulrich		27 April 1896 Ste. Genevieve Co.	Baden

Education: Could read and write.
Occupation: Stonemason, Night watchman at Shaw Gardens in St. Louis, Missouri
Religious Affiliation: Roman Catholic

Comments:
Ulrich Burkart was a stonemason. He brought his young family to the United States and settled in Ste. Genevieve County, Missouri where some distant relatives had already settled. He and his wife had four sons and four daughters, of whom two sons died young. As the children grew to adulthood, they moved to St. Louis, Missouri. Eventually, Ulrich and his wife Regina both moved to St. Louis where Ulrich worked as a night watchman in the Shaw Gardens. Ulrich bled to death from a self-inflicted wound to his throat on 28 December 1918 in St. Louis. Regina died of uremia and chronic interstitial nephritis on 10 September 1920. They were both buried in the Sts. Peter and Paul Cemetery in St. Louis, Missouri.

Note: This family is distantly related to the Gregor Burkart family, and to the Gerstner, Heil, Benedict Huber, Joseph Rehm and Weiler families of Ste. Genevieve County, Missouri.

Alexander Burle Family
Surname Variations: Berle, Borley, Burhle
European Origin: Ebersweier, Baden, Germany
Family:
Father: Joseph Burle, born 5 September 1790 in Baden, Germany.
Mother: Maria Anna Ganter, born 1 August 1801 in Baden, Germany.
   Children:
       i. Maria Eva, born 23 December 1826 in Ebersweier, Baden, Germany. She married Joseph Meier on 28 May 1866 in Ebersweier. Joseph was the son of Simon Meier and Barbara Glanzmann.
*   ii. Alexander, born 16 July 1829 in Ebersweier, Baden, Germany. [See sketch below.]
    iii. Agnes, born 7 January 1831 in Ebersweier, Baden, Germany. She married Roman Eisenmann on 7 January 1867 in Ebersweier. Roman was the son of Joseph Eisenmann and Katharina Gisi, born 14 August 1835 in Baden, Germany.
†   iv. Ludwig "Louis," born 22 August 1833 in Ebersweier, Baden, Germany. [See Ludwig "Louis" Burle sketch.]
    v. Rosa, born 16 September 1836 in Ebersweier, Baden, Germany. She died on 17 July 1904 in Germany.
    vi. Wilhelm, born 21 May 1839 in Ebersweier, Baden, Germany. He married Theresia Lebert on 19 October 1874 in Ebersweier. Theresia was the daughter of Ziriack Lebert and Maria Anna Streif.
‡   vii. Johann Baptist "John," born 24 June 1842 in Ebersweier, Baden, Germany. He was a tailor. He followed his two older brothers to Missouri and settled in St. Louis. John married Elizabeth

"Lizzie" Zimmermann on 7 June 1870 in St. Louis. Lizzie was the daughter of Henry Zimmermann and Agnes Bohn, born in August 1848 in Germany. The couple had five sons and one daughter. John died of stomach cancer on 5 November 1905 and Lizzie died of lobar pneumonia on 15 November 1908, both in St. Louis. They were both buried in the Sts. Peter and Paul Cemetery in St. Louis, Missouri.

Immigration:
Arrived 26 December 1857 from Le Havre, France to New Orleans aboard the *Ann Washburn*:
    Burle, Alesandre, 26
        Louis, 24
Arrived 29 May 1867 from Le Havre, France to New York aboard the *Tampico*:
    Burle, Johann, 26   Tailor

Biographical:
Husband: Alexander Burle
   Birth – 16 July 1829 in Ebersweier, Baden, Germany.
   Death/Burial – 9 June 1911 in Ste. Genevieve County, Missouri. He was buried in the Our Lady Help of Christians Cemetery in Weingarten, Ste. Genevieve County, Missouri.
Wife: Magdalena Feist, daughter of Joseph Faist and Theresia Faist. [See Michael Feist sketch.]
   Birth – 12 July 1821 in Diersburg, Baden, Germany.
   1) Marriage – 6 September 1838 in Hofweier, Baden, Germany to Mathias Stutz. [See Mathias Stutz sketch.]
   2) Marriage – 14 May 1857 in Zell, Ste. Genevieve, Ste. Genevieve County, Missouri to Joseph Ganter. [See Joseph Ganter sketch.]
   3) Marriage – 30 August 1859 in Zell, Ste. Genevieve County, Missouri to Alexander Burle.
   Death/Burial – 14 January 1887 in Ste. Genevieve County, Missouri. She was buried in the Our Lady Help of Christians Cemetery in Weingarten, Ste. Genevieve County, Missouri.
Children:
   i.   William, born 27 August 1860 in Ste. Genevieve County, Missouri. He was baptized on 14 October 1860 in the Sts. Philip and James Catholic Church in River aux Vases, Ste. Genevieve County. William died on 28 April 1861 in Ste. Genevieve County. He was buried in the St. Joseph Cemetery in Zell, Ste. Genevieve County, Missouri. No issue.
   ii.   William, born 10 April 1862 in Ste. Genevieve County, Missouri. He was baptized on 11 May 1862 in the Sts. Philip and James Catholic Church in River aux Vases, Ste. Genevieve County, Missouri. He died young. No issue.
   iii.   John, born 10 November 1863 in Ste. Genevieve County, Missouri. He was baptized on 25 December 1863 in the Sts. Philip and James Catholic Church in River aux Vases, Ste. Genevieve County. John was a farmer. He married Ursula Burgert on 15 November 1887 in Ste. Genevieve County, Missouri. Ursula was the daughter of Simon Burgert and Louisa Fitzkam, born 22 October 1863 in Ste. Genevieve County, Missouri. The couple had five sons and two daughters, of whom two sons died in early childhood. John died of pulmonary tuberculosis on 6 January 1922 and Ursula died of an apoplexy on 19 May 1925, both in Ste. Genevieve County, Missouri. They were both buried in the Our Lady Help of Christians Cemetery in Weingarten, Ste. Genevieve County, Missouri.

Land Patents:
Ste. Genevieve County, Missouri

Patentee	Issue Date	Land Office	Cert. No.	Serial No.	Twp	Rng	Sec	Acres
Burle, Alex	30 Sep 1882	Ironton	44502	MO4230 .070	37-N	7-E	26	39.62
Burle, John	9 Jun 1905	Ironton	47276	MO6260 .197	37-N	7-E	23	5.06

Naturalization:

Name	Declaration	Naturalization	Origin
Burle, Alexander	21 November 1853	11 November 1865 Ste. Genevieve Co.	Baden

Military:
Served in the U.S. Civil War for the Union:
Private, Company F, 78th Enrolled Missouri Militia
    Alexander Burle enlisted on 30 April 1864 in Ste. Genevieve County, Missouri. He was ordered into service on 16 October 1864 and was relieved from duty on 25 November 1864. He served a total of 41 days of actual service.

Education: Could read and write
Occupation: Farmer
Religious Affiliation: Roman Catholic
Comments:
Alexander Burle came to the United States with his younger brother, Ludwig "Louis" in 1857. They both came directly to Missouri and settled in Ste. Genevieve County. A younger brother, Johann "John," followed them to Missouri, but settled in St. Louis. Alexander married Mrs. Magdalena Ganter on 30 August 1859 in Zell, Ste. Genevieve County. Magdalena had been widowed twice before she married Alexander and had at least five surviving children from those marriages. Alexander bought a farm near the town of Ste. Genevieve where they raised their family. Alexander and Magdalena had three sons, of whom two died in infancy. During the Civil War, Alexander enlisted in the 78th Enrolled Missouri Militia. In the spring of 1884 Magdalena suffered a series of paralytic strokes which left her partially paralyzed. She eventually became so weak that she was completely bedridden. Magdalena died of hemiplegia on 14 January 1887 in Ste. Genevieve County. After his wife's death, Alexander lived with his son who had taken over the operation of the family farm. Alexander died of testicular cancer on 9 June 1911 in Ste. Genevieve, Ste. Genevieve County, Missouri. He and Magdalena were both buried in the Our Lady Help of Christians Cemetery in Weingarten, Ste. Genevieve County, Missouri.

Ludwig "Louis" Burle Family
Surname Variations: Berle, Borley, Burhle
European Origin: Ebersweier, Baden, Germany
Family:
Father: Joseph Burle, born 5 September 1790 in Baden, Germany.
Mother: Maria Anna Ganter, born 1 August 1801 in Baden, Germany

    Children:

Note: For a comprehensive discussion of Joseph Burle's children see the Alexander Burle sketch.

Immigration:
Arrived 26 December 1857 from Le Havre, France to New Orleans aboard the *Ann Washburn*:
    Burle, Alesandre, 26
        Louis, 24

Biographical:
Husband: Ludwig "Louis" Burle
    Birth – 22 August 1833 in Ebersweier, Baden, Germany.
    Death/Burial – 14 March 1914 in Ste. Genevieve, Ste. Genevieve County, Missouri. He was buried in the Valle Spring Cemetery in Ste. Genevieve, Ste. Genevieve County, Missouri.
Wife: Balbina Burgert, daughter of Michael Burgert and Apollonia Fischer [See Simon Burgert sketch.]
    Birth – 24 April 1837 in Bohlsbach, Baden, Germany.

Marriage – 15 February 1859 in Zell, Ste. Genevieve County, Missouri.

Death/Burial – 7 May 1910 in Ste. Genevieve County, Missouri. She was buried in the Valle Spring Cemetery in Ste. Genevieve, Ste. Genevieve County, Missouri.

Children:
  i. Child. Died young.
  ii. Child. Died young.
  iii. Jules Henry Louis, born 11 January 1863 in Louisiana. He was a tailor. Henry married Mary Ann Elizabeth Schlattmann on 9 June 1891 in Ste. Genevieve County, Missouri. Mary was the daughter of Anton Schlattmann and Maria Eva Roth, born 23 February 1871 in Ste. Genevieve County, Missouri. The couple had three sons and five daughters. Henry died of colon cancer on 30 September 1935 in St. Louis, Missouri. Mary died of a cerebral hemorrhage on 16 May 1951 in St. Louis. They were both buried in the Valle Spring Cemetery in Ste. Genevieve, Ste. Genevieve County, Missouri.
  iv. Mary Caroline, born 10 January 1866 in Ste. Genevieve County, Missouri. She was baptized on 18 February 1866 in the Ste. Genevieve Catholic Church in Ste. Genevieve, Ste. Genevieve County, Missouri. She married John Xavier Schlattmann on 8 September 1891 in Ste. Genevieve County, Missouri. John was the son of Anton Schlattmann and Maria Eva Roth, born 27 May 1867 in Ste. Genevieve County, Missouri. [See Anton Schlattmann sketch.]
  v. Theresa Apollonia, born 20 January 1868 in Ste. Genevieve County, Missouri. She was baptized on 23 February 1868 in the Ste. Genevieve Catholic Church in Ste. Genevieve, Ste. Genevieve County, Missouri. She died young. No issue.
  vi. Joseph A. , born 18 August 1870 in Missouri. When he was about two years old, Joseph suffered an attack of meningitis which left him deaf and mute. As an adult, he worked as a general laborer. On 14 April 1905, Joseph was run over by a train and, among other injuries, one of his legs was badly broken. The injured leg became infected within a week and had to be amputated. Unfortunately, septicemia had already set in. Joseph died of blood poisoning on 28 April 1905 in Ste. Genevieve. He was buried in the Valle Spring Cemetery in Ste. Genevieve, Ste. Genevieve County, Missouri. He never married and had no known issue.
  vii. Emma Ann Louise, born 5 February 1874 in Ste. Genevieve County, Missouri. She was baptized on 8 March 1874 in the Ste. Genevieve Catholic Church in Ste. Genevieve, Ste. Genevieve County, Missouri. Emma died on 30 August 1876 in Ste. Genevieve County. She was buried in the Memorial Cemetery in Ste. Genevieve, Ste. Genevieve County, Missouri. No issue.

U.S. residence other than Ste. Genevieve County, Missouri:
[New Orleans?], Louisiana
St. Louis, Missouri

Naturalization:

Name	Declaration	Naturalization	Origin	Remarks
Burle, Louis			Baden	1900 Census

Military:
Served in the U.S. Civil War for the Confederacy:
Private, Company E, 1st Louisiana Infantry
  Louis Burle served from 1862 to 1863 [approximately one and a half years]. He was taken prisoner at Fort Butler near Donaldsonville, Louisiana [during the second Battle of Donaldsonville, 28 June 1863?]. Then he enlisted in the 41st Regiment Missouri Infantry Volunteers.
Served in the U.S. Civil War for the Union:
Private, Company F, 41st Regiment Missouri Infantry Volunteers
  Louis Burle [He enlisted using the alias "Louis Ganter"] enlisted on 19 September 1864 in St. Louis, Missouri. He served active duty until 11 July 1865 when he was mustered out.

Education: Could read and write
Occupation: Tailor, employed by Rozier & Jokerst and Jokerst-Yealy Merchantile Co.
Religious Affiliation: Roman Catholic
Political Affiliation and/or Any Offices Held:
   Junior Vice Commander, J. Felix St. James Post, G.A.R [elected 1897]
Comments:
Ludwig "Louis" Burle came to the United States with his older brother, Alexander in 1857. They both came directly to Missouri and Alexander settled in Ste. Genevieve County. Louis married Balbina Burgert in Ste. Genevieve County and shortly after their marriage, the couple moved to Louisiana. Louis served both the Confederacy and the Union during the Civil War. He enlisted in the 1st Louisiana Infantry (CSA) in 1862. He was captured by Union troops at Fort Butler near Donaldsonville, Louisiana, most likely during the second battle of Donaldsonville in June 1863. Louis apparently made his way back to Missouri by the fall of 1864 when he enlisted in the 41st Regiment Missouri Infantry Volunteers. He served in that unit under the alias "Louis Ganter" until he was mustered out in July 1865. After the war ended, Louis moved his family back to Ste. Genevieve County, Missouri. The couple had seven children, of whom only two sons and one daughter survived to adulthood. The couple celebrated their fiftieth wedding anniversary with family and friends on 15 February 1909 in Ste. Genevieve. Shortly after this event, Balbina who had suffered from chronic kidney ailments for over thirty years, died of chronic cystitis on 7 May 1910 in Ste. Genevieve. Louis died of asthma and bronchitis on 14 March 1914 in Ste. Genevieve County, Missouri. They were both buried in the Valle Spring Cemetery in Ste. Genevieve, Ste. Genevieve County, Missouri.

Michael Burtcher Family
Surname Variations: Bertcher, Burcher, Butcher, Burtscher
European Origin: Germany
Family:
Father: Unknown
Mother: Unknown
   Children:
†   i.   Bartholomew, born about 1772 in Germany. He was a stonemason. He married Elizabeth Bloom about 19 September 1795 in Baltimore, Maryland. Elizabeth was born about 1770 in Maryland. Elizabeth died on 30 August 1797 in Ste. Genevieve. Bartholomew died on 24 July 1802 at Mine La Motte, Madison County, Missouri. They were both buried in the Memorial Cemetery in Ste. Genevieve. The couple does not appear to have had any surviving children.
*   ii.   Michael, born about 1777 in Germany. [See sketch below.]
†   iii.   Sebastian, born about 1782 in Germany. He was a stonemason. He was a member of the Louisiana Lodge No. 109 of the Freemasons in Ste. Genevieve. He remained in Ste. Genevieve County Missouri until at least 1840. His date and place of death are unknown. Sebastian does not appear to have ever married and had no known issue.

Immigration:
Arrived from Germany some time before September 1795 aboard an unknown vessel:
   Burtcher, Bartholomew
      Michael
      Sebastian

Biographical:
Husband: Michael Burtcher
   Birth – about 1777 in Germany.
   Death/Burial – 24 May 1829 in Kaskaskia, Randolph County, Illinois.
Wife: Margaret "Peggy" Hayden, daughter of William Bolemus Hayden and Hannah Ramsey
   Birth – about 1800 in Bourbon County, Kentucky.

Marriage – about 1812 in Cape Girardeau County, Missouri. Divorced in June 1821.
Death/Burial – about 1833, most likely in Missouri.
Children:
    i. Margaret Catherine, born 6 February 1813 in Ste. Genevieve County, Missouri. She was baptized on 26 September 1814 in the Ste. Genevieve Catholic Church in Ste. Genevieve, Ste. Genevieve County, Missouri. Margaret was educated at the convent school of the Church of the Immaculate Conception in Kaskaskia, Randolph County, Illinois. She married Mathew Gray on 25 December 1832 in Kaskaskia, Randolph County, Illinois. He was a farmer. Matthew was born on 23 September 1809 in Belfast, Waldo County, Maine. His father died when he was four years old and his mother moved to Kaskaskia, Illinois. He was a veteran of the Blackhawk War. The couple first lived in Montebello, Hancock County, Illinois and then, in 1876, they moved to Ida Grove, Ida County, Iowa. They had three sons and seven daughters, of whom two daughters died in infancy and one daughter died in early childhood. Matthew died on 23 August 1881 and Catherine died on 2 November 1896, both in Ida Grove, Ida County, Iowa. They were both buried in the Ida Grove Cemetery in Ida Grove, Ida County, Iowa.

    ii. Michael, born 17 January 1815 in Ste. Genevieve County, Missouri. He was baptized on 23 April 1815 in Ste. Genevieve Catholic Church in Ste. Genevieve, Ste. Genevieve County, Missouri. He was a farmer. It is possible that Michael was involved in a shooting about 1845 which may be the reason he left Missouri and went to Texas. Michael served in the Mexican War as a private in the company led by Captain Ben F. Hill in Bell's Regiment Texas Mounted Volunteers commanded by Colonel J. C. Hayes. He enlisted in San Antonio, Bexar County, Texas on 15 April 1847 and was honorably discharged on 2 June 1848 on order of Major General Zachary Tayler. He purchased land in Smith County, Texas in December 1848. Michael married Sarah Ann Keegans on 22 March or April 1849 in Tyler, Smith County, Texas. Sarah was the daughter of James Keegans and Nancy Eades, born 1 October 1831 in Washington County, Texas. After their marriage the couple moved to Bastrop County, Texas where they resided for several years. In 1859 they moved up the Colorado River to the Perdernales River in Blanco County, Texas. Michael traded Wiley B. Waldrop two double yokes of oxen and their wagon for 107 acres of land. The couple had six sons and one daughter. Michael was ambushed and murdered on 18 January 1864 in Blanco County, Texas. The circumstances of his death are very vague, but may have been related to Civil War sympathies. Sarah died on 25 February 1901 in San Antonio, Bexar County, Texas. She was buried in the City Cemetery No. 4 in San Antonio, Bexar County, Texas.

    iii. Bolemus August "Gus," born about 1818 in Illinois. He was a farmer. He married Mary Ellen Ricketts on 3 June 1841 in Gasconade County, Missouri. Mary Ellen was the daughter of Benjamin R. Ricketts and Rachel Griffee, born 27 September 1828 in Muskingum County, Ohio. Gus and Mary Ellen lived on a farm in Osage County, Missouri that was very close to that of Mary Ellen's parents. The couple had six sons and six daughters. Gus died in 1870 in Osage County, Missouri. Mary Ellen died on 18 May 1872 in Osage County, Missouri. Their burial location is unknown.

U.S. residence other than Ste. Genevieve County, Missouri:
Baltimore, Maryland
Randolph County, Illinois

Land Patents:
Osage County, Missouri

Patentee	Issue Date	Land Office	Cert. No.	Serial No.	Twp	Rng	Sec	Acres
Burtcher, Bolemus	10 Jun 1857	St. Louis	22929	MO1040_.161	44-N	7-W	36	90.97
Burtcher, Bolemus	2 May 1859	St. Louis	29617	MO1100_410	44-N	7-W	36	40.00

Education: Could read and write
Occupation: Stonemason
Religious Affiliation: Roman Catholic
Comments:
The three Burtcher brothers, Bartholomew, Michael and Sebastian, came to the United States from Germany some time before September 1795. A probate record in Ste. Genevieve County, Missouri indicates that they had sisters but the sisters were not named and their location not given. The brothers lived in Baltimore, Maryland until about 1796 when they went west to Kaskaskia, Illinois where their skills as stonemasons were highly sought after. They were accompanied by their brother-in-law, Peter Bloom, and by the Woolford family with whom they had business dealings. By August of 1797, the brothers were living in Ste. Genevieve, Ste. Genevieve County, Missouri. The brothers are known to have built homes and buildings in Ste. Genevieve and did much work in the area on fireplaces, hearths, retaining walls and more. Sebastian Burtcher's residence is still standing in Ste. Genevieve. From the numerous lawsuits which appear in the records of Ste. Genevieve between 1797 and 1830, the brothers appear to have been fairly contentious. Sebastian and Michael were constantly being sued for not having paid their debts, for allowing other people to play billiards on their table on Sunday, for land claim disputes and so on. Michael and his wife Margaret were living in less than wedded bliss. In March 1819, Margaret filed for divorce in the Circuit Court of Ste. Genevieve County. In her petition, she stated that her husband had treated her with cruelty over a period of several years and that on the 20th of December 1817 had violently beaten her and thrown her out of the house. Michael responded with a countersuit, claiming that Margaret had committed adultery, but his named witnesses failed to appear in court. The jury found that Michael was the guilty party and granted the divorce in June 1821. Michael died in Randolph County, Illinois on 24 May 1829. Margaret is said to have died in 1833, most likely in Missouri.

Bernhard Busam Family
Surname Variations: Boosam
European Origin: Rammersweier, Baden, Germany
Family:
Father: Franz Michael Busam, born 6 June 1780 in Rammersweier, Baden, Germany. He died on 24 May 1857 in Rammersweier.
Mother: Maria Magdalena May, born 17 April 1774 in Weierbach, Baden, Germany.
   Children:
   i. Joseph, born 23 February 1802 in Rammersweier, Baden, Germany.
   ii. Benedikt, born 21 March 1803 in Rammersweier, Baden, Germany.
   iii. Elisabeth, born 30 October 1804 in Rammersweier, Baden, Germany. She married Bartholomaus Litterst on 12 September 1831 in Weingarten Church, Baden, Germany. Bartholomaus was the son of Johann Nepomuk Litterst and Magdalena Kiefer, born 15 August 1799 in Rammersweier. The couple had three sons and three daughters. Bartholomaus died on 1 April 1876 and Elisabeth died 6 October 1887, both in Rammersweier.
   iv. Caecilia, born 16 November 1806 in Rammersweier, Baden, Germany.
   v. Euphrosina, born 1 February 1809 in Rammersweier, Baden, Germany. She married Blasius Ott on 16 January 1832 in Weingarten Church, Baden, Germany. Blasius was the son of Andreas Ott and Catharina Basler, born 1 February 1800 in Zell-Offenburg, Baden, Germany. Blasius died on 11 January 1880 in Zell-Offenburg and Euphrosina died on 7 January 1883 in Rammersweier.
*   vi. Bernhard, born 15 July 1811 in Rammersweier, Baden, Germany. [See sketch below.]
   vii. Hieronimus, born 18 September 1813 in Rammersweier, Baden, Germany.
   viii. Benedikt, born 21 February 1816 in Rammersweier, Baden, Germany. He married Franziska Hauser on 24 November 1846 in Weingarten Church, Baden, Germany. Franziska was the daughter of Anton Hauser and Genovefa Hauser, born 28 May 1825 in Rammersweier. The couple had two sons and two daughters. Benedikt died on 15 December 1871 and Franziska died on 22 February 1876, both in Rammersweier.

ix. Theresia, born 16 October 1817 in Rammersweier, Baden, Germany.
x. Michael, born 19 September 1821 in Rammersweier, Baden, Germany. He married Juliana Viktoria Falk on 4 May 1852 in Weingarten Church, Baden, Germany. Juliana was the daughter of Valentin Falk and Genovefa Hospmann, born 17 February 1830 in Weierbach, Baden, Germany. The couple had one son and one daughter. Juliana died on 24 March 1899 and Michael died on 2 June 1899, both in Rammersweier.

Immigration:
Arrived 24 January 1857 from Le Havre, France to New Orleans aboard the *Wurtemberg*:
    Busam, Bernhard, 45   Baden
        Johanna, 44
        Sophie, 15
        George, 14
        Monica, 8
        Helene, 6

Biographical:
Husband: Bernhard Busam
    Birth – 15 July 1811 in Rammersweier, Baden, Germany.
    Death/Burial – 3 September 1858 in Ste. Genevieve County, Missouri. He was buried in the St. Joseph Cemetery in Zell, Ste. Genevieve County, Missouri.
Wife: Johanna Basler, daughter of Peter Basler and Maria Anna Sifferle
    Birth – 7 May 1812 in Fessenbach, Baden, Germany.
    Marriage – 11 May 1840 in Rammersweier, Baden, Germany.
    Death/Burial – Unknown. No mention of her has been found after the 1870 census.
    Children:
i. Sophia, born 11 May 1841 in Rammersweier, Baden, Germany. Before her marriage she lived in the household of Nicholas Munsch and worked as a domestic servant. Sophia married Franz Xavier Geiler on 9 December 1861 in Ste. Genevieve, Ste. Genevieve County, Missouri. Xavier was the son of Augustin Gailer and Theresia Haas, born 4 December 1828 in Durbach, Baden, Germany. [See Franz Xavier Geiler sketch.]
ii. George, born 24 March 1843 in Rammersweier, Baden, Germany. After his father's death, he was fostered first in the household of Nicholas Hauck and later with Jacob Stuppy. No further mention of him has been found after the 1870 census.
iii. Monica, 17 April 1848 in Rammersweier, Baden, Germany. After the death of her father, Monica and her mother lived in the household of John Braun. No further mention of her has been found after the 1860 census.
iv. Helena, born 24 August 1850 in Rammersweier, Baden, Germany. She died on 21 August 1868 in Ste. Genevieve County, Missouri. She was buried in the Memorial Cemetery in Ste. Genevieve, Ste. Genevieve County, Missouri. No issue.

Naturalization:

Name	Declaration	Naturalization	Origin
Busam, Bernhard	22 September 1857 Ste. Genevieve Co.		Baden

Occupation: Farmer
Religious Affiliation: Roman Catholic
Comments:
Bernhard Busam brought his family to the United States in 1857 and settled in Ste. Genevieve County, Missouri. Unfortunately, he died about a year and a half after he arrived and his family could not stay together. The older children were sent to live and work with neighboring families and Johanna and her youngest

daughter lived with the John Braun family. After 1870, the only member of the family who remained in Ste. Genevieve County was the oldest daughter, Sophia. No record has been found of the other members of the family after 1870.

Michael Busam Family
Surname Variations: Boosom, Bosom
European Origin: Rammersweier, Baden, Germany
Family:
Father: Lorenz Busam, born in July 1776 in Rammersweier, Baden, Germany. He died on 5 May 1862 in Weierbach, Baden, Germany.
Mother: Maria Anna Hoschmann, born 13 August 1769 in Rammersweier, Baden, Germany. She died on 21 February 1817 in Rammersweier.
Children:
- i. Bartholomäus, born 13 August 1795 in Rammersweier, Baden, Germany. He died on 15 August 1795 in Rammersweier. No issue.
- ii. Valentin, born 1 February 1797 in Rammersweier, Baden, Germany. He married Theresia Hansmann on 24 November 1823 in Weingarten, Baden, Germany. Theresia was the daughter of Franz Anton Hansmann and Maria Magdalena Neger, born 7 October 1798 in Rammersweier. The couple had five sons and four daughters. Theresia died on 16 July 1866 and Valentin died on 20 October 1875, both in Rammersweier.
- iii. Joseph, born 15 April 1799 in Rammersweier, Baden, Germany. He died on 30 March 1800 in Rammersweier. No issue.
- iv. Katharina, born 10 November 1800 in Rammersweier, Baden, Germany. She married Michael Litterst on 27 November 1826 in Weingarten, Baden, Germany. Michael was the son of Johannes Michael Litterst and Anna Maria Wigant, born 13 September 1795 in Weierbach, Baden, Germany. The couple had three sons and seven daughters, all born in Weierbach. Michael died on 28 January 1855 and Katharina died on 25 October 1875, both in Weierbach.
- v. Anton, born 11 May 1804 in Rammersweier, Baden, Germany.
- * vi. Michael, born 15 September 1805 in Rammersweier, Baden, Germany. [See sketch below.]
- vii. Maria Magdalena, born 16 December 1806 in Rammersweier, Baden, Germany. She married Simon Amandus Kern on 24 May 1831 in Weingarten, Baden, Germany. Simon was born on 26 October 1806 in Fessenbach, Baden, Germany. The couple had nine sons and five daughters, all born in Fessenbach.
- viii. Elisabeth, born 16 November 1810 in Rammersweier, Baden, Germany.

Immigration:
Arrived 24 February 1855 from Le Havre, France to New Orleans aboard the *Lexington*:
Busam, Michel, 45
    Maria Anna, 36
    Severin, 12
    Friedrich, 9
    Caroline, 5

Biographical:
Husband: Michael Busam
  Birth – 15 September 1805 in Rammersweier, Baden, Germany.
  Death/Burial – 26 December 1864 in River aux Vases, Ste. Genevieve County, Missouri.
Wife: Maria Anna Kiefer, daughter of Philip Jacob Kiefer and Maria Magdalena Omeis
  Birth – 19 May 1810 in Rammersweier, Baden, Germany.
  Marriage – 6 February 1832 in Weingarten, Baden, Germany.
  Death/Burial – 11 October 1891 in Weingarten, Ste. Genevieve County, Missouri. She was buried in the

Our Lady Help of Christians Cemetery in Weingarten, Ste. Genevieve County, Missouri.

Children:
    i. Genovefa, born 4 January 1833 in Rammersweier, Baden, Germany. She died on 19 January 1834 in Rammersweier. No issue.
    ii. Viktoria, born 20 December 1834 in Rammersweier, Baden, Germany. She died on 19 August 1836 in Rammersweier. No issue.
    iii. Luitgard, born 6 June 1837 in Rammersweier, Baden, Germany. She died on 12 November 1837 in Rammersweier. No issue.
    iv. Simon, born 2 January 1839 in Rammersweier, Baden, Germany. He died on 23 December 1842 in Rammersweier. No issue.
    v. Rosa, born 16 September 1840 in Rammersweier, Baden, Germany. She died on 28 December 1842 in Rammersweier. No issue.
    vi. Severin, born 8 October 1842 in Rammersweier, Baden, Germany. During the Civil War, Severin enlisted in the 78th Enrolled Missouri Militia. Severin married Catherina Jokerst on 1 September 1866 in Ste. Genevieve County, Missouri. Catharina was the daughter of Andreas "Andrew" Jokerst and Kunigunda Grass, born 12 January 1844 in Ste. Genevieve County, Missouri. The couple had at one son who died at the age of two years. Severin died on 20 May 1878 in River aux Vases, Ste. Genevieve County. Catharina married Simon Burgert as her second husband on 22 February 1881 in Ste. Genevieve County, Missouri. [See Simon Burgert sketch.]
    vii. Friedrich, born 11 November 1844 in Rammersweier, Baden, Germany. No further mention of him has been found after he appears on the ship's manifest with his family.
    viii. Andreas, born 29 November 1847 in Rammersweier, Baden, Germany. He died on 20 February 1849 in Rammersweier. No issue.
    ix. Carolina, born 5 February 1850 in Rammersweier, Baden, Germany. She married Wendelin Weiler on 26 November 1872 in Ste. Genevieve County, Missouri. Wendelin was the son of Anton Weiler and Salome Deck, born 17 February 1849 in Ste. Genevieve County, Missouri. [See Anton Weiler sketch.]
    x. Karl, born 30 January 1854 in Rammersweier, Baden, Germany. He died on 14 April 1854 in Rammersweier. No issue.

Naturalization:

Name	Declaration	Naturalization	Origin
Busam, Michael	14 May 1858	9 May 1861 Ste. Genevieve Co.	Baden

Military:
Served in the U.S. Civil War for the Union:
Private, Company F, 78th Enrolled Missouri Militia
    Severin Busman [Busam] enlisted in August 1862 in Ste. Genevieve, Missouri. He was ordered into service on 16 October 1864 and was relieved from duty on 25 November 1864. Total of 41 days of actual service

Occupation: Farmer
Religious Affiliation: Roman Catholic
Comments:
Michael Busam was a farmer in Rammersweier, Baden, Germany. He and his wife had ten children, of whom only two sons and one daughter survived beyond infancy. Michael moved his family to the United States in 1855 and they settled in Ste. Genevieve County, Missouri where Michael bought a farm. Michael died on 26 December 1864 in River aux Vases, Ste. Genevieve County. His burial location is unknown. After her husband's death, Maria lived with her surviving son until his death in 1878. She then moved into her daughter Caroline's household and remained there until her death on 11 October 1891 in Weingarten, Ste. Genevieve

County, Missouri. She was buried in the Our Lady Help of Christians Cemetery in Weingarten, Ste. Genevieve County, Missouri.

C

Carl Felix "Charles" Carssow Family

Surname Variations: Carsaw, Carso, Carsow, Cars[s]on,
European Origin: Ellrich, Nordhausen, Thuringia, Germany
Family:
Father: Julius Carssow, born about 1805 in Prussia. He is said to have died in 1844 on the British island of Heligoland [now a German possession].
Mother: Rosalia Fischer
   Child:
*   i. Carl Felix "Charles," born 25 January 1835 in Ellrich, Nordhausen, Thuringia, Germany. [See sketch below.]

Immigration:
Arrived about 1853 from Germany to New Orleans aboard an unknown vessel:
    Carssow, Carl Felix

Biographical:
Husband: Carl Felix "Charles" Carssow
   Birth – 25 January 1835 in Ellrich, Nordhausen, Thuringia, Germany.
   Death/Burial – 1 May 1905 in Lewiston, Nez Perce County, Idaho.
Wife: Anna Schwartz, daughter of Adam Schwartz and Marie Louise Belbeau [See Adam Schwartz sketch.]
   Birth – 10 January 1847 in Ste. Genevieve County, Missouri.
   Marriage – 19 July 1863 in Ste. Genevieve County, Missouri.
   Death/Burial – 21 January 1922 in Lewiston, Nez Perce County, Idaho.
   Children:
    i. Felix Hugo, born 4 September 1864 in Ste. Genevieve County, Missouri. He studied engineering at the School of Mines in Rolla, Missouri in the late 1880s. He moved to California about 1887 to attend the University of California at Berkley where he earned a civil engineering degree in 1891. After he graduated, he moved to San Francisco and worked as a city engineer. In 1893, he traveled to several major cities in the U.S., studying the construction of their waterworks. About 1900, he moved east and lived about three years in Camden, New Jersey. In 1903 he went to Germany, returning in August of that year. By 1910, Felix was again living in San Francisco where he was employed as a city engineer. In 1919, he moved to Honolulu, Hawaii where he opened his own engineering firm. He remained there until about 1923 when he moved to San Diego, California and went to work as a draftsman for the Navy. Felix does not appear to have ever married and has no known issue. His date and place of death are unknown at present.
    ii. Eugene Julius, born in December 1866 in Ste. Genevieve County, Missouri. He studied law at the University of Missouri and earned his degree there in 1888. He returned to Ste. Genevieve and practiced for a time in Ste. Genevieve in partnership with Henry S. Shaw, a prominent attorney, in the firm of Shaw & Carssow. In early 1889, Eugene dissolved his law partnership and moved to Spokane Falls, Washington Territory. By 1910, he had traveled north to Ophir, Alaska and joined the rush to the gold fields. He does not appear to have had much success as a miner. About 1916, Eugene moved to Big Sandy, Chouteau County, Montana where he owned and operated a billiard hall and confectionary shop until the early 1940's. He died on 8 September 1948 in Lewiston, Nez Perce County, Idaho. He does not appear to have ever

married and had no known issue.

iii. Mary Julia, born about 1868 in Ste. Genevieve County, Missouri. She died in 1870 in Ste. Genevieve County, Missouri. No issue.

iv. Otto Charles, born 2 January 1871 in Ste. Genevieve County, Missouri. When he first moved to the western states, he lived on a farm near Spokane, Spokane County, Washington. Otto married Jessie O. Cameron on 2 January 1893 at Sprague, Lincoln County, Washington. Jessie was the daughter of George W. Cameron and Lucinda Bell, born about 1871 in Iowa. The couple does not appear to have had any children. No record of Jessie has been found after her marriage, but she may have died before November 1898. Otto began to teach school and then moved to Moscow, Latah County, Idaho. He married Rhoda Belle Estes as his second wife in Moscow on 9 November 1898. Belle was the daughter of James Karr Estes and Virginia Pendleton Goodwin, born 7 June 1874 in Sharp County, Arkansas. After their marriage, Otto was the principle of the Russell school near Moscow for two years. Then he moved his family to Mt. Idaho in Idaho County where he was superintendent of the city schools. The family later moved back to Moscow where Otto established a grocery business and Belle worked in the store as the book keeper. The couple had four sons and two daughters, of whom one daughter died in infancy. Otto's health began to fail in early 1912 and the daily running of the grocery store fell to Belle. Otto died from inflammatory rheumatism and Bright's disease on 2 January 1913 in Moscow. He was buried in the Moscow Cemetery in Moscow. Belle continued to run the store after her husband's death, but closed it and retired in the 1940s. She died in February 1964 in Moscow and was buried in the Moscow Cemetery.

v. Rudolph Benton, born 26 January 1873 in Ste. Genevieve County, Missouri. He studied at the University of Michigan School of Pharmacy, graduating in 1892. He and his brothers Oscar and Arthur established the Carssow Pharmaceutical Company in St. Louis, Missouri in the late 1890s, but after several years, the two younger brothers moved west to rejoin their parents and Rudolph tried to keep the business going by himself. He married Harriet Frances Timbermann about 1907 in Missouri. Harriet was the daughter of John Davis Timbermann and Mary Emma Bishop, born 25 July 1879 in Cotton Plant, New Madrid County, Missouri. The couple moved to San Antonio, Bexar County, Texas where Rudolph first worked as a chemist for a pharmaceutical company and then he started his own drug store in San Antonio. The couple had three sons and one daughter, of whom one son died as a teenager. Rudolph died on 22 March 1953 and Harriet died on 31 July 1974, both in Bexar County, Texas. They were both buried in the Mission Burial Park in San Antonio, Bexar County, Texas.

vi. George Charles, born 28 July 1875 in Ste. Genevieve County, Missouri. He moved west and settled on a ranch north of Lamona, Lincoln County, Washington. He married Anna Luiten on 20 October 1900 at Ritzville, Adams County, Washington. Anna was the daughter of Jacob E. Luiten and Elisabeth "Elisa" Kuhlman, born 13 August 1880 in Glencoe, McLeod County, Minnesota. The couple had two sons and four daughters. Anna died of supperative peritonitis on 20 December 1915 in Harrington, Lincoln County, Washington. She was buried in the Odessa Cemetery in Odessa, Lincoln County, Washington. George seems to have lived an aimless life after his wife's death. He remained on the ranch until 1921 and then moved to Lewiston, Idaho for a few years. From there he went to California in 1923. He later went to Big Sandy, Chouteau County, Montana and lived with his brother Eugene in the 1930s. He visited at the homes of various relatives until World War II broke out, and he took a defense job at a California shipyard. In January 1945 he suffered a heart attack and was hospitalized for three weeks but returned to his duties until ill health forced him to quit. He decided to visit his brother, Rudolph, in San Antonio to recuperate. He died there in May 1945. His body was shipped back to Washington and he was buried beside his wife in the Odessa Cemetery in Odessa, Lincoln County, Washington.

vii. Oscar Christian, born 20 October 1878 in Ste. Genevieve County, Missouri. He graduated from the St. Louis University School of Medicine [Marion-Sims Medical College] in 1898. He and his brothers Rudolph and Arthur established the Carssow Pharmaceutical Company in St.

Louis, Missouri in the late 1890s, but he resigned from the company after several years. In 1912, Oscar traveled to Austria to study surgery and returned to the United States in late 1913. He moved to Lewiston, Nez Perce County, Idaho and established a medical practice. He later purchased a building in downtown Lewiston which became known as the Carssow Building to house his office. He was a charter member of the American College of Surgeons and was a member of the North Idaho Medical Society, the Idaho State Medical Society, the Nez Perce Masonic Lodge and the Lewiston Elks Lodges. He also served as vice-president of the American Bank & Trust Company which was also located in the Carssow Building. Oscar served as mayor of Lewiston in 1911 when the then-Mayor, Ben F. Tweedy resigned after a dispute with the city council over option law. He was married to Anna Weir Eaves on 15 December 1925 in Lewiston. Anna was the daughter of Elliott Weir Eaves and Julia May Gregory, born 13 July 1890 in Lewiston. The couple had no children. Oscar died after a prolonged illness on 18 August 1941 in Spokane, Spokane County, Washington. His burial location is unknown at present. His widow eventually moved to San Francisco, California where she died of breast cancer on 17 June 1972. She was buried in the Cypress Lawn Cemetery in Colma, San Mateo County, California. No issue.

viii. Arthur Eric, born 4 January 1881 in Ste. Genevieve County, Missouri. He and his brothers Oscar and Rudolph established the Carssow Pharmaceutical Company in St. Louis, Missouri in the late 1890s, but after several years, he left to rejoin his family in Idaho. In Lewiston, Arthur established the Carssow Drug Company [pharmaceutical]. He was arrested on a bootlegging charge in March 1913 when he was caught pouring out illegal liquor. Arthur appears to have been married as early as 1912 to Maria A. _____. She was born of unknown parents about 1893 in Kansas. The couple does not appear to have had any children. No record of Maria has been found after about 1924. There is an indication that the couple had been divorced in the 1940 census. Arthur moved to Colville, Stevens County, Washington by the mid-1930s and opened another drug store. He was shot twice in the abdomen and seriously wounded when he intervened in a domestic dispute. He recovered from the incident, but died on 17 October 1949 in Colville, Stevens County, Washington. Arthur was buried in the Normal Hill Cemetery in Lewiston, Nez Perce County, Idaho.

ix. Grace Rosalie, born 26 February 1883 in Ste. Genevieve County, Missouri. She attended the Normal School at Cape Girardeau [now Southeast Missouri State University]. She later moved to Lewiston, Idaho to join her parents. She married Milo R. Bartlett on 18 November 1903 in Lewiston. Milo was the son of William Bartlett and Ida Drew, born about 1879 in Iowa. The couple had no children together and were divorced before 1920. After her divorce, Grace supported herself by working as a bookkeeper in her brother Oscar's medical office. She married August Swanson Frost as her second husband on 22 June 1924 in Moscow, Latah County, Idaho. August was born of unknown parents on 6 August 1880 in Skone, Sweden. He came to the United States in May 1903. He lived in Chicago, Cook County, Illinois for a number of years after his arrival. He was married there to Olive Magnuson as his first wife on 9 March 1907. He and Olive appear to have had one daughter, born in Illinois. August moved to Idaho with his family by 1920. Olive died on 7 February 1924 in Moscow, Latah County, Idaho. There were no children born to August and Grace and they were divorced by 1930. Grace remained single for the rest of her life. She moved to Vallejo, Solano County, California after her second divorce where she worked as a chemical technician in the Navy yard hospital. She lived for a while in San Francisco before retiring to Coldwater, Branch County, Michigan. She died on 24 April 1969 in Coldwater and was buried in the Lake View Cemetery in Quincy, Branch County, Michigan. No issue.

x. Hedwig Ida, born 12 November 1888 in Ste. Genevieve County, Missouri. She moved to Lewiston, Nez Perce County, Idaho with her parents as a young girl. She attended the University of Idaho for two years and then moved to Seattle, Washington to attend the University of Washington, graduating two years later. She taught school in Asotin County,

Washington for a year after she graduated and then moved to San Juan, Puerto Rico to teach. She was married in San Juan on 9 September 1914 to John J. "Jack" Murrell. Jack was in Puerto Rico working as an electrical engineer when the couple met. He was born of unknown parents about 1882 in Missouri. The couple lived in Alabama where they raised their two daughters. Jack's date and place of death are unknown. Ida died on 1 January 1970 in San Bernardino, California.

U.S. residence other than Ste. Genevieve County, Missouri:
Louisiana
Minnesota
Cedar County, Iowa
St. Louis, Missouri
Lewiston, Nez Perce County, Idaho

Naturalization:

Name	Declaration	Naturalization	Origin	Remarks
Carssow, Charles F.			Germany	1900 Census Info

Military:
Served in the U.S. Civil War for the Union:
Felix Carssow reportedly served a short time as an assistant hospital surgeon in the Union Army.
[1890 Veterans Census, Ste. Genevieve County, Missouri].

Education:
Carl Felix Carrsow is said to have attended several years of medical school in Louisiana.
He graduated from the St. Louis Medical College on 1 March 1863.
Occupation: Medical Doctor and Druggist
Religious Affiliation: Lutheran
Political Affiliation and/or Any Offices Held:
Ste. Genevieve City Alderman, elected July 1884
Member, Ste. Genevieve Board of Education
Ste. Genevieve County Physician [Health Inspector], appointed 1885
Comments:
Carl Felix "Charles" Carssow was the son of Julius Carssow and Rosalia Fischer. His father was a District Inspector of Customs under the Prussian government. He is said to have died on the British island of Heligoland at the age of 39 years [about 1844]. Charles is said to have come to the United States in 1853, landing in New Orleans where he stayed for several years. He apparently began to study medicine in this city. After about three years, he reportedly went first to Minnesota and then Iowa before moving south to St. Louis, Missouri where he resumed his medical studies. He graduated from the St. Louis Medical College on 1 March 1863. He served a short time as an assistant hospital surgeon in the Union Army. In the summer of 1863 he moved to Ste. Genevieve County near the small village of New Offenburg where he opened his first practice. He married Anna Schwartz on 19 July 1863 in Ste. Genevieve County. The Carssows remained in New Offenburg until the early 1870s when they moved into the city of Ste. Genevieve. The couple had eleven children, although records for only seven sons and three daughters have been found. Of these ten, one daughter died in infancy. Charles soon built up a large practice in Ste. Genevieve and began to accumulate considerable property. Aside from his medical practice, Carl also served as a city alderman and was a member of the Board of Education. He also served as county physician, providing medical care to the inmates of the Ste. Genevieve County Poor Farm and conducting health inspections of various public institutions. In the summer of 1899, he moved with his wife and youngest children to Lewiston, Nez Perce County, Idaho. In spite of being 65 years old, he soon built up a good practice there. Charles died at his home in Lewiston on 1 May 1905. Anna lived in Lewiston with a widowed son and her two youngest daughters. She died on 21 January 1922 in Lewiston.

Johann Georg Cromer Family

Surname Variations: Cramer, Kramer, Kromer, Krummer
European Origin: Baden, Germany
Family:
Father: Unknown
Mother: Unknown
   Child:
*   i.   Johann Georg [See sketch below.]

Immigration:
Arrived about October or November 1817 from Germany to Philadelphia aboard an unknown vessel:
    Cromer, Johann Georg
        Rosine
        Andrew

Biographical:
Husband: Johann Georg Cromer
   Birth – in Germany.
   Death/Burial – 4 July 1834 in Ste. Genevieve, Ste. Genevieve County, Missouri.
Wife: Rosine Ziegler
   Birth – about 1799 in Germany.
   Marriage – about 1815 in Germany.
   Death/Burial – 4 August 1851 in Ste. Genevieve, Ste. Genevieve County, Missouri. She was buried in the Memorial Cemetery in Ste. Genevieve, Ste. Genevieve County, Missouri.
Children:
    i.   Andrew, born about 1816 in Baden, Germany. He worked in Ste. Genevieve County as a farm laborer and was living in the household of Pius Palmer in 1860. Andrew died on 2 February 1879 in Ste. Genevieve County. He was buried in the Sts. Philip and James Cemetery in River aux Vases, Ste. Genevieve County, Missouri. He does not appear to have ever married and had no known issue.
    ii.   Francis Joseph, born about 1819 in Pennsylvania. He married Catherine Pfeiffer on 22 November 1842 in Ste. Genevieve County, Missouri. She was the daughter of Philip Pfeiffer and Catherine _____, born on 8 April 1826. The couple had one son and two daughters, all born in Ste. Genevieve. By 1850, Francis had moved to St. Louis where he worked as a clerk for a steamboat office. In 1854 they moved to Dubuque, Dubuque County, Iowa where Francis worked as a grocer and then was hired as the deputy city manager. He was a member of the Masonic Fraternity and belonged to the Dubuque Lodge. Francis died some time between 1865 and 1870, most likely in Dubuque. By 1870, after her husband's death, Catherine moved to Black Hawk County, Iowa with her two daughters. They supported themselves by working as milliners. Catherine died on 26 May 1883 in Hamilton County, Iowa. She was buried in the Graceland Cemetery in Webster City, Hamilton County, Iowa.
    iii.   Xavier, born 22 May 1824 in Pennsylvania. Xavier was a cooper by trade. He married Paulina Fitzkam on 9 April 1850 in Ste. Genevieve County, Missouri. She was the daughter of Simon Fitzkam and Maria Scholastika Hurst, born 25 June 1829 in Rammersweier, Baden, Germany. The couple had two sons, both of whom died in infancy. Paulina died on 5 June 1852 in Ste. Genevieve. She was buried in the Memorial Cemetery in Ste. Genevieve, Ste. Genevieve County, Missouri. After his wife's death, Xavier may have followed his older brother to Iowa. He married Barbara Wilber as his second wife about 1858 most likely in Dubuque County, Iowa. Barbara was the daughter of ____ Wilber and Catherine _____, born 16 July 1834 in Hesse-Darmstadt, Germany. About 1859, Xavier moved his family to Galena, Jo Daviess County, Illinois where he continued his trade as a cooper. The couple had four sons and three

daughters. Xavier died on 8 March 1888 and Barbara died on 2 March 1889, both in Galena, Jo Daviess County, Illinois. They are both buried in the St. Marys Cemetery in Jo Daviess County, Illinois.

   iv. Maria Anna, born about 1826 in New York. She married John Wittmore on 3 February 1847 at Ste. Genevieve, Ste. Genevieve County, Missouri. He was the son of Joseph Wittmore and Barbara Weininger, born about 1821 in Bavaria, Germany. [See John Wittmore sketch.]

   v. George, born about 1828 most likely in Ste. Genevieve County, Missouri. He died in February 1837 in Ste. Genevieve County, Missouri. No issue.

   vi. Lucy, born 15 February 1833 most likely in Ste. Genevieve County, Missouri. She was baptized in the Ste. Genevieve Catholic Church in Ste. Genevieve on 10 March 1833. Lucy died on 1 July 1834 in Ste. Genevieve, Ste. Genevieve County, Missouri. No issue.

U.S. residence prior to Ste. Genevieve County, Missouri:
Pennsylvania
New York

Naturalization:

Name	Declaration	Naturalization	Origin
Krummer, Andres [Cromer, Andrew]		22 October 1866 Ste. Genevieve Co.	Baden

Religious Affiliation: Roman Catholic

Comments:

Johann Georg Cromer and his wife, Rosine Ziegler came to the United States with their infant son in 1817. They landed in Philadelphia and, according to the law of that time, within thirty days of his arrival, Johann had indentured himself for a period of two years to pay for the cost of the voyage. The family moved to Ste. Genevieve County, Missouri before 1833 and Johann purchased a lot in the city of Ste. Genevieve. It is possible that Rosine was a sister to Mathias and Sebastian Ziegler. Johann Georg died of cholera on 4 July 1834 in Ste. Genevieve County, Missouri. Sebastian Ziegler and Jacob Yealy were present and received George's verbal last will and testament which they registered in the County Court on 17 July 1834. Rosine was left to raise her four surviving children by herself. She was living in the household of her son, Xavier, in 1850. Rosine died on 4 August 1851 in Ste. Genevieve County and was buried in the Memorial Cemetery in Ste. Genevieve, Ste. Genevieve County, Missouri.

D

Christopher Dallas Family

Surname Variations: Dalles, Del[l]es[s]e, Delisse
European Origin: Hombourg-Haut, Lorraine, France
Family:
Father: Jean Delles
Mother: Marguerite Boussert [or Bieser]
   Children:
†   i. Jean "John," born 2 June 1819 in France. [See John Dallas sketch.]
*   ii. Christopher, born 15 April 1831 in France. [See sketch below.]

Immigration:
Arrived some time before October 1858 aboard an unknown vessel:
    Delles, Christopher

Biographical:
Husband: Christopher Dallas
   Birth – 15 April 1831 in France.
   Death/Burial – 2 December 1874 in Ste. Genevieve County, Missouri. He was buried in the Sts. Philip and James Cemetery in River aux Vases, Ste. Genevieve County, Missouri.

1) Wife: Felicity Schmiederer, daughter of Augustin Schmiederer and Catherine Hermann [See August Schmiederer sketch.]
   Birth – about 1840 in Germany.
   Marriage – 5 October 1858 in Zell, Ste. Genevieve County, Missouri.
   Death/Burial – before August 1870 in Ste. Genevieve County, Missouri.
   Children:
      i. John C., born 22 September 1864 in Ste. Genevieve County, Missouri. He was baptized on 23 October 1864 in the Ste. Genevieve Catholic Church in Ste. Genevieve, Ste. Genevieve County, Missouri. As a young man, John moved to San Antonio, Bexar County, Texas where he worked as a saloon barkeeper and later he managed a cafe. He married Margaret C. "Maggie" Eiserloh about 1896 most likely in San Antonio, Bexar County, Texas. Maggie was the daughter of Peter Eiserloh and Margaret Mary Kraus, born 20 July 1874 in San Antonio, Bexar County, Texas. The couple had two sons, of whom one died in early childhood. John died of a cerebral hemorrhage complicated by a diabetic coma on 23 October 1931 in San Antonio. Maggie died of leukemia on 9 May 1942 in San Antonio. They were both buried in the St. Joseph Society Catholic Cemetery in San Antonio, Bexar County, Texas.
      ii. Rosine, born 5 January 1869 in Ste. Genevieve County, Missouri. She was baptized on 9 February 1869 in the Ste. Genevieve Catholic Church in Ste. Genevieve, Ste. Genevieve County, Missouri. Rosine died on 1 February 1874 in Ste. Genevieve County. She was buried in the Saints Philip and James Cemetery in River aux Vases, Ste. Genevieve County, Missouri. No issue.

2) Wife: Franziska "Frances" Kiefer, daughter of Franz Bartholomew Kiefer and Helena Basler
   Birth – 30 March 1849 in Fessenbach, Baden, Germany.
   1) Marriage – Marriage – 16 August 1870 in River aux Vases, Ste. Genevieve County, Missouri to Christopher Dallas

2) Marriage – 29 March 1875 in River aux Vases, Ste. Genevieve County, Missouri to Joseph Rudloff. [See Johann Georg Rudloff sketch.]

Death/Burial – 14 May 1941 in St. Louis, Missouri. She was buried in the Calvary Cemetery in St. Louis, Missouri.

Children:
- iii. Francis Joseph "Frank," born 19 June 1871 in Ste. Genevieve County, Missouri. He was baptized on 15 August 1871 in the Sts. Philip and James Catholic Church in River aux Vases, Ste. Genevieve County, Missouri. Frank died of pneumonia on 8 November 1883 in Ste. Genevieve County. He was buried in the Immaculate Conception Cemetery in St. Mary, Ste. Genevieve County, Missouri. No issue.
- iv. Helena Josephine "Lena," born 19 April 1873 in Ste. Genevieve County, Missouri. She was baptized on 25 May 1873 in the Ste. Genevieve Catholic Church in Ste. Genevieve, Ste. Genevieve County, Missouri. She married Joseph M. Bader on 12 September 1893 in Ste. Genevieve, Ste. Genevieve County. Joseph was the son of Joseph Bader and Mary Witty, born 29 September 1871 in Ste. Genevieve County, Missouri. [See Joseph Bader sketch.]

Naturalization:

Name	Declaration	Naturalization	Origin
Dallas, Christopher	7 November 1860	5 November 1863 Ste. Genevieve Co.	France

Military:
Served in the U.S. Civil War for the Union:
Private, Company D, 78th Enrolled Missouri Militia
  Christopher Dallas [or Delles] enlisted on 30 April 1864 in St. Mary's, Missouri. He was ordered into service on 16 October 1864 and was relieved from duty on 25 November 1864. He served a total of 41 days of actual service.

Occupation: Farmer
Religious Affiliation: Roman Catholic
Comments:
Christopher Dallas was the much younger brother of Johann "John" Dallas who came to Ste. Genevieve County, Missouri in 1847. Christopher followed his older brother to Ste. Genevieve County some time between 1850 and October 1858 when he married Felicity Schmiederer in Ste. Genevieve County. Christopher was a farmer and bought a farm near River aux Vases. The couple had one son and one daughter, of whom the daughter died in early childhood. Felicity died some time before August 1870, most likely in Ste. Genevieve County. Her burial location is unknown. Christopher married Franziska "Frances" Kiefer as his second wife. The couple had one son and one daughter, of whom the son died in early adolescence. Christopher died on 2 December 1874 in Ste. Genevieve County. He was buried in the Sts. Philip and James Cemetery in River aux Vases, Ste. Genevieve County. Frances married Joseph Rudloff as her second husband on 29 March 1875 in River aux Vases, Ste. Genevieve County, Missouri. Joseph was a widower with two children of his own. Frances died of heart disease on 14 May 1941 in St. Louis, Missouri. She was buried in the Calvary Cemetery in St. Louis.

John Dallas Family
Surname Variations: Dalles, Del[l]es[s]e, Delisse
European Origin: Hombourg-Haut, Lorraine, France
Family:
Father: Jean Delles
Mother: Marguerite Boussert or Bieser
  Children:

Note: For a comprehensive discussion of Jean Delles' children see the Christopher Dallas sketch.

Immigration:
Arrived 15 April 1847 from Le Havre, France to New York aboard the *Amulet*:
    Delisse [Dalles], J[ohn], 28
        Barbara, 29
        Johann, 2 – son of John
        Barbara, 1 – daughter of John

Biographical:
Husband: John Dallas [aka Jean Delles]
    Birth – 2 June 1819 in Elsass-Lothringen [German name for Alsace-Lorraine], France.
    Death/Burial – 11 August 1902 in Ste. Genevieve County, Missouri. He was buried in the Valle Spring Cemetery in Ste. Genevieve, Ste. Genevieve County, Missouri.
Wife: Barbara Reichert, daughter of Peter Reichert and Catherine Jeannot
    Birth – 19 September 1817 in Hombourg-Haut, Lorraine, France.
    Marriage – 14 January 1845 in Hombourg-Haut, Lorraine, France.
    Death/Burial – 3 December 1885 in Ste. Genevieve County, Missouri. She was buried in the Valle Spring Cemetery in Ste. Genevieve, Ste. Genevieve County, Missouri.
    Children:
        i. John, born 23 April 1845 in France. He was a farmer. John married Catherine Monck [aka Mank] on 20 February 1871 in St. Clair County, Illinois. Catherine was the daughter of unknown parents, born about 1850 in Illinois. The couple had two sons and one daughter, of whom one son and one daughter died in infancy. Catherine died 30 March 1876 in Ste. Genevieve County, Missouri. She was buried in the Memorial Cemetery in Ste. Genevieve, Ste. Genevieve County. John married Maria Anna "Mary" Siebert, widow of Henry Eichenlaub on 7 June 1880 in Ste. Genevieve County, Missouri. [See Gervais Eichenlaub sketch.] Mary was the daughter of Henry Siebert and Mary Ann Sucher, born 6 November 1853 in Ste. Genevieve County, Missouri. She had two sons and one daughter with her first husband, of whom only one son survived infancy. John and Mary had seven sons and five daughters. Mary died of dysentery on 22 July 1916 and John died of cystitis and cholera morbus on 25 September 1918, both in Ste. Genevieve County. They were both buried in the Sacred Heart Cemetery in Ozora, Ste. Genevieve County, Missouri.
        ii. Barbara, born 14 December 1846 in France. She married Joseph Sucher on 19 April 1870 in Ste. Genevieve, Ste. Genevieve County, Missouri. Joseph was the son of Lorenz "Lawrence" Sucher and Anna Regina Kirchner, born 23 September 1844 in Ste. Genevieve County, Missouri. [See Lorenz Sucher sketch.]
        iii. Catherine, born 9 June 1848 in [Berks County?], Pennsylvania. She married Franz Xavier Lipp on 27 November 1866 in Ste. Genevieve County, Missouri. Xavier was the son of Ignatius Lipp and Brigitta Schnurr, born 22 September 1835 in Sasbach, Achern, Baden, Germany. [See Franz Xavier Lipp sketch.]
        iv. Peter, born in February 1850 in [Berks County?], Pennsylvania. He was baptized on 5 May 1850 in the Ste. Genevieve Catholic Church in Ste. Genevieve, Ste. Genevieve County, Missouri. Peter married Mary Ann Gittinger on 10 November 1874 in River aux Vases, Ste. Genevieve County, Missouri. Mary Ann was the daughter of Franz Anton Gittinger and Maria Victoria Baelzer, born about 1853 in France. The couple had one stillborn infant and a daughter who died in infancy. Mary Ann died of childbed fever on 7 March 1877, less than two weeks after the birth of her second child. She was buried in the Sts. Philip and James Cemetery in River aux Vases, Ste. Genevieve County, Missouri. Peter's date of death and burial location are unknown.
        v. Mary Anna, born 24 June 1851 in Ste. Genevieve County, Missouri. She was baptized on

14 August 1851 in the Ste. Genevieve Catholic Church in Ste. Genevieve, Ste. Genevieve County, Missouri. Mary married Joseph Gittinger on 5 September 1871 in Ste. Genevieve County, Missouri. Joseph was the son of Franz Anton Gittinger and Maria Victoria Baelzer, born 5 February 1843 in Alsace-Lorraine, France. [See Franz Anton Gittinger sketch.]

vi. Anna, born 18 September 1852 in Ste. Genevieve County, Missouri. She was baptized on 9 December 1852 in the Ste. Genevieve Catholic Church in Ste. Genevieve, Ste. Genevieve County, Missouri. Anna married Aloysius Anton "Anthony" Trautmann on 30 September 1873 in Ste. Genevieve, Ste. Genevieve County. Anthony was the son of Peter Paul Trautmann and Monica Fallert, born 11 January 1851 in Ste. Genevieve County, Missouri. [See Peter Trautman sketch.]

vii. Sarah, about 1853 in Missouri. No further information.

viii. Christopher, 3 April 1856 in Ste. Genevieve County, Missouri. He married Maria Theresia Bahr on 12 June 1877 in Ste. Genevieve County, Missouri. Maria was the daughter of Bartholomew Bahr and Regina Friedmann, born 6 May 1857 in Ste. Genevieve County, Missouri. The couple had seven sons and four daughters, of whom two sons died in childhood. Christopher died of typhus of 8 June 1906 and Maria died of pneumonia on 21 March 1914, both in Ste. Genevieve County, Missouri. They were both buried in the Sacred Heart Cemetery in Ozora, Ste. Genevieve County, Missouri.

ix. Charles, born 28 October 1857 in Ste. Genevieve County, Missouri. He was baptized on 8 August 1858 in the Ste. Genevieve Catholic Church in Ste. Genevieve, Ste. Genevieve County, Missouri. Charles died on 10 October 1858 in Ste. Genevieve County, Missouri. He was buried in the St. Joseph Cemetery in Zell, Ste. Genevieve County, Missouri. No issue.

x. Eliza, about 1860 in Missouri. No further information.

xi. Pauline, born 10 September 1859 in Ste. Genevieve County, Missouri. She was baptized on 30 October 1859 in the Ste. Genevieve Catholic Church in Ste. Genevieve, Ste. Genevieve County, Missouri. Pauline married Lawrence Rechert on 25 August 1879 in Ste. Genevieve County, Missouri. Lawrence was the son of Jacob Rechert and Maria Bucher, born about 1855 in Scott County, Missouri. He was a carpenter. The couple moved to Oran, Scott County, Missouri shortly after they were married. They are said to have had seven children, of whom one son and three daughters survived to adulthood. Lawrence is said to have died on 12 March 1893 in Scott County, Missouri. He is buried in the St. Lawrence Catholic Cemetery in New Hamburg, Scott County, Missouri. Pauline died of heart disease on 12 November 1958 in St. Louis, Missouri. She was buried in Cape Girardeau, Cape Girardeau County, Missouri

U.S. residence prior to Ste. Genevieve County, Missouri:
[Berks County?], Pennsylvania

Land Patents:
Ste. Genevieve County, Missouri

Patentee	Issue Date	Land Office	Cert. No.	Serial No.	Twp	Rng	Sec	Acres
Dallas, John	1 Oct 1880	Ironton	43645	MO4220_.265	37-N	9-E	28/22	8.41
Deelles, John	15 Nov 1854	Jackson	15800	MO3670_.324	37-N	9-E	27	68.20

Naturalization:

Name	Declaration	Naturalization	Origin
Dallas, John	21 May 1855	23 May 1857 Ste. Genevieve Co.	France

Military:
Served in the U.S. Civil War for the Union:
Private, Company D, 78th Enrolled Missouri Militia
John Dallas [or Delles] enlisted on 30 April 1864 in St. Mary's, Missouri. He was ordered into service on

16 October 1864 and was relieved from duty on 25 November 1864. He served a total of 41 days of actual service.

Education: Could read and write.
Occupation: Farmer
Religious Affiliation: Roman Catholic
Comments:
John Dallas brought his wife and two children to the United States from Alsace-Lorraine, France. The village where his wife was born was only a few miles from the German town Saarbruken. The Dallas [or Delles] family was of German origin. The Dallases appear to have moved slowly west from New York once they arrived in America. They spent several years in Pennsylvania before they eventually arrived in Ste. Genevieve County, Missouri. John bought land and began to farm. John's younger brother, Christopher, followed him to Ste. Genevieve County some time between 1850 and 1858. John and Barbara had four sons and seven daughters, of whom one son and two daughters died in infancy or early childhood. Barbara died of capillary bronchitis on 5 December 1885 in Ste. Genevieve County. After his wife's death, John traveled to Texas to visit his daughter and nephew. He stayed for a couple of years and then returned to Missouri. John suffered a paralytic stroke during the first week of August 1902 and due to his advanced age, he did not recover. He died on 16 August 1902 in Ste. Genevieve County. Both Barbara and John were buried in the Valle Spring Cemetery in Ste. Genevieve, Ste. Genevieve County, Missouri.

Franz Sales Deck Family
Surname Variations: None
European Origin: Weierbach, Baden, Germany
Family:
Father: Simon Deck, born 30 October 1812 in Weierbach, Baden, Germany. He died on 18 May 1883 in
   Weierbach.
Mother: Anna Maria Kiefer, born 19 December 1816 in Weierbach, Baden, Germany. She died on
   23 May 1875 in Weierbach.
   Children:
       i.   Barbara, born 7 December 1837 in Weierbach, Baden, Germany.
*   ii. Franz Sales, born 27 January 1839 in Weierbach, Baden, Germany. [See sketch below.]
      iii. Andreas, born 16 November 1840 in Weierbach, Baden, Germany.
      iv. Veronica, born 27 August 1843 in Weierbach, Baden, Germany.
      v.   Wendelin, born 14 October 1846 in Weierbach, Baden, Germany.
      vi. Nicolaus, born 27 November 1848 in Weierbach, Baden, Germany. He died on 3 February
           1878 in Weierbach. No further information.
      vii. Sophie, born 5 May 1853 in Weierbach, Baden, Germany. She died on 1 October 1854 in
           Weierbach. No issue.
      viii. Valentin, born 4 February 1847 in Weierbach, Baden, Germany. He died on 5 May 1859 in
            Weierbach. No issue.

Immigration:
Arrived some time before January 1871 aboard an unknown vessel:
   Deck, Franz Sales

Biographical:
Husband: Franz Sales "Frank" Deck
   Birth – 27 January 1839 in Weierbach, Baden, Germany.
   Death/Burial – 19 December 1892 in Ste. Genevieve County, Missouri. He was buried in the Valle
      Spring Cemetery in Ste. Genevieve, Ste. Genevieve County, Missouri.
Wife: Sophia Pfaff, daughter of Peter Pfaff and Maria Magdalena Stoeckle [See Anton Pfaff sketch.]
   Birth – about 1830 in Baden, Germany.

1) Marriage – 9 August 1853 in Ste. Genevieve County, Missouri to Anton Vogt. [See Anton Vogt sketch.]
2) Marriage – 1 January 1871 in Ste. Genevieve County, Missouri to Franz Sales Deck.

Death/Burial – 26 September 1893 in Ste. Genevieve County, Missouri. She was buried in the Valle Spring Cemetery in Ste. Genevieve, Ste. Genevieve County, Missouri.

Child:

i. Maria Anna, born 27 December 1872 in Ste. Genevieve County, Missouri. She was baptized on 2 February 1873 in the Ste. Genevieve Catholic Church in Ste. Genevieve, Ste. Genevieve County, Missouri. Maria married Thomas D. Godfrey on 15 April 1895 in Chester, Randolph County, Illinois. Thomas was the son of Jacob Godfrey and Margaret Beck, born 26 August 1868 in Grafton, Jersey County, Illinois. He worked various jobs for the government fleet which operated on the Mississippi River and was stationed in the city of Ste. Genevieve. After he retired from the fleet, he worked as a clerk in one of the Ste. Genevieve County lime kilns. The couple had two sons and two daughters, of whom one daughter died in early childhood. Thomas died of chronic myocarditis and pneumonia on 11 December 1946 and Maria died of cerebral thrombosis and arterio sclerosis on 27 November 1950, both in Ste. Genevieve. They were both buried in the Valle Spring Cemetery in Ste. Genevieve, Ste. Genevieve County, Missouri.

Occupation: Flour mill worker and night watchman at Cone Mills
Religious Affiliation: Roman Catholic
Comments:

Franz Sales "Frank" Deck appears to be the only member of his family to have come to the United States. He arrived some time before his January 1871 marriage to Mrs. Sophia Vogt in Ste. Genevieve County, Missouri. Frank was employed in the Cone Mills in Ste. Genevieve as a miller and later as a night watchman. Frank and Sophia had one daughter together and Frank helped raise Sophia's children from her first marriage. In September 1881, an unknown man stopped at the Deck home and asked for a drink of water. Frank's nine-year-old daughter was home alone and she started to get the water when the man reportedly drew a pistol and told her to hurry up. The frightened girl ran screaming into the house and up the stairs. Her cries drew the attention of some neighbors who chased the stranger away with no harm done. Frank died of congestion on 19 December 1892 and Sophia died of dysentery on 26 September 1893, both in Ste. Genevieve. They were both buried in the Valle Spring Cemetery in Ste. Genevieve, Ste. Genevieve County, Missouri.

Johann Ulrich "John" Denler Family

Surname Variations: Dänller, Dendler, Denlar, Dennler, Dentler
European Origin: Bleienbach, Canton Bern, Switzerland
Family:
Father: Friedrich M. Dennler, born 19 April 1801 in Switzerland. He is said to have died of cholera in 1851 in St. Louis, Missouri.
Mother: Katharina Bruegger, born 15 August 1802 in Switzerland. She is said to have died of cholera in 1851 in St. Louis, Missouri.

Children:

‡ i. Anna Barbara, born 30 December 1823 in Bleienbach, Canton Bern, Switzerland. She married Friedrich Ulrich Geiser on 7 November 1848. The couple had two sons and three daughters. Friedrich died in Switzerland some time between 1859 and 1878. In 1878, Barbara brought her family to Madison County, Illinois to live near her sister, Mary Schwend. Barbara married Samuel Bircher [aka Bucherer] as her second husband on 16 February 1895 in Madison County. The couple had no children together. Barbara died on 19 February 1898 in Highland, Madison County, Illinois. She was buried in the Highland Cemetery in Highland, Madison County, Illinois. After his wife died, Samuel lived with his widowed sister-in-law, Mary Schwend. He died on 11 September 1907 in Madison County and was buried in the Highland

‡ ii. Maria Anna "Mary," born 29 August 1829 in Bleienbach, Canton Bern Switzerland. She married Joseph Anton Schwendemann on 22 August 1851 in St. Louis, Missouri. Joseph was the son of Joseph Anton Schwendemann and Anna Maria Joggerst, born 1 October 1810 in Offenburg, Baden, Germany. Shortly after his marriage, Joseph shortened his surname to "Schwend" and his descendants are all known by that name. The young couple moved to Black Jack, Madison County, Illinois, where they purchased a farm. In 1863, they moved to Highland, Madison County. The couple had three sons and four daughters. Joseph died on 26 April 1873 in Saline Township, Madison County, Illinois. About 1877, Mary and her oldest son, Joseph, returned to Switzerland to visit family. They returned to the United States in October 1878 with Mary's widowed sister, Barbara, and her two youngest daughters. Mary suffered a stroke on 6 August 1904. She died on 17 August 1904 in Highland, Madison County, Illinois. Mary was buried in the Highland City Cemetery in Highland, Madison County, Illinois.

Cemetery in Madison County, Illinois.

‡ iii. Elisabeth, born about 1831 in Switzerland. She is said to have died of cholera in 1851 in St. Louis, Missouri. She may never have married and had no known issue.

‡ iv. Jacob, born about 1835 in Switzerland. No further information has been found after he appeared on the arrival manifest of the *Leonidas*.

‡ v. Verona "Fannie," born 1 September 1839 in Switzerland. She married Martin Arth about 1857 in Madison County, Illinois. Martin was the son of unknown parents, born 12 October 1835 in Alsace-Lorraine, France. He had come to the United States aboard the *Heidelberg*, landing at New Orleans on 5 December 1854. Martin was a farmer. The couple had four sons and seven daughters. Verona died on 12 June 1909 in Collinsville, Madison County, Illinois. Martin died on 24 January 1913 in Black Jack, Madison County, Illinois. They were both buried in the St. John the Baptist Catholic Cemetery in Madison County, Illinois.

‡ vi. Johann, born about 1842 in Switzerland. No further information has been found after he appeared on the arrival manifest of the *Leonidas*.

‡ vii. Anna, born about 1843 in Switzerland. She is said to have died of cholera in 1851 in St. Louis, Missouri. No issue.

‡ viii. Rosina, born 21 May 1844 in Bleienbach, Canton Bern, Switzerland. She married George John Liekert on 25 December 1862 in Black Jack, Madison County, Illinois. George was born about 1840 in Germany. He is said to have been a Catholic priest who was excommunicated when he married Rosina. The couple had one son and one daughter. George died about 1868 in Madison County, Illinois. Rosina married Jacob Renner as her second husband on 8 April 1868 in St. Clair County, Illinois. Jacob was the son of John Renner and Susan _____, born on 11 April 1835 in Bavaria, Germany. The couple had one daughter. Jacob died on 28 March 1869 in Lebanon, St. Clair County, Illinois. Rosina married Richard Snell as her third husband on 17 November 1870 in Madison County, Illinois. Richard was born in 1840 in Switzerland. The couple had one son and one daughter. Richard died about 1880 in Illinois. Rosina married Hubert Ruff as her fourth husband on 6 July 1880 in Madison County, Illinois. Hubert was born in March 1845 in Germany. The couple had three sons. Hubert died after 1910, most likely in Illinois. Rosina died on 5 November 1925 in St. Jacob, Madison County, Illinois. She was buried in the Greenwood Cemetery in East St. Louis, St. Clair County, Illinois.

‡ ix. Friedrich, born about 1845 in Switzerland. No further information has been found after he appeared on the arrival manifest of the *Leonidas*.

‡ x. Samuel, born about 1847 in Switzerland. He is said to have died of cholera in 1851 in St. Louis, Missouri. No issue.

* xi. Johann Ulrich "John," born 24 May 1848. [See sketch below.]

Immigration:
Arrived 26 May 1851 from Le Havre, France to New Orleans aboard the *Leonidas*:
    Dänller [Dennler], Friederic, 50
        Catharina, 49
        Marie, 22
        Elisabeth, 20
        Jacob, 16
        Johann, 9
        Anna, 8
        Verona, 7
        Friederic, 6
        Rosina, 5
        Samuel, 4
        [Johann Ulrich, 2]

Arrived 5 December 1854 from Le Havre, France to New Orleans aboard the *Heidelberg*:
    Arth, Martin, 19

Arrived 28 October 1878 from Antwerp, Belgium to Philadelphia aboard the *Switzerland*:

Schwend, Maria, 49	Tailoress	from the U.S.
Joe, 25	Farmer	
Gieser, Barbara, 56		from Switzerland
Lena, 20		
Susanna, 18		

Biographical:
Husband: Johann Ulrich "John" Denler
    Birth – 24 May 1848 [Said to have been born in Switzerland, Germany, France or at sea, depending on which record is consulted.]
    Death/Burial – 20 October 1911 in Ste. Genevieve County, Missouri. He was buried in the Lutheran Cemetery in Ste. Genevieve, Ste. Genevieve County, Missouri.
Wife: Magdalena Wilhelmina "Lena" Eberhardt, daughter of J. Eberhardt and Magdalena Huise [See Peter Schaaf sketch.]
    Birth – 14 April 1852 in New Orleans, Orleans Parish, Louisiana.
    Marriage – 2 June 1873 in Ste. Genevieve County, Missouri.
    Death/Burial – 2 January 1933 in Ste. Genevieve County, Missouri. She was buried in the Lutheran Cemetery in St. Genevieve, Ste. Genevieve County, Missouri.
    Children:
        i.   Katie, born 13 September 1874 in Bloomsdale, Ste. Genevieve County, Missouri. She married Amos Cleophus Carron on 30 April 1895 in Ste. Genevieve County. Amos was the son of Joseph Charles Carron and Philomena Drury, born 10 June 1872 in Ste. Genevieve County, Missouri. He was a farmer. The couple had three sons and seven daughters, of whom one son and one daughter died in early childhood. About 1915, the family moved to Crystal City, Jefferson County, Missouri where Amos worked in the Pittsburgh Plate Glass Company. Amos died of chronic myocarditis and heart disease on 12 December 1937, and Katie died of a cerebral apoplexy on 18 January 1952, both in Crystal City. They were both buried in the Sacred Heart Cemetery in Crystal City, Jefferson County, Missouri.
        ii.   Louisa, born in March 1877 in Bloomsdale, Ste. Genevieve County, Missouri. She died some time between 1900 and 1910, most likely in Ste. Genevieve County, Missouri. She may never have married and had no known issue.
        iii.   John Gottlieb, born 2 August 1879 in Bloomsdale, Ste. Genevieve County, Missouri. He was a general laborer. John died of cerebral sclerosis on 30 November 1958 in Ste. Genevieve County, Missouri. He was buried in the Lutheran Cemetery in Ste. Genevieve, Ste. Genevieve

County, Missouri. John never married and had no known issue.

iv. Elizabeth Veronica, born 16 March 1882 in Bloomsdale, Ste. Genevieve County, Missouri. She married Theodore Francis Staechle [aka Stackley] on 15 November 1904 in Ste. Genevieve, Ste. Genevieve County. Theodore was the son of Joseph Staechle and Regina Grass, born 29 January 1880 in Ste. Genevieve County, Missouri. He was an engineer at the Pittsburgh Plate Glass Company in Crystal City, Jefferson County, Missouri. The couple had two sons and five daughters, of whom two daughters died in childhood. Theodore died of pneumonia on 1 October 1959 in St. Louis, Missouri. Elizabeth died on 11 April 1970. They were both buried in the Sacred Heart Cemetery in Crystal City, Jefferson County, Missouri.

v. Henry, born in February 1885 in Bloomsdale, Ste. Genevieve County, Missouri. He died some time between 1900 and 1910, most likely in Ste. Genevieve County, Missouri. He never married and had no known issue.

vi. Caroline Wilhelmina, born 24 May 1887 in Bloomsdale, Ste. Genevieve County, Missouri. She married Joseph John Staeckle on 25 September 1914 in Crystal City, Jefferson County, Missouri. Joseph was the son of Francis Xavier Staeckle and Clara Helena Siebert, born 2 June 1877 in Ste. Genevieve County, Missouri. He worked at the Pittsburgh Plate Glass Company in Crystal City. The couple had two daughters. Joseph died of hemorrhagic pachymeningitis [inflammation and bleeding of the membranes surrounding the brain, spinal cord and nerves] on 1 February 1923 in Jefferson County, Missouri. He was buried in the Sacred Heart Cemetery in Crystal City, Jefferson County, Missouri. After her husband's death, Caroline supported herself and her two daughters by taking in laundry to wash. Caroline died on 29 December 1968 in Ste. Genevieve County, Missouri. She was buried in the Sacred Heart Cemetery in Crystal City, Jefferson County, Missouri.

vii. Mary Anna, born 22 August 1889 in Bloomsdale, Ste. Genevieve County, Missouri. She married Joseph Anton Wolk on 25 October 1910 in Ste. Genevieve County. Joseph was the son of Peter Wolk and Rosina Zerwig, born 18 November 1879 in Ste. Genevieve County, Missouri. He was a farmer. The couple had four sons and three daughters, of whom one son died in infancy. Joseph died on 6 March 1965 and Mary Anna died on 17 December 1972, both in Ste. Genevieve County, Missouri. They were both buried in the Valle Spring Cemetery in Ste. Genevieve, Ste. Genevieve County, Missouri.

viii. Josephine R. , born 21 July 1893 in Bloomsdale, Ste. Genevieve County, Missouri. She married Charles August Stuppy on 28 October 1919 in Ste. Genevieve County, Missouri. Charles was the son of Peter Stuppy and Genevieve Roth, born 16 June 1888 in Ste. Genevieve County, Missouri. He was a farmer. The couple had five daughters, two of whom died in early childhood. Charles died on 20 April 1969 and Josephine died on 30 January 1993, both in Missouri. They were both buried in the Valle Spring Cemetery in Ste. Genevieve, Ste. Genevieve County, Missouri.

ix. Mathilda "Tillie, " born 16 April 1899 in Bloomsdale, Ste. Genevieve County, Missouri. She married William Jacob Stuppy on 16 February 1930 in Ste. Genevieve County, Missouri. William was the son of Peter Stuppy and Genevieve Roth, born 10 July 1886 in Zell, Ste. Genevieve County, Missouri. He was a farmer. The couple had two sons. William died of chronic myocarditis and a cerebral hemorrhage on 16 December 1960 in Ste. Genevieve County, Missouri. Tillie died on 28 January 1987. They were both buried in the Valle Spring Cemetery in Ste. Genevieve, Ste. Genevieve County, Missouri.

Education: Could read and write
Occupation: Farmer
Religious Affiliation: Lutheran
Comments:
Johann Ulrich "John" Denler came to the United States with his parents and siblings in 1851. From their landing in New Orleans, they appear to have gone directly up the Mississippi River to St. Louis, Missouri.

They arrived just as one of the great cholera epidemics in that city began to rage. John's parents and more than half of his siblings are said to have died of the disease shortly after they arrived. The surviving members of the family fled across the Mississippi River into Illinois, as did many other St. Louis residents. It is uncertain where John resided between 1851 and 1873. He may have been raised in the household of one of his older sisters or fostered with some other family. By June 1873, he was a resident of Ste. Genevieve County, Missouri, where he married Magdalena Wilhelmina "Lena" Eberhardt, daughter of J. Eberhardt and Magdalena Huise and step-daughter of Peter Schaaf. The couple lived on a farm near Bloomsdale, Ste. Genevieve County. They had two sons and seven daughters, of whom one son and one daughter died in childhood. John died of chronic Bright's disease on 20 October 1911 in Ste. Genevieve County, Missouri. Magdalena died of chronic heart disease on 2 January 1933 in Ste. Genevieve County, Missouri.

Peter Dietzer Family
Surname Variations: Ditzer, Duetzer
European Origin: Germany
Family:
Father: Unknown
Mother: Unknown
   Child:
*   i.   Peter, born about 1820 in Germany.

Immigration:
Arrived before October 1855 aboard an unknown vessel:
    Dietzer, Peter

Biographical:
Husband: Peter Dietzer
   Birth – about 1820 in Germany.
   Death/Burial – 30 March 1887 in St. Louis, Missouri. He was buried in the Calvary Cemetery in St. Louis, Missouri.
Wife: Catherine 'Kate" Schumaecher
   Birth – about 1821 in Germany.
   Marriage – 10 October 1855 in St. Louis, Missouri.
   Death/Burial – after 1880, most likely in Missouri.
   Children:
     i.   Mary Elisabeth "Lizzie," born 5 August 1855 in Missouri. She married John Henry Wille as his second wife on 29 May 1884 in St. Louis, Missouri. John was the son of Johann Herman Wille and Anna Maria Stigge, born 2 February 1838 in Oldenburg, Niedersachsen, Germany. He had come to the United States about 1852. John was a grocer and saloon keeper in St. Louis. He married Bertha Emilia Heitmann as his first wife on 9 January 1862 in St. Louis, Missouri. John and Bertha had six sons and five daughters. Bertha died of complications from childbirth on 9 January 1882 in St. Louis. She was buried in the Calvary Cemetery in St. Louis, Missouri. Henry and Lizzie had no children together. Henry died of heart disease on 23 September 1904 and Lizzie died of breast cancer on 9 February 1914, both in St. Louis. They were both buried in the Calvary Cemetery in St. Louis, Missouri.
     ii. Peter, born 18 February 1857 in Missouri. He was baptized on 18 April 1858 in the Ste. Genevieve Catholic Church in Ste. Genevieve, Ste. Genevieve County, Missouri. Peter was a teamster. As an adult, Peter used the surname "Ditzer." He married Minnie Goettemann. Minnie was the daughter of Henry Goettemann and Sophia Kline, born 11 November 1861 in St. Louis, Missouri. The couple had one son and two daughters of whom the son died in infancy. The couple appears to have separated some time before 1900 when Minnie was living with her brother, Louis Goettemann in St. Louis, Missouri. She remained in his household for

the rest of her life. Minnie died of bronchio pneumonia on 7 February 1923 in St. Louis, Missouri. She was buried in the Bethany Cemetery in Wellston, St. Louis County, Missouri. Peter died of chronic myocarditis and hypertension on 18 July 1934 in St. Louis, Missouri. He was buried in the Bethany Cemetery in Wellston, St. Louis County, Missouri.

U.S. residence other than Ste. Genevieve County, Missouri:
St. Louis, Missouri

Naturalization:

Name	Declaration	Naturalization	Origin
Dietzer, Peter		8 May 1863 Ste. Genevieve Co.	Prussia

Occupation: Farmer, [House?] painter
Religious Affiliation: Roman Catholic
Comments:
Peter Dietzer came to the United States before 1855 and settled in St. Louis, Missouri. He married Catherine Schumaecher on 10 October 1855 in St. Louis, Missouri. The couple had one son and one daughter. Some time before 1857, Peter and Catherine moved to Ste. Genevieve County, Missouri where Peter worked as a farmer. The family stayed in Ste. Genevieve County for at least fifteen years and then they returned to St. Louis, Missouri where Peter took a job as a [house?] painter. Peter died of pneumonia on 30 March 1887 in St. Louis, Missouri. He was buried in the Calvary Cemetery in St. Louis, Missouri. Catherine died some time after March 1887, but her date and place of death are unknown.

Bernard Difani Family
Surname Variations: Dafani[e], Def[f]ani, Def[f]any, Diffany, Divane
European Origin: Zusenhofen, Baden, Germany
Family:
Father: Xavier Difani, born 20 December 1791 in Zusenhofen, Baden, Germany. He died on
   3 October 1848 in Zusenhofen.
Mother: Maria Anna Winkler, born 1 January 1800 in Zusenhofen, Baden, Germany. She died on
   14 December 1860 in Perry County, Missouri. She was buried in the St. Joseph Cemetery in
   Apple Creek, Perry County, Missouri.
   Children:
‡   i.   Joseph, born 6 March 1820 in Zusenhofen, Baden, Germany. He was a shoemaker and farmer in Perry County, Missouri. He bought a farm known as "Bumble Nook" where he was very successful raising and training horses. Joseph married Mary Reutilia Luttrell on 16 May 1850 in Perry County. Reutilia was the daughter of unknown parents, born 28 November 1825 in Tennessee. The couple had seven sons. Joseph served in the 64th Enrolled Missouri Militia during the Civil War. Reutilia died on 14 January 1866 in Perry County. After his wife's death, Joseph's health began to fail, but he married Leah Isabelle Milster as his second wife on 31 May 1866 in Perry County. Leah was the daughter of David Milster and Mary "Polly" Cline, born 14 May 1826 in Concord, Cabarrus County, North Carolina. Joseph died on 6 November 1866 in Perry County, Missouri. Both he and his first wife were buried in the Mount Hope Cemetery in Perryville, Perry County, Missouri. Leah married Henry Frasier as her second husband on 2 June 1870 in Perry County. Henry was born of unknown parents about 1826 in Missouri. Leah died of neurasthemia on 5 January 1890 in Missouri. She was buried in the Brown Cemetery in Perry County, Missouri.
‡   ii. Franziska T., born 27 August 1821 in Zusenhofen, Baden, Germany. She accompanied her brother George when he moved to Chariton County, Missouri to settle. Franziska married Valentine George Kahler about 1854 in Chariton County, Missouri. He was a farmer in Chariton County. Valentine was the son of Johann Valentine Kahler and Anna Elisabeth

Klingman, born 28 January 1824 in Oberhochstadt, Bavaria, Germany. Franziska was Valentine's third wife. His first wife was said to have been Elisabeth Cooper. Elisabeth was the daughter of unknown parents, born about 1824 in Germany. She died in 1850 in Chariton County, Missouri, leaving no surviving children. Valentine married Nancy Pruett as his second wife about 1852, most likely in Chariton County. The couple had one surviving daughter. Nancy presumably died before 1854. Valentine and Franziska had four sons and one daughter. Franziska died on 27 August 1899 and Valentine died of pneumonia on 11 February 1905, both in Chariton County. They were both buried in the Newcomer Cemetery in Menden Township, Chariton County, Missouri.

‡ iii. Francis Xavier, born 28 September 1823 in Zusenhofen, Baden, Germany. He married Catherine Renner on 23 July 1854 in St. Louis, Missouri. Catherine was the daughter of Johann Martin Renner and Letitia Flanagan, born about 1827 in Maryland. The couple had two sons and two daughters, of whom one son died in infancy. Xavier died on 29 August 1859 in Perry County, Missouri. He was buried in the Mount Hope Cemetery in Perryville, Perry County, Missouri. After her husband's death, Catherine raised her surviving children by herself. By the late 1860s she began to show signs of mental instability and by 1880, she was no longer able to care for herself. She was sent to the Perry County Poor Farm by 1880. She died some time after 1880, most likely in Perry County, Missouri.

‡ iv. Georg[e] Mauritius, born 21 September 1825 in Zusenhofen, Baden, Germany. He was a shoemaker. George married Annie Knothe on 21 April 1852 in Missouri. Annie was the daughter of Anthony Knothe and Anna Riechte, born in Canton Berne, Switzerland in April 1831. The couple moved with George's sister, Franziska, to Chariton County, Missouri shortly after they were married. The couple had one son and two daughters and three other children who died young. George died on 11 April 1904 and Annie died on 9 April 1912, both in Chariton County, Missouri. They were both buried in the Elliott Grove Cemetery in Brunswick Township, Chariton County, Missouri.

† v. Maria Anna, born 31 December 1827 in Zusenhofen, Baden, Germany. She married Johann Georg "John G." Jordan on 3 August 1853 in St. Louis, Missouri. John was the son of Johann Georg Jordan and Anna Maria Straehl, born 23 August 1830 in Boeblingen, Neckarkreis, Württemberg, Germany. [See Johann Georg Jordan sketch.]

* vi. Bernard [aka Benjamin], born 12 April 1830 in Zusenhofen, Baden, Germany. [See sketch below.]

‡ vii. Andreas "Andrew," born 16 November 1832 in Zusenhofen, Baden, Germany. He was a shoemaker. He married Wilhelmina Christina Willi on 11 November 1860 in St. Louis, Missouri. Christina was the daughter of Jacob Willi and Elisabeth Winkleman, born 9 October 1840 in Hermann, Gasconade County, Missouri. Andrew moved his family to Montgomery City, Montgomery County, Missouri about 1864, where he established a shoemaking business. The couple had six sons and four daughters, of whom one son and one daughter died in infancy. In the late 1880s, Andrew moved his family to Riverside County, California, possibly for health reasons. Christina died on 31 July 1889 in Murrieta, Riverside County, California. She was buried in the Laurel Cemetery in Murrieta. After his wife's death, Andrew returned to Montgomery County, Missouri with his youngest children. He died of la grippe and pneumonia on 11 March 1891 in Mongtomery City, Montgomery County, Missouri. He was buried in the Montgomery City Cemetery in Montgomery City, Montgomery County, Missouri.

‡ viii. Lorenz, born 9 August 1835 in Zusenhofen, Baden, Germany. He was a shoemaker. He lived in Perry County, Missouri with his siblings until the outbreak of the Civil War. Lorenz enlisted as a private in Company A of the 3rd Regiment Missouri Volunteers on 8 June 1861 in St. Louis, Missouri. He took part in the Battle of Carthage and the Battle of Wilson's Creek. On 1 October 1861, he was transferred to Company F of the 17th Missouri Volunteer Infantry Regiment. He served in the Battle of Pea Ridge and in the skirmishing at Searcy Landing, Arkansas. He was killed in action during the Battle of Whitney's Lane in Searcy, White County, Arkansas on

	19 May 1862. The dead from that action were originally buried near Searcy. They are thought to have been recovered after the war and reburied at the National Cemetery in Little Rock as unknowns. Lorenz never married and had no known issue. After the war, the Perry County, Missouri Grand Army of the Republic Defani Post No. 273 was named in his honor.
‡ ix.	Theresa, born 18 January 1838 in Zusenhofen, Baden, Germany. She married Frederick Philip Weisbrod on 6 October 1856 in Perry County, Missouri. Frederick was the son of Johann L. Weisbrod and Maria Magdalena Steinbach, born 25 July 1835 in Nassau, Main-Tauber Kreis, Baden, Germany. Frederick was a farmer. The couple had seven sons and four daughters. Theresa died on 16 November 1900 and Frederick died of a stroke complicated by pneumonia on 30 January 1915, both in Perry County, Missouri. They were both buried in the St. Joseph Cemetery in Apple Creek, Perry County, Missouri.
† x.	Sophia, born 7 April 1841 in Zusenhofen, Baden, Germany. She married Christian Meyers about 1868, most likely in Missouri. Christian was born of unknown parents about 1840 in Ohio. He was a cooper. The couple had two sons and one daughter. Sophia may have died some time before 1880 in Missouri. Christian died of pneumonia on 5 January 1900 in St. Mary, Ste. Genevieve County, Missouri.

Immigration:
Arrived about 1850 aboard an unknown vessel:
    Difani, Joseph
        Franz Xavier
Arrived 18 April 1850 from Le Havre, France to New Orleans aboard the *Holyoke*:
    Divane, Georg, 25   Baden   St. Louis   Shoemaker
        Bernard, 20   Shoemaker
        Marianne, 22   Servant
    [Note: their surname was indexed as Dirane]
Arrived 17 April 1851 from Le Havre, France to New Orleans aboard the *Lexington*:
    Diffang, Francesca, 29   Baden
        Marianne, 51
    Diffanny, Andre, 18   Baden   New Orleans   Farmer
        Lorenz, 14
        Therese, 11
        Sophie, 9

Biographical:
Husband: Bernard [aka Benjamin] Difani
  Birth – 12 April 1830 in Zusenhofen, Baden, Germany.
  Death/Burial – 7 February 1895 in St. Mary, Ste. Genevieve County, Missouri. He was buried in the St.
    Mary Cemetery in St. Mary, Ste. Genevieve County, Missouri.
Wife: Mary E. Redford
  Birth – 24 February 1839 in Perry County, Missouri.
  Marriage – About 1862 in Missouri.
  Death/Burial – 24 February 1901 in St. Mary, Ste. Genevieve County, Missouri. She was buried in the
    St. Mary Cemetery in St. Mary, Ste. Genevieve County, Missouri.
  Children:
    i. Lawrence Joseph, born 1 April 1864 in Missouri. He worked at the flour mill in St. Mary. Lawrence married Emma E. Solf on 27 December 1888 in St. Mary, Ste. Genevieve County, Missouri. Emma was the daughter of Ernst August Solf and Caroline Wilhelmina Ruschmeyer, born 25 December 1865 in Union, Franklin County, Missouri. The couple had five sons and two daughters, of whom one son died in infancy. Emma died of a stomach ailment and heart disease on 6 November 1921 and Lawrence died of heart disease on 4 July 1937, both in St.

Mary, Ste. Genevieve County, Missouri. They were both buried in the St. Mary Cemetery in St. Mary, Ste. Genevieve County, Missouri.

ii. Louis F. , born 7 January 1866 in Missouri. He married Annie Reed on 22 August 1892 in St. Mary, Ste. Genevieve County, Missouri. Annie was the daughter of Evaristus Reed and Loretta Tucker, born 9 February 1865 in Perry County, Missouri. Louis was a farmer. Within seven years of their marriage, Louis moved his family to Pocahontas, Randolph County, Arkansas where he bought a farm. The couple had four sons and one daughter. Annie died on 12 July 1940 and Louis died on 2 January 1953, both in Pocahontas. They were both buried in the St. Paul Cemetery in Pocahontas, Randolph County, Arkansas.

iii. Rowena E. , born 29 March 1868 in Missouri. She married Henry Stuart Mattingly on 4 January 1888 in St. Mary, Ste. Genevieve County, Missouri. Henry was the son of George Mattingly and Mary B. Powell, born 18 December 1862 in Ste. Genevieve County, Missouri. He was a druggist. The couple lived in Phelps County, Missouri where Henry worked in a drug store. They had three sons and two daughters, of whom the two oldest sons died in early childhood. Henry suffered from asthma and that may have led him to experiment with drugs and alcohol. He soon became addicted to morphine and alcohol. He became a patient at the Keeley Institute, an early rehabilitation clinic for addicts, in Newburg, Phelps County, Missouri. He died there of cardiac arrest during an asthma attack on 26 March 1908. After her husband's death, Rowena moved her family to Tucson, Pima County, Arizona where she was a music teacher. She stayed there until about 1935 and then moved to Santa Ana, Orange County, California with her youngest son. She died on 23 April 1947 in Orange County, California.

iv. Genevieve H. , born 24 April 1870 in Missouri. She married Thomas McCurgan Hudson on 24 October 1895 in Perryville, Perry County, Missouri. He was a physician. Thomas was the son of Joshua A. Hudson and Mary Ann Erwin, born 13 November 1865 in Perry County, Missouri. The couple had seven sons and one daughter, of whom two sons and one daughter died in infancy or early childhood and one son died as a teenager. Thomas died of pulmonary tuberculosis on 8 June 1914 in Perryville, Perry County. Genevieve died of myocardial infarction [heart attack] on 30 November 1956 in St. Louis, Missouri. They were both buried in the Mount Hope Cemetery in Perryville, Perry County, Missouri.

v. Bernard G. , born 17 March 1872 in Missouri. He was baptized on 14 April 1872 in the Immaculate Conception Catholic Church in St. Mary, Ste. Genevieve County, Missouri. Bernard was a farmer. He married Julia Lenz on 26 December 1893 in St. Mary, Ste. Genevieve County, Missouri. Julia was the daughter of Henry Lenz and Louise Weigert, born 11 October 1869 in Perryville, Perry County, Missouri. The couple had three daughters. Some time in the early 1920, Bernard and Julia moved to Jefferson County, Missouri. Julia died of pulmonary tuberculosis on 10 October 1924 in Crystal City, Jefferson County, Missouri. Bernard died of coronary thrombosis and heart disease on 24 April 1940 in St. Louis, Missouri. They were both buried in the Mount Hope Cemetery in Perryville, Perry County, Missouri.

vi. Mary Ann, born 3 November 1874 in Missouri. She was baptized on 6 December 1874 in the Immaculate Conception Catholic Church in St. Mary, Ste. Genevieve County, Missouri. She was born with some form of congenital mental deficiency. After her parents died, she lived with her sister Genevieve. She was later moved to the Missouri State Hospital No. 4 in Farmington, St. Francois County, Missouri. Mary Ann died of chronic heart disease on 23 April 1943 in Farmington. She was buried in the St. Mary Cemetery in St. Mary, Ste. Genevieve County, Missouri. Mary Ann never married and had no known issue.

vii Julius Xavier, born 20 March 1877 in Ste. Genevieve County, Missouri. He was baptized on 10 May 1877 in the Immaculate Conception Catholic Church in St. Mary, Ste. Genevieve County, Missouri. For most of his life, Julius worked as a general laborer in the flour mill in St. Mary. He died of stomach cancer on 15 January 1939 in Ste. Genevieve County. He was buried in the St. Mary Cemetery in St. Mary, Ste. Genevieve County, Missouri. He never married and had no known issue.

    viii. Theresa Matilda, born 21 April 1880 in Missouri. She was baptized on 7 May 1880 in the Immaculate Conception Catholic Church in St. Mary, Ste. Genevieve County, Missouri. She married Alben Joseph Rosati Cissell on 14 May 1902 in Perry County, Missouri. Joseph was the son of Vincent Cissell and Mary Caroline French, born 30 December 1866 in Perryville, Perry County, Missouri. He was a farmer. The couple had four sons and four daughters, of whom one daughter died in infancy. Joseph died from acute dilation of the heart on 21 September 1927 and Theresa died from burns and smoke inhalation when her garden burn pile got away from her on 20 November 1943. They both died in Perryville, Perry County, and were both buried in the Mount Hope Cemetery in Perryville, Perry County, Missouri.

U.S. residence prior to Ste. Genevieve County, Missouri:
St. Louis, Missouri

Land Patents:
Perry County, Missouri

Patentee	Issue Date	Land Office	Cert. No.	Serial No.	Twp	Rng	Sec	Acres
Difani, Joseph	20 Aug 1867		2816		36	11	24	40.0
				Swampland Patents Vol. 5				

Naturalization:

Name	Declaration	Naturalization	Origin
Difani, Andreas	8 January 1855 Perry County		Baden

Military:
Served in the U.S. Civil War for the Union:
Private, Company D, 78th Enrolled Missouri Militia
    Bernard Difani enlisted 25 August 1862 in St. Mary, Ste. Genevieve County, Missouri. He was enrolled 30 April 1864 as 1st Lieutenant. He was ordered into service on 16 October 1864 and was relieved from duty on 25 November 1864. He served a total of 41 days of actual service.
Private, Company E, 35th Regiment, Enrolled Missouri Militia
    George Difani enlisted 26 July 1862 in Brunswick, Missouri. He was ordered into service on 2 August 1862 and was relieved from duty on 6 December 1862. He served a total of 95 days of actual service.
Sergeant, Company C, 64th Enrolled Missouri Militia
    Joseph Difani enlisted 9 August 1862 in Perry County, Missouri. He was ordered into service on 23 April 1863 and was relieved from duty on 20 May 1863. He served a total of 27 days of actual service. He was ordered into service on 29 September 1864 and was relieved from duty on 1 December 1864. He served a total of 31 days of actual service.
Private, Company C, 64th Enrolled Missouri Militia
    Andrew Difani enlisted on 9 August 1862 in Perry County, Missouri.
Private, Company A, 3rd Regiment Missouri Volunteers
    Lorenz Defani enlisted 8 June 1861 in St. Louis, Missouri. On 1 October 1861, he was transferred to Company F of the 17th Missouri Volunteer Infantry Regiment. He was killed in action during the Battle of Whitney's Lane in Searcy, White County, Arkansas on 19 May 1862.

Education: Could read and write
Occupation: Master Shoemaker
    Proprietor, Difani Hall and Saloon in St. Mary, Ste. Genevieve County, Missouri
Religious Affiliation: Lutheran and Roman Catholic
Comments:
Bernard Difani was born in Zusenhofen, Baden, Germany on 12 April 1830. After his father's death he and his mother and siblings came to the United States. From New Orleans, he went to St. Louis, where he engaged

in the shoe business until about 1857, when he moved to St. Mary, Ste. Genevieve County, Missouri. His mother and siblings had already moved to Perry County, Missouri to settle. In the 1860 census of Ste. Genevieve County, Bernard was listed with a woman named Caroline Difani in his household. It is possible that he was married in St. Louis before he came to Ste. Genevieve County. She may have died before 1862. About 1862 Bernard married Mary E. Redford who bore him eight children. Bernard had fought in the Revolutionary Army under Fritz Hecker in Baden, Germany in 1848, and at the outbreak of the Civil War, he enlisted as a private in Company D in the 78th Enrolled Missouri Militia. In May 1863, he was promoted to 1st Lieutenant. On October 16, 1864, he was ordered into active service to help repulse Price's raid into Missouri and relieved from duty on November 25, 1864. During the last years of his life, Bernard owned and operated the Difani Hall and Saloon in St. Mary, Missouri. He was a member of the J. Felix St. James Grand Army of the Republic Post #326 in St. Genevieve, Missouri. He died of heart trouble on 7 February 1895, the age of sixty-four years. After her husband's death, Mary moved to Perry County with her youngest daughters. She died on 24 February 1901 in St. Mary, Ste. Genevieve County, Missouri. Bernard and Mary were both buried in the St. Mary Cemetery in St. Mary, Ste. Genevieve County, Missouri.

Bertha Doerge Family
Surname Variations: Straubi
European Origin: Berlin, Germany
Family:
Father: Ludwig "Louis" Straube, born about 1807 in Germany. He is said to have died about 1856 in
   St. Louis, Missouri.
Mother: Emilia Koehler, born about 1811 in Germany. She is said to have died about 1849 in St. Louis,
   Missouri.
   Children:
‡   i.   Mathilde, born in February 1835 in Germany. She married Adelbert Loehr on 2 October 1858 in St. Louis, Missouri. Adelbert was born of unknown parents about 1829 in Bavaria, Germany. He was an editor and advertising agent for several St. Louis newspapers. The couple had two daughters. Adelbert died on 27 July 1867 in St. Louis. He was buried in Holy Ghost Cemetery in St. Louis. After her husband's death, Mathilde supported herself and her two daughters by working as a clerk in a general store. She died in 1909 in St. Louis.
*   ii. Bertha M., born 14 November 1836 in Berlin, Germany. [See sketch below.]
‡   iii. Theodor, born about 1838 in Germany. He is said to have died in St. Louis, Missouri in 1854. He never married and had no known issue.
‡   iv. Rudolph F., born 9 March 1841 in Berlin, Germany. As a young man he learned the printing business and worked for the *St. Louis Christian Advocate* from about 1855 to 1871. He was married to Julia A. Teschemacher on 8 February 1866 in St. Louis, Missouri. Julia was the daughter of Emil Teschemacher, a well-known lithographer, and Catherine Rothert, born 22 September 1844 in Louisville, Jefferson County, Kentucky. The couple had three sons and four daughters, of whom one son and one daughter died in early childhood. About 1870, Rudolph began to have health problems and a physician recommended that he leave the city and live a more healthy country life. He moved his family to Warren County, Missouri and bought a farm. Rudolph died on 16 June 1907 and Julia died on 8 June 1924, both in Warren County, Missouri. They were both buried in the Wright City Cemetery in Wright City, Warren County, Missouri.
‡   v.   Emilia, born about 1843 in Germany. She married Gustav Schuetz on 7 May 1864 in St. Louis, Missouri. Gustav was born of unknown parents about 1834 in Germany. Emilia died from the complications of childbirth on 26 March 1865 in St. Louis. The infant daughter died of convulsions on 25 June 1865 and Gustav died of phthisis pulmonalis [a form of tuberculosis] on 3 December 1865 in St. Louis. They were all buried in the Holy Ghost Cemetery in St. Louis.
‡   vi. Ludwig Gustav Arthur "Louis," born about 1845 in Germany. Like his older brother, Rudolph, he became a printer as a young man. He married Maria Theresa "Mamie" Boileau on

9 February 1871 in St. Louis, Missouri. Mamie was the daughter of Etienne Boileau, a perfumer, and Euphrosine _____, born 20 May 1851 in Missouri. The couple had four sons and two daughters, of whom one daughter died in infancy. About 1885, Louis moved his family to Los Angeles County, California, possibly for health reasons. He found work as a carpenter. Louis died on 17 September 1899 in Los Angeles County. After her husband's death, Mamie worked as a nursemaid for a private family to support her children. Mamie died on 25 September 1942 in Los Angeles County, California.

   vii. Herman, born in Germany. He died in infancy in Germany. No issue.

Immigration:

Arrived 8 November 1847 from Hamburg, Germany to New Orleans aboard the *James N. Cooper*:
   Straube, Ludwig, 40
        Emilie, 36
        Mathilde, 11
        Bertha, 9
        Theodor, 8
        Emilie, 5
        Rudolph, 4
        Louis, 2
        Fried., 42

Biographical:
Husband: Carl Ernst Ludwig "Charles" Doerge [See the Carl "Charles" Doerge family sketch.]
  Birth – 11 September 1823 in Hornberg, Baden, Germany.
  Death/Burial – 25 January 1917 in St. Louis County, Missouri. He was buried in the St. Paul Cemetery in Fenton, St. Louis County, Missouri.
Wife: Bertha M. Straube
  Birth – 14 November 1836 in Berlin, Germany.
  1) Marriage – 27 May 1856 in St. Louis, Missouri to Charles Doerge. [Filed for divorce in September 1873 in Jefferson County, Missouri. Final decree was granted on 6 June 1878.]
  2) Marriage – 19 February 1894 in Ste. Genevieve County, Missouri to Christopher Darien [aka Gustav Heinrich Samuel Doerge. See Carl "Charles" Doerge sketch.] Marriage ended in divorce by 1898.
  Death/Burial – 5 March 1926, Ste. Genevieve, Ste. Genevieve County, Missouri. She was buried in the Valle Spring Cemetery in Ste. Genevieve, Ste. Genevieve County, Missouri.

See the Carl "Charles" Doerge sketch for a complete discussion of the children of the marriage between Charles Doerge and Bertha Straube.

There were no children born to Christopher Darien and Bertha Straube.

U.S. residence prior to Ste. Genevieve County, Missouri:
  St. Louis, Missouri
  Jefferson County, Missouri

Education: Graduate, St. Louis School of Midwives, 1876
Occupation: Midwife
Religious Affiliation: Roman Catholic
Comments:
Bertha Straube was born in Berlin, Germany. Her father, Louis Straube, was a guilder of picture frames and architectural moldings. About 1843, the Straube family moved to Hamburg, Germany where Louis went to help rebuild the city after a large portion of it was destroyed by fire. In 1847, the Straube family came to the United States and settled in St. Louis, Missouri. The Friedrich Straube who came with the family may have

been Louis' older brother. Both of Bertha's parents and one of her brothers died within a few years of their arrival in America and the five surviving Straube children lived together in St. Louis until they married. Bertha married Charles Doerge on 27 May 1856 in St. Louis, Missouri. He was working as a wallpaper hanger in St. Louis at the time of their marriage. Shortly before the Civil War erupted, Charles and Bertha moved their young family to Jefferson County, Missouri. Bertha bought a farm from her brother-in-law, Herman Doerge, for the sum of one dollar and that is where she and her children lived while Charles went to war. After the war, relations between Bertha and Charles were apparently strained to the point that Bertha filed for divorce in September 1873 in Jefferson County, Missouri. She and her children moved to St. Louis where she attended the St. Louis School of Midwives, graduating in 1876. Her divorce from Charles was final in June 1878, by which time, Bertha had moved her family to Ste. Genevieve, Ste. Genevieve County, Missouri, where she established a midwifery practice. In Ste. Genevieve, Bertha prospered as her reputation grew. By 1881, she had built a house of her own on Main Street. On 19 February 1894, Bertha was married to Christopher Darien [Gustav Heinrich Samuel Doerge, her former brother-in law] in Ste. Genevieve County, Missouri. The marriage ended in divorce by 1898. By the time she retired, Bertha had attended more than 1,000 maternity cases in her career and the people in the town affectionately called her "Grandma" Doerge. One of the last babies she delivered was her own great-great-grandchild in 1925. Bertha died of asthma and chronic bronchitis on 6 March 1926 in Ste. Genevieve. She was buried in the Valle Spring Cemetery in Ste. Genevieve, Ste. Genevieve County, Missouri.

Carl "Charles" Doerge Family

Surname Variations: Darien, Darrier, Derria, Dearrin, Dirge, Dirke, Dörge, Dürgen
European Origin: Hornberg, Baden, Germany
Family:
Father: Johann Hartwig Daniel Dörge, born 17 January 1788 in Hornberg, Baden, Germany. He died on 29 September 1868 in Rock Township, Jefferson County, Missouri.
Mother: Johanna Dorothea Justine Engelmann, born 24 March 1796 in Aschersleben, Magdeburg, Sachsen, Germany. She died in 1873 in St. Louis, Missouri.
Children:

‡ i. Carl Friedrich Wilhelm "William", born 18 October 1816 in Hornberg, Baden, Germany. He married Christine Dorothea Lohrs in Germany. Christine was born about 1811 in Hanover, Germany. William brought his family to America about 1841. They settled in Cincinnati, Hamilton County, Ohio, where William worked in a brewery. By 1860, the family had moved to Madison County, Illinois, where William purchased a farm. The couple had two sons and three daughters. Christine died some time between 1860 and 1867, most likely in Madison County, Illinois. William married Mrs. Dorothea E. Backs [née Menschieus] as his second wife on 2 June 1867 in Madison County, Illinois. Dora was the widow of Gottlieb Bachs [aka Backs], a weaver, who had died in Germany about 1851. She was born in May 1826 in Germany. Gottlieb and Dora had five children, of whom at least three were sons and one a daughter, all born in Germany. Dora and her children had come to the United States in 1866. William died on 12 February 1901 in Edwardsville, Madison County, Illinois. Dora's date and place of death are unknown.

‡ ii. Charlotta Wilhelmina Carolina, born 5 October 1818 in Hornberg, Baden, Germany. She married Fredrich August Frost in Germany. Friedrich was born on 21 August 1815 in Berlin, Germany. The couple had at least one son and two daughters who were born in Berlin. Frederich died after 1879 in St. Louis, Missouri. Carolina died on 2 March 1903 in Covington, Kenton County, Kentucky. No further information.

‡ iii. Emilia Rosalia Bertha Mathilda "Matilda", born 9 May 1821 in Hornberg, Baden, Germany. She married John William Schiffmann. John was born about 1814 in Bavaria, Germany. He was a tailor in St. Louis, Missouri. The couple had at least four sons and one daughter, all born in Missouri. Matilda died of stomach cancer in St. Paul, Minnesota on 26 July 1880. She was buried in the Holy Ghost Cemetery in St. Louis but was later reinterred in the New St. Marcus

                Cemetery in Affton, St. Louis County, Missouri. John died some time after 1880 and was buried in the New St. Marcus Cemetery in Affton, St. Louis County, Missouri.

*   iv. Carl Ernst Ludwig "Charles," born 11 September 1823 in Hornberg, Baden, Germany. [See sketch below.]

‡   v. Carl Christopher Herman, born 23 March 1827 in Hornberg, Baden, Germany. Herman was a farmer. He married Christine Wilhelmina Caroline Riechman on 18 October 1849 in St. Louis, Missouri. Caroline was the widow of Heinrich Christian Friedrich Rohlfing who had died in 1849. She had one daughter with her first husband. Caroline was the daughter of Johann Conrad Heinrich Christian Riechman and Anna Maria Sophia Margarethe Roethemeier, born in Nordhemmern, Minden-Lubbecke, Nordrhein-Westfalen, Germany. For the first years of their marriage, Herman and Caroline lived in Jefferson County, Missouri. About 1865, they moved to Madison County, Illinois, but by 1880, they had returned to Missouri, settling on a farm in Newton, County. The couple had three sons and four daughters, of whom one daughter died in infancy. Caroline died on 26 April 1892 and Herman died on 19 July 1904, both in Newton County, Missouri. They were both buried in the Stone Cemetery in Diamond, Jasper County, Missouri

‡   vi. Johanna Louisa Augusta, born 23 November 1830 in Hornberg, Baden, Germany. She married Franz Heinrich Rose on 8 August 1850 in St. Louis, Missouri. No further information.

‡   vii. Augusta Sophia Dorothea, born 1 August 1837 in Hornberg, Baden, Germany. She married Rudolph W. [aka Reuben] Bruesselbach on 16 April 1854 in Jefferson County, Missouri. Rudolph was the son of unknown parents, born 17 April 1824. The couple had three sons and six daughters. Rudolph died on 5 January 1891 in Jersey County, Illinois. He was buried in the St. Francis Xavier Cemetery in Jerseyville, Jersey County, Illinois. Augusta died of chronic hepatitis and cholecystitis on 27 October 1918 in St. Louis, Missouri. She was buried in the New St. Marcus Cemetery in Affton, St. Louis County, Missouri.

‡   viii. Gustav Heinrich Samuel [aka Christopher Darien], born 25 July 1839 in Hornberg, Baden, Germany. Christopher came to the United States with his parents about 1841. During the Civil War, he served for the Union in the 10th Regiment, Missouri Volunteer Infantry, using the alias Christopher Darien. After the war, he married Sophia Feiks on 31 March 1867 in Carondelet, St. Louis County, Missouri. Sophia was born of unknown parents about 1850 in Darmstadt, Hesse, Germany. The couple had one son who used the surname "Darian" all of his life. Sophia died on 10 March 1892. Christopher married his former sister-in-law, Bertha Doerge [née Straube], on 19 February 1894 in Ste. Genevieve County, Missouri. The marriage appears to have ended in divorce by 1898. There were no children born to this couple. Christopher married Barbara Schweitzer on 28 September 1899 in St. Louis, Missouri. Barbara was the daughter of Joseph Schweitzer and Barbara Schindelmeyer, born on 27 December 1851 in Germany. They do not appear to have had any children. Christopher died of dry gangrene of the feet and back [bedsores?] on 10 February 1932 and Barbara died of colon cancer on 1 December 1935 both in Carondelet, St. Louis County, Missouri. They were both buried in St. Paul's Churchyard Cemetery in St. Louis, Missouri.

Immigration:
Arrived about 1841 [1900 census] aboard an unknown vessel:
    Doerge, Daniel and wife Johanna Engelmann
        Augusta
        Christophe [Gustav]
    Doerge, William and wife Christina Lohrs
        Wilhelmina
Arrived 1849 from Germany to Galveston, Texas aboard an unknown vessel:
    Dirke [Doerge], Hermann, 19

Arrived 7 May 1855 from Bremen, Germany to New York aboard the *Corliolan*:
    Dörge [indexed as Doege], Carl, 32   book binder   from Prussia   going to St. Louis

Biographical:
Husband: Carl Ernst Ludwig "Charles" Doerge
  Birth – 11 September 1823 in Hornberg, Baden, Germany.
  Death/Burial – 25 January 1917 in St. Louis County, Missouri. He was buried in the St. Paul Cemetery in Fenton, St. Louis County, Missouri.
Wife: Bertha M. Straube [See Bertha Doerge sketch.]
  Birth – 14 November 1836 in Berlin, Germany.
  1) Marriage – 27 May 1856 in St. Louis, Missouri [Filed for divorce in September 1873 in Jefferson County, Missouri. Final decree was granted on 6 June 1878.]
  2) Marriage – 19 February 1894 in Ste. Genevieve County, Missouri to Christopher Darien. [aka Gustav Heinrich Samuel Doerge. Marriage ended in divorce by 1898.
  Death/Burial – 5 March 1926, Ste. Genevieve, Ste. Genevieve County, Missouri. She was buried in the Valle Spring Cemetery in Ste. Genevieve, Ste. Genevieve County, Missouri.
Children:
    i. Louis, born 17 May 1860 in St. Louis, Missouri. Louis worked as a miller all of his life. He started as a sweeper at the Cone Mills in Ste. Genevieve as a very young man. He later worked at mills at Staabtown, Brickey's and Bloomsdale in Ste. Genevieve County and ended his career at a mill in Fenton, St. Louis County, Missouri. He married Anna Nora Beauchamp on 26 December 1883 in Ste. Genevieve County. Anna was the daughter of Thomas Beauchamp and Mary Bequette, born 14 January 1861 in Ste. Genevieve County. The couple had two sons and five daughters and two children who died in infancy. Louis died of bronchio pneumonia on 29 February 1940 in Clayton, St. Louis County, Missouri. Anna died of chronic myocarditis on 3 October 1944 in Ste. Genevieve County, Missouri. They were both buried in the St. Agnes Cemetery in Bloomsdale, Ste. Genevieve County, Missouri.
    ii. Charles, born 3 June 1863 in Jefferson County, Missouri. He was a shy and reticent man who lived most of his life with his mother. As a young man he worked various odd jobs around Ste. Genevieve County to earn a living. He eventually bought a ferry boat named the *Dewey* and operated a transfer business. In November 1906, he took his boat down the Mississippi River to New Madrid County and while he was there, he became ill. He was only partially recovered when he went back out on the river in a skiff a few days later. While he was bailing the boat out, he was overcome by dizziness and fell into the icy water. Charles suffered a relapse and was taken home to Ste. Genevieve where his mother nursed him to no avail. He died on 12 January 1907 in Ste. Genevieve. He was buried in the Valle Spring Cemetery in Ste. Genevieve, Ste. Genevieve County, Missouri. Charles never married and had no known issue.
    iii. Rudolph, born 9 April 1868 in Jefferson County, Missouri. He owned and operated a paint and wallpaper business in Ste. Genevieve called the Main Street Decorator. He married Bertha Mischke on 9 September 1896 in St. Louis, Missouri. Bertha was the daughter of Albert Mischke and Anna Dollnick, born 2 April 1877 in Chicago, Cook County, Illinois. The couple had four sons and one daughter. Rudolph died of heart disease and chronic bronchitis on 8 January 1918 in Ste. Genevieve County. He was buried in the Valle Spring Cemetery in Ste. Genevieve, Ste. Genevieve County, Missouri. After her husband's death, Bertha continued to run the paint and paper store and eventually turned it over to one of her sons. She is said to have moved to Chester, Randolph County, Illinois after 1940. She died there on 31 January 1953 after a long illness. She was buried in the Valle Spring Cemetery in Ste. Genevieve, Ste. Genevieve County, Missouri.
    iv. Emily, born in December 1869 in Jefferson County, Missouri. No record of her has been found after the 1870 census. It is said that she died about 1875, possibly in St. Louis. No issue.
    v. Helena B. "Lena," born 9 August 1872 in Jefferson County, Missouri. She married Charles

Timothy Dempsey on 30 June 1897 in Ste. Genevieve County, Missouri. Charles was the son of John Dempsey and Margaret Gallager, born 28 October 1872 in St. Louis, Missouri. He worked as a steward and clerk on a riverboat that ferried between St. Louis, Missouri and Cairo, Illinois. The couple had two sons and one daughter. Charles died of arterio sclerosis on 17 March 1955 and Helena died of colon cancer on 15 February 1959, both in Ste. Genevieve County. They were both buried in the Valle Spring Cemetery in Ste. Genevieve, Ste. Genevieve County, Missouri.

U.S. residence prior to Ste. Genevieve County, Missouri:
St. Louis, Missouri
Jefferson County, Missouri

Land Patents:
Jefferson County, Missouri

Patentee	Issue Date	Land Office	Cert. No.	Serial No.	Twp	Rng	Sec	Acres
Doerrie, Daniel	1 Oct 1852	St. Louis	19458	MO0900_.492	43-N	5-E	28	40.0
Dorrea, Hermann	3 Jun 1851	St. Louis	4519	MW-0965-263	42-N	5-E	9	40.0

Naturalization:

Name	Declaration	Naturalization	Origin	Remarks
Darien, Christopher		18 September 1896 St. Louis, MO	Germany	C-25795 Vol. 15, p. 344

Military:
Served in the U.S. Civil War for the Union:
Sergeant, Company C, Rifle Battalion, 2nd Missouri Infantry
   Doerge, Charles enlisted 18 April 1861 in St. Louis, Missouri. He mustered out in August 1861.
Lieutenant, Company F, 12th Regiment Missouri Volunteer Infantry
   Doerge, Charles enlisted 13 August 1861 in St. Louis, Missouri. He was wounded in right leg above the ankle at Fourteen Mile Creek on 11 May 1863; almost completely deafened by cannon fire. He was transferred to the 30th Company, 1st Battalion, Invalid Corps 11 March 1864. Returned to active service with the 12th Regiment Missouri Volunteer Infantry on 24 May 1864. He was mustered out on 8 August 1864 near Atlanta, Georgia

Education: Could read and write both English and German
Occupation: Wallpaper Hanger / Farmer / Odd jobs
Religious Affiliation: Unknown
Comments:
Carl Ernst Ludwig "Charles" Doerge came to the United States in 1855. His parents and youngest siblings came to the United States about 1841 and settled in Jefferson County, Missouri. Charles followed his family to the United States in 1855. He was working as a wallpaper hanger in St. Louis at the time of his marriage to Bertha Straube. The couple lived in St. Louis for the first few years of their married life. Shortly before the Civil War erupted, Charles and Bertha moved their young family to Jefferson County, Missouri. Bertha bought a farm from her brother-in-law Herman Doerge, for the sum of one dollar and that is where she and her children lived while Charles went to war. He served for the Union as a Lieutenant in Company F of the 12th Regiment Missouri Volunteer Infantry. This unit served in some of the most intense campaigns of the Trans-Mississippi Theater. Charles received a gunshot wound in his right leg just above the ankle at Fourteen Mile Creek near Raymond, Mississippi on 11 May 1863 during the Vicksburg Campaign. He refused medical aid and continued to fight with his unit. The untreated wound eventually became infected and Charles was ordered to seek treatment in a military hospital. He was temporarily transferred to the 30th Company, 1st Battalion, Invalid Corps in March 1864. Charles managed to recuperate sufficiently to return to active duty in his former unit in time to take part in General Sherman's march through Georgia. He was mustered out of active service

near Atlanta, Georgia in August of 1864. The wound he received during the war continued to plague him for the rest of his life, often causing his leg to swell up and become lame. After the war Charles returned to Jefferson County, but relations between Bertha and Charles were apparently strained to the point that Bertha filed for divorce in September 1873 in Jefferson County. The divorce was final in June 1878. Charles moved around the midwestern United States after his divorce. He moved to Jerseyville, Jersey County, Illinois in the late 1870s where he kept a dry goods store. He may also have married a much younger woman named Maizie D. _____ as his second wife. Maizie was born of unknown parents about 1865 in Frankfurt am Main, Germany. No record of her has been found after the 1880 census. By 1890, Charles appears to have moved south to Navasota, Grimes County, Texas for a short time and then he moved into the Home for Disabled Volunteer Soldiers in Milwaukee, Milwaukee County, Wisconsin where he remained until about 1908. His last years were spent in Missouri with his oldest son, Louis. Charles died of valvular heart disease on 25 January 1917 in St. Louis County, Missouri. He was buried in the St. Paul Cemetery in Fenton, St. Louis County, Missouri.

Johann Georg Dold Family
Surname Variations: Dalts, Doldt, Dole, Doll, Dolt
European Origin: Baden, Germany
Family:
Father: Unknown
Mother: Unknown
   Child:
*   i.   Johann Georg, born 4 December 1821 in Baden, Germany. [See sketch below.]

Immigration:
Arrived 4 November 1848 from Antwerp, Belgium to New York aboard the *Floridian*:
     Dold, George, 27   tinker   from Germany
          Andreas, 25   [relative of George's?]

Biographical:
Husband: Johann Georg Dold
   Birth – 4 December 1821 in Baden, Germany.
   Death/Burial – 18 April 1876 in Ste. Genevieve County, Missouri. He was buried in the Sts. Philip and
      James Cemetery in River aux Vases, Ste. Genevieve County, Missouri.
1) Wife: Catherine Litterst, daughter of Caspar Simon Litterst and Ursula Lehmann [See Caspar Simon
     Litterst sketch.]
   Birth – about 1834 in Baden, Germany.
   Marriage – 3 June 1851 in Ste. Genevieve County, Missouri.
   Death/Burial – 30 December 1852 in Ste. Genevieve County, Missouri. She was buried in the St. Joseph
     Cemetery in Zell, Ste. Genevieve County, Missouri.
   Child:
     i.   Sophie, born 16 May 1852 in Ste. Genevieve County, Missouri. She died of smallpox on
        8 December 1872 in Ste. Genevieve County, Missouri. Sophie was buried in the Sts. Philip and
        James Cemetery in River aux Vases, Ste. Genevieve County, Missouri. No issue.

2) Wife: Eleanora Seitz, daughter of Joseph Seitz and Maria Josepha Rheinhardt [See Joseph Seitz sketch.]
   Birth – 20 February 1824 in Oberweier bei Lahr, Baden, Germany.
   1) Marriage – 25 September 1843 in Oberweier bei Lahr, Baden, Germany to Lorenz Nock.
   2) Marriage – 15 April 1853 in Ste. Genevieve County, Missouri to Johann Georg Dold.
   Death/Burial – 1901 in Ste. Genevieve County, Missouri. She was buried in the Sts. Philip and James
     Cemetery in River aux Vases, Ste. Genevieve County, Missouri.
   Children of Lorenz Nock and Eleanora Seitz:
     i.   Katharina, born 14 March 1844 in Oberweier bei Lahr, Baden, Germany. She died on

15 January 1847 in Oberweier. No issue.
 ii. Eleanora, born 24 October 1846 in Oberweier bei Lahr, Baden, Germany. She died on 11 December 1847 in Oberweier. No issue.
 iii. Eleanora, born 18 October 1848 in Oberweier bei Lahr, Baden, Germany. She married Charles "Carl" Raumschuh on 2 March 1869 in Ste. Genevieve County, Missouri. Carl was the son of Bernard Raumschuh and Barbara Müller, born 28 March 1847 in Grossweier, Baden, Germany. [See Bernard Raumschuh sketch.]

Children of Johann Georg Dold and Eleanora Seitz:
 ii. George, born 31 January 1854 in Ste. Genevieve County, Missouri. As a young man, he moved to St. Louis to work and returned home for a visit in late 1872. He soon sickened and died of smallpox on 25 November 1872 in Ste. Genevieve County. He infected most of his siblings with the disease. George was buried in the Sts. Philip and James Cemetery in River aux Vases, Ste. Genevieve County, Missouri. No issue.
 iii. Paulina, born 30 November 1855 in Ste. Genevieve County, Missouri. She was baptized on 9 March 1856 in the Sts. Philip and James Catholic Church in River aux Vases, Ste. Genevieve County, Missouri. Paulina married Joseph Basler on 19 February 1878 in Weingarten, Ste. Genevieve County, Missouri. Joseph was the son of Valentine Basler and Maria Anna Cleopha Falk, born 19 March 1852 in Ste. Genevieve County, Missouri.[See Valentine Basler sketch.]
 iv. Charles "Carl", born 6 November 1857 in Ste. Genevieve County, Missouri. He died of smallpox on 6 December 1872 in Ste. Genevieve County, Missouri and was buried in the Sts. Philip and James Cemetery in River aux Vases, Ste. Genevieve County, Missouri. No issue.
 v. Mary, born 29 September 1860 in Ste. Genevieve County, Missouri. She was baptized on 11 November 1860 in the Sts. Philip and James Catholic Church in River aux Vases, Ste. Genevieve County, Missouri. No further information after the 1870 census. She may have died of smallpox in December 1872.
 vi. Catherine Eleanor, born 30 July 1862 in Ste. Genevieve County, Missouri. She married Andrew Basler on 9 August 1881 in Weingarten, Ste. Genevieve County, Missouri. Andrew was the son of Valentine Basler and Maria Anna Cleopha Falk, born 6 February 1856 in Ste. Genevieve County, Missouri. [See Valentine Basler sketch.]
 vii. Philip, born 5 January 1864 in Ste. Genevieve County, Missouri. He was baptized on 14 February 1864 in the Sts. Philip and James Catholic Church in River aux Vases, Ste. Genevieve County, Missouri. No further information after the 1870 census. He may have died of smallpox in December 1872.
 viii. Edward, born 4 September 1866 in Ste. Genevieve County, Missouri. He was baptized on 14 October 1866 in the Sts. Philip and James Catholic Church in River aux Vases, Ste. Genevieve County, Missouri. He died of smallpox on 10 December 1872 in Ste. Genevieve County and was buried in the Sts. Philip and James Cemetery in River aux Vases, Ste. Genevieve County, Missouri. No issue.
 ix. Joseph, born about 1868 in Ste. Genevieve County, Missouri. No further information after the 1870 census. He may have died of smallpox in December 1872

Land Patents:
Ste. Genevieve County, Missouri

Patentee	Issue Date	Land Office	Cert. No.	Serial No.	Twp	Rng	Sec	Acres
Dolt, John G.	1 Sep 1856	Jackson	16551	MO3730_.386	36-N	8-E	15	80.00

Naturalization:

Name	Declaration	Naturalization	Origin	Remarks
Dold, Charles		21 November 1856 Ste. Genevieve Co.	Baden	First name should be John George.

Military:
Served in the U.S. Civil War for the Union:
Private, Company F, 78th Enrolled Missouri Militia

Dolt, George enlisted 30 April 1864 in Ste. Genevieve County, Missouri. He was ordered into service on 16 October 1864 and was relieved from duty on 25 November 1864. He served a total of 41 days of actual service.

Occupation: Farmer
Religious Affiliation: Roman Catholic
Comments:

Johann Georg "George" Dold came to the United State in 1848. He appears to have gone directly to Missouri and settled in Ste. Genevieve County on a farm near the village of River aux Vases. He was married twice. George's first wife, Catherine Litterst, died within six months of the birth of her only child. George married Mrs. Eleanora Nock as his second wife. Eleanora's first husband had died in Germany before she had come to the United States with her parents, siblings and young daughter in 1852. George and Eleanora had eight children together. The family was comfortably prosperous until the winter of 1872. Their oldest son, George, had come home from St. Louis for a visit and soon fell ill with smallpox. Within a week, the entire family had come down with the disease and at least six of the children died. Only the parents and two daughters survived for certain. George died on 18 April 1876 in Ste. Genevieve County, Missouri. He was buried in the Sts. Philip and James Cemetery in River aux Vases, Ste. Genevieve County, Missouri. After her husband's death, Eleanora lived with her daughter Paulina. She died in 1901 and was buried in the Sts. Philip and James Cemetery in River aux Vases, Ste. Genevieve County, Missouri.

Bernard Doll Family
Surname Variations: Dall
European Origin: Sasbach, Achern, Baden, Germany
Family:
Father: Johann Georg Doll, born 16 April 1806 in Sasbach, Achern, Baden, Germany.
Mother: Gertrud Ebler, born 21 February 1810 in Sasbachwalden, Achern, Baden, Germany.
Children:
* i. Bernard, born 9 August 1832 in Sasbach, Achern, Baden, Germany. [See sketch below.]
  ii. Joseph, born 29 August 1835 in Sasbach, Achern, Baden, Germany.
  iii. Victoria, born 13 May 1837 in Sasbach, Achern, Baden, Germany. She married Ignaz Vierthaler on 1 July 1862 in Sasbachwalden, Achern, Baden, Germany. Ignaz was the son of Joseph Vierthaler and Franziska Ruh, born 1 February 1823 in Sasbach.
  iv. Amalia, born 12 July 1840 in Sasbach, Achern, Baden, Germany. She married Leonard Buehler on 27 February 1865 in Durbach, Baden, Germany. Leonard was the son of Johann Buehler and Anna Maria _____, born about 1822 in Germany.
  v. Carolina, born 7 January 1843 in Sasbach, Achern, Baden, Germany. She married Andreas Zink on 23 January 1866 in Sasbachwalden, Achern, Baden, Germany. Andreas was the son of Anton Zink and Richardis Späth, born 30 November 1835 in Sasbachwalden, Achern, Baden, Germany.
  vi. Sophia, born 10 May 1844 in Sasbach, Achern, Baden, Germany. She died on 21 May 1844 in Sasbach. No issue.
  vii. Cecilia, born 7 October 1849 in Sasbach, Achern, Baden, Germany. She died on 27 October 1849 in Sasbach. No issue.

Immigration:
Arrived 17 March 1858 from Le Havre, France to New Orleans aboard the *B. D. Metcalf*:
  Doll, Bernard, 25   Baden   Farmer
  Decker, Catherine, 26

Biographical:
Husband: Bernard Doll
  Birth – 9 August 1832 in Sasbach, Achern, Baden, Germany.
  Death/Burial – 30 November 1875 in Ste. Genevieve County, Missouri. He was buried in the Memorial
    Cemetery in Ste. Genevieve, Ste. Genevieve County, Missouri.
1) **Wife:** Catherine Decker, daughter of Anton Decker and Magdalena Baumer
  Birth – 12 February 1831 in Sasbachwalden, Achern, Baden, Germany.
  Marriage – about 1858.
  Death/Burial – 16 January 1866 in Ste. Genevieve, Ste. Genevieve County, Missouri. She was buried in
    the Memorial Cemetery in Ste. Genevieve, Ste. Genevieve County, Missouri.
  Child:
  i. Elizabeth, born about 1859 in Ste. Genevieve County, Missouri. She married a man named
    George Kempf on 29 March 1879 in Ste. Genevieve, Ste. Genevieve County, Missouri. No
    further information has been found after the record of their marriage.

2) **Wife:** Magdalena "Lena" Kempf, daughter of Frederick Kempf and Magdalena _____ [See Frederick
    Kempf sketch.]
  Birth – about 1846 in Baden, Germany.
  1) Marriage – 14 May 1866 in Ste. Genevieve, Ste. Genevieve County, Missouri to Bernard Doll.
  2) Marriage – 12 September 1876 in Ste. Genevieve, Ste. Genevieve County, Missouri to Joseph
    Fitzkam.
  Death/Burial – 19 September 1892 in St. Louis, Missouri. She was buried as "Lena Doll" in the Sts. Peter
    and Paul Cemetery in St. Louis, Missouri.
  Children of Bernard Doll and Magdalena Kempf:
  ii. Francis Joseph "Frank," born 1 October 1867 in Ste. Genevieve County, Missouri. He was
    baptized on 8 December 1867 in the Ste. Genevieve Catholic Church in Ste. Genevieve. Frank
    was a laborer in the Anheuser Busch Brewery. He was married to Cecilia F. Weber about 1903,
    most likely in St. Louis, Missouri. Cecilia was born of unknown parents on 25 October 1870 in
    Missouri. The couple had three sons and two daughters. Frank died of hypertrophic cirrhosis of
    the liver and alcoholism on 13 March 1917 in St. Louis, Missouri. He was buried in Sts. Peter
    and Paul Cemetery in St. Louis, Missouri. After her husband's death, Cecelia worked as a
    seamstress to support herself and her five children. She never remarried. Cecelia died of
    cerebral thrombosis and heart disease on 7 January 1960 in St. Louis, Missouri. She was buried
    in the Sts. Peter and Paul Cemetery in St. Louis, Missouri.
  iii. Mary Anna, born 14 May 1871 in Ste. Genevieve County, Missouri. She was baptized on
    18 June 1871 in the Ste. Genevieve Catholic Church in Ste. Genevieve. Anna was a nurse. She
    married Henry C. Uphoff on 26 March 1898 in St. Clair County, Illinois. Henry was born of
    unknown parents in November 1865 in Illinois. He was a machinist in a brickyard. Anna was
    his second wife, but nothing is known of his first wife. The couple does not appear to have had
    any children. The couple divorced some time between 1910 and 1920. Anna died of
    asphyxiation after inhaling gas fumes [suicide] on 17 April 1920 in St. Louis, Missouri. She
    was buried in the Saints Peter and Paul Catholic Cemetery in St. Louis, Missouri. No further
    mention of Henry has been found after the 1910 census. He may have returned to Illinois.
  iv. Johanna Theresa, born 3 April 1873 in Ste. Genevieve County, Missouri. She was baptized on
    27 April 1873 in the Ste. Genevieve Catholic Church in Ste. Genevieve. She married Gottfried
    Beckman about 1901. He was a horse and cattle trader. Gottfried may have been the son of
    Chris Beckmann and Lydia Einig, and was born about 1867 in Illinois. The couple had one son
    and one daughter. Johanna died on 29 July 1923 in Alton, Madison County, Illinois. She was
    buried in the Highland Cemetery in Highland, Madison County, Illinois. Gottfried married
    Lydia Einig [possibly a cousin] as his second wife in 1926 in Bond County, Illinois. Lydia was
    the daughter of Daniel Einig and Margaret Feinenn, born about 1875 in Missouri. Gottfried and

Lydia had no children together. Gottfried died in 1949 and Lydia died in 1958. They were both buried in the Highland Cemetery in Highland, Madison County, Illinois.
- v. Caroline Louisa, born 25 January 1875 in Ste. Genevieve County, Missouri. She was baptized on 28 March 1875 in the Ste. Genevieve Catholic Church in Ste. Genevieve. Louise married Henry George about 1897. He was a cooper in a brewery in St. Louis, Missouri. Henry was the son of Henry George and Alvina Lehmann, born 30 July 1874 in Belleville, St. Clair County, Illinois. The couple had three sons. Louise died of heart failure on 23 March 1947 in St. Louis, Missouri. Henry died of a heart attack on 22 October 1963 in Valley-Park, St. Louis County, Missouri. They were both buried in St. Paul's Churchyard in Affton, St. Louis County, Missouri.

Children of Joseph Fitzkam and Magdalena Kempf:
- i. John Bernard [aka Bernard Doll], born 2 October 1877 in Ste. Genevieve County, Missouri. He was baptized on 11 October 1877 in the Ste. Genevieve Catholic Church in Ste. Genevieve. Bernard was a teamster and worked as a miller in St. Louis, Missouri. He married Lillian Wier about 1899. Lillian was the daughter of _____ Wier and Martha _____, born 21 May 1876 in Milwaukee, Wisconsin. Her father died when she was very young and her mother married a man named Frank J. Bowman. Bernard and Lillian had two sons and one daughter. Bernard died of bronchio pneumonia complicated by ulcers and rectal abscesses on 31 May 1937 in St. Louis. Lillian died of cardiovascular heart disease on 11 October 1954 in St. Louis. They were both buried in the Sunset Memorial Park in Affton, St. Louis, County, Missouri.
- ii. Clara Sophie [aka Clara Doll], born 12 October 1879 in Ste. Genevieve County, Missouri. She was baptized on 9 November 1879 in the Ste. Genevieve Catholic Church in Ste. Genevieve. She married John Fey about 1898. He was a printer and paper dealer. John was the son of Henry Fey and _____, born 11 August 1872 in St. Louis, Missouri. The couple had one daughter. Clara died of acute diverticulitis, appendicitis and peritonitis on 3 March 1936 in St. Louis, Missouri. After his wife's death, John may have married for a second time in October 1936 to a woman named Margaret _____. Nothing is known of her. John died of myocarditis on 30 October 1939 in St. Louis. He and his first wife were both buried in the Sunset Memorial Park in Affton, St. Louis County, Missouri.
- iii. Lena [aka Lena Doll], born 2 July 1882 in Missouri. After the death of her mother, Lena lived with her older sister Clara. She married Ernst Stark about 1901, most likely in St. Louis, Missouri. Ernst was the son of Johann Ernst Starkjohann [later shortened to Stark] and Paulina Seitzinger, born 24 September 1876 in St. Louis, Missouri. He was a bookbinder. The couple had two daughters. Ernst and Lena divorced before 1920 and Ernst quickly remarried to a woman named Elizabeth _____. Lena, who had custody of the two children, worked as a seamstress and took in boarders to support her family. She married _____ Miller some time before 1930, but according to the 1930 census, he had died by 1930. Lena married for a third time to George Berberich some time before 1940. George was born on 25 June 1878 in Missouri. He was a shipping clerk for a candy factory in St. Louis and was a widower with two grown children of his own. Lena died of coronary thrombosis and congestive heart failure on 12 February 1951 in St. Louis, Missouri. She was buried as "Lee Berberich" in the Sts. Peter and Paul Cemetery in St. Louis. George died of heart failure on 25 October 1957 in St. Louis. He was buried in the Park Lawn Cemetery in Lemay, St. Louis County, Missouri.

U.S. residence prior to Ste. Genevieve County, Missouri:
Possibly St. Louis, Missouri

Land Patents:
Ste. Genevieve County, Missouri

Patentee	Issue Date	Land Office	Cert. No.	Serial No.	Twp	Rng	Sec	Acres
Doll, Bernard	5 Nov 1874	Ironton	566	MO4280_.059	37-N	9-E	14,15	118.43

Military:
Served in the U.S. Civil War for the Union:
Private, Company G, 78th Enrolled Missouri Militia
> Bernard Doll enlisted on 4 October 1862 in Ste. Genevieve, Missouri. He was ordered into service on 16 October 1864 and was relieved from duty on 25 November 1864. He served a total of 41 days of actual service.

Occupation: Shoemaker
Religious Affiliation: Roman Catholic
Comments:
Bernard Doll came to the United States with his fiancé Catherine Decker in 1858. They were married shortly after their arrival and appear to have come directly to Ste. Genevieve County. Bernard was a shoemaker. During the Civil War, Bernard enlisted in the 78th Enrolled Missouri Militia. Catherine died on 16 January 1866 in Ste. Genevieve, Ste. Genevieve County, Missouri, leaving Bernard with a small daughter to raise. He married Magdalena Kempf as his second wife just five months after Catherine's death. There is some confusion about Magdalena's maiden name. In her marriage record to Bernard and in the Ste. Genevieve *Herald* notice of her death, her name is given as Kempf. However, on her death certificate, a family member gave it as Kientzle. But it was most definitely Kempf. Bernard and Magdalena had one son and three daughters. Bernard died on 30 November 1875 in Ste. Genevieve County. He was buried in the Memorial Cemetery in Ste. Genevieve, Ste. Genevieve County, Missouri. Magdalena married Joseph Fitzkam as her second husband on 12 September 1876 in Ste. Genevieve, Ste. Genevieve County, Missouri. Joseph was the son of Johannes "John" Fitzkam and Brigitta Hauck, born 8 March 1854 in Ste. Genevieve County, Missouri. He was a farmer. [He is not to be confused with Joseph F. Fitzkam, son of Philip Jacob Fitzkam and Theresia Gallus, born 1 January 1856 in Ste. Genevieve County, Missouri. That Joseph was a barber.] Magdalena and Joseph had one son and two daughters. Joseph Fitzkam died of acute dysentery on 19 September 1885 in Ste. Genevieve County, Missouri. He had been ill for about 4 weeks prior to his death. He was buried in St. Mary, Ste. Genevieve County, Missouri. After Joseph's death, Magdalena moved her family to St. Louis, Missouri where she worked as a domestic servant in order to support her children. She reverted to using her first husband's surname and all of her children were also known by the Doll surname. Magdalena died of typhoid pneumonia on 19 September 1892 in St. Louis, Missouri. She was buried as "Lena Doll" in the Sts. Peter and Paul Cemetery in St. Louis, Missouri.

Note: Bernard Doll was a nephew to Joseph Doll (1793-1880), and first cousin to George, Joseph, Catherine, Pauline and Lawrence Doll who also settled in Ste. Genevieve County, Missouri.

Johann Georg "George" Doll Family
Surname Variations: Dall
European Origin: Sasbach, Achern, Baden, Germany
Family:
Father: Bernard Doll, born in Sasbachwalden, Achern, Baden, Germany.
Mother: Magdalena Hodapp, born 22 March 1804 in Kappelrodeck, Baden, Germany.
  Children:
	i.	Bernard, born 19 August 1826 in Baden, Germany. He died in 1864 in Baden, Germany.
	ii.	Joseph, born 1 November 1827 in Baden, Germany. He died on 25 January 1828 in Baden, Germany. No issue.
*	iii.	Johann Georg "George," born 14 October 1829 in Sasbach, Achern, Baden, Germany. [See sketch below.]
†	iv.	Joseph, born 26 June 1831 in Sasbach, Achern, Baden, Germany. [See Joseph Doll sketch.]
†	v.	Catherine, born 13 January 1833 in Sasbach, Achern, Baden, Germany.
†	vi.	Lorenz "Lawrence," born 30 July 1834 in Sasbach, Achern, Baden, Germany. [See Lawrence Doll sketch.]

vii. Child, born and died on 2 February 1837 in Sasbach, Achern, Baden, Germany. No issue.
viii. Karl, born 23 January 1840 in Sasbach, Achern, Baden, Germany. He died on 28 January 1840 in Sasbach. No issue.

† ix. Paulina, born 20 November 1841 in Achern, Bühl, Baden, Germany. She married Joseph Christian Willi on 2 April 1861 in Ste. Genevieve, Ste. Genevieve County, Missouri. Joseph was the son of Jacob Willi and Catherine Manchert, born 25 December 1834 in Canton Bern, Switzerland. [See Joseph Christian Willi sketch.]

x. Silverius, born 5 September 1843 in Baden, Germany.

Immigration:
Arrived 17 January 1854 from Le Havre, France to New Orleans aboard the *Milan*:
    Doll, George, 24
        Catherine, 21
        Pauline, 13

Biographical:
Husband: Johann Georg "George" Doll
  Birth – 14 October 1829 in Sasbach, Achern, Baden, Germany.
  Death/Burial – 21 February 1878 in Ste. Genevieve County, Missouri. He was buried in the Valle Spring Cemetery in Ste. Genevieve, Ste. Genevieve County, Missouri.
Wife: Clothilda Palmer, daughter of Isfried Palmer and Rosa Heitz [See Isfried Palmer sketch.]
  Birth – 3 June 1836 in Ebersweier, Baden, Germany.
  Marriage – 16 September 1856 in Zell, Ste. Genevieve County, Missouri.
  Death/Burial – 27 July 1891 at the County Poor Farm in Ste. Genevieve County, Missouri. She was buried in the Valle Spring Cemetery in Ste. Genevieve, Ste. Genevieve County, Missouri.
Children:
i. Mary Rosalia, born 21 June 1857 in Ste. Genevieve County, Missouri. She was baptized on 16 August 1857 in the Ste. Genevieve Catholic Church in Ste. Genevieve, Ste. Genevieve County, Missouri. She married Louis Peter Moser on 26 April 1881 in Ste. Genevieve. Louis was the son of John Peter Moser and Mary Meyer, born about 1866 in Missouri. The couple had one daughter. Louis and Mary divorced before January 1897. Louis died of bronchio pneumonia on 2 June 1932 in St. Louis, Missouri. Mary married James William Bell on 6 January 1897 in St. Mary, Ste. Genevieve County. William was the son of Josiah Bell and Celeste _____, born January 1858 in Missouri. He was a farmer. The couple had one son. According to the 1910 census, William and Mary were divorced by 1910. Mary died of cirrhosis of the liver on 18 June 1915 in Ste. Genevieve County, Missouri. She was buried in the Valle Spring Cemetery in Ste. Genevieve, Ste. Genevieve County, Missouri.

ii. William, born 11 December 1858 in Ste. Genevieve County, Missouri. He died on 26 September 1860 in Ste. Genevieve County. William was buried in the Memorial Cemetery in Ste. Genevieve, Ste. Genevieve County, Missouri. No issue.

iii. Josephine, born 30 October 1860 in Ste. Genevieve County, Missouri. She died on 15 September 1880 in Ste. Genevieve County when she was fatally burned after a can of coal oil exploded when she was filling a lamp. She never married and had no issue.

iv. Charles, born 17 January 1862 in Ste. Genevieve County, Missouri. He was baptized on 3 April 1862 in the Ste. Genevieve Catholic Church in Ste. Genevieve, Ste. Genevieve County, Missouri. He was a general laborer. According to his death certificate, Charles was a widower at the time of his death. However, no marriage record for him has been found. Charles died of chronic myocarditis and nephritis on 5 September 1931 in St. Louis, Missouri. He was buried in the Sts. Peter and Paul Catholic Cemetery in St. Louis, Missouri. He had no known issue.

v. Wilhelmina "Mina," born 27 April 1865 in Ste. Genevieve County, Missouri. She was baptized on 20 June 1865 in the Ste. Genevieve Catholic Church in Ste. Genevieve, Ste. Genevieve

County, Missouri. Mina married Francis William "Frank" Linderer on 11 September 1888 in Ste. Genevieve. Frank was the son of Joseph Linderer and Regina Fallert, born 23 October 1863 in Baltimore, Maryland. He was a farmer. The couple had four sons and six daughters. Mina died of pneumonia and chronic heart disease on 26 October 1930 in Ste. Genevieve County, Missouri. Frank died of chronic valvular heart disease on 5 November 1934 in St. Louis, Missouri. They were both buried in the Valle Spring Cemetery in Ste. Genevieve, Ste. Genevieve County, Missouri.

vi. Francis Xavier, born 12 April 1867 in Ste. Genevieve County, Missouri. He was baptized on 12 June 1867 in the Ste. Genevieve Catholic Church in Ste. Genevieve, Ste. Genevieve County, Missouri. Frank was a general laborer. He died of uremia on 29 March 1932 in St. Louis, Missouri. He was buried in the Calvary Cemetery in St. Louis. Frank never married and had no known issue.

vii. Caroline Euphrosine, born 28 April 1870 in Ste. Genevieve County, Missouri. She was baptized on 12 June 1870 in the Ste. Genevieve Catholic Church in Ste. Genevieve, Ste. Genevieve County, Missouri. She married Nicholas A. Klein on 11 September 1894 in Ste. Genevieve. Nicholas was the son of Anton Klein and Catherina Kohm, born 8 February 1869 in Zell, Ste. Genevieve County, Missouri. The couple had six sons and one daughter. Caroline died on 30 March 1923. Nicholas died of heart failure on 3 September 1925 in Ste. Genevieve County, Missouri. They were both buried in the Valle Spring Cemetery in Ste. Genevieve, Ste. Genevieve County, Missouri.

viii. Rose Anna, born 10 May 1872 in Ste. Genevieve County, Missouri. She was baptized on 7 July 1872 in the Ste. Genevieve Catholic Church in Ste. Genevieve, Ste. Genevieve County, Missouri. She may have married a man named George Sapp and was living in St. Louis, Missouri in 1915. No further information.

ix. Catherine Regina, born 11 February 1876 in Ste. Genevieve County, Missouri. She was baptized on 19 May 1876 in the Ste. Genevieve Catholic Church in Ste. Genevieve, Ste. Genevieve County, Missouri. She married Lawrence Joseph Ruh on 11 April 1899 in Ste. Genevieve. Lawrence was the son of Lawrence Ruh and Sophia Bieser, born 28 February 1878 in Ste. Genevieve County, Missouri. [See Lawrence Ruh sketch.]

x. Paulina Barbara, born 15 March 1878 in Ste. Genevieve County, Missouri. She was baptized on 20 May 1878 in the Ste. Genevieve Catholic Church in Ste. Genevieve, Ste. Genevieve County, Missouri. She married Brasier Marcel Thomure on 10 January 1899 in Ste. Genevieve. Brasier was the son of George Thomure and Amelia Griffard, born 28 January 1876 in River aux Vases, Ste. Genevieve County, Missouri. He was a farmer. The couple had two sons and three daughters. Paulina died on 7 October 1925 and Brasile died on 26 August 1959, both in East St. Louis, St. Clair County, Missouri. They were both buried in the Valle Spring Cemetery in Ste. Genevieve, Ste. Genevieve County, Missouri.

Land Patents:
Ste. Genevieve County, Missouri

Patentee	Issue Date	Land Office	Cert. No.	Serial No.	Twp	Rng	Sec	Acres
Doll, George	15 Aug 1860	Jackson	52917	MW-0393-482	37-N	9-E	10	160.0

Naturalization:

Name	Declaration	Naturalization	Origin
Doll, George		5 November 1863 Ste. Genevieve Co.	Baden

Military:
Served in the U.S. Civil War for the Union:
Private, Company G, 78th Enrolled Missouri Militia
   George Doll enlisted on 4 October 1862 in Ste. Genevieve, Missouri. He was ordered into service on 16 October 1864 and was relieved from duty on 25 November 1864. He served a total of 41 days of actual service.
Private, Company K, 21st Missouri Volunteer Infantry
   George Doll [drafted recruit] enlisted 22 December 1864 in Ironton, St. Francois County, Missouri. Mustered out on 3 October 1865 in Mobile, Alabama.

Occupation: Farmer
Religious Affiliation: Roman Catholic
Comments:
Johann Georg "George" Doll came to the United States in 1854 with his two youngest sisters. His brothers Joseph and Lawrence followed later. George and his sisters appear to have come directly to Ste. Genevieve County, Missouri after they landed. He married Clothilda Palmer in 1856. George bought land between the towns of Ste. Genevieve and St. Mary where the couple raised their family. George and Clothilda had three sons and seven daughters, of whom one son and one daughter died young. George died on 21 February 1878 in Ste. Genevieve County, Missouri. After her husband's death, Clothilda began to suffer from bouts of melancholy and eventually was not able to care for herself or her children. She was taken to the County Poor Farm where she died of a bowel complaint on 27 July 1891. Both George and Clothilda were buried in the Valle Spring Cemetery in Ste. Genevieve, Ste. Genevieve County, Missouri.

Note: George and his siblings were nephews and nieces of Joseph Doll (1793-1880), who also settled in Ste. Genevieve County, Missouri with his family. [See Joseph Doll sketch.]

Joseph Doll Family
Surname Variations: Dold
European Origin: Obersasbach, Sasbach and Sasbachwalden, Achern, Baden, Germany
Family:
Father: Bernard Doll
Mother: Lutgard Decker
   Children:
   i. Bernard. He married Magdalena Hodapp on 17 October 1826 in Sasbachwalden, Achern, Baden, Germany. Magdalena was the daughter of Joseph Hodapp and Magdalena Huber, born 22 March 1804 in Kappelrodeck, Baden, Germany. [See George Doll sketch.]
* ii. Joseph, born about 1793 in Sasbach, Achern, Baden, Germany. [See sketch below.]
   iii. Johann Georg, born 16 April 1806 in Sasbach, Achern, Baden, Germany. He married Gertrud Ebler on 29 February 1832 in Sasbachwalden, Achern, Baden, Germany. Gertrud was the daughter of Joseph Ebler and Gertrud Grechtler, born 21 February 1810 in Sasbachwalden. [See Bernard Doll sketch.]
   iv. Maria Anna, born 19 October 1808 in Sasbach, Achern, Baden, Germany.
   v. Gertrud, born 14 March 1812 in Sasbach, Achern, Baden, Germany.
   vi. Michael, born 8 October 1813 in Sasbach, Achern, Baden, Germany. He died on 10 March 1814 in Sasbach. No issue.
   vii. Brigitta, born 30 January 1815 in Sasbach, Achern, Baden, Germany. She died on 2 February 1815 in Sasbach. No issue.
   viii. Lorenz, born 10 August 1816 in Sasbach, Achern, Baden, Germany.
   ix. Magdalena, born 6 November 1819 in Sasbach Achern, Baden, Germany. She died on 13 November 1819 in Sasbach. No issue.

Immigration:
Arrived 21 July 1847 from Le Havre, France to New Orleans aboard the *Lyons*:
    Doll, Joseph, 40   Farmer   Baden
        Johanna, 50
    [Hug] Marianna, 22
    [Hug] Johanna 21
    [Hug] Josephine [Genevieve], 16
    [Hug] Johann [Roman], 12
        Theresa, 10
        Sophia, 8
        Victoire [Eleanore], 5

Biographical:
Husband: Joseph Doll
    Birth – about 1793 in Sasbachwalden, Achern, Baden, Germany.
    Death/Burial – 10 February 1880 in Ste. Genevieve County, Missouri. He was buried in the Memorial Cemetery in Ste. Genevieve, Ste. Genevieve County, Missouri.
Wife: Johanna Lang, daughter of Alois Lang and Maria Anna Ernst
    Birth – 21 January 1795 in Neusatz amt Bühl, Baden, Germany.
    1) Marriage – 10 August 1823 in Obersasbach, Achern, Baden, Germany to Johannes Hug. [See Roman Huck sketch.]
    2) Marriage – 18 November 1834 in Obersasbach, Achern, Baden, Germany to Joseph Doll.
    Death/Burial – 18 March 1879 in Ste. Genevieve County, Missouri. She was buried in the Memorial Cemetery in Ste. Genevieve, Ste. Genevieve County, Missouri.
Children:
    i. Theresia, born 16 October 1835 in Obersasbach, Achern, Baden, Germany. She married Bernard Schmitt on 9 November 1852 in Ste. Genevieve, Ste. Genevieve County, Missouri. Bernard was the son of Johann Schmitt and Elisabetha Bohnert, born 29 April 1832 in Kappelrodeck, Baden, Germany. [See Bernard Schmitt sketch.]
    ii. Sophia, born 20 January 1839 in Obersasbach, Achern, Baden, Germany. She married William Baumann on 17 June 1856 in Zell, Ste. Genevieve County, Missouri. William was the son of Franz Anton Baumann and Catherine Armbruster, born 15 February 1832 in Canton, Stark County, Ohio. [See Franz Anton Baumann sketch.]
    iii. Eleanora, born 22 February 1841 in Obersasbach, Achern, Baden, Germany. She married her cousin Lawrence Doll on 18 January 1862 in Ste. Genevieve, Ste. Genevieve County, Missouri. Lawrence was the son of Bernard Doll and Magdalena Hodapp, born 30 July 1834 in Sasbach amt Achern, Baden, Germany. [See Lawrence Doll sketch.]

Land Patents:
Ste. Genevieve County, Missouri

Patentee	Issue Date	Land Office	Cert. No.	Serial No.	Twp	Rng	Sec	Acres
Doll, Joseph	15 Aug 1860	Jackson	65176	MW-0393-483	37-N	9-E	11	151.66

Naturalization:

Name	Declaration	Naturalization	Origin
Doll, Joseph	23 November 1848	20 November 1852 Ste. Genevieve Co.	Baden

Occupation: Farmer
Religious Affiliation: Roman Catholic

Comments:
Joseph Doll was born in Sasbachwalden, Achern, Baden, Germany. He married Mrs. Johanna Hug on 18 November 1834 in Obersasbach, Achern, Baden, Germany. Johanna was the widow of Johannes Hug and had one son and four daughters from her first marriage. The couple had three daughters together. Joseph brought his large family to the United States in 1847. They endured an unusually long voyage and eventually landed in New Orleans, Louisiana. They traveled up the Mississippi River to Ste. Genevieve County, Missouri where Joseph rented land about five miles south of the city of Ste. Genevieve. He farmed that land for a number of years and later purchased government land in the same vicinity. The family was almost completely destitute for the first years they lived in Missouri. Bad weather lead to poor harvests and the winter of 1848-1849 was one of the worst on record. Joseph had only been able to build a small, one-room cabin to shelter his family and they suffered terribly from cold and hunger. Eventually, Joseph was able to enlarge the house, improve their living conditions and become more financially stable. Johanna died on 18 March 1879 and Joseph died a year later on 10 February 1880, both in Ste. Genevieve County, Missouri. They were both buried in the Memorial Cemetery in Ste. Genevieve, Ste. Genevieve County, Missouri.

Note: Joseph Doll was uncle to Bernard, George, Joseph, Catherine, Pauline and Lawrence Doll who also settled in Ste. Genevieve County, Missouri.

Joseph Doll Family
Surname Variations: Dall
European Origin: Sasbachwalden, Achern, Baden, Germany
Family:
Father: Bernard Doll, born in Sasbachwalden, Achern, Baden, Germany.
Mother: Magdalena Hodapp, born 22 March 1804 in Kappelrodeck, Baden, Germany.
    Children:

Note: For a comprehensive discussion of Bernard Doll's children see the Johann Georg "George" Doll sketch.

Immigration:
Arrived about 1854 to New York aboard an unknown vessel:
    Doll, Joseph

Biographical:
Husband: Joseph Doll
    Birth – 26 June 1831 in Sasbach, Achern, Baden, Germany.
    Death/Burial – 2 March 1888 in Ste. Genevieve County, Missouri. He was buried in the St. Mary Cemetery in St. Mary, Ste. Genevieve County, Missouri.
Wife: Francisca Klumpp, daughter of Anton Klumpp and Christine Hund
    Birth – 14 January 1828 in Kappelrodeck, Achern, Baden, Germany.
    Marriage – 5 March 1860 in Zell, Ste. Genevieve County, Missouri.
    Death/Burial – 8 March 1900 in Ste. Genevieve County, Missouri. She was buried in the St. Mary Cemetery in St. Mary, Ste. Genevieve County, Missouri.
    Children:
        i.   Joseph, born 30 April 1862 in Ste. Genevieve County, Missouri. Joseph was a farmer. He married Mrs. Louise Yeagle on 27 November 1895 in St. Mary, Ste. Genevieve County. Louise was the daughter of Herman Buehler and Amelia Roth, born 16 November 1855 in Missouri. She had married Conrad Yeagle as her first husband on 3 October 1888 in Ste. Genevieve County, Missouri. [See Conrad Yeagle sketch.] Joseph and Louise had no children. Louise died of pneumonia on 26 February 1905 in Ste. Genevieve County. She was buried in the St. Mary Catholic Cemetery in St. Mary, Ste. Genevieve County, Missouri. Joseph married Mrs. Mary Louise Wolf as his second wife on 14 July 1907 in St. Mary, Ste. Genevieve County. Mary was the daughter of Theodore Roulette and Catherine Rond, born 26 September 1862 in Ste.

Genevieve County. She was the widow of Andrew Wolf whom she had married on 12 May 1885 in St. Mary. Andrew had died on 11 June 1906 in Ste. Genevieve County and was buried in the St. Mary Catholic Cemetery in St. Mary. [See John Wolf sketch.] Joseph and Mary had no children together. Joseph died of pulmonary thrombosis on 22 January 1927 and Mary died of bronchial pneumonia caused by influenza on 27 January 1943, both in St. Mary. They were both buried in the St. Mary Catholic Cemetery in St. Mary, Ste. Genevieve County, Missouri.

ii. Mary, born April 1865 in Ste. Genevieve County, Missouri. She lived for a time with her older brother, Joseph. No further information has been found after the 1900 census.

iii. Sophia, born about 1866 in Ste. Genevieve County, Missouri. She died on 12 October 1870 in Ste. Genevieve County. Sophia was buried in the St. Mary Cemetery in St. Mary, Ste. Genevieve County, Missouri. No issue.

iv. Charles H., born 4 March 1869 in Ste. Genevieve County, Missouri. He was a saloon keeper in St. Mary. Charles married Elizabeth Ann Faser on 25 May 1897 in St. Mary, Ste. Genevieve County, Missouri. Elizabeth was the daughter of Ignatius Faser and Elizabeth Hagen, born 21 November 1878 in Ste. Genevieve County, Missouri. The couple had three sons and five daughters, of whom one daughter died in early childhood. Charles died of coronary thrombosis and possibly gall bladder cancer on 20 March 1940 in St. Louis, Missouri. Elizabeth died in February 1964 in Ste. Genevieve County, Missouri. They were both buried in the St. Mary Cemetery in St. Mary, Ste. Genevieve County, Missouri.

v. John, born 25 February 1875 in Ste. Genevieve County, Missouri. He was baptized on 27 March 1875 in the Immaculate Conception Catholic Church in St. Mary, Ste. Genevieve County, Missouri. John died on 16 October 1876 in Ste. Genevieve County. He was buried in the St. Mary Catholic Cemetery in St. Mary, Ste. Genevieve County, Missouri. No issue.

U.S. residence prior to Ste. Genevieve County, Missouri:
Pennsylvania, 1854 to 1856

Naturalization:

Name	Declaration	Naturalization	Origin
Doll, Joseph		5 November 1863 Ste. Genevieve Co.	Baden

Military:
Served in the U.S. Civil War for the Union:
Private, Company D, 78th Enrolled Missouri Militia
  James [Joseph] Doll enlisted 25 August 1862 in St. Mary, Ste. Genevieve County, Missouri.

Occupation: Farmer
Religious Affiliation: Roman Catholic
Comments:
According to his obituary, Joseph Doll came to the United States about 1854. He is said to have landed in New York and then moved to Pennsylvania where he lived for about two years. By about mid-1856, he had settled in Ste. Genevieve County, Missouri near the town of St. Mary's Landing [present-day St. Mary]. He married Francisca Klumpp in March 1860 in Zell, Ste. Genevieve County. During the Civil War, Joseph enlisted in the 78th Enrolled Missouri Militia, but he does not appear to have served any active duty. Joseph died of malarial fever complicated by heart failure due to excessive drinking on 2 March 1888 in Ste. Genevieve County, Missouri. Francisca died on 8 March 1900 in Ste. Genevieve County, Missouri. They were both buried in the St. Mary Cemetery in St. Mary, Ste. Genevieve County, Missouri.

Julius Joseph Doll Family

Surname Variations: None
European Origin: Prussia, Germany
Family:
Father: Unknown
Mother: Unknown
   Child:
*   i.   Julius Joseph, born 30 April 1830 in Germany. [See sketch below.]

Immigration:
Arrived 2 November 1857 from Liverpool, England to New York aboard the *Australia*:
    Doll, [Julius] Joseph, 27   Gardner   from Germany   to St. Louis
        Catherine, 21

Biographical:
Husband: Julius Joseph Doll
    Birth – 30 April 1830 in Germany.
    Death/Burial – 25 March 1878 in Ste. Genevieve County, Missouri. He was buried in the Valle Spring Cemetery in Ste. Genevieve, Ste. Genevieve County, Missouri.
Wife: Catherine Nau, daughter of _____ Nau and Barbara Cornely
    Birth – 7 February 1836 in Bingen am Rhein, Germany.
    Marriage – about 1855 in Bingen am Rhein, Germany.
    Death/Burial – 29 April 1913 in Ste. Genevieve County, Missouri. She was buried in the Valle Spring Cemetery in Ste. Genevieve, Ste. Genevieve County, Missouri.
    Children:
        i.   Child. Died in infancy. No issue.
        ii.   Child. Died in infancy. No issue.
        iii.   Child. Died in infancy. No issue.
        iv.   Child. Died in infancy. No issue.
        v.   Johanna Mary, born 21 March 1864 in Ste. Genevieve County, Missouri. She was baptized on 17 April 1864 in the Ste. Genevieve Catholic Church in Ste. Genevieve, Ste. Genevieve County, Missouri. Johanna married Felix Isreal Bequette on 20 September 1881 in Ste. Genevieve, Ste. Genevieve County, Missouri. Felix was the son of Augustine Bequette and Marie Louise Carron, born 9 August 1859 in Ste. Genevieve County, Missouri. Felix was a farmer. The couple two sons and three daughters, of whom one child died in infancy and one daughter died in early childhood. Felix died of acute interstitial nephritis on 17 October 1928 and Johanna died of a cerebral hemorrhage on 22 January 1948, both in Ste. Genevieve, Ste. Genevieve County, Missouri. They were both buried in the Valle Spring Cemetery in Ste. Genevieve, Ste. Genevieve County, Missouri.

U.S. residence prior to Ste. Genevieve County, Missouri:
    St. Louis, Missouri, 1857 – 1861

Occupation: Farmer
Religious Affiliation: Roman Catholic
Comments:
Julius Joseph Doll and Catherine Nau were married in Bingen am Rhein, Germany in 1855. They came to the United States in 1857 and settled in St. Louis, Missouri. Four years later they moved to Ste. Genevieve County, Missouri, where Joseph bought a farm. The couple had five children, but only one daughter survived to adulthood. The other children all died in infancy. Joseph died on 25 March 1878 in Ste. Genevieve County, Missouri. He was buried in the Valle Spring Cemetery in Ste. Genevieve, Ste. Genevieve County, Missouri. After her husband's death, Catherine hired a man to work the family farm. After her daughter's marriage, her

son-in-law took over the farm operation. Catherine died of hemiplegia on 29 April 1913. She was buried beside her husband in the Valle Spring Cemetery in Ste. Genevieve, Ste. Genevieve County, Missouri.

Lorenz "Lawrence" Doll Family
Surname Variations: None
European Origin: Sasbachwalden, Achern, Baden, Germany
Family:
Father: Bernard Doll, born in Sasbachwalden, Achern, Baden, Germany.
Mother: Magdalena Hodapp, born 22 March 1804 in Kappelrodeck, Baden, Germany.
 Children:

Note: For a comprehensive discussion of Bernard Doll's children see the Johann Georg "George" Doll sketch.

Immigration:
Arrived about 1856 [1900 census] aboard an unknown vessel:
 Doll, Lawrence

Biographical:
Husband: Lawrence Doll
 Birth – 30 July 1834 in Sasbachwalden, Achern, Baden, Germany.
 Death/Burial – 6 February 1906 in St. Louis, Missouri. He was buried in the Sts. Peter and Paul
  Cemetery in St. Louis, Missouri.
Wife: Eleonora Doll, daughter of Joseph Doll and Johanna Lang [See Joseph Doll sketch.]
 Birth – 22 February 1841 in Obersasbach, Achern, Baden, Germany.
 Marriage – 18 January 1862 in Ste. Genevieve, Ste. Genevieve County, Missouri.
 Death/Burial – 18 March 1922 in St. Louis, Missouri. She was buried in the Sts. Peter and Paul
  Cemetery in St. Louis, Missouri.
 Children:
  i. Paulina, born 22 January 1863 in Ste. Genevieve County, Missouri. She was baptized on
   1 March 1863 in the Ste. Genevieve Catholic Church in Ste. Genevieve, Ste. Genevieve
   County, Missouri. She married John Bamberger about 1907 in Missouri. He was the proprietor
   of a restaurant and saloon in St. Louis, Missouri. John was born 19 February 1839 in Germany.
   He had come to the United States about 1856 with his brother Philip and married his first wife,
   Elisabeth _____ about 1863, most likely in Missouri. Paulina worked in the Bamberger
   household as a domestic servant before John's wife Elisabeth died of heart disease on 24 March
   1905 in St. Louis, Missouri. There were no children from John's first marriage and he and
   Pauline had no children. John died of aortic heart disease on 17 October 1915 in St. Louis,
   Missouri. His body was cremated in the Missouri Crematory in St. Louis. Paulina died of
   peritonitis after her appendix ruptured on 7 January 1926 in St. Louis, Missouri. She was buried
   in the Sts. Peter and Paul Cemetery in St. Louis, Missouri.
  ii. Mary Magdalena, born 10 May 1865 in Ste. Genevieve County, Missouri. She was baptized on
   16 July 1865 in the Ste. Genevieve Catholic Church in Ste. Genevieve, Ste. Genevieve County,
   Missouri. Mary died on 29 March 1879 in Ste. Genevieve County. No issue.
  iii. Emma Elenora, born 2 September 1867 in Ste. Genevieve County, Missouri. She was baptized
   on 13 October 1867 in the Ste. Genevieve Catholic Church in Ste. Genevieve, Ste. Genevieve
   County, Missouri. She married Henry W. Weiser on 24 November 1891 in St. Louis, Missouri.
   He was a bricklayer in St. Louis. Henry was born in August 1867 in Missouri. He may be the
   Henry Weiser, son of Gallus Weiser and Mary _____ who were living in Perryville, Perry
   County, Missouri in 1870. Rather late in life, Henry and Emma had one son. Emma died of
   acute bronchitis on 13 October 1933 in St. Louis. She was buried in the Resurrection Cemetery
   in Affton, St. Louis County, Missouri. After his wife's death, Henry and his son moved to East

iv. Catherine, born 10 April 1870 in Ste. Genevieve County, Missouri. She was baptized on 22 May 1870 in the Ste. Genevieve Catholic Church in Ste. Genevieve, Ste. Genevieve County, Missouri. No further information has been found after the 1880 census.

v. Emile Joseph, born 2 June 1872 in Ste. Genevieve County, Missouri. He was baptized on 20 July 1872 in the Ste. Genevieve Catholic Church in Ste. Genevieve, Ste. Genevieve County, Missouri. Joseph was a brewery fireman. Joseph died on 4 November 1941 from injuries he sustained when he was hit by a bus when he was crossing a street in St. Louis. His skull was fractured and multiple ribs were broken when the wheels of the bus passed over his chest. He was buried in the Sts. Peter and Paul Cemetery in St. Louis, Missouri. He never married and had no known issue.

vi. Anna Theresa, born 22 August 1875 in Ste. Genevieve County, Missouri. She was baptized on 4 October 1875 in the Ste. Genevieve Catholic Church in Ste. Genevieve, Ste. Genevieve County, Missouri. She married Charles P. Moore. Charles was the son of Peter Moore and Bertha Mittenbach, born 23 September 1868. He was a railroad car repairman. The couple did not have children together, but they raised a young girl who may have been a child of an earlier marriage of Charles' or she may have been Charles' sister. Charles died of diabetes mellitus and heat prostration on 13 July 1930 in St. Louis, Missouri. After her husband's death, Annie lived with her foster daughter and her family. Annie died of arteriosclerotic heart disease on 21 September 1954 in St. Louis. Both she and her husband were buried in the Sts. Peter and Paul Cemetery in St. Louis, Missouri.

vii. Lawrence, born 28 January 1877 in Ste. Genevieve County, Missouri. He was baptized on 16 March 1877 in the Ste. Genevieve Catholic Church in Ste. Genevieve, Ste. Genevieve County, Missouri. No further mention of Lawrence has been found after the 1880 census.

viii. Infant, born about April 1879 in Ste. Genevieve County, Missouri. The child died on 21 April 1879. No issue.

ix. Edwin, born 29 October 1880 in Ste. Genevieve County, Missouri. He was baptized on 13 December 1880 in the Ste. Genevieve Catholic Church in Ste. Genevieve, Ste. Genevieve County, Missouri. Edwin died on 24 January 1881 in Ste. Genevieve County, Missouri. No issue.

x. Philip James, born 1 May 1882 in Ste. Genevieve County, Missouri. He was baptized on 22 June 1882 in the Ste. Genevieve Catholic Church in Ste. Genevieve, Ste. Genevieve County, Missouri. He worked as an upholstery fitter in a furniture factory. Philip married Mary Ann Mabes. Mary Ann was the daughter of John Mabes and _____, born 13 January 1882 in St. Louis, Missouri. The couple had two sons and one daughter. Philip died of thrombo phlebitis of the right leg and pulmonary embolism on 22 May 1938 in St. Louis, Missouri. Mary Ann died of acute myocarditis and chronic nephritis on 13 November 1938 in St. Louis. They were both buried in the new Sts. Peter and Paul Cemetery in St. Louis, Missouri.

U.S. residence other than Ste. Genevieve County, Missouri:
St. Louis, Missouri

Naturalization:

Name	Declaration	Naturalization	Origin
Doll, Lorentz		5 November 1863 Ste. Genevieve Co.	Baden

Military:
Served in the U.S. Civil War for the Union:
Corporal, Company G, 78th Enrolled Missouri Militia
Lorenze Doll enlisted 30 April 1864 at Ste. Genevieve County, Missouri. He was ordered into

service on 16 October 1864 and was relieved from duty on 25 November 1864. He served a total of 41 days of actual service.

Private, Company K, 21st Missouri Volunteer Infantry
Lorenzo Doll [drafted recruit] enlisted 22 December 1864 in Ironton, St. Francois County, Missouri. Mustered out on 3 October 1865 in Mobile, Alabama.

Education: Could read and write
Occupation: Farmer, Teamster
Religious Affiliation: Roman Catholic

Comments:
Lawrence Doll came to the United States as a young man about 1856. He married his first cousin, Eleonora Doll, in Ste. Genevieve County, Missouri in 1862. During the Civil War, Lawrence served in the 78th Enrolled Missouri Militia as a corporal in Company G. Several companies, including G, of the 78th EMM were called to active service in October 1864, to take part in the pursuit of General Sterling Price's Army of Missouri after the Battle of Fort Davidson near Pilot Knob, Missouri. Lawrence was drafted into the 21st Missouri Volunteer Infantry at Ironton and remained in active service until the end of the war. He returned to Ste. Genevieve County, Missouri after the war was over and went back to farming. By the late 1890s, Lawrence had moved his family to St. Louis, Missouri where he worked as a teamster. Lawrence died of paralysis due to a cerebral hemorrhage on 6 February 1906 in St. Louis, Missouri. Eleonora died of apoplexy on 18 March 1922 in St. Louis, Missouri. They were both buried in the Sts. Peter and Paul Cemetery in St. Louis, Missouri.

Meinrad Donze Family

Surname Variations: Doncie, Donzé, Donzi, Dorsey, Douzie, Dunzie
European Origin: Pfaffenheim, Haut-Rhin, Alsace, France
Family:
Father: Simon Meinrad Donzé, born 27 October 1786 in Pfaffenheim, Haut-Rhin, Alsace, France.
   He died on 2 September 1837 in Pfaffenheim.
Mother: Anna Maria Freudenreich, born 17 August 1790 in Pfaffenheim, Haut-Rhin, Alsace, France.
   She died on 17 April 1844 in Pfaffenheim.
   Children:
†   i. Seraphin, born 4 June 1827 in Pfaffenheim, Haut-Rhin, Alsace, France. [See Seraphin Donze sketch.]
*   ii. Meinrad, born 29 May 1829 in Pfaffenheim, Haut-Rhin, Alsace, France. [See sketch below.]

Immigration:
Arrived 15 October 1849 from Le Havre, France to New Orleans aboard the *Cromwell*:
   Donze, Meinrath, 19   from Germany
         Louisa, 2
   Munsch, Gertrude, 26

Biographical:
Husband: Meinrad Donze
   Birth – 29 May 1829 in Pfaffenheim, Haut-Rhin, Alsace, France.
   Death/Burial – 9 December 1907 in Ste. Genevieve, Ste. Genevieve County, Missouri. He was buried in the Valle Spring Cemetery in Ste. Genevieve, Ste. Genevieve County, Missouri.
Wife: Wilhelmina Joggerst, daughter of Franz Ignatz Joggerst and Maria Johanna Brischle [See Franz Ignatz Joggerst sketch.]
   Birth – 23 September 1841 in Badenweiler, Baden, Germany.
   Marriage – 19 August 1858 in Zell, Ste. Genevieve County, Missouri.
   Death/Burial – 23 April 1922 in Ste. Genevieve, Ste. Genevieve County, Missouri. She was buried in the

Valle Spring Cemetery in Ste. Genevieve, Ste. Genevieve County, Missouri.

Children:
- i. Johanna, born about 1858 in Ste. Genevieve County, Missouri. She died on 26 July 1865 in Ste. Genevieve County. She was buried in the St. Joseph Cemetery in Zell, Ste. Genevieve County, Missouri. No issue.
- ii. Anna Maria, born 18 August 1860 in Ste. Genevieve County, Missouri. She married her first cousin, John Nicholas Donze on 22 October 1881 in Lawrenceton, Ste. Genevieve County. John was the son of Seraphin Donze and Gertrude Munsch, born 29 August 1861 in Ste. Genevieve County, Missouri. [See Seraphin Donze sketch.]
- iii. Josephine L., born 16 March 1862 in Ste. Genevieve County, Missouri. Josephine married Henry Joseph Gisi in a double wedding, with her brother Frank and Henry's sister Anna Maria Gisi, on 11 February 1890 in Ste. Genevieve, Ste. Genevieve County, Missouri. Henry was the son of Valerian Gisi and Caroline Litterst, born 23 July 1864 in River aux Vases, Ste. Genevieve County, Missouri. He was a farmer. The couple had three sons and three daughters. Some time after 1900, Henry and Josephine moved their family south to Perry County, Missouri where they bought a farm near the small town of Cinque Hommes. Henry died of cirrhosis of the liver on 13 June 1936 in Perry County, Missouri. Josephine died on 10 June 1948, in West Branch, Ogemaw County, Michigan. They were both buried in the St. Boniface Cemetery in Perryville, Perry County, Missouri.
- iv. Lawrence, born 3 September 1863 in Ste. Genevieve County, Missouri. He was baptized on 25 October 1863 in the Sts. Philip and James Catholic Church in River aux Vases, Ste. Genevieve County. Lawrence died on 7 August 1865 in Ste. Genevieve County. He was buried in the St. Joseph Cemetery in Zell, Ste. Genevieve County, Missouri. No issue.
- v. Carolina, born 4 March 1865 in Ste. Genevieve County, Missouri. She was baptized on 26 March 1865 in the Sts. Philip and James Catholic Church in River aux Vases, Ste. Genevieve County. Carolina died on 19 July 1865 in Ste. Genevieve County. She was buried in the St. Joseph Cemetery in Zell, Ste. Genevieve County, Missouri. No issue.
- vi. Francis Xavier "Frank," born 26 November 1866 in Ste. Genevieve County, Missouri. He was a farmer. Frank married Anna Maria Gisi in a double wedding with Anna's brother Henry and Frank's sister Josephine, on 11 February 1890 in Ste. Genevieve, Ste. Genevieve County, Missouri. Anna was the daughter of Valerian Gisi and Sophia Burgert, born 11 July 1867 in Ste. Genevieve County, Missouri. The couple had two sons and two daughters. Frank died of acute Bright's disease and a kidney stone on 28 March 1926 at his son's home in St. Francois County, Missouri. Anna died of a cerebral embolism and phlebitis in her right leg on 27 June 1944 in Ste. Genevieve County. They were both buried in the Our Lady Help of Christians Cemetery in Weingarten, Ste. Genevieve County, Missouri.
- vii. Meinrad Seraphin, born 15 October 1868 in Ste. Genevieve County, Missouri. He was a farmer. Meinrad married Anna Mary Hurst on 31 January 1893 in Ste. Genevieve, Ste. Genevieve County, Missouri. Anna was the daughter of Joseph Hurst and Wilhelmina Dora Otte, born 29 August 1873 in Ozora, Ste. Genevieve County, Missouri. The couple had three sons. Anna died of consumption of the throat on 12 December 1900 in Ste. Genevieve County, about five weeks after the birth of her third child. She was buried in the Sacred Heart Cemetery in Ozora, Ste. Genevieve County. Meinrad married Theresia Bieser as his second wife on 16 November 1903 in Weingarten, Ste. Genevieve County, Missouri. Theresia was the daughter of Bartholomew Bieser and Catherine Baumann, born 15 December 1881 in Weingarten, Ste. Genevieve County. The couple had three sons and two daughters. For the last several years of her life, Theresia suffered from a disease which lead to progressive paralysis. She died of pulmonary edema and acute cardiac dilation on 9 February 1940 in Ste. Genevieve County. Meinrad died of chronic myocarditis and nephritis on 24 April 1955 in Ste. Genevieve County. They were both buried in the Valle Spring Cemetery in Ste. Genevieve, Ste. Genevieve County, Missouri.

viii. Wilhelmina C., born 15 June 1870 in Ste. Genevieve County, Missouri. She married Francis Xavier "Frank" Stuppy on 19 July 1892 in Ste. Genevieve, Ste. Genevieve County, Missouri. Frank was the son of Jacob Stuppy and Francisca Huck, born 14 October 1862 in Ste. Genevieve County, Missouri. [See Jacob Stuppy sketch.]

ix. Maria Tharsilla "Mary," born 29 December 1871 in Ste. Genevieve County, Missouri. She was baptized on 28 January 1872 in the Sts. Philip and James Catholic Church in River aux Vases, Ste. Genevieve County. She married George Menk on 25 April 1893 in St. Louis, Missouri. George was the son of Wilhelm Menk and Anastasia "Anna" Baurentischel, born 2 February 1857 in St. Louis, Missouri. He was a lithographer and a junior partner in the St. Louis firm of Foerstel, Menk & Co. The couple had three sons and two daughters. Mary died of puerperal septicemia [childbed fever] on 30 May 1905 in St. Louis after the birth of her fifth child. George was left to raise the children on his own. He never remarried. George died of angina pectoris on 18 March 1934 in St. Louis. He and his wife were both buried in the Sts. Peter and Paul Cemetery in St. Louis, Missouri.

x. Louisa Johanna [aka Jane], born 9 December 1873 in Ste. Genevieve County, Missouri. She was baptized on 10 January 1874 in the St. Lawrence Catholic Church in Lawrenceton, Ste. Genevieve County. Louisa died of consumption on 7 November 1896 in Ste. Genevieve County, Missouri. She had caught the measles about sixteen months before her death, a disease from which she never fully recovered before she succumbed to tuberculosis. She was buried in the Valle Spring Cemetery in Ste. Genevieve, Ste. Genevieve County, Missouri. Louisa never married and had no issue.

xi. Sophia Theresa, born 18 March 1875 in Ste. Genevieve County, Missouri. She was baptized on 4 April 1875 in the St. Lawrence Catholic Church in Lawrenceton, Ste. Genevieve County. Sophia married Henry Charles Gittinger on 24 April 1900 in Ste. Genevieve, Ste. Genevieve County. Henry was the son of George Gittinger and Marie Ann Valle, born 25 January 1874 in Ste. Genevieve County, Missouri. Henry was a farmer. The couple had three sons and five daughters. Sophia died of an intestinal obstruction complicated by gall stones and diabetes on 19 August 1933 in St. Louis, Missouri. Henry married Josephine Emily Bequette as his second wife about 1934. Josephine was the daughter of August Bequette and Marie Louise Carron, born on 8 November 1873 in Missouri. The couple had no children together. Josephine died of heart disease and a throat infection on 8 January 1953 in St. Louis. Henry died on 15 April 1970 in St. Louis, Missouri. Henry and both of his wives were buried in the Valle Spring Cemetery in Ste. Genevieve, Ste. Genevieve County, Missouri.

xii. Emily Catherine, born 5 April 1877 in Ste. Genevieve County, Missouri. She was baptized on 6 May 1877 in the Our Lady Help of Christians Catholic Church in Weingarten, Ste. Genevieve County. Catherine married Henry George Hurst on 29 July 1901 in Ste. Genevieve County, Missouri. Henry was the son of Joseph Hurst and Wilhelmina Maria Theresa Otte, born 20 February 1879 in Ste. Genevieve County, Missouri. Henry was a farmer. Between 1910 and 1920, Henry moved his family to Clay County Arkansas where he purchased a farm. The couple had five sons and three daughters. Emily died of heart disease on 28 September 1958 in Cape Girardeau, Cape Girardeau County, Missouri. She was buried in the New Guardian Angel Cemetery in Oran, Scott County, Missouri. Henry is said to have died in Henryetta, Okmulgee County, Oklahoma.

xiii. Valentine Seraphin, in October 1878 in Ste. Genevieve County, Missouri. He was baptized in November 1878 in the Our Lady Help of Christians Catholic Church in Weingarten, Ste. Genevieve County. Valentine was a farmer and later an auto mechanic. He was married to Genevieve Josephine Scherer on 25 November 1901 in Ste. Genevieve, Ste. Genevieve County. Josephine was the daughter of John Scherer and Sophia Mary Bahr, born 3 January 1884 in Missouri. The couple had two sons and three daughters. Valentine died of heart disease and pneumonia on 25 February 1943 in Ste. Genevieve County, Missouri. Josephine died on 4 April 1974. They were both buried in the Valle Spring Cemetery in Ste. Genevieve, Ste. Genevieve

County, Missouri.

xiv. Joseph Henry, born 22 March 1881 in Ste. Genevieve County, Missouri. He was baptized on 24 April 1881 in the St. Lawrence Catholic Church in Lawrenceton, Ste. Genevieve County. Joseph was a barber and as a young man he moved to East St. Louis, St. Clair County, Illinois where he owned and operated a barber shop. He married Mary Schrantz on 28 July 1903 in East St. Louis, St. Clair County. Mary was the daughter of Louis Schrantz and Mary Ann Masserang, born in June 1876 in Illinois. The couple had three sons and six daughters. Joseph died of a heart attack on 17 December 1958 in East St. Louis, St. Clair County, Illinois. Mary died on 4 September 1966 in Freeburg, St. Clair County, Illinois.

xv. Andrew Martin [twin], born 8 November 1883 in Ste. Genevieve County, Missouri. He was baptized on 17 November 1883 in the Our Lady Help of Christians Catholic Church in Weingarten, Ste. Genevieve County. Andrew was a barber. He married Mary Lorena Christian Gisi on 20 November 1911 in Ste. Genevieve, Ste. Genevieve County, Missouri. Lorena was the daughter of Valerian Gisi and Mary Johanna "Jane" Rigdon, born 3 November 1880 in Ste. Genevieve County, Missouri. The couple had three sons, of whom the oldest died in infancy. Andrew died on 10 July 1966 in Fletcher, Jefferson County, Missouri, and Lorena died on 14 August 1971 in Ste. Genevieve. They were both buried in the Valle Spring Cemetery in Ste. Genevieve, Ste. Genevieve County, Missouri.

xvi. Lawrence William [twin], born 8 November 1883 in Ste. Genevieve County, Missouri. He was baptized on 17 November 1883 in the Our Lady Help of Christians Catholic Church in Weingarten, Ste. Genevieve County. After he left school, Lawrence rambled around the Midwestern and Western United States for a number of years. He spent two years in Denver, Colorado working as a bookkeeper for an auto dealership. He spent his nights attending a school to learn auto mechanics and eventually opened his own garage. He returned to Missouri and went to work as a wholesale grocery salesman for the firm of Geldahaus-Wulfing & Co. of St. Louis. He married Mrs. Elisabeth Mary Rottler on 17 January 1916 in Ste. Genevieve, Ste. Genevieve County, Missouri. Elisabeth was the widow of Fridolin Andrew "Fred" Rottler and had one daughter from her first marriage. [See Valentine Rottler sketch.] Elisabeth was the daughter of Bernard Huck and Maria Figge, born 6 October 1886 in Ste. Genevieve County, Missouri. The couple had five sons and three daughters. Lawrence died of a heart attack on 7 February 1960 at Perryville, Perry County, Missouri, and Elizabeth died on 2 December 1984. They were both buried in the Valle Spring Cemetery in Ste. Genevieve, Ste. Genevieve County, Missouri.

xvii. Rose Carolina, born 22 October 1886 in Ste. Genevieve County, Missouri. She was baptized in November 1886 in the Our Lady Help of Christians Catholic Church in Weingarten, Ste. Genevieve County. Rose married Leo August Klein on 19 October 1909 in Ste. Genevieve, Ste. Genevieve County, Missouri. Leo was the son of Ignatius Klein and Magdalena Lipp, born 26 October 1881 in Ste. Genevieve County, Missouri. He was the proprietor of a dry goods store. The couple had three sons and one daughter, of whom one son died in infancy. Rose died of a heart attack on 27 August 1962 in Farmington, St. Francois County, Missouri. Leo died of injuries he received in an automobile accident on 5 September 1963 in St. Louis, Missouri. They were both buried in the Valle Spring Cemetery in Ste. Genevieve, Ste. Genevieve County, Missouri.

xviii. John Seraphin, born and died on 13 November 1887 in Ste. Genevieve County, Missouri. He lived for only an hour. The baby was buried in the Our Lady Help of Christians Cemetery in Weingarten, Ste. Genevieve County, Missouri. No issue.

U.S. residence prior to Ste. Genevieve County, Missouri:
Gold fields of California

Land Patents:
Ste. Genevieve County, Missouri

Patentee	Issue Date	Land Office	Cert. No.	Serial No.	Twp	Rng	Sec	Acres
Dorsey, Meinrat	30 Oct 1857	Jackson	246003	MO3840_.102	37-N	7-E	17	35.69
Dunsey, Minerot	1 Mar 1860	Jackson	37009	MO4080_.328	37-N	7-E	18	80.00

Naturalization:

Name	Declaration	Naturalization	Origin	Remarks
Donze, Meinrad			France	1900 census

Military:
Served in the U.S. Civil War for the Union:
Private, Company I, 78th Enrolled Missouri Militia
   Minerad Donze enlisted 12 June 1863 at New Offenburg, Ste. Genevieve County, Missouri.

Education: Could read and write
Occupation: Farmer
Religious Affiliation: Roman Catholic
Comments:
Meinrad Donze followed his older brother, Seraphin, to the United States in 1849, bringing with him Seraphin's wife and young daughter. Shortly after his arrival in Ste. Genevieve County, Missouri, Meinrad went west to California and Colorado where he spent several years mining for gold. He returned to Ste. Genevieve County, Missouri and went to work with his brother, farming land near the present-day town of River aux Vases. Meinrad was married to Wilhelmina Joggerst in 1856. By 1881, Meinrad had purchased his own farm and was living with his family near Weingarten, Ste. Genevieve County. Meinrad and Wilhelmina had eight sons and ten daughters, of whom one son and two daughters died in the summer of 1865 of an unknown contagion, one daughter died of tuberculosis as a teenager in 1896, and their youngest son died within an hour of birth. The family prospered and their descendants are numerous. Meinrad died on 9 December 1907 in Ste. Genevieve. Wilhelmina died of stomach cancer on 23 April 1922 in Ste. Genevieve County, Missouri. They were both buried in the Valle Spring Cemetery in Ste. Genevieve, Ste. Genevieve County, Missouri.

Seraphin Donze Family
Surname Variations: Doncie, Donzé, Donzi, Douzie, Dunzie
European Origin: Pfaffenheim, Haut-Rhin, Alsace, France
Family:
Father: Simon Meinrad Donzé, born 27 October 1786 in Pfaffenheim, Haut-Rhin, Alsace, France.
   He died on 2 September 1837 in Pfaffenheim.
Mother: Anna Maria Freudenreich, born 17 August 1790 in Pfaffenheim, Haut-Rhin, Alsace, France.
   She died on 17 April 1844 in Pfaffenheim.
   Children:

Note: For a comprehensive discussion of Simon Meinrad Donzé's children see the Meinrad Donze family sketch.

Immigration:
Arrived 3 January 1848 from Le Havre, France to New Orleans aboard the *Chesapeak*:
   Dunze, Serevius [Seraphin], 21   farmer   from France
Arrived 15 October 1849 from Le Havre, France to New Orleans aboard the *Cromwell*:
   Donze, Meinrath, 19   from Germany
      Loulsa, 2
   Munsch, Gertrude, 26

Biographical:

Husband: Seraphin Donze

    Birth – 4 June 1827 in Pfaffenheim, Haut-Rhin, Alsace, France.

    Death/Burial – 19 April 1879 in Ste. Genevieve County, Missouri. He was buried in the Our Lady Help of Christians Cemetery in Weingarten, Ste. Genevieve County, Missouri.

Wife: Gertrude Munsch, daughter of Joseph Munsch and Gertrude Schmitt [See Nicholas Munsch sketch.]

    Birth – 20 March 1823 in Fellering, Haut-Rhin, Alsace, France.

    Marriage – 10 April 1846 in Fellering, Haut-Rhin, Alsace, France.

    Death/Burial – 25 December 1893 in Ste. Genevieve County, Missouri. She was buried in the Our Lady Help of Christians Cemetery in Weingarten, Ste. Genevieve County, Missouri.

Children:

    i. Louisa, born 17 March 1847 in Alsace, France. She married Henry Schilli on 20 November 1866 in Zell, Ste. Genevieve County, Missouri. Henry was the son of Joseph Schilli and Anna Maria Jaeger, born 5 July 1845 in Ste. Genevieve County, Missouri. [See Joseph Schilli sketch.]

    ii. Maria Caroline, born about 1850 in Missouri. She died on 29 March 1861 in Ste. Genevieve County and was buried in the St. Joseph Cemetery in Zell, Ste. Genevieve County, Missouri. No issue.

    iii. Valentine, born 14 February 1852 in Ste. Genevieve County, Missouri. Valentine died on 27 July 1871 in Ste. Genevieve County, Missouri. He was buried in the St. Joseph Cemetery in Zell, Ste. Genevieve County, Missouri. No issue.

    iv. Henry, born 30 June 1856 in Ste. Genevieve County, Missouri. He was a carpenter. Henry married Justine Stutz about 1877. Justine was the daughter of Mathias Stutz and Magdalena Feist, born 27 December 1856 in Ste. Genevieve County, Missouri. The couple had three sons. In the late 1890s, Henry moved his family to East St. Louis, St. Clair County, Illinois where he worked as a contract carpenter. Justine died of a lingering illness on 19 December 1918 in East St. Louis, St. Clair County, Illinois in St. Clair County, Illinois. Henry died on 2 April 1941 in East St. Louis, St. Clair County, Illinois. He was buried in the Mount Carmel Cemetery in Belleville, St. Clair County, Illinois.

    v. Seraphin B., born 23 December 1857 in Ste. Genevieve County, Missouri. As a young man, Seraphin taught school for about four years. He moved to Greeley, Colorado where he worked as a carpenter for several years. Seraphin returned to Ste. Genevieve County about 1880 and he and his brother, Henry, opened a general store near Weingarten. He married Maria Anna "Mary" Koller on 3 October 1882 in Weingarten, Ste. Genevieve County, Missouri. Mary was the daughter of Francis Xavier Koller and Salome Jaeger, born 25 October 1858 in Ste. Genevieve County, Missouri. The couple had two sons and two daughters. Seraphin eventually bought out his brother's share in the store at Weingarten and became the sole proprietor. He later went into partnership with his son-in-law, John A. Kettinger. Seraphin served as the first postmaster of the town of Weingarten. He apparently also liked to tinker with machinery. In January 1894, he registered a patent for an improved design for a cider press. Mary died of chronic heart disease on 22 March 1930 in Ste. Genevieve County. Seraphrin died of coronary thrombosis on 29 December 1940 in Ste. Genevieve County, Missouri. They were both buried in the Our Lady Help of Christians Cemetery in Weingarten, Ste. Genevieve County, Missouri.

    vi. John Nicholas, born 29 August 1861 in Ste. Genevieve County, Missouri. He was a farmer. John married his first cousin, Anna Maria Donze on 22 October 1881 in Lawrenceton, Ste. Genevieve County, Missouri. Anna was the daughter of Meinrad Donze and Wilhelmina Joggerst, born 18 August 1860 in Ste. Genevieve County, Missouri. The couple had five sons and five daughters, of whom two sons died in infancy. Anna died of chronic interstitial nephritis and heart disease on 23 September 1928 and John died of pulmonary tuberculosis and heart disease on 24 October 1936, both in Ste. Genevieve County. They were both buried in the Our Lady Help of Christians Cemetery in Weingarten, Ste. Genevieve County, Missouri.

vii. Joseph M. , born 11 June 1868 in Ste. Genevieve County, Missouri. He died 6 January 1873. He was buried in the Our Lady Help of Christians Cemetery in Weingarten, Ste. Genevieve County, Missouri. No issue.

Land Patents:
Ste. Genevieve County, Missouri

Patentee	Issue Date	Land Office	Cert. No.	Serial No.	Twp	Rng	Sec	Acres
Donze, John N.	31 Aug 1907	Twp / School land purchase			37-N	7-E	26	25.94
Donze, S. B.	27 Nov 1907	Twp / School Land purchase			34-N	7-E	16	88.39
Dousey, Serafin	1 Jul 1869	Ironton	43269	MO4210_.006	37-N	7-E	36	40.0
Douze, Serafin	30 Jun 1875	Ironton	44038	MO4220_.186	37-N	7-E	36	80.0
Douze, Seraphin	1 Dec 1853	Jackson	14839	MO3650_.296	37-N	7-E	25	40.0
Douze, Seraphin	1 Sep 1859	Jackson	35130	MO4000_.406	37-N	7-E	36	40.0
Douze, Seraphin	1 Mar 1860	Jackson	36706	MO4080_.038	37-N	7-E	36	80.0

Naturalization:

Name	Declaration	Naturalization	Origin
Donzie, Seraphine	15 November 1852	24 November 1854 Ste. Genevieve Co.	France

Military:
Served in the U.S. Civil War for the Union:
Private, Companies F & I, 78th Enrolled Missouri Militia
  Seraphine Donze enlisted 12 June 1863 in Ste. Genevieve County, Missouri.

Education: Could read and write
Occupation: Farmer
Religious Affiliation: Roman Catholic
Comments:
Seraphin Donze and Gertrude Munsch were married in Fellering, Haut-Rhin, Alsace, France in 1846. Seraphin left France in late 1847 and arrived in the United States in January 1848. His wife and newborn daughter remained in France and followed with Seraphin's brother, Meinrad, about a year later. The family settled in Ste. Genevieve County, Missouri where Seraphin purchased land and began to farm. During the Civil War, Seraphin enlisted in the 78th Enrolled Missouri Militia, but it is doubtful that he ever saw active service. Seraphin died of what was described as "colic" on 19 April 1879 and Gertrude died of pneumonia on 25 December 1893, both in Ste. Genevieve County. They were both buried in the Our Lady Help of Christians Cemetery in Weingarten, Ste. Genevieve County, Missouri.

Jacob Duffner Family
Surname Variations: Dufner
European Origin: Elzach, Freiburg, Baden, Germany
Family:
Father: Anton Duffner
Mother: Agatha Blessing
  Children:
    i. Catharina, born 22 October 1793 in Gutenbach, Villingen, Baden, Germany.
    ii. Maria, born 25 November 1794 in Gutenbach, Villingen, Baden, Germany.
    iii. Elisabeth, born about 1795 in Gutenbach, Villingen, Baden, Germany.
    iv. Martin, born about 1795 in Gutenbach, Villingen, Baden, Germany.
  ‡ v. Vincenz, born about 1797 in Gutenbach, Villingen, Baden, Germany. He was a cabinet maker. He came to the United States some time before May 1828. Vincenz married Anastasia Jock [aka Yeack or Yake] on 17 May 1828 in Baltimore, Maryland. Anastasia was the daughter of Johann

Baptist Jeck and Anna Maria Broclin, born 28 April 1806 in Zeiningen, Canton Aargau, Switzerland. The couple lived the first few years of their married life in Virginia and then they moved to Cincinnati, Hamilton County, Ohio. The couple had four sons and four daughters, of whom one son died at the age of three weeks. Vincent died on 12 July 1860 in Cincinnati. Anastasia died on 8 January 1868 in Hamilton County, Ohio. They were both buried in the St. John Cemetery in St. Bernard, Hamilton County, Ohio.
- vi. Mathias, born about 1798 in Gutenbach, Villingen, Baden, Germany.
- vii. Victoria, born 25 August 1799 in Gutenbach, Villingen, Baden, Germany.
- * viii. Jacob, born 16 July 1801 in Gutenbach, Villingen, Baden, Germany. [See sketch below.]
- ix. Sylvester [twin], born 28 December 1802 in Furtwangen, Villingen, Baden, Germany.
- x. Genovefa [twin], born 28 December 1802 in Furtwangen, Villingen, Baden, Germany. She is said to have died on 30 May 1851.

Immigration:
Arrived 22 July 1847 from Le Havre, France to New Orleans aboard the *Timoleon*:
Duffnoor [Duffner], Jacob, 46
    Marie, 31
    Euphrosina, 10
    Christine [Crescentia], 6
    Walbourg, 1

Biographical:
Husband: Jacob Duffner
- Birth – 16 July 1801 in Gutenbach, Villingen, Baden, Germany.
- Death/Burial – 29 September 1851 in Cincinnati, Hamilton County, Ohio.

Wife: Maria Anna Kopp, daughter of Johann Kopp and Walburga Pfaff
- Birth – 8 December 1815 in Elzach amt Waldkirch, Baden, Germany.
- 1) Marriage – 17 October 1836 in Elzach, Freiburg, Baden, Germany to Jacob Duffner.
- 2) Marriage – 27 July 1852 in Zell, Ste. Genevieve County, Missouri to Simon Hurst [See Simon Hurst sketch.]
- 3) Marriage – 13 March 1863 in Ste. Genevieve County, Missouri to Andreas "Andrew" Wipfler. [See Andrew Wipfler sketch.]
- Death/Burial – 7 August 1894 in Ste. Genevieve County, Missouri. She was buried in the Valle Spring Cemetery in Ste. Genevieve, Ste. Genevieve County, Missouri.

Children:
- i. Euphrosina, born 30 October 1836 in Elzach, Freiburg, Baden, Germany. Her mother's obituary indicates that she died of cholera in 1851 in Cincinnati, Hamilton County, Ohio. No issue.
- ii. Maria Anna, born 26 July 1838 in Elzach, Freiburg, Baden, Germany. She died on 27 April 1843 in Germany. No issue.
- iii. Crescentia "Grace," born 26 February 1840 in Elzach, Freiburg, Baden, Germany. She married Lawrence Schmiederer on 14 December 1857 in Zell, Ste. Genevieve County, Missouri. Lawrence was the son of Augustin Schmiederer and Catherine Hermann, born about 1835 in Germany. [See August Schmiederer sketch.]
- iv. Edwald, born 28 November 1841 in Elzach, Freiburg, Baden, Germany. He died on 27 February 1843 in Germany. No issue.
- v. Maria Anna, born 2 June 1843 in Elzach, Freiburg, Baden, Germany. She may have died before 1847 in Germany.
- vi. Walburga, born about 1846 [in Strasbourg, Alsace, France?]. Her mother's obituary indicates that she died of cholera in 1851 in Cincinnati, Hamilton County, Ohio. No issue.

U.S. residence prior to Ste. Genevieve County, Missouri:
Cincinnati, Hamilton County, Ohio, 1847-1851

Occupation: Watchmaker
Religious Affiliation: Roman Catholic
Comments:
Jacob Duffner was a watchmaker in Germany. He married Maria Anna Kopp in 1836. The couple is said to have had seven children, but records for only six children have been found. Of those six, one son and two daughters died in Germany. About 1845, the Duffners moved to Strasbourg, Alsace, France. Jacob brought his family to the United States in 1847. His older brother, Vincent, had already settled in Hamilton County, Ohio and Jacob followed him there. In 1851, cholera swept through the city of Cincinnati and Jacob and two of his three surviving children died in the epidemic. His widow, Maria, and only surviving daughter moved south to Ste. Genevieve County, Missouri in early 1852. Maria married Simon Hurst as her second husband on 27 July 1852 in Zell, Ste. Genevieve County. Maria married Andreas "Andrew" Wipfler as her third husband on 13 March 1863 in Ste. Genevieve County, Missouri.

E

Jacob Echle Family

Surname Variations: Backle, Echtle, Eckle
European Origin: Baden, Germany
Family:
Father: [Andreas?] Echle
Mother: [Cecilia Breig?]
Note: The parents' names were obtained from Jacob's marriage record, but they were very difficult to decipher.
   Children:
*   i. Jacob, born about 1829 in Baden, Germany. [See sketch below.]
       ii. Andreas, born 2 October 1832 in Baden, Germany. He married Cecilia Fischer on 31 August 1868 in Biberach amt Offenburg, Baden, Germany. Cecilia was the daughter of Sylvester Fischer and Catharina Armbruster, born 20 October 1842 in Biberach amt Offenburg, Baden, Germany. The couple had two sons and four daughters, all born in Biberach.

Immigration:
Arrived after 1850 and before May 1854 aboard an unknown vessel:
     Echle, Jacob

Biographical:
Husband: Jacob Echle
    Birth – about 1829 in Baden, Germany.
    Death/Burial – about 1861, most likely in Missouri.
Wife: Caroline Fallert, daughter of Franz Anton Fallert and Regina Oberle [See Franz Anton Fallert sketch.]
    Birth – 8 December 1839 in Ste. Genevieve County, Missouri.
    1) Marriage – 17 January 1856 in Zell, Ste. Genevieve County, Missouri to Jacob Echle
    2) Marriage – 19 May 1863 in Zell, Ste. Genevieve County, Missouri to Bernard Baumann [See Franz Anton Baumann sketch.]
    Death/Burial – 27 May 1915 in Ste. Genevieve County, Missouri. She was buried in the Sts. Philip and James Cemetery in River aux Vases, Ste. Genevieve County, Missouri.
    Children:
       i. Mary Ann, born 25 October 1856 in Ste. Genevieve County, Missouri. She married Charles Sucher on 23 August 1875 in Ste. Genevieve County. Charles was the son of Lawrence Sucher and Anna Regina Kirchner, born 31 May 1854 in Ste. Genevieve County. [See Lorenz Sucher sketch.]
       ii. Joseph, born 29 January 1858 in Ste. Genevieve County, Missouri. He died on 27 October 1858 in Ste. Genevieve County. He was buried in St. Joseph's Cemetery in Zell, Ste. Genevieve County, Missouri. No issue.
       iii. John, born about 1859 in Ste. Genevieve County, Missouri. He died in infancy. No issue.
       iv. Clara Philomena, born 6 July 1860 in Ste. Genevieve County, Missouri. She was baptized in the Ste. Genevieve Catholic Church, Ste. Genevieve, Ste. Genevieve County, on 24 August 1860. She married George Grass as his second wife on 12 June 1888 in Ste. Genevieve County. George was the son of George Grass and Maria Anna Siebert, born 24 April 1854 in Ste. Genevieve County, Missouri. [See George Grass sketch.]

Naturalization:

Name	Declaration	Naturalization	Origin
Echtle, Jacob	15 May 1854	23 May 1857 Ste. Genevieve Co.	Baden

Occupation: Brewer
Religious Affiliation: Roman Catholic
Comments:
Jacob Echle came to Ste. Genevieve County, Missouri after 1850 but before May 1854 when he declared his intention to become a citizen of the United States. He was married to Caroline Fallert in 1856 in Ste. Genevieve County. Jacob was a brewer and lived in the city of Ste. Genevieve. He and his wife had two sons who both died in infancy and two daughters. Jacob reportedly died by drowning in the Mississippi River in 1861. Caroline married for a second time on 19 May 1863 in Zell, Ste. Genevieve County, Missouri to Bernard Baumann. Caroline died on 26 May 1915 in Ste. Genevieve County and was buried in the Sts. Philip and James Cemetery in River aux Vases, Ste. Genevieve County, Missouri.

Severin Eckenfels Family
Surname Variations: Ekenfels, Ekenfeltz
European Origin: [Rammersweier?], Baden, Germany
Family:
Father: [Nicholaus?] Eckenfels
Mother: Franziska _____, born about 1796 in Baden, Germany. She died on 19 May 1861 in Ste. Genevieve County, Missouri. She was buried in the St. Joseph Cemetery in Zell, Ste. Genevieve County, Missouri.
  Child:
*   i.   Severin, born 2 October 1824 in Baden, Germany. [See sketch below.]

Immigration:
Arrived 23 March 1846 from Le Havre, France to New Orleans aboard the *Monument*:
    Eckenfels, Severin, 21   Farmer   from Baden   going to Missouri

Biographical:
Husband: Severin Eckenfels
  Birth – 2 October 1824 in Baden, Germany.
  Death/Burial – 2 January 1888 in Ste. Genevieve County, Missouri. He was buried in the St. Joseph Cemetery in Zell, Ste. Genevieve County, Missouri.
Wife: Catherine Kiefer, daughter of Joseph Kiefer and Maria Anna Basler [See Joseph Kiefer sketch.]
  Birth – 30 October 1824 in Rammersweier, Baden, Germany.
  Marriage – 31 July 1848 in Ste. Genevieve County, Missouri.
  Death/Burial – 9 September 1912 in Ste. Genevieve County, Missouri. She was buried in the St. Joseph Cemetery in Zell, Ste. Genevieve County, Missouri.
  Children:
    i.   Josephine, born 6 May 1849 in Missouri. She married Anton Braun as his third wife on 3 September 1888 in Zell, Ste. Genevieve County, Missouri. Anton was the son of Johann Nepomuk Braun and Thekla Hauser, born 18 January 1839 in Rammersweier, Baden, Germany. [See Johann Nepomuk Braun sketch.]
    ii.   Mary Anna, born 28 March 1851 in Ste. Genevieve County, Missouri. She married Silvester Braun on 23 November 1869 in Ste. Genevieve County, Missouri. Silvester was the son of Johann Nepomuk Braun and Francisca Basler, born 6 January 1848 in Rammersweier, Baden, Germany. He was the half-brother of Anton Braun, above. [See Johann Nepomuk Braun sketch.]
    iii.   Francis Xavier, born 2 February 1853 in Ste. Genevieve County, Missouri. He was a farmer. Xavier married Rosina Kohler on 23 November 1875 in Ste. Genevieve County. Rosina was the

daughter of Simon Kohler and Johanna Guethle, born 29 August 1853 in Ste. Genevieve County. The couple had one son and one daughter, both of whom died in early childhood. Rosina died on 25 January 1880 in Ste. Genevieve County. She was buried in the St. Joseph Cemetery in Zell, Ste. Genevieve County, Missouri. Xavier married Mrs. Wilhelmina Schaaf as his second wife on 7 June 1880 in Ste. Genevieve. Wilhelmina was the daughter of Ludwig "Louis" Armbruster and Euphrosine Siefert, born 23 October 1856 in Ste. Genevieve County, Missouri. Her first husband, Wilhelm "William" Schaaf had died on 22 May 1879. [See Wilhelm "William" Schaaf sketch.] Xavier and Wilhelmina had no children together but fostered several nieces and nephews over the years. Xavier died of heart disease and arthritis on 26 August 1931 and Wilhelmina died of pneumonia on 26 May 1936, both in Ste. Genevieve County, Missouri. They were both buried in St. Joseph Cemetery at Zell, Ste. Genevieve County, Missouri.

iv. Elizabeth, born 23 March 1854 in Ste. Genevieve County, Missouri. She married Charles Peterson. Nothing is known of Charles other than his name and that he died some time between 1893 and 1900, most likely in St. Louis, Missouri. The couple had three daughters. Elizabeth died of a cerebral hemorrhage on 3 August 1941 in St. Louis, Missouri. She was buried in the Sts. Peter and Paul Cemetery in St. Louis, Missouri.

v. Theresa, born 4 March 1856 in Ste. Genevieve County, Missouri. She died on 6 February 1865 in Ste. Genevieve County, Missouri. No issue.

vi. Joseph Emanuel, born 8 February 1858 in Ste. Genevieve County, Missouri. He was a farmer. He married Mary Magdalena Braun on 24 November 1884 in Perryville, Perry County, Missouri. Mary was the daughter of William Braun and Caroline Renard, born 2 March 1865 in Perry County, Missouri. The couple lived on a farm in Perry County where they raised their family. They are said to have had twelve children, but records for only three sons and six daughters have been found. Mary died of influenza on 14 June 1935 and Joseph died of cerebral thrombosis on 19 August 1955, both in Perryville, Perry County, Missouri. They were both buried in St. Boniface Cemetery in Perryville, Perry County, Missouri.

vii. Francisca Anna, born 8 January 1860 in Ste. Genevieve County, Missouri. She married Peter Henry William Wilder on 17 October 1879 in Zell, Ste. Genevieve County, Missouri. Peter was the son of Peter Nicolaj Georg Wilder and Ludwina Klein, born 4 November 1855 in Ste. Genevieve County, Missouri. [See Peter Wilder sketch.]

viii. John Chrisostomus, born 28 March 1862 in Ste. Genevieve County, Missouri. He died in February 1865 in Ste. Genevieve County, Missouri. No issue.

ix. Charles Theodore, born 13 February 1864 in Ste. Genevieve County, Missouri. He was a farmer. Theodore married Anna Catherine "Katie" Braun on 3 April 1894 in Zell, Ste. Genevieve County. Catherine was the daughter of Anton Braun and Maria Eva Jacob, born 28 December 1874 in Ste. Genevieve County. The couple had two sons and four daughters, of whom one daughter died in early childhood. Katie died of exophthalmic goiter [possibly caused by Grave's Disease] and heart disease complicated by pneumonia on 21 February 1935 in Ste. Genevieve County. Theodore died of pneumonia and acute myocarditis on 1 March 1935 in Ste. Genevieve County, Missouri. They were both buried in the St. Joseph Cemetery in Zell, Ste. Genevieve County, Missouri.

x. Anna Maria Theresa, born 26 August 1865 in Ste. Genevieve County, Missouri. She died on 30 July 1866 in Ste. Genevieve County, Missouri. No issue.

xi. Anna Katherine, born and died on 30 April 1870 in Ste. Genevieve County, Missouri. She was buried in the St. Joseph Cemetery at Zell, Ste. Genevieve County, Missouri. No issue.

Land Patents:
Ste. Genevieve County, Missouri

Patentee	Issue Date	Land Office	Cert. No.	Serial No.	Twp	Rng	Sec	Acres
Ekenfels, John	2 May 1859	St. Louis	29682	MO1100_.448	38-N	6-E	4	96.33
Eckenfels, Severin	3 Jan 1856	Jackson	17745	MO3690_.378	37-N	8-E	1	39.60
Ekenfels, Severin	1 Dec 1851	Jackson	12279	MO3600_.417	37-N	8-E	1	38.41
Ekenfelts, Severen	1 Jul 1857	Jackson	10318	MO3660_.157	37-N	8-E	1	39.46

Naturalization:

Name	Declaration	Naturalization	Origin
Eikenfelsz, Servin	7 May 1850	21 May 1853 Ste. Genevieve Co.	Baden

Military:
Served in the U.S. Civil War for the Union:
Sergeant, Company K, 78th Enrolled Missouri Militia
    Seaveren Ekenfelts enlisted on 1 August 1863 in Ste. Genevieve, Missouri.

Education: Could read and write
Occupation: Farmer
Religious Affiliation: Roman Catholic
Political Affiliation and/or Any Offices Held: Secretary, Germania Verein [social club], 1874-5
Comments:
Severin Eckenfels is said to have been born near Rammersweier, Baden, Germany. He came to the United States in company with Joseph Kiefer who eventually became his father-in-law. He married Catherine Kiefer in 1848 in Ste. Genevieve County, Missouri. Severin worked as a laborer for Benedict Huber for a time and then he worked for a while in the government rock quarry near the town of Ste. Genevieve until he had earned enough money to buy his own land. During the Civil War, Severin enlisted as a sergeant in Company K of the 78th Enrolled Missouri Militia. It is doubtful that he ever saw active service. Severin died of dropsy on 2 January 1888 at his home near Zell. After her husband's death, Catherine lived with her youngest son Theodore and his family. She died of heart failure on 9 September 1912 in Ste. Genevieve County, Missouri. Severin and Catherine were both buried in the St. Joseph Cemetery in Zell, Ste. Genevieve County, Missouri.

Anton Eckert Family
Surname Variations: Eckart, Echert, Egert, Ekkert
European Origin: Baden, Germany
Family:
Father: Unknown
Mother: Unknown
    Child:
*   i.   Anton, born 5 January 1834 in Baden, Germany. [See sketch below.]
‡   ii.   Daughter. She came to the United States and was living in Detroit, Wayne County, Michigan in August 1891. No further information.

Immigration:
Arrived 13 April 1854 from Le Harvre, France to New York aboard the *Salletile*:
    Eckert, Anton, 21   from Baden   Farmer

Biographical:
Husband: Anton Eckert
    Birth – 5 January 1834 in Baden, Germany [from tombstone].
    Death/Burial – 13 January 1923 in Ste. Genevieve County, Missouri. He was buried in the St. Joseph

Cemetery in Zell, Ste. Genevieve County, Missouri.

Wife: Mary Magdalena Eichenlaub, daughter of Gervais Eichenlaub and Catherine Jokerst [See Gervais Eichenlaub sketch.]

Birth – 22 July 1836 in Zell, Ste. Genevieve County, Missouri.

Marriage – 28 April 1856 in Zell, Ste. Genevieve County, Missouri.

Death/Burial – 27 October 1906 in St. Louis, Missouri. She was buried in the Saints Peter and Paul Catholic Cemetery in St. Louis, Missouri.

Children:

i. Maria Anna "Mary," born 18 September 1857 in Ste. Genevieve County, Missouri. She died on 16 September 1863 in Ste. Genevieve County. Mary was buried in the St. Joseph Cemetery in Zell, Ste. Genevieve County, Missouri. No issue.

ii. Henry, born 1 April 1861 in Ste. Genevieve County, Missouri. He was a farmer. Henry married Mary Anna Francisca Huber on 20 November 1888 in Ste. Genevieve County. Mary was the daughter of Francis Xavier Huber and Ursula Bieser, born 1 January 1867 in Ste. Genevieve County, Missouri. The couple had two sons and two daughters. In early April 1899, Henry had suffered a bout of pneumonia. He had recovered but was still weak when he went out to catch up on some field work. He was caught in a cold spring rain while he was working and suffered a relapse. Henry died of pneumonia on 29 April 1899 in Ste. Genevieve County. He was buried in the St. Joseph Cemetery in Zell, Ste. Genevieve County, Missouri. Mary married John George Huber as her second husband on 15 May 1900 in Zell, Ste. Genevieve County. John was the son of Andreas "Andrew" Huber and Agatha Harter, born 14 April 1867 in Missouri. [See Andreas Huber sketch.]

iii. Joseph Anton, born 6 October 1863 in Ste. Genevieve County, Missouri. As a young man, Joseph moved to St. Louis, Missouri and worked in a brewery. About 1896, he suffered a rupture [hernia] while at work. The injury was never treated and only got worse. In early 1898, Joseph finally went to a hospital where he was operated on. But by then he had developed testicular cancer of which he died on 18 February 1898 in St. Louis, Missouri. Joseph was buried in Potters Field in St. Louis, Missouri. Joseph never married and had no known issue.

iv. Barbara, born 6 October 1865 in Ste. Genevieve County, Missouri. She married Francis A. "Frank" Harter on 10 April 1883 in Zell, Ste. Genevieve County. Frank was a farmer. He was the son of John Frederick "Fred" Harter and Theresia Kiefer, born 22 October 1857 in Buffalo, Erie County, New York. [See Fred Harter sketch.]

v. Maria Katherine, born about 1868 in Ste. Genevieve County, Missouri. She married David Huber on 5 November 1889 in Zell, Ste. Genevieve County. He was a farmer. David was the son of Francis Xavier Huber and Ursula Bieser, born 14 March 1864 in Ste. Genevieve County. The couple had two sons and two daughters, of whom one daughter died in early childhood. Katherine died of pneumonia on 10 April 1899 in Zell, Ste. Genevieve County, Missouri. She was buried in the St. Joseph Cemetery in Zell. David was left to raise three small children by himself. He married Mary Theresa Schmelzle as his second wife on 3 November 1903 in Ste. Genevieve. Mary was the daughter of Joseph Schmelzle and Theresa Gieser, born 17 September 1874 in Ste. Genevieve County, Missouri. The couple had one son and four daughters. Mary died of spinal cancer on 24 March 1932 in Ste. Genevieve County, Missouri. David died of chronic heart disease on 23 May 1946 in Ste. Genevieve County. They were both buried in the St. Joseph Cemetery in Zell, Ste. Genevieve County, Missouri.

vi. Caroline, born about 1877 in Ste. Genevieve County, Missouri. Caroline died of pseudo membranous croup on 14 December 1882 in Ste. Genevieve County, Missouri. No issue.

Land Patents:

Ste. Genevieve County, Missouri

Patentee	Issue Date	Land Office	Cert. No.	Serial No.	Twp	Rng	Sec	Acres
Eckert, Anthony	1 Dec 1858	Jackson	24737	MO3850_.185	37-N	8-E	3	97.90

Naturalization:

Name	Declaration	Naturalization	Origin
Eckert, Anton		10 May 1866 Ste. Genevieve Co.	Baden

Military:
Served in the U.S. Civil War for the Union:
Sergeant, Company K, 78 Enrolled Missouri Militia
    Anton Eckert enlisted 24 September 1864 and mustered out in December 1864.

Occupation: Farmer
Religious Affiliation: Roman Catholic
Political Affiliation and/or Any Offices Held:
    Republican
    Ran for County Assessor in 1884 but withdrew the October before the election

Comments:
Anton Eckert came to the United States in 1854 and appears to have come directly to Ste. Genevieve, County, Missouri. It is possible that he is the Anton Eckert who was a nephew to Gervais Eichenlaub and that he followed his uncle to America. At least one of Anton's sisters came to the United States since Anton was noted in the *Fair Play* as having gone to visit her in Detroit, Wayne County, Michigan in August 1891. Anton married Mary Magdalena Eichenlaub in 1856 in Zell, Ste. Genevieve County. They bought land about six miles west of the town of Ste. Genevieve and established a farm. During the Civil War, Anton served as a sergeant in Company K of the 78th Enrolled Missouri Militia. Anton and Magdalena dealt with a number of personal tragedies. Of their six children, only one daughter outlived her parents. On the morning of 2 February 1900, just after the family finished breakfast, a chimney flue fire caused their home and most of its contents to burn to the ground. The family stayed with the Charles Roth family until they could rebuild. Magdalena died of chronic rheumatism on 27 October 1906 in St. Louis, Missouri. [The dates on her tombstone are incorrect.] She was buried in the Saints Peter and Paul Cemetery in St. Louis, Missouri. Anton died of chronic valvular heart disease on 13 January 1923 in Ste. Genevieve County, Missouri. He was buried in the St. Joseph Cemetery in Zell, Ste. Genevieve County, Missouri.

Bernard Benjamin Effrein Family
Surname Variations: Efferin[e], Effrain, Effren[e], Effrin, Ephron, Everine, Evering
European Origin: Germany
Family:
Father: Bernard Effrein [aka Evering from son's marriage record in Ste. Genevieve County, Missouri.]
Mother: Elisabeth _____
    Child:
*   i.   Bernard Benjamin, born about 1844 in [St. Louis?], Missouri or in Germany. [See sketch below.]

Immigration:
Arrived 8 November 1866 from Le Havre, France to New York aboard the *Fulton*:
    Oberle, Justine, 20   Servant   Germany

Biographical:
Husband: Bernard Benjamin Effrein
    Birth – about 1844 in [St. Louis?], Missouri or Germany.
    Death/Burial – 14 December 1895 in Ste. Genevieve, Ste. Genevieve County, Missouri. He was buried in the Valle Spring Cemetery in Ste. Genevieve, Ste. Genevieve County, Missouri.
Wife: Justina "Augusta" Oberle, daughter of Joseph Oberle and Franziska Schmelzle
    Birth – 16 June 1845 in Sasbachwalden, Baden, Germany.
    Marriage – 29 April 1867 in Ste. Genevieve, Ste. Genevieve County, Missouri.

Death/Burial – 20 June 1939 in Ste. Genevieve, Ste. Genevieve County, Missouri. She was buried in the Valle Spring Cemetery in Ste. Genevieve, Ste. Genevieve County, Missouri.

Children:
  i. Joseph Herman, born 27 January 1868 in Ste. Genevieve County, Missouri. He was baptized on 15 March 1868 in the Ste. Genevieve Catholic Church in Ste. Genevieve, Ste. Genevieve County, Missouri. He was a blacksmith and operated a wagon shop in the city of Ste. Genevieve. Joseph married Mary Josephine Samson on 16 November 1891 in Ste. Genevieve, Ste. Genevieve County. Mary was the daughter of Anton Samson and Magdalena Roth, born 10 February 1868. The couple had two sons and one daughter, of whom one son who died within hours of birth. Joseph died on 7 March 1925 in Ste. Genevieve when he shot himself with a revolver in the left side. Mary died of carcinoma of the lungs and breast on 26 December 1948 in Ste. Genevieve, Ste. Genevieve County, Missouri. They were both buried in the Valle Spring Cemetery in Ste. Genevieve, Ste. Genevieve County, Missouri.
  ii. Peter Henry, born 16 December 1869 in Ste. Genevieve County, Missouri. He was baptized on 23 January 1870 in the Ste. Genevieve Catholic Church in Ste. Genevieve, Ste. Genevieve County, Missouri. He worked for the War Department Engineers at Large in Ste. Genevieve County between 1895 and 1899. By 1900, Peter was living in Yavapai County, Arizona where he worked as a mine laborer. He moved to Muscatine County, Iowa about 1908 where he worked for the C.R.L. & P. Railroad as a tank man. He was accidently crushed to death between two railroad cars in the Muscatine rail yards in Muscatine, Muscatine County, Iowa on 10 July 1910. His body was brought back to Missouri and buried in Ste. Genevieve County [cemetery unknown at present]. He may never have married and had no known issue.
  iii. Bernard Benjamin "Ben," born 25 March 1872 in Ste. Genevieve County, Missouri. He was baptized on 5 May 1872 in the Ste. Genevieve Catholic Church in Ste. Genevieve, Ste. Genevieve County, Missouri. He married Anna Mary Karl on 27 November 1893. Anna was the daughter of David Karl and Magdalena Grieshaber, born 21 April 1875 in Ste. Genevieve County, Missouri. The couple had two sons and five daughters. The family lived in Farmington, St. Francois County, Missouri where Ben worked for the wagon manufacturing firm of Lang & Brothers. He later left that firm and moved to Ste. Genevieve where he went into business with his brother, Joseph, who operated a wagon manufacturing shop. Ben suffered a stroke on the afternoon of 6 August 1925 while he was at work. He died on 11 August 1925 without ever having regained consciousness. He was buried in the Valle Spring Cemetery in Ste. Genevieve, Ste. Genevieve County, Missouri. Anna married August William Henry Menge as her second husband on 25 February 1927. August was the son of Christopher Carl Menge and Mary Griner, born 16 October 1863 near Palmyra, Marion County, Missouri. August was a clerk in the Klein & Brother grocery store in Farmington which was owned and operated by his cousins J. E. and Ed Klein. August and Anna had no children together. In 1934, August fell ill with influenza which weakened his heart. He died of heart failure on 11 February 1934 in Farmington, St. Francois County, Missouri. He was buried in the St. Paul Lutheran Cemetery in Farmington, St. Francois County, Missouri. Anna died of a cerebral hemorrhage on 27 September 1955 in Bonne Terre, St. Francois County, Missouri. She was buried in the New Calvary Cemetery in Farmington, St. Francois County, Missouri.
  iv. Louisa Frances, born 4 July 1875 in Ste. Genevieve County, Missouri. She was baptized on 8 August 1875 in the Ste. Genevieve Catholic Church in Ste. Genevieve, Ste. Genevieve County, Missouri. She married Henry Joseph Cocolise on 5 November 1895 in Ste. Genevieve, Ste. Genevieve County. He worked as a sales clerk for John Boverie's general store in St. Genevieve until his health began to fail. Henry was the son of Virgil Cocolise and Antoinette Maurice, born 24 September 1875 in Ste. Genevieve County, Missouri. The couple had one daughter. Henry developed health issues and he moved to Denver, Colorado. Henry died suddenly in Las Vegas, San Miguel County, New Mexico on 13 June 1918. His body was brought back to Missouri and was buried in the Valle Spring Cemetery in Ste. Genevieve, Ste.

Genevieve County, Missouri. After her husband's death, Louise remained in Ste. Genevieve with her daughter Thelma. After Thelma was widowed, she became a nurse and Louise and her daughter and grandchildren moved to Colorado Springs, El Paso County, Colorado about 1939. Louise died in Colorado Springs on 7 December 1941. She was buried in the Evergreen Cemetery in Colorado Springs, Colorado.

v. John Edward, born 11 May 1878 in Ste. Genevieve County, Missouri. He was baptized on 7 July 1878 in the Ste. Genevieve Catholic Church in Ste. Genevieve, Ste. Genevieve County, Missouri. He was an implement dealer. He married Alice Maria Lelie on 8 October 1906 in Ste. Genevieve. Alice was the daughter of Emile Cornelius Lelie and Mary Catherine Schumert, born 13 January 1884 in Ste. Genevieve, Ste. Genevieve County, Missouri. The couple had two sons. John died of chronic myocarditis and chronic nephritis on 10 February 1933 in Ste. Genevieve County, Missouri. Alice died on 24 December 1965 in St. Louis, Missouri. They were both buried in the Valle Spring Cemetery in Ste. Genevieve, Ste. Genevieve County, Missouri.

vi. Maria Clara "Mary," born 9 April 1884 in Ste. Genevieve County, Missouri. She was baptized on 8 May 1884 in the Ste. Genevieve Catholic Church in Ste. Genevieve, Ste. Genevieve County, Missouri. She married George Joseph Sexauer on 25 September 1906 in Ste. Genevieve. George was the son of George Sexauer and Elizabeth Sauer, born 8 December 1880 in Ste. Genevieve County, Missouri. George was a bartender and saloon keeper until Prohibition. Later he became a salesman for a soft drink company. The couple had one son and one daughter. George died of acute pancreatitis and pancreatic necrosis on 9 November 1954 in St. Louis, Missouri. Mary died in 1968. They were both buried in the Valle Spring Cemetery in Ste. Genevieve, Ste. Genevieve County, Missouri.

U.S. residence prior to Ste. Genevieve County, Missouri:
[St. Louis?], Missouri

Education: Could read and write
Occupation: Blacksmith
Religious Affiliation: Roman Catholic
Comments:
The first record of Bernard Benjamin Effrein in Ste. Genevieve County is in the 1850 census when he appears as a 6-year-old foster child in the household of George Falk, a master blacksmith who had come to the United States with his parents in 1842. [See George Falk sketch.] Bernard did not travel with this family, but was born in either Germany or Missouri to German parents. Both the 1850 and 1860 census records show him as having been born in Germany. In both the 1870 and 1880 census records, Bernard was noted as having been born in Missouri. According to two of his children's death certificates, Bernard may have been born in St. Louis, Missouri. The 1880 census does indicate that both of his parents were German. Bernard became a blacksmith like his foster father and at least two of his own sons followed the same profession. He was widely known for the excellent quality of his work. Bernard's health began to decline when a sore that wouldn't heal developed on one of his feet. He suffered for several years before he was finally unable to work. Bernard died on 14 December 1895 in Ste. Genevieve after having been a home-bound invalid for at least a year. He was buried in the Valle Spring Cemetery in Ste. Genevieve, Ste. Genevieve County, Missouri. After her husband's death, Augusta lived with her youngest daughter, Clara, and her family in Ste. Genevieve. Augusta died of chronic myocarditis on 20 June 1939 in Ste. Genevieve. She was buried in the Valle Spring Cemetery in Ste. Genevieve, Ste. Genevieve County, Missouri.

Note: Justina "Augusta" Oberle was a niece to Bernard Oberle with whom she came to the United States aboard the *Fulton*. She was also a first cousin to Bernard Schmelzle.

William Ehe Family

Surname Variations: Eke
European Origin: Hesse-Darmstadt, Germany
Family:
Father: Wilhelm "William" Ehe, born about 1807 in Hesse-Cassel, Germany. He died some time after June 1880, most likely in Missouri.
Mother: Catherine "Kate" _____, born about 1814 in Hesse-Darmstadt, Germany. She died some time between 1870 and June 1880, most likely in Missouri.
Children:

‡   i. Philipp, born about 1842 in Hesse-Darmstadt, Germany. As a young man he worked in the printing trade in St. Louis, Missouri. He married Augustina Zimmermann on 7 October 1860 in St. Louis. Philipp served as a private in Company D of the 6th Regiment Enrolled Missouri Militia during the Civil War. He later served as a private in Battery C, 1st Illinois Light Artillery. No further information has been found for either Philipp or his wife after his Civil War service.

‡   ii. Catharina Louisa, born 20 April 1846 in Hesse-Darmstadt, Germany. She married Edward Riehl on 30 May 1865 in St. Louis, Missouri. Edward was born about 1843 in Missouri. He worked in a feed store. The couple had two sons and two daughters, of whom one daughter died in early childhood. Louisa and Edward may have been divorced some time before June 1889. Edward died on 31 March 1897 in St. Louis, Missouri. He was buried in the Bellefontaine Cemetery in St. Louis. Louisa married Frederick F. Miller on 15 June 1889 in Madison County, Illinois. The couple had one son. Louisa died of an obstruction of the bowels on 3 November 1914 in Webster Groves, St. Louis County, Missouri. She was buried in the Bellefontaine Cemetery in St. Louis, Missouri.

*   iii. William Godfried, born 30 August 1855 in St. Louis, Missouri. [See sketch below.]

Immigration:
Arrived 10 September 1853 from Bremen, Germany to New York aboard the *Diana*:
    Eke [Ehe], W[ilhelm], 47
        C[atherina], 40
        P[hilipp], 11   [male child]
        C[atherina], 7 [female child]

Biographical:
Husband: William Godfried Ehe
    Birth – 30 August 1855 in St. Louis, Missouri.
    Death/Burial – 25 July 1931 in Carondelet, St. Louis County, Missouri. He was buried in the Sts. Peter and Paul Cemetery (Old) in St. Louis, Missouri.
Wife: Mary Eva Ritter, daughter of Paul Ritter and Catharina Metz [See Paul Ritter sketch.]
    Birth – 28 December 1859 in Ste. Genevieve County, Missouri.
    Marriage – 1 March 1878 in Ste. Genevieve County, Missouri.
    Death/Burial – 25 April 1929 in St. Louis, Missouri. She was buried in the Sts. Peter and Paul Cemetery (Old) in St. Louis, Missouri.
    Children:
        i. Louisa Anna, born 20 December 1878 in Ste. Genevieve County, Missouri. She was baptized on 12 January 1879 in the Ste. Genevieve Catholic Church in Ste. Genevieve. Louisa married John Adolphus Roussin on 3 October 1899 in Ste. Genevieve County, Missouri. John was the son of Francis Adolphe Roussin and Julia Celeste Bequette, born 3 December 1876 in Ste. Genevieve County, Missouri. John was a farmer. For the first few years of their married life, the couple lived on a farm in Warren County, Missouri. They had three sons. By 1920, the family moved to St. Louis, Missouri where John worked as a carpenter. His father Francis lived with

them for the last few years of his life. John died in June 1968 and Louisa died in March 1972, both in St. Louis, Missouri. They were both buried in the Resurrection Cemetery in Affton, St. Louis County, Missouri.

ii. Catherine, born 9 February 1881 in Ste. Genevieve County, Missouri. She was baptized on 2 March 1881 in the Ste. Genevieve Catholic Church in Ste. Genevieve. After dinner on Wednesday, 23 January 1883, Catherine and her older sister Louisa were amusing themselves by poking straws into the fire of the kitchen stove to see them burn. Their mother stepped out to do some household chore when Louise ran to her, screaming that her little sister was burning. Mary found the toddler ablaze on the kitchen floor. The child lived for about an hour before she succumbed to her injuries. She was buried in the Valle Spring Cemetery in Ste. Genevieve, Ste. Genevieve County, Missouri. No issue.

iii. William John, born 27 December 1883 in Ste. Genevieve County, Missouri. He was baptized on 21 January 1884 in the Ste. Genevieve Catholic Church in Ste. Genevieve. He married Mary Magdalena Donze on 26 October 1909 in Ste. Genevieve County, Missouri. Mary was the daughter of John Nicholas Donze and Anna Maria Donze, born 16 April 1884 in Ste. Genevieve County, Missouri. William worked as a farmer, a miller and as a carpenter. The couple had two daughters who they may have adopted from Illinois. The family moved back and forth between Ste. Genevieve County and St. Louis several times before finally settling near Weingarten, Ste. Genevieve County. John died on 11 April 1967 and Mary died a week and a half later on 23 April 1967, both in Ste. Genevieve County. They were both buried in the Our Lady Help of Christians in Weingarten, Ste. Genevieve County, Missouri.

iv. Mary Catherine, born 27 April 1889 in Ste. Genevieve County, Missouri. She was baptized on 19 May 1889 in the Ste. Genevieve Catholic Church in Ste. Genevieve. She married Felix William Jokerst about 1908 in Missouri. Felix was the son of Henry Jokerst and Sophia Winter, born 27 January 1882 in Ste. Genevieve County, Missouri. Felix worked a variety of jobs, including coffee roaster in a coffee factory, carpenter and millwright. The couple had three sons. Felix died of heart failure on 21 April 1958 in St. Louis, Missouri. Catherine died on 19 September 1988 in St. Louis. They were both buried in the Resurrection Cemetery in Affton, St. Louis County, Missouri.

v. Emma Genevieve, born 1 January 1892 in Ste. Genevieve County, Missouri. She was baptized on 24 January 1892 in the Ste. Genevieve Catholic Church in Ste. Genevieve. As a young woman Emma worked as a basket maker. She married William H. Siebert about 1914. William was the son of Charles Aloysius Siebert and Josephine Zerwig, born 20 May 1887 in Ste. Genevieve County, Missouri. William had a truck garden business in St. Louis. The couple had one son and two daughters. William died of lung cancer on 7 October 1935 in St. Louis, Missouri. Emma died in September 1965 in St. Louis, Missouri. They were both buried in the Resurrection Cemetery in Affton, St. Louis County, Missouri.

U.S. residence other than Ste. Genevieve County, Missouri:
St. Louis, Missouri

Land Patents:
Osage County, Missouri

Patentee	Issue Date	Land Office	Cert. No.	Serial No.	Twp	Rng	Sec	Acres
Ehe, William	10 Jun 1857	St. Louis	26465	MO1070_.025	41-N	8-W	9	80.00

Naturalization:

Name	Declaration	Naturalization	Origin
Ehe, William		31 March 1859 St. Louis City Circuit Court	Germany

Military:
Served in the U.S. Civil War for the Union:
Private, Company D, 6th Regiment Enrolled Missouri Militia
   Phillip Ehe enlisted 9 September 1862 in St. Louis, Missouri. He was ordered into active service on 16 June 1863 in St. Louis. Relived from active duty 15 July 1863 in St. Louis.
Private, Battery C, 1st Illinois Light Artillery
   Phillip Ehe, enlisted 24 February 1864 in Illinois.

Education: Could read and write
Occupation: Farmer
Religious Affiliation: Roman Catholic
Comments:
William Godried Ehe was born in St. Louis, Missouri in 1855. His father, Wilhelm Ehe, brought his wife and two children to the United States in 1853 from Hesse-Darmstadt, Germany and the family settled in St. Louis, Missouri. Wilhelm was a weaver in Germany, but he worked as a watchman in a foundry in St. Louis. His oldest son worked for a printer in St. Louis before the outbreak of the Civil War. Wilhelm bought land in Osage County, Missouri, but it is doubtful that he ever lived there. By 1870, Wilhelm, his wife and youngest son had moved to Ste. Genevieve County, Missouri where they lived on a farm near the city of Ste. Genevieve. William's mother, Katharina, appears to have died some time between 1870 and June 1880, perhaps in Ste. Genevieve County. William married Mary Eva Ritter in 1878 in Ste. Genevieve County. William's father lived with them. William and Mary had one son and four daughters. William enjoyed taking part in marksmanship competitions and was often among the top prize-winning shooters. Some time before 1910, William and Mary moved to St. Louis with their daughter Emma. Mary died of chronic interstitial nephritis and myocarditis on 25 April 1929 and William died of chronic myocarditis and nephritis on 25 July 1931, both in St. Louis. They were both buried in the Sts. Peter and Paul Cemetery in St. Louis, Missouri.

Gottfried Ehler Family
Surname Variations: Aller, Eler, Öhler, Ohler, Oehler, Oeler
European Origin: Bühl amt Offenburg, Baden, Germany
Family:
Father: Thomas Öhler
Mother: Francisca Gärtner
   Children:
   i. Joseph, born 11 December 1811 in Bühl amt Offenburg, Baden, Germany. Joseph married Anna Maria Gärtner on 7 January 1835 in Bühl. Anna Maria was the daughter of Simon Gärtner and Anna Maria Kempf.
   ii. Anton, born 18 January 1813 in Bühl amt Offenburg, Baden, Germany.
   iii. Laurentz, born 17 July 1814 in Bühl amt Offenburg, Baden, Germany.
   iv. Paul, born 23 January 1816 in Bühl amt Offenburg, Baden, Germany. He married Eleonora Schläfle on 25 July 1842 in Bühl. Eleonora was the daughter of Raimond Schläfle and Magdalena Lapp, born about 1821. He married Adelheid Bahr as his second wife on 11 August 1857 in Bühl. Adelheid was the daughter of Jakob Bahr and Anna Maria Vetter, born 25 March 1835 in Baden, Germany.
* v. Gottfried, born 7 May 1818 in Bühl amt Offenburg, Baden, Germany. [See sketch below.]
   vi. Leo, born 6 October 1819 in Bühl amt Offenburg, Baden, Germany.

Immigration:
Arrived 30 January 1843 from Le Havre, France to New Orleans aboard the *Mozart*:
>Mehler [Oehler], Gottfried, 24
>>Adelheid, 26
>>Clotilda, 2
>>Friedrich, 1/4

Biographical:
Husband: Gottfried Ehler
>Birth – 7 May 1818 in Bühl amt Offenburg, Baden, Germany.
>Death/Burial – 25 May 1892 in Ste. Genevieve County, Missouri. He was buried in the Valle Spring Cemetery in Ste. Genevieve, Ste. Genevieve County, Missouri.

Wife: Adelheide [aka Adelaide] Anti, daughter of Jacob Anti and Theresia Brischle
>Birth – about 1817 in Weier, Baden, Germany.
>Marriage – about 1840 in Baden, Germany.
>Death/Burial – 22 July 1894 1892 in Ste. Genevieve County, Missouri. She was buried in the Valle Spring Cemetery in Ste. Genevieve, Ste. Genevieve County, Missouri.

Children:
>i. Clothilde, born 14 June 1841 in Baden, Germany. She married Benjamin Hauck [aka Haug] on 21 August 1859 at Zell, Ste. Genevieve County, Missouri. Benjamin was the son of Joseph Hauck and Rosalia Duffner, born 23 June 1830 in Hechingen, Germany. [See Benjamin Hauck sketch.]
>ii. Friedrich Reinhold, born 10 September 1842 in Baden, Germany. He worked as a general laborer. He married Mathilde Flieg on 23 December 1863 in Zell, Ste. Genevieve County, Missouri. Mathilde was the daughter of Anton Flieg and Catharina Strobel, born 11 January 1843 in Weilheim, Hohenzollern-Hechingen, Germany. The couple had one son, one daughter and a child who died young. Mathilde died of pneumonia on 20 October 1908 in Ste. Genevieve County, Missouri. She was buried in the Valle Spring Cemetery in Ste. Genevieve, Ste. Genevieve County, Missouri. Reinhold died of accidental asphyxiation when a gas jet was left partially open on 26 February 1922 in St. Louis, Missouri. He is said to have been buried in Ste. Genevieve County, Missouri.
>iii. Charles Thomas, born 16 December 1845 in Ste. Genevieve County, Missouri. He was baptized on 11 January 1846 in the Ste. Genevieve Catholic Church in Ste. Genevieve, Ste. Genevieve County, Missouri. Charles was a farmer. He married Catherine Stoeckle. Catherine was the daughter of Johann "John" Stoeckle and Magdalena Rehm, born 6 June 1855 in Ste. Genevieve County, Missouri. The couple had five sons and six daughters. Charles died of a cancer on the right side of his face on 20 February 1914 in Ste. Genevieve County, Missouri. Catherine died of heart disease on 3 September 1934 in Ste. Genevieve County, Missouri. They were both buried in the St. Joseph Cemetery in Zell, Ste. Genevieve County, Missouri.
>iv. Simon, born 1 January 1848 in Ste. Genevieve County, Missouri. He was baptized on 1 February 1848 in the Ste. Genevieve Catholic Church in Ste. Genevieve, Ste. Genevieve County, Missouri. Simon died on 3 December 1866 in Ste. Genevieve County, Missouri. Simon was buried in the St. Joseph Cemetery in Zell, Ste. Genevieve County, Missouri. No issue.
>v. Andrew, born about 1851 in Missouri. He died on 29 July 1861 in Ste. Genevieve County. He was buried in the St. Joseph Cemetery in Zell, Ste. Genevieve County, Missouri. No issue.
>vi. Rosina, born in Missouri. She died before 1860 in Missouri. No issue.
>vii. Theresa, born in Missouri. She died before 1860 in Missouri. No issue.
>viii. Fridolin "Fritz," born 1 February 1858 in Missouri. He worked as a general laborer. Fritz married Josephine Grieshaber on 10 January 1882 in Ste. Genevieve County, Missouri. Josephine was the daughter of Fabian Grieshaber and Amelia Baumann, born 22 April 1862 in Ste. Genevieve County, Missouri. The couple had no children. Fritz committed suicide by

hanging himself on 6 June 1925 in Ste. Genevieve County, Missouri. Josephine died of heart disease and chronic nephritis on 8 November 1935 in Festus, Jefferson County, Missouri. They were both buried in the Valle Spring Cemetery in Ste. Genevieve, Ste. Genevieve County, Missouri.

Land Patents:
Ste. Genevieve County, Missouri

Patentee	Issue Date	Land Office	Cert. No.	Serial No.	Twp	Rng	Sec	Acres
Ochler, Godfried	1 Jul 1848	St. Louis	14711	MO0810_.429	38-N	8-E	19	44.08
Oeler, Godfrey	1 Jun 1849	St. Louis	16067	MO0840_.348	38-N	8-E	22	80.00
Oeler, Godfrey	1 Mar 1854	St. Louis	21570	MO0940_.416	38-N	8-E	22	40.00

Naturalization:

Name	Declaration	Naturalization	Origin
Oehler, Godfried	22 May 1849	24 May 1851 Ste. Genevieve Co.	Baden

Military:
Served in the U.S. Civil War for the Union:
Private, Company K, 78th Enrolled Missouri Militia
  Reinold Ohler enlisted on 1 August 1863 in Ste. Genevieve, Missouri.
Private, Company K, 78th Enrolled Missouri Militia
  Thomas Ohler enlisted on 30 April 1864 in Ste. Genevieve, Missouri. He was ordered into active service on 16 October 1864. He was relieved from duty on 25 November 1864. He served a total of 41 days of active service.

Education: Could read and write
Occupation: Carpenter / Builder / Farmer
Religious Affiliation: Roman Catholic
Comments:
Gottfried Ehler was born in Bühl amt Offenburg, Baden, Germany, and as a young man, he became a carpenter and house builder. He married Adelheide Anti about 1840 and their first two children were born in Germany. In 1843, Gottfried brought his family to Ste. Genevieve County, Missouri where he bought land and farmed. He also continued to do carpentry work on the side. One of the last building projects he accomplished was the building of the Kehl school house, several miles north of the town of Ste. Genevieve. During the Civil War, two of Gottfried's sons enlisted in the 78th Enrolled Missouri Militia, but only Thomas saw active duty. Gottfried died of a liver complaint on 25 May 1892 in Ste. Genevieve County, Missouri. Adelheide lived the last years of her life with her daughter Clothilde. She died on 22 July 1894 in Ste. Genevieve County, Missouri. Both Gottfried and Adelheide were buried in the Valle Spring Cemetery in Ste. Genevieve, Ste. Genevieve County, Missouri.

Charles Ehrhard Family
Surname Variations: Earhart, Ehrhardt, Ehrherdt
European Origin: Hanover, Germany
Family:
Father: August Ehrhard, born about 1806 in Hanover, Germany.
Mother: Regina _____, born about 1807 in Hanover, Germany.
  Children:
*   i.   Charles, born about 1838 in Prussia. [See sketch below.]
†   ii.   Johanna Augusta, born about 1846 in Hanover, Germany. She married John Holstein. He died some time before October 1877. Augusta married Joseph Kohm as her second husband on 16 October 1877 in Ste. Genevieve, Ste. Genevieve County, Missouri. Joseph was the son of

Nicolaus Kohm and Anastasia Henhoffer, born 13 April 1840 in Waldprechtsweier, Baden, Germany. [See Joseph Kohm sketch.] Augusta married Michael Jokerst as her third husband on 11 January 1889 in Ste. Genevieve, Ste. Genevieve County, Missouri. Michael was the son of Ferdinand Jokerst and Agnes Siebert, born 23 September 1853 in Bohlsbach, Baden, Germany. [See Michael Jokerst sketch.]

Immigration:
Arrived before January 1861 aboard an unknown vessel:
    Ehrhard, Charles

Biographical:
Husband: Charles Ehrhard
    Birth – about 1838 in Hanover, Germany.
    Death/Burial – after June 1892.
1) Wife: Louisa Reike [surname from son, Charles' marriage record]
    Birth – 13 November 1837 in Germany.
    Marriage – about 1860.
    Death/Burial – 11 November 1868 in Randolph County, Illinois. She was buried in the Trinity Lutheran Church Cemetery in Red Bud, Randolph County, Illinois.
    Children:
        i. Minnie C., born 19 January 1861 in Randolph County, Illinois. She married John B. Cochran on 16 December 1880 in Chester, Randolph County, Illinois. John was the son of William Barnett Cochran and Mary Ann Douglas, born 31 December 1844 in Illinois. The couple had at least one daughter. John died on 14 April 1895. He was buried in the Evergreen Cemetery in Chester, Randolph County, Illinois. Minnie married Alfred M. Gludey as her second husband on 13 May 1898 in Randolph County, Illinois. Alfred was the son of Rudolph Gludey and Maria _____, born about 1862. After her second husband died, Minnie ran a hotel and restaurant in Chester. Minnie married A.F. Staffey as her third husband on 11 May 1910 in Cape Girardeau County, Missouri. Minnie died of lobar pneumonia and interstitial nephritis on 22 April 1927 in Webster Groves, St. Louis County, Missouri. She was buried in the Evergreen Cemetery in Chester, Randolph County, Illinois beside her first husband.
        ii. Charles, born 17 April 1863 in Illinois. He married Mollie Schrader on 15 May 1889 in Chester, Randolph County, Illinois. Mollie was the daughter of Ernst Wilhelm Diedrich Schrader and Dorothea Louisa Roeder, born 30 September 1865 in Chester, Randolph County, Illinois. The couple moved to St. Louis, Missouri where Charles worked as a grocer. They do not appear to have had any children together. Charles died of lobar pneumonia and acute rheumatism on 27 November 1913 in St. Louis, Missouri. He was buried in Chester, Randolph County, Illinois. After her husband's death, Mollie operated a boarding house on Spring Avenue in St. Louis. Mollie married Aloysius Froehly as her second husband on 20 April 1926 in Hillsboro, Jefferson County, Missouri. Aloysius was a tuck pointer in a bricklaying business. Mollie died of chronic myocarditis on 13 September 1936 in St. Louis, Missouri. She was buried in the Calvary Cemetery in St. Louis, Missouri.
        iii. John, born about 1865 in Illinois. He was deaf and mute. He died on 1 October 1886 in Chester, Randolph County, Illinois. He does not appear to have ever married and had no known issue.

2) Wife: Catherine Schroeder
    Birth –
    Marriage – 28 January 1869 in Randolph County, Illinois
    Death/Burial – before June 1870, most likely in Randolph County, Illinois.
    Children:

    There were no known children born to Charles Ehrhard and Catherine Schroeder.

3) **Wife:** Sophia Sackmann
   Birth – about 1846 in Baden, Germany.
   Marriage – 11 September 1871 in St. Louis, Missouri.
   Death/Burial – 21 July 1900 in St. Louis, Missouri. Her body was cremated in the Missouri Crematory in St. Louis, Missouri.
   Children:
   - iv. Joseph, born 2 June 1873 in Missouri. He was a paper hanger. Joseph died of tuberculosis on 27 October 1905 in St. Louis, Missouri. He was buried in the Evangelical Lutheran Cemetery in St. Louis, Missouri. He does not appear to have ever married and had no known issue.

U.S. residence prior to Ste. Genevieve County, Missouri:
Randolph County, Illinois

Occupation: Farmer / Stonemason
Religious Affiliation: Lutheran
Comments:
Charles Ehrhard came to the United States some time before 1860 and settled in Randolph County, Illinois. It is uncertain whether he and his first wife, Louisa, were married before they arrived. Charles purchased land near the town of Red Bud, Randolph County, Illinois and began to farm. The couple had two sons and one daughter. Louisa died in late 1868 and Charles married a woman named Catherine Schroeder the following year. Catherine died before June 1870, by which time Charles had moved his family across the Mississippi River to Ste. Genevieve County, Missouri where he worked as a stonemason. He married Sophia Sackmann in St. Louis, Missouri in 1871. By 1880, Charles had moved his family back to Randolph County, Illinois, this time locating near the town of Chester. By 1892, Charles was living in St. Louis, Missouri, where both his son and daughter had moved. Sophia died in St. Louis, Missouri on 21 July 1900. Charles' date of death is unknown.

Gervais Eichenlaub Family
Surname Variations: Eichenlaus, Eigenlaub, Ichenlaub
European Origin: Staufen, Freiburg, Baden, Germany
Family:
Father: Peter Eichenlaub, born about 1768 in Germany. He died on 28 June 1836 in Staufen, Freiburg, Baden, Germany.
Mother: Catherine Dorgler, born about 1767 in Germany. She died after 1816 in Germany.
   Children:
   - i. Maria Anna, born 29 May 1796 in Staufen, Freiburg, Baden, Germany. She died on 25 June 1875 in Staufen.
   - ii. Elisabetha, born 25 June 1798 in Staufen, Freiburg, Baden, Germany. She died before January 1804. No issue.
   - iii. Katherine, born 27 November 1799 in Staufen, Freiburg, Baden, Germany. She married Franz Joseph Eckert on 28 December 1835 in Staufen. He was the son of Thomas Eckert and Theresia Behrle. They had one son and four daughters, all born in Staufen. Katherine died on 30 April 1877 in Staufen.
   - iv. Johann Peter, born 27 January 1802 in Staufen, Freiburg, Baden, Germany. He died on 26 January 1865 in Staufen.
   - v. Elisabetha, born 30 January 1804 in Staufen, Freiburg, Baden, Germany.
   - * vi. Gervais, born 4 April 1806 in Staufen, Freiburg, Baden, Germany
   - vii. Bartholomaus, born 24 August 1810 in Staufen, Freiburg, Baden, Germany. He married Rosa Kreid on 20 June 1836 in Staufen. Rosa was the daughter of Jakob Kreid and Theresia Albrecht. The couple had at least four sons, of whom one died in infancy. Bartholomaus died

on 13 January 1894 in Staufen. A man named Constantine Eichenlaub, who may have been their son, died in Ste. Genevieve County, Missouri and a will dated 11 September 1871 was registered in the Probate Court for him on 23 September 1871. This Constantine mentions his father Bartholomew of Stauffen, Grand Dukedom of Baden, and a brother, Martin in his will.

Immigration:
Arrived some time before May 1835 marriage in Ste. Genevieve County, Missouri:
> Eichenlaub, Gervais

Biographical:
Husband: Gervais Eichenlaub
> Birth – 4 April 1806 in Staufen, Freiburg, Baden, Germany.
> Death/Burial – 30 December 1855 in Ste. Genevieve County, Missouri. He was buried in the St. Joseph Cemetery at Zell, Ste. Genevieve County, Missouri.

Wife: Catherine Jokerst, daughter of Franz Anton Jokerst and Anna Marie Siebert [See Franz Anton Jokerst sketch.]
> Birth – 29 October 1812 in Bohlsbach, Baden, Germany.
> Marriage – 4 May 1835 in Ste. Genevieve, Ste. Genevieve County, Missouri.
> Death/Burial – 2 October 1882 in Ste. Genevieve County, Missouri and was buried in the St. Joseph Cemetery at Zell, Ste. Genevieve County, Missouri.

Children:
i. Mary Magdalena, born 22 July 1836 in Ste. Genevieve County, Missouri. She was baptized on 1 August 1836 in the Ste. Genevieve Catholic Church at Ste. Genevieve. She married Anton Eckert on 28 April 1856 in Zell. Anton was born 5 January 1834 in Baden, Germany. [See Anton Eckert sketch.]

ii. Catherine, born 5 November 1837 in Ste. Genevieve County, Missouri. She was baptized on 27 November 1837 in the Ste. Genevieve Catholic Church at Ste. Genevieve. She married Joseph Armbruster on 2 August 1853 in Ste. Genevieve County, Missouri. [See Joseph Armbruster sketch.]

iii. Robert, born 23 May 1840 in Ste. Genevieve County, Missouri. He was baptized on 18 June 1840 in the Ste. Genevieve Catholic Church at Ste. Genevieve. During the Civil War, he served as a private in Battery C of the 2nd Regiment, Missouri Light Artillery. The unit was primarily tasked with the security of the river front in Cape Girardeau County until May 1864. The battery was sent to Jefferson City to defend against General Sterling Price in October 1864 and then sent to various postings. The unit was mustered out in December 1865. Robert married Rebecca Steimle on 12 May 1865 in River aux Vases, Ste. Genevieve Co., Missouri. Rebecca was the daughter of Ignatz Steimle and Maria Anna Oberle, born 29 May 1842 in Obersasbach, Achern, Baden, Germany. The couple had one son. Robert died of tuberculosis on 11 January 1868 in St. Louis, Missouri. He was buried in Ste. Genevieve County, Missouri. Rebecca married Charles Gerhard Guethle [aka Gidley] as her second husband on 29 April 1869 in French Village, St. Francois County, Missouri. [See Henry Guethle sketch.]

iv. Joseph, born 9 April 1842 in Ste. Genevieve County, Missouri. He was baptized on 15 May 1842 in the Ste. Genevieve Catholic Church at Ste. Genevieve. He was a farmer. Joseph married Theresa Siebert on 8 August 1865 in Ste. Genevieve County, Missouri. Their wedding was a double ceremony with Theresa's brother Henry who married Joseph's sister Barbara. Theresa was the daughter of Heinrich "Henry" Siebert and Maria Anna Sucher, born 23 September 1846 in Ste. Genevieve County, Missouri. Joseph and Theresa had three sons and one daughter, of whom the daughter died in infancy. Joseph was chopping wood in his yard when he suddenly died of a heart attack on the afternoon of 13 November 1875 in Ste. Genevieve County, Missouri. He was buried in the St. Joseph Cemetery in Zell, Ste. Genevieve County, Missouri. Theresa married Henry Armbruster as her second husband on 23 October

1876 in River aux Vases, Ste. Genevieve County, Missouri. [See Ludwig Armbruster sketch.]
- v. Carolina, born 18 February 1844 in Ste. Genevieve County, Missouri. She was baptized on 5 May 1844 in the Ste. Genevieve Catholic Church at Ste. Genevieve. She married Leon Herzog on 26 September 1865 in Zell, Ste. Genevieve Co., Missouri, He was a shoemaker. Leon was the son of Joseph Herzog and Maria Anna Trautmann, born 28 June 1842 in Ste. Genevieve County. Leon and Caroline had five sons and five daughters. Leon died of heart disease and bronchitis on 24 August 1932 and Caroline died of heart disease and asthma on 6 January 1933, both in Ste. Genevieve County. They were both buried in the Valle Spring Cemetery in Ste. Genevieve, Ste. Genevieve County, Missouri.
- vi. Barbara, born about 1846 in Ste. Genevieve County, Missouri. She married Henry Siebert on 8 August 1865 in Ste. Genevieve County, Missouri. Their wedding was a double ceremony with Henry's sister Theresa who married Barbara's brother Joseph. Henry was the son of Heinrich "Henry" Siebert and Maria Anna Sucher, born 4 May 1842 in Ste. Genevieve County. Henry died on 20 February 1870 in Ste. Genevieve County and was buried in St. Joseph Cemetery at Zell, Ste. Genevieve County, Missouri. [See Heinrich "Henry" Siebert sketch.] Barbara married Joseph Muelhaeusler as her second husband on 9 August 1870 in Ste. Genevieve County, Missouri. Joseph was the son of Andreas Muelhaeusler and Franziska Kocher, born 22 May 1847 in Oberweier bei Lahr, Baden, Germany. [See Joseph Muelhaeusler sketch.]
- vii. Henry, born 20 February 1848 in Ste. Genevieve County, Missouri. He was baptized on 26 March 1848 in the Ste. Genevieve Catholic Church at Ste. Genevieve. He married Maria Anna Siebert on 2 June 1874 at River aux Vases, Ste. Genevieve County, Missouri. Maria Anna was the daughter of Heinrich "Henry" Siebert and Mary Ann Sucher, born 6 November 1853 in Missouri. Henry and Maria had two sons and one daughter. Henry died on 22 September 1879 and was buried at Sts. Philip and James Cemetery at River aux Vases, Ste. Genevieve County, Missouri. Mary married John Dallas as her second husband on 7 June 1880 in Ste. Genevieve County, Missouri. [See John Dallas sketch.]
- viii. Johannes "John," born 26 April 1850 in Ste. Genevieve County, Missouri. He died on 6 August 1856 and was buried in the St. Joseph Cemetery at Zell, Ste. Genevieve County, Missouri. No issue.
- ix. Mary Elisabeth, born 17 November 1852 in Ste. Genevieve County, Missouri. She married William Hurst on 11 April 1871 at River aux Vases, Ste. Genevieve County, Missouri. William was the son of George Hurst and Maria Anna Palmer, born 1 November 1849 in Ste. Genevieve County, Missouri. [See George Hurst sketch.]

Land Patents:
Sainte Genevieve County, Missouri

Patentee	Issue Date	Land Office	Cert. No.	Serial No.	Sec	Twp	Rng	Acres
Eichenlaub, Gervas	10 Apr 1849	Jackson	10601	MO3570_.308	23	7-N	8-E	101.44
Eichenlaub, Katharina	1 Mar 1860	St. Louis	30785	MO1130_..108	35	38-N	8-E	9.28

Naturalization:

Name	Declaration	Naturalization	Origin
Eichenlaub, Gervais		30 July 1838 Ste. Genevieve Co.	Baden

Military:
Served in the U.S. Civil War for the Union:
Private, Company K, 78th Enrolled Missouri Militia
   Joseph Eichenlaub enlisted on 1 August 1863 in Ste. Genevieve, Missouri.

Private, Battery C, 2nd Regiment, Missouri Light Artillery
>Robert Eigenlaub [Eichenlaub] enlisted on 14 September 1861 in St. Louis, Missouri. He was mustered out on 24 August 1863 in Benton Barracks, Missouri.

Private, Company K, 78th Enrolled Missouri Militia
>Robert Eichenlaub enlisted on 30 April 1864 in Ste. Genevieve, Missouri. He was ordered into active service on 16 October 1864. He was relieved from duty on 25 November 1864. He served a total of 41 days of active service.

Occupation: Farmer
Religious Affiliation: Roman Catholic
Comments:
Gervais Eichenlaub came to the United States some time before his 1835 marriage to Catherine Jokerst in Ste. Genevieve County, Missouri. He bought land and soon began to farm. He and his wife had nine children, of whom one son died in early childhood. Gervais died on 30 December 1855 in Ste. Genevieve County, Missouri. He was buried in the St. Joseph Cemetery at Zell, Ste. Genevieve County, Missouri. After her husband's death, Catherine remained on the farm, eventually buying additional land. As she got older, Catherine began to suffer from heart disease. She went to live in her oldest daughter's household where she helped with the chores and children. Catherine died in her sleep 2 October 1882 in Ste. Genevieve County, Missouri and was buried by her husband in the St. Joseph Cemetery at Zell, Ste. Genevieve County, Missouri.

Ferdinand Eisenbeis Family

Surname Variations: Eisenbein, Eisenbice, Eisenbise, Eisenberg
European Origin: Oberweier bei Lahr, Baden, Germany
Family:
Father: Fridolin Eisenbeis, born 5 March 1809 in Oberweier bei Lahr, Baden, Germany. He died on 26 June 1884 in Oberweier.
Mother: Elisabeth Rieder [aka Riether], born 15 June 1815 in Oberweier bei Lahr, Baden, Germany. She died on 6 July 1872 in Oberweier.
Children:

‡   i.   Maria Anna, born 17 December 1837 in Oberweier bei Lahr, Baden, Germany. She came to the United States with her cousin, Maria Anna Muelhaeusler in 1864. She married Jacob Schuler on 13 October 1864 in Ste. Genevieve County, Missouri. Jacob was the son of Johann Jacob Schuler and Carolina Sparmeyer, born about 1836 in Barr, Bas-Rhin, Alsace, France. [See Johann Jacob Schuler sketch.]

*   ii.   Ferdinand, born 3 August 1839 in Oberweier bei Lahr, Baden, Germany. [See sketch below.]

iii. Katharina, born 20 November 1841 in Oberweier bei Lahr, Baden, Germany. No further information.

iv. Elisabeth, born 12 February 1845 in Oberweier bei Lahr, Baden, Germany. She married Adolf Seitz on 20 July 1876. He was a wagon maker. Adolf was the son of Matthias Seitz and Genovefa Feist, born 22 February 1852 in Oberweier. The couple had six sons and four daughters, all born in Oberweier. Elisabeth died on 25 May 1916 and Adolf died on 16 August 1919, both in Oberweier.

v. Josef, born 29 June 1847 in Oberweier bei Lahr, Baden, Germany. He died on 5 July 1847 in Oberweier. No issue.

vi. Viktoria, born 18 February 1849 in Oberweier bei Lahr, Baden, Germany. She married Valentin Köninger on 17 August 1881 in Oberweier. He was a shoemaker and clockmaker. Valentin was the son of Krescenz Köninger, born 15 July 1851 at Nussbach bei Offenburg, Baden, Germany. The couple had four sons and one daughter, all born in Oberweier. Viktoria died on 11 November 1904 and Valentin died on 15 October 1926, both in Oberweier.

vii. Josef, born 24 October 1853 in Oberweier bei Lahr, Baden, Germany. He was a farmer in Oberweier. Josef married Albertina Schätzle on 17 February 1877 in Oberweier. Albertina was the daughter of Anton Schätzle and Barbara Hammerle, born 7 June 1854 in Niederwinden, Baden, Germany. The couple had five sons and 3 daughters, all born in Oberweier. Joseph died on 1 January 1905 and Albertina died on 22 December 1921, both in Oberweier.

Immigration:
Arrived 6 July 1860 from Le Havre, France to New York aboard the *American Union*:
    Esenbeis, Ferdinand, 21   from Baden
Arrived 7 April 1864 from Le Havre, France to New York aboard the *Arabian*:
    Eisenbeis, Marie, 26 – sister of Ferdinand
    Mulhaeuser, Marianne, 23

Biographical:
Husband: Ferdinand Eisenbeis
  Birth – 3 August 1839 in Oberweier bei Lahr, Baden, Germany.
  Death/Burial – 7 December 1916 in Bloomsdale, Ste. Genevieve County, Missouri. He was buried in the St. Philomena's Cemetery in Bloomsdale, Ste. Genevieve County, Missouri.
Wife: Elisabeth Isenmann, daughter of Johann Baptist "John" Isenmann and Maria Anna Littenecker [See Johann Baptist "John" Isenmann sketch.]
  Birth – 11 August 1845 in Ste. Genevieve County, Missouri.
  Marriage – 12 September 1865 in Weingarten, Ste. Genevieve County, Missouri.
  Death/Burial – 6 January 1913 in Bloomsdale, Ste. Genevieve County, Missouri. She was buried in the St. Philomena's Cemetery in Bloomsdale, Ste. Genevieve County, Missouri.
Children:
  i. Joseph Ferdinand [twin], born 22 January 1867 in Bloomsdale, Ste. Genevieve County, Missouri. He was a farmer. Joseph married Maria M. Kertz on 25 November 1890 in Bloomsdale. Maria was the daughter of Johann "John" Kertz and Apollonia Grade, born 24 November 1868 in Missouri. The couple had nine sons and three daughters, of whom two sons and one daughter died in infancy. Joseph was a member of the Bloomsdale Council No. 1848, Knights of Columbus. He was a stockholder of the Bank of Bloomsdale and was elected to serve as a director in January 1921. Maria died of acute hyperthyroidism and heart disease on 26 May 1930 in St. Louis, Missouri. Joseph died of chronic heart disease and hemiplegia on 5 May 1950 in Ste. Genevieve County. They were both buried in St. Philomena's Cemetery in Bloomsdale, Ste. Genevieve County, Missouri.
  ii. Mary Elizabeth [twin], born 22 January 1867 in Bloomsdale, Ste. Genevieve County, Missouri. She married Nicholas Kertz on 24 September 1889 in Bloomsdale. Nicholas was the son of Johann "John" Kertz and Apollonia Grade, born 11 April 1866 in Germany. [See Johann Kertz sketch.]
  iii. John H., born 8 July 1869 in Bloomsdale, Ste. Genevieve County, Missouri. He appears to have suffered from some sort of mental or physical debility. In the 1880 census he is listed as insane. According to the 1900 census, he was both deaf and dumb and does not appear to have ever held a job. He died of chronic diarrhea on 28 October 1913 in Ste. Genevieve County, Missouri. He never married and had no known issue.
  iv. Theresa, born 18 July 1870 in River aux Vases, Ste. Genevieve County, Missouri. She was baptized on 4 September 1870 in the Sts. Philip and James Catholic Church in River aux Vases, Ste. Genevieve County, Missouri. Theresa married Michael Kertz on 18 April 1898 at Weingarten, Ste. Genevieve County. Michael was the son of Johann "John" Kertz and Apollonia Grade, born 9 April 1874 in Ste. Genevieve County, Missouri. [See Johann Kertz sketch.]
  v. Catherine, born 10 March 1872 in River aux Vases, Ste. Genevieve County, Missouri. She married Henry Jacob Basler on 5 November 1895 in Weingarten, Ste. Genevieve County. Henry was the son of Joseph Basler and Maria Anna "Mary" Schweiss, born 16 July 1872 in

Zell, Ste. Genevieve County. Henry was a farmer. The couple had five sons and two daughters and a child who died in infancy. Henry died of heart disease and a cerebral hemorrhage on 3 October 1944 in St. Louis, Missouri. Catherine died of ovarian cancer on 24 May 1959 in Jefferson County, Missouri. They were both buried in St. Philomena's Cemetery in Bloomsdale, Ste. Genevieve County, Missouri.

vi. William Ferdinand, born 27 May 1873 in Ste. Genevieve County, Missouri. He was baptized on 15 June 1873 in the St. Lawrence Catholic Church in Lawrenceton, Ste. Genevieve County, Missouri. William moved to Oklahoma City, Oklahoma County, Oklahoma in the early 1900s with several of his siblings. He went into partnership with his brother Charles in a blacksmithing and horse shoeing business. He married Mary Rusha C. Heflin on 5 May 1909 in Oklahoma City. Rusha was the daughter of William H. Heflin and Eunice F. Ward, born 18 October 1883 in Grayson County, Texas. The couple had two daughters, of whom one died in infancy. Rusha died on 24 July 1913 in Oklahoma City. She was buried in the Fairlawn Cemetery in Oklahoma City. After his wife's death, William sold his home and lived in various boarding houses. He began to speculate in land and at one time owned the Jefferson Hotel in downtown Oklahoma City. His brother, Charles, and his wife, who had no children of their own, raised William's surviving daughter. William died on 2 July 1941 in Oklahoma City. He was buried in the Fairlawn Cemetery in Oklahoma City, Oklahoma County, Oklahoma.

vii. Valentine, born 11 February 1875 in Lawrenceton, Ste. Genevieve County, Missouri. He was baptized on 25 March 1875 in the St. Lawrence Catholic Church in Lawrenceton, Ste. Genevieve County, Missouri. He married Veronica Theresa Basler on 6 November 1899. Veronica was the daughter of Joseph Basler and Mary Schweiss, born 10 September 1879 in Zell, Ste. Genevieve County. Valentine was a farmer. The couple had six sons and four daughters. In the late 1920s, Valentine sold his farm and moved his family to Festus, Jefferson County, Missouri, where he worked as a rock crusher for a road crew and his sons worked in the Pittsburgh Plate Glass Company. Veronica died of heart disease and diabetes on 9 May 1952 in Festus, Jefferson County, Missouri. Valentine died of heart disease and Parkinson's' disease on 2 December 1960 in Festus, Jefferson County, Missouri. They were both buried in the Sacred Heart Cemetery in Crystal City, Jefferson County, Missouri.

viii. Elisabeth Anna Margarethe, born 8 July 1876 in Lawrenceton, Ste. Genevieve County, Missouri. She was baptized on 6 August 1876 in the St. Lawrence Catholic Church in Lawrenceton, Ste. Genevieve County, Missouri. She moved to Oklahoma City, Oklahoma County, Oklahoma in the early 1900s with several of her siblings. She married William H. Butcher on 18 September 1905 in Oklahoma City. He was a butcher and meat packer. William was the son of Thomas Butcher and Martha Elizabeth Mills, born 16 January 1878 in Pratt County, Kansas. The couple had one son and one daughter. William died on 3 August 1958 and Anna died on 4 November 1965, both in Oklahoma City. They were both buried in the Rose Hill Burial Park in Oklahoma City, Oklahoma County, Oklahoma.

ix. Charles William Ferdinand, born 27 May 1878 in Lawrenceton, Ste. Genevieve County, Missouri. He was baptized on 15 June 1878 in the Our Lady Help of Christians Catholic Church in Weingarten, Ste. Genevieve County, Missouri. He moved to Oklahoma City, Oklahoma County, Oklahoma in the early 1900s with several of his siblings. Charles became an auto mechanic and machinist. He married Anna Mary Zurline. Anna was born 22 April 1888 in Tennessee. The couple had no children of their own, but raised a niece, the daughter of Charles' brother, William. Charles died on 16 December 1972 Anna died on 22 June 1974, both in Oklahoma. They were both buried in the Rose Hill Burial Park in Oklahoma City, Oklahoma County, Oklahoma.

x. Julianna M. , born 11 June 1880 in Weingarten, Ste. Genevieve County, Missouri. She was baptized on 4 July 1880 in the Our Lady Help of Christians Catholic Church in Weingarten, Ste. Genevieve County, Missouri. She married Edward Joseph Mergenthaler on 4 May 1910 in St. Louis, Missouri. Edward was the son of Christian Mergenthaler and Mary A. Klein, born

9 March 1885 in New Haven, Franklin County, Missouri. He worked for the streetcar railway in the city of St. Louis, Missouri. The couple had five daughters, of whom one died in early childhood. Edward died on 8 June 1964. Julia died on 8 November 1973. They were both buried in the St. Peter Cemetery in Kirkwood, St. Louis County, Missouri.

xi. Peter Henry, born 19 July 1881 in Weingarten, Ste. Genevieve County, Missouri. He was baptized on 31 July 1881 in the Our Lady Help of Christians Catholic Church in Weingarten, Ste. Genevieve County, Missouri. He moved to Oklahoma City, Oklahoma County, Oklahoma in the early 1900s with several of his siblings. By 1917, Peter was a fireman in Okmulgee, Okmulgee County, Oklahoma. He married Violet Martha Way on 4 November 1917 in Okmulgee, Okmulgee County, Oklahoma. Violet was the daughter of Isaac P. Way and Ida M. Crays, born April 1896 in Indiana. Her parents were divorced when she was a toddler and she and her mother lived with an aunt in Martin County, Indiana. Her mother later married a man named Ira Stephens. Pete and Violet had two sons. The couple eventually moved to Tulsa, Tulsa County, Oklahoma. Pete died in March 1969 and Violet died in October 1983, both in Tulsa, Tulsa County, Oklahoma.

xii. Andrew, born 17 September 1882 in Weingarten, Ste. Genevieve County, Missouri. He was baptized on 24 September 1882 in the Our Lady Help of Christians Catholic Church in Weingarten, Ste. Genevieve County, Missouri. He died of "black croup" on 26 December 1882 in Weingarten. Andrew was buried in Our Lady Help of Christians Cemetery in Weingarten, Ste. Genevieve County, Missouri. No issue.

xiii. Sophia, born 23 May 1884 in Weingarten, Ste. Genevieve County, Missouri. She was baptized on 8 June 1884 in the Our Lady Help of Christians Catholic Church in Weingarten, Ste. Genevieve County, Missouri. She died of la grippe [influenza] on 4 April 1892 in Weingarten. Sophia was buried in Our Lady Help of Christians Cemetery in Weingarten, Ste. Genevieve County, Missouri. No issue.

xiv. Rosina M., born 7 January 1887 in Weingarten, Ste. Genevieve County, Missouri. She never married but had one son. She worked as a laundress to support herself and her child. She died of pneumonia and influenza on 7 May 1936 in Lawrenceton, Ste. Genevieve County. She was buried in the St. Philomena's Cemetery in Bloomsdale, Ste. Genevieve County, Missouri.

xv. Anton Raymond, born 14 July 1889 in Weingarten, Ste. Genevieve County, Missouri. He was baptized on 11 August 1889 in the Our Lady Help of Christians Catholic Church in Weingarten, Ste. Genevieve County, Missouri. He married Emma R. Karl on 8 September 1914 in Zell, Ste. Genevieve County. Emma was the daughter of John Karl and Elisabeth Weiler, born 18 November 1891 in Weingarten. Anton was a farmer. The couple had two sons and two daughters. Anton died of a heart attack on 27 March 1958 in Ste. Genevieve County. Emma died on 29 September 1988. They were both buried in the Sacred Heart Cemetery in Ozora, Ste. Genevieve County, Missouri.

xvi. Felix Nicholas Peter, born 3 June 1891 in Weingarten, Ste. Genevieve County, Missouri. He was baptized on 28 June 1891 in the Our Lady Help of Christians Catholic Church in Weingarten, Ste. Genevieve County, Missouri. He married Elizabeth Mary Hoog. Elizabeth was the daughter of Simon Hoog and Mary Anne Naeger, born 26 October 1892 in Ste. Genevieve County, Missouri. After their marriage, Felix and Elizabeth moved to St. Louis, Missouri, where Felix worked as a clerk in a steel mill. The couple had two sons and one daughter. About 1926, the family moved to Los Angeles, Los Angeles County, California, where Felix worked as an insurance sales agent and then as a clerk in the charity department for the County of Los Angeles. Felix died on 2 February 1985 in Lynwood, Los Angeles County, California. Elizabeth died on 4 January 1988 in Stockton, San Joaquin County, California.

Naturalization:

Name	Declaration	Naturalization	Origin
Eisenbeis, Ferdinand		27 April 1887 Ste. Genevieve Co.	Baden

Military:
Served in the U.S. Civil War for the Union:
Private, Company F, 78th Enrolled Missouri Militia
    Ferdinand Eisenbeis enlisted in August 1862 in Ste. Genevieve County, Missouri.

Education: Could read and write
Occupation: Farmer
Religious Affiliation: Roman Catholic
Comments:
Ferdinand Eisenbeis was born in Germany. He came to the United States in 1860 and settled in Ste. Genevieve County, Missouri near the town of Weingarten. He was the nephew of Katharina Eisenbeis Rottler and a distant cousin of the Seitz and Muelhaeusler families. He is definitely *not* the Ferdinand Eisenbeis who came to the United States in 1848 aboard the *Archelaus*, landing in New York. That person came to the United States with his parents and siblings and eventually settled in Pottowatomi County, Kansas. Ferdinand married Elisabeth Isenmann in 1864 and for the first few years of their married lives, the couple lived near Bloomsdale, Ste. Genevieve County. About 1879, Ferdinand moved his family back to Weingarten and remained there until about the mid-1890s when they returned to Bloomsdale. Elisabeth died of pneumonia and pericarditis on 4 January 1913 and Ferdinand died of pneumonia on 7 December 1916, both in Ste. Genevieve County, Missouri. They were both buried in the St. Agnes' Cemetery [old St. Philomena's] in Bloomsdale, Ste. Genevieve County, Missouri.

Note: The families of those children of Ferdinand Eisenbeis who moved to Oklahoma before 16 November 1907 and their descendants are eligible for membership in the First Families of the Twin Territories through the Oklahoma Genealogical Society.

Joseph Endres Family
Surname Variations: Anders, Andres, Andrews, Enders, Endress
European Origin: Freudenberg amt Wertheim, Baden, Germany
Family:
Father: Valentin Endres, born 24 June 1786 in Freudenberg amt Wertheim, Baden, Germany. He died on
    28 December 1829 in Freudenberg amt Wertheim, Baden, Germany.
Mother: Maria Anna Kunzmann, born 25 February 1788 in Freudenberg amt Wertheim, Baden, Germany.
    She died on 28 November 1865 in Freudenberg amt Wertheim, Baden, Germany.
    Children:
        i. Johann Peter, baptized on 13 September 1815 in the Catholic Church at Freudenberg amt Wertheim, Baden, Germany. No further information.
        ii. Catherine, born in Freudenberg amt Wertheim, Baden, Germany. She was married to Carl Walz on 30 June 1844 in Freudenberg. Carl was the son of Jacob Walz and Margaretha Hummel. No further information.
        iii. Valentin, born 21 December 1823 in Freudenberg amt Wertheim, Baden, Germany. He was baptized in the Catholic Church at Freudenberg on 22 December 1823. Valentin died on 4 March 1827 in Freudenburg. No issue.
*   iv. Joseph Michael, baptized on 5 February 1827 in the Catholic Church at Freudenberg amt Wertehim, Baden, Germany. [See sketch below.]

Immigration:
Arrived about 1857 aboard an unknown vessel:
> Endres, Joseph Michael

Biographical:
Husband: Joseph Michael Endres
> Birth/Baptism – Baptized on 5 February 1827 in the Catholic Church at Freudenberg amt Wertehim, Baden, Germany.
> Death/Burial – 3 July 1889 in Lawrenceton, Ste. Genevieve County, Missouri. He was buried in the St. Lawrence Cemetery at Lawrenceton, Ste. Genevieve County, Missouri.

Wife: Maria Theresa Bechtold, daughter of Bernard Bechtold and Margaretha Knapp [See Bernard Bechtold sketch.]
> Birth – 13 October 1831 in Freudenberg amt Wertheim, Baden, Germany.
> Marriage – 9 May 1858 in Little Canada [aka Petite Canada; present-day French Village], St. Francois County, Missouri.
> Death/Burial – 20 March 1919 in Ste. Genevieve County, Missouri. She was buried in the St. Lawrence Cemetery at Lawrenceton, Ste. Genevieve County, Missouri.

Children:
i. Theckla, born 13 February 1859 in Ste. Genevieve County, Missouri. She was baptized on 6 March 1859 in St. Philomena's Catholic Church at Bloomsdale, Ste. Genevieve County, Missouri. She may have died after 1860.
ii. Anna Maria, born 1 June 1860 in Ste. Genevieve County, Missouri. She married Louis G. Long on 7 June 1881 in Lawrenceton, Ste. Genevieve County, Missouri. Louis was the son of Frederick Gabriel Long and Maria Kleopha Gegg, born 6 September 1855 in Lancaster County, Pennsylvania. Louis was a grocer and came to Ste. Genevieve County from Pennsylvania to visit his Gegg cousins. After his marriage, he and Anna Maria lived in Ste. Genevieve County until about 1897. The family moved to Lancaster County, Pennsylvania and lived near Louis' parents. The couple had seven sons and six daughters, of whom two sons and a daughter died in infancy. All but the youngest four children were born near Lawrenceton in Ste. Genevieve County, Missouri. One of Louis and Anna's sons, Edward Vincent, returned to Ste. Genevieve to help his grandmother run her farm. Anna Maria died on 19 October 1904 and Louis died on 11 October 1924, both in Lancaster County, Pennsylvania.
iii. Theresa, born about 1868 in Ste. Genevieve County, Missouri. No further mention after the 1880 census.

Military:
Served in the U.S. Civil War for the Union:
Private, Company I, 78th Enrolled Missouri Militia
> Joseph Andres enlisted 12 June 1863 at New Offenburg, Missouri.

Private, Company F, 78th Enrolled Missouri Militia
> Joseph Andrews transferred from Company I on 18 October 1864. He was ordered into active service on 18 October 1864 and relieved from service on 25 November 1864. He served a total of 39 days of active duty.

Occupation: Farmer
Religious Affiliation: Roman Catholic
Comments:
Joseph Michael Endres was born in Freudenberg amt Wertheim, Baden, Germany. He came to the United States about 1857, possibly at the same time as his future wife, Maria Theresa Bechtold, and her family. Joseph and Theresa were married in 1858, after they arrived in the United States. They settled on a farm in Union Township in northern Ste. Genevieve County near present-day Lawrenceton. During the Civil War, Joseph served as a private in Companies I and F of the 78th Enrolled Missouri Militia. After the war, Joseph

and his wife remained on the farm. The couple had three daughters, all born in Ste. Genevieve County. Theresa's older, unmarried brother Dominic lived with them and helped Joseph work the land. Joseph died on 3 July 1889 and was buried in the St. Lawrence Cemetery in Lawrenceton. Dominic died nearly a year later and Theresa was left to run the farm with the help of her grandson, Edward V. Long. Theresa died of chronic dysentery and senile dementia on 20 March 1919. She was buried in the St. Lawrence Cemetery at Lawrenceton, Ste. Genevieve County, Missouri.

Joseph A. Ernst Family

Surname Variations: Ernest, Earnst
European Origin: Lütgeneder, Westphalia, Germany
Family:
Father: Franz Joseph Ernst
Mother: Anna Maria Wilmer
    Child:
*   i.   Joseph Aloysius, born 10 December 1836 in Lütgeneder, Westphalia, Germany. [See sketch below.]

Immigration:
Arrived in late 1858 from Germany to New York aboard an unknown vessel:
    Ernst, Joseph A.

Biographical:
Husband: Joseph Aloysius Ernst
    Birth – 10 December 1836 in Lütgeneder, Westphalia, Germany.
    Death/Burial – 20 February 1920 in Ste. Genevieve County, Missouri. He was buried in the Valle Spring Cemetery in Ste. Genevieve, Ste. Genevieve County, Missouri.
Wife: Mary Magdaline "Adeline" Hechinger, daughter of Protase Hechinger and Abigail Lord
    Birth – 17 March 1843 near Cincinnati, Hamilton County, Ohio.
    Marriage – 26 September 1865 in Cincinnati, Hamilton County, Ohio.
    Death/Burial – 8 October 1901 in Ste. Genevieve County, Missouri. She was buried in the Valle Spring Cemetery in Ste. Genevieve, Ste. Genevieve County, Missouri.
    Children:
        i.   Francis Joseph Adam "Frank," born 23 September 1866 in Saint Peter, Highland Township, Franklin County, Indiana. He married Louisa Bertha Valle on 23 March 1889 in Hillsboro, Jefferson County, Missouri. Bertha was the daughter of Louis August Bertolemé "L. Bert" Valle and Philomena Janis, born 9 September 1867 in Ste. Genevieve County, Missouri. Frank was a printer and eventually took over the management of the Ste. Genevieve *Herald* from his father. The couple had four sons and one daughter. Frank died of pneumonia and chronic heart disease on 3 December 1941 in Ste. Genevieve. Bertha died of heart disease on 26 March 1950 in Ste. Genevieve. They were both buried in the Valle Spring Cemetery in Ste. Genevieve, Ste. Genevieve County, Missouri.
        ii.   John Edward, born 5 November 1868 in Ste. Genevieve County, Missouri. He was a credit manager and bookkeeper for Sonnenfeld's Millinery Store in St. Louis. He married Elizabeth Ella Luer on 10 February 1897 in St. Louis, Missouri. Elizabeth was the daughter of Charles Luer and Elizabeth Mawe, born 21 October 1873 in St. Louis, Missouri. The couple had two sons and three daughters. John died of coronary occlusion on 30 January 1945 in Maplewood, St. Louis County, Missouri. He was buried in the Sts. Peter and Paul Cemetery in St. Louis, Missouri. Elizabeth died on 27 April 1965 in Maplewood, St. Louis County, Missouri.
        iii.   William Anthony, born 26 November 1870 in Ste. Genevieve County, Missouri. He died on 12 June 1871 in Ste. Genevieve County. William was buried in the St. Joseph Cemetery in Zell, Ste. Genevieve County, Missouri. No issue.

iv. Mary Alice, born 3 May 1872 in Ste. Genevieve County, Missouri. She died of pneumonia and epilepsy on 13 March 1886 in Ste. Genevieve County, Missouri. She was buried in the Valle Spring Cemetery in Ste. Genevieve, Ste. Genevieve County, Missouri. No issue.

v. Florence Agatha "Flora," born 10 November 1874 in Ste. Genevieve County, Missouri. She was baptized on 3 December 1874 in the Ste. Genevieve Catholic Church in Ste. Genevieve, Ste. Genevieve County, Missouri. She married Edward Cross on 28 October 1902 in Ste. Genevieve, Ste. Genevieve County, Missouri. Edward was the son of Samuel Cross and Cordelia Hyde, born 23 August 1877 in Perryville, Perry County, Missouri. The couple had one son and one daughter. Flora died of a cerebral vascular accident on 30 July 1947 in St. Louis, Missouri. Edward died of a stroke on 17 September 1950 in St. Louis, Missouri. They were both buried in the Valle Spring Cemetery in Ste. Genevieve, Ste. Genevieve County, Missouri.

vi. Henry, born 13 January 1877 in Ste. Genevieve County, Missouri. He died before 1880. No issue.

vii. Ida Rosine, born 17 September 1878 in Ste. Genevieve County, Missouri. She was baptized on 14 October 1878 in the Ste. Genevieve Catholic Church in Ste. Genevieve, Ste. Genevieve County, Missouri. She died on 1 May 1879 in Ste. Genevieve County, Missouri. No issue.

viii. Adaline, born about December 1881 in Ste. Genevieve County, Missouri. She died on 1 June 1882 in Ste. Genevieve County, Missouri. No issue.

ix. Girl, born 19 February 1890 in Ste. Genevieve, Ste. Genevieve County, Missouri. She died young.

U.S. residence prior to Ste. Genevieve County, Missouri:
Alton, Madison County, Illinois, 1858-
Cincinnati, Hamilton County, Ohio
Franklin County, Indiana, 1865-1868

Naturalization:

Name	Declaration	Naturalization	Origin
Ernst, Joseph A.		2 May 1872 Ste. Genevieve Co.	Prussia

Education: Attended the Jesuit College at Paderborn, Westphalia, Germany. Graduated in 1857.
Occupation: Teacher / School principal; Founder and Editor, Ste. Genevieve *Herald*, May 1882
Religious Affiliation: Roman Catholic
Political Affiliation and/or Any Offices Held: Joseph A. Ernst, Republican
Ste. Genevieve County, Assessor, 1873-74
Postmaster, New Offenburg, Ste. Genevieve County, 1871
Postmaster, Ste. Genevieve, Ste. Genevieve County, Missouri, 1889

Comments:
Joseph A. Ernst was born in Lütgeneder, Westphalia, Germany in 1836. His father was a carpenter and builder and must have been fairly well-to-do since he was able to send Joseph to study at the Jesuit College at Paderborn, Westphalia, Germany. Joseph graduated in 1857 and the following year left home for America. He traveled first to Alton, Madison County, Illinois where he stayed a short while. Then he traveled north to Cincinnati, Ohio where he became a school teacher. He married Mary Magdaline "Adeline" Hechinger there in 1865. The couple remained in Ohio for the first years of their lives together, then moved to Franklin County, Indiana where Joseph again worked as a school teacher. About 1868, the family moved to Ste. Genevieve, Ste. Genevieve County, Missouri where he taught until 1887. In 1882, Joseph founded the Ste. Genevieve *Herald*, a weekly newspaper published in both English and German. He ran the newspaper with spirit and humor until he retired in 1916, turning the newspaper over to his son, Frank. Members of the Ernst family continued to run the newspaper until 1969. The newspaper remains one of the few independent weekly newspapers in Missouri to this day. Joseph and Adeline are said to have had ten children, of whom only two sons and one daughter survived to adulthood. Adeline died of consumption aggravated by influenza on 8 October 1901 in Ste.

Genevieve. Joseph died of senile gangrene and uremia on 29 February 1920 in Ste. Genevieve, Ste. Genevieve County, Missouri. They were both buried in the Valle Spring Cemetery in Ste. Genevieve, Ste. Genevieve County, Missouri.

Francis "Frank" Esselman Family
Surname Variations: Asselman, Eselman
European Origin: Hanover, Germany
Family:
Father: Johann Bernard "Bennet" Esselman, born about 1821 in Hanover, Germany. He died on 3 December 1869 in Randolph County, Illinois.
Mother: Anna Adelaide Catherine Sinker [aka Sunker], born 30 November 1827 in Germany. She died on 26 March 1900 in Randolph County, Illinois. She was buried in the St. Marys Cemetery in St. Mary, Ste. Genevieve County, Missouri.
Children:
  i. Joseph, born 23 December 1850 in Randolph County, Illinois. He was a farmer. Joseph married Mrs. Lucinda Schneider on 27 July 1880 in Randolph County, Illinois. Lucinda was the daughter of Michael Grott and Juliana Zanter, born 11 November 1849 in [Berlin, Germany or Posen, Poland?]. She was the widow of Valentine Schneider. Valentine and Lucinda were married on 24 October 1876 in Randolph County, Illinois and had one daughter. Valentine died in 1879 in Randolph County, Illinois. Joseph Esselman and Lucinda had two sons and two daughters, of whom one daughter died in early childhood. Lucinda died of a "nervous attack" on 24 September 1924 in Chester, Randolph County. Joseph died on 29 March 1925. They were both buried in the St. Marys of Help Catholic Cemetery in Chester, Randolph County, Illinois.
  ii. George, born about 1853 in Randolph County, Illinois. He married Louvina Riney on 18 September 1883 in Perry County, Missouri. Louvina was the daughter of Thomas Edward Riney and Mary Ann Stewart, born 15 August 1866 in Perry County, Missouri. The couple had seven sons and five daughters, of whom three sons and one daughter died in infancy or early childhood. Louvina died on 17 December 1909 in Missouri. She was buried in the St. Marys Cemetery in St. Mary, Ste. Genevieve County, Missouri. George married Mrs. Theresa R. Thieret as his second wife on 17 February 1914 in Perry County. Theresa was the widow of John Peter [aka Jean Pierre] Thieret and had five sons and three daughters from her first marriage. Theresa was the daughter of John Sutterer and Rosella Flora, born 24 January 1866 in St. Louis, Missouri. George and Theresa had no children together. George farmed for most of his life until about 1922 when an infected foot became gangrenous and he had both legs amputated near the hips. Theresa died of influenza on 2 May 1926 in Perryville, Perry County, Missouri. She was buried in the Mount Hope Cemetery in Perryville, Perry County, Missouri. After his wife's death, George lived first with his son Pat in Bois Brule Bottom and then made his home with his son Leonard. George died of arteriosclerosis on 19 September 1934 in Bois Brule, Perry County, Missouri. He was buried in the St. Marys Cemetery in St. Mary, Ste. Genevieve County, Missouri.
  iii. Catherine [twin], born 10 February 1858 in Randolph County, Illinois. She married Robert Anastazy Dreska [aka Dreczka] on 8 November 1876 in Claryville, Perry County, Missouri. Robert was born 28 July 1850 in Poland. He was a well-known tailor in Chester. The couple had four sons and one daughter. Robert died on 17 May 1927 in Chester, Randolph County, Illinois. After her husband's death, Catherine sold her home and went to live with her children in turn. Catherine died on heart disease on 20 April 1935 while living with her daughter in Detroit, Wayne County, Michigan. They were both buried in the St. Marys Catholic Cemetery in Chester, Randolph County, Illinois.
  iv. Elizabeth [twin], born 10 February 1858 in Randolph County, Illinois. She married Ernst Heinrich "Henry" Brinkmann on 18 November 1880 in Chester, Randolph County, Illinois. Henry was born 11 April 1856 in Randolph County, Illinois. The couple had one son and two

daughters, of whom the two daughters died in infancy and their son died as a young man with no known issue. Henry died on 6 December 1908 in Randolph County, Illinois. Elizabeth died of pulmonary tuberculosis on 26 December 1925 in Kankakee, Kankakee County, Illinois. They were both buried in the Evergreen Cemetery in Chester, Randolph County, Illinois.

    v. Mary, born 27 November 1861 in Randolph County, Illinois. She married Edward J. Rhodes on 26 January 1885 in Claryville, Perry County, Missouri. Edward was born 16 August 1860 in Missouri. He was a farmer. The couple had three sons and two daughters. Mary died on 7 April 1902 and Edward died on 10 March 1908, both in Perry County, Missouri. They were both buried in the St. Marys Cemetery in Chester, Randolph County, Illinois.

*   vi. Francis John Nepomuk "Frank," born 25 April 1863 in Randolph County, Illinois. [See sketch below.]

    vii. William Henry, born 16 January 1866 in Randolph County, Illinois. He died on 13 October 1866 in Chester, Randolph County, Illinois. No issue.

    viii. Anna [twin], born 11 December 1867 in Randolph County, Illinois. She married Edward Everett Pearson on 29 January 1890 in Claryville, Perry County, Missouri. Edward was born about 1861 in Illinois. The couple had one son and two daughters. Edward died on 21 May 1898 in Claryville. Anna married William J. Caho as her second husband on 10 January 1901 in Claryville. William was born on 28 May 1875 in Claryville. Anna and William had one son. William died in 1918. Anna died of heart disease on 4 September 1946 in Claryville. She was buried in the St. Marys Cemetery in Chester, Randolph County, Illinois.

    ix. Susanna [twin], born about 1868 in Randolph County, Illinois. She married Thaddeus Faye Young on 16 July 1892 in Claryville, Perry County, Missouri. Thaddeus was born on 1 November 1869 in Fort Smith, Arkansas. The couple had three sons and one daughter. Thaddeus died on 21 August 1940 in Perry County, Missouri. Susanna died of asthma on 9 June 1951 in Perry County, Missouri. They were both buried in the St. Marys Cemetery in St. Mary, Ste. Genevieve County, Missouri.

    x. Bernard, born 5 July 1870 in Randolph County, Illinois. He died before 1880 in Randolph County, Illinois. No issue.

Immigration:
Arrived 18 December 1845 from Bremen, Germany to New Orleans aboard the *Zebra*:
    Esselman, B[ernard], 26   Farmer

Biographical:
Husband: Francis John Nepomuk Esselman
    Birth – 25 April 1863 in Randolph County, Illinois.
    Death/Burial – 15 October 1927 in St. Mary, Ste. Genevieve County, Missouri. He was buried in the St. Marys Cemetery in St. Mary, Ste. Genevieve County, Missouri.
Wife: Matilda Gertrude "Tillie" Layton, daughter of Fredric Layton and Elizabeth Ellen Sadler
    Birth – 14 January 1867 in Perry County, Missouri.
    Marriage – 3 September 1888 in Perry County, Missouri [civil ceremony]. The marriage was sanctified on 26 August 1917 in the Immaculate Conception Catholic Church in St. Mary, Ste. Genevieve County, Missouri.
    Death/Burial – 27 August 1917 in Perry County, Missouri. She was buried in the St. Marys Cemetery in St. Mary, Ste. Genevieve County, Missouri.
    Children:
        i. Earl Francis, born 12 February 1889 in Claryville, Perry County, Missouri. He was a farmer. Earl married Emily Louisa "Emma" Breig on 17 October 1910 in St. Mary, Ste. Genevieve County, Missouri. Emma was the daughter of Joseph Breig and Catherina "Katie" Braun, born 20 November 1891 in Perry County, Missouri. The couple had four sons and two daughters. Earl died on 1 August 1972 and Louisa died on 22 February 1982 in Ste. Genevieve County,

Missouri. They were both buried in the Catholic Cemetery in St. Mary, Ste. Genevieve County, Missouri.

ii. Mary Grace, born 30 January 1891 in Claryville, Perry County, Missouri. She married Joseph Clarence Elder on 23 November 1915 in St. Mary, Ste. Genevieve County, Missouri. Joseph was the son of Augustine Guy Elder and Mary Jane Miles, born 9 July 1889 in Perry County, Missouri. He was a foreman in a stove manufacturer in St. Louis, Missouri. He later worked as a retail sales clerk. The couple had two sons and one daughter. Mary died on 28 March 1973 and Joseph died in January 1976, both in St. Louis, Missouri. They were both buried in the Calvary Cemetery in St. Louis, Missouri.

iii. Elizabeth "Bessie," born 11 April 1894 in Claryville, Perry County, Missouri. She married Arthur Francis Elder on 10 November 1913 in St. Mary, Ste. Genevieve County, Missouri. Arthur was the son of Augustine Guy Elder and Mary Jane Miles, born 24 January 1893 in Perry County, Missouri. He was a farmer. The couple had three sons and one daughter, of whom two sons died in infancy. The couple later adopted a boy named Andrew Adams. Arthur died on 19 May 1971 and Elizabeth died on 2 March 1975, both in Perryville. They were both buried in the Mount Hope Cemetery in Perry County, Missouri.

iv. Magdalena "Maggie," born 12 May 1896 in Perry County, Missouri. She was baptized on 16 December 1900 in the Immaculate Conception Catholic Church in St. Mary, Ste. Genevieve County, Missouri. Maggie married John Augustin Breig on 26 November 1917 in St. Mary, Ste. Genevieve County, Missouri. John was the son of Joseph Breig and Catherina "Katie" Braun, born 22 August 1896 in Perry County, Missouri. [See Joseph Breig sketch.]

v. Frederick Dewey, born 28 January 1899 in Perry County, Missouri. He died on 11 December 1900 in Perry County. He was buried in the St. Marys Cemetery in St. Mary, Ste. Genevieve County, Missouri. No issue.

vi. Albert Joseph, born 8 April 1901 in Perry County, Missouri. He was baptized on 7 September 1901 in the Immaculate Conception Catholic Church in St. Marys, Ste. Genevieve County, Missouri. Albert was a farmer. He later worked as a salesman in a drugstore. He married Alice Loretta Pound on 22 June 1926 in St. Louis, Missouri. Alice was the daughter of William C. Pound and Barbara _____, born 25 November 1907 in St. Louis, Missouri. The couple had one son. Alice died 22 November 1967. Albert died 8 September 1968 in Omaha, Douglas County, Nebraska. They were both buried in the St. Marys Cemetery in St. Mary, Ste. Genevieve County, Missouri.

vii. Alfreda Marie "Alpha," born 7 December 1903 in Perry County, Missouri. She was baptized on 3 June 1904 in the Immaculate Conception Catholic Church in St. Mary, Ste. Genevieve County, Missouri. Alpha married Richard Leon Cole. Richard was the son of Sam Cole and Sarah Ada _____, born 8 January 1907 in Oklahoma. He was a house painter and paper hanger. The couple had one son. Richard died on 15 December 1978 and Alpha died on 11 May 1995, both in Tulsa, Tulsa County, Oklahoma. They were both buried in the St. Marys Cemetery in St. Mary, Ste. Genevieve County, Missouri.

viii. Francis Oriel "Frank," born 10 November 1907 in Perry County, Missouri. He was baptized on 15 May 1909 in the Immaculate Conception Catholic Church in St. Mary, Ste. Genevieve County, Missouri. Frank was an auto mechanic. He married Nelma E. Cambron on 27 April 1937 in Chester, Randolph County, Illinois. Nelma was the daughter of Curby Bernard Cambron and Nola Allen, born 18 December 1919 in Perry County, Missouri. The couple had no children. Frank died after a long illness on 3 July 1972 in St. Louis, Missouri. He was buried in the St. Marys Cemetery in St. Mary, Ste. Genevieve County, Missouri. Nelma married Ivan Carl Rodebush as her second husband about 1974.

U.S. residence prior to Ste. Genevieve County, Missouri:
Randolph County, Illinois
Perry County, Missouri

Education: Could read and write
Occupation: Farmer
Religious Affiliation: Roman Catholic
Comments:
Frank Esselman, the son of German immigrant parents, was born in Randolph County, Illinois. He married Matilda Gertrude "Tillie" Layton on 3 September 1888 by a Justice of the Peace in Randolph County, Illinois. The couple lived near the town of Claryville in Perry County, Missouri where Frank owned and operated a farm. The family attended the Immaculate Conception Catholic Church in St. Mary, Ste. Genevieve County, and did a lot of business in that town. Most of Frank's siblings also moved into Perry County. Apparently, the fact that their marriage had never been blessed by the Catholic Church was an issue for the couple. The day before Tillie died, the priest from St. Mary came to their home to sanctify their marriage and to give Tillie the Last Rites. She died of yellow jaundice the next day on 27 August 1917 in Perry County, Missouri. Frank died of dropsy and kidney disease on 15 October 1927 in Perry County, Missouri. They were both buried in the St. Marys Cemetery in St. Mary, Ste. Genevieve County, Missouri.

Benjamin Etter Family
Surname Variations: Edder
European Origin: Canton Thurgau, Switzerland
Family:
Father: Johann Etter
Mother: Susanna Huber
    Child:
*   i.   Benjamin, born 29 October 1822 in Canton Thurgau, Switzerland.

Immigration:
Arrived some time before 1844 aboard an unknown vessel:
    Etter, Benjamin

Biographical:
Husband: Benjamin Etter
    Birth – 29 October 1822 in Canton Thurgau, Switzerland.
    Death/Burial – 5 November 1889 in Ferndale, Humboldt County, California.
Wife: Wilhelmina Kern, daughter of John Dominic Kern and Regina Kettinger [See John Dominic Kern sketch.]
    Birth – 28 July 1835 in Germany.
    Marriage – 12 October 1854 in Ste. Genevieve County, Missouri.
    Death/Burial – 17 January 1913 in Ferndale, Humboldt County, California.
    Children:
        i.   Charles Benjamin, born 19 January 1856 in Ste. Genevieve County, Missouri. He was baptized on 6 April 1856 in the Ste. Genevieve Catholic Church in Ste. Genevieve, Ste. Genevieve County, Missouri. He died on 14 January 1862 in Ste. Genevieve County, Missouri. He was originally buried in the Memorial Cemetery in Ste. Genevieve, Ste. Genevieve County. A memorial stone was later installed in the Valle Spring Cemetery in Ste. Genevieve, Ste. Genevieve County, Missouri. No issue.
        ii.   Mary Louisa, born 23 March 1858 in Ste. Genevieve County, Missouri. She was baptized on 18 May 1858 in the Ste. Genevieve Catholic Church in Ste. Genevieve, Ste. Genevieve County, Missouri. Louisa never married. She lived with her parents until they died and then lived with one of her younger brothers. She died on 6 September 1935 in Humboldt County, California. No issue.
        iii   John Edward Emile, born 6 January 1861 in Ste. Genevieve County, Missouri. He was baptized on 31 March 1861 in the Ste. Genevieve Catholic Church in Ste. Genevieve, Ste. Genevieve

County, Missouri. He married Minnie J. Schallard on 3 November 1887 in Humboldt County, California. Minnie was the daughter of _____ Schallard and Barbara _____, born in 15 May 1867 in Switzerland. Emile and Minnie had four sons and two daughters. John died on 11 May 1943 and Minnie died on 4 October 1945, both in Humboldt County, California.

iv. Henry Julius, born 4 August 1863 in Ste. Genevieve County, Missouri. He was baptized on 20 September 1863 in the Ste. Genevieve Catholic Church in Ste. Genevieve, Ste. Genevieve County, Missouri. He was a rancher. He married Genieve M. Haley about 1900 in California. Genieve was the daughter of Elisha Haley and Ella F. West, born 15 February 1877 in Table Bluff, California. The couple had two sons and four daughters. The couple may have been divorced. Genieve married a man named Henry Wildie Morse on 10 December 1934 in Marin County, California. It was a second marriage for both of them. Henry was the son of Henry Clay Morse and Eliza Jane Caldwell, born 5 March 1875 in Humboldt County, California. Henry Etter died on 2 July 1937 in Humboldt County, California. Henry Morse died in January 1956. Genieve died on 22 May 1956 in Humboldt County, California. She was buried in the Ocean View Cemetery in Eureka, Humboldt County, California.

v. George Benjamin, born 1 February 1866 in Ste. Genevieve County, Missouri. He was baptized on 7 May 1866 in the Ste. Genevieve Catholic Church in Ste. Genevieve, Ste. Genevieve County, Missouri. He married Margaret Ellen Hogan about 1892 in California. Margaret was the daughter of James Edward Hogan and Sarah Anne McGovern, born 31 January 1873 in McKinleyville, Humboldt County, California. The couple had three sons and seven daughters, of whom two daughters died young. George went into partnership with his brothers, Fred, August and Albert in the agricultural firm of Etter Brothers. The brothers worked together to carve their operation from unsettled land. Eventually, each brother turned to a line in the operation for which his talents especially suited him. George managed most of the stock raising operations of the firm. He was also in charge of transportation and home farm management. Margaret died on 17 April 1929 and George died on 4 January 1930, both in Humboldt County, California.

vi. James William "Willie," born October 1868 in Missouri. He is said to have died about 1886 in Humboldt County, California. He never married and had no known issue.

vii. Joseph Frederick "Fred," born October 1870 in Shingle Springs, El Dorado County, California. He married Margaret Ellilian Bailey about 1911 in California. Margaret was the daughter of John V. Bailey and Mary Allen Clark, born 1 February 1880 in Hamilton County, Iowa. The couple had three sons. Fred went into partnership with his brothers, George, August and Albert in the agricultural firm of Etter Brothers. The brothers worked together to carve their operation from unsettled land. Eventually, each brother turned to a line in the operation for which his talents especially suited him. Fred was a particularly clever machinist and took over the lumber operation on the ranch. All of the wood used to build the ranch buildings at Ettersburg was milled by Fred right on the ranch. He also helped keep all of the ranch equipment serviced and running. Fred died on 30 July 1938 in Humboldt County, California. Margaret died on 20 September 1952 in Humboldt County, California. They were both buried in the Ettersburg Cemetery in Ettersburg, Humboldt County, California.

viii. Albert Felix, born 27 November 1872 in El Dorado County, California. By the time he was twelve, Albert demonstrated a genius for developing, hybridizing and propagating fruit varieties, especially apples, peaches and strawberries. He was encouraged and supported in this pursuit by his parents, especially his mother, who was reputed to have had a "green thumb." Albert attended public school but never received any formal education in his chosen pursuit. He was almost entirely self-taught. By the end of his teens, he was looking out for a site where he could continue his plant-breeding experiments. On a fishing trip to the Mattole River Valley, he found a section of land above Bear Creek and in 1894 he staked a claim to it. This area along the Pacific coast in the King Range has wet winters and hot summers, and Albert later attributed his success partly to his choice of location. The site where he developed his ranch was subsequently named after him, first as Etter and then as Ettersburg. Albert managed the ranch with three of his brothers, George, Fred, and August, as the firm of Etter Brothers. While Albert focused on plant breeding, his brothers oversaw other kinds of farming, stock raising and lumber operations. In 1940, Albert began a partnership with George Roeding Jr.'s California Nursery Company (CNC) in Fremont with the goal of patenting and then marketing Etter's best apple varieties. CNC introduced six Etter varieties in its 1945 catalog. He also experimented with breeding over a hundred varieties of forage plants, grasses, and clovers. His research showed that some of the large white clovers from southern Europe were suitable for Humboldt County dairy farmers to use for forage because they put on a great deal of growth during the winter. Albert later undertook some experiments with tree nut crops such as English walnuts, chestnuts and filberts. Albert was a member of the California Nurserymen's Association and the American Pomological Society, and he was president of the Ettersburg Farm Center (a branch of the Humboldt County Farm Bureau). He married Katherine Ann McCormick rather late in life after 1920 in California. Catherine was born 26 February 1892 in New Jersey. She was noted in one source as having been a mail order bride. The couple had no children. Albert died on 12 November 1950 and Katherine died on 22 February 1979, both in Humboldt County, California. Albert's agricultural legacy continues to this day. In 1928, Albert donated all of his strawberry research material to the University of California, where his Ettersburg 121 became an ancestor of various commercially important varieties. In the 1970s, apple fancier Ram Fishman visited the remains of the Etter experimental orchard and found over one hundred apple trees still thriving. On many of these trees, multiple test varieties were represented, often by a single grafted branch. Fishman ultimately located about half of Etter's pink-fleshed varieties in the test orchard and in nearby areas, and in 1983 he founded the Greenmantle Nursery to make seven of them available to the public. They were given new names since the old names could not be firmly determined and are marketed under the Rosetta series title.

ix. August Anthony, born 21 February 1875 in California. He went into partnership with his brothers, Fred, George and Albert in the agricultural firm of Etter Brothers. The brothers worked together to carve their operation from unsettled land. Eventually, each brother turned to a line in the operation for which his talents especially suited him. August was primarily involved in raising cattle and horses on the ranch. August never married and has no known issue. August died on 15 December 1960 in Humboldt County, California. He was buried in the St. Mary's Cemetery in Ferndale, Humboldt County, California.

x. Francis Xavier [twin], born 22 July 1878 in Ferndale, Humboldt County, California. He was a rancher and cattleman. He married Dora May Hill on 21 September 1904 in Ferndale, Humboldt County. Dora was the daughter of George Russell Hill and Bertha Jane Roscoe, born 16 October 1882 in Humboldt County, California. The couple had three sons and two daughters. Frank died on 1 March 1952 in Humboldt County, California. He was buried in the St. Mary's Cemetery in Ferndale, Humboldt County, California. Dora died on 28 February 1981 in Petrolia, Humboldt County, California. She was buried in the Roscoe Cemetery in Honeydew, Humboldt County, California.

xi. Louis Simeon [twin], born 22 July 1878 in Ferndale, Humboldt County, California. He was a rancher. Louis never married and has no known issue. Louis died on 21 February 1937 in Humboldt County, California.

xii. Walter Edward, born 20 November 1882 in Ferndale, Humboldt County, California. He married Anna M. McAllister in May 1931 in California. Anna was the daughter of _____ McAllister and Rose _____, born 20 November 1896 in California. Although he was not a member of the Etter Brothers firm, Walter was closely involved in its operation. He was an engineer and mechanic and ran the engines and saws, the blacksmith shop and other machinery on the ranch. He and his wife had no known issue. Walter died on 23 March 1946 in Humboldt County, California.

U.S. residence other than Ste. Genevieve County, Missouri:
Siskiyou County, California, 1850-1854
El Dorado County, California, 1866-1876
Humboldt County, California, 1877-

Land Patents:
Humboldt County, California

Patentee	Issue Date	Cert. No.	Serial No.	Twp	Rng	Sec	Acres
Etter, Albert F.	12 Oct 1900	1469	CACAAA149332	4-S	1-E	12, 7	161.45
Etter, Albert F.	10 Jan 1901	8522	CACAAA149394	4-S	1-E	13	160.00
Etter, August A.	10 Jan 1901	8532	CACAAA149397	4-S	1-E	14	160.00
Etter, August A.	31 Dec 1904	1720	CACAAA149400	4-S	1-E	13	160.00
Etter, Emile J.	10 Jan 1901	8531	CACAAA149362	3-S	1-E	7	160.00
Etter, Emile J.	10 Jan 1901	8536	CACAAA149363	3-S	1-E	5	40.00
Etter, Frank X.	10 Jan 1901	8527	CACAAA149396	4-S	1-E	2, 11	160.00
Etter, Frank X.	12 Dec 1901	8811	CACAAA149398	4-S	1-E	12	40.00
Etter, Frank X.	19 Nov 1906	10392	CACAAA149404	4-S	1-E	12	160.00
Etter, Fredrick J.	9 Apr 1901	8593	CACAAA149365	3-S	1-E	7,8,18	160.00
Etter, Fredrick J.	31 Dec 1904	1721	CACAAA149401	4-S	1-E	13, 14	160.00
Etter, George B.	17 Dec 1900	1483	CACAAA149392	4-S	1-E	12	160.00
Etter, George B.	17 Dec 1900	8526	CACAAA149385	4-S	1-E	2, 3	160.00
Etter, Henry A.	17 Dec 1900	1482	CACAAA149964	4-S	2-E	7	160.00
Etter, Henry J.	10 Jan 1901	8519	CACAAA149966	4-S	2-E	17, 18	160.00
Etter, Henry J.	12 Mar 1903	8539	CACAAA149973	4-S	2-E	7	40.00
Etter, Louis S.	10 Jan 1901	8521	CACAAA149393	4-S	1-E	3	162.12
Etter, Louis S.	19 Nov 1906	10393	CACAAA149405	4-S	1-E	11, 12	160.00

Naturalization:

Name	Declaration	Naturalization	Origin
Etter, Benjamin		3 April 1854 St. Louis Court of Common Pleas	Switzerland

Military:
Served in the U.S. Mexican American War:
3rd Infantry, Private, Company A
    Benjamin Etter enlisted on 23 February 1847 in Chicago, Illinois. He was mustered out 25 July 1848 when his enlistment term expired.

Education: Could read and write
Occupation: [House] Painter / Miner / Farmer
Religious Affiliation: Roman Catholic

Comments:
Benjamin Etter came to the United States as a young man about the mid-1840s. He is said to have settled in Missouri where he farmed for a few years. In 1847, he enlisted in the United States Army during the Mexican American War and served until the hostilities were over. He returned to Missouri for a short time and then went west to Siskiyou County, California where he worked as a miner. Benjamin remained there for four years and then went back east to Chicago, Illinois and then on to Missouri. He had settled in Ste. Genevieve County by late 1854 when he married Wilhelmina Kern. The couple lived with Wilhelmina's parents and Benjamin worked as a farm hand with his father-in-law. About 1866, the family moved back to California, traveling first to Chicago then on to New York City by railroad. From New York, they took a ship to Aspinwall [now Colon], Panama. They crossed the isthmus by rail and then took passage aboard a steamship to Sacramento,

California. Benjamin settled his family in Latrobe, El Dorado County, California where he farmed and mined until March 1876. He then moved his family one last time to Humboldt County, California to a tract of land on the Eel River near what is now the town of Ferndale. He was the first man in Humboldt County to grow lentils and made quite a success of the venture. Wilhelmina was also active in managing a cattle operation, specializing in beef and dairy herds. Benjamin died on 5 November 1889 in Ferndale, Humboldt County, California. After her husband's death, Wilhelmina continued to operate her dairy with the assistance of her son, Walter. Wilhelmina died on 17 January 1913 in Humboldt County, California.

Appendix A

States of the German Confederation, 1815 – 1866

State		Rank	Capital
Austria	*Österreich*	Empire	Vienna
Bavaria	*Bayern*	Kingdom	Munich
Hanover	*Hannover*	Do.	Hanover
Prussia	*Preußen*	Do.	Berlin
Brandenburg			Berlin
Bas Rhin			Cologne
Jülich-Cleves-Berg			Düsseldorf
Pomerania	*Pommern*		Stettin
Saxony	*Sachsen*		Magdeburg
Silesia	*Schlesien*		Breslau
Westphalia	*Westfalen*		Essen
East Prussia (after 1866)	*Ostpreußen*		Königsberg
Posen (after 1866)			Posen
West Prussia (after 1866)	*Westpreußen*		Danzig
Saxony	*Sachsen*	Do.	Dresden
Württemberg		Do.	Stuttgart
Hesse-Cassel		Electorate	Kassel
Baden		Grand Duchy	Karlsruhe
Hesse-Darmstadt		Do.	Darmstadt
Mecklenburg-Schwerin		Do.	Schwerin
Mecklenburg-Strelitz		Do.	New Strelitz
Oldenburg		Do.	Oldenburg
Hesse Homburg		Landgraviate	Homburg
Anhalt Bernburg		Duchy	Bernburg
Anhalt Cothen		Do.	Cothen
Anhalt Dessau		Do.	Dessau
Brunswick	*Braunschweig*	Do.	Brunswick
Holstein-Lauenburg		Do.	Gluckstadt
Luxemburg & Limburg		Do.	Luxemburg
Nassau		Do.	Wiesbaden
Saxe-Altenburg	[Thuringia]	Do.	Altenburg
Saxe-Coburg and Gotha	[Thuringia]	Do.	Gotha
Saxe-Lauenburg	[Thuringia]	Do.	Ratzeburg
Saxe-Meiningen	[Thuringia]	Do.	Meiningen
Saxe-Weimar-Eisenach	[Thuringia]	Do.	Weimar
Hohenzollern Hechingen		Principality	Hechingen
Hohenzollern Sigmaringen		Do.	Sigmaringen
Lichtenstein		Do.	Vaduz
Lippe		Do.	Detmold
Reuss Greitz	[Thuringia]	Do.	Greitz
Reuss Schleitz	[Thuringia]	Do.	Lobenstein
Schaumburg Lippe		Do.	Bückeburg
Schwarzburg Rudolstadt	[Thuringia]	Do.	Rudolstadt
Schwarzburg Sondershausen	[Thuringia]	Do.	Sondershausen
Waldeck		Do.	Arolsen
Lübeck		Free City	
Hamburg		Do.	
Bremen		Do.	
Frankfurt [am Main]		Do.	
Alsace-Lorraine	*Elsass Lothringen*	Imperial Territory [after 1871]	Strasbourg

Appendix B

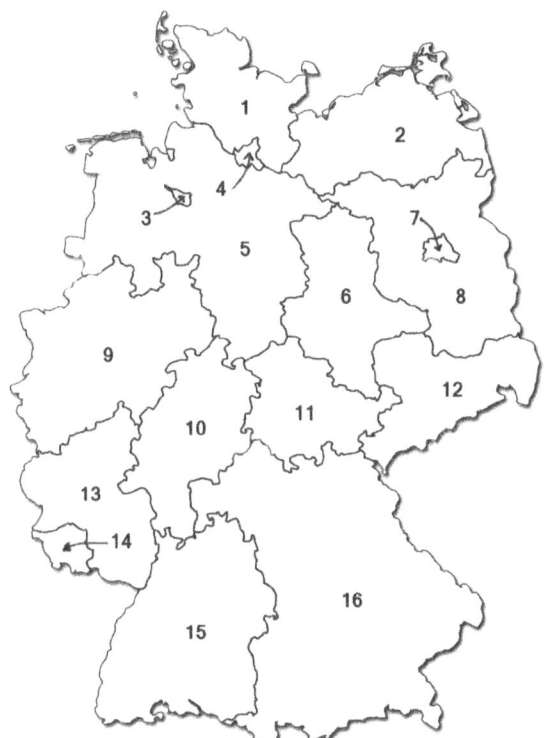

Germany After 1990

State	Capital
1. Scheswig-Holstein	Kiel
2. Mecklenburg-Vorpommern	Schwerin
3. Bremen	Bremen
4. Hamburg	Hamburg
5. Lower Saxony	Hanover
6. Saxony-Anhalt	Magdeburg
7. Berlin	Berlin
8. Brandenburg	Potsdam
9. North Rhine-Westphalia	Düsseldorf
10. Hesse	Wiesbaden
11. Thuringia	Erfurt
12. Saxony	Dresden
13. Rhineland-Palatinate	Mainz
14. Saarland	Saarbrücken
15. Baden-Württemberg	Stuttgart
16. Bavaria	Munich

Appendix C

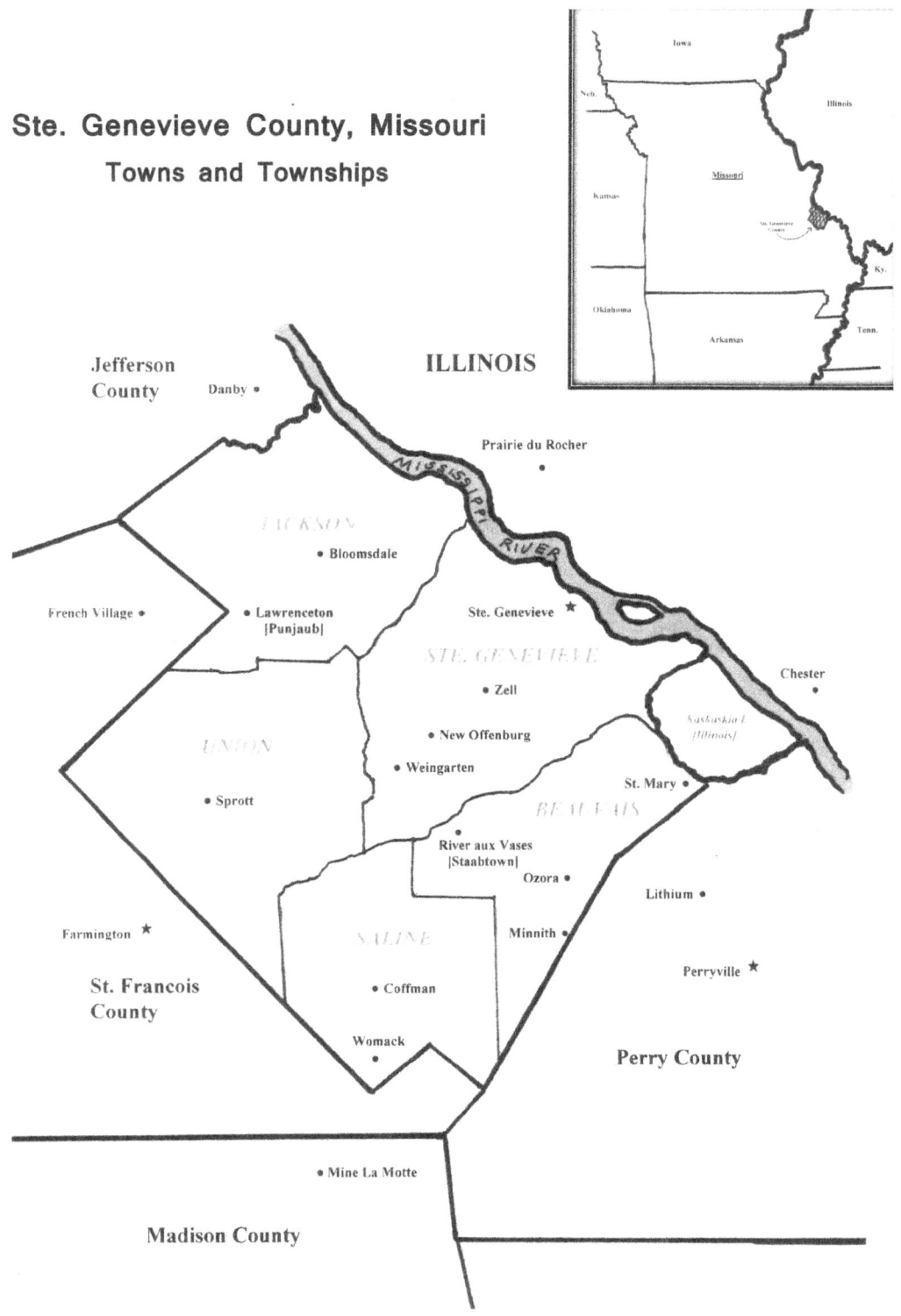

Bibliography

Collections and Papers

Missouri State Archives, Jefferson City, Missouri.
    Ste. Genevieve County Wills, C-6217, C-6218
Missouri State Historical Archives, St. Louis, Missouri.
    Delassus-St. Vrain Family Collection, 1544-2001
State Historical Society of Missouri, Columbia, Missouri.
    Missouri, Ste. Genevieve. Archives, 1756-1930. C-3636
Western Historical Manuscript Collection, University of Missouri – Rolla.
    Lohman, Marcine, transcriber. *Church Register, 1861-1982, Immanuel Evangelical Lutheran Church of Pilot Knob, Missouri.* Folder R383.

Printed Sources

Beckerman, Rob. *Baum Family Tree II*. Ste. Genevieve, Missouri : Rob Beckerman. 1983.
_____. *Ste. Genevieve County Tombstone Inscriptions*, Vols. 1-5, Ste. Genevieve, MO (1021 Market St., Ste. Genevieve 63670) : R. Beckerman, [1982-1984]
Bennion Family of Utah, Volume 2. Salt Lake City, Utah : Bennion Family Association, [1962].
Bernays, Thekla. *Augustus Charles Bernays: A Memoir*. St. Louis : C. V. Mosby Company, 1912.
Boernstein, Heinrich. *Memoirs of a Nobody: The Missouri Years of an Austrian Radical, 1849-1866.* St. Louis : Missouri Historical Society Press, 1997.
Elllinghouse, Cletis R. *Mingo*. Philadelphia, Pennsylvania : Xlibris Corporation. 2008.
Grubb, Farley. *German immigrant Servant Contracts Registered at the Port of Philadelphia, 1817-1831.* Baltimore : Genealogical Publishing Co., Inc. 1994.
Henson, Anna Marie Dieckmann. *St. Clement Parish, Bowling Green, Missouri: Family of Faith, 1871 – 1996*, [Bowling Green, Missouri?] 1996
History of the Archdiocese of Saint Louis. St. Louis, MO : Western Watchman Publishing Co., 1924.
Hombourg Mag, Le Magazine de Votre Ville. "Notre Histoire – Des Hombourgeios en Amerique" L'ueurs et Senteurs d'Avent 2011. No. 12 – Janvier 2012 (French language). Directeur de la publication – Jacques Furlan. Hombourg-Haut, Lorraine, France. p. 18-19
Köbele, Albert and Fritz Schleicher. *Ortssippenbuch Oberweier, Kreis Lahr in Baden*, Selbstverlag des Verfassers : Grafenhausen bei Lahr, Baden [Germany], 1964.
Koerfer, Maria. *Ortsfamilienbuch der katholischen Pfarrgemeinde St. Johannes d. T. Ottersweier, 1641-1940 : mit Neusatz, Waldmatt, Breithurst, Niederhofen und Aspich bis 1783 [Vol. 1, A– K; Vol. 2, L – Z]* / Lahr-Dinglingen : Interessengemeinschaft Badischer Ortssippenbücher, 2009. Vols. 1 & 2.
Missouri. Office of the Secretary of State. *Official Manual of the State of Missouri. 1907-1908.* Jefferson City, Missouri : The Hugh Stephens Printing Co.
Moursund, John Stribling. *Blanco County [Texas] History*. Burnet, Texas : Nortex Press. 1979.
Okenfuss, Dick and Julie Roerkohl Okenfuss. *Okenfuss Family History and Genealogy*. May 1985.
Porter, Carol. S. *Meeting Louis At The Fair: The Projects & Photographs of Louis Clemens Spiering, World's Fair Architect*. St. Louis : Virginia Publishing Co., 2004.
Ries, Johann Georg. *Familienbuch Gamshurst : mit Litzloch, Michelbuch, Ziegelhütte und dem ehemaligen Holzhof*. Lahr, Germany : Interessengemeinschaft Badischer Ortssippenbucher, 2007.
Rozier, Firmin A. *150th Celebration of the Founding of Ste. Genevieve* [St. Louis, MO : G. A. Pierrot & Son, Printers, 1885.]

Schaal-Lustig, Marie Louise. *Niederseebach État-Civil, 1793-1902: Naissances, Mariages, Décès.* (French language) [S.I.] : Atelier Généalogique de l'Arrondissement de Wissembourg et Environs, 2002.

Schmidt, Bob. *Veterans and Events in the Civil War in Southeast Missouri, Volume II.* French Village, MO : B. Schmidt, 2000.

Ste. Genevieve County Family Histories. Ste. Genevieve Historical/Genealogical Society, [S.I. : s.n., 1988?].

Valley of The Upper Maumee River : With Historical Account of Allen County and The City of Fort Wayne, Indiana : The Story of Its Progress From Savagery to Civilization. Vol.1. Madison, Wisconsin : Brant & Fuller, 1889.

Microform Records

Kirchenbuch, 1608-1900, Katholische Kirche Offenburg (A. Offenburg), [includes records from Zell-Weierbach, Ortenberg, Elgersweier, Bohlsbach, Fessenbach, Rammersweier, Durbach, Gengenbach and Walterweier] manuscript (microfilm), German language, Salt Lake City, Utah : Gefilmt durch The Genealogical Society of Utah, 1974. Taufen, Konfirmation, Heiraten, Tote [FHL films 957712-957720; 949950-949955].

Kirchenbuch, 1631-1907, Katholische Kirche Freudenberg, (A. Wertheim), Germany. (manuscript on microfilm), Salt Lake City, Utah : Genealogical Society of Utah, 1975 [FHL films 1044071 – 1044077].

Kirchenbuch, 1642-1899, Katholische Kirche Hofweier (A. Offenburg), manuscript (microfilm), German language, Salt Lake City, Utah : Gefilmt durch The Genealogical Society of Utah, 1974. Familienbuch, 1670-1887 [FHL film 957702].

Kirchenbuch, 1655-1900, Katholische Kirche Durbach (A. Offenburg), manuscript (microfilm), German language, Salt Lake City, Utah : Gefilmt durch The Genealogical Society of Utah, 1973; Taufen, Tote, Heiraten, 1655-1744 [FHL film 949375], Taufen, Tote, Heiraten 1744-1823 [FHL film 949376], Taufen 1805-1860 [FHL film 949377], Taufen 1861-1881 [FHL film 949378], Heiraten 1824-1900 [FHL film 949379] and Tote 1744-1900 [FHL film 949380].

Kirchenbuch, 1656-1900, Katholische Kirche Harthausen a. Scheer (OA. Gammertingen), manuscript (microfilm), German language, Salt Lake City, Utah : Fefilmt durch the Genealogical Society of Utah, 1972. Taufen 1819-1884, Heiraten 1819-1886 [FHL Film 920474].

Kirchenbuch, 1558-1906, Evangelische Kirche Fellbach (OA. Cannstatt), manuscript (microfilm), German language, Salt Lake City, Utah : Gefilmt durch The Genealogical Society of Utah, 1967; Parish register of baptisms, marriage, burials, confirmations, family registers and parish members for Fellbach, Wuerttemberg, Germany. [FHL films 1055978 – 1055983].

Kirchenbuch, 1697-1900, Katholische Kirche Lauf (A. Bühl), Manuscript (microfilm), German language, Salt Lake City, Utah: Gefilmt durch The Genealogical Society of Utah, 1971; Taufen 1812-1853, [FHL film 890563]; Taufen 1854-1900 [FHL film 890564]; Heiraten 1698-1900 [FHL film 890565], Tote, 1748-1832 [FHL film 890566]; Tote, 1833-1861 [FHL film 890567].

Kirchenbuch, 1697-1930, Katholische Kirche Sasbach (A. Achern), Manuscript (microfilm), German language, Salt Lake City, Utah: Gefilmt durch The Genealogical Society of Utah, 1971; Taufen 1782-1803, Tote 1795-1830 [FHL film 865516]; Taufen 1803-1841 [FHL film 865516]; Heiraten 1817-1923 [FHL film 865517].

Kirchenbuch, 1703-1901. Katholische Kirche Ebersweier (A. Offenburg), manuscript (microfilm), German language, Salt Lake City, Utah : Gefilmt durch The Genealogical Society of Utah, 1974; Taufen, Heiraten, Tote, 1704-1901 [FHL films 1054224, 1054225].

Kirchenbuch, 1703-1901, Katholische Kirche Windschläg (A. Offenburg). Manuscript (microfilm), German language, Salt Lake City, Utah : Gefilmt durch The Genealogical Society of Utah; Taufen, Heiraten, Tote 1703-1901 [FHL films 958333, 958334, 1055898, 1055899], Familienbuch 1870 [FHL film 1055900].

Kirchenbuch, 1724-1900, Katholische Kirche Fautenbach (A. Achern), manuscript (microfilm), German language, Salt Lake City, Utah : Gefilmt durch The Genealogical Society of Utah, 1974; Taufen 1724-1833 [FHL film 995503], Taufen 1827-1900 [FHL film 995504], Heiraten 1735-1900, Tote 1735-1762 [FHL film 995505], Tote 1763-1900 [FHL film 958347].

Kirchenbuch, 1787-1889, Katholische Kirche Gengenbach (A. Offenburg), Salt Lake City, Utah : Gefilmt durch the Genealogical Society of Utah, 1972. Taufen 1810-1834 [FHL film 891250], Heiraten 1773-1832 [FHL film 891256]

Kirchenbuch, 1788-1900, Katholische Kirche Ortenberg (A. Offenburg), manuscript (microfilm), German language, Salt Lake City, Utah : Gefilmt durch The Genealogical Society of Utah, 1974, 1976. Taufen, Heiraten, Tote [FHL films 949956-94998]; Familienbuch, 1873 [FHL film 949958, Item 3].

Kirchenbuch, 1790-1900, Katholische Kirche Bohlsbach (A. Offenburg), manuscript (microfilm), German language, Salt Lake City, Utah : Gefilmt durch The Genealogical Society of Utah, 1973. Taufen, Heiraten, [FHL film 957362]; Tote, Familienbuch [FHL film 957363].

Missouri, Ste. Genevieve County – Circuit Court Records, Naturalization (manuscript on microfilm), Salt Lake City, Utah : Filmed by the Genealogical Society of Utah, 1973. [FHL film 1986572, Items 3-7]

Missouri, Ste. Genevieve County – Recorder of Deeds, Marriage Records, 1805-1959 (manuscript on microfilm), Salt Lake City, Utah : Filmed by the Genealogical Society of Utah, 1973. Marriage Books A and B [FHL film 915668], Books C and D [FHL film 915669], Books E – G [FHL film 1986236].

Missouri, Ste. Genevieve County, Bloomsdale and Lawrenceton – Church Records, 1848-1993, Catholic Church. St. Philomena and St. Agnes (Bloomsdale) and St. Lawrence (Lawrenceton) and *Missouri, St. Francois County, French Village – Church Records, 1848-1993,* Catholic Church. St. Anne (manuscript on microfilm), Salt Lake City, Utah : Filmed by the Genealogical Society of Utah, 1994. [FHL films 1939896, 1939897]

Missouri, Ste. Genevieve County, Ozora – Church Records, 1898-1993, Catholic Church. Sacred Heart (Ozora). (manuscript on microfilm), Salt Lake City, Utah : Filmed by the Genealogical Society of Utah, 1994. [FHL film 1939726]

Missouri, Ste. Genevieve County, River aux Vases – Church Records, 1850-1993, Catholic Church. SS. Philip and James (River aux Vases). (manuscript on microfilm), Salt Lake City, Utah : Filmed by the Genealogical Society of Utah, 1994. [FHL films 1939724, 1939725]

Missouri, Ste. Genevieve County, St. Marys – Church Records, 1759-1993, Catholic Church. Immaculate Conception (St. Marys) (manuscript on microfilm), Salt Lake City, Utah : Filmed by the Genealogical Society of Utah, 1994. [FHL film 1939724]

Missouri, Ste. Genevieve County, Ste. Genevieve – Church Records, 1759-1993, Catholic Church of Ste. Genevieve. (manuscript on microfilm), Salt Lake City, Utah : Filmed by the Genealogical Society of Utah, 1994. [FHL films 1939897, 1938898, 1939899, 1939900, 1939901]

Missouri, Ste. Genevieve County, Weingarten – Church Records, 1875-1993, Catholic Church. Our Lady Help of Christians (Weingarten). (manuscript on microfilm), Salt Lake City, Utah : Filmed by the Genealogical Society of Utah, 1994. [FHL film 1939725]

Missouri, Ste. Genevieve County, Zell – Church Records, 1848-1993, Catholic Church. St. Joseph (Zell). (manuscript on microfilm), Salt Lake City, Utah : Filmed by the Genealogical Society of Utah, 1994. [FHL film 1939726]

Newspapers

Alton Evening Telegraph (Alton, Illinois)
Daily Missouri Republican (St. Louis, Missouri)

Iron County Register (Ironton, Missouri)
Montgomery City Standard (Montgomery County, Missouri)
The Morning Oregonian (Portland, Oregon)
Perry County Republican (Perryville, Missouri)
Pocahontas Star Herald (Pocahontas, Arkansas)
Rockdale Messenger (Milam County, Texas)
Rockdale Reporter (Milam County, Texas)
St. Louis Enquirer (St. Louis, Missouri)
St. Louis Globe Democrat (St. Louis, Missouri)
St. Louis Post-Dispatch (St. Louis, Missouri)
St. Louis Republic (St. Louis, Missouri)
Ste. Genevieve Fair Play (Ste. Genevieve, Missouri)
Ste. Genevieve Herald (Ste. Genevieve, Missouri)
Ste. Genevieve Plaindealer (Ste. Genevieve, Missouri)
Southeast Missourian (Cape Girardeau, Missouri)
Southern Cross [Savanah, Georgia, Catholic newspaper]
The Spokesman-Review (Spokane, Washington)
The Fort Scott Tribune (Fort Scott, Kansas)
Weekly Tribune and the Cape County Herald (Cape Girardeau, Missouri)

Online Resources

Archives
Ancestry.com
> http://www.ancestry.com (accessed 1 October 2015)
>> 1890 Oklahoma First Territorial Census
>> Missouri Marriage Records, 1805-2002 [Missouri State Archives]
>> Missouri, Wills and Probate Records, 1766-1988 [Missouri State Archives]
>> St. Louis City Death Records, 1850-1902
>> St. Louis, Missouri Marriages, 1804-1876
>> Texas, Death Certificates, 1903-1982
>> U.S. Bureau of the Census, Census Records 1790-1940
>> U.S. Civil War Pension Files
>> U.S. Customs Service, Passenger Arrival Records, 1820-1948
>> U.S. Social Security Death Index, 1935-2014

Missouri State Archives, Missouri Digital Heritage
> http://www.sos.mo.gov/archives/ (accessed 12 September 2015)
>> Missouri Death Certificates, 1910-1964
>> Soldiers' Records: War of 1812 – World War I

Landesarchiv Baden-Württemberg: Deutsche Digitale Bibliothek
> https://www2.landesarchiv-bw.de/ (accessed 7 April 2015)
>> Mörsch, Baden, Germany – Standesbücher [Birth, Marriage, Death, 1797 – 1869]

Burials
Allen County Public Library, Genealogy Center, Fort Wayne, Indiana
> http://www.genealogycenter.info/otherstates/ (accessed 9 August 2015)
>> Ste. Genevieve County, Missouri Cemetery headstone photographs

Find A Grave
> http://www.findagrave.com/ (accessed 27 September 2015)

National Park Service, Vicksburg National Military Park, Mississippi, Interments
> http://www.nps.gov/vick/historyculture/inter-b.htm (accessed 3 June 2014)

St. Mary's Cemetery listing, Galena, Jo Daviess County, Illinois
   http://jodaviess.illinoisgenweb.org/cemeteries/StMary1.htm (accessed 7 August 2013)

Genealogical Records
FamilySearch, Family History Library, Salt Lake City, Utah
   https://familysearch.org/ (accessed 2 October 2015)

Family Histories
Kaye, Catherine. *William Roth Family Album*
   https://picasaweb.google.com/108577528655430334021/WilhelmRoth18291901 (accessed 8 October 2015)

Land Records
U.S. Bureau of Land Management, General Land Office Records, 1796-1907
   http://www.glorecords.blm.gov/ (accessed 30 September 2015)

Marriages
Allen County, Indiana Marriage Records
   http://vitalrecords.accessgenealogy.com/indiana/allen/page1.htm (accessed 9 June 2014)
Illinois State Archives. Illinois Statewide Marriage Index online
   http://www.ilsos.gov/isavital/marriagesrch.jsp (accessed 13 August 2015)

Newspapers
Chronicling America, Historic American Newspapers, Library of Congress
   http://www.chroniclingamerica.loc.gov (accessed 8 October 2015)
      Ste. Genevieve *Fair Play*

Obituaries
Mackley Genealogy, Obituaries [primarily St. Francois and Ste. Genevieve Counties]
   http://www.mackleygenealogy.com/ (accessed 8 October 2015)
Suntimes Obits, Ste. Genevieve, Missouri
   http://www.suntimesnews.com/stegen/obits/index.htm (accessed 2 February 2015)

Index of Names

——
- Anna 164
- Anna Maria 230
- Barbara 87, 280, 282
- Caroline 133
- Catherine 205, 261
- Celeste 234
- Dora 40
- Edith 107
- Elisabeth 23, 24, 53, 54, 241
- Elise 23
- Elizabeth 89, 232
- Elizabeth May 62
- Emma 89
- Esther 166
- Euphrosine 223
- Eva 166, 168
- Frances 72
- Franziska 254
- Lucille 129
- Magdalena 231
- Maizie D. 228
- Margaret 189, 232
- Maria 266
- Maria A. 203
- Maria Ann 18
- Martha 232
- Mary 81, 241
- Regina 265
- Rose 283
- Sarah Ada 280
- Susan 213
- Theresia 47
- Tiney 138

Able
- Francisca 35

Abt
- Agatha 1
- Alphonse Paul 3
- Andreas 1
- Anton Austin 2
- Child 2
- Clara A. 1
- Engelbert 1
- Gerald Francis 3
- Jacob 1
- Joseph C. 1
- Joseph Charles 2
- Margaret Catherine 2
- Maria Hedwig 2
- Paul 1, 3
- Peter John 2

Ackerman
- Wilhelmina 186

Adams
- Andrew 280

Adelmann
- Amelia 96, 97

Akers
- Mary 63

Albrecht
- Theresia 267

Albright
- Henrietta 101

Alexandre
- Mary L. 117

Allen
- John P. 164, 165
- Maria .... *See* Maria Katherina Guschwa
- Nola 280

Allerding
- Catherine 140

Alley
- Susan Day 23

Allgeier
- Agatha 3
- Anton 4
- Francisca 4
- Franz Carl 4
- Franz Ignatius 4
- Johann Evangelist 4
- Joseph .... 4, 173, *See* Joseph Allgire
- Lorenz 3
- Maria Barbara 4
- Regina 173
- Stephen 4

Allgire
- Bernard 5
- Elisabeth 5

    John 5
    Joseph 3, 4, 5, 6
    Mary 5
Ams
    Maria Elisabetha 11
Amsler
    Baby boy 7
    John 6, 7
    Josephine G. 7
    Lorena Caroline 7
    Mary Louise 6
    William John 6
Anderson
    Andreas 8
    Andreas A. 8, 102
    Andrew 8, 103
    Brooks 61
    Mary Anna 60
André
    Jean Jacques Louis 96
    Maurice 96
Anstedt
    Johanna 72
Anti
    Adelheide 264, 265
    Jacob 264
Armbruster
    Amelia 17
    Andreas 9, 10, 11, 66, 70, 126, 247
    Andrew 10
    Anna Catherine 172
    Anthony 17
    Bernard 9, 11, 12, 66
    Bernhard 12
    Caroline 12
    Catharina 253
    Catherine 9, 10, 13, 52, 66, 120, 172, 237
    Catherine Theresa 12
    Charles William 17
    Elisabeth 12, 39, 40
    Euphrosine 11
    Franz Michael 9
    Franz Xavier 16
    Georg 16
    Gottfried 15
    Gottfried Boniface 15
    Helena 12
    Henry 14, 16, 268

    Ignatius 10, 13, 50
    Ignatius [aka Nicholas] 13
    Ignatz 9, 11, 39, 70
    Johann Baptist 16
    Johanna 15
    John 14, 110
    Joseph 9, 13, 14, 15, 16, 18, 110, 268
    Josephine 10
    Louis 16, 17, 18
    Louisa 12, 50
    Ludwig 10, 15, 16, 18, 255, 269
    Maria Anna 9
    Mary 14
    Mary Theresia 13
    Mathias 11, 172
    Melchior 15
    Nicholas 14
    Philippine 14
    Rosine 17
    Theresia 15
    Wilhelm Michael 10
    Wilhelmina 17, 255
    William 14
Arnold
    Cornelius 19, 50
    Franz Joseph 18
    Henry Francis 19
    John Michael 19, 50
    Joseph 18, 19
    Joseph Anton 18
    Maria Anna [aka Nancy] 19
    Maria Antoinette 18, 49
    Michael 18, 20, 49, 50
    Sophia 18
Arth
    Martin 213
Asher
    Jacob 5
Aubuchon
    Alice M. 14
    Leo 14
Auer
    Anna 21
    Elisabeth Helen 21
    Georg 21
    Ignatius 21, 22
    John Nicholas 21
    Mary 21

Theresa 21
Baader
  Johann Baptist 28, 30
Bach
  Frances 23
  Johann 23, 24, 142
  John 23, 24
  Sophia Fredricka 23, 142
  Theodore C. 24
Bachle
  Anthony August 26
  August 25, 27
  Augustus 25, 35, 93
  Lawrence Alexander 27
Bächlé
  Conrad 25, 34, 35, 93
Bachs
  Gottlieb 224
Backs
  Dorothea E. .... See Dorothea E. Menschieus
Bader
  Anna Mary 33
  Anton 32
  August Edwin 33
  Caroline 28, 30, 31, 145
  Charles Joseph 33
  Crescentia 28
  Friedrich 28
  Jessie Josephine 33
  John Baptist 28
  Joseph 28, 30, 31, 32, 34, 79, 114, 145, 208
  Joseph M. 29, 208
  Josepha 28
  Jules Vincent 33
  Karl 28
  Laura Blanche 2, 28
  Ludwig 28, 30, 31, 79
  Magdalena 32
  Mary Caroline 29
  Mary Helen Regina 34
  Maximilian 30, 32, 34, 145
  Maximilian Joseph 29
  Oliver John 33
  Susan Elisabeth 33
  Theresia 32, 145, 147
  Viktoria 32
  Wilhelm 28
  William Frederick 32

William Leo 29
Baechle
  Adeline Helen 35
  Anselm 94
  August 26
  Bernard George 26
  Catherine 178
  Conrad 26
  Conrad August 35
  Emma K. 36
  Francis Joseph 25
  Francisca Catherine 35
  Henry 35
  Johanna Philomena 26
  Joseph 25, 34, 35, 36
  Maria Magdalena 25
  Mary Louise 26, 35
  Regina R. 26
  Rosine Magdalena 35
  William Joseph 35
Baechlé
  Anselm .... 25, *See* Anselm Begley
  Anthony August ..... *See* Anthony August Bachle
  Augustus .... 25, 26, 27, *See* Augustus Bachle
  Catherine 25
  Elisabeth 25
  Helena 25
  Joseph 25, 36
  Lawrence Alexander *See* Lawrence Alexander Bachle
Baechle?
  Bernard 118
Baelzer
  Maria Victoria 209, 210
Bahr
  Adelheid 263
  Agatha 38
  Barthololmew 210
  Bartholomew 37
  Cecilia 38
  Charles Joseph 2
  Frances Carolyn 142
  Franciska 38
  Franziska 37
  Friedrich 37
  Helena Agnes 2
  Jakob 263
  Johann Nepomuk 38

Klara 37
Lorenz 38
Maria Theresia 210
Martin 37, 38, 39, 142
Mathias 38
Sophia 180
Sophia Mary 245
Bailey
   John V. 282
   Margaret Ellilian 282
Baird
   Elizabeth 93
Ball
   Anton 74
   Maria Eva 74
Bamberger
   John 241
   Philip 241
Bangelmann
   Heinrich Andreas 23
   Wilhelmina 24
   Wilhelmina Theresia 23, 142
Bantz
   Anna Mary Magdalena 40
   Benedict 12, 39, 40
   Catherine Euphrosine 39
   Francis Henry 39
   M. 47
   Susanna 47, 48
Barnett
   Sarah Jane 186
Barnum
   _____ 63
   George Henry 63
Bartels
   August Frederick 41
   Charles Robert 41
   Frederick 40, 42
   Johann Frederick 40
   John Frederick 41
Barth
   Josephine 67
Bartlett
   Milo R. 203
   William 203
Baschob
   Johann 4
   Mary 4
Basher

Sarah Jane 137
Basler
   Agatha 53, 54
   Andreas 52
   Andrew 55, 229
   Anna Maria 45
   Bernhard 53
   Caroline 56
   Catharina 196
   Catherine 45
   Cornelius 53, 55
   Crescentia 85
   Delia .... 14, *See* Odelia Bieser
   Elisabeth 47
   Euphrosina 43
   Fabian 45
   Francis 48
   Francis Xavier 158
   Francisca 68, 254
   Franz Michael 53, 55
   Franziska 43, 46, 52, 149, 150
   Genevieve 53
   Georg 54
   George 56
   George Philip 47
   Gottfried 19, 49
   Helena 51, 207
   Henry 55, 56
   Henry Jacob 271
   Isidor 52
   Isidore 50
   Jacob 42, 43, 44, 45, 149
   Johann Baptist 43, 44, 45, 46, 48, 149
   Johann Georg 51, 179
   Johanna 43, 197
   John 56
   John Baptist 43
   Joseph43, 44, 47, 48, 49, 51, 52, 54, 56, 229, 271, 272
   Juliana 45
   Katharina 42
   Katherine 47
   Louise Ursula 57
   Maria Anna 42, 54, 254
   Maria Antonia 47
   Maria Eva 14
   Maria Victoria 42
   Mary Ann 47

Michael 43
Nicholas 47
Norbert 46
Pancratius 43
Peter 12, 13, 14, 19, 43, 48, 49, 51, 197
Regina 44, 45
Roberta Agnes 158
Sebastian 42, 44, 48, 149
Severin 12, 50
Simon 52
Sophia 19, 50, 54
Sophia [aka Josephine] 56
Theresa 49
Theresia 43, 51
Ursula 53
Valentin 51, 52, 53, 68, 179
Valentine 53, 54, 55, 57, 229
Veronica 52
Veronica Theresa 272
Wilhelm 54, 55, 56, 57
Wilhelmina 19, 50
William 54, 55
William V. 54
Bassler
   John 57, 58
Basso
   Elisabeth 110
Bauer
   Andrew F. 59
   Barbara 59
   Charles Lawrence 60
   Elizabeth 59
   Emile William 60
   George 58, 61
   George A. B. 58
   George H. 60
   Henry B. 59
   John Peter 60
   Katharina 60
   Magdalena 58
   Margarethe Mary 59
   Maria Anna 68
   Mary Agnes 60
   Michael John 59
Baum
   Alma Josephine 65
   Anna Caroline 63
   Anthony Christian 62
   Charles Albert 62
   Christian 61, 63, 65
   Frieda Gertrude 64
   Genevieve Catherine 63
   George Francis 63
   Hedwig Olympia Maria 63
   Henry 62
   Hilda Helen 64
   Johann Kaspar 61
   John Francis Xavier 64
   Louisa Anna 62
   Mary Odelia 63
   Odelia Estella 64
   Oliver Louis 64
   Robert Joseph 65
   Walter Joseph 64
Baumann
   Amelia 71, 264
   Andreas 52, 59, 67
   Anna Elisabeth 132
   Anton 67, 69
   Bernard 67, 253, 254
   Brigitta 68, 120, 121
   Catharina 66
   Catherine 109, 244
   Dora Theresa 159
   Francis Anthony 146
   Francis Xavier 69
   Francisca 66
   Franz Anton 9, 52, 66, 70, 120, 237, 253
   Gustav 146
   Johanna 68
   Johannes 66
   John 68
   John B. 68
   Joseph 66, 69
   Joseph F. 132
   Leona Louise 132
   Leonard 67, 109, 112, 131
   Leonhard 9, 66
   Louisa 68
   Louisa Frances 131
   Louise 59
   Maria Anna 66
   Maria Magdalena 66
   Mary Anna 156
   Nicholas 132
   Paulina 71

    Peter 70, 71
    Victoria 71
    William 68, 146, 237
    William S. 112
Baumer
    Magdalena 231
Baumgartner
    Anna C. 72
    Anton 72
    Augustus 72
    Clara Therese 72
    Eva 73
    Henry John 72
    Johann 71, 73
    John Henry 72
    Lena 72
    Sophia M. 73
    Ursuala 72
    William 72
Baumstark
    Ameliana 74
    Anna Helena 77
    Anton 74
    Augusta Maria Theresa 76
    Augustin 74
    Boniface 73, 76
    Emile Valentine 74
    Eulalia Margaret 77
    Frank 75, 76
    Franz 73, 74
    Genevieve Lorina 75
    Herbert Friedrich 75
    Irene Catherine 75
    Ludwig 74
    Marie Antoinette 76
    Mary Theresa 74
    Olivia Theresa 77
    Thomas 74
    Wilhelm 74, 76, 77
    William 74, 75, 76, 77, 78
Baurentischel
    Anastasia 245
Bayer
    Amand 78
    Charles 79, 124
    Edward 124
    Fridolin Mathias 79
    Margarette 31, 79

    Philippine 160
    Simon 78
    Valentine 79
    Vincent 31, 78, 79, 80, 151, 152
    William 146
Beauchamp
    Anna Nora 226
    Michael Andrew 64
    Thomas 226
    Tossie Mary 64
Bebion
    Anna Elisabetha 81
    Anna Louisa 80
    Euphrosine Caroline 81
    Georg Friederich 81
    Gottlob 80, 81, 82
    Johann Georg 81
    Johann Michael 81
    Johanna Friedericka 81
    Michael 80
Bechtold
    Andreas 82
    Barbara 82
    Bernard 82, 84, 275
    Clara Barbara 83
    Dominic 276
    Dominicus 83
    Johann Andreas 83
    Johann Bernard 82, 83
    Johann Nicholas 83
    Johann Sebastian 83
    Maria Elisabetha 83
    Maria Theresa 275
    Maria Theresia 83
    Thecla 83
Beck
    Ameilia 85
    Anselm 84
    Anton 85
    Apollonia 84
    Bonifaz 84
    Elisabeth 85
    Franz Anton 84
    Georg 85
    George 84, 85, 86
    Joseph 85
    Juliana 86
    Karl 85

Liborius 85
Margaret 212
Maria Magdalena 86
Mathias 85
Ottilia 85
Rosina 86
Sophia 86

Beckemeyer
Carl 87
Charles F. 88
Edward August 88
George Philipl 89
Heinrich 87
James Aral 89
John W. 88
Margaret Theresa 88
Martin Luther 88
Mary Elizabeth 88
Mary Ella Sarah 89
Richard Franklin 88
Robert Samuel 89
Rose Annl 89
Val 89
Wilhelm 87, 90
William 87, 89

Beckermann
Antoinette Sophia 92
Emma Clothilde 91
George 90, 91, 92
George Edward 92
Henrietta Catherine 91
Henry 92
Hermann 90, 92, 93
Johann Heinrich 90, 92
John Nicholas 91
Louise 92
Margaret 90
William 90
William Henry 91

Beckman
Gottfried 231

Beckmann
Chris 231

Begley
Anselm 25, 93, 94
Child 93
George 93
Theresa 93

Behrle
Theresia 267

Belbeau
Marie Louise 201

Belieu
Mary 5

Belken
Caspar 98
Elizabeth Catherine 98

Bell
James William 234
Josiah 234
Lucinda 202

Bellisime
Charles 87
Mary A. 87, 90

Benham
Mary 170

Bennett
Hattie A. 129

Benz
Agatha 12, 39
Benedict 39
Felix 39
Florian 12, 39
Georg 39
Kreszentia 39
Maria Anna 54
Walburga Apollonia 25, 34

Bequette
August 245
Augustine 181, 240
Felix Isreal 240
Josephine Emily 245
Julia Celeste 261
Mary 226
Mary Clara 181

Berberich
George 232
Lee 232

Berger
Genovefa 177
John 36
Wilhelmina 36

Berke
Salome 57

Berkemeier
Anna Maria 131

Bernays

Adolphus 97
Amalia Mathilde 96
Anna Cecilia 97
Clemens 94
Clementine 96
Francis J. 97
Franz Jacob 94, 95, 96, 97
Friedrich Bernard 95
Helen 96
Helen Genevieve 97
Jacob 97
Johann Georg 95
Karl Ludwig 95
Martha 97
Michael 95
Son 95

Berninger
Maria Eva 149

Berry
Martha Ann 139
Mary Genevieve 64

Bertrand
Louisa 96

Betten
Christoph 98
Christopher F. 98
Clara Ernestina 99
Elizabeth 99
Emma Louise 99
Francis J. 99
Johann 98, 100
Johannes Christoph 98
John 98, 100
Joseph 99
Maria Anna 98, 99
Maria Catherina 98

Beule
Maria 98

Biel
Carl Heinrich 101
Charles Henry 8, 9, 100, 102, 103
Frances A. 101
Jennie Ruth 101
Minnie Ida 101
Wilhelm 100
William 102

Bieser
Anastasia 103

Andrew 107
Anthony 105
Anton 103, 104, 106, 109
August 106, 107, 110, 114
Bartholomew 103, 109, 244
Bernard 112
Bernhard 108, 109
Carolina 103
Caroline 109, 115
Catherine 110
Cecilia 103
Charles Joseph 107
Charles Michael 114
Charles Paul 105
Child 105
Edward Henry 105
Elisabeth Maria 111
Elizabeth 107
Ellen 104
Emma 114, 175
Ferdinand 104, 106
Francis William 105
Georg 106, 110, 111, 113, 114
George Joseph 111
Helena 103, 108, 109
Jacob 108, 109, 111
Johann Baptist 103
Johann Evangelist 109
John 107
Joseph 14, 49, 104, 106, 108, 110, 111, 112, 113, 153
Katharina 112
Katherine Josephine 105
Louisa 104
Louise 112
Magdalena 108
Maria Anna 103, 104, 109
Maria J. 111
Maria Theresa 105
Mathias 112
Michael 106, 107, 111, 113, 114, 115
Monica 108
Odelia 14, 49, 110
Philip August 110
Richardis 103
Rosina 103
Rosina Caroline 105
Sabina 103

Sophia	104, 235
Sophia Caroline	110
Theresia	104, 112, 153, 154, 244
Ursula	109, 257
Valentine	112
Victoria	103
Wendolin George	107
Wilhelm	108
Willam M.	114
William	31, 107

Biggs
- Lucinda Adaline ... 137
- Nettie ... 137
- William ... 137

Billy
- Delma Rose ... 31
- Joshua ... 31

Binder
- _____ ... 189

Bircher
- Samuel ... 212

Birsner
- August John ... 77
- John Nepomuk ... 77

Bisch
- Albert ... 115, 116, 118
- Andreas ... 115
- Charles ... 117
- Henry ... 117
- Maria Anna ... 115
- Mary Ann ... 116
- Theodore ... 116

Biser
- Catharina ... 43, 148
- Franz Anton ... 103
- Johannes Georg ... 108, 111

Bishop
- Mary Emma ... 202

Bleckler
- Gerald Joseph Martin ... 119
- Henry Dudley ... 119
- Joseph Edgar ... 119
- Martin B. ... 118, 119, 120
- Mary Myrtle ... 119
- Russel Francis Benedict ... 119

Bleifuss
- Mary Louise ... 121
- Mathaus ... 68, 120, 121

- Michael ... 68, 120, 121

Blessing
- Agatha ... 249

Bliler
- Emereuth ... 140
- Margaret M. ... 140

Bloom
- Catherine ... 5
- Elizabeth ... 194
- Peter ... 196

Bloss
- George ... 33
- Helen A. ... 33

Bockenkamp
- August Gustav ... 123
- Bertha ... 123
- Blanche Agnes ... 124
- Caroline ... 122
- Edwin ... 123
- Elizabeth Jane ... *See* Elizabeth Jane Reed
- Elva Leona ... 123
- Emma ... 122
- Georgiana Edith ... 124
- Gustave ... 122
- Helena ... 121
- Henry Julius ... 123
- Herman ... 121, 176
- Herman Frederick ... 121, 122
- Irene Virgie ... 124
- Jessie Ellen ... 123
- Julius ... 121, 124
- Leonard ... 123
- Mary Bertha ... 121
- Richard J. ... 122, 176, 177
- Wilhelmina ... 121, 123

Bockers
- Henry B. ... 7

Bodner
- Lydia ... 175, 177

Boehle
- Agnes ... 125
- Anna Maria ... 125
- Balbina ... 126
- Elisabetha ... 125
- Francisca ... 125
- Franz ... 126
- Johann ... 10, 125
- Joseph ... 126

Lucas 10, 125, 127
Mathais 125
Michael 126
Paul 126
Regina 126
Boernstein
Heinrich 95
Bogy
John L. 34
Leon 23
Bohise
John 71
Böhle
Martin 125
Bohn
Agnes 191
Bohnert
Elisabetha 237
Boileau
Etienne 223
Maria Theresa 222
Bolle
Augusta Elisabeth 129
Bertha Alvina Alma 129
Felix Frederick 129
Flora Eleonora 128
Frederick 127, 130
Frederick G. A. 128
George Henry 128
Heinrich Christoph 127
Herman Thomas 129
Nicholas Frederick 128
Bonarens
Anna Margaretha 130
Franz Ignatius 130
Gerhard Herman 130
Johann Bernard 131
Johann Franz 131
Johann Heinrich 131
Maria Adelheid 130, 131
Maria Elisabeth 130
Martin 130
Bonnarens
Bernard John 132
Edward Bernhard 132
Frank 131
Johann Franz 130, 131, 133
John Henry 132

John Herman 132
Joseph Nicolaus 132
Martin Herman 132
Mary Anna 132
Theodore George 131
Bönniger
Balthasar 175
Boos
Ambrose 133, 134
August 133
Emilia 134
Frances A. 60
Franz Xavier 133, 134
George 60
Infant 134
Joseph 133, 134
Mary Josephine 134
Botz
Franz Jacob 134, 135, 136
Johanna Christine 135
Boussert
Marguerite 207, 208
Boverie
John 259
Bowling
Margaret 61
Bowman
Frank J. 232
Boyer
Celeste 162
Eli P. 62
George Francis 89
Hattie 89
Mary Alice 62
Solomon C. 89
Theodule Cyprian 89
Braching
Walburga 112, 153
Brackenbusch
Charles 147
Bradfield
Charles R. 88
Robert Theodore 88
Brandel
Ann Myrtle 138
Anton 136
August 137
George Bernard 138

Heinrich	136, 137, 139
John Henry	138
Joseph	136
Joseph Andrew	137
Josephine	122
Katharina	136
Louisa	136, 137
Maria Anna	136
Mary Louisa	138
Matilda Elizabeth	138
Philipp	136
Richard	138
Rowena	138

Brands
Albert Lorenzo	140
Catharina Margaretha	130
Franklin Wolcott	139
Harmony	139, 141
Harmony Thomas	139
Peter Herman	140

Brandt
Adam	26
Charles E.	26

Bransch
Franz	110
Maria Anna	14, 49, 110, 111

Braun
Andreas	43
Andrew	142
Angelina Paulina	144
Anna Catherine	255
Anton	148, 254, 255
Bernard	24, 141, 143, 144, 156
Bernhard	148
Catharina	141
Catherina	279, 280
Catherine	142, 151, 156, 157
Catherine Ursula	147
Child	151
Christina	141, 142
Elizabeth	151
Emma	145
Francis Charles	144
Francis Ignatius	142
Francis Xavier	146
Franz Anton	141, 143, 144, 167
Franz Ignatius	23, 141, 143
Franz Joseph	32, 144
Franziska	148
Georg	144
George	32, 34, 144, 145, 146, 147
Gertrud	148
Hedwig	145
Henry George	147
Ignaz	141
Infant	144
Johann	43, 150
Johann Martin	43, 148
Johann Nepomuk	43, 46, 148, 150, 254
John	152, 197, 198
Joseph	141, 145
Joseph Henry	142
Josephine	145, 147
Karl	148
Karolina	144
Kunigunda	150
Louisa Maria	151
Maria	151
Maria Anna	38, 43, 141, 148
Maria Magdalena	45, 149
Martin	79, 150, 151, 152
Mary Ann	142, 146, 181, 182
Mary Elisabeth	144, 167
Mary Magdalena	255
Mary Theresia	144
Maximillian Anthony Sylvester	147
Michael	148
Moritz	181
Regina	141, 144, 145
Regina Euphemia	144
Salome	3
Silvester	149
Sophia	151
Sylvester	254
Theresa	146
Valentin Constantin	149
Valentine	151
Victoria	149
Victoria	151
Victoria Rosine	146
Viktoria	148
Wendelin	151
William	142, 255
Xavier Bernard	142

Breckle
Anna Catherine	153

August William 154
  Bernard 153
  Child 154
  Elisabeth 153
  Francis 112, 153
  Frank 153
  Joseph Henry 154
  Louise 154
  Maria Magdalena 153
  Sophia 153
Breig
  Agatha 155
  August Lorenz 158
  Augustine 155
  Cecilia 67, 155, 253
  Clara 157
  Clara Genevieve 157
  Edward 157
  Edward Laurence 157
  Elizabeth Bridget 156
  Emily Louisa 156, 279
  Emma Catherine 159
  Francis Joseph 158
  George William 158
  Henry Joseph 156
  John Augustin 156, 280
  Joseph 142, 155, 156, 157, 279, 280
  Joseph Xavier 158
  Josephine Catherine 156
  Josephine Cecilia 159
  Karolina 155
  Katharina 155
  Leonard 155
  Leonard Edgar 159
  Ludwig 155
  Magdalena 155
  Mary Magdalena 156, 158
  Michael 155, 157
  Michael Joseph 142
  Rosa 159
  Stephan 155
  Wilhelm 157, 158, 159
  William 155, 157
  William Matthew 157
Brichle
  Francis 112, 153, 154
  Franz Xavier 153
Brinkmann

  Ernst Heinrich 278
Brischle
  Clara 160
  Ignatius 160, 161
  Joseph 161
  Linus 160
  Magdalena 160
  Maria Johanna 159, 243
  Sophia 160, 161
  Theresa 160
  Theresia 264
  Veronica 160
  Victoria 126, 160
  Vincent 159, 160, 161
Broclin
  Anna Maria 250
Bross
  Agatha 125
  Amandus 161
  Anna Christina Catherine 163
  Benedict 161, 162, 164
  Benedict Xavier 163
  Catherine Victoria Felicity 163
  Dominicus 162
  Eleanora 162
  Francis Joseph 162
  Franz Joseph 161
  Johannes Chrysostomus 161
  Joseph 162
  Josephine Emily 162
  Maria Anna 162
  Maria Barbara 162
  Maria Rosalie 162
  Priscilla Margaretha 162
Brown
  Lila Anna 59
  Mariah Ann 138
  William 59
Bruederlie
  Amalie 16
  Martin 16
Bruegger
  Katharina 212
Brueschle
  Caspar 159
Bruesselbach
  Rudolph W. 225
Brunner

Amalia 173
　　Felix 173
Bruns
　　Anna Margaretha 131
Bube
　　Adam 164, 165
　　Adam Johann Gottfried 164
　　Caroline 165
　　Catherine Elizabeth 165
　　Emma 164
　　Henry 164
　　Mary Johanna 165
　　Mary Theresa 165
　　Peter Joseph 165
Bucher
　　Maria 210
Buchholtz
　　Catherine 166
　　Charles 144, 167
　　Franciska 167
　　Franz Wendelin166, 168, *See* Frank Wallace
　　　　Buckholt
　　George 167
　　Joseph 167
　　Lawrence 168
　　Mary Philippine 167
　　Moritz 166
　　Morris 144, 166, 168
　　Peter 167
　　Sophia Catherine 167
Buckholt
　　Frank Wallace 166
Buehler
　　Adelgunde 174
　　Alois 173
　　Anton 168
　　Arnold Willibald 169
　　Charles A. 169
　　Charles Francis 172
　　Eduard 169
　　Edward 170
　　Emily Sophia 170
　　Francis Charles 168, 171
　　Franz Karl 169, 170
　　Henry Herman 171
　　Herman 169, 170, 171, 172, 238
　　Ignaz 173
　　Johann 230

　　John George 172
　　Joseph 168, 169, 173, 174, 175
　　Josephine 169
　　Julius 170
　　Katharina 174
　　Kornelius 173
　　Leonard 230
　　Leopold 168, 174
　　Louisa 171
　　Louise 238
　　Louise Wilhelmina Mary 174
　　Maria Anna 173
　　Mary 170
　　Mary Ann Elisabeth 172
　　Mary Louise Catherine 174
　　Nikolaus 173
　　Pauline 171
　　Pauline Amelia 170
　　Pauline Elisabeth 169
　　Philomena Josephine 172
　　Rosina 171
　　Stillborn Child 174
　　Theresia 174
　　Viktor 173
　　William 169
　　William E. 169, 170
Buenniger
　　Adam 122, 175, 176, 177
　　Balthasar 177
　　Christian John 175
　　Edward Adam 176
　　Elsabeth 175
　　Garfield 176
　　Hobart George 176
　　Lydia E. 176
　　Mary 175
Bühler
　　Georg 168, 171
　　Joseph 173
Buhlinger
　　Charles 105
　　Cyriac 105
Bürck
　　Franziska 112
Burgert
　　Andreas 179
　　Anna Maria 184
　　Balbina 183, 192, 194

Bartholomaus 177
Bartholomew 1, 2, 177, 179
Bertinus 180
Charles 181
Charles B. 178
Evariste 181
Frances Philomena 1, 3
Francis Charles 181
Francis Joseph 184
Franziska 163
Genovefa 179, 180
Gustav 178
Infant 183
Jacob 183
Johannes 179
Joseph 1, 2, 52, 177, 178, 179, 181
Karl 52, 53, 179, 180, 181, 182
Ludwig 183
Magdalena 179
Maria Anna 180
Maria Apollonia 183
Maria Elizabeth 183
Mary Ann 181
Mary Josepha 2, 3
Mary Josephine 181, 184
Mary Louisa 184
Mary Magdalena 181
Mathias 180
Michael 182, 192
Monica Barbara 184
Paul 179
Pauline Catherine Theresa 181
Rosalie 181
Simon 182, 183, 184, 185, 191, 192, 199
Sophia 178, 179, 244
Theresa 183
Theresia 52, 53, 68, 179, 181
Ursula 183, 191
Burgess
Elza B. 101
Gilliam Washington 101
Burkart
Alice Cecilia 189
Aloisia 188
Anton 188
Barbara 185
Caroline 186
Clementine 185

Cornel 188
Cornelius Xavier 189
Crispin 188
Felix 186
Franziska 188
George Aloisius 189
George Anthony 189
Gregor 185, 188, 190
Jacob 185
Joseph 185
Josephine Mary 187
Julia L. 186
Katharina 185, 188
Katherine Philomena 186
Leo Joseph 189
Ludwig 185
Magdalena 188
Maria Luisa 185
Maria Magdalena 189
Mary Louise 189
Mary Theresa 187
Odile Genevieve 189
Peter Paul Aloysius 186
Regina 186
Theresa 186
Ulrich 188, 190
Burkdorf
Dora 186
Burke
Charles A. 186
Burlbaw
Adeline 104
Katherine Barbara 105
Nicholas 104, 105
Burle
Agnes 190
Alexander 183, 190, 191, 192
Child 193
Emma Ann Louise 193
Johann 192
Johann Baptist 190
John 183, 191
Joseph 183, 190, 192
Joseph A. 193
Jules Henry Louis 193
Louis 183
Ludwig 183, 190, 192, 194
Maria Eva 190

Mary Caroline 193
Rosa 190
Theresa Apollonia 193
Wilhelm 190
William 191
Burleigh
Harry F. 122
Burley
Samuel W. 122
Burmann
Regina Elisabeth 128
Burtcher
Bartholomew 194, 196
Bolemus August 195
Margaret Catherine 195
Michael 194, 195, 196
Sebastian 194, 196
Busam
Andreas 199
Anton 198
Bartholomäus 198
Benedikt 196
Bernhard 196, 197
Caecilia 196
Carolina 199
Caroline 105
Elisabeth 196, 198
Euphrosina 196
Franz Michael 196
Friedrich 199
Genovefa 199
George 197
Helena 197
Hieronimus 196
Johann Evangelist Karl 177
Joseph 196, 198
Karl 199
Katharina 198
Lorenz 198
Luitgard 199
Maria Magdalena 198
Michael 47, 184, 197, 198, 199
Monica 197
Rosa 199
Severin 184, 185, 199
Simon 199
Sophia 197
Theresia 197

Valentin 198
Victoria 177, 179
Viktoria 199
Bush
Wilhelmina 91
Buss
Peter 103
Xavier 103
Butcher
Thomas 272
William H. 272
Buyatte
Louise 5
Byington
James 87
Rachel 87, 90
Cagle
Elizabeth 187
Caho
William J. 279
Caine
Eva 189
Caldwell
Eliza Jane 282
Cambron
Christina Mary 156
Curby Bernard 280
Nelma E. 280
Cameron
George W. 202
Jessie O. 202
Carr
Charles S. 189
Clyde McCann 189
Carron
Amos Cleophus 214
Ida Agnes 88
Joseph Charles 214
Josephine 88
Marie Ida 158
Marie Louise 181, 240, 245
Mary Louise 89
Nora E. 14
Theodore F. 88
William Felix 87, 88
Carson
Kit 116
Carssow
Arthur Eric 203

Carl Felix 201, 204
Eugene Julius 201
Felix Hugo 201
George Charles 202
Grace Rosalie 203
Hedwig Ida 203
Julius 201
Mary Julia 202
Oscar Christian 202
Otto Charles 202
Rudolph Benton 202
Catticoath
Catherine 28
Charleville
Mary Clementine 89
Cimijotti
Frank 26
Mary 26
Cissell
Alben Joseph Rosati 221
Clement 180
Elizabeth 180, 181, 182
Vincent 221
Clark
Mary Allen 282
William 116
Cleveland
Grover 99
Clevlen
Charles 101
George Grant 101
Cline
Mary 217
Coats
Edward 166
Cochran
John B. 266
William Barnett 266
Cocolise
Henry Joseph 259
Virgil 259
Cole
Richard Leon 280
Sam 280
Collier
Eliza Clara 138
Conrad?
Catherine 45
Cooper
Elisabeth 218
Cornely
Barbara 240
Correck
Elisabeth 98
Cottner
Susan 167
Courtois
Henry 119
Margaret 119, 120
Coyle
Mary 36
Cramer
Susanna Maria 130
Crawford
Anna Lualen 138
William Washington 138
Crays
Ida M. 273
Creizenach
Theresia 94, 97
Cromer
Andrew 205
Francis Joseph 205
Johann Georg 205, 206
Lucy 206
Maria Anna 206
Xavier 205
Cross
Edward 277
Samuel 277
Cureton
Minnie 137
Richard 137
Dallas
Anna 210
Barbara 209
Catherine 209
Charles 210
Christopher 29, 207, 208, 209, 210, 211
Eliza 210
Francis Joseph 208
Helena Josephine 29, 208
Jean 207
Johann 208
John 207, 208, 209, 210, 211, 269
John C. 207
Maria Anna 209
Pauline 210

Peter 209
Rosine 207
Sarah 210
Damers
Maria 118
Darien
Christopher 223, 224, 225, 226
Dauer
Magdalena 49
Dawson
Frederic 63
Mary Elizabeth 63
Dean
Amanda Red 136
Deck
Andreas 211
Barbara 211
Franz Sales 211, 212
Maria Anna 212
Nicolaus 211
Regina 188
Salome 45, 148, 199
Simon 211
Sophie 211
Thekla 62
Valentin 211
Veronica 211
Wendelin 211
Xavier 188
Decker
Anton 231
Catherine 231, 233
Magdalena 168
Deckert
John 72
Mary Elizabeth 72
Delcour
Carrie A. 76
Delles
Jean 207, 208, 209
Dempsey
Charles Timothy 227
John 227
Demsky
Johann 73
John 73
Denler
Anna 213
Anna Barbara 212

Caroline Wilhelmina 215
Elisabeth 213
Elizabeth Veronica 215
Friedrich 213
Henry 215
Jacob 213
Johann 213
Johann Ulrich 212, 213, 214, 215
John Gottlieb 214
Josephine R. 215
Katie 214
Louisa 214
Maria Anna 213
Mary Anna 3, 215
Mathilda 215
Rosina 213
Samuel 213
Verona 213
Dennler
Friedrich M. 212
Derrick
Amanda Jane 88
Deters
Maria Catherine 130
Dicus
Amanda Elizabeth 101
Dietmeyer
Magdalena 142
Dietzer
Mary Elisabeth 216
Peter 216, 217
Difani
Andreas 218
Bernard 217, 218, 219, 221
Bernard G. 220
Caroline 222
Francis Xavier 218
Franziska T. 217
Genevieve H. 220
George Mauritius 218
Joseph 217
Julius Xavier 220
Lawrence Joseph 219
Lorenz 218
Louis F. 220
Maria Anna 218
Mary Ann 220
Rowena E. 220

Sophia 219
Theresa 219
Theresa Matilda 221
Xavier 217

Doerge
Bertha 222, 225, 226
Carl 223, 224
Carl Christopher Herman 225
Carl Ernst Ludwig 223, 225, 226
Carl Friedrich Wilhelm 224
Charles 223, 224, 226
Charlotta Wilhelmina Carolina 224
Emilia Rosalia Bertha Mathilda 224
Emily 226
Gustav Heinrich Samuel 223, 224, 225, 226
Helena B. 226
Herman 224, 227
Johanna Louisa Augusta 225
Louis 226
Rudolph 226

Doering
Andrew 73
Friedrich 96
Heinrich 96
Ignatz 73
Wilhelmina 95

Dold
Catherine Eleanor 55, 229
Charles 229
Edward 229
George 229
Johann Georg 54, 55, 228, 229, 230
Joseph 229
Mary 229
Paulina 54, 229
Philip 229
Sophie 228

Doll
Amalia 230
Anna Theresa 242
Bernard 144, 230, 231, 232, 233, 236, 237, 238, 241
Brigitta 236
Carolina 230
Caroline Euphrosine 235
Caroline Louisa 232
Catherine 144, 167, 233, 238, 242
Catherine Regina 235
Cecilia 230
Charles 234
Charles H. 239
Child 234, 240
Clara 232
Edwin 242
Eleanora 237
Eleonora 241, 243
Elizabeth 231
Emile Joseph 242
Emma Elenora 241
Francis Joseph 231
Francis Xavier 235
George 233, 236, 238
Gertrud 236
Infant 242
Johann Georg 230, 233, 234, 236, 238, 241
Johanna Mary 240
Johanna Theresa 231
John 239
Joseph 68, 171, 230, 233, 236, 237, 238, 239, 241
Josephine 234
Julius Joseph 240
Karl 234
Lawrence 233, 236, 237, 238, 241, 242, 243
Lena 232
Lorenz 233, 236, 241
Magdalena 236
Maria Anna 236
Mary 239
Mary Anna 231
Mary Magdalena 241
Mary Rosalia 234
Michael 236
Paulina 234, 241
Paulina Barbara 235
Pauline 233, 238
Philip James 242
Rose Anna 235
Silverius 234
Sophia 68, 146, 230, 237, 239
Theresia 60, 237
Victoria 230
Wilhelmina 234
William 234

Dollnick
Anna 226

Donnelly
  Frank S. 36
  James 33
  Michael 36
  Winifred B. 33
Donnerberg
  Wilhelmina 121, 124
Donze
  Andrew Martin 246
  Anna Maria 244, 248, 262
  Carolina 244
  Emily Catherine 245
  Franz Xavier 244
  Henry 248
  Johanna 244
  John Nicholas 244, 248, 262
  John Seraphin 246
  Joseph Henry 246
  Joseph M. 249
  Josephine L. 244
  Lawrence 244
  Lawrence William 246
  Louisa 248
  Louisa Johanna 245
  Maria Caroline 248
  Maria Tharsilla 245
  Mary Magdalena 262
  Meinrad 243, 247, 248, 249
  Meinrad Seraphin 244
  Rose Carolina 246
  Seraphin 243, 244, 247, 248, 249
  Seraphin B. 248
  Sophia Theresa 245
  Valentine 248
  Valentine Seraphin 245
  Wilhelmina C. 245
Donzé
  Simon Meinrad 243, 247
Dörge
  Johann Hartwig Daniel 224
Dorgler
  Catherine 267
Douglas
  Mary Ann 266
Downs
  James Jonathan 75
  Michael 75
Dreska
  Robert Anastazy 278
Drew
  Ida 203
Drury
  Charles 31
  Charles Albert 186
  Jules 31
  Philomena 214
  William Martin 186
Dudley
  Mary Catherine 69
Duebner
  Barbara 81
Duffner
  Anton 249
  Catharina 249
  Crescentia 250
  Edwald 250
  Elisabeth 249
  Euphrosina 250
  Genovefa 250
  Jacob 249, 250, 251
  Maria 249
  Maria Anna 250
  Martin 249
  Mathias 250
  Rosalia 264
  Sylvester 250
  Victoria 250
  Vincent 251
  Vincenz 249
  Walburga 250
Dufour
  Parfait 118
Eades
  Nancy 195
Eaves
  Anna Weir 203
  Elliott Weir 203
Eberhardt
  J. 214, 216
  Magdalena Wilhelmina 214, 216
Ebinger
  August 122
  Lizetti 122
Ebler
  Gertrud 230, 236
  Joseph 236

Echle
   Andreas 253
   Andreas? 67, 253
   Clara Philomena 253
   Jacob 67, 253, 254
   John 253
   Joseph 253
   Mary Ann 253

Eckenfels
   Anna Katherine 255
   Anna Maria Theresa 255
   Charles Theodore 255
   Elizabeth 255
   Francis Xavier 17, 254
   Francisca Anna 255
   John Chrisostomus 255
   Joseph Emanuel 255
   Josephine 149, 254
   Mary Anna 149, 254
   Nicholaus? 254
   Severin 17, 149, 254, 256
   Theresa 255

Eckert
   Anton 256, 258, 268
   Barbara 257
   Caroline 257
   Franz Joseph 267
   Friedrich 123
   Henry 257
   Joseph Anton 257
   Maria Anna 257
   Maria Katherine 257
   Thomas 267

Eder
   Anton 104
   Louisa 104

Effrein
   Bernard Benjamin 258, 259, 260
   John Edward 260
   Joseph Herman 259
   Louisa Frances 259
   Maria Clara 260
   Peter Henry 259

Ehe
   Catharina Louisa 261
   Catherine 262
   Emma Genevieve 262
   Louisa Anna 261
   Mary Catherine 262
   Philipp 261
   Wilhelm 261, 263
   William 261
   William Godfried 261, 263
   William John 262

Ehler
   Andrew 264
   Charles Thomas 264
   Clothilde 264, 265
   Fridolin 264
   Friedrich Reinhold 264
   Gottfried 263, 264, 265
   Rosina 264
   Simon 264
   Theresa 264
   Thomas 265

Ehlinger
   Leo 97

Ehret
   Rosina 55

Ehrhard
   August 265
   Charles 265, 266, 267
   Johanna Augusta 265
   John 266
   Joseph 267
   Maria Lutgardis 42
   Minnie C. 266

Eichenlaub
   Barbara 17, 269
   Bartholomaus 267
   Carolina 269
   Catherine 14, 15, 110, 268
   Constantine 268
   Elisabetha 267
   Gervais 14, 16, 209, 257, 258, 267, 268, 270
   Henry 209, 269
   Johann 269
   Johann Peter 267
   Joseph 16, 268, 269
   Katherine 267
   Maria Anna 267
   Mary Elisabeth 269
   Mary Magdalena 257, 258, 268
   Peter 267
   Robert 268

Einig

Daniel 231
Lydia 231
Eisenbeis
   Andrew 273
   Anton Raymond 273
   Catherine 271
   Charles William Ferdinand 272
   Elisabeth 270
   Elisabeth Anna Margarethe 272
   Felix Nicholas Peter 273
   Ferdinand 270, 271, 274
   Fridolin 270
   John H. 271
   Josef 270
   Joseph Ferdinand 271
   Julianna M. 272
   Katharina 78, 79, 151, 270, 274
   Maria Anna 270
   Mary Elizabeth 271
   Peter Henry 273
   Rosina M. 273
   Sophia 273
   Theresa 271
   Valentine 272
   Viktoria 270
   William Ferdinand 272
Eisenmann
   Joseph 190
   Maria Anna 168, 171
   Roman 190
Eiserloh
   Margaret C. 207
   Peter 207
Elder
   Arthur Francis 280
   Augustine Guy 280
   Joseph Clarence 280
   Leonard 138
End
   Elisabeth 108
   Franz Joseph 108
   Maria Sophia 38
Endres
   Anna Maria 275
   Barbara 173
   Catherine 274
   Johann Peter 274
   Joseph 83, 274

   Joseph Michael 83, 274, 275
   Theckla 275
   Theresa 275
   Valentin 83, 274
Engelmann
   Johanna Dorothea Justine 224
Engelmeier
   William 169
Ernst
   Adaline 277
   Anna 80
   Florence Agatha 277
   Francis Joseph Adam 276
   Franz Joseph 276
   Girl 277
   Henry 277
   Ida Rosine 277
   John Edward 276
   Joseph A. 276, 277
   Joseph Aloysius 276
   Maria Anna 9, 66, 237
   Mary Alice 277
   William Anthony 276
Erwin
   Mary Ann 220
Esselman
   Albert Joseph 280
   Alfreda Marie 280
   Anna 279
   Bernard 279
   Catherine 278
   Earl Francis 156, 279
   Elizabeth 278, 280
   Francis 278
   Francis John Nepomuk 156, 279
   Francis Oriel 280
   Frank 281
   Frederick Dewey 280
   George 278
   Johann Bernard 278
   Joseph 278
   Magdalena 156, 280
   Mary 279
   Mary Grace 280
   Susanna 279
   William Henry 279
Estes
   James Karr 202

    Rhoda Belle 202
Etter
    Albert Felix 282
    August Anthony 283
    Benjamin 281, 284
    Charles Benjamin 281
    Francis Xavier 283
    George Benjamin 282
    Henry Julius 282
    James William 282
    Johann 281
    John Edward Emile 281
    Joseph Frederick 282
    Louis Simeon 283
    Mary Louisa 281
    Walter Edward 283
Eversole
    Barry Abraham 29
    Harriet Kristie 29
Ewel?
    Henrietta 100
Faessler
    Maria Anna Elisabetha 15
Faist
    Joseph 191
    Theresia 191
Falk
    Anna Mary 62
    Franziska 108
    George 26, 27, 260
    Jacob 62
    Juliana Viktoria 197
    Maria Ann .... 27, *See* Maria Anna Fallert
    Maria Anna Cleopha 54, 55, 229
    Peter 54
    Valentin 197
Fallert
    Caroline 67, 253, 254
    Christina 66
    Elisabetha 141
    Franz Anton 26, 45, 67, 253
    Joseph 45
    Katherine 144
    Maria Anna 26
    Maria Barbara 67
    Monica 178, 210
    Regina 235
Faser

    Elizabeth Ann 239
    Ignatius 239
Faulkner
    Caroline 101, 103
Fautz
    Catherine Anastasia 16
Feiks
    Sophia 225
Feinenn
    Margaret 231
Feist
    Genovefa 270
    Josephine 134
    Katharina 9, 104
    Magdalena 104, 183, 191, 248
    Michael 71, 104, 191
Felling
    Gerhardt 137
    Henry G. 137
Fey
    Henry 232
    John 232
    Maria Ursula 177
Figge
    Maria 246
Fischer
    Apollonia 182, 192
    Cecilia 253
    Charles Brandon 97
    George W. 97
    Johann Paul 67
    Juliana Eleanora 133
    Maria Ursula 68
    Rosalia 201, 204
    Sylvester 253
Fisher
    Joseph 134
Fishman
    Ram 283
Fitterer
    Juliana 186
Fitzkam
    Clara Sophie 232
    Helena 42, 44, 48, 149
    Johannes 233
    John Bernard 232
    Joseph 231, 232, 233
    Joseph F. 233
    Lena 232

Louisa 183, 185, 191
Maria Catherine 24
Paulina 205
Philip 183
Philip Jacob 183, 233
Simon 205
Flanagan
Letitia 218
Flieg
Andreas 59
Anton 59, 264
Mathilde 264
Thomas 159
Wilma Magdalena 159
Flora
Rosella 278
Flori
Conrad 129
Wilhelmina 129
Foell
Maria Eva 125, 127
Forthuber
Joseph 96
Franck
Emelie 75
Frasier
Henry 217
Frederich
Maria 73
Frederick
Sophia 5, 6
Freiburg
Gertrud 98
French
Mary Caroline 221
Frent
Sarah Elizabeth 88
Freud
Sigmund 97
Freudenreich
Anna Maria 243, 247
Frezensunski
Amelia 128
Friedman
Christina 19
John 19
Mary Catherine A. 20
Theresia 19
Friedmann

Joseph 37
Regina 37, 210
Friedrich
Johann 55
Maria Anna 55
Fritsch
Crescentia 161
George 85, 87
Froehly
Aloysius 266
Frost
August Swanson 203
Fredrich August 224
Frueh
Joseph 141
Raimund 141
Früh
Maria Anna 66
Fuerth
Charles Christian 99
Joseph 99
Joseph Francis 99
Funk
Annie Lillie 140
Christian 140
Fuson
James C. 136
Sylvester James 136
Gailer
Augustin 197
Gallager
Margaret 227
Gallus
Theresia 183, 233
Gamel
Elias Theodore 123
Harry Robert 123
Ganter
Joseph 191
Louis 193, 194
Maria Anna 183, 190, 192
Ganther
Genovefa 16
Michael 16
Gärtner
Anna Maria 263
Francisca 263
Simon 263
Gass

Lorenz 125
Gebhardt
　　　Amelia Sephronia 129
Geck
　　　Johann Adam 160
　　　Karl 160
Gegg
　　　Albert 56
　　　Catherine .... *See* Catherine Yonk
　　　Francis Joseph 55
　　　Francis Xavier 56
　　　Joseph 85, 126, 160
　　　Maria Adelaide 105
　　　Maria Albertina 85, 86
　　　Maria Kleopha 275
　　　Severin 55
　　　William 126
Geiler
　　　Franz Xavier 197
Geiser
　　　Friedrich Ulrich 212
George
　　　Henry 232
Gerstner
　　　Anton 146
　　　Joseph 146
Gibbar
　　　James Nicholas 180
　　　Peter James 180
Gibel
　　　Eva 126
Gibson
　　　Marguerite 50
Gieser
　　　Theresa 257
Giesler
　　　Dora Agnes 156
　　　Georg 45
　　　George 45
　　　Gideon 156
　　　Maria Anna 45, 149
　　　Mary 58
　　　Sophia 103
Gisi
　　　Anna Maria 244
　　　Henry Joseph 244
　　　Joseph 56, 178
　　　Katharina 190
　　　Mary Lorena Christian 246

　　　Ursula 56
　　　Valerian 178, 244, 246
Gittinger
　　　Alexius 3
　　　Franz Anton 4, 209, 210
　　　George 245
　　　George Felix 29
　　　Henry Charles 245
　　　Mary Ann 209
Glanzmann
　　　Barbara 190
Glaser
　　　Franz 151
　　　John Wendolin 2
　　　Joseph 151
　　　Leonard C. 2
　　　Martin J. 153
　　　Rosalia 151
Gludey
　　　Alfred M. 266
　　　Rudolph 266
Glynn
　　　Bridget 75
Godfrey
　　　Jacob 212
　　　Thomas D. 212
Godfried
　　　Rosalia 174
Goering
　　　Barbara 178
　　　Walburga 56
Goettemann
　　　Henry 216
　　　Louis 216
　　　Minnie 216
Gooch
　　　Frances A. 137
Goodwin
　　　Virginia Pendleton 202
Govro
　　　Emelie Marcelite 5
　　　Etienne 5
　　　Francis Xavier 5
　　　Mary 5
Grade
　　　Apollonia 271
Graf
　　　Emma Rosina 24
　　　Fidel 169

 Pauline 169, 171
 Simon 24
Grass
 George 253
 Kunigunda 184, 199
 Regina 215
 Walburga 77
Gray
 Araminta 122
 Mathew 195
Grechtler
 Gertrud 236
Gregoire
 Marie Pauline 116
Gregory
 Julia May 203
Gremminger
 Franz Matthias 43
 Heinrich 43
Grieg
 Magdalena 145
Grieshaber
 Anastasia 68
 Anna Agnes 74
 Anthony 183
 Brigitta 71
 Charles Andrew 184
 Elizabeth M. 184
 Fabian 71, 264
 John 74
 Josephine 264
 Kilian 183, 184
 Magdalena 259
Griffard
 Amelia 235
Griffee
 Rachel 195
Griffey
 Letty Lucille 158
Grifford
 _____ 158
Grimm
 Catharina Maria 14
Griner
 Mary 259
Grither
 Catherine 12
 Johann Baptist 41
 John 41

 Maria Anna 56
 Mary Louisa 41, 42
Grott
 Lucinda 278
 Michael 278
Guethle
 Andreas Saturnin 85
 Barbara .... *See* Barbara Huber
 Charles Gerhard 268
 Clara 85
 Felix 47
 Gerhard Charles 83
 Heinrich 83
 Henry 268
 Johann 19, 38, 49
 Johanna 255
 Juliana 19
 Louisa 49
 Maria Philippine 167
 Maria Sophia 142
 Maria Sophina 38
 Regina 84
 Regina Johanna 47
Guilloz
 Catherine 102, 135
Guitar
 James L. 87
 Josephine 87
 Mary Elizabeth 87, 88
 Minerva 87
 Missouri Ellen 87
 Rachel .... *See* Rachel Byington
 Samuel 87, 90
Guschwa
 Maria Eva .... *See* Maria Eva Hendrich
 Maria Katherina 164, 165
 Peter 164
Haas
 Agatha 85
 Franziska 84
 Michael 84, 85
 Theresia 197
Habig
 Frances 181
Hacke
 Fred 114
 Selma Clare 114
Haeffner

Elisabeth 45
Haefner
   Anna Maria 68, 120
Hagan
   Emily 9
Hagen
   Elizabeth 239
Hahn
   John 129
   Louise 129
   Theresa 54
Haley
   Elisha 282
   Genieve M. 282
Hambel
   Charles 122
   Charles G. 121
Hamm
   C. W. 179
Hammensteadt
   Anna Sophia Elisabeth 110, 111
Hammer
   Jane M. 62
Hammerle
   Barbara 271
Hammert
   Henry F. 49
Hannauer
   Charles Edward 76
   Lydia Josephine 76
Hans
   Anna Maria 173
   Georg Jacob 173
Hansmann
   Franz Anton 198
   Theresia 198
Harris
   Louisa Belle 69
   Oliver 69
   Peter B. 129
Harter
   Agatha 7, 86, 257
   Barbara 63
   Francis A. 257
   John Frederick 257
Hauck
   Andreas 35
   Benjamin 264
   Brigitta 233

Joseph 264
Maria Brigita 35
Mary C. 91, 93
Nicholas 91, 197
Hauk
   Margaretha 82
Hauser
   Anton 196
   Augusta 4
   Franz Anton 148
   Franz Joseph 4
   Franziska 196
   Genovefa 196
   Maria Brigida 9, 11, 66
   Thekla 148, 150, 254
Hauser?
   Wilhelmina 4
Hawkins
   David Lewis 99
   Mary Julia 98
Haxel
   Mary 50
   Peter Ludwig 49, 50
Hayden
   Margaret 194
   William Bolemus 194
Hayes
   J. C. 195
Healy
   James Joseph 123
   Michael 123
Hechinger
   Mary Magdaline 276, 277
   Protase 276
Hecker
   Fritz 222
Heflin
   Mary Rusha C. 272
   William H. 272
Heid
   Regina 16
Heidel
   Elisabeth 169
Heil
   John 186
   Joseph 186
   Maria Anna 186
Heitmann
   Bertha Emilia 216

Heitz
- Genevieve 38
- Rosa 28, 234
- Valerian Joseph 38

Helbig
- Pauline 114

Henderson
- Cora Alice 34
- Elizabeth Ann 5
- Jane D. 123
- Stokely 5

Hendrich
- Maria Eva 164, 165

Henhoffer
- Anastasia 266

Henn
- Luzia 43

Henry
- Jennie J. 33

Hering
- Mary Ann 169

Hermann
- Anna Maria 11, 163
- Catherine 207, 250
- Elizabeth 10

Herr
- Catherine 181

Herrmann
- Verena 114

Herter
- Robert 48
- Sybilla 41

Hertich
- Charles 96

Hertig
- Cecilia 142, 155, 157

Herz
- Ludgardis 84

Herzog
- Agatha 56
- Bonaventure 6, 56
- Emerencia 6
- Fidelia 59, 67
- Joseph 67, 163, 269
- Laurence 163
- Leon 269
- Maria Anna 47

Hess
- Frank 54
- Ludgardis 84
- Marquart 54
- Peter 84

Hettig
- Fidel 34
- Theresia Regina 64

Hickey
- Robert 190
- Robert W. 190

Hicks
- William A. 15

Hill
- Ben F. 195
- Dora May 283
- George Russell 283

Hiney
- Constantine 71

Hipes
- Bartholomew 170
- Peter Edward 170

Hirsch
- Eva Margaretha 135

Hirt
- Bernard 146
- Karl 146

Hodapp
- Joseph 236
- Magdalena 233, 236, 237, 238, 241
- Mary Ann 133
- Paul Joseph 133

Hoferer
- Maria Anna 39
- Michael 39
- Theresa 39

Hoffman
- Catherine .... *See* Catherine Schnurr
- Paul 174
- Paul Peter 174, 175

Hogan
- James Edward 282
- Margaret Ellen 282

Hogenmiller
- Johanna 161
- Joseph 161
- Theresia 160

Hohmann
- Caspar 81
- Henry 81, 82

Holliday

Gertrude Catherine 138
Lucinda Adaline ...... *See* Lucinda Adaline Biggs
Milton 137
Thomas King 138
Holst
Johann Friedrich 14
John 14
Holstein
John 265
Hoog
Amelia 68
Elizabeth Mary 273
Regina 59
Simon 273
Thomas 68
Hootselle
Joseph N. 187
Thomas Green 187
Höpf
Walburga 51, 179
Hoschmann
Maria Anna 198
Hospmann
Genovefa 197
Höss
Andreas 11
Maria Anna 11, 39
Huber
Andreas 86, 257
Andrew 7
Barbara 83, 84
Benedict 10, 109, 188, 190, 256
David 257
Francis Xavier 108, 109, 257
Johanna 12
John George 257
Joseph 3
Magdalena 236
Mary 3
Mary Anna 6
Mary Anna Francisca 257
Philip 3
Rosalia 41
Susanna 281
Veronica Josephine 132
William Andrew 86
William Anton 132
Hubert

Anthony 189
Joseph 189
Huck
Bernard 246
Elisabeth Mary 246
Florian 68
Francis John Florian 77
Francisca 178, 245
Genevieve 6
George Washington 77
Johanna 69
Joseph 68
Roman 68, 237
Hudson
Joshua A. 220
Thomas McCurgan 220
Huff
Margaret 10
Hug
Johann 68
Johanna .... 52, *See* Johanna Lang
Johannes 237, 238
Magdalena 84, 85
Hugelmann
Magdalena 84
Huise
Magdalena 214, 216
Hultrop
Frederick 187
Rose 187
Humke
Catherine 123
Hummel
Margaretha 274
Humpert
Charles 54, 55
Franz Michael 54
Hieronymus 35
John Charles William 35
Hund
Christine 238
Hunt
Anna Paulina 181
Cornelius 181
Hurka
Ignatius 104
Jacob 104
Hurley
Charles 189

Hurst
- Agatha 46
- Anna Mary 244
- Franziska 150
- George 269
- Helena 43
- Henry George 245
- Isidore 86
- Joseph 244, 245
- Karl Joseph Franz 103
- Maria Anna 109
- Maria Scholastika 205
- Simon 103, 250, 251
- William 86, 269

Hyde
- Cordelia 277

Hynds
- David Henry 154
- Laura Alta 154

Isenmann
- Conrad 112, 153, 154
- Elisabeth 271, 274
- Johann Baptist 160, 271
- John 161
- Joseph 112, 160
- Maria Anna 74
- Theresa 158
- Ursula 25
- Wendel 126

Jacob
- Franz Kilian 149
- Maria Eva 149, 255

Jacobs
- Christian 175, 177

Jaeger
- Anna Maria 68, 248
- Catherina 106, 110, 113
- Catherine 113
- Salome 248

Janis
- Emilie Reine 117

Jarrard
- Eunice 128

Jeannot
- Catherine 209

Jeck
- Anastasia 249
- Johann Baptist 250

Jennings
- Margaret 59

Jenny
- Frank 9

Joggerst
- Anna Maria 213
- August William 7
- Franz Ignatz 159, 243
- Joseph 159
- Nicholas 7
- Tharsilla 86
- Wilhelmina 243, 247, 248

John
- Katherine 34

Jokerst
- Andreas 184, 199
- Anna Catherine 158, 159
- Bernard 10, 11, 163
- Catherina 199
- Catherine 14, 184, 257, 268, 270
- Cecilia 180
- Charles Conrad 64
- Charlotte Louisa 64
- Felix William 262
- Ferdinand 266
- Francis Xavier 158
- Francisca 132
- Franz Anton 10, 11, 268
- Genevieve 158
- Henry 149, 262
- Henry B. 163
- Joseph 149
- Laurence 38
- Ludgard 72
- Maria Magdalena 44, 67, 104, 160
- Mary Cecilia 158
- Mary Helena 2
- Michael 38, 266
- Sophia .... *See* Sophia Winter

Jones
- [Vernon?] 77
- _____ 117
- Frances Elizabeth 154

Jordan
- Johann Georg 218

Jungling
- Franziska 74

Kahler

    Johann Valentine 217
    Valentine George 217
Kaiser
    Mary 137
Kaltenbach
    Theresia 4
Karl
    Anna Mary 259
    Caspar 161
    David 161, 259
    Emma R. 273
    Henry 161
    John 273
    Mary 161
Kast
    Aloysius 162
    Maria Anna 162, 164
    Victoria 164
Kastner
    Hermann 135, 136
    Mary Josephine ...... *See* Mary Josephine Schmidt
Katke
    Marie J. 187
Kauflin
    Josephine 169, 170
Keck
    Catherine Barbara 91
Keegans
    James 195
    Sarah Ann 195
Keil
    Henry 118
Kelleher
    Anna B. 35
Keller
    Augusta 41
    Herman 41
    Joseph 18
    Magdalena 18
    Theresia 18, 20, 49, 50
Keller?
    Magdalena 18
Kelly
    Annie Elizabeth 163
Kemp
    Jennie 91
Kempf
    Agatha 154
    Anna Maria 263

    Christina 44, 109
    Frederick 231
    Genovefa 52, 179
    George 231
    Magdalena 71, 231, 232, 233
    Michael 78
    Simon 78, 80
    Theresa 80
Kennard
    Blanche 154
    James 154
Kenner
    George W. 41
    Nora M. 41
Kenosha
    Bernard 126
Kerchner
    Eva Clara 83
Kern
    Charles C. 19
    Helena 183
    John Dominic 19, 32, 281
    Julia Margaretha 32, 34
    Simon Amandus 198
    Wilhelmina 281, 284
Kertz
    Johann 271
    Maria M. 271
    Michael 271
    Nicholas 271
Kessler
    Peter 162
    Simon 162
Ketterer
    Engelbert 85
    Maria Josephine 85
Kettinger
    John A. 248
    Joseph 68
    Regina 19, 32, 281
Kidd
    Clarence Henderson 138
Kiefer
    Anna Maria 211
    Catharina 17, 149
    Catherine 254, 256
    Ferdinand 108
    Franciska 29

Franz	43
Franz Bartholomew	51, 207
Franziska	51, 207, 208
Genovefa	44, 45
Johann Michael	42
Joseph	42, 43, 254, 256
Joseph Sebastian	72
Leona Cornelia	2
Louisa	51
Magdalena	196
Maria Anna	198
Peter	2, 28
Philip	28
Philip Jacob	108, 198
Philomena Mary	72
Theresia	257

Kieffer
Katharina	108, 111
Maria Ursula	148

King
William J.	50

Kirchner
Anna Regina	209, 253
Christina Josephine	60
Lawrence	45
Mary Ann	78
Michael Anton	45
Peter	78, 86
Regina	86

Kirklin
Eliza Ann	13

Kist
Stephanie	10, 125
Victoria	86

Klagus
Bertha	187

Klassner
Elisabeth	12, 21

Kleibecker
Maria	90, 92

Klein
Anton	6, 235
Bertha	174
Caroline	62, 65
Christian	81
Helen A.	91
Ignatius	246
Joseph	6
Leo August	246
Ludwina	255
Ludwina Johanna	47
Mary A.	272
Michael	62
Nicholas A.	235
Rosina	32
Wilhelmina	7
William F.	32

Kleinberg
Andrew	21
Charles T.	21

Kline
Sophia	216

Klingman
Anna Elisabeth	218

Klumpp
Anton	238
Frances	171
Francisca	238, 239
Lawrence	54, 55
Rosa	37

Knapp
Margaretha	83, 84, 275
Nikolaus	83

Knothe
Annie	218
Anthony	218

Knott
Tiporah S.	99

Kobel
Jacob	10
Mary Eliza	10

Koch
Gottlieb	81

Kocher
Franziska	269

Koehler
Emilia	222

Koeneman
William	100

Koenig
Maria Anna	26

Koester
Augusta Rosetta	111
John Charles Edward	110, 111
Margaret	60
Wilhelmina	110

Kohler

Catherine 149
Joseph 105
Joseph Nicholas 105
Rosina 254
Simon 255
Kohm
Catherina 6, 235
Franz 174
Henry Ignatius 174
Joseph 265, 266
Nicolaus 266
Koller
Francis Xavier 248
Maria Anna 248
Köninger
Krescenz 270
Valentin 270
Kopf
Elisabeth 84
Kopp
Johann 250
Maria Anna 250, 251
Köppel
Elisabetha 173
Sylvester 173
Kraenzle
Elizabeth 132
Kraft
Johann 183
Johanna 116, 118
Krauch
Matilda 105
Kraus
Margaret Mary 207
Kreid
Jakob 267
Rosa 267
Kreitler
Daniel 86
Ferdinand 54
Francis 54
Leo 86
Krieger
Gertrude 131, 133
Theodore 131
Krummer
Balbina 10, 125
Mathias 125
Kuehn

Meinrad 115
Theresia 1
Kuehne
Ferdinand 58, 59
Kuest
Ignatz 9, 126
Joseph Friedrich 9
Stephanie .... 10, *See* Stephanie Kist
Kuhlman
Elisabeth 202
Kuntz
Ernestine 140
Maria Elisabeth 52
Kunz
Maria Anna 171
Kunzmann
Maria Anna 83
Maria Anna 274
Kurfurst
Magdalena 160
Labruyere
Leocadia 50
Louis Anton Bernard 59
Laible
Agnes 167
Laier
Lucia 185
Laigast
Maria Ursula 32, 144
Lalumondiere
Edward F. 112
Henry 112
Judithe Zoe 59, 112
Mary Jane 31
Lane
Harry Russell 138
Lang
Alois 237
Johanna 68, 237, 238, 241
Margaret 129
Lange
Caroline W. 122
Langelier
Cornelia Josephine 112
Jean Baptist 112
Jean Baptiste 59
Louisa Rosalie 59
Pelagie Juliette 59
Lapp

Magdalena 263
Larkin
Edith J. 33
Hugh 33
LaRose
Eleanora 119
Felix 31
Joseph Stanislaus 119, 120
LaVielle
Mary Adelaide 41
Lawbaugh
Ella Adelaide 41
Emanuel Sylvester 41
Mary Catherine 41
Layton
Anne 180
Bertha 89
Clement 89
Fredric 279
Mary Irene 182
Matilda Gertrude 156, 279, 281
Thomas A. 182
Lebert
Theresia 190
Ziriack 190
Lehmann
Alvina 232
Franz Michael 54
Helena 69, 141, 148
Theresia 53
Ursula 228
Lehr
George 145
William 145
Leiner
Anna Margaretha 174
Leitermann
Maria Cecilia 37
Mathias 37
Leitterman
Joseph 163
Mary Ann 163
Lelie
Alice Maria 260
Emile Cornelius 260
Lenz
Henry 220
Julia 220
Léon

Joseph Amabile 50
Mary Suzanne Felicite 50
Lett
Hedwig 33
Liekert
George John 213
Lienert
Anton 180
Paul 180
Theodor 180
Lienhard
Catharina 15
Lincoln
Abraham 95
Linderer
Francis William 235
Joseph 235
Linn
Louis 118
Linnertz
Anton 22
Julius William 22
Lipp
Anna Maria 31
Franz Xavier 209
Ignatius 209
Magdalena 246
Maria Anna 121
Littenecker
Gertrud 67
Maria Anna 160, 271
Litterst
Bartholomaus 196
Caroline 244
Caspar Simon 228
Catherine 228, 230
Franziska 49
Gertrud 53, 55
Jacob 108
Johann Nepomuk 196
Johannes Michael 198
Joseph 47, 48
Maria Anna 108
Michael 198
Loeb
Edward 92
Loehr
Adelbert 222
Loehring

Frederick 186
William Frederick 186
Lohmann
Josephine 169, 170
Mary 170
William 169, 170
Lohrs
Christine Dorothea 224
Loida
Albert 184
Maria 104
William 184
Long
Edward V. 276
Edward Vincent 275
Frederick Gabriel 275
Louis G. 275
Lucinda 117
Lord
Abigail 276
Lotspeich
Franz 162
Walburga 161
Lucas
Christine Louise 147
Lucas?
Anna 26
Luer
Charles 276
Elizabeth Ella 276
Luiten
Anna 202
Jacob E. 202
Lusk
Charles Hana 65
Salmon Brooks 65
Lutman
Artemissa Martha Jane 88, 90
Jacob Franklin 88
Luttrell
Mary Reutilia 217
Lutz
Dorothea 8, 101
Maas
Joducus 98
Peter 98
Mabes
John 242
Mary Ann 242

Maennle
Heinrich 164
Magnuson
Olive 203
Manchert
Catherine 11, 234
Christoph 115
Walburga 115
Marlen
Mary E. 21
Marquis
John G. 33
William Andrew 33
Marshall
Jacob Blake 23
Lowell Jacob 23
Martin
Emma 36
Marx
Karl 95
Masserang
Mary Ann 246
Mathes
Delilah 60
Mattingly
George 220
Henry Stuart 220
Lena Margaret 138
Mary 180
Matz
Maria Eva 159
Maurice
Antoinette 259
Felix 119
Josephine 91
Odile Philomena 119, 120
Mawe
Elizabeth 276
May
Johann 42
Maria 182
Maria Magdalena 196
Martha 43
Simon 42
McAllister
_____ 283
Anna M. 283
McCarthy
Florence 124

334

McCormick
  Katherine Ann 283
McDaniel
  James 101
  Lou V. 101
McDonnell
  Sarah J. 123
McFarland
  Clara A. 33
McGee
  Mabel E. 91
  Robert W. 91
McGovern
  Sarah Anne 282
McNabb
  _____ 59
Medley
  Mary Jane 123
Meier
  Joseph 190
  Simon 190
Menge
  August William Henry 259
  Christopher Carl 259
Menk
  George 245
  Wilhelm 245
Menn
  Anna Caroline 147
  Ludwig 147
Menschieus
  Dorothea E. 224
Mentier
  Mary Elizabeth 91
  Robert 91
Mergenthaler
  Christian 272
  Edward Joseph 272
Messberger
  Cecilia 162
Messenger
  Georg 12
  George Adam 12
Metz
  Catharina 49, 261
Meyer
  Bernard Everhard 130
  Conrad 91
  Emma 147
  Frank Jacob 92
  Franz Anton 173
  George 109
  Gerard Heinrich 130
  Hilarius 25
  Jacob 25
  Johann Heinrich 130
  Martin 76, 77
  Mary 234
  Regina C. 91
  Rosamunda 173
  Stella Martha 92
Meyers
  Christian 219
  John 172
  John Christian 172
  Joseph Henry 172
Miles
  Mary 182
  Mary Jane 280
Miller
  _____ 232
  Benjamin Harrison 34
  Edna Mae 119
  Eliza M. 101
  Franciska 25, 27
  Frederick F. 261
  Harold 101
  Hugh H. 119
  John Henry 34
  Leslie Earl 76
  William H. 76
Mills
  Martha Elizabeth 272
Milster
  David 217
  Leah Isabelle 217
Milz
  Sophie 122
Minks
  Susan Elizabeth 119
Mischke
  Albert 226
  Bertha 226
Mitchell
  John 128
  Theodore 128
Mittenbach

Bertha 242
Mohr
  Elisabeth 174
Monahan
  Mary 33
Monck
  Catherine 209
Moody
  Alta Mavis 123
  William 123
Moon
  James 117
  Liona 117
Moore
  Charles P. 242
  Mary 139
  Peter 242
Moorman
  Helena 130
  Lambert 130
Moran
  Catherine 123
Moreau
  Marie Louise 64
Morebock
  Jennie L. 122
Morse
  Henry Clay 282
  Henry Wildie 282
Moser
  John Peter 234
  Louis Peter 234
Muelhaeusler
  Andreas 269
  Joseph 269
  Maria Anna 270
Mueller
  Katharina 37
  Regina 32, 145
Muessig
  Sophia Clara 132
Müller
  Barbara 47, 229
  Elisabeth 126
  Maria Anna 179
Mundi
  Catharina 173
Munsch
  Gertrude 244, 248, 249

  Joseph 248
  Nicholas 197, 248
Murrell
  John J. 204
Myers
  Ignatius 45
  Joseph 45
Naeger
  Anna Maria Theresa 132
  Mary Anne 273
  Mathias 38
  Wendelin 38
Nau
  _____ 240
  Catherine 240
Neff
  Margaretha 78
Neffon
  Rosalia 160
Neger
  Maria Magdalena 198
  Maria Ursula 54
Neidhardt
  Johanna 77
Nesselbosch
  Franziska 9, 10, 126
  Stefan 9
Nesselhof
  Walburga 141
Nock
  Aloisia 84
  Eleanora .... 229, *See* Eleanora Seitz
  Josef 84
  Katharina 228
  Lorenz 228
Norman
  John Sylvester 93
  Willis 93
Norwein
  Conrad 115
Norwine
  Conrad 115, 118
Oberle
  Bernard 31, 121, 260
  Catherine 141, 143
  Joseph 258
  Justina 258, 260
  Maria Anna 31, 79, 268
  Mary Ann 79

Paul 121
Regina 26, 45, 67, 253
Ockenfuss
Monica 108
Oehler
Elisabeth 112, 153
Joseph 112
Theresia 103
Öhler
Anton 263
Joseph 263
Laurentz 263
Leo 263
Paul 263
Thomas 263
Okenfuss
Adolph Christian 63
Maximilian 63
Omeis
Maria Magdalena 108, 198
Osstheimer
Barbara 4
Ott
Andreas 196
Blasius 196
Otte
August 42
August Friedrich 158
Dorothea 42
Edward Albert 158
Heinrich 40, 42
Henry 42
Wilhelmina Dora 244
Wilhelmina Maria Theresa 245
Ottenad
Mary L. 76
Owens
Caroline 138
Palmer
Anna Maria 69
Caroline 145
Catherine 72
Clothilda 234, 236
Genevieve 172
Isfried 28, 234
Johanna 52
Maria Anna 269
Paul 28, 145
Pius 52, 69, 205
Panter
Joseph 57, 58
Panther
Lorenz 58
Magdalena 58
Pariset
Julia 21
Parker
Timothy 88
William M. 88
Patrick
Angie 65
Pauleke
Wilhelmina 35
Pearson
Edward Everett 279
Peiser
Ernst 146
Selma 146
Perkins
Elizabeth Ann 88
Perman
Clara 119
Perret
Francisca 35
Peterson
Charles 255
Petrequin
Adolph 135
Frederick 102, 135
Sophia 102, 103
Petrie
Christine 122, 123, 176
Pfaff
Anton 211
Francis 2
Peter 211
Sophia 211, 212
Walburga 250
Xavier Charles 2
Pfeiffer
Catherine 205
Philip 205
Pförtner
Heinrich 100
Henrietta 100
Pfundstein
Anton 84

    Joseph 84
Phegley
    Emily 21
Pieper
    Anna Theodora 98
Ploeger
    Ernst 91
    Henry Ernest 91
Pohlmann
    Mary 107
Ponder
    Joseph 58
Poston
    Felix Grundy 139
    Nancy A. 139
Pound
    Alice Loretta 280
    William C. 280
Powell
    Mary B. 220
Pratte
    Pierre Auguste Bernard 117
    Theresa Orilla 117
Price
    Sterling 117, 243, 268
Primo
    Clyde 124
    Louis Valle 124
    Ralph Claude 124
Proctor
    George Powell 138
    Lloyd F. 138
Pruett
    Nancy 218
Pullen?
    Ellen M. 88
Pustmueller
    Clarence C. 159
Pyle
    Victoria Adelaide 63
Radloff
    Anna Margaretha 61
Ramsey
    Hannah 194
Rauch
    Henry 21
    Olivia M. 21
Raumschuh
    Bernard 9, 47, 229

    Charles 229
    Franz Joseph 9
    Josef 9
    William 47
Rechert
    Jacob 210
    Lawrence 210
Redford
    Mary E. 219, 222
Reed
    Annie 220
    Eliza 176
    Elizabeth Jane 122, 176, 177
    Evaristus 220
    James 122, 123, 176
    Mary Ann 123, 125
Reeder
    William Brent 87
Rehm
    Francis 109
    Gottlieb 33
    Joseph 109, 188, 190
    Joseph Gottlieb 33
    Joseph Richard 44
    Magdalena 264
    Mary 44
Reichert
    Barbara 209
    Peter 209
Reike
    Louisa 266
Renard
    Caroline 255
Rendler
    Andrew 167
    Balbina 125
    Francis 167
Renner
    Catherine 218
    Jacob 213
    Johann Martin 218
    John 213
Revillod
    Marie Francoise 96
Reynolds
    Benjamin F. 93
    George 10
    Mary A. 93

Vianna 10
Rheinhardt
   Maria Josepha 80, 228
Rhodes
   Edward J. 279
Ricketts
   Benjamin R. 195
   Estelle 117
   Mary Ellen 195
Rieble
   Ottilia 103
Riechman
   Christine Wilhelmina Caroline 225
   Johann Conrad Heinrich Christian 225
Riechte
   Anna 218
Rieder
   Elisabeth 270
Riehl
   Edward 261
Riehle
   Anastasia 52
Rigdon
   James Abijah 60
   Lucinda Julia 60
   Mary Johanna 246
Rinehart
   Joseph 162
Riney
   Louvina 278
   Thomas Edward 278
Ringwald
   Franz Xavier 63
   Louisa 65
   Louise Genevieve 63
Ritter
   Maria Eva 49
   Mary Eva 261, 263
   Paul 49, 261
   Victoria 14, 49
Roberts
   Edmund 118
Röck
   Rosalia 168
Rodebush
   Ivan Carl 280
Roeder
   Dorothea Louisa 266
Roeding
   George 283
Roethemeier
   Anna Maria Sophia Margarethe 225
Rohlfing
   Heinrich Christian Friedrich 225
Rolffes
   Arthur 76
Rond
   Catherine 238
Roscoe
   Bertha Jane 283
Rose
   Franz Heinrich 225
Rosebach
   Maria Anna 55
Roseman
   Heinrich 174
   Herman Gerhardt 174
Rosener
   Mary Susan 167
   Valentine 167
Rossmann
   August Mathias 187
   Mathias Henry 187
Roth
   Amelia 171, 172, 238
   Anton 52, 56
   Brigitta 142
   Catherine Elisabeth 154, 155
   Charles 258
   Christian 6
   Christina 32
   Esther Mary 158
   Franz Joseph 171
   Genevieve 215
   George 17
   Heinrich 154
   Jacob 17
   Johanna 17
   Louis Wendel 158
   Louise .... 6, 7, *See* Louise Baumann
   Magdalena 145, 259
   Maria Eva 56, 193
   Peter 59
   Roman 142
   Sophia 56
   William 52, 299
Rothert

    Catherine 222
Rottler
    Elisabeth 31, 78, 80
    Elisabeth Mary .... *See* Elisabeth Mary Huck
    Fridolin Andrew 246
    Katharina 79, 80, 151
    Rosina 74, 75
    Valentine 74, 78, 79, 80, 151, 246
    Wendelin 78, 79, 151
Roulette
    Mary Louise 238
    Theodore 238
Roussin
    Francis Adolphe 261
    John Adolphus 261
Rozier
    Felix 118
    Firmin A. 118
    Francis C. 118
Rudloff
    Francis 5
    Genevieve Rosine 59
    George 137
    Henry 5
    Johann Georg 5, 59, 137, 208
    Joseph 29, 208
    Mary Mildred 5
    Sophia 137, 139
    Sophia Louisa 29
Rudolphi
    Fidel 66
    Ignatz 66
Rueff
    Maria Francisca 37
Ruf
    Elisabeth 162
Ruff
    Charles B. 75
    Hubert 213
Rugg
    Josephine Rogers 88
Ruh
    Anton 104
    Conrad 46
    Franziska 230
    Lawrence 104, 235
    Lawrence Joseph 235
    Maria Theresa 46
Ruschmann
    Anastasia 173
Ruschmeyer
    Caroline Wilhelmina 219
Russell
    John Alfred 129
    Samuel Campbell 129
Rutledge
    George M. 65
    Mildred C. 65
Ryan
    John H. 186
    Thomas 186
Saar
    Caroline 104, 106
    Mathias 104
Sackmann
    Sophia 267
Sadler
    Elizabeth Ellen 279
Samson
    Anton 145, 259
    Charles Albert 145
    Karl 134
    Mary Josephine 259
    Richard 134
Sapp
    George 235
Satory
    Joseph 53, 179
Sauer
    Elizabeth 64, 260
Sauers
    Joseph 10
Schaaf
    Mathilda 169, 171
    Peter 214, 216
    Wilhelm 17, 169, 255
    Wilhelmina .... *See* Wilhelmina Armbruster
    William 17
    Wolfgang 17, 169
Schaefer
    Margaretha 25
Schaf
    Magdalena 115
Schallard
    _____ 282
    Minnie J. 282
Schätzle
    Albertina 270

Anton 271
Schaub
Josephine C. 28
Scheer
Maria Antonia 173
Scherer
Anton 119
Emerentia 10
Genevieve Josephine 245
John 245
Louise Elizabeth 119
Maria Anna 101
Schiffmann
John William 224
Schilli
Catherine 68, 69
Henry 248
Joseph 68, 248
Paulina 183, 184
Schilly
Valentine 31
Schimpf
Maria Richardis 112
Schindelmeyer
Barbara 225
Schindler
Helena Catherina 62
Schläfle
Eleonora 263
Raimond 263
Schlattmann
Anton 193
John Xavier 193
Mary Ann Elizabeth 193
Schlicht
Anna E. 187
Schlichter
_____ 135
Alexander 135
Francisca .... *See* Francisca Spietz
Schmelzle
August 128
Bernard 26, 260
Franziska 258
Joseph 257
Lena 128
Louisa Philomena 26
Mary Theresa 257
Schmiderer

Katharina 133
Schmidt
Barbara 105
Catherine 158
Cecilia 2
Lawrence 132
Lawrence Joseph 132
Maria Josephine 135
Mary Josephine 136
Michael 135
Schmiederer
Anthony Joseph 158
Apollonia 6, 56
August 207
Augustin 207, 250
Felicity 207, 208
Hildagarde Apollonia 158
Lawrence 250
Magdalena 17, 169
Schmitt
Bernard 60, 237
Gertrude 248
Gustave Joseph 60
Harriet Elizabeth 88
Johann 237
Nikolaus 173
Schmoll
Karoline 136
Louisa 136
Schmutz
Mary Ann 26
Schneider
Clara 76, 128
Fred 154, 155
John Friedrich 36
John N. 63, 65
Louisa .... *See* Louisa Ringwald
Lucinda .... *See* Lucinda Grott
Maria Anna 104
Ursula 159
Valentine 278
Viktoria 160
Schnurr
Anton 174
Brigitta 209
Catherine 174, 175
Johann Evangelist 168
Joseph 66

Maria Anna 9, 66
Rosalia 168
Schoenfeld
Amelia 8
Amelia Sophia 8, 101, 103
William 8, 101
Schonder
Margaret E. 187
Martin 187
Schönfeld
Karl Friedrich 8, 101
Schott
Catherine 146
Magdalena 154
Schrader
Ernst Wilhelm Diedrich 266
Mollie 266
Schrantz
Louis 246
Mary 246
Schroeder
Catherine 266, 267
Henry 169
Wilhelmina Bertha 169
Schröer
Maria Helena 130
Schubert
Johanna Josephine 146
Schuetz
Gustav 222
Schuler
Charles 72
Jacob 270
Johann Jacob 72, 270
Schulte
Johann 98
Schultz
Frank 99
Mary T. 99
Richard 99
Schulz
Carl 186
Lillian P. 186
Schumaecher
Catherine 216, 217
Schumert
Mary Catherine 260
Schwaab
Anton 126

Joseph 126
Schwartz
Adam 201
Anna 201, 204
Scholastica 93
Schwarz
Bernard Leo 33
Joseph 33
Schweigert
Andreas 69, 141, 148
Crescentia 24, 141, 156
Justine 69
Mary 2
Mathias 148
Schweiss
Anastasia 78, 86
Catherine 45
Francis Xavier 44, 45
Maria Anna 44, 271
Mary 272
Schweitzer
Barbara 225
Joseph 225
Schwend
Joseph Anton 213
Schwendemann
Joseph Anton ... 213, *See* Joseph Anton Schwend
Schwent
Anna Regina 105
August 160
Francisca 67, 109, 112, 131
John 132
Joseph 44, 67, 104, 105, 149, 160
Kunigunda 149
Lawrence 149
Nicholas 104
Theresia Sophia 132
William 44
Seals
Esther 87
Seckinger
Theresia 85
See
Maria Anna 54
Seewald
Anton 114
Selbold
Anna Barbara 58, 61
Seiler

Joseph 4
Meinrad 4
Seitz
Adolf 270
Eleanora 54, 55, 228, 229, 230
Joseph 78, 80, 228
Matthias 270
Seitzinger
Paulina 232
Sellinger
Bernard 49, 167
Elisabeth 144, 167, 168
George 49, 167
Helena 13, 19, 49, 51
Maria Anna 63
Serrer
Joseph 39
Paula 39
Sewald
Andreas 31, 32
Andrew 31, 79
Andrew Elias 175
Caroline 79, 124
Charles Frederick 175
Elizabeth M. 79
Mary Ann 79, 175
Michael 114, 175
Valentine 175
Sexauer
Edward Leo 64
George 35, 64, 260
George Joseph 260
Joseph 35
Shappo
Isabelle 119
Shearlock
George Walter 60
Shine
Clara 187
Shuppe
Caroline 100
Sickburg
A. W. 129
Siebert
Agnes 266
Anna Maria 11
Augustin 72
Carl Aloysius 109
Cecilia 19, 38, 49
Charles Aloysius 262
Clara Helena 215
Heinrich 268, 269
Henry 16, 17, 209, 269
Joseph Firmin 109
Josephine Mary 17
Maria Anna 209, 253, 269
Maria Eva 72, 73
Theresa 16, 268
Theresia 38
Veronica 172
William H. 262
Siebler
Ottilia 134
Siefert
Euphrosine 16, 255
Johannes Peter 16
Siegrist
Catharina 160
Sifferle
Maria Anna 197
Simpson
Mary Melissa 119
Singer
Elisabeth 171
Sinker
Anna Adelaide Catherine 278
Sinz
Augustin 160
Johann 160
Skaggs
Jeremiah P. 166
Nancy Ellen 166
Snell
Richard 213
Solf
Emma E. 219
Ernst August 219
Spaeth
Creszentia 150
Spann
Helen Louise 75
John Naill 75
Sparmeyer
Carolina 270
Caroline 72
Späth
Richardis 230

343

Speak
Edna Earle 75
Spietz
Francisca 135, 136
Spitzmiller
Michael 93
Theresia 93, 94
Splettstoser
Minna Amelia 112
Spradling
Arthur Marion 89
George Lincoln 89
Spring
Catharina 162
St. Vrain
Ceran de Hault de Lassus 116
Felix Auguste de Hault de Lassus 116
Marie Felicite 116
Staab
Philippine 57
Staechle
Joseph 215
Theodore Francis 215
Staeckle
Francis Xavier 215
Joseph John 215
Staffey
A.F. 266
Stamm
Christian 12
Stanford
Lola Hester 88
Thomas 88
Stanton
Eugene Beauregarde Joseph 64
Samuel Stewart 64
Stark
Ernst 232
Starkjohann
Johann Ernst 232
Stauss
Charles Anton 72
Walburga 99
Steffan
Francis Xavier 105
Sylvester 105
Steimle
Ignatz 268
Rebecca 268

Steinbach
Maria Magdalena 219
Steinle
Magdalena 114
Stephens
Ira 273
Stevens
John S. 100
Melissa Jane 29
Stewart
Mary Ann 278
Stigge
Anna Maria 216
Stirnaman
Lawrence 21
Peter 21
Stock
Johanna Maria Theresia 23
Stocker
Andreas 18
Francis 18, 50
Stoeckle
Catherine 264
Johann 264
Maria Magdalena 211
Stoetzle
Franziska 105
Stoll
Michael 57
Theodore Joseph 57
Stolzer
Ferdinand 160
Martin 160
Straehl
Anna Maria 218
Straube
Bertha 223, 227
Bertha M. 222, 223, 226
Emilia 222
Friedrich 223
Herman 223
Louis 223
Ludwig 222
Ludwig Gustav Arthur 222
Mathilde 222
Rudolph F. 222
Theodor 222
Streif
Maria Anna 190

Streule
　Franz Xavier 12
　Theresia 12, 50
Striebel
　August William 142
　Stephen 142
Strobe
　Theresia 21
Strobel
　Catharina... 59, 264
Stumpf
　Katherine 129
Stuppy
　Anton Reinhard 1
　Charles August 215
　Francis Xavier 1, 245
　Jacob 178, 197, 245
　Mary Anna 178
　Peter 215
　William Jacob 215
Stutz
　Justine 248
　Maria Anna 104, 106
　Mathias 104, 191, 248
Sucher
　Charles 253
　Joseph 209
　Lawrence 253
　Lorenz 209, 253
　Maria Anna 268, 269
　Mary Ann.............................. 16, 209, 269
　Sophia 19
Suhm
　Georg 150
　Michael 150
Sullivan
　Adelia Bridget 99
Summers
　Susan... 123
Sutterer
　John.. 278
　Theresa R. 278
Swafford
　Dorsey T. 119
Tayler
　Zachary 195
Terry
　Carlyle Marshall 129
　Eugene P. 129

Teschemacher
　Emil 222
　Julia A. 222
Thieret
　John Peter 278
　Theresa R. .... *See* Theresa R. Sutterer
Thomann?
　Fred. Wm. 162
Thompson
　Charles Raymond 114
　Fred C. 189
Thomure
　Brasier Marcel 235
　George 235
　Joseph 162
　Mary Judith 120
Thyen
　Johann Bernard.. 131
　Maria Gesina 131
Timbermann
　Harriet Frances 202
　John Davis 202
Tinker
　James 119
　Margaret Pearl 119
　Sarah 94
Tlapek
　John W. 42
Tränkle
　Luitgard 84
Trautmann
　Aloysius Anton... 210
　Caroline 176
　Clara 1, 2, 178
　Constantine... 43, 44
　Maria 163
　Maria Anna 269
　Peter Paul.. 178, 210
Tucker
　Catherine 180
　Clement Camilus 180
　Leo Severin 180
　Loretta 220
　Martin Francis 180
　Martina 180
　Michael 180, 182
　Nicholas 182
Tweedy
　Ben F. 203

345

Uding
  Caroline Maria 122, 125
  Friedrich 122
  Friedrich Wilhelm August 122
Ullrich
  Maria Anna 141
Ulrich
  Susan 18
Uphoff
  Henry C. 231
Vaeth
  Bernard 82
  Josephine 25
  Peter 82
  Peter Andrew 25
  Theresa 27
Valle
  Eulalia 112
  Francis Joseph 156
  Francis L. 100
  L. Bert 100
  Leo August 156
  Louis August Bertolemé 276
  Louisa Bertha 276
  Marie Ann 245
  Mary Ann 29
  Melanie P. 34
Vallet
  Celine 190
Vaughn
  Elizabeth Sephronia 114
  James Edward 114
Vetter
  Anna Maria 263
Vierthaler
  Ignaz 230
  Joseph 230
Vineyard
  Ernest S. 123
  Steve 123
Viox
  John 146
  Mary Ann 146
Vogelsang
  Ervin C. R. 75
  Vernice Alvina 75
Vogt
  Anton 21, 59, 85, 212
  Henry 59
  Roman 85, 87
Vogt Sophia .... *See* Sophia Pfaff
Volk
  Mathias 37
Vorst
  Joseph 101
  Joseph Henry 101
Waggener
  Alice Harriet 139
  Reuben Garnett 139
Waldrop
  Wiley B. 195
Waller
  Catharina Magdalena 49, 50
  Joseph Anton 49
Walter
  Joseph 145, 147
  Magdalena 15
  Peter 145
Walton
  Isabelle 65
Walz
  Carl 274
  Jacob 274
Ward
  Eunice F. 272
  Samuel Adolph 138
Way
  Isaac P. 273
  Violet Martha 273
Weber
  Anna R. 182
  Cecilia F. 231
  Elsabeth 175
  Emma R. 182
  Francis Anthony 182
  Frank 181, 182
  Henry 165
  Henry W. 166, 182
  Herman 183
  Ignatius 183
  J. A. 100
  John Henry 165
  John J. 88
  Joseph August 182
  Rose Regina 88
Wehner
  George 27, 128, 130
  Mary 76, 77, 78

Nicholas 76, 128
 Theresa 128, 130
 Ursula Bertha 27
Wehrle
 Annie 89
Weiberg
 Henrietta 156
Weide
 Peter Nicolaj Georg 47
Weiger
 Maria 145
Weigert
 Louise 220
Weiler
 Anton 45, 148, 199
 Elisabeth 273
 Elizabeth Theresa 105
 Franziska 10, 109
 Gertrude 45
 Magdalena 188
 Mathilda 148
 Salome Katherine 105
 Wendelin 105, 199
Weininger
 Barbara 206
Weis
 Isabella 173
 Magdalena 173
 Maria Elisabetha 173
Weisbrod
 Frederick Philip 219
 Johann L. 219
Weiser
 Gallus 241
 Henry W. 241
Weiss
 Francis Xavier 121
 Louisa 104
Weisskopf
 Apollonia 161
Weitmann
 Elisabeth 107
Weldesofer
 Monica 104, 105
Wells
 Emeline 139, 141
Wenger
 Charles 72
Wengert

 Charles Ambrose 156
 Martin 23, 24
 Martin Lewis 156
Werner
 George 49
 George Marx 167
 Ignatz 66
 Joseph 66
 Lawrence 49
 Mary Helena 167
Wessner
 Agnes 1
West
 Ella F. 282
White
 Erwin 119
Whitehead
 George E. 62
 Martha Ann 114
 Maud Union 62
Wieberg
 Christina 11, 172
 Elizabeth Veronica 172
 John 12, 21
 Mary 21, 22
 Nicholas 172
Wier
 ____ 232
 Lillian 232
Wigant
 Anna Maria 198
Wilber
 ____ 205
 Barbara 205
Wilder
 Henry 8
 Louis Andrew 47
 Peter 47, 255
 Peter Henry William 255
 Peter Nicolaj Georg 255
 Sophia Catherina 33
Will
 George 178
 Johann Georg 25
 Johann Martin 25
 Maria Anna 82
 Mary Ann 74
 Mary Emily 178

Wi...
Johann Herman 216
John Henry 216
Willi
Jacob 11, 218, 234
Joseph Christian 11, 12, 234
Wilhelmina Christina 218
Williams
Elizabeth 92
Wilmer
Anna Maria 276
Winkleman
Elisabeth 218
Winkler
Cecilia 5, 59, 137
Maria Anna 121, 217
Winn
Jane 62
Winter
Caroline 132
Leopold 149, 174
Rosine 28, 30
Sophia 149, 262
Wipfler
Andreas 250, 251
Andrew 250
Theresia 73, 76, 115
Wirtner
Franziska Helena 4
Wittmore
John 206
Joseph 206
Witty
Mary 28, 30, 208
William or John? 28
Wolf
Andrew 239
John 239
Josephine 95
Mary Louise .... *See* Mary Louise Roulette
Wilhelmina .... *See* Wilhelmina Flori
Wolk
Anna Mary 3
Joseph A. 3
Joseph Anton 215
Leona Catherine 3
Peter 215
Philip Jacob 144
Wood
Edith G. 97
Henry H. 62
Woolford
Nancy Ann 5
Worajeck
Anna 184
Worley
Anna Katherine 13
Jacob 13
Wörner
Jonas 141
Joseph 141
Ottilia 141
Wörter
Josepha 85, 160
Wright
David 137
Wulf
Caroline 186
Wunning
Frederick 100
Wussler
Theresia 16
Yeagle
Conrad 171, 238
Henry 171
Louise .... *See* Louise Buehler
Yealy
Jacob 121, 206
Leon Sebastian 121
Yonk
Catherine 126
Friedrich 126
Young
Maria D. 189
Otto Joseph 114
Thaddeus Faye 279
Zanter
Juliana 278
Zerwig
Josephine 262
Rosina 215
Ziegler
Johanna 73
Mathias 206
Rosine 205, 206
Sebastian 206
Zimmermann
Augustina 261

Christina 3
  Elizabeth 191
  Henry 191
Zink
  Andreas 230
  Anton 230
  Ignaz 141
  Joseph 141
  Meinrad 141

Zoellner
  Antoinette 98
  Wilhelm 98
Zopf
  Jacob 53
  Mary Magdalena 53
Zurline
  Anna Mary 272

www.ingramcontent.com/pod-product-compliance
Lightning Source LLC
Chambersburg PA
CBHW080725300426
44114CB00019B/2494